A World of Whose M

Order al:

Hist

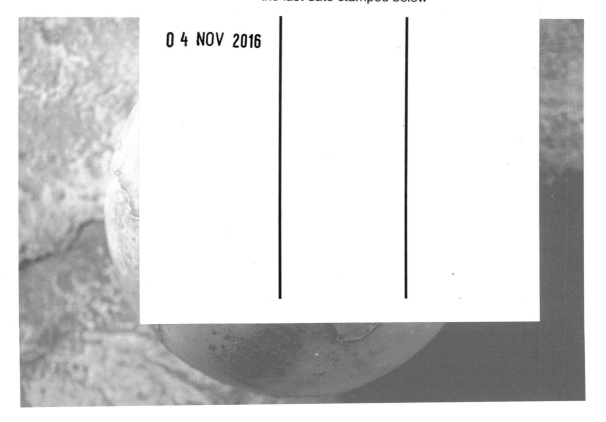

Project team

Dr Simon Bromley, Course team chair

Dr William Brown, Co-chair

Course team

Dr Suma Athreye
Dr George Callaghan
Dr Ranjit Dwivedi
Ann Garnham
Dr Jef Huysmans
Dr Bob Kelly
Professor Maureen Mackintosh
Dr Giles Mohan
Professor Chandan Mukherjee

Dr Raia Prokhovnik
Dick Skellington
Dr Mark Smith
Hedley Stone
Professor Grahame Thompson
Professor David Wield
Dr Gordon Wilson
Professor Marc Wuyts
Dr Helen Yanacopulos

The OU would like to acknowledge the valuable contribution made to the course team and the development of *A World of Whose Making?* by Dr Robert Garson of the University of Keele.

Dr Hazel Johnson, critical reader
Maria Ana Lugo, St Antony's College, Oxford, critical reader
Kirsten Adkins, BBC
Sally Baker, OU Library
Brenda Barnett, secretary
Pam Berry, composition services
Karen Bridge, project manager
Maurice Brown, software development
Lene Connolly, materials procurement
Mick Deal, software QA
Marilyn Denman, course secretary
Wilf Eynon, audio-visual
Fran Ford, Politics and Government Secretary
Sarah Gamman, rights adviser
Carl Gibbard, designer

Richard Golden, production and presentation administrator
Dr Mark Goodwin, lead editor
Gill Gowans, copublishing advisor
Celia Hart, picture research
Avis Lexton, Economics Secretary
Lisa MacHale, BBC
Vicki McCulloch, designer
Magda Noble, media consultant
Eileen Potterton, course manager
Andrew Rix, audio-visual
David Shulman, BBC
Kelvin Street, OU Library
Colin Thomas, software development
Gill Tibble, BBC
Gail Whitehall, audio-visual
Joanne Osborn, editor

Contributors to this volume

Dr Suma Athreye, Lecturer in Economics, Faculty of Social Sciences, The Open University.
Dr Simon Bromley, Senior Lecturer in Government and Politics, Faculty of Social Sciences, The Open University.
Dr William Brown, Lecturer in Government and Politics, Faculty of Social Sciences, The Open University.
Dr Robert Garson, Reader in American Studies, University of Keele.
Dr Jef Huysmans, Lecturer in Government and Politics, Faculty of Social Sciences, The Open University.
Dr Tim Jordan, Lecturer in Sociology, Faculty of Social Sciences, The Open University.
Dr Giles Mohan, Lecturer in Development Studies, Faculty of Technology, The Open University.
Dr Raia Prokhovnik, Senior Lecturer in Government and Politics, Faculty of Social Sciences, The Open University.
Dr Rafal Rohozinski, Director, Advanced Network Research Group, Programme for Security in International Society, Cambridge University.
Dr Roberto Simonetti, Senior Lecturer in Economics, Faculty of Social Sciences, The Open University.
Dr Mark J. Smith, Senior Lecturer in Government and Politics, Faculty of Social Sciences, The Open University.
Dr Benno Teschke, Lecturer in International Relations, Department of International Relations and Politics, University of Sussex.
Professor Grahame Thompson, Professor of Political Economy, Faculty of Social Sciences, The Open University.
Dr Helen Yanacopulos, Lecturer in Development Studies, Faculty of Technology, The Open University.
Professor Sami Zubaida, Professor of Politics and Sociology, Birkbeck College, University of London.

A World of Whose Making?

Ordering the International:
History, Change and Transformation

Edited by
William Brown, Simon Bromley
and Suma Athreye

Pluto  Press
LONDON • ANN ARBOR, MI

in association with

The Open
University

This publication forms part of the Open University course DU301 *A World of Whose Making? Politics, Economics, Technology and Culture in International Studies*. Details of this and other Open University courses can be obtained from the Course Information and Advice Centre, PO Box 724, The Open University, Milton Keynes MK7 6ZS, United Kingdom: tel. +44 (0)1908 653231, email general-enquiries@open.ac.uk.

Alternatively, you may visit the Open University website at http://www.open.ac.uk, where you can learn more about the wide range of courses and packs offered at all levels by The Open University.

Copyright © 2004 The Open University
First published 2004 by Pluto Press in association with The Open University.

The Open University
Walton Hall
Milton Keynes
MK7 6AA
United Kingdom
www.open.ac.uk

Pluto Press
345 Archway Road   11030 South Langley Avenue
London   Chicago
N6 5AA   IL 60628, USA
www.plutobooks.com

Library of Congress Cataloguing-in-Publication Data
A catalogue record for this book is available from the Library of Congress.
British Library Cataloguing-in-Publication Data
A catalogue record for this book is available from the British Library.
Edited, designed and typeset by The Open University.
Printed and bound in the United Kingdom by The Bath Press, Bath.
ISBN 0 7453 2138 0 (hbk)
ISBN 0 7453 2137 2 (pbk)
1.1

To purchase a selection of Open University course materials visit the webshop at www.ouw.co.uk, or contact Open University Worldwide, Michael Young Building, Walton Hall, Milton Keynes MK7 6AA, United Kingdom for a brochure: tel. +44 (0)1908 858785; fax +44 (0)1908 858787, email ouwenq@open.ac.uk

Contents

Preface

Ordering the International: History, Change and Transformation is part of *A World of Whose Making? Politics, Economics, Technology and Culture in International Studies*, a course from The Open University's Faculty of Social Sciences.

As with other Open University texts, *Ordering the International* has been produced by a 'course team' of academics and support staff. This volume, and the course itself, would not have been possible without the contributions of the whole course team who played a vital role in writing, preparing and refining successive drafts and in shaping the book and the course. We are also extremely grateful to those authors from outside The Open University – Benno Teschke, Sami Zubaida and Rafal Rohozinski – who wrote or contributed to chapters for this volume. Theirs are rich contributions indeed. We also wish to thank our two external assessors, Professor Anthony Payne and Professor Rhys Jenkins, who reviewed draft chapters and other course materials and provided valuable advice on how to improve them.

The academic staff of The Open University are particularly fortunate to benefit from the work of skilled, efficient (and patient!) administrative, production and support staff. Marilyn Denman and Fran Ford prepared successive drafts of the text speedily and accurately, despite formidable workloads. Marilyn Denman also gave us valuable and cheerful support as course secretary. Mark Goodwin, the lead editor for all the course materials, oversaw the composition of the book with his customary attention to detail, care and good humour, making our lives so much easier despite the perennial difficulties academics have with deadlines. Thanks also to designers Vicki McCulloch and Carl Gibbard for their work on the book. Gill Gowans oversaw the copublication process with Pluto Press, and our thanks go to her and to Pluto for their support in this project. Last, but definitely not least, we owe a huge debt of thanks to Eileen Potterton, our Course Manager on *A World of Whose Making?* Eileen oversaw the production of *Ordering the International*, as well as the course as a whole, with such unflappable efficiency, energy and all round goodwill that even the difficult bits were easy.

Ordering the International is the second of a two book series. Its companion volume (which forms the first half of the course *A World of Whose Making?*) is *Making the International: Economic Interdependence and Political Order*, also copublished with Pluto Press. *Ordering the International* is oriented towards studying and analysing international order through the perspectives of International Studies, whereas *Making the International* teaches the core viewpoints, concepts and models needed to analyse international political economy.

William Brown, Simon Bromley and Suma Athreye

Chapter 1 The subject and scope of International Studies

Simon Bromley and William Brown

1 Introduction

This book is about the modern international system and about what International Studies (IS) has to say about that system. Few areas of our social world have more importance, or more claim on our attention, than the international. Hardly a day can go by without us being aware of some 'international event' that affects our lives. If it only provided a better understanding of the forces shaping the world in which we live, studying the international system would be a worthy endeavour. However, we concur with Fred Halliday when he writes that the international is not just 'something "out there", an area of policy that occasionally intrudes, in the form of bombs or higher oil prices' (1994, p.20). The international is also a constitutive element of our social world. We live in an 'international' world every bit as much as a 'domestic' or 'national' one, and how the international is ordered and how it changes are inextricably linked to what may appear, on the surface, to be closer-to-home, 'domestic' concerns. The two go hand in hand. In an era in which politicians, activists and commentators try to grapple with rapid global change and divine the tectonic shifts that underlie the mêlée of everyday international affairs, we need some tools and ideas to make sense of this aspect of our lives.

The principal aim of this book is to use a theoretical and historical understanding of the modern international system to improve our comprehension of contemporary events and developments. To help with this, we have defined three framing questions to guide our investigations. These questions are addressed in different ways in the chapters that follow, and we shall return to them systematically in the concluding section of the book (Part 4). Here we identify these questions and outline some of the groundwork needed to pursue them.

1: Is it possible to analyse the international system as a whole?

We believe this to be a meaningful question. However, one of the tasks of this chapter is to establish some of the foundations for an answer by defining precisely what we mean by the term 'international'.

2: How can we best characterize, understand and explain the processes of international interaction and the kinds of order and disorder with which they are associated?

3 (which stems from 2): Is the contemporary international system changing and, if so, by whose agency?

To answer these questions we need a framework within which to analyse the international system and identify the different areas, and agents, of change. Specifically, we need both a historical perspective from which to analyse and judge the contemporary world and some delineation of the different sectors of the international to which these questions can be directed. In this chapter we shall offer one way of approaching this task.

The structure of this chapter is as follows. First, in Section 2 we begin by outlining an understanding and definition of 'the international', and hence try to delineate the subject matter of International Studies. In doing this we seek to identify a *general* meaning of 'the international' as well as two different ways in which it is also necessary to locate the specificity of *particular* international systems. In undertaking this second task we also offer a framework for identifying the different sectors of the international. In Section 3 we outline our approach to identifying the historical specificity of the 'modern' international system – the perspective from which claims about contemporary change can, and should, be judged. We conclude by briefly looking forward to the rest of the book.

2   What is the 'problematic of the international'?

The discipline of International Studies aims to study international systems. But what, exactly, do we mean by 'the international'? To answer this question we follow what is – to the best of our knowledge – the most successful elucidation of what its author, Justin Rosenberg, calls 'the problematic of the international' (2000, pp.65–85). A 'problematic', in this context, is simply a set of related questions, or areas of inquiry, that forms a coherent object of study. Rosenberg aims to define a 'successful general abstraction of "the international"' (2000, p.77), that is, a conception which can apply universally to all human societies, abstracted from the particular form and content of any actual societies in any given time and place. If successful, International Studies can then be said to have a general problematic to which it addresses itself.

Rosenberg makes a strong case, one which we endorse, that defines the international primarily in political terms. The problematic of the international, according to Rosenberg, addresses the characteristic issues that arise from geopolitics, that is, relations between politically organized societies. Let us see how he comes to this conclusion.

The first thing to note is that this political definition of the international 'presupposes a prior general abstraction of "the political"' (2000, p.77). Fortunately, the latter is rather easy to provide. All societies – certainly all societies that have maintained regular and ordered relations with other societies – have established and maintained forms of social control for the maintenance of social order, for making and enforcing collectively binding decisions and rules, and for protecting themselves against (real and imagined) external challenges. That is to say, all societies discharge certain *political* functions. Now, the scope of these political functions varies from one society to another, as do the extent to which they are performed as specialized activities and the extent to which they are institutionalized. But in all societies there is something that can be identified as 'the political' aspect of social life.

Notice that, while this definition picks out some generic, universal aspects of social life; that is, it identifies a 'general abstraction' of politics, it does not presuppose any particular account of how politics operates in any given society. It is what Karl Marx, from whom this kind of methodology is derived, called a 'rational' or 'reasonable' abstraction 'in so far as it really brings out and fixes the common element' (1973, p.85). In order to apply a general concept of politics, we have to specify, for any given society, its particular content as well as the form in which it occurs – and these vary from one historically given society to another.

The empirical fact that 'in the known field of human history, social orders have always *co*-existed' (Rosenberg, 2000, p.80) means that the existence of politics immediately implies the existence of *relations between and among politically organized societies, that is, geopolitics*. Thus, politics, and a fortiori geopolitics, are transhistorical features of all human societies and their interrelations. William Polk, for example, argues that the 'fundamentals of foreign affairs', that is, things such as 'trade, defence, warfare, diplomacy, espionage, exclusion, and conversion' have been in existence at least since the emergence of interacting societies based on settled agriculture (Polk, 1997, p.10).

It is important to stress that, while the geopolitical arises from the coexistence of politically organized societies, the relations between and among these societies may themselves be political (war, diplomacy, international law), economic and technological (trade, investment, technological diffusion, forms of communication and transport), and socio-cultural (shared or contested norms, ideas and cultures). What defines the geopolitical is not the idea that relations between and among societies are exclusively, or even primarily, political but rather that politically organized societies coexist (and hence interact) with one another. To repeat, such interactions and the social relations thereby established can be political, economic, technological or socio-cultural.

Drawing on considerations of this kind, Rosenberg (2000) argues that there is indeed a transhistorical, general 'problematic of the international'. This problematic comprises three fundamental elements: 'the political regulation of ungoverned interaction, the differentiated moral standing of insiders and outsiders, and the intellectual (and philosophical) issue of the whole made up by the parts' (Rosenberg, 2000, p.79). He proceeds to explain it thus:

> [G]iven that no social order has ever yet been coextensive with humanity as a whole, it certainly follows that the collectively binding rules we would identify have always had a limited remit in terms of who is bound by them. This means too that there will always be an inside and an outside; and if the binding rules of political association specify rights and obligations, then how could the moral standing of insiders and outsiders not differ? Moreover, if the collectively binding rules are what demarcate the inside, how could these be the same as the (causal, moral, legal) rules of interaction among these insides (of which, it follows from their non-universal character, there must be more than one)? And if they are not, then the question of the interrelation of these, and of the parts to the superordinate whole, arises also as a *general* question which must be answered in each instance.

(Rosenberg, 2000, p.79)

This book endorses the position forcefully defended by Rosenberg, the idea that there is a problematic of the international, or the geopolitical: it is what constitutes the core disciplinary focus of International Studies. (Rosenberg uses the term 'international' where we sometimes use the term 'geopolitical'. Nothing turns on this, and in much of the rest of the book the two terms will be used interchangeably. However, some authors use geopolitics as a more general term, reserving 'international' for the geopolitics of the modern international system in which the political organization of society takes the form of a nation state.)

2.1   Identifying the specificity of particular international systems

The above exposition establishes the general abstractions of politics and geopolitics, and hence the problematic of the international. However, like Rosenberg, we also believe that the *forms* taken by politics and geopolitics have varied enormously throughout history and across different societies and patterns of inter-societal interaction. Concrete instances of politics and geopolitics are always manifested in historically specific forms, as concrete particulars. There are two senses to this specificity.

The first sense we have already alluded to: namely, the need for historical specificity in the use of general abstractions. Immediately after introducing the idea of general abstractions, Marx goes on to say that they are 'abstract moments with which no real historical stage ... can be grasped' (1973. p.88). Marx argues that understanding and explaining the history and workings of any concrete society – and, by extension, any inter-societal system – involve combining the transhistorical and the historically specific in coherent ways. This is not always an easy balance to maintain, but it is essential if we are to avoid falsely reading back into the past features that are specific to contemporary circumstances, or surreptitiously including transhistorical elements in concepts designed to capture the particular features of the modern.

Let us consider the following example as a way of illustrating the argument so far. The first several hundred years – the Spring and Autumn years – of the era of Chinese history known as the Eastern Zhou period (c.770–221 BCE) were followed by an age known as that of 'the Warring States'. During the time of the Warring States, seven large states in northern China contended for power. They were all Chinese in the sense of speaking and writing mutually intelligible languages and sharing a common culture. 'But', writes Warren Cohen, 'they considered themselves to be independent states and preserved their separateness with military fortifications and customs restrictions. Each had its own army, led by professional generals. Each had professional diplomats ... and a nascent system of international law came into existence' (2000, p.12). Interestingly, for our purposes:

> two themes gained centrality in the writings of Chinese intellectuals during the Warring States era ... One argument, for which the classic exponent was Mozi (c.480–390 [BCE]), a contemporary of Socrates, focused on the need for a balance of power to protect small and weak states against potential aggressors. The other, expounded by Mencius (c.371–289 [BCE]), a contemporary of Aristotle, and perhaps even earlier by Laozi (c. 6th century BCE), was universalist, seeking a unified world state, specifically the unification of the known world under one Chinese government.

(Cohen, W., 2000, p.13)

We don't know whether these exchanges amounted to the first glimmerings of proto-realist thought or the idea of world government, but they are a testament to the longevity of the discourses of geopolitics. That is, they show the existence of the political in the form of each of the seven states (social controls aimed at providing social order, collectively binding decisions and rules, and protection against external challenges). They also show the existence of the geopolitical in the relations between those politically organized societies. In this instance, for example, forms of war and trade, diplomacy and international law: economic and political relations within a single cultural order. But if we look closely, we also see that the forms taken by politics, and particularly geopolitical competition, were very different from those with which we are familiar in, say, modern European history (see Chapter 2). To give just one example: in the incessant warfare that characterized the period of the Warring States, large states devoured small states until the different politically organized societies were eventually subsumed in one unified government under the rule of Qinshi Huangdi, the Qin Emperor, in 221 BCE. This is precisely the point. General concepts – say, of geopolitical competition – must always be filled out with historically specific content.

If historical concreteness is the first sense of specificity, the second arises directly from this and refers to the need to think about the relations between politics and other areas of social life. We have already noted that geopolitics – that is, relations between and among politically organized societies – can include economic, technological and socio-cultural interaction as well as politics itself. As we said above, the general abstraction of geopolitics is designed to pick out relations between and among politically organized societies, not to confine our attention solely to the political aspects of international relations, as if this analytically distinct category exists in splendid isolation from other areas of social interaction. Indeed, the nature of politics in any given society as well as the geopolitics among interacting societies may themselves be strongly shaped by these other – economic, technological or socio-cultural – areas of social life and kinds of interaction.

The theory that most obviously attends to the general determinations of the international is realism. It *does* make a claim that the geopolitical is autonomous from other sectors and it *does* claim a transhistorical applicability. This is both its strength and its weakness. By focusing on the general abstraction common to all inter-societal interaction (geopolitics), it positions itself at the very centre of International Studies. This is one important reason for its centrality, or intellectual dominance, in the field of International Studies. However, it could be argued that realism fails to combine an analysis of the general with an analysis of the particular in both the senses identified above. It tends to emphasize the transhistorical at the expense of the historically specific, and it maintains that the realm of politics is sufficiently autonomous from other dimensions of society and inter-societal interaction to be theorized in its own terms. 'Realism is wrong,' writes Rosenberg, 'whenever it attempts to assemble these general determinations into a free-standing explanatory theory which can be applied in an unmediated way to the real world of international politics' (2000, p.81; see also Rosenberg, 1994). You will have an opportunity to make your own judgement of realism later in this book, but for now we want to echo Rosenberg's subsequent comment that 'like it or not, there is no way beyond realism by going around it. For, however misconceived it may be, it is sitting on the intellectual foundations (the general determinations) which we too need to make sense of international relations' (2000, p.81). These general determinations, to repeat, are the generic and irreducible facts of the political moment of social life and geopolitical coexistence.

Thus far this section has covered a lot of ground in a rather compressed manner. To help you grasp the main points here is a brief reconstruction of the argument.

- We started with a general concept of politics that is common to all societies and we defined this in terms of social controls aimed at providing social order, collectively binding decisions and rules, and some protection against external challenges. This concept of politics is general, it applies universally to all human societies (or at least all those since the development of settled agriculture) and it abstracts from the particular content and form taken by politics in any given society.
  It is possible to formulate a general, abstract concept of politics.

- Given that politically organized societies have always coexisted with one another (we take this to be an empirical, historical fact), we said that politics inevitably gives rise to geopolitics, that is, relations between and among these societies. There is, therefore, another general abstract concept – a 'general abstraction' of geopolitics.
  Given the coexistence of societies, it is also possible to have a general, abstract concept of geopolitics.

- We noted that geopolitics encompasses different 'sectors' of relations between societies: political relations, economic and technological relations and relations of socio-cultural interaction.
  Geopolitics includes economic, technological and socio-cultural, as well as political, relations of interaction between societies.

- Following Rosenberg, we argued that these geopolitical relations between politically organized orders routinely pose three questions: 'the political regulation of ungoverned interaction, the differentiated moral standing of insiders and outsiders, and the intellectual (and philosophical) issue of the whole made up of the parts' (Rosenberg, 1990, p.79). The study of these three questions constitutes the general 'problematic of the international', or the geopolitical; they are the focus of attention of the discipline of International Studies.
  Three recurring issues of geopolitics define the problematic of the international.

- The abstract concepts of politics and geopolitics pick out general features that exist across societies at different moments in history, that is, they are transhistorical concepts. But the features they identify always occur in particular, historical forms with their own specific content. So, we suggested that in order to use a general abstraction to explain any given society or inter-societal system we must specify its particular characteristics in any given historical instance.

General, abstract concepts are transhistorical and must be filled in with particular detail relevant to the case in hand.

■   We then said, finally, that filling in the historically particular characteristics of the general abstraction of geopolitics involves attending, first, to the ways in which it is realized in particular forms, and second, to the relations between the different sectors – political, economic, and technological and socio-cultural – subsumed under this particular abstraction.

Filling in historical specificity involves both saying something about the form that the general abstraction takes in a particular historical instance and stating how its component sectors relate to one another.

2.2   Analysing particular geopolitical systems

With these methodological preliminaries established, we can now turn to the task of developing a framework for the analysis of particular patterns of geopolitics, exhibited by different forms of international system, in the light of their general determinations *and* in the light of historical specificity and other dimensions of social life. As we do not want to prejudge the merits of any particular model of the international (such as realism or Marxism), we will employ a framework that identifies certain general features of all international systems, allows for historical specificity in defining those features, and is open-ended as to the relations between politics and geopolitics and other dimensions of societies and inter-societal systems. There are several such frameworks, but the one developed by Barry Buzan and Richard Little (2000) has the twin virtues of simplicity and clarity. Not every international system can be neatly squeezed into this construction but it does provide a rough and ready set of tools for analysis. In what follows, we present a (slightly modified) framework based on the work of Buzan and Little.

The idea of an international system presupposes a number of parts (in International Studies these are often called 'units') that interact with one another and that maintain relations with one another on a regular and reasonably patterned or ordered basis. The parts, or units, are the coexisting politically organized societies that we spoke of above. The *units* of an international system, say Buzan and Little, are 'sufficiently cohesive to have actor quality ... and sufficiently independent to be differentiated from others' (2000, p.69). To the extent that the parts of an international system relate to one another in a regular and ordered manner, we can say that the system has structure – the *structure* of the relations among the parts is simply the way in which those relations are ordered. Clearly, the idea of a system assumes that its parts interact with one another in some fashion. Buzan and Little define the *interaction capacity* of a system as the technological and organizational means of transportation and communication by which this is made possible: it tells us about the possibilities for interaction between and among the units. And finally, there are the *processes* of interaction that actually take place, that is, 'the patterns of action and reaction that can be observed among the units that make up a system' (Buzan and Little, 2000, p.79). It is important to remember that, while this gives us a serviceable framework for analysing international systems in general, the identification of the units, structure, interaction capacity and processes is always a matter of concrete historical investigation.

Before we can proceed with our historical investigations, however, we must attend to the second aspect of specificity mentioned above and situate the political dimension in relation to other dimensions of social life and inter-societal interaction. We have already said that we accept the idea of a transhistorical problematic of the international, that is, the existence of an irreducible realm of geopolitics given by the coexistence of politically organized societies. Yet, we also seek to situate politics in relation to other dimensions of social life such as the economic, the technological and the socio-cultural. Following Buzan and Little, we shall refer to these dimensions as 'sectors': sectors provide 'views of the whole system [seen] through an analytical lens which selects one particular type of relationship and highlights the type of unit, interaction, and structure most closely associated with it' (2000, p.72).

This book will focus on three such sectors: the political sector of authoritative rule, the socio-cultural sector of collective identities and conceptions of rights and justice, and the economic and technological sector of production, trade and innovation. If we bring together a focus on the elements of international systems and an analysis of sectors we shall have a framework like the one shown in Table 1.1 (overleaf).

Table 1.1   A framework for analysing (changes in) the international system

Elements of the international system	Sectors of the international system		
	Political sector of authoritative rule	Socio-cultural sector of collective identities and conceptions of rights and justice	Economic and technological sector of production, trade and innovation
Principal units in the international system			
Structure of relations among units			
Interaction capacity			
Dominant processes of interaction			

The problematic of the international is committed to the irreducibility of the political sector in any international system – as it is the coexistence of politically organized units that defines the geopolitical – but it is not committed to the (implicitly realist) idea that a theory of the international can be built solely from that point of view. 'Sectors bring a selected type of activity into clearer view,' write Buzan and Little, 'but they do not establish grounds for thinking that in reality these activities are autonomous, and organized independently from what goes on in other sectors' (2000, p.75). Even the strictly political aspects of the international may be best explained in terms of causes operating in other areas of social life. All the authors of this book share the view that a purely political account of geopolitics is wanting. In addition to considering the political sector of the international (in Part 1), this book will also investigate the socio-cultural dimensions of societies and inter-societal systems (Part 2), the dimension of economic and technological interactions (Part 3), as well as the connections between all of these (Parts 1 to 3 and, especially, Part 4).

3   The specificity of the modern international system

We have defined the problematic of the international, following Rosenberg, in terms of the generic issues or questions inevitably posed by geopolitics, in any situation involving the coexistence of more or less independent politically organized societies. This is what constitutes the general object of study in International Studies. And we emphasized the importance of focusing on the twofold specificity of any international system: first, in terms of attending to both transhistorical and historically specific determinations at work in ordering politics and geopolitics; and second, in asking how politics and the strictly political aspects of geopolitics relate to other areas of social life and inter-societal interaction (remember that geopolitics refers to the totality of relations between and among politically organized societies).

It is a moot point among historians as to how many international systems there have been before the present international system established itself as the first fully global order somewhere between the sixteenth and nineteenth centuries (see Buzan and Little, 2000). Certainly, the Chinese Warring States referred to earlier constituted a 'regional' international system, as did the Greek city-states. In turn, there was an interaction between Carthage, Rome, the Greek city-states and the Persian Empire in the fourth century BCE, although it has been argued that this system was 'linear' in the sense that one unit interacted with another that in turn interacted with a third and so on. Linear systems can be contrasted with multiordinate systems – such as the Warring States, the Greek city-states in their dealings with one another, the early modern European states-system and, of course, the present international system – in which each unit interacts directly with all the others.

However, the modern international system is the first and only international system that has been truly global, encompassing, absorbing and subordinating all its older, smaller forerunners. It is the modern international system that is the focus of much of contemporary International Studies, and the focus of this book, and we want to offer some preliminary thoughts on the specificity (in the terms discussed above) of this particular international system.

Dating the rise of the modern system is a hotly contested issue, as you will see in Chapter 2, which argues strongly in favour of one particular interpretation of its rise. We are not going to pre-empt that debate here. However, we do need to say something to indicate the broad historical compass of what follows. For the purposes of this book, we have identified three different ways of specifying the modernity of the international system: first, the development and expansion of sovereign states and the states-system; second, the development, expansion and universalization of capitalist social relations of production, including the emergence of industrial capitalism; and third, the culture and politics of liberal (and imperial) enlightenment. That is, the modern international system had its origins in early modern European history and was bound up with a complex series of changes that included: the gradual consolidation of sovereign states and a states-system premised on the mutual recognition and formal equality of its members; the emergence and subsequent dynamic expansion of capitalism with its characteristic forms of capital accumulation, technological innovation and periodic crises; the industrial revolution based on new ways of organizing production and markets and the application of inanimate energy to productive activities in industry and then agriculture; and the development of an increasingly secular, scientific, liberal (but, as we shall see, also imperial) culture as opposed to religious and magical cosmologies and patterns of belief. We think it is important to think carefully about the connections between all of these aspects of modernity when studying the modern international system.

Our starting point for analysing the international system is the crystallization of the states-system in early modern Europe, as this defined the political and geopolitical context in which the subsequent transformations associated with modernity were to occur. There is a sense in which sovereign states form the core of the modern international system, because they are the predominant units in which political functions have been organized and institutionalized in the period since the seventeenth century in Europe. Complex processes of colonial imposition and defensive imitation, followed by selectively invited incorporation, have steadily brought other (non-European) regions and societies into the framework of the sovereign state and the states-system.

Although we begin with the consolidation of the sovereign states-system, and specifically with the reworking of early modern forms of rule and geopolitics by the development of capitalism, we shall also consider the other dimensions of the modern international system thereby established. For, as Alexander Wendt has pointed out:

> in the past two centuries ... the international system has experienced substantial institutional differentiation, first into political and economic spheres, and more recently, arguably, into a nascent sphere of global civil society as well. The ultimate cause of these changes is the spread of capitalism, which unlike other modes of production is constituted by institutional separations between spheres of social life. The transposition of this structure to the global level is far from complete, but already it is transforming the nature of international life.
>
> (Wendt, 1999, p.14)

That is to say, the contemporary international system is a states-system but it is also an expanding capitalist world economy marked by economic interdependence, technological innovation and massive inequalities. It is also an emerging realm of socio-cultural engagement in which non-state actors operate on an increasingly transnational basis. So, as well as viewing the international from the point of view of sovereign states, the states-system, the impact of capitalist social property relations on these, and the expansion of both capitalism and the states-system into the non-European world (Part 1), we also consider the international from the point of view of the socio-cultural sector of collective identities and conceptions of rights and justice (Part 2), and in terms of the economic and technological sector of production, trade and innovation as well as the social movements that mobilize around these issues (Part 3).

4   Looking forward

In answering our three framing questions, therefore, the authors in this book address these three sectors of the modern international system and they do so by drawing on a variety of approaches and debates. As a result, we shall not prejudge any of these questions. In response to the first question – 'Is it possible to analyse the international system as a whole?' – we clearly believe that it is, although it remains to be seen what kinds of answer can be given to the question of the historical specificity of the modern international system as well as to the relations between politics (and the political aspects of geopolitics) and other socio-cultural, economic and technological features of social life. In response to the second question – 'How can we best characterize, understand and explain the processes of international interaction and the kinds of order and disorder with which they are associated?' – the authors explore a wide range of different concepts and models, viewing the international system from a range of different perspectives. Along the way, they provide the materials for assembling several different models of, and narratives about, contemporary world order, which we return to in Part 4. In response to the third question – 'Is the contemporary international system changing and, if so, by whose agency?' – a central premise of this book is that it is only by attending to the historically specific features of the modern, in the light of a general problematic of the international, that the question of transformation can be coherently posed. This means that our third question is aimed primarily at an investigation of whether contemporary events represent a transformation of one form of geopolitics into another.

We do, however, want to nail our colours to the mast here in one respect. In relation to our third question, we do consider, if somewhat sceptically, the thesis that the advent of *global* social relations is bringing an end to the problematic of the international by transcending the historically given condition of geopolitics. The issue of how globalization comes about – that is, a movement towards ever more extensive and intensive social relations of global scope, operating at increasing speed and with greater effect – is discussed in this book. However, if globalization *theory* is something more than this, then it is a very bold claim indeed. In effect, it proposes that technological change at the level of the interaction capacity of the international system – essentially the ability to co-ordinate geographically dispersed activities in real-time by means of electronically mediated flows of knowledge and communication – is overcoming the plurality of politically organized societies that has existed since the advent of settled agriculture and provides the substrate of geopolitics. This book has much to say about the first of these alternatives, that is, about explanations for the globalization of processes of interaction and social relations. Given what we have already said about the problematic of the international and how we propose to study it, it is perhaps not surprising that the second alternative – that is, that digital information communication technologies are rendering the problematic of the international obsolete – is viewed rather circumspectly in these pages.

Indeed, we do not believe that globalization is about to render International Studies redundant. As Rosenberg wrote in an earlier work: 'To say that [International Studies] should be reconstituted as a social science does not entail that it either should or would disappear into sociology' (1994, p.46). This book is an attempt to present International Studies as a social science without subsuming it into sociology: the world is not yet a single society. The problematic of the international, we believe, has much life left in it.

Each part of what follows has its own introduction that sets out the key elements and details the specific contents of the individual chapters. We won't repeat that material here. Part 4 seeks to consolidate the major models that contend in debates around the problematic of the international and returns to some of the considerations sketched out in this chapter. We have provided a range of questions for you to think about as you study the text, as well as a range of study activities for you to complete. These elements are designed to encourage you to engage actively with the material and to develop the ability and confidence to apply what you have learnt for yourself. We hope that you enjoy studying this book.

Part 1 States and the states-system

A 1792 satirical cartoon of Lord Macartney 'kowtowing' to the Emperor of China (top), and Chris Patten at a ceremony to mark the handover of Hong Kong to China in 1997 (bottom)

These two photos represent either end of one particular story about how states come to be members of the states-system. The first is a cartoon imagining the first British diplomatic meeting with the Emperor of China in 1793. Britain was the most powerful, and economically the most developed, European state at the time, yet the Chinese Empire received the British as 'tribute emissaries' and demanded that they 'kowtow'. The British envoy, Lord Macartney, did kowtow, but only on one knee – signalling the beginning of a long struggle over the terms on which China would deal with other states. The Chinese Emperor, Qianlong, sent an edict to George III saying: 'We have never valued ingenious articles, nor do we have the slightest need of your country's manufactures. ... Hence we ... have commanded your tribute envoys to return safely home. You, O King, should simply act in conformity with our wishes by strengthening your loyalty and swearing perpetual obedience' (quoted in Brzezinski, 1997, pp.14–15; see also Spence, 1999). For his part, Macartney wrote in his journal that China's opposition was ultimately futile, since it was 'in vain to attempt arresting the progress of human knowledge' (cited in Spence, 1999, p.123).

The second photo shows a more recent moment in the same story: the end of British imperial control of Chinese territory in 1997 as the last Governor of Hong Kong, Chris Patten, handed the territory back to China.

In between, the British and other European powers treated China as a subordinate polity, using their power in the nineteenth century to stipulate the terms on which other polities would or would not be admitted to the club of 'modern states'. At the core of this process of sovereign recognition was 'the standard of civilization' applied by European states to other states. Using this 'test', sovereign recognition would be accorded only to states that could, among other things, guarantee basic rights such as life, property, freedom of travel and commerce, especially to foreign nationals; demonstrate an organized bureaucracy, able to provide for the state's defence; adhere to international law; participate in international diplomatic interchange; and conform to 'accepted' civilized norms such as the prohibition of slavery (Gong, 2002, p.80). Those that failed the test would not be treated as equals by European states.

In the mid-nineteenth century, China was treated as a sovereign state but was subjected to a series of 'unequal treaties' (as the Chinese called them). In 1842 China signed the Treaty of Nanking based on the civilization test, conceding that British nationals in China would be subject to British concepts of law. In 1858 China conceded further rights to Europeans over trade in the Tientsin treaties. European military superiority was confirmed when the Chinese fleet, unchanged since the fifteenth century, confronted the 'iron-clad, steam-driven' ships of the British in 1860: the entire Chinese fleet 'was reduced to matchwood. All the English suffered was the death of one sailor, struck by a stray cannonball' (Pagden, 2001, p.67). As a result, China gave foreign powers the rights to run 36 'concession' territories. At the end of the First World War China was still denied the same rights as other Western sovereign states; it was recognized as an equal only after the Japanese attack on Pearl Harbor, when the unequal treaties were ended. From the Communist revolution of 1949 until the early 1970s, the country's relationship with the West was antagonistic, but by 1971 the Peoples' Republic of China had taken up its place as a permanent member of the UN Security Council. In the 1980s and 1990s China developed extensive trade and investment relations with Western countries; in 1997 it regained Hong Kong (and in 1999 the Portuguese-controlled territory of Macao); and in 2002 it joined the World Trade Organization and committed itself to a fundamental reform of its legal system to bring it into conformity with commercial and trade practices in the wider international, capitalist economy.

Contrast this with the story of the rise of Japan, China's neighbour, to Great Power status. From the Meiji Restoration (1868) onwards, Japan sought to conduct itself in accordance with existing norms of international relations, rather than trying to resist them as China had done. Japan's attempts to act as a Great Power in the European fashion included conflict with China (1894–95), in which the Japanese were careful to conform to the laws of war; participation with Western powers in the suppression of the Boxer rebellion in China (1900–01); the Anglo-Japanese alliance of 1902; war against Russia (1904–05); and the colonial annexation of Korea (1910) and parts of China (1915). By the early twentieth century, when it started to build its empire in Asia, 'Japan had begun to behave like a Great Power and to be accepted by the Western Great Powers as a member of the ruling directorate of international society' (Suganami, 1984, pp.192–3). This seemed to be confirmed by Japan's membership of the Council of the League of Nations in 1920, yet its proposal for a clause on racial equality to be added to the League's Covenant was rejected. Only after the Second World War did the Western powers accept the principles of racial equality and sovereign equality embodied in the right to national self-determination expressed in the UN Charter. Even then, and despite becoming one of the most developed economies in the world, the legacy of Japan's defeat in the Second World War meant that it remained outside the club of the permanent members of the Security Council.

Through these different routes, both China and Japan became 'full' members of the international system. But what do these stories say about the history and nature of the states-system into which they were accepted? Do they demonstrate the creation of an indelibly European system, an imperial order based on European conceptions of what international relations should be? Are they a demonstration of the importance of power relations as the determinants of how states will treat one another? Do they show the gradual expansion and spread of a capitalist international economy? Or are they stories about the formation and gradual expansion of a universal system of accepted norms and institutions on which states and their relations with one another are constructed?

We think that these stories illustrate both the complex character of the development of the contemporary international system – the mix of the expansion of the states-system, the growth of the world economy and the role of empire – and the contested universality of the states-system. It is these issues, and the basic transformations that they involve, which are the subject matter of Part 1.

We begin, in Chapter 2, by looking at the origins and evolution of the European states-system. Benno Teschke challenges the conventional claim that the origins of the modern states-system lie in the Peace of Westphalia of 1648 – the treaties which brought to an end the Thirty Years War and which, for some, consolidated the rise of the multi-actor, territorially-fixed states-system characteristic of the modern era. Instead, Teschke argues that this system remained pre-modern and that the first truly modern state was born with the rise of capitalism in England. Thus, he traces the evolution of the modern European states-system from feudalism and the rise of the absolutist states to the eventual emergence and spread of capitalist states in the eighteenth and nineteenth centuries. He contrasts the forms taken by economic and political life in feudal Europe, and the characteristic kinds of international relations that they produced, with the development of capitalism in England and the emergence of a separate sphere of economic accumulation and interaction.

In Chapter 3, Simon Bromley explores some of the features of the European states-system that developed during the eighteenth, nineteenth and early twentieth centuries, noting that they were coincident with the establishment of European empires in most of the rest of the world. In addition to detailing some of the key rules and institutions of the 'society of states', the central question he addresses is the extent to which contemporary claims that there is a single international community, based on universally shared values, can be sustained in the light of the history of European imperialism and colonialism and continuing debates about the importance of cultural difference. The European standard of civilization was widely viewed in the non-Western world as a racist instrument of domination, which distributed sovereignty unequally based on considerations of power rather than right. It was regarded as a product of *European* civilization that was imposed upon other equally legitimate civilizations. How have things changed since then?

In Chapter 4, William Brown examines one particular interpretation of the development of the modern international system: namely, the notion that it represents the consolidation of a liberal international order. Outlining the key features of a liberal international order, he examines how it differs from systems based on either imperial control or a traditional balance of power. He examines the nature of political relations between states in a liberal order and the extent to which these transcend the condition of anarchy, the forms of economic co-operation among states, and the multilateral institutions that help to bind the liberal order together. Brown presents the idea of a liberal international order in its own terms, but he also develops two lines of criticism: first, that it rests upon a particular distribution of power and, second, that it is a product of a particular form of capitalist development. On any reading, the role of the USA is an important part of any account of liberal order.

In Chapter 5, the final chapter in Part 1, Simon Bromley considers some aspects of the role of US power in the international system and, specifically, the prospects that it will extend the liberal order it has been associated with since the end of the Second World War. He considers US power in a number of settings – in the transatlantic arena, in relation to Russia and China, and in new asymmetric conflicts involving terrorism and the doctrine of pre-emption – and draws upon Marxist (and other) theories to speculate about how the USA might shape the future of international order.

Chapter 2 The origins and evolution of the European states-system

Benno Teschke

1   Introduction

This chapter begins by discussing the origins of the modern states-system and, in doing that, puts forward a particular view of what it is that determines the character of the states-system. From this basis, subsequent chapters in Part 1 go on to assess the nature of the European states-system, its geographical spread, and debates about the contemporary character of, and changes to, the international system.

The predominant approach to understanding the structure of international politics in the states-system is realism (discussed in Bromley, 2004). It operates with a sharp distinction between the hierarchical character of (domestic) politics within states and the anarchical nature of (international) politics between and among states. The structure of international politics is determined by the distribution of power among states. The realist approach describes changes in the states-system in terms of alterations in the distribution (or balance) of power as the resources available to states (or to coalitions of states) changes. What is sometimes called the 'polarity' of the system, that is, the number of major or great powers, may change in what remains an otherwise unaltered anarchical international political structure.

Question

What features of the international system's political structure does realism leave out in describing change?

I want to identify two features in particular: changes in the nature of the societies that make up the system, and transformations in the character of international relations even while the system as a whole remains 'anarchic'.

According to realists, the political structure of an international system is defined by the anarchic character of relations between and among the units (or states) comprising the system, and by the distribution of power resources across those states. Realists see anarchy as a constant, invariant feature of all international politics and contend that the nature of the societies and economies over which states rule is irrelevant for an understanding of international interaction and behaviour, since all states are driven to behave similarly by a common concern with security and power in a self-help system. In effect, this only leaves the distribution of power as a marker distinguishing one international system from another.

Realist theory, at least in the form adumbrated by Kenneth Waltz (1979), is a relatively transhistorical kind of theory. It aims to apply to any system where there is a plurality of independent interacting political units. Realists often argue that their theory of the balance of power can apply just as much to the city-states of ancient Greece, the rise and fall of the Roman Empire, and the myriad political forms of feudal Europe as it can to the contemporary world of nation states. It is a theory of international politics that has constant change (of the distribution of power) within an invariant structure (anarchy), with a never-ending mechanism (the balance of power).

This chapter will present a very different analysis. I argue:

■ that there is more than one form of geopolitics consistent with a formally anarchical states-system, that is, a system in which the member states recognize no sources of authority above themselves

■ that the precise character of the dominant geopolitical logic in any plurality of states is best explained by the character of the configuration between the political and the economic that organizes production in the states concerned.

I shall argue that different ways of organizing the economic life of society – what I shall call, following Karl Marx, different social property relations – are systematically related to different forms of state and, correspondingly, different patterns of geopolitical interaction and behaviour.

1.1 The theory and history of the states-system: the 'myth' of Westphalia

My argument is informed by a different theoretical perspective from that of realism – it is a Marxist approach – and it is based on close attention to different historical forms of state and society. To explain the historical changes taking place at the level of politics and geopolitics, I shall argue that we need to relate these to the economic character of the societies concerned, to the forms of property and class relations involved in historically specific ways of organizing economic life.

Thus, the key theoretical claim of this chapter is that a Marxist approach, which looks at the relations between social property relations, forms of state and patterns of geopolitical interaction, is better able to account for the historically specific features of the modern states-system than the timeless generalizations of realism.

Geopolitics
Geopolitics as used here refers to politics between and among political communities, whatever the nature of those communities – for example, lordships, kingdoms, empires, city-states. It is, therefore, a more general term than international politics, which refers to politics between and among territorial states.

Social property relations
Brenner defines social property relations as 'the relationships among the direct producers, among the class of exploiters (if any exists), and between the exploiters and producers, which specify and determine the regular and systematic access of the individual economic actors (or families) to the means of production *and* to the economic product' (Brenner, 1986, p.26).

Specifically, I aim to show that many of the generalizations made in realist arguments gloss over important differences and involve false generalizations from one set of circumstances to another. Features of states, and of inter-state interaction and behaviour, are often presented as transhistorical, as operating across different times and places, when they are in fact, on closer inspection, seen to be historically specific to a particular time and set of circumstances. Chief among the circumstances that matter, I believe, are how states relate to societies and most especially how political power relates to the organization of economic life. Consequently, an important part of what follows involves taking a very close look at some issues of European economic life that are often passed over in debates about the European states-system. It is only by attending to this underlying detail that we shall be able to uncover the changing nature of such things as 'states' and 'sovereignty', thereby seeing that different forms of organizing economic and political power can have very different consequences for the logic of the system as a whole.

Since I am concerned to illuminate the character of the contemporary (modern) states-system, I shall focus my historical critique on what is widely taken to be a founding moment of that system: namely, the Peace of Westphalia (1648), which ended the catastrophic Thirty Years War in early modern Europe. The Peace Treaties of Westphalia occupy a central place in the discourse of the modern states-system; indeed it is often called the Westphalian system, signifying for many analysts an epochal turning point in the history of modern international relations. In this classical perspective, shared by realism, the Westphalian Peace Congress marked the end of claims to primacy within Europe of the Catholic Church and the Holy Roman Empire, and the beginning of the codification of the core principles for a modern system of states which came to conceive itself as a society comprised of plural and legally independent entities (the self-conception of this 'society' of states is explored in more detail in Chapter 3). This view argues that Europe moved from an international order marked by hierarchy, with the Catholic Church and the Holy Roman Empire (which made claims to authority over Christendom and a large swathe of Western Europe) at the top, to one of anarchy among formally equal sovereign territorial states.

The principal historical argument of this chapter is that while Westphalia did indeed mark something of a turning point in the development of the European states-system, it did not mark the origins of the *modern* system. That came later. Rather, I shall argue that we have to understand the modern international system as the result of two transitions. The first, in which Westphalia did play a role, was the consolidation of a system of absolutist, dynastic states out of the complex and fragmented political world of feudalism. In this system, the patterns of co-operation and conflict were tied to the state as the personal property of a hereditary monarch, and while state territory became politically and juridically more consolidated, it continued to shift geographically. The second transition, which established the patterns of co-operation and conflict familiar in the modern international system (discussed in detail in Chapter 3), involved the emergence and spread of a specifically capitalist form of sovereign statehood and a corresponding form of territoriality and inter-state system. This second and later transition, from absolutist to capitalist geopolitics, was associated above all with developments in seventeenth and eighteenth-century England and offered a different model of diplomacy and geopolitics to that associated with the leading absolutist state of the time – France.

To anticipate the argument to follow, Westphalia codified a set of pre-modern, absolutist practices of statecraft. It was only the second transition – from feudalism to capitalism in England – that established the beginning of the essential features of a modern system: impersonal public authorities recognizing one another's sovereign independence and formal equality.

1.2 A preview

It is likely that the following historical ground will be unfamiliar to you, and the theoretical argument is new, so I shall try to set out the main things to look out for before we begin. You might find it useful to return to this at the end of each section.

Section 2 sets out the basic features of economic and political life in feudal Europe and argues that the central institution of that society – lordship – was both a way of organizing the agrarian economy and the basis of political rule. It also argues that because the means of coercion (and hence political power) were dispersed among many, hierarchically related lords, with geographically over-lapping and variable rights and powers, there was no clear distinction between domestic and international affairs. Together, these features meant that the feudal 'state' consisted of an association of lords and that geopolitical competition involved the conquest of territories and peoples based on investment in the means of coercion. Section 2 aims to provide a general introduction to the basic character of the feudal economy, state and geopolitics.

This feudal world emerged out of the collapse of the Carolingian Empire, which takes its name from the Frankish King and Emperor, Charlemagne, who ruled most of present-day France, Germany, Austria, Italy, and northeast Spain, that is, most of the lands of the former Roman Empire in the West. Section 3 looks at the nature of the Empire and examines how, as it disintegrated, political power was privatized and fragmented resulting in feudalism. It shows that there were two important legacies of these developments for the future of European geopolitics: first, henceforth Europe's geopolitics would always comprise a multi-actor system with rival centres of political power; and second, there were pronounced regional differences in the balance of forces between peasants, lords and princes in the feudal world, which gave rise to different trajectories of future development.

These diverging trajectories of development, particularly the different patterns of state formation that they gave rise to, are the subject of Section 4. I take two states that are often held to be exemplars of the modern state – France and England – and argue that, because of the different character of feudal institutions in each, they in fact exhibited radically different patterns of state formation. In France, between the eleventh and fourteenth centuries, a comparatively weak French monarchy gradually and slowly extended its rule over France in competition with local lords. In England a strong, centralized state emerged, based on close collaboration between lords and monarchy.

This initial divergence in the patterns of state formation in France and England conditioned how each responded to the major economic and demographic crises that convulsed Europe in the fourteenth and fifteenth centuries. Section 5 explores these differences and argues that France saw the consolidation of a form of absolutism, in which the state was the patrimonial property of the ruling dynasty and where lords became absorbed into the absolutist state apparatus, while the independent peasantry became subject to centralized taxation. By contrast, in England peasants were driven from the land and became property-less workers, while lords became landed property owners, employing tenant farmers, in an increasingly capitalist economy. Instead of dynastic absolutism, England saw the development of a constitutional monarchy, in which the state increasingly served as a general political framework for the capitalist economy.

Sections 6 and 7, respectively, show that the typical geopolitics associated with the French-style absolutist state and the English model of a capitalist polity are very different. The former Westphalian order was characterized by a fundamentally pre-modern form of geopolitics, based on a fusion of economic and political competition and on a direct link between the 'private' fortunes of the ruling dynasty and the 'public' activities of the state. Section 7 argues that it was the growing dominance and example of the latter, the capitalist–parliamentary state that developed in the late seventeenth century in England, that transformed this system into modern geopolitics based on a separation of 'private' economic and 'public' political affairs, and a clear distinction between domestic and international realms.

In Section 8 I briefly reflect on the implications of my argument for characterizing change in the international system.

This historical storyline is summarized in Figure 2.1, and you may find it a useful reference point while studying the more detailed sections that follow.

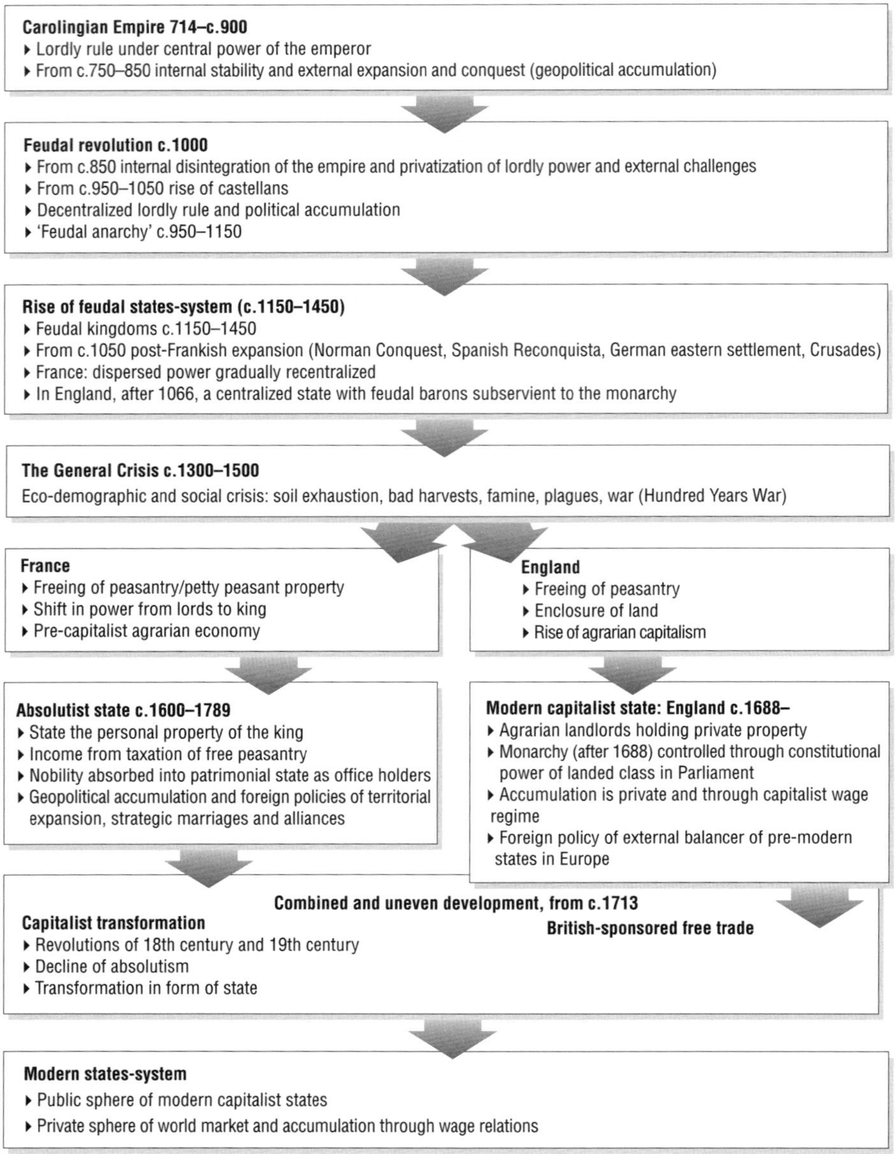

Carolingian Empire 714–c.900
▸ Lordly rule under central power of the emperor
▸ From c.750–850 internal stability and external expansion and conquest (geopolitical accumulation)

Feudal revolution c.1000
▸ From c.850 internal disintegration of the empire and privatization of lordly power and external challenges
▸ From c.950–1050 rise of castellans
▸ Decentralized lordly rule and political accumulation
▸ 'Feudal anarchy' c.950–1150

Rise of feudal states-system (c.1150–1450)
▸ Feudal kingdoms c.1150–1450
▸ From c.1050 post-Frankish expansion (Norman Conquest, Spanish Reconquista, German eastern settlement, Crusades)
▸ France: dispersed power gradually recentralized
▸ In England, after 1066, a centralized state with feudal barons subservient to the monarchy

The General Crisis c.1300–1500
Eco-demographic and social crisis: soil exhaustion, bad harvests, famine, plagues, war (Hundred Years War)

France
▸ Freeing of peasantry/petty peasant property
▸ Shift in power from lords to king
▸ Pre-capitalist agrarian economy

England
▸ Freeing of peasantry
▸ Enclosure of land
▸ Rise of agrarian capitalism

Absolutist state c.1600–1789
▸ State the personal property of the king
▸ Income from taxation of free peasantry
▸ Nobility absorbed into patrimonial state as office holders
▸ Geopolitical accumulation and foreign policies of territorial expansion, strategic marriages and alliances

Modern capitalist state: England c.1688–
▸ Agrarian landlords holding private property
▸ Monarchy (after 1688) controlled through constitutional power of landed class in Parliament
▸ Accumulation is private and through capitalist wage regime
▸ Foreign policy of external balancer of pre-modern states in Europe

Combined and uneven development, from c.1713

Capitalist transformation
British-sponsored free trade
▸ Revolutions of 18th century and 19th century
▸ Decline of absolutism
▸ Transformation in form of state

Modern states-system
▸ Public sphere of modern capitalist states
▸ Private sphere of world market and accumulation through wage relations

Figure 2.1 The origins of the modern states-system in Europe

2 Politics and geopolitics in medieval Europe

What does it mean to talk about geopolitical relations in medieval Europe prior to Westphalia (Teschke, 1998)? The modern state, and states-system, involves an evident separation between domestic and international politics, the former hierarchically organized within the state and the latter anarchically ordered between states. At the same time, this system involves a division, defined in law, between the 'public' and the 'private', a central aspect of which is the separation of a 'private' economic realm of markets and property rights and a 'public' political realm of the state and government. Compared to this, the medieval social order was neither characterized by a clear demarcation between the domestic and the international spheres, nor by the institutional separation of politics and economics. In fact, the fundamental problem with the medieval world is to determine the nature of the political (and the geopolitical) and to specify the actors that were qualified to conduct 'international' relations at the time.

As we shall see, the central institution of feudal life – that is, lordship – was both economic and political, and relations among lords were both hierarchical and anarchical. Medieval politics and geopolitics contained vertical relations of subordination and horizontal relations of co-ordination among highly differentiated carriers of political power. It is, therefore, misleading to analyse the range of these diverse political authorities – pope, emperor, kings, dukes, counts, bishops, cities, lords – as if they were state-like units, because none of them enjoyed the modern state's monopoly of the means of violence guaranteeing exclusive control over a bounded territory. Political authority was dispersed, fragmented and overlapping, unlike the bounded, unified and exclusive authority claimed by modern sovereign states. That is to say, the people in a given territory might owe allegiance to a range of different authorities, both political and religious, on different matters.

2.1 The basic character of feudalism

Classically, the literature on feudalism follows either Max Weber (1968), who conceptualized feudal politics as a type of patrimonial power (or 'personal rule'), or the French historian, Mark Bloch (1961), who studied feudalism as a specific form of agrarian economy based on a dependent peasantry. Patrimonial power, according to Weber, is a form of rule that is an extension of the rulers' extended household, in which administration and force are under the direct, personal control of a ruler. Feudalism was patrimonial rule dispersed geographically among subordinates (vassals), based on personal ties between the overlord and his vassals. A dependent peasantry, in Bloch's sense, is one that has access to the means of subsistence, the land and its

Feudalism
Feudalism can be defined politically as a personalized and geographically decentralized system of rule, and economically as the local and coercive extraction of surplus from a dependent peasantry, the two dimensions being fused in the institution of lordship and the feudal vassalic pyramid.

produce, but from which a ruling class is able to extract coercively a share of the total output. Thus, Weber defines feudalism primarily in political terms, as a form of rule, whereas Bloch sees it as a type of agrarian economy and set of class relations.

Question

Can you think of a connection between Weber's feudal politics and Bloch's feudal economy?

Hint: Think about what might happen in circumstances where the means of violence are dispersed among a range of power centres rather than monopolized by a centralized, territorial state.

Compared with the modern state and states-system, the most striking feature of the feudal world was the absence of a state monopoly in the means of violence. Instead, the means of violence were distributed among the members of the dominant class, typically in a pyramid of lord–vassal–sub-vassal relations. The means of violence and the political power they supported simultaneously served as a mode of dominating and exploiting the mass of direct producers – the peasantry – in a predominantly agrarian economy. Since these direct producers were, as a rule, in possession of the means of subsistence, feudal lords had to force access to peasant production by coercive political means, backed by their personal share in the means of violence. This was how they reproduced themselves as political lords. In short, Weber's political powers and Bloch's economic powers were fused together in the institution of feudal lordship.

Karl Marx spoke about the connections between the economic and political aspects of this form of society as follows:

> It is clear, too, that in all forms where the actual worker himself remains the 'possessor' of the means of production and the conditions of labour needed for the production of his own means of subsistence, the property relationship must appear at the same time as a direct relationship of domination and servitude, and the direct producer therefore an unfree person. ... Under these conditions, the surplus labour for the nominal landowner can only be extorted from them by extra-economic compulsion, whatever the form this might assume.

(Marx, 1981, p.926)

This is a difficult passage, but Marx is saying that because peasant producers have a degree of control over the land and its produce, and are thereby able to reproduce themselves (that is, provide the food and shelter necessary for themselves and their families), those seeking property rights in peasant output must stake their claim by force. The Marxist historian Robert Brenner

(1986 and 1987) has argued that these relations gave rise to a particular set of dynamics quite different from capitalist societies. Access to peasant surpluses (that is, output over and above that necessary to reproduce the peasantry) required coercive political means – Marx's 'extra-economic compulsion' – and so lords engaged in political accumulation, that is, they attempted to build up their political and coercive power in order to ensure their own economic security and expansion. The economic (or class) power of lords, the power to extract economic resources from the peasantry, depended on access to political power, which in turn gave access to property rights, including rights over the produce and labour of the direct producers themselves. Feudal ruling-class power meant investment in the means of coercion. Whereas growth in a capitalist economy requires investment in the means of production, or capital accumulation, the ability of lords to expand their economic output required 'investment' in the means of coercion – hence Brenner's term 'political accumulation'.

Political accumulation
Political accumulation refers to the strategy of feudal lords to build up greater coercive powers, political domination and control over territory in order to extract greater surplus out of dependent peasant producers, leading over time to the development of stronger 'states'.

Question

How would you describe the class relations of a feudal society?

As a rule, the class relations between producers (peasants) and non-producers (lords and their vassals) took the form of a 'rent-regime', in which serfs were compelled either to hand over part of their produce to a lord, in cash or in kind, to work for the lord on his demesne (the part of an estate worked directly for the lord), or to rent land. These relations were embodied in the institution of the lordship –both a unit of authority and an agrarian economic enterprise – that constituted the basic building block of the medieval 'state'. Therefore, the producers in a feudal economy, the peasants, had part control over their means of production and their ability to work as did the feudal lords, and class relations were both economic and political. This is represented in Tables 2.1 and 2.2 overleaf. In Table 2.1, I have added two other kinds of producer for comparison. Slaves own no property, they are the property of others, and they have no control over their labour power. An independent producer owns his or her means of production and controls his or her labour power. In Table 2.2, I have presented idealized descriptions of three types of social property relations.

Class
A class is a set of individuals with the same relationship of ownership, part ownership or non-ownership to the factors of production, which include the means of production (the material things that are needed in order to produce) and the labour power (the ability to work) of the producers.

Table 2.1   Class relations

		Does the producer own his or her labour power?		
		Yes	Partly	No
Does the producer own his or her means of production?	Yes	Independent producer		
	Partly		Serfdom	
	No			Slavery

Table 2.2   Types of social property relations

Mode	What is the purpose of production?	What is the form in which the surplus is extracted from the direct producers?	What are the means by which the surplus is extracted?
Slavery	Use and market, depending on context	Direct appropriation by the slave-owner	Slave-owner has control over the life of the slave
Feudalism	Largely for use, some for market	Peasant works on lord's land, or peasant hands some output (in kind or money) to lord, or peasant pays rent to lord	Through coercion: the lord has local monopoly over the means of violence and hence political power
Capitalism	Largely for market	Surplus value extracted in the process of production and realized as profits reaped by earnings from sale on markets after payment of costs, including the cost of employing labour power	Workers have no ownership of the means of production and hence must offer their labour power to property owners in return for wages

2.2   The feudal 'state' and its geopolitics

This fusion of political domination and economic exploitation in the Middle Ages had a direct impact on the structure of medieval political authority. The sharing of power among the individual members of the ruling class who presided in their lordships over dependent peasants implied that the 'feudal state', viewed as an ensemble of lordships, was geographically decentralized, institutionally personalized, and inherently subject to inter-lordly competition over their relative share in land and labour. This is expressed in Perry Anderson's (1974) notion of 'parcellized sovereignty'. Unlike the modern state's monopoly over the legitimate use of force, the feudal state was more an association of lords, each of whom had personal control over a part of the means of legitimate force. Land was not owned by lords as private property, but as a rule held as a fief from an overlord. Overlords granted fiefs – that is, conditional control over land – in return for obligations to perform certain military and administrative services. In other words, even the property rights of lords were never absolute but conditional upon the performance of certain obligations, laid down in a mutual vassalic 'contract'. This was directed upwards to whoever occupied the apex of the feudal pyramid, usually the king. Yet this relation between lord and overlord – often stretching over various levels – did not imply absolute hierarchy and subordination precisely because lords were not civil servants or functionaries of the state but arms-bearing land-holders and, in that capacity, full political lords. For these reasons, German medieval historians refer to this phenomenon as 'a state of associated persons' (*Personenverbandsstaat*) (Mayer, 1963; Mitteis, 1975).

As bearers of arms, which were necessary both for the subjection of the peasantry and for the provision of military and advisory services to their overlords, lords had the right to carry out feuds (Brunner, 1992) both against their overlords, if they felt injured, and against rival lords. The peculiar institution of the 'feud' straddled the boundaries between the private and the public, the domestic and the international, the legitimate and the criminal recourse to arms. In other words, because the means of violence were distributed among lords throughout the feudal pyramid in the context of an agrarian political economy based on a lord/peasant rent-regime, medieval polities were neither internally completely pacified and governed by an impersonal law, nor purely anarchical and governed by considerations of the balance of power. Consequently, just as the economic and the political were fused together, so too were the domestic and the 'international'. It is not possible to partition feudal politics into a bounded domestic realm of internal hierarchy on the one hand, and external anarchy on the other. There was, therefore, no distinct sphere of anarchical 'international' relations in which power balancing among distinct polities could operate (see Chapter 3).

What, then, drove medieval political and geopolitical relations? I noted above that the building block of feudal society was the institution of lordship. Access to property was politically established, and every individual lord stood in a double-edged antagonistic position between a dependent but resisting peasantry and competing rival lords. As a result of this, lordly strategies of reproduction required systematic investment in the means of violence, rather than in the means of production, to control land and labour. This is what Brenner means by the phrase 'political accumulation'. This imperative produced a series of military technological innovations, while stalling innovations in economically productive technology. Peasants produced mainly for subsistence purposes, that is, for their own consumption, and thus their incentives were to diversify production rather than to specialize; lords extracted a surplus mainly for non-productive consumption (military equipment and conspicuous consumption), and so the long-term economic dynamic was relatively static. In capitalist societies, capital accumulation is generally associated with technological innovation – more efficient ways of using economic inputs to produce outputs (see Chapter 10). In the feudal economy, political accumulation resulted primarily in military innovations because peasants had little incentive to specialize along the lines of comparative advantage and lords had to maintain their security and coercive positions.

However, the systematic build-up of military power was also the precondition for, as well as a consequence of, intensifying the exploitation of labour, the conquest of neighbouring regions, direct internecine warfare with overlords and co-vassals, the reclamation, cultivation and defence of new lands, and the successful conduct of marital policies and inheritance conflicts to acquire land. The acquisition of land translated directly into a geographical extension of state territory, and thus feudal territoriality was – in contrast to modern territoriality – always shifting, contracting and expanding according to the martial and marital fortunes of its noble class. Not only did political accumulation imply an absence of fixed territorial borders, but any given territory comprised various layers of lord–vassal–sub-vassal relations; one patch of land could have several political masters with differentiated claims to it.

This meant that the ground of feudal territory was constantly shifting and fragmented and that political space was not clearly delineated by frontiers but by 'marches', or border zones. Precisely because these zones were permanently contested, they also enjoyed special liberties and privileges of military command granted by the king and exercised by marcher lords who thus established semi-autonomous marcher lordships – strongholds that posed as much threat to the neighbouring feudal kingdom as to the kingly overlord himself. The rights to war were not monopolized by the state, but oligopolistically enjoyed by the hierarchy of lords, and so peace was a variegated affair, sponsored by differentiated actors in the form of the 'peace of the land', the 'peace or truce of God', or the 'peace of towns'.

Question

To contemporary eyes, the feudal world can look very strange. Based on the features described above, how would you describe the key differences between feudalism and the contemporary world?

Whereas in the contemporary world there is a relative separation of a 'private' economy and the 'public' sphere of politics and the state (discussed further in Section 5.3), in the feudal era these were fused in the institution of lordship. The ability of a lord to pursue private gain relied on possession of political resources, especially the use of force. Force was used both to extract surplus from the peasantry and to pursue feuds with other lords and overlords. This had two consequences. Unlike modern states, the legitimate use of force was dispersed among many lords and overlords. 'States' as such were not the clearly territorially-defined units under a unified, exclusive authority, but shifting associations of lords with complex and overlapping territorial boundaries. Secondly, economic development was relatively static as lords pursued political accumulation (greater military power, territory and political power) rather than investment in the means of production. Geopolitics, then, consisted of competition over feudal property relations in the form of political and geopolitical accumulation and feuding, and warfare embraced both aspects of 'civil' war and war between polities. Realist attempts to describe this as a struggle for security in a self-help environment (for example, Fischer, 1992) gloss over these fundamental differences.

3 From the Carolingian Empire to a multi-actor system

The previous section established in general terms one crucial part of my argument, that is, that the specific class characteristics of a specific property regime (feudalism) produce a certain kind of geopolitics (geopolitical accumulation of territory and the means of coercion). In this section I want to look more closely at the historical detail of the rise of the feudal system.

So far, in describing the central institution of feudal society as lordship, and in tracing some of its implications, I have talked of lordship in general. In other words, I have been generalizing about feudal society. However, the historical literature distinguishes three dominant types of lordship that were different in the ways in which they were institutionalized (Duby, 1974; Rösener, 1992). First, *banal lordship* referred to the general royal power of command, taxation, decreeing and jurisdiction. Second, *domestic lordship* conferred absolute power over personal dependants (ranging from serfdom to slavery). Third, *landlordship* involved land ownership, tenant freedom and only limited rights of service. The long-term institutional dynamic of feudal power in Western Europe can be traced in terms of different constellations of these three kinds of lordship, that is, institutions which regulated both lordly power and inter-lordly relations. In brief outline, this was a trajectory from an imperial formation (c.750–950), via the times of feudal anarchy (c.950–1150), to the reconsolidation of multiple feudal kingdoms (c.1150–1450). In this section, I chart the first of these shifts in European geopolitical order, from the imperial hierarchy of the Carolingian Empire to the period of feudal anarchy. This shift is synonymous with the transition from the early to the late Middle Ages.

The exposition of the general character of feudal social property relations, state and geopolitics presented above remains incomplete without a demonstration of how these 'forms' were expressed in the actual history of medieval Europe. In what follows, I shall argue that since the geopolitical dynamics of the medieval order derived from lordly strategies of political accumulation, we can understand this history as the result of conflicting strategies of reproduction (a) between the lordly class and the peasantry, (b) amongst the members of the lordly class, and (c) between feudal polities and external communities.

3.1   The Carolingian Empire

At its zenith (during the eighth and ninth centuries), the Carolingian Empire embraced the whole of Gaul (including Septimania and Brittany), western and southern Germany (including Saxony, Frisia and parts of the middle Danube region), the north-eastern Iberian Peninsula, and Lombardian Italy (see Figure 2.2 for details). Its heyday came with the coronation of Charlemagne (King of the Franks 768–814), who was crowned Emperor by Pope Leo II in 800. The Carolingian polity was remarkable for the pronounced public office structure on which it was based. Here, significant elements of an imperial system of public governance and central control existed, operated by counts, vice-counts and *missi* (landless royal inspectors) (Ganshof, 1971; Nelson, 1995). *Missi* were temporary but plenipotentiary royal inspectors originally entrusted with the judicial, fiscal and military supervision of landed counts. They were empowered to override the decisions of regional counts and to penalize abuses of power. In shuttling between the peripatetic imperial court and their local districts, these landless *missi* formed the main pillar of imperial public governance, central control and statehood around the year 800. This office structure was directly dependent upon a strong institution of kingship, epitomized by the *king's monopoly of the ban* – the power to tax, command, decree and adjudicate. Kingship itself was dynastic, hereditary, and personal, that is patrimonial in character. The kingdom was regarded as the king's private property.

Figure 2.2   The geographical extent and nature of territoriality and borders of the Carolingian Empire

The class relations of the Empire combined elements of public power inherited from the Roman Empire with more feudal interpersonal 'Germanic' elements. On the one hand, local lords had absolute authority, that is, domestic lordship, over their dependants. The classical Carolingian manor was bi-partite. It was divided into the lord's demesne, worked by slaves and serfs personally bound to the lord, and tenements cultivated by those same peasants for their own subsistence (Duby, 1968). On the other hand, there was a substantial though decreasing number of free and arms-bearing peasants exclusively subject to, and taxed by, royal counts who were recruited from the privileged imperial Frankish aristocracy and who exercised royal banal lordship (Goetz, 1995). These two forms of lordship (domestic and banal) were associated with a distinct division of political competencies and powers in which a local lordly class, extracting rents in labour and in kind from slaves and serfs on their manors, sat alongside the king/Emperor, directly taxing (through his counts) his free peasantry. This afforded the free peasantry a degree of protection from the ambitions of local lords and generated resources for the king that left the estates of the lords untouched. This had the effect of moderating lordly competition for access to peasant surpluses.

The comparatively extraordinary degree of internal stability, peace and public order during Charlemagne's reign was predicated upon this two-tiered class structure which fostered the conditions for successful external aggression. Indeed, the relative stability of the Carolingian polity was also underwritten by the state-consolidating implications of Frankish strategies of political accumulation within the wider system of geopolitical relations. The latent conflict between the imperial aristocracy and lesser lords over access to peasant surpluses was cushioned by the relentless cycles of conquest, pegging the landholding class to a supreme warlord continuously engaged in the systematic redistribution of conquered land and the wider spoils of war (tribute, treasure, women, slaves, arms, cattle) amongst his contented and loyal imperial and local aristocracy (Haldon, 1993). The Empire was a conquest state, its economy to a large degree a 'war economy', so that the authority of the kingly ban remained unchallenged as long as the Emperor succeeded in providing his aristocratic followers with extended opportunities for personal enrichment.

3.2 The break-up of the Carolingian Empire and the 'feudal revolution'

Around 850, however, the opportunities for external conquest dried up. Offensive campaigns turned into defensive wars. Vikings, Hungarians and Saracens made deep inroads into the heartlands of the Carolingian Empire and turned the logic of plunder against the Frankish lords. Under conditions of weakened imperial authority, a profound crisis of ruling class solidarity led to the disintegration of the imperial state (Teschke, 2003). Dissatisfied lords started to usurp public offices as a counter-strategy to offset lost income opportunities, build up personal entourages of warriors holding land from them, and began to patrimonialize 'their' fiefs, that is, to treat conditional grants of land from the king as personal property to be held in the family. To the degree that the spoils of war dwindled and that the Franks were now themselves constrained to pay tributes to the Normans, the nobility had to rely more and more on land and the peasantry as primary sources of income. In this context, the malcontent, local nobility developed an interest in 'privatizing' public political powers in order to strengthen its political hold on the peasant population. Regional lords entered into a period of open conflict with their nominal overlords, the post-imperial states. Internal redistribution of titles to wealth became the logical alternative to external conquest.

The result of this was that between circa 900 and 1050, the centralized political powers of the empire were broken up and decentralized. In particular, the royal power of the ban was appropriated by lords all the way down the ladder of political units – from dukes to margraves, counts, vice-counts – until even the least landed lord, the castellan, had appropriated powers previously reserved by the king (Duby, 1953). Castellans, often exercising control over a tiny territory of a few villages and half a dozen small lordships, transformed their banal lordships into quasi-sovereign mini-states (Hilton, 1990). This meant the 'privatization' of public justice, the localization of fiefs, arbitrary taxation, and the general subjection of the remaining free peasantry to the status of serfdom (Bonnassie, 1991a/b). During the critical period of general political disintegration around the millennium, the protective link between the hitherto free peasantry and royal public power was cut, delivering the peasantry to the mercy of their immediate castellans. Independent peasants were turned into serfs; this was the process known to historians as the 'feudal revolution' (Poly and Bournazel, 1991).

For around 200 years, from 950 to 1150, castellans became the prime actors in medieval political life, forming henceforth the territorial nuclei on the power–political, geo-strategic map. Once public power was completely individualized, castellans turned upon themselves in fierce inter-lordly competition over the appropriation and enforcement of lucrative former public rights, unleashing the general 'feudal anarchy' and violence associated with post-Carolingian Europe. This new constellation of lordly power went hand in hand with changes in the military order and innovations in military technology during the tenth and eleventh centuries (Bartlett, 1993). Local, banal lordship necessitated a heavy militarization of encastled lords by means of the formation of mounted executive forces – the knights – and ushered in a breakdown in ruling class solidarity in the form of sharpened competition over land, labour and privileges. The old Carolingian light cavalry and the free peasant armies gave way to the rise of the heavy cavalry of the knightly class, the demilitarization of the formerly free peasantry, and the widespread appearance of new small, but high, stone castles designed for local power protection.

Although the feudal revolution was a highly uneven process, geographically and historically, it produced profound changes in noble proprietary consciousness, inheritance law and family forms. Changing property titles led to a heightening of aristocratic family consciousness over inheritance patterns and a corresponding tightening of lineage in favour of agnatic primogeniture, that is, to firstborn son. This was a means of safeguarding property against further division and guaranteeing the territorial integrity of the ancestral family seat. Hereditability of lordships and fiefs spawned constrictions in the rules of land succession and changes to family law. Kindreds turned into dynasties. Henceforth, we find the particle of origin 'de', 'von', and 'of' in dynastic family names next to the adoption of the toponymic surnames, indicating where they came from, and heraldic emblems, even among the lower landed nobility. This was a clear pointer to the making of a new distinct social identity of the noble class hereafter rooted in ancestral family seats.

In the context of the population growth of the eleventh century, the effect of primogeniture (the right of succession of the firstborn), combined with growing land scarcity in the post-Carolingian heartlands, produced two typical responses in economies based upon coerced agrarian production. Internal expansion, the conquest of nature, was coupled with external expansion, the conquest of people. Frankish Europe entered into an important phase of internal colonization and large-scale land reclamation and land clearances, vastly expanding the total area under cultivation in the Frankish heartlands of Europe (Bloch, 1966). However, given that the scope for land reclamations within the borders of the old Frankish Empire was finite, internal colonization was accompanied and supplemented by external colonization, the conquest of foreign peoples (Wickham, 1994). The closure of the lineage in favour of the eldest son immediately posed the chronic question of the provision of the wherewithal for other noble sons. And it was precisely these younger sons, the 'youths', who most 'naturally' began to look beyond the narrow confines of their homelands (Duby, 1977).

The very extension and diversification of the ruling strata, featuring now a knightly class itself aspiring to land as the economic basis of maintenance and status, added a particularly restless, highly militarized, and aggressive element to the composition of the nobility. These knightly cadets were the most decisive executioners of late eleventh-century geopolitical expansion, for by around 1050 the redistribution of arable land within the post-Carolingian core areas came to a halt. Warlords had to look elsewhere to satisfy their thirst for land and booty, either for themselves or for their growing numbers of knights. This phase marks the origins of feudal expansion based on a radically feudalized and militarily fragmented, that is, politically decentralized, society.

Finally, it is this dynamic context of heightened inter-lordly competition over land and labour that provides the explanation for four great expansionary movements of the time. The post-Frankish knights asserted their land hunger by setting out to conquer the British Isles (Norman Conquest, 1066); southern Italy and the eastern Mediterranean (Italy in 1061 and the First Crusade, 1096–99); the Iberian peninsula (*Reconquista*, 1035); and large stretches of the Slavonic lands east of the Elbe–Saale line (*Deutsche Ostsiedlung*, 1110). Out of the millennial crucible of the 'feudal revolution', lordship-based political communities spread all over Europe with a lasting influence on the various regional processes of state formation throughout late medieval and early modern times. These knight-led expansionary movements were not completed until the fifteenth century, and established the institutional and geographical parameters for the subsequent geopolitical organization of the European early modern system of states.

In summary, the 'feudal revolution' of the year 1000 established a new mode of political domination and economic exploitation, spawning a series of closely interrelated novel phenomena.

- Socially, it changed the status of virtually all direct producers to that of serfdom.

- Politically, it ushered in a prolonged crisis of public governance resulting in the feudalization of political power.

- Militarily, it gave rise to an internal differentiation within the nobility associated with the emergence of the knightly class.

- Geopolitically, it marked the point of departure for an extraordinary display of noble 'political accumulation', resulting in four expansionary outward movements driving the late Frankish lords over the borders of the Carolingian core lands into hitherto unconquered regions.

Activity 2.1

To check your understanding of feudal geopolitics and the break-up of the Carolingian Empire, explain why these expansionary movements took place.

The 'transnational' Frankish nobility set out to conquer Europe and the resulting feudalism created a world, or at least a European world, in its own image.

These developments had two important consequences for the subsequent course of European political and geopolitical history. First, the destruction of the Carolingian Empire around the year 1000 had the effect of creating *multiple* centres of political power. Future attempts by late medieval kings to recentralize feudal power took place in the context of the widespread dynastic management of land (and the associated dependent peasantry) by feudal lords and an absence of any overarching, imperial public power. Second, the break-up of the Frankish Empire led to regionally diverging, long-term trajectories of European state formation, especially in the two important cases of France and England. These were based on variations in the balance of class forces in different local areas. The end result, after the general crisis of the fourteenth and fifteenth centuries, was two radically different state–society complexes. These diverging trajectories of state formation in England and France, and their consequences for the European states-system, are examined in Section 4.

4 Diverging feudal state formation in France and England

The decline of the Carolingian Empire outlined above imposed a new property settlement on large parts of Europe, extended the reach of feudal relations of exploitation into the European periphery, and established the basis for a non-imperial, territorially divided, system of feudal polities headed by dynasties. Yet the specific trajectories of state formation in the high and late Middle Ages in various regions of Europe diverged considerably. This section exemplifies these divergences with regard to England and France, the two archetypical cases of modern state building that are often (falsely) assumed to be the same. I shall argue that these divergences had profound implications for the nature of the Westphalian system of states, revolving around absolutist France; and the modern system of states, revolving around capitalist Britain.

In the French case, class conflicts between the peasantry, the nobility and the king resulted in a transition from feudalism to absolutism, whereas class conflicts in England resulted in a transition from feudalism to capitalism. The outcome of these divergent, long-term trajectories meant that the French absolutist state–society complex structured the 'Westphalian' system of dynastic states, whereas the English capitalist state–society complex challenged that order and gradually imposed a different logic of international relations on continental Europe during the eighteenth and nineteenth centuries. There was, thus, not one system-wide 'medieval-to-modern' shift (Ruggie, 1986), but two shifts. These were yoked together in a long-term process of geographically combined and socially uneven development. Here I shall look at the first of these shifts; I shall comment on the second shift in Section 5.

4.1 Demographic growth and the urban revival

Before I take the case of France, I want to make some comments about the general economic situation up to the fourteenth century. For, despite economic prosperity, the feudal nature of social relations meant that there was no dynamic transformation of the economy and geopolitics remained geared to political accumulation. Indeed, between the eleventh and fourteenth centuries, feudal Europe underwent a remarkable period of economic recovery, based on population growth, reclamation of new arable land, and an intensification in the exploitation of labour following the general imposition of serfdom. Growing lordly incomes translated into growing lordly demand and this fanned an urban revival (a growth in the size and number of towns) in the twelfth and thirteenth centuries. Lordly demands for military equipment and conspicuous consumption established a system of Europe-wide, long-distance trade.

The political organization of towns took three different forms, depending on their relations with territorial lords. First, where territorial lords were strong as in France and England, towns never gained autonomy but had to co-operate with central rulers. Second, where territorial lords were weak as in northern Italy, towns gained full political autonomy and organized themselves as independent city-states (oligarchic merchant republics). Third, where power relations between territorial lords and towns were balanced as in Germany and parts of the Low Countries/Flanders, they organized themselves as semi-independent city-leagues, while also being represented in the German Imperial diet (the legislative assembly or administrative council of the Holy Roman Empire).

Inter-urban trading networks, managed by merchants operating commercial monopolies, remained entirely dependent upon aggregate lordly demand and embedded in a labour-intensive agrarian economy. The growth of commercial exchange did not alter the pre-capitalist property relations in the countryside (Dobb, 1946). In fact, inter-urban trading networks and towns eventually diminished during the fourteenth century in line with the erosion of lordly incomes during the decline of the wider agrarian economy. The feudal economy, based on political relations of exploitation, did not generate a self-sustaining cycle of economic growth. Producers continued to produce primarily for subsistence purposes and non-producers continued to reproduce themselves by customary means, that is, by trying to increase the rate of exploitation rather than by trying to increase the rate of productivity by reinvesting in the means of production. Investment in the means of violence and coercion, enabling successful political and geopolitical accumulation, remained the preferred strategy of reproduction for the noble class. Nevertheless, while this general economic pattern prevailed throughout Western Europe, regional trajectories of state formation diverged substantially during this period (Brenner, 1985b). Moreover, it was the regionally specific, lordship-based property relations that emerged from the tenth-century crisis which largely conditioned these divergences. I now consider, in turn, the trajectories of France and England.

4.2   France

The pattern of feudal state formation in Capetian France (from 'Capet', the family name of French monarchs) was determined by the complete post-millennial fragmentation of political power in the form of the banal regime (Brenner, 1996). From the late eleventh century onwards, and indeed throughout the twelfth and thirteenth centuries, the princes and the king tried to regain control over their territories. Internally this meant seeking to regain power lost to the castellans during the break-up of the Carolingian Empire and externally by competing with one another. The logic of French state building consequently unfolded under the constant pressures of geopolitical competition within the ruling class, driving smaller lords into the hands of greater lords, concentrating the political power of lords and their control of the peasantry. In this process, the Capetian monarchy deployed the whole arsenal of feudal expansionary techniques of political accumulation to establish its suzerainty (over-lordship) over *Francia* during the course of four centuries. These ranged from outright war and annexation, through dynastic marriage policies, alliance building and bribery to simple confiscation and enfeoffment (the process by which a lord was turned into a vassal), so that the local aristocracy was either suppressed, co-opted, intermarried, bought or tied to the king by unstable bonds of vassalage (Given, 1990).

However, precisely because the concentric expansion of the Capetian monarchy was a gradual, piecemeal and protracted process, the political organization of the French kingdom never achieved a unitary character. Most importantly, French 'mediatization' ('the vassal of my vassal is not my vassal') meant that there was no simple hierarchy from the king down through the ranks of the nobility. As a result, the authority of the king was only weakly recognized. Due to this absence of organization within the ruling class, the regional French nobility competed with the king for the powers to tax and control the peasantry. These competing claims to final jurisdiction were decisive for the improving status of the French peasantry (Brenner, 1985a/b). In spite of unfavourable demographic pressures, the peasantry succeeded during the course of the twelfth and thirteenth centuries in shaking off serfdom – labour rents were commuted to money rents – and in establishing by the early fourteenth century *de facto*, though not *de jure*, property rights over customary tenures, including the right to inherit. Lords in need of cash sold charters of liberty to peasant communes, thereby regulating lordly exactions and curbing their arbitrary character. Rents (*cens*), and also other dues (fines, death dues, transfer dues), that still weighed on the plots became fixed and remained unadjusted for inflation. Over time, lords were obliged to lease out demesne lands to peasants or to sell land directly (Duby, 1968). Declining rents and alienation of property brought lords to an increasingly precarious financial situation. Many castellans and knights were driven into debt and were drawn into the service of greater noble households. Alternatively, they sold themselves as mercenaries or went directly 'abroad' to carve out lordships in the non-Frankish periphery.

Meanwhile, the peasantry exploited the weakened status and disorganization of their direct lords to appeal immediately to royal courts to uphold the concessions that had been wrought from their erstwhile banal lord. In this process, the king tended to side with the peasants, for their loss of serfdom was his gain as a freed peasant paid tax to the king rather than rent to a lord, giving the monarchy a new income base and weakening the noble rival. Charters of liberty for rural communes and individual franchises dislodged much of the direct noble hold on the rural population. Wherever the local nobility tried to re-impose arbitrary taxation or customary levies to counteract their losses, a combination of peasant revolts and the French king's strategy of supporting petty peasant proprietorship in public courts, led to the long-term decline of the decentralized banal regime.

By the beginning of the fourteenth century, the French 'state' came to rest on a new constellation of social classes. The king, in theory and in practice, had become a feudal suzerain engaged in the contested establishment of a rudimentary layer of public offices in the provinces to supervise public taxation and jurisdiction. The territorial princes had become integrated into the feudal hierarchy. The independent class of banal lords and knights had vanished or had turned into a petty nobility of service for the king. Many towns had emancipated themselves from control by lords and enjoyed royal liberties. Finally, the peasantry had gained personal freedom and *de facto* property rights. Yet for all the tendencies toward administrative centralization and territorial concentration, the realm remained thoroughly feudal, that is, political power was personalized and 'parcellized' in character.

4.3   England

England after the Norman Conquest, in striking contrast to France, constituted a uniquely centralized, internally organized and socially homogenous feudal state. The specific cohesion of medieval England was the direct result of the rapid imposition of Norman rule upon Anglo-Saxon England, replicating the feudal system of ducal Normandy (Brenner, 1985b). Within two decades, the Anglo-Saxon landholding class was dispossessed and killed, its lands redistributed by William the Conqueror amongst his leading warriors – the barons. The sweeping nature of the Conquest resulted in the imposition of Norman dominion over England. In terms of the ownership, size and constitutional status of lordships, a revolution in land tenure steamrolled the country. Lords came to hold their estates 'of the king', in possession and hereditary in character, but not as private patrimonies. The king remained the supreme landowner of the entire territory. As Frankish

Gaul disintegrated into countless independent banal lordships, England was unified *en bloc*. The Norman and Plantagenet kings succeeded, despite regular baronial contestations, in retaining the *king's monopoly of the ban* after 1066. All landholding Norman nobles had to swear direct fealty to the king (Oath of Salisbury, 1086) so that the decentralizing consequences of vassalic 'mediatization' – truly detrimental for Capetian France – were blocked. The 'King's Peace', predicated upon the power of the ban, minimized the continental practices of private feuding by providing recognized and legitimate institutions for the settling of disputes over questions of land, property and privileges amongst the members of the Anglo-Norman ruling class (Kaeuper, 1988).

The sudden imposition of the tightly organized manorial regime meant that domestic lordship was closely associated with the large-scale enserfment of the Anglo-Saxon peasantry (Brenner, 1985b; 1996). Due to the self-organization of the noble class, the English peasantry was unable to shake off serfdom during the twelfth and thirteenth centuries. Noble self-organization and co-operation in the form of a centralized feudal state meant that royal law mitigated latent inter-lordly conflicts, left serfs to the exclusive jurisdiction of manorial lords (dampening thereby lord–king tensions) and free men to the exclusive royal jurisdiction under Common Law. Institutionally, revocable sheriffs staffed this supplementary layer of public legal power which operated next to the traditional inter-lordly bonds of vassalage. In a way, post-1066 authority relations were based on a dual structure which resembled the Carolingian polity described in Section 3. Norman lords held free rein to deal with their villains (serfs) on their manors, whereas the remaining free peasants (freeholders) were taxed by the king and enjoyed free access to public courts. Not surprisingly, class struggle typically took the form of peasants contesting their social status – villain or free – which acted as criterion for access to different courts: manorial or public (Hilton, 1976).

Furthermore, due to the vast landed resources of the British Isles and the overarching authority of William the Conqueror and his successors, the expansionary phase for the dynamic of political and geopolitical accumulation and, therewith, the internal cohesion of the ruling class, could be sustained well into the fourteenth century. It was only broken by the onset of an economic and demographic crisis which intensified inter-noble competition over declining revenues, setting off the Hundred Years War and the subsequent 'civil' Wars of the Roses. Between the eleventh and fourteenth centuries, Anglo-Norman lords not only conquered the Celtic fringes (conquests of Wales, Ireland, and Scotland), but also turned their acquisitiveness against the various fragmented duchies in western France, to create under the Plantagenets a realm that reached from the Hebrides to the Pyrenees (Davies, 1990). Simultaneously, martial superiority was both cause and effect of the extraordinary degree of centralization of the English kingdom, expressed in the unchallenged monopoly of the royal ban.

Activity 2.2

How would you summarize the differences in feudal state formation in France and England?

Hint: Consider the degree of control enjoyed by the central state, the relationship of the king to lords and the position of the peasantry.

---

5 The general crisis of the fourteenth and fifteenth centuries

During the fourteenth and fifteenth centuries, large parts of Europe, including France and England, entered into a deep and prolonged period of general crisis. This crisis was multi-dimensional, encompassing a massive reduction in population, poor harvests, famines and plague (the Black Death). Geopolitically it was registered in the upheaval of the Hundred Years War. However, although the crisis was general across Europe, it impacted in very different ways on different regions. In particular, the different class relationships and class conflicts of different regions meant that responses to the crisis varied. As we have just seen, the balance of class forces in fifteenth-century France and England were very different. Accordingly, the differentiated outcomes of the general crisis have to be read through the lenses of these diverging class balances. This is what I now attempt to do, again following the story as it developed in France and then England.

5.1 France: from feudalism to absolutism

I have argued that prior to the onset of the general crisis there was a gradual decline in the French lords' capacity for surplus extraction, caught between peasant resistance and royal support for petty peasant property. When the demographic crisis struck the French countryside, the lords' reaction failed due to the persistence of the pattern of peasant resistance and kingly protection of peasant freehold. As an alternative, lords turned against each other to recover income and increasingly took up offices in the 'state' during and after the Hundred Years War. Private property in the state's extractive apparatus in the form of venal offices, that is, offices of state sold to the nobility, provided new income opportunities for an increasingly de-feudalized nobility. The old sword-carrying nobility (*noblesse d'épée*) based on control of land and a dependent peasantry turned gradually into the new office nobility (*noblesse de robe*) based on service to the state. The result was the consolidation of petty peasant property, now taxed by a centrally organized *noblesse de robe* rather than owing rents to the local lord. The absolutist state now revolved around the kingly court as the centre of intrigue, faction and inter-noble rivalries. Sixteenth and seventeenth-century France saw the growing consolidation of the absolutist tax/office state, notwithstanding sporadic waves of noble resistance. The general crisis had accelerated the transformation of a feudal lord–peasant rent regime into an absolutist king–peasant tax regime.

> **Absolutist state**
> The features of the absolutist state include the fact that the state is the personal property of the king; the nobility is transformed from a land-based class into an office-holding class; and extraction of surplus from a freed peasantry mainly takes place through the royal tax system.

After the general crisis, France (and much of Europe) experienced a renewed period of economic and commercial recovery. However, this commercial upswing, the discovery of trading routes to the Americas and India, and the growth of long-distance trade did not represent a breakthrough to capitalism, but merely replicated, if on a larger scale, the nexus between growing lordly incomes and the urban revival of the twelfth century. As before, growing royal income was, as a rule, not reinvested in the means of production, but spent primarily on military equipment and conspicuous courtly consumption. This pattern drove the build-up of the permanent war state, while sapping the viability of the agrarian economy. The sixteenth-century spurt in commercial capitalism was predicated on growing kingly demand. In this process, the towns did not become laboratories of proto-capitalism. Rather, they struck a close alliance with the king who sold royal charters to privileged royal monopoly companies. Trade was predicated on politically and militarily protected trading routes to the exclusion of competitors. The king provided the military protection of overseas commerce (convoys, ports, armed merchant fleets and so on). Out-gunning, not out-pricing, characterized the logic of the great maritime–mercantile empires of the epoch.

The absolutist state did not establish the conditions for capitalist economic development and perpetuated the logic of political and geopolitical accumulation, since taxation resembled a centralized rent. A combination of punitive peasant taxation, diversified peasant production for subsistence and the subdivision of plots by inheritance, rather than specialization on markets and the concentration of land ownership, prevented an economic breakthrough. The proceeds of taxation, in turn, were pumped back into the apparatus of coercion and domination and royal conspicuous consumption. When economic and political crisis struck again in the early seventeenth century, intensified class conflict over the distribution of income led to peasant revolts, noble unrest and royal repression. This crisis may also explain the new system-wide attempts of geopolitical accumulation in the form of the Wars of Religion and the Thirty Years War, in which France, of course, played a leading role. The absolutist French state/society complex, caught between punitive taxation and spiralling military expenditures, underwent a series of fiscal crises during the course of the eighteenth century, until it collapsed during the French revolution.

5.2   Absolutist sovereignty and its dynamic

 Question

France was one of the key powers involved in the Peace of Westphalia. Can the French absolutist state claim to constitute a modern state?

The question is crucial, precisely because France is often singled out as the classical case of modern state formation and because France played, next to Sweden, the leading role in determining the content of the Peace of Westphalia and the post-1648 general nature of the Westphalian system of states.

You have seen that the centralization of sovereignty in the absolutist tax/ office state did not entail a separation of public and private realms, of politics and economics, as sovereignty was henceforth personalized by the king who regarded the realm as his patrimonial property. In this context, sovereignty meant proprietary kingship or 'generalized personal domination' (Gerstenberger, 1990). Politically, the transformation of France from a feudal realm into an absolutist monarchy did not entail the establishment of modern sovereignty. The aristocracy were incorporated into the patrimonial state as office-holders and thus lost their feudal autonomy; nevertheless, office-holding recreated new privileges within the state. Absolutism never implied unlimited royal power, but institutionalized a new and ultimately unstable *modus vivendi* between king and aristocracy. Recent historical research has shown convincingly that office venality, patronage and clientelism blocked the establishment of a modern bureaucracy in Weber's sense (Parker, 1996). Taxation remained non-uniform. Noble exemption from taxation was associated with a failure to establish permanent representative assemblies (as the demand for 'no taxation without representation' made elsewhere did not apply). The court became the centre of patronage, intrigue and faction. Diverse law codes operated in various regions and for differentiated status groups. No modern system of public finance was set up. The means of violence were not monopolized by the state but personalized by the king, yet re-alienated to patrimonial officers through the sale of army posts. The widespread reliance on mercenaries further undermined royal claims to the monopoly of violence. External and internal trade were extensively politically controlled. In short, all the institutional trappings of the modern state and a capitalist economy were absent in early modern France.

Some have argued that military rivalry in the geopolitical sphere led to permanent warfare, intensified resource extraction by the state from society, the development of new modes of taxation and organization to accomplish this, a general centralization of the state, and a growing monopolization of the means of violence in the hands of the state. In this way, absolutist geopolitical competition is seen as producing modern sovereign states. As the enlightenment thinker Montesquieu originally put the point: states made war as war made states. But early modern state building was, in fact, a desperate and ultimately self-destructive attempt by pre-capitalist landed classes to consolidate their positions in a relatively stagnant, and sometimes contracting, agrarian economy. *Pre-capitalist states made war, but war unmade states.* In developmental terms, absolutism was not a society in transition, but a dead end.

5.3   England: from feudalism to capitalism

When the general crisis struck England after the Black Death (1348), lords tried to recuperate falling income by trying to increase rents despite a fall in the population. However, this failed due to a long period of peasant resistance (Hilton, 1988). The English peasantry removed many of the feudal controls and gained full freedom. However, rather than gaining property rights to their plots (freeholds) as in France, the English peasantry during the sixteenth and seventeenth centuries was gradually evicted from its customary lands by landlords. Landlords drove peasants from their lands, consolidated and enclosed their holdings, and leased these out to large capitalist tenants who engaged in commercial farming by employing wage labour (Brenner, 1985a/b). In this process, English peasants were not protected by the monarchy, and the French pattern of a peasant–king alliance did not arise, derailing the establishment of absolutism in the form of the tax/office state. The result was the destruction of the old lordly powers of political surplus extraction.

Question

Using Table 2.3, where would you place the English peasantry subsequent to the process just described?

Table 2.3   Class relations

		Does the producer own his or her labour power?		
		Yes	Partly	No
Does the producer own his or her means of production?	Yes	Independent producer		
	Partly		Serfdom	
	No	English peasantry after eviction from, and enclosure of, common lands (wage labour)		Slavery

The English peasantry lost the partial control it had over the means of production (essentially the land) under serfdom but gained full control over its labour power because it was no longer subjected to feudal lords. In contrast, lords gained full property rights over land but lost direct, coercive control over the labour of a dependent peasantry. Private property owners now had to employ property-less workers, and markets played a much larger role in allocating resources in the economy. This set of arrangements – a transformation of property relations that entails the need to produce for market exchange, in conditions of private ownership of the means of production and free wage labour – is what Marx meant by capitalism. According to Marx, once capitalism becomes dominant in an economy, markets no longer represent an opportunity where surplus product can be sold, but an economic compulsion in which the propertied and the property-less have to reproduce themselves. Producers do not simply produce *for* the market, but have to reproduce themselves *in* the market.

As Robert Brenner argues, the establishment of agrarian capitalism was the unintended outcome of class conflicts between peasants and lords over property rights. The subjection of labour and capital to market competition meant that market success came to depend on economic competitiveness. Cost-cutting and innovation became the new mechanisms to increase productivity in commercial farming. Systematic reinvestment in the means of production (not coercion) engendered agricultural improvements in the countryside and the beginning of self-sustaining economic development in the form of the 'Agricultural Revolution' (Beckett, 1990). Dramatic productivity increases in agriculture combined with the development of industry, led to sustained economic growth, the creation of a nation-wide home market and eventually the industrial revolution. As population growth and urbanization continued apace, the general crisis of the seventeenth century had relatively little effect on England. Thus, whereas state formation in France resulted in a centralization of political accumulation in the hands of the absolutist state, in England a new social property regime involving economic accumulation in the private sphere of a market-based civil society developed.

Capitalism

Capitalism is based on a set of social property relations in which property-less direct producers are compelled to sell their labour-power to the owners of the means of production in return for wages. Given that both producers and capitalists are subjected to market competition, production is for sale in the market. While surplus value is created and extracted in the process of production itself, profits are realized from earnings from sale in markets after payment of costs including payment of labour power.

5.4 Capitalist (modern) sovereignty

Politically, the transformation of a militarized and decentralized lordly class into a demilitarized class of capitalist landlords in England provided the social base for the new constitutional monarchy. The self-organization of these capitalist landlords in Parliament meant that sovereignty came to be centralized and pooled in a state that was no longer directly involved in processes of political accumulation. After the revolutions of the seventeenth century, in which agrarian private property owners came to consolidate their political power over and against the monarchy, sovereignty took on the formula 'King-in-Parliament'. A capitalist aristocracy came to dominate Parliament and determined the affairs of the state (Brenner, 1993). In a series of royal concessions – the 1689 Bill of Rights, the 1694 Triennial Act, and the 1701 Act of Settlement – the 'committee of landlords' that made up Parliament secured essential control over taxation, the army, jurisdiction, foreign policy and the right of self-convocation (Brewer, 1989). This also guaranteed the security of the new private property regime and binding contract. Furthermore, the 'financial revolution' combined a new system of taxation – national, uniform and effective – with a modern system of public credit (the creation of the National Debt 1693 and the Bank of England 1694), while office venality and corruption gradually gave way to a rationalized bureaucracy. Capitalism rose in conjunction with the first modern state – but this was capitalism in one country only.

Question

What is the difference between political accumulation and economic accumulation under capitalism?

Hint: Take another look at Table 2.2 in Section 2.1.

Following Marx, I have defined capitalism as a social property regime in which direct producers are separated from their means of subsistence. It follows that producers are compelled to sell their labour power to owners of the means of production to make a living. Workers are paid a wage and property owners keep any profits generated by the production and sale of goods and services. Markets represent a compulsion to which both workers and capitalists (property owners) are subjected. This compulsion to survive in the market produces a series of interlocked phenomena. As a rule, market dependence entails inter-capitalist competition, creating incentives for systematic reinvestment in the means of production (rather than in the means of violence), driving technological innovation, raising productivity, and accounting for a dynamic process of economic growth. Out-pricing (not out-gunning) economic accumulation (rather than political) denotes the dominant mode of capitalist dynamics. The historical precondition for the emergence of this form of capitalism was the separation of direct producers from their means of production, the making of 'free' wage labour. In the English agrarian economy, this process began in the sixteenth century and intensified dramatically in the seventeenth. It led to the transformation of bonded peasants into agrarian wage labour and of the militarized class of feudal lords into a demilitarized class of capitalist landlords, renting out land to tenants subject to market competition.

Economic accumulation
Owners of the means of production compete in markets in pursuit of private profits which are then re-invested as capital in the development of the means of production which, through innovation (see Chapter 10), raises productivity. In this sense, capital is self-expanding value leading to expanded accumulation.

Question

What are the implications of the establishment of capitalism for modern sovereignty?

The transition from feudalism to capitalism engenders a shift from a regime of political accumulation based on a feudal rent regime (or an absolutist tax/ office regime), to a regime of economic accumulation, based on a capitalist wage regime. Feudalism involved the decentralization and personalization of political power by lords, creating the 'parcellized sovereignty' of the medieval 'state', and absolutism involved the centralization and persisting personalization of political power by dynasties.

By contrast to both, capitalism makes possible the centralization and depersonalization of political power in the form of the modern state. In capitalism, the power of the ruling class resides in its private ownership of, and control over, the means of production, and the state is no longer required to interfere directly in economic processes. The state's central function can be confined to the internal maintenance and external defence of a regime of private property. This involves the legal enforcement of what become civil contracts among politically (though not economically) equal and free citizens, subject to civil law. This, in turn, is consistent with a public monopoly in the means of violence, while enabling the build-up of an 'impartial' public bureaucracy. Political power and, particularly, the means of violence, can now be pooled in a public state set over and above the economy. While these features do not, of course, exhaustively define the role of the modern state, the link between capitalist property relations and what Marx called the 'purely political' state is a strong one, especially in the English case. I turn now to the implications of these different trajectories of state formation in France and England for the development of the European states-system.

6   The Westphalian system of states

Question

How does the story recounted in Sections 4 and 5 above differ from the view outlined in Section 1.1, that Westphalia represented a key moment in the formation of the modern states-system?

The short answer is that the interpretation presented above offers a direct challenge to the conventional account of the modernity of the Peace Treaties of Westphalia (Teschke, 2002). If France was a typical Westphalian state, then Westphalia represented dynastic states that operated on the basis of political and geopolitical accumulation, a form of centralized but still personalized power, organized in absolutist states. However, in the seventeenth and eighteenth centuries, very different types of state co-existed in the European states-system (see Figure 2.3). France, Austria, Spain, Portugal, Sweden, Russia, the Ottoman Empire, Denmark–Norway, Brandenburg–Prussia, Naples and the Papal state were all absolutist states. The Holy Roman Empire maintained its status as a confederal elective monarchy until 1806, though its constituent polities had gained greater, though not complete, independence after 1648. The Dutch General Estates established an independent oligarchic merchant republic. Poland was a 'crowned aristocratic republic' and Switzerland a free confederation of cantons. The Italian merchant republics struggled against their transformation into monarchies. Yet most importantly for the future of the system, England turned into a parliamentary and constitutional monarchy presiding over the first capitalist economy. Significantly, as Justin Rosenberg (1994) pointed out, England was the one major European power that was *not* represented at the Westphalia settlement.

Activity 2.3

Study Figure 2.3 and note down the main characteristics of the Westphalian system which it illustrates.

Hint: Compare this map with the earlier map of the Carolingian Empire (Figure 2.2) and think about the main argument about Westphalia that this chapter has put forward.

It is true that the Westphalian system came to be dominated by the numerical and power-political preponderance of dynastic–absolutist states. But dynastic sovereignty, as I established in the French case, had little in common with modern sovereignty. In dynastic states, sovereignty was personalized in the monarch who regarded and treated the state as the private patrimonial property of the reigning dynasty. Seventeenth-century kingship was no longer feudal, that is, a 'contractual' affair mediated by vassalage between the mightiest lords in the country, but an institution that had appropriated the powers of command in a sovereign fashion (Beik, 1985). It was sovereign, but this was personalized, dynastic sovereignty, not the impersonal sovereignty of most modern states.

Proprietary kingship meant that public policy and, *a fortiori*, foreign policy were not conducted in the name of the interest of the state or the national interest, but in the name of dynastic interests. *Raison d'etat* (reason of state) meant *raison de roi* (reason of the king). It was expressly in diplomatic and foreign affairs that monarchs were most eager to impose their 'personal rules' in order to negotiate their private titles to sovereignty with fellow monarchs. Under agrarian class relations based on political accumulation, the strategies

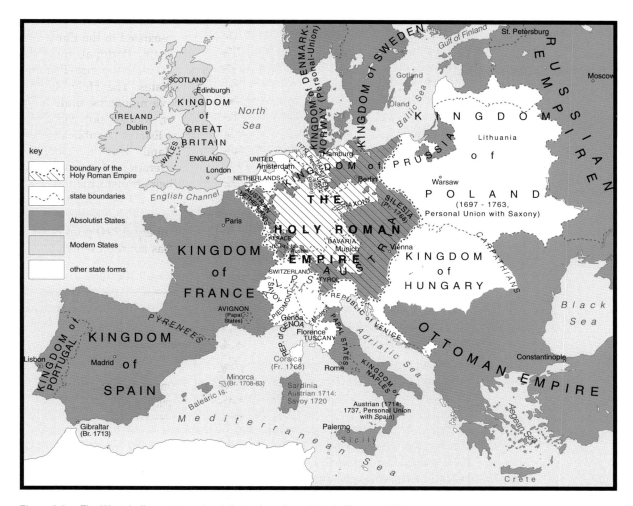

Figure 2.3   The Westphalian system: absolutist and modern states in Europe, 1721

of the ruling classes, organized in the patrimonial state, remained tied to the logic of geopolitical accumulation predicated upon investment in the means of coercion.

As you have seen in Section 4.2, these strategies can be divided into (1) the arbitrary and often punitive taxation of the peasantry by the king, mediated by (2) the sale of offices to a landless *noblesse de robe*. These were matched by (3) geopolitical accumulation through war and dynastic marriage policies, and (4) politically maintained and enforced trade organized through royal sales of monopoly trading charters to privileged merchants. Consequently, the two main contemporary war issues, as has been empirically catalogued by Holsti (1991), were struggles over dynastic territorial claims and commercial monopolies and exclusive trading routes.

Specifically because absolutist states remained trapped in the logic of geopolitical accumulation, the tendency towards territorial expansion remained endemic in international relations. Parity based on sovereign equality was time and again betrayed by territorial designs expressed in the nomenclature of the diverse heads of state. A scale of ranks placed sovereigns on a descending ladder. The Holy Roman Emperor was given pride of first place followed by the 'Most Christian King', the king of France. Hereditary monarchs were, as a rule, placed above elective ones, and republics ranked lower than monarchies followed by non-royal aristocrats and free cities. The standing of England was seriously weakened as a result of the various Commonwealth governments, and serious conflict over precedence occurred wherever there was a mismatch between *de facto* importance and the title of state. Peter the Great's adoption of the imperial title in 1721, for example, aroused not only considerable resentment in Vienna (the seat of the Holy Roman Empire), which would not tolerate a second imperial title in Europe, but also in Britain which recognized the title only in 1742, and in France which followed suit as late as 1772. Towards the end of the seventeenth century, many German actors sought to gain a royal title upon realizing that ducal status or *Kurfürsten* (Elector) status tended to exclude them from international politics.

Moreover, the nexus between centralized public power and patrimonial property meant that the politics of 'international' relations were largely identical to the 'private' family affairs of reigning monarchs. Since sovereignty was transmitted by birth, royal sex, as Marx argued, was directly political: 'The highest constitutional act of the king is therefore his sexual activity, for through this he makes a king and perpetuates his body' (Marx, 1975, p.40). The implication was that all the rather biologically-determined play of dynastic genealogy and family reproduction – like problems of succession, marriage, inheritance and childlessness – determined the very nature of early modern geopolitics. Given the persisting personalization of sovereignty, two conflicting practices dominated early modern patterns of co-operation and conflict. First, proprietary kingship induced systematic policies of dynastic intermarriage as a political instrument for the aggrandizement of territory as well as for securing and enhancing wealth. Inter-dynastic marriages not only characterized 'international' relations, they constituted the single most cost-effective and rapid strategy of expanded personal reproduction of absolutist rulers. Consequently, this was a geopolitical order in which 'states' could marry 'states'. Second and inversely, the resulting European-wide web of dynastic family relations and alliances simultaneously contained the seeds of disorder, partition and destabilization. 'Private' inter-family and intra-family disputes, physical accidents and pathological calamities were immediately translated into 'public' international conflicts. Claims to genealogical–hereditary precedence were usually resolved by war. Next to mercantilist trade wars (that is wars over the political and military control of international trade), wars of succession and, more broadly, wars over hereditary pretensions became the dominant forms of international conflict. Thus, the Wars of the Spanish Succession (1702–13/14), the Polish Succession (1733–38), the Austrian Succession (1740–48), and the Bavarian Succession (1778–79) patterned early modern international conflict. In each case, precisely because dynastic family disputes mediated by the web of intra-dynastic family relations inevitably affected almost all European states, every succession crisis turned immediately into a general European-wide conflict.

Considering the imperative to expand territory typical of absolutist geopolitics, power balancing was not a stabilizing mechanism that guaranteed the independence and survival of smaller states (see Chapter 3), but rather a predatory foreign policy technique operated by the great dynasties to eliminate smaller polities and to maximize territory and wealth. This technique demanded a consensus among the leading powers – *convenance* – and invited bandwagoning rather than balancing (Schroeder, 1994). Dynastic power balancing meant 'equality in aggrandizement' (Wight, 1966a, p.156) leading to a system of eliminatory and compensatory equilibrium amongst the bigger powers.

The dynastic structure of inter-state relations also had direct implications for contemporary territoriality. The politics of inter-dynastic family relations led to supra-regional territorial constructions – especially dynastic unions – which defined the logic of territorial (dis-)order and defied the logic of territorial contiguity and stability. Marital policies and inheritance practices, mediated by violent conflict, led to frequent territorial redistributions among European princes. Territorial unity meant nothing but the unity of the ruling House, personified in its dynastic head. Nevertheless, the unity of the House was not coterminous with the geographical contiguity of its lands. Although these territories were nominally 'bounded' as they belonged to one sovereign, they constituted geographical conglomerates, governed by diverse law codes and tax regimes, crisscrossing the dynastic map of Europe. Early modern Europe was a states-system of 'composite monarchies' (Elliott, 1992). At the same time, the ever-changing territorial size of early modern 'states' intensified the problem of internal administrative cohesion. Austria, Spain, Sweden, Russia or Prussia exemplified the scattered and disjointed mosaic character of early modern territoriality, combining multi-ethnic provinces with different law traditions which had little in common except the family house of their rulers.

Question

Question

In the light of the discussion in Section 6, identify the main features of absolutist, dynastic geopolitics.

I would summarize the key features of Westphalian geopolitics as follows:

- Sovereignty was personalized in the monarch who regarded and treated the state as the private patrimonial property of the reigning dynasty.

- Public policy, especially foreign policy, was therefore conducted in the name and interests of the ruling dynasty.

- The ruling classes were politically organized in patrimonial states and pursued their economic interests by directly political means, involving investment in the means of coercion.

- Externally, this meant that policy was shaped by wars to acquire territory and populations; by dynastic marital alliances – states could marry states; and by politically controlled trade, including trade wars.

- 'Private' family matters – divorces, the absence of a legitimate heir, illness and so forth – became causes of public international conflict as in the many wars of 'succession'.

- The tendency to territorial expansion remained endemic and belied the notion of sovereign equality.

- States were often 'composite monarchies' of scattered, heterogeneous territories and peoples, rather than contiguous and homogeneous realms.

- The balance of power did not mean a balancing that preserved the independence of states but rather a predatory technique by which big powers removed smaller ones from the map while maintaining a compensatory equilibrium among themselves.

In sum, given the diverse yet overwhelmingly dynastic nature of the constitutive units of the Westphalian system, it featured a series of system-defining phenomena that set it structurally apart from its modern successor. These phenomena were bound up with the persistence of political and geopolitical accumulation which blocked the emergence of modern sovereignty. The idea that the Westphalian settlement marks the beginning of the modern states-system thus rests on an erroneous conflation of absolutist and capitalist forms of sovereignty. It was an anarchic system but this anarchy did not revolve around the security interests of states but around the competitive proprietary interests of kings.

7   Towards the modern system of states

Question

How were dynastic inter-state relations transformed into modern international relations?

In my view, this instance of change, the second transition I referred to in Sections 1 and 4, is directly linked to the formation of capitalism and the growth of the modern state in England. In the period between the end of the Glorious Revolution in 1688 and the accession in 1714 of the first Hanoverian king, George I, the pattern of British foreign policy shifted as a result of the consolidation of capitalism. This, in turn, revolutionized the institutional set-up of the British state (Wood, 1991). Henceforth, this new state–society complex would play a pivotal role in reshaping the European system of states.

7.1   British foreign policy: the balance of power

If this thesis is correct, if capitalism does not involve a logic of political accumulation, we should also expect to see a decline of external geopolitical (territorial) accumulation that defined the war-driven international conduct during the feudal and absolutist ages. At the end of the seventeenth century, English sovereignty lay no longer with the king but with Parliament in the context of a constitutional monarchy. The historical basis of England's new attitude towards Europe was the decoupling of foreign policy from dynastic interests brought about by Parliament's right – established in the Act of Settlement of 1701 – to jointly determine foreign policy.

Britain's role, strategy, and foreign policy objectives changed decisively as a result of its new domestic socio-political arrangements. Parliament adopted a unique dual foreign policy, based on the blue-water policy in overseas waters and on power balancing in the continental theatre. 'For almost three centuries (from about 1650 to 1920) Great Britain had available to it a highly distinctive system of national security' (Baugh, 1988, p.33). Blue-water policy meant opposing European powers by technologically and numerically superior naval forces, withdrawing from continental territorial ambitions, and establishing oceanic commercial hegemony overseas. In this context, the old dynastic tie between the Hanoverians and their German stemlands was seen as a disturbing legacy by Parliament. It stood in direct contradiction to Britain's overall strategic interests – its national interest.

After the Treaty of Utrecht in 1713, British (England and Scotland had become Great Britain after the 1707 Act of Union) foreign policy no longer operated on the principle of 'natural allies' – known as the 'Old System' which allied England, the Dutch Republic and Austria against France – but on the fluid principle of rapidly changing coalitions which earned it, on the continent, the epithet 'Perfidious Albion'. This nickname was due to a failure by dynasts both to grasp the nature of changing majorities in a parliamentary system and to understand the logic of a post-dynastic foreign policy of active balancing in the context of an overwhelmingly dynastic system of continental states.

The result was that, during the eighteenth century, a very specific balance of power came into operation in Europe. As absolutist states continued their policies of territorial expansion driven by geopolitical accumulation, parliamentary Britain sought to manage the balance of the European states-system by indirect interventions in the form of loans to smaller powers, while also operating a balance of threat to counter any imperial–hegemonic ambitions. In other words, Britain became the balancer of the balance. Its ability to play this role was based on a productive capitalist economy that financed naval supremacy. Britain was not the accidental insular exception of dynastic rivalry, but the conscious regulator of a system of European politics from which it was socio-economically, but not geographically, set apart.

In this context, the fundamental break with the old territorially accumulative logic of the absolutist states-system arose because of the rise of capitalism in England. The onset of agrarian capitalism in sixteenth-century England, the conversion of dynastic sovereignty into parliamentary sovereignty in the late seventeenth century, and the adoption of a new foreign policy resulted in the gradual de-territorialization of British interests on the continent. At the same time, Britain began to manipulate the old inter-dynastic rivalries by a new conception of active balancing. In terms of the operation of the absolutist inter-dynastic system, Britain was the power that consciously balanced the respective pretensions of largely absolutist states.

7.2   Uneven development

Nonetheless, developmentally, the eighteenth-century world was not yet a capitalist system. As long as the majority of the dominant European powers were dynastic, absolutist states, Britain remained engulfed in a hostile world of politically accumulating states. This explains why Britain's struggle overseas with Spain and France retained a military-mercantilist character. It also shows why Britain was centrally involved in all major eighteenth-century conflicts, from the War of Spanish Succession to the American War of Independence (1775–83). Likewise, geopolitical pressure also reflected back on post-1688 British state formation; a smooth transition to a minimalist liberal state was not possible (Brewer, 1989). The key difference with contemporary continental states, however, was that the eighteenth-century British build-up of a 'military–fiscal' state could be sustained: it was based on a productive capitalist economy and an increasingly rationalized state apparatus that operated a system of taxation and public finance that was national, uniform, and effective. On the continent, the military–fiscal state led to recurrent and deep crises (and finally collapse) – most notably in France.

Powered by its expanding capitalist economy and ample public revenues, and due to its new dual foreign policy with commercial interests overseas and security interests in Europe, Britain established itself during the eighteenth century as the world's major power. While active balancing was initially a defensive measure designed to safeguard the power of Parliament, the new constitutional settlement and the Protestant Succession against the absolutist Catholic powers, the policy of playing states off against each other increasingly had the effect of undermining the military and financial viability of the continental absolutist states. As it thrived on its expanding capitalist economy, Britain continued to play off continental actors against each other in a process of geopolitically combined and socially uneven development until they were financially and economically exhausted. The French Revolution of 1789 was only the most dramatic result of this process. For in the case of conflict between France and Britain, the result was a militarily defeated and bankrupt state which faced dramatic class conflicts at home, eventually forcing a violent transformation of class relations. Across Europe, further wars and revolutions went hand in hand with agrarian reform, peasant liberation and transformations in the basic character of the state. Only after the series of European revolutions during the late eighteenth and nineteenth centuries – many of them 'revolutions from above' or 'passive revolutions' – and the 'freeing' of markets in favour of a world market, did the new logic of British-sponsored free trade amongst capitalist states impose a non-territorial logic of international economic competition based on economic contracts between private citizens. At least, this was increasingly the case in Europe and the Americas; elsewhere in Asia and Africa forms of geopolitical accumulation persisted in the form of the European Empires (see Chapter 3).

Question

In the light of Sections 6 and 7, how should we conceive the relationship between capitalism and the modern states-system?

As I have argued above, the political organization of the modern world in the form of a territorially divided system of states is not a function of capitalism. Rather, capitalism was 'born into' a system of dynastic polities that had consolidated their territories and overcome feudal fragmentation during the absolutist period. Consequently, capitalism emerged in a geopolitical system that was already configured as a system of many states. However, once agrarian capitalist property relations were institutionalized and consolidated in the British state towards the end of the seventeenth century, a new form of economic and political order emerged and began to reshape the older inter-dynastic order based on logics of political and geopolitical accumulation. The making of capitalist (modern) sovereignty, originally in one country, reshaped Europe and, then, the world.

Any account of capitalist expansion on a global scale must not only register its uneven development, but also recognize that it was geopolitically mediated, that is, refracted through the existence of societies organized in the form of territorial states. Capitalist expansion had to 'work itself through' multiple, pre-established sovereignties.

This working through was not merely an economic process, it was a political and, a fortiori, geopolitical process too. Pre-capitalist classes, organized in patrimonial states, had to design new strategies to defend their position in an international environment which put them at a comparative economic *and* coercive disadvantage. Capitalism outperformed such states economically and challenged their ability to pursue political accumulation. These strategies were not uniform; they ranged from the intensification of domestic relations of exploitation and the build-up of an increasingly repressive state apparatus for military and fiscal mobilization, via 'enlightened' absolutism, policies of neo-mercantilism and imperialism, to the adoption of liberal economic policies. Yet in one way or another, on pain of extinction, pre-capitalist states had to accommodate, assimilate, or adjust – or invent radical new strategies, most notably socialism.

Kees van der Pijl (1998) conceives this process as a three-century cycle in which the British (and later Anglo-American) liberal 'heartland' was repeatedly challenged by a series of 'contender states'. Contender states are characterized by the active role of the state, closely linked to ruling classes, in assuming many of the functions exercised in liberal capitalist societies by the private sector. State-led projects of centralized and rationalized public planning attempt to mobilize society 'hot-house fashion' to catch up with and challenge the hegemony of the heartland. Schematically speaking, this cycle opposed eighteenth-century absolutist France and nineteenth-century Napoleonic France and the German Empire to Britain; early twentieth-century Germany and Japan to Britain, the USA and France; and the Soviet Union and China to the USA-led West in the second half of the twentieth century.

Although the initial impetus towards state modernization and capitalist transformation was geopolitical, state responses to this pressure were refracted through respective class relations in different national contexts, including class resistance. If Britain showed its neighbours the image of their future, it did so in a highly distorted way. Conversely, Britain never developed a pristine culture of liberal capitalism because it was, from the first, dragged into an international environment that inflected its domestic politics and long-term development. The 'distortions' were mutual.

7.3   Capitalist geopolitics

While the productive advances generated by the expansion of capitalism entailed a series of transformations to the dynastic polities of continental Europe (and later other kinds of polities across the world), it did not challenge the existence of multiple polities. Rather, capitalism transformed the nature of territoriality within that system, ending geopolitical and, therefore, territorial accumulation. States no longer married one another; ruling families did not preside over composite monarchies; and inter-state competition was not primarily about control of territory. Capitalism did not produce the European states-system, but it transformed it and has proved to be eminently compatible with it, as well as with the expansion of that system to the rest of the world (see Chapter 3).

As a rule, capitalism can expand on a wider and wider geographical scale through the creation of property rights and wage labour in new regions, and through trade and investment, without the need for direct political control over production. As Marx once said, the bourgeoisie (that is, property owners employing wage labour) carries its social power in its pocket. Contracts can be concluded and money can move between private actors in different parts of the world, across the borders of states, without the need for one state to control another. The functioning of a capitalist world market is predicated, at a minimum, on the existence of states that maintain a rule of law, that is, that guarantee contracts and rights, especially pertaining to property, between 'private' individuals, as well as on the legal security of international transactions to maintain open national economies.

In time, the key principle of modern international relations was transformed from the war-assisted accumulation of territories to the management of an increasingly worldwide capitalist economy and the regulation of an open international economy by the leading capitalist states. A 'private', universalized world market now co-exists with a 'public' system of states based on fixed territoriality (for discussions of this and of how, after Britain, the USA came to pursue this agenda, see Chapters 4 and 5). The logic of political and geopolitical accumulation in the form that was systematically built into the absolutist dynastic states was replaced by a world in which, in principle, economic activity is competitive and mobile while politics takes place in a context of fixed and unified territorial states.

Activity 2.4

Fill in the boxes in Table 2.4 (overleaf) that have been left blank.

Table 2.4 Feudal, absolutist and capitalist geopolitics compared

	Feudalism	Absolutism	Capitalism
Nature of sovereignty	'Parcellized sovereignty'; personalized and decentralized among lords sharing an oligopoly in the means of violence	Personalized and centralized in the monarch; the state is the private patrimonial property of the ruling dynasty	Centralized and de-personalized; residing in the state as an impersonal legal order with a monopoly in the means of coercion
Public and private/ political and economic		Public affairs of the state directly linked with and fused to the private interests of the ruling dynasty	Separation in law between a private realm and a public sphere; differentiation between state and market
Relationship of the ruling class to the state	Ruling class *is* 'the state'; the feudal polity forms an ensemble of lordships or a 'state of associated persons'		Ruling classes rely on the state indirectly to uphold their private rights to property and contract
Nature of accumulation	Political and geopolitical based on investment in the means of coercion	Political and geopolitical based on investment in the means of coercion	
Economic development	Relatively lethargic and cyclical; governed by eco-demographic cycles	Relatively lethargic and cyclical; governed by eco-demographic cycles	

Military development	Dynamic; governed by permanent re-investment in the means of coercion	Dynamic; governed by permanent re-investment in the means of coercion	Conjunctural, sustained by dynamic market competition, but dependent on political conjunctures and threats to open world market
Character of external policy	Feuding, territorial expansion, land reclamation, conquest, strategic marriages		Dependent on the conjectures and crises of capitalism. Multilateral policies to promote and manage an international economy open to trade and investment among private parties, but also periods of economic nationalism and inter-imperialist war
Nature of the balance of power	No balance of power	Big powers eliminate smaller powers, while a compensatory equilibrium maintains a dynamic balance among the big powers	Active balancing by Britain on the continent combined with imperial dominance of the oceans, followed by an extended period of geopolitically mediated, uneven development of capitalism on a worldwide basis
Form of territoriality	Shifting, fragmented, overlapping, non-contiguous, internally differentiated (marches)	Internally consolidated but shifting in scope	

8 Conclusion

The origins and evolution of the European states-system lie in a twofold transition. The first of these was the transition from feudalism to the world of multiple, absolutist states – the world of Westphalia. The second was the development of a capitalist economy and state in England. The transfer of capitalism to the continent, and then to the rest of the world, was riddled with social conflicts, civil and international wars, social revolutions and counter-revolutions. However, its essential mechanism was the geopolitically combined and socio-economically uneven development of a new regime of social property relations – capitalism.

It was a long and bloody transformation – a transitional period – in which the processes of capitalist expansion, state transformation and integration into the 'West' was generalized, schematically speaking, from 1688 to the First World War in Europe, and from the First World War via the Second World War and the period of decolonization for the rest of the non-socialist world. From 1917 in Russia, 1945 in Eastern Europe and from 1949 in China, a socialist model of economy and state sought to offer an alternative course of development, in opposition to the capitalist world. After 1989 and the end of the Cold War, this model was abandoned almost everywhere. Thereafter, a fully, if unevenly, integrated capitalist world economy may be said to have come into existence.

International relations during this long period were not modern but *modernizing* and this modernization has been a deeply contested and conflict-ridden process. International relations, from the late seventeenth century onwards, were not a continuation of the rise and fall of great powers in an otherwise unchanging structure of anarchy, as realism proposes, but rather expressed the unfolding of this gigantic human drama which transformed the nature of the international system.

Further reading

A powerful Marxist critique of realism and a discussion of the connections between capitalist social property relations and the anarchical states-system can be found in Rosenberg, J. (1994) *The Empire of Civil Society: A Critique of the Realist Theory of International Relations*, London, Verso.

For a detailed historical and theoretical critique of the myth of Westphalia and an elaboration and extension of the argument presented in this chapter, see Teschke, B. (2003) *The Myth of 1648: Class, Geopolitics, and the Making of Modern International Relations*, London, Verso.

For a provocative essay about the character of English socio-economic and political development compared with the absolutist systems of continental Europe, see Wood, E. (1991) *The Pristine Culture of Capitalism: A Historical Essay on Old Regimes and Modern States*, London, Verso.

For the 'Brenner Thesis' on the transition from feudalism to capitalism in England and the diverging Anglo-French long-term patterns of state formation and economic development, see Aston, T.H. and Philpin, C.H.E. (eds) (1985) *The Brenner Debate: Agrarian Class Structure and Economic Development in Pre-Industrial Europe*, Cambridge, Cambridge University Press.

Chapter 3 Universalism and difference in international society

Simon Bromley

1 Introduction

... in compliance with God's order, we issue the following fatwa to all Muslims. The ruling to kill the Americans and their allies – civilians and military – is an individual duty for every Muslim who can do it in any country in which it is possible to do it, in order to liberate the al-Aqsa Mosque [in Jerusalem] and the Holy Mosque [Mecca] from their grip, and in order for their armies to move out of all the lands of Islam, defeated and unable to threaten any Muslim. This is in accordance with the words of Almighty God, 'and fight the pagans all together as they fight you all together', and 'fight them until there is no more tumult or oppression, and there prevail justice and faith in God'.

(Founding statement of al-Qaeda, 23 February 1998)

The SECURITY COUNCIL,

REAFFIRMING the principles and purposes of the Charter of the United Nations,

DETERMINED to combat by all means threats to international peace and security caused by terrorist acts,

RECOGNIZING their inherent right of individual or collective self defense in accordance with the Charter ...

CALLS on all states to work together urgently to bring to justice the perpetrators, organizers and sponsors of the terrorist attacks and STRESSES that those responsible for aiding, supporting or harbouring the perpetrators, organizers and sponsors of these acts will be held accountable ...

EXPRESSES its readiness to take all necessary steps to respond to the terrorist attacks of 11 September 2001 ...

(United Nations Security Council Resolution 1328, passed unanimously on 12 September 2001)

After the events of 11 September 2001 in the USA, the United Nations (UN) was unanimous in condemning the al-Qaeda attacks as a threat to international peace and security, and as a challenge to the principles and purposes of the UN Charter. The attacks were, according to the resolutions of the Security Council, a threat to the international community as a whole, a community whose members are sovereign states recognizing the authority of international law. The language of the UN Charter (the founding document of the UN) is explicitly universal and appeals to two broad principles that claim a general validity. The first begins with the idea of 'we the peoples' (from the preamble to the UN Charter) and proclaims a universal right of different peoples to self-government, expressed in the notion of sovereign equality in international law. The second is the Universal Declaration of Human Rights, a set of rights said to be owed to all people by virtue of their common humanity. These commitments underpin the idea that there are some universally acknowledged principles or norms that should govern the conduct of all peoples and people at the international level. These principles and norms are what make the different political communities in the states-system a single 'international community'. Using a somewhat older language to that of the UN Charter, President George W. Bush invoked a similar imagery when he said that the events of 11 September represented an attack on 'civilization'.

The founding statement of al-Qaeda indicates, however, that there are groups which do not recognize the authority of these norms. The adherents of al-Qaeda would not accept President Bush's implicit characterization of their actions as 'barbaric', the 'other' to civilization, rather they claim adherence to a different civilization. Specifically, al-Qaeda rejects the secular claim to political authority embodied in the notion of a right to self-government as well as the idea that there are universal norms binding all – its appeal is to Muslims, not to humanity, even if Islam is a religion open to all who are willing to convert. From the point of view of al-Qaeda, it is the policies and actions of the USA that represent, at best, a different and hostile civilization and, at worst, barbarism.

Thus, while the UN and President Bush spoke of a single 'civilized' international community, others argued that the different political and religious communities of the world represent either a 'clash of civilizations' or a 'clash of barbarisms'. Some time before the events of 11 September 2001, the American political scientist, Samuel Huntington, wrote that:

> The underlying problem for the West is not Islamic fundamentalism. It is Islam, a different civilization whose people are convinced of the superiority of their culture and are obsessed with the inferiority of their power. The problem for Islam ... is the West, a different civilization whose people are convinced of the universality of their culture and believe that their superior,

if declining, power imposes on them the obligation to extend that culture throughout the world.

(Huntington, 1996, pp.217–18)

For Huntington it was simply misleading to speak of a single international community. Rather, there was a single international system – that is, a world of interacting societies, cultures and states in which all affected one another – but there were no universally agreed norms. Universal norms, Huntington maintained, were the product of a universal power, in this case the power of the West. This single international system encompasses *different* civilizations, particular ways of ordering collective affairs among peoples – Islamic, Western and so on – but its putatively universal international law is, in fact, the product of Western norms.

An assault on civilization or a clash of barbarisms? The attack on the World Trade Center, 11 September 2001

On the other hand, Gilbert Achcar argued that al-Qaeda no more represented an authentic expression of Islamic civilization than the USA's military actions in Afghanistan in 2002 and Iraq in 2003 represented a defence of civilized values, Western or otherwise. Achcar was pointing to the fact that no culture has a monopoly of civilized values and all cultures embody a diversity of competing interpretations over what values to uphold. Along with many critics of the wars in Afghanistan and Iraq, Achcar spoke of:

> Murdering civilians ... when it is an ineluctable consequence, known in advance, of an attack on combatants that is not required as a matter of imperative necessity. ... When there is any possible alternative to such attacks, and when they destroy more human lives than they save, such attacks are simply criminal. ... when two barbarisms clash, the strongest, the one that acts as the oppressor, is still more culpable.

> (Achcar, 2002, p.67)

For Achcar the prospect was less one of contending civilizations than a general descent into barbarism, a simple assertion of might is right, an untrammelled exercise of power without reference to any kind of legitimating norms save those of the most particular kind (such as the defence of national self-interest).

1.1 The perennial questions of international political theory

In Chapter 2, Benno Teschke argued that social transformations in Europe and the rise of the modern state were the basis of the modern international system. In the twentieth century, this states-system came to encompass virtually the entire inhabited world. Yet does this mean that we can speak of the international system in the kind of universalist terms used by the UN? Is there any such thing as the international community or, as some have called it, 'an international society', and if so on what shared norms and institutions is it based? These are perennial questions in international political theory and have been posed in new and especially stark form following the events of 11 September 2001 and the debates and conflicts that have ensued.

In this chapter I am going to investigate this issue through three key questions:

1   Can we speak of an international community, or an international society, based on shared, universal norms and institutions and, if so, what are they?

2   How did something that started as a European international society spread outwards to the rest of the world, and what is the contemporary relevance of this process?

3   How do different ideas about the nature of political communities lead to different ideas about universalism and difference in the international system?

Let me unpack these three questions a little and say something about how I am going to address them in the rest of this chapter.

The first question asks whether the UN really does speak for a single international society in which different communities share in the workings of certain common norms and institutions and, if this is the case, what are these norms and institutions? Or is there, rather, a system formed by interacting societies, in which each society sustains its own norms and institutions, and in which relations between societies are basically motivated by the pursuit of self-interest on the basis of power? Do such norms and institutions that exist in the international system simply reflect the interests of the powerful?

Next, given that the modern states-system originated in Europe, the second question asks how that system expanded to cover the whole globe. However, we also need to consider how the norms and institutions of the European states-system dealt with societies outside Europe and how this changed over time. Indeed, in the course of this development and expansion, European norms and institutions were themselves transformed by contact, conflict and co-operation with other parts of the world. Therefore, we are not dealing with an unchanging set of European practices. And even if the norms of today's international society have European origins, does this matter? Does this mean the norms are nothing more than the expression of the interests of the most powerful states, or are they of universal value?

Finally, the third question demonstrates that how we answer the first and second questions partly depends on how we understand the political aspects of society. That is to say, how do individual people relate to 'their' collectivity and also to those outside their collectivity, to 'others'? Are those outside 'our' group, particular 'strangers' (members of other political communities) or universal 'friends' (members of a common humanity)? This theme of universalism versus particularism was originally posed in religious terms, since it was the great world religions that first provided a form of identity wider than the locality in which peoples lived. In view of the fact that modern European states are secularized Christian polities, does this mean that claims to universalism are, in effect, secularized Christian claims? What might be the force of a universal and secular morality?

Questions like these have been at the centre of international political theory for hundreds, if not thousands, of years, and they go to the heart of contemporary debates about how different peoples can and should live together in an increasingly crowded and interdependent world. In their contemporary form, they were first posed with any clarity and substance in the development and subsequent global expansion of the European states-system. This is not to say that these questions have not been posed in other cultures at other times – they have – but rather to recognize that contemporary debates and conflicts over these issues operate in a historical and cultural context massively shaped by developments centred in Europe and the expansion of European society into the non-European world.

I shall begin in Section 2 by considering a group of scholars, collectively known as the 'English School', who were particularly concerned to identify the norms and institutions of what one of the School's leading members, Hedley Bull, called the 'anarchical' international society (the School's term for what is nowadays called the 'international community'). (The English School scholars were (and are) closely associated with International Studies as it developed as an academic discipline in Britain, although not all are English or even British.) While many others have written about these issues (and I shall draw on some of this work below), the English School has, I believe, a special claim on our attention because it has been preoccupied with exactly the themes that I have just identified – do different communities share enough to form an international community? How has an international society that was originally European become universal? And how do particular political communities, and the individual collective identifications that they encompass, relate to each other?

In Section 3, I shall take a more historical look at these issues by focusing on the problems raised by the fact that contemporary international society has European and colonial origins. I discuss some of the issues that arise from this history. In fact, adherents of the English School have disagreed among themselves about the degree to which present-day international society, to the extent that it exists, can claim a universal validity as well as disagreeing about the arguments on which such a claim of universality might be based. This is the subject of Section 4, in which I outline contending positions in the analysis of universalism and difference in the contemporary world by looking at different ways that scholars have tried to define the nature of political communities and the relations between them.

2   The idea of an international society

The main work of the English School has been concerned with studying the practice of states in order to uncover the norms and institutions of international society, and to give a description of them and their workings which is as close to that of the actual practice of states as possible. In this way, the English School seeks to make explicit the often implicit workings of international society in much the same way that an anthropologist might seek to make one culture transparent to another.

Question

While you might have an idea of what 'society' refers to, what is an *international* society?

According to the English School, an international society is a society whose members are states. A state is a compulsory form of political rule with a common government, territory and people. A collection of states forms a *system* when there are significant relations among them, patterns of causal interconnection in which the actions of one affect another. An international system is, by definition, anarchic because states are sovereign and there is no overarching authority above states. By contrast, a *society* of states is an anarchical system in which states share in the workings of norms and institutions (formal and informal rules) that guide conduct, and patterns of expectations that states hold about one another and which organize significant elements of their interaction.

According to the English School, international society is one route to achieving international order, that is, a regular pattern of action and reaction that maintains the basic goals of social life. These goals are those of peace and security, the idea that agreements should be kept, and the existence of rules for protecting and transferring property. Even in the absence of rules, norms and institutions, order may result from a stable balance of power arising from common interests in these primary goals. An international society, however, has rules, norms and institutions shared among states and aimed at achieving these ends. It is still, formally speaking, an anarchy since there is no government above the state, but there are durable elements of collective action and identity between its member states.

What transforms a group of independent states into a collectivity with shared interests and an identity of its own? For the English School, the answer is that the rules of international society are in part 'constitutive'. What do they mean by this? An international society is a *society* (rather than just an anarchical *system*) because the rules on which it is based go beyond those that states might subscribe to based on the interests that individual states have in common – say, a concern with survival. They do not only regulate interactions between self-interested actors but, at least in part, are constitutive of its members and their relations with one another – they are constitutive rules. These are difficult ideas and I shall return to them in Section 2.7. For now, I shall offer you an example to indicate what is meant.

Constitutive rules serve to create the possibility of the activity they govern. They can be distinguished from regulative rules which seek to regulate a pre-existing state of affairs. Consider an example given by the philosopher, John Searle:

International society
An international society is a society of states in which states 'conceive themselves to be bound by a common set of rules in their relations with one another, and share in the workings of common institutions' (Bull, 1995, p.13).

Constitutive rules
Constitutive rules serve to create the activity, and in part the actors, that they govern.

Regulative rules
Regulative rules regulate a pre-existing state of affairs among pre-existing actors.

> ... the rules of chess do not regulate an antecedently existing activity. It is not the case that there were a lot of people pushing bits of wood around on boards, and in order to prevent them from bumping into each other all the time and creating traffic jams, we had to regulate the activity. Rather, the rules of chess create the very possibility of playing chess.

(Searle, 1995, pp.27–8)

Activity 3.1

Consider the two examples of rules from the international sphere below and identify whether they are regulative or constitutive rules.

1   The rules of deterrence (discussed in Chapter 4) allow states, in a world of nuclear weapons capable of bringing human life on the planet to an end, to ensure that they survive by each threatening to retaliate in the event of an attack.

2   The rules of sovereignty (discussed further below) identify the legitimate actors in the game of international politics as sovereign states – states will only conduct diplomatic or other international relations with other sovereign states (and not nomadic tribes, multinational firms or terrorist networks).

Rules or norms and institutions of international society
According to Bull, the rules (or norms) of an international society prescribe the patterns of behaviour that sustain security, agreements and property in the international system. The institutions of an international society make those rules effective.

The English School identified a number of rules or norms and institutions of international society and in the following sections I shall go through each of these. As you will see, some of these can be interpreted both as regulative and constitutive of international society

2.1   Sovereignty and mutual recognition

The first rule (or rather complex of rules) of an international society is that of the mutual recognition of the sovereign claims among states. Domestic or internal sovereignty is claimed in relation to a given territory and population and can be asserted independently of other states. External or international sovereignty – the recognition of sovereignty claims by other states – can arise in one of two ways.

First, mutual recognition may arise simply as a result of a prudent calculation of interests: one state recognizes the external sovereignty of another because the domestic sovereignty of the latter is an accomplished fact – a fact that might be costly to ignore or try to reverse. 'The existence of what is recognized,' says Martin Wight, 'determines the act of recognition, and not the other way round' (1986, p.46).

Second, recognition may be a constitutive act: the mutual recognition of states as sovereign by one another may serve to empower each against other potential claimants for political authority. Recognition in this active sense is what complements and thereby completes a domestic claim to sovereign authority. A claim to rule that is recognized by other states in this way is a vastly more efficient means of governing than one that has to be defended, by either force or fraud, against rival claimants for political power such as religious or economic organizations. In short, active mutual recognition between the members of the society of states can serve, in part, to create the sovereignty of those states (that is, it is constitutive) and can thus bring great benefits.

The institutions of an international society are those things that function in order to make the rules effective. Since international society is, in Bull's terms, an anarchical society, the primary institutions of the society of states are 'the members of the society themselves – sovereign states – which are chiefly responsible for performing the functions of helping to make the rules effective' (Bull, 1995, p.68). However, the European society of states also developed certain collective institutions for upholding its rules. According to Bull these included the balance of power, international law, diplomacy, the special rights and duties of the great powers, and war. I shall consider these below as well as an institution that Bull does not mention – colonialism. Some of these require a little more explanation than others.

2.2   The balance of power

I have noted that the external recognition of sovereignty can simply be a recognition of an established fact based on self-interest or it can be a more active, mutually empowering, constitutive process. Similarly, the balance of power can be thought of either in terms of a mechanism that arises directly from independent states acting on the basis of self-interest or as a shared norm among states. Historically, the emergence of an international society of sovereign states, in which each recognized the sovereign prerogatives of the others, rested on a balance of power in Europe between a plurality of states. However, 'only in the eighteenth century,' say Bull and Watson, 'was the idea firmly implanted among European states that an attempt by any one of them to establish hegemony over the others was a violation of the rules of their international society' (1984, p.6). As a result, the 'balance of power' assumed a central importance as one of the key institutions of that society.

In the mechanical sense, power balancing is as old an interaction among separate political communities as the eighteenth-century philosopher and political theorist, David Hume, pointed out in his essay 'Of the balance of power':

... the maxim of preserving the balance of power is founded so much on common sense and obvious reasoning, that it is impossible it could altogether have escaped antiquity, where we find, in other particulars, so many marks of deep penetration and discernment. If it was not so generally known and acknowledged as at present, it had, at least, an influence on all the wiser and more experienced princes and politicians. And indeed, even at present, however generally known and acknowledged among speculative reasoners, it has not, in practice, an authority much more extensive among those who govern the world.

(Hume, 1994, pp.157–8; first published 1752)

At the level of 'common sense and obvious reasoning', the balance of power describes a situation where, amidst a plurality of powers, states that seek to maintain their independence align with one another to counteract the power of the strongest, since this is the steadiest means of avoiding subordination. One alternative to 'balancing' is known as bandwagoning, in which states seek to align themselves with the strongest power, an inherently dangerous course of action since the strong cannot be trusted not to misuse their power (another alternative – 'co-binding' – is discussed in Chapter 4).

However, the balance of power is not just a description of the behaviour of interacting states; it is also, as Hume says, a 'maxim', that is, a rule of conduct in the society of states. Conducting foreign policy according to the balance of power was, for the major European states of the eighteenth and nineteenth centuries, an expected and acknowledged procedure, a principle by which policy could be fashioned, a way of anticipating the actions and reactions of others.

It is important to emphasize that the aim of the balance of power was not peace as such, but the preservation of the dominant members of the society of states as independent political entities. Indeed, war is an instrument for maintaining the balance of power, and the maintenance of peaceful interstate relations is only a secondary aim of the balance of power. Nevertheless, the possibility of war, and the potential extinction of sovereign independence that goes with it, is why the balance of power is necessary. As Chris Brown has rightly pointed out, 'War and the balance of power stand together – or, perhaps, fall together' (1997, pp.103–4). Of course, intelligently played, the balance of power ought to serve to reduce the level of conflict, since it should deny likely aggressors the margin of superiority needed for victory in war. Yet the collective aim that it served was primarily the preservation of the members of the society of states. The order produced by the institution of the balance of power was, therefore, an order based on states, considered as the legitimate monopolists over territorial rule and the means of physical coercion, sharing in a common rule for a common aim.

After the Treaty of Utrecht (1713), territorial states – that is, states that derived their legitimacy from an ability to control a territory and govern its people – and the balance of power increasingly dominated European international society. Writing about this order in about 1750, the French philosopher, political thinker and satirist, Voltaire, said:

> For some time now it has been possible to consider Christian Europe, give or take Russia, as '*une espece de grande republique*' – a sort of great commonwealth – partitioned into several states, some monarchic, the others mixed, some aristocratic, others popular, but all dealing with one another; all having the same basic religion, though divided into various sects; all having the same principles of public and political law unknown in the other parts of the world. Because of these principles the European [states] never enslave their prisoners, they respect the ambassadors of their enemies, they jointly acknowledge the pre-eminence and various rights of [legitimate rulers], and above all they agree on the wise policy of maintaining an equal balance of power between themselves so far as they can, conducting continuous negotiations even in times of war, and exchanging resident ambassadors or less honourable spies, who can warn all the courts of Europe of the designs of any one, give the alarm at the same time and protect the weaker.

> (quoted in Bobbitt, 2002, p.131)

2.3 International law

International law is, arguably, the critical institution of an international society and the mark that relations among states embody shared rules and norms. In the contemporary era, the UN has, above all, been a framework for conducting international affairs according to international law. However, two issues arise in trying to define the nature of international law: (1) can it claim a universal validity? and (2) does it have the same legal force as a legal order within states? Because international law is so critical to claims of an international society, and because the arguments surrounding these two issues are rather tangled, I need to spend a little more time discussing this institution.

Question

Is international law universal?

To take the first issue, it has been argued that international law is not in fact a shared universal but rather the imposition of rules by the powerful. Thus, Anthony Pagden has argued that the origins of international law lie in the Roman Empire: 'The law of nations' (an old term for international law),

Pagden argued, 'like all forms of universalism, was once created to make a group of peoples into an empire' (2001, p.176). For Pagden, international law's particular imperial origins thus belie the universal claims now made for it. In fact, Pagden goes on to argue that the subsequent development of international law has always been carried forward by some power – by the Catholic Church after the fall of the Roman Empire; by the 'civilizing mission' of European states in the age of exploration and colonialism; and latterly by the USA.

However, I would challenge this argument on two grounds. First, in terms of the understanding of the history of international law, there are reasons to question the importance of the Roman Empire (and of the other subsequent powers) in the origins and development of international law. Pagden draws our attention to the Roman's *ius gentium* (law of nations), which the Romans held to be common to all civilized peoples. However, the *ius gentium* mainly concerned commercial relations between peoples (what is now called *private* international law) rather than public international law. The latter is the proper title for contemporary international law and its subject matter is not groups of peoples or communities, or even people as individuals, but peoples as organized under the legal personality of a sovereign state, and its object is the relations – diplomatic, commercial, military, and other – among sovereign states.

Perhaps more importantly, the root idea behind the Roman law of nations was that it was universally recognized because it was based 'on the common sense, or "natural reason", which all men shared as part of their human nature. Thus the [Roman] "law of nations" was sometimes characterized as natural law (*ius naturale*)' (Stein, 1999, p.13). Yet this idea is not originally Roman but Greek, and can be traced to early Greek (Stoic) thought and the belief that human beings constituted a single genus, distinguished by the possession of reason. This formed the basis of the notion that there could be objective, universal normative standards, knowable and accessible to all, regardless of the particular culture that they came from. The origin of international law, therefore, may not lie in empire but in reason.

The subsequent development of international law should also lead us to question Pagden's claims. While the mediating roles of the Roman empire, Christianity and European colonialism are certainly important, the development of secular states in early modern Europe also drew upon Roman law for their legal apparatus and defended it on the basis that it was authoritative *non ratione imperii, sed imperio rationis* (not by reason of power, but by the power of reason). My first objection to Pagden, therefore, is that there are good reasons to doubt the historical claim that international law has always been in essence an institution in the service of the powerful; it may have some more objective, universal basis.

My second objection to Pagden's argument about the particular origins (and therefore non-universality) of international law is a more general point. For even if the origins of international law do lie in the Roman Empire, does it matter? All human institutions and ideas have an origin in some history and culture. Some – civilization in the sense of settled agriculture, cities and literacy – seem to have been invented independently more than once in different historical and cultural settings. However, it does not follow that something's claim to universal validity is necessarily negated by a particular historical or cultural origin. To assume that the universal validity of something is indelibly tainted by its particular origins is a genetic fallacy. Nobody supposes that this is true for, say, mathematics. Did the West reject the decimal number system because of its Hindu-Arabic origins? Even if certain notions first arose in the course of European history, this in no way prevents them from contributing to the common heritage of humanity. At the most, it indicates that the heritage has a history and may continue to have one. In principle, this might be the case with international law.

Question

Is international law actually law?

The second issue that challenges the idea that international law is a universal institution of international society is the debate about whether it is *law*, that is, about whether it has the same force as a legal order within the state. This is a complex debate that turns, in part, on different accounts of the force of domestic law. Suppose we accept that domestic law has a genuine normative component, that it is not simply commands backed up by force, then what is the normative force of international law? To answer this we need to look again at the origins of modern international law.

By the seventeenth century, natural law was beginning to lose the underlying religious world view that gave it imaginative force in Catholic Europe. This was, in some measure, because of the religious strife associated with the Reformation and Counter-Reformation. It was also a response to the scepticism that arose from a greater awareness of cultural and religious difference occasioned by the European 'voyages of discovery' to the non-European world, and as a result of the scientific revolution. Natural law, in the hands of such early Enlightenment thinkers as Thomas Hobbes (1588–1679), was transformed from a divinely ordained external standard into the idea of subjective natural rights – universal rights that are duplicated in every individual and which no one can rationally deny to another. Thus, natural law was understood as the basis of a universal moral theory.

These individual rights – broadly to seek peace and uphold agreements – can be alienated to a collective body. Hobbes, of course, is famous for his theory of domestic sovereignty, in which people contrive an artificial agreement to subordinate their individual rights of self-judgement to an overarching power with the authority to judge for all, providing others do likewise. This effects a transition from the moral to the legal level. On Hobbes's account:

> What matters is not just that one will is substituted for many wills: the key point is that it is an authorized will. It is endowed with a special kind of open-ended authority: sovereignty, the power to legislate, potentially on any aspect of life, for the whole community. For those who live within the realm of this authority, a new [legal] situation has been created. ... [People] are now linked in a network of mutual rights and duties.

(Malcolm, 2002, pp.443–4)

Domestically, thus, there is a legal basis for law. International law, by contrast, remains at the moral level and is, therefore, subject to the law of nature. Indeed, Hobbes called international law the *ius inter gentium* (the law between peoples) in order to distinguish it clearly from the Roman *ius gentium*. There is no analogous authority in the society of states to the sovereign state, there is no authorized legislative body, and hence there is no *general* legal order at the international level. States can sign particular treaties, covenants, agreements, and so forth, and the law of nature obliges them to uphold these but the only authority at the international level is that provided by the law of nature. Relations among states are subject to the law of nature; morality applies, but there is not, on this account, a general legal order at the international level.

Once again, there is a general point to note. If one starts from some notion of a universal morality that applies to individuals, it is easy to see how the legal authority of the state *domestically* can be justified. More precisely, that authority will be more or less tightly constrained depending on how broadly one specifies the rights which individuals can reasonably claim. The narrower (or broader) conception one has of individual rights, the more absolute (or conditional) is the sovereignty that can reasonably be claimed by the state. But on this account, there is no general legal order between states until states collectively authorize it.

The alternative to Hobbes's line of reasoning is to seek to claim that international law is *law* in that it is based on custom and practice and derives some authority from that fact. If one grounds the legitimacy of general norms and rules not, like Hobbes, in reasoned assent but in some customary practice, then one can quite properly accord normative force to international law even in the absence of explicit authorization.

The idea of international law plays a central role in distinguishing an international society from a system of states for the English School. It is, therefore, worth reflecting briefly on the significance of the ideas we have just reviewed. Hedley Bull thought that international law (and thus international society) rested 'upon a common culture or civilization, or at least some of the elements of such a civilization' (1995, p.15). Contemporary international law was based on the culture of the 'dominant Western powers' and, according to Bull, this culture had shallow roots in many non-Western societies. Huntington makes a similar point more bluntly: the universal claims of institutions such as international law represent 'the ideology of the West for confrontations with non-Western cultures. ... The non-West sees as Western what the West sees as universal' (1996, p.66). In this view, international law is an imposition by the powerful; it is universal insofar as the powerful can make it so. It is less clear whether this view sees international law as truly *law*. If domestic law is regarded also as a product of power, then maybe international law is lawful in a similar way.

Against this kind of view, Hobbes was insistent that universalism was a consequence of a general reason, not a particular culture or power. In Hobbes's time, the principal claimant to universal truth was the Roman (Catholic) Church, what Hobbes called a 'Confederacy of Deceivers' whose aim, while preaching universal salvation, was 'to obtain dominion over men in this present world'. According to the most perceptive account of Hobbes's international political theory:

> He was convinced that the amalgam of Graeco-Roman philosophy and biblical doctrine, developed over the centuries by the Roman Church and taught in all European universities, was the biggest single threat to the stability of states. ... It was responsible for fomenting rebellions within states, and wars between them. ... The aim [of Hobbes's work] was to clear out of people's minds the false metaphysical assumptions, bogus religious doctrines, and pernicious political principles that had accumulated there as the products of centuries of priestcraft. Once this cultural lumber had been removed, people could easily be taught the true principles of political science – Hobbes's principles – and would then clearly understand their duties as citizens and subjects.

(Malcolm, 2002, pp.453–4)

But while Hobbes maintained that the law of nature was universal by virtue of the power of reason, he did not believe that international law has the *legislative authority* of domestic law within a state. Rather, the particular agreements of international law only have the *moral* force of the law of nature, since no sovereign power has been established over the members of international society. In Hobbes's understanding, international law is a universal moral order that underpins particular agreements among states; it lacks the collective authorization given to the sovereign in domestic law.

2.4   The special rights and duties of the great powers

The privilege and responsibility for maintaining the balance of power inevitably falls to the most powerful states. After the conclusion of the Napoleonic wars in 1815, there was an explicit, *de jure* recognition of this fact. The resulting 'Concert of Europe' was based on two connected principles:

> The first of these was the formal assertion of the unique privileges and responsibilities of the Great Powers in the maintenance of international order. The second, made necessary by the first, was that if the special managerial role of the Great Powers was to be recognised, it would be necessary to order more formally the relationships between the powers themselves.

> (Clark, 1989, p.114)

Specifically, the Concert involved the elaboration of a new diplomatic norm among the great powers, namely, that of 'formal and common consent' to changes to the status quo regarding European geopolitics. The use of the term 'Europe', Watson writes, 'as a diplomatic entity, in the sense of a group of states having common interests and duties and in whose name member states could take joint decisions' dates from this time (1984, p.72). How far the Concert of Europe represented a genuine element of collective management of the international system, and how far it was merely an expedient rationalization of a temporary equilibrium amidst a plurality of powers, is much debated. Nonetheless, it does illustrate the general point that the great powers claim special privileges and responsibilities.

2.5   War

The contention that war is an institution of the society of states is at first sight perplexing – surely warfare is a breakdown of society? However, sovereign states claim a monopoly over the legitimate use of organized force within their territories and, as a corollary of mutual recognition, expect others to do likewise. That is to say, collectively, international society arrogates to states – rather than, say, firms, religious organizations, pirates or whoever – the right to deploy force. (Compare this with the dispersal of the means of violence in feudal 'international' society described by Benno Teschke in Chapter 2.) Until the UN Charter, the right to use force in the pursuit of paramount state interests was part of the toolkit of every self-respecting, and other-regarding, state.

However, not only did states, individually and collectively, attempt to monopolize the use of force, they also sought to elaborate mutual understandings of the 'rules' of war. The most ambitious attempt to specify rules to govern, and limit, the use of force, is, of course, the UN. Since the establishment of the UN Charter, international law provides that states 'shall refrain in their international relations from the threat or use of force against the territorial integrity or political independence of any state' [Article 2(4)], subject to 'the inherent right of individual or collective self-defence if an armed attack occurs against a Member of the United Nations, until the Security Council has taken measures necessary to maintain international peace and security' (Article 51). The fundamental idea was that states would foreswear the unilateral right to resort to force because the Security Council would, collectively, exercise a monopoly over the use of force in order to uphold international peace and security. However, the overall settlement was fundamentally incoherent and resulted, perhaps as intended, in the permanent members of the Council – that is, the USA, Russia, China, France and Britain – operating outside the framework of the Charter.

The right to individual self-defence is the basic principle of an anarchical system and the possibility of collective self-defence is essential to the operation of the balance of power. These principles would operate in the event of the Security Council being unable to maintain international peace and security, something that it could accomplish only if there were agreed norms of action between the permanent members as to the nature of 'international peace and security'. To date, these powers have been unable to agree any such norms. Thus, as Martin Wight points out, 'Article 51 "turned the veto inside out" ... by recognizing that a majority of powers cannot be prevented from cooperating to pursue *outside* an international organization a policy which the unanimity rule prevents them from pursuing *inside* the organization' (1986, p.218). In short, in the absence of a concert among the permanent members of the Security Council, the great powers continued to assert their independent rights and duties. On the other hand, if the Security Council was unanimous, it could impose the law on smaller powers.

2.6   Colonialism

The English School's identification of the institutions of international society focuses on the norms and institutions between European states as they developed from the seventeenth century onwards. However, Europe's international society rapidly expanded to encompass the whole of the known and inhabited world, and this expansion was based on a deep paradox, even on hypocrisy. For while the European states-system was the first such set of arrangements explicitly based on principles of sovereign rather than imperial (or hegemonial) rule – it was in that sense the first properly inter-national society – it achieved its global ascendancy precisely as a result of imperialism. Europe's hegemony over the rest of the world was achieved by empire building and colonialism. Naturally, this meant in practice that there were two sets of rules (at least): one for the dealings among European polities

Colonialism
Colonialism is, in general, the policy and practice of establishing colonies, that is, the settlement of people in new lands who retain some forms of allegiance to their country of origin. Most European colonialism was also a form of imperialism, that is, the extension of power through conquest so as to create empires.

and another for those between European and non-European polities. As Bull and Watson point out: 'the European states, as they evolved this non-hegemonial system in their relations with one another, at the same time established a number of empires, which, while they were rival and competing, taken together amounted to a European hegemony over the rest of the world' (1984, p.6).

Question

How do we explain the difference between sovereign systems, imperial systems and hegemonial systems?

Earlier (pre-modern) European geopolitics and other 'regional' international systems 'were all, at least in the theory that underlay them, hegemonial or imperial' (Bull and Watson, 1984, p.3). In an imperial system, many political communities may co-exist but one of them claims and exercises a higher authority at least over certain core matters, usually relating to the use of force and the economic bases of state power. Within these limits, local states may exercise considerable autonomy but they remain *de jure* and *de facto* subordinate to the imperial power. In a sovereign system, by contrast, there are no relations of *de jure* authority: each state is constitutionally independent.

Thus, as Chris Brown says, in an imperial system 'autonomy is contingent', but between sovereign states autonomy 'is built into the rules of the game, it is a constitutive rule which defines the nature of the relationship' between states (2002, p.5). In the practice of relations among and between states, things have rarely been as tidy as a simple division between sovereign and imperial orders might suggest. In many cases, formally sovereign states have accepted the *de facto* authority of another, more powerful, state, and the English School typically refer to the latter as a hegemonial system based on hegemonial authority. Empire and fully independent sovereign statehood might usefully be thought of as two poles of a continuum, with hegemony as the median point.

For the English School, the notion of international order was one in which the units are different polities, and their concern is the relationships between polities. This means a clear distinction can be drawn between sovereign and imperial principles based on whether or not formal independence of those polities exists or not. Recognition of hegemony is given as something in between these two, with hegemony understood in its general meaning of 'influence over'. In Chapters 4 and 5 you will come across other approaches to international order which extend the units of the international system to include transnational actors and processes – the economy and economic actors such as firms and social groups such as classes. This leads to different ways of interpreting actual instances of hegemony in terms of the ways that influence can be exercised. Furthermore, it leads to some views of empire and

---

Imperial system
An imperial system or empire is based on the formal exercise of authority by one or more state(s) over other subordinate polities.

Sovereign system
A sovereign system is based on the recognized constitutional independence and formal equality of the states which comprise it.

Hegemonial system
A hegemonial system is formally based on sovereign independence, but one or more state(s) exercise(s) *de facto* influence over the others.

The expansion of Europe: British colonial administrators meeting local representatives in Lagos, Nigeria, circa 1910

imperialism that are not limited to formal political control but may be based also on power exercised through the economic and social spheres.

For our purposes in this chapter we shall stick with the English School's approach and note that the notion of sovereign equality – that is, the idea that sovereignty, and with it the right to participate in the institutions of international society, might apply to all, and not just to European peoples, and that sovereigns are formally equal parties to any agreements in international law – made an appearance after the First World War. Yet it only received something like universal endorsement after the Second World War. For this reason, some analysts have argued that colonialism should be regarded as an additional institution of Europe's international society. I consider some of the implications of this in more detail in Section 3.

2.7   Where is the 'We' in international society?

The mutual recognition of sovereignty, the balance of power, international law, the special rights and duties of the great powers and war are all, according to the English School, rules or institutions of the society of states – things that endow that society and its members with a genuinely collective identity. I have suggested that, at least until the end of the Second World War, it is reasonable to see colonialism as an additional institution of European international society. We can think of these rules and institutions as forming a 'constitution' for the society of states. The society of states is not merely an aggregate of independent states, each acting on the basis of self-interest, but also a collective body with shared rules and institutions in which the identities and actions of its members – that is, sovereign states – are shaped by their participation in that anarchical society. There are, therefore, two key ideas here. First, the rules and institutions of international society are, in part, constitutive: what states are, their identities, and what they do, the games they play, are, to some extent, created by the rules and institutions of that society. Second, in some respects international society acts as a collective body with its own forms of decision making which are irreducible to an aggregation of individual decisions by its member states.

Activity 3.2

To check your understanding of my survey of the norms and institutions of international society (Sections 2.1 to 2.6), make sure that you can identify some examples of the first of these two key ideas (that is, that the norms and institutions are, in part, constitutive of the members of international society).

Now, a crucial question in any constitutional order is who gets to interpret the constitution. What happens when there are competing, possibly conflicting, interpretations of the constitution? How is the constitution changed as circumstances change? I have argued that international law is not a general legal order of the kind found within the state, there is no authorized legislative body operating at an international level (see Section 2.3), at best it is an accumulation of widely accepted custom and practice. The only body that might in principle perform such a role, the UN and, especially, the Security Council, has failed to develop a genuine concert among the major powers, let alone among the membership as a whole.

There is, then, no generally recognized body that can speak authoritatively for the 'we', from the 'we the peoples' mentioned in the preamble to the UN Charter. Nevertheless, Alexander Wendt, has argued that:

> Not only do modern states see themselves as a We bound by certain rules, but since at least the Congress of Vienna in 1815 they have been evolving a collective, second-order awareness of how that collective identity functions, and of what is required to keep it orderly. This emerging collective self-consciousness is found and expressed in the 'public sphere' of international society where states appeal to public reason to hold each other accountable and manage their joint affairs.

(Wendt, 1999, p.376)

Neither the English School nor Wendt have provided a clear account of the idea that international society has a constitution in which 'states appeal to public reason to hold each other accountable and manage their joint affairs'. Nevertheless, the basic point they are making is, I think, a simple and important one.

Any group of actors that embraces a set of common purposes faces a dilemma about how to take decisions. One possibility is for each member to make an independent individual decision about the issue in question and then to form a collective judgement directly, using some kind of voting procedure. In the society of states this might involve, for example, taking decisions in the Security Council or the General Assembly of the UN. (One can imagine alternative principles such as weighting the votes based on the population of the member states.) Another possibility is to have some basic rules and institutions that specify the collective decisions to be taken in response to similar kinds of issues. This subordinates individual decision making to some collective procedures, and those procedures determine the collective judgement. Acting on the basis of the balance of power, and recognizing the special rights and duties of the great powers, might be examples in the anarchical society of states.

The first option individualizes judgements, the second collectivizes judgements. If the group faces a range of connected decisions over time, it will face a choice of whether to individualize or collectivize decision making. The central difference is that the second option constrains individual decisions so that the group's collective decisions are consistent. Moreover, if the group wishes to implement its common purposes consistently over time, it has no option but to employ the second mode of decision making. Adopting the first procedure will produce inconsistencies in judgements of similar issues on different occasions, thereby undermining the ability of the group to be an effective promoter of its common purposes.

Question

Under what circumstances might you expect states to accept collective forms of decision making?

Presumably, states will accept collective decision making when the common purposes thereby served are sufficiently important compared with the loss of freedom involved in the accompanying constraints on individual decisions. States are likely to accept collective forms of decision making when the benefits that flow from this exceed the costs associated with the loss of independent initiative. This suggests that the acceptance of collective decision making in the society of states is likely to be one of degree. Different states are likely to be more or less willing to accept collective decision making on different issues.

By way of illustration, consider the example of whether to intervene militarily in another state. If states were to adopt the first method and vote (say in the UN) each time an issue of intervention arose, the likelihood is that there would be inconsistent judgements and intervention would sometimes be sanctioned, particularly if powerful states were in favour of it. But if states had a general interest in preventing intervention from happening, it would be more effective to construct a basic rule or institution which outlawed intervention. The loss for states would be the restriction on their freedom to intervene in other states. The gain would be a general rule protecting them from intervention by others.

The key point, however, is that the decisions of a collectivity which seeks a degree of rationality over time in its common purposes are not the same as the aggregate decisions of its individual members taken independently. There is an irreducible tension between collective and individual decision making. In circumstances of collective decision making, Philip Pettit has argued, 'individual intentions will follow on the formation of the group intention ... since the group can only act through the actions of its members. But they are not the stuff out of which the group intention is constructed; on the contrary, they are effects that the group intention plays a role in bringing about' (Pettit, 2001, p.115). An anarchical society can only act through the actions of its members but the interests and intentions of those members are, in some measure, shaped by their membership of a collectivity which has decided to collectivize elements of its decision making. That, at least, is one way to make sense of the English School's arguments and Wendt's notion that modern states 'see themselves as a We'.

3   Europe and the wider world

I now want to turn from the analysis of the norms and institutions that order international society to a more historical focus and look at the process by which the international society among European states became a universal international society. The core of this process was the expansion of European states outwards. Yet this raises a whole series of questions about whether the 'universal' international society that it led to, given its origins, is really universal at all.

American independence at the end of the eighteenth century marked the beginning of a shift from an exclusively European international society, which self-consciously distinguished the 'civilized' affairs of Europe from the norms of the non-European world, to the universal recognition of national self-determination and universal human rights after the Second World War. At first, the newly independent nations were confined to areas of European settlement but later embraced the whole world. During the course of this history, the rules and institutions of international society have changed as a result of a deeply contested process.

I noted in Section 2.6 that, in effect, colonialism amounted to one of the key institutions of Europe's international society. The fact that the European state eventually became the global state form is in large part a product of the global expansion of European society that began in the late fifteenth century. This was symbolized by Christopher Columbus's 'discovery' of the Americas in 1492 and Vasco Da Gama's arrival at the port of Calicut on the southwest coast of India in 1498. Thus began the creation of what were to become the first world empires – truly global in their compass, spanning several continents across the oceans.

Previous empires in Europe, Asia and the Americas had been regionally focused, none had been truly global and none had managed to extend their control across significant stretches of sea. For the Americas, this was the beginning of what Alfred Crosby called the 'Columbian exchange', in which the Spanish conquests brought devastation to the meso-American societies by means of the spread of infectious diseases and armed conflict, and large amounts of silver to mainland Europe. In Asia it began what the Indian historian, K.M. Panikkar, referred to as the Vasco Da Gama epoch of Asian history, where Portuguese trade and settlement involved the formation of mixed communities of European and Asian merchants just like the Dutch and English that followed them.

In Sections 3.1–4, I want to look at aspects of this expansion. First and most generally, I shall look at the idea that the spread of the European states-system was one aspect of a more general spread of modernity across the globe. This raises the question as to whether modernity is indelibly 'European' and whether that means that today's international society also bears this European birthmark. Second, I shall look at how the Europeans squared the circle between the adherence to norms of sovereign equality between states in Europe and imperial domination over other non-European societies. I shall then go on to assess how ideas of nation and race not only changed Europe's relations with the wider world but also had far-reaching and tragic consequences within European international society.

3.1   The Enlightenment and Eurocentrism

Dipesh Chakrabarty has argued that:

> The phenomenon of 'political modernity' – namely, the rule by modern institutions of the state, bureaucracy, and capitalist enterprise – is impossible to *think* of anywhere in the world without invoking certain categories and concepts, the genealogies of which go deep into the intellectual and even theological traditions of Europe. ... These concepts

entail an unavoidable – and in a sense indispensable – universal and secular vision of the human. ... It has historically provided a strong foundation on which to erect – both in Europe and outside – critiques of socially unjust practices. ... This heritage is now global.

(Chakrabarty, 2000, p.4)

Given this, a central question for Chakrabarty, as for other scholars attempting to 'think' in terms of post-colonial political theory, is whether many of the typical features of modernity represent 'a genuinely universal [heritage] ... or whether world capitalism represented a forced globalization of a particular fragment of European history' (Chakrabarty, 2000, p.69).

Question

In what ways did Enlightenment liberalism represent, in Chakrabarty's terms, 'a forced globalization of a particular fragment of European history'?

Enlightenment thinking often presented modernity as a specifically, indeed uniquely, European achievement. This view is Max Weber's 'old question': 'to what combination of circumstances the fact should be attributed that in Western civilization, and in Western civilization only, cultural phenomena have appeared which (as we like to think) lie in a line of development having *universal* significance and value' (Weber, 1920, p.13). Weber himself was 'inclined to think the importance of biological heredity very great' (Weber, 1920, p.30).

Not only did Enlightenment thinkers tend to portray modernity as distinctively European, they also claimed a universal significance for it, as Weber's comment also makes clear: the formation of modernity, though unique to Europe, is a moment 'having universal significance and value'. That is to say, Enlightenment thinkers held that the principles and institutions of modernity were of universal relevance because they represented a form of progress, an irreversible achievement of potential benefit to all humanity. Writing shortly after the climax of the age of European imperialism and the First World War, Weber was already less than certain of this judgement. In the quotation above (Weber, 1920, p.13) note the explicit loss of nerve in the parentheses, 'as we like to think'. Subsequent commentators have been reluctant to endorse it in an unqualified form, even when separated from Weber's enthusiasm for 'comparative racial neurology and psychology' as the explanation for European uniqueness.

Nevertheless, it was the combination of these two views (that modernity was distinctively European and that it represented progress of universal validity) that gave Eurocentrism its particular historical force, making it something more than the banal, provincial ethnocentrism common to all cultures. For, as

Eurocentrism
As used here, Eurocentrism refers to the view that the advent of modernity was *both* a distinctively European achievement *and* a form of universal progress, an irreversible achievement of benefit to all humanity. Critics of Eurocentrist views question both the identification of modernity with specifically European achievements and the idea that any one form of society and politics is equally relevant for all cultures.

Samir Amin pointed out, the claim that a Western model represented a form of progress of universal applicability implied 'a theory of world history and, departing from it, *a global political project*' (1988, p.75, emphasis added). This political project constitutes one major theme of modern world politics. However, it has always been, as it remains today, deeply contested. The narratives of modernity and the rise of the West continue to be the subject of deep disagreements in international politics. These critical discourses take many different forms but I want to distinguish three rather different ways of challenging the alleged universality of Western modernity.

In the first place, the equation or conflation of modernity with Europe and the West can be questioned. This view holds fast to the idea that modernity represents a form of universal progress but denies that this was a uniquely Western achievement. The Indian economist Amartya Sen (1999 and 2000), for example, has argued that the preconditions for the development of the universal principles of modernity were widely distributed across the major centres of culture and civilization on the Eurasian landmass; they are not specifically Western. Sen questions Huntington's assertion that 'the West was the West long before it was modern' (Huntington, 1996, p.69), pointing to the fact that the principles of modernity were the outcome of struggles and conflicts within the West, not a simple expression of some Western essence.

On account of this, the particular inflection given to the universal principles of modernity by the rise of the West are destined to pass as modernities develop elsewhere. This view, consequently, says that many aspects of modernity are part of a shared heritage of humanity, that there was a modernity in the West which came first, pre-empting other potential *modernities* for a time; and that as the temporary Western dominance passes, these other modernities will become more visible, making a more genuinely universal modernity possible.

The second way to question the idea of the universality of modernity is to point to its contradictory character. This might be termed the radical critique of modernity from 'within'. For example, socialist, feminist and anti-racist challenges to the dominant liberal narratives of individual and collective autonomy raise deep questions about just how universal the promises of modernity are: can genuine autonomy be extended to all, or is the freedom of some bought at the price of the unfreedom of others? This is still a narrative about modernity, about the possibility of universal progress, but one that emphasizes the limited and contradictory character of developments to date.

And third, there is a critique of modernity from 'without', which points to the necessity of its 'dark side'. Nietzsche diagnosed this as modernity's particular will-to-power, stressing what is lost, excluded or suppressed in the formation of modernity. Again, there is nothing very new in this. The dark side of modernity is a constant refrain of Enlightenment thought from at least Montesquieu's *Persian Letters* (1721):

> You wrote at some length, in one of your letters, about the development of the arts, science and technology in the West. You will think me a barbarian, but I do not know whether the utility that we derive from them compensates mankind for the abuse that is constantly made of them. ... I am always afraid that they will eventually succeed in discovering some secret which will provide a quicker way of making men die, and exterminate whole countries and nations.

> (Letter 105: from Rhedi, in Venice, to Usbek, in Paris, the 5th moon of Ramadan, 1717)

In the second half of the nineteenth century, this line of thought developed into a 'crisis of reason' narrative, which was extended to thinking about the international sphere by historians such as Oswald Spengler and Arnold Toynbee. From this viewpoint, the historical ascendancy of the West represents one particular historical experience, and systematic processes of exclusion and injustice perpetrated against 'outsiders' or 'others' undermine its claims to universality. These discourses suggest that difference and particularity may be permanent, even desirable, features of the human condition and that a singular ideal of progress may itself be part of the problem, not the solution.

The modern heirs of imperial thinking, says Pagden, 'tend to assume that a rule of law which respects individual rights and liberal democratic government ... is a universal and not, as it most surely is, the creation of Graeco-Roman Christendom' (2001, p.175). 'The West won the world not by the superiority of its ideas or values or religion,' says Huntington, 'but rather by its superiority in applying organized violence. Westerners often forget this fact; non-Westerners never do' (1996, p.51).

In Chakrabarty's terms, both the first and second kind of critique of modernity noted above concur with the thought that the Enlightenment represents 'an unavoidable – and in a sense indispensable – universal and secular vision of the human' (Chakrabarty, 2000, p.4), while the third critique is more consistent with the idea that it represents a 'forced globalization of a particular fragment of European history' (Chakrabarty, 2000, p.69).

3.2 Ideologies of empire

Whatever view one takes of the spread of modernity, the history of European expansion produced an encounter between the European states-system and the wider world. Where did the non-European, non-Christian peoples, who were encountered in the course of empire, fit into the framework of Europe's international society? In fact, we can trace a changing ideology of empire that attempted to deal with the paradox, or hypocrisy I noted in Section 2.6, of one set of norms for European international society and another for non-European peoples.

One powerful idea underpinning claims to political and territorial authority outside of Christian Europe was that of spreading the faith and saving souls. Following the *Reconquista* of Muslim Spain, this was the basis of the Spanish monarchy's claims to rule in the Americas. It sought and obtained authorization from the Pope. This was the idea 'that just as the *civitas* had ... become coterminous with Christianity [as Christianity became the official faith of the Roman Empire], so to be human – to be, that is, one who was 'civil', and who was able to interpret correctly the law of nature – one had now also to be a Christian' (Pagden, 1995, p.24).

However, as religious legitimation of rule was challenged in Europe, both by internecine religious strife among Christians and by the rise of essentially secular, humanist and republican ideas, so the basis on which colonization might be justified also shifted. The basis of political authority was thereby conceptualized in effectively secular terms, in terms of autonomous individuals, rights-bearing agents, who transfer some of their rights to the state, in order that the latter may protect their remaining freedoms. Liberal thinkers, John Locke (1632–1704) for example, gave an account of the rights that individuals could reasonably claim and, consequently, made the legitimacy of sovereignty contingent on law conforming to private morality. Within Europe, these ideas constituted a powerful liberal attack on the arbitrary power of rulers whose claim to legitimacy was either religious or absolutist.

Nonetheless, societies that did not uphold these rights in this way were, according to these liberal theorists, in a sense 'pre-political'. Considered as individuals, their people were entitled to moral considerations as was everyone else, but they had no legal–political status as *peoples*. When applied to the peoples of the non-European world, to the Indians of north America, for example, which were said to be living in a 'state of nature', Locke's *Second Treatise of Government* 'vindicate[d] a private right of punishment against people or nations which break the law of nature; ... allow[ed] arbitrary powers of life and death to the masters of slaves taken in war; and ... allow[ed] settlers to occupy the lands of native peoples without consulting their wishes in any way' (Tuck, 1999, p.133).

Even as the range of moral considerations that might be given to individuals expanded, liberalism continued to resist the idea that different kinds of peoples had rights. Even John Stuart Mill wrote, in his essay 'A Few Words on Non-Intervention' (1859), that 'barbarians have no rights as a *nation*, except a right to such treatment as may, at the earliest possible period, fit them for becoming one. The only moral laws for the relation between a civilized and a barbarous government, are the universal rules of morality between man and man.'

By these means, liberal thinkers sought to reconcile notions of individual rights, limited government and the rule of law at home with capitalist colonial expansion and settlement in foreign lands. These ideas represented an important shift in the ruling mores and discourses of empire. In contrast to conquest empires based on force and religious conversion, trading empires would be based on wealth and common interests – what the English in the eighteenth century liked to call 'empires of liberty'. This was no longer an expanding military culture of a force-wielding, feudal aristocracy, but rather a commercial and increasingly capitalist process of economic expansion. This shift was accompanied by the Enlightenment's 'powerful celebration of the civilizing and humanizing power of commerce' (Pagden, 2001, p.92). 'Civilization', rather than evangelization, thus became the official discourse of the European empires. And to be civil was to be someone who knew how to interpret the natural law correctly, nowadays extended to include the full panoply of free markets, liberal democracy and human rights.

Thus, from the time of the proto-liberal thought of Hobbes, through the more expansive notions of rights and self-government in Locke, to the comments of Mill on the rights of intervention of 'civilized' peoples against 'barbarians', liberalism has been a theory of liberty *and* empire. That is to say, liberal imperialism has deep roots and a more or less continuous presence in the history of capitalist development since the late seventeenth century.

By the early nineteenth century, the idea that empire and civilization marched hand in hand had struck sufficiently firm roots that an influential textbook, Wheaton's *Elements of International Law* (1836), could declare that international public law was limited to the 'civilized and Christian people of Europe'. Whether other peoples, nations or sovereigns passed the 'standard of civilization' test for entry into international law as full legal persons, and so enjoyed a formal equality of status with the European powers, was for its existing – that is, European – members to decide. Legal personality in international law had, by the middle of the nineteenth century, come to depend 'upon recognition by the European States and recognition was not dependent upon any objective legal criteria' (Brownlie, 1984, p.361).

Although the language of empire was one of civilization, and the standard of civilization test was set in terms of notions of individual rights, justice and the rule of law, this 'change of doctrine interacted with an increase in European cultural chauvinism and racial theories' (Brownlie, 1984, p.362). In effect, the European states regarded themselves as civilized and thought of their dealings with one another in one set of terms, while the relationship between Europe – which in the eighteenth century came to be conceptualized as in some senses a single order – and the rest of the world was increasingly conceived in racial terms. "Civilization,' like Christianity,' writes Pagden, 'was a world open to all who chose to enter it. In the early nineteenth century, however, a darker and more lasting way of understanding difference began to make an appearance: racism. ... It assumed the human family was not one but many' (2001, p.146).

3.3 Empire and nation

Until the end of the Second World War, the European powers did not accept the principle of self-government for the non-European world. The territorial and national states of European international society were imperial and colonial states outside Europe. As David Chandler says, 'the major powers either regulated their territorial acquisitions directly – as in Africa and India – or, as in China, Japan and the Ottoman empire, insisted that their own actions could not be fettered by local domestic legislation, claiming the right of extraterritoriality' (2000, p.56). As a universal principle, sovereign equality in international law is a post-Second World War phenomenon, legitimated by an appeal to racial equality and a right to (national) self-government.

Even within Europe, the principle of national self-determination played no formal role in thinking about international order until the later stages of the First World War, though nationalism had been a powerful force in European geopolitics since the French Revolution. The First World War brought about the collapse of the three large, multi-ethnic empires – the Austro-Hungarian, the Tsarist and the Ottoman – and posed the question of how the successor states could be integrated into the European states-system. Until that time, the only new entrants to the states-system aside from Japan had been states formed essentially by European settlement in the new world. During the First World War, however, the President of the USA, Woodrow Wilson, proclaimed national self-determination as a principle of international legitimacy, while in revolutionary Russia the Bolsheviks asserted anti-colonialism as a key aim of the international communist movement.

After the First World War, it was evident that the principles by which the major powers sought to order the international system would have to come to terms with the force of popular nationalism. Taken to its logical conclusion, this idea would imply one state for every people. Not only was this a complete non-starter considering the intermingling of peoples and the realities of power, but it also failed to confront the question of how to individuate peoples in the first place. What constituted a people? Was it a common territory, a shared language, common descent, shared religious belief, a shared history and sense of destiny, subjection to the authority of a state, or fate? Were all nations, however defined, equally deserving of self-determination?

Nationalism
Nationalism is the principle
that each nation should have
a state of its own.

As far as international society is concerned, the idea that nationalism – that is, the principle that each nation should have a state of its own – is a principle of political legitimacy represented a novel departure that was difficult to accommodate. As Philip Bobbitt explains:

> It is one thing to suppose that a vote of the people legitimates a particular policy or ruler; this implies that, within a state, the people of that state have a say in the political direction of the state. It is something else altogether to say that a vote of the people legitimates a state within the society of states. That conclusion depends on not simply a role for self-government, but a right of self-government.

(Bobbitt, 2002, p.180)

The standard of civilization test had presupposed that new states seeking admission to the European 'family of nations' would uphold freedom of worship and abolish religious and civil disabilities in domestic legal systems. In this respect, its focus was the religious beliefs and private interests of individuals. After the First World War, minority rights treaties replaced this test as the way in which the great powers sought to deal with questions of international legitimacy (minority rights treaties are also discussed in Chapter 6). 'What was new in 1919,' according to Mark Mazower, 'was the concern for "national" rather than exclusively religious rights, and for collective rather than individual liberties, as well as the provision for international deliberation by a supranational body [the League of Nations] rather than a conclave of Great Powers' (1998, p.54). The basic idea was that since nations could not be aligned on a one-to-one basis with states, and since most actual nations contained significant minorities who did not identify with the prevailing definition of the national identity, national self-determination was compatible with international order only in so far as states respected the claims of minorities. In the absence of such respect, internal conflicts were likely to become international as majorities in one state tried to support minorities in others, just as the European powers in the nineteenth century sought to support their co-religionists abroad.

The more or less complete failure of this framework to stem the rise of exclusively ethnic and racial forms of nationalism in Europe, and the destructive consequences of this for the states-system, were to play an important role in the development of the human rights regime in the UN after the Second World War. The most extreme instance of the destructive effects of this potential was, of course, the development of National Socialism in Germany during the inter-war years. It was no accident that Germans living outside Germany constituted the largest collection of minorities in inter-war Europe.

3.4   Empire and race

European fascism was by no means a specifically German phenomenon, and similar movements of the authoritarian, modernizing right can be found outside Europe, most notably in Japan. Nevertheless, when compared with Italian fascism, for example, there were two distinctive features of the German experience that were to have profound repercussions for the future. The first was the prominence of racial ideology in the ethnic identification and definition of German nationalism. 'The second,' says Mark Mazower, 'was that while [Italian] Fascism – like older imperialisms – saw its civilizing burden lying chiefly outside Europe, National Socialism did not: and just here, no doubt – by turning Europeans back into barbarians and slaves – lay the Nazi's greatest offence against the sensibility of the continent' (1998, p.73).

The ideology of race: Nazi soldiers parade in a mass rally at Nuremberg, 6 September 1938

This twofold character of National Socialism – that is, the centrality of 'race' in the definition of the nation and the application of the politics of empire to Europe – has given rise to an important debate about the links between European civilization, especially as it related to the non-European world, and the culture and politics of fascism within Europe. Aime Cesaire's *Discourse on Colonialism* (1955) represents a powerful statement of the idea that the barbarism of fascism within Europe, on the one side, and the expansion of European civilization without, on the other, were intimately linked. Cesaire argued that the racist legitimation of colonialism was directly connected to fascism:

> First we must study how colonization works to decivilize the colonizer, to brutalize him in the true sense of the word, to degrade him, to awaken him to buried instincts, to covetousness, violence, race hatred, and moral relativism ... a poison has been instilled into the veins of Europe and, slowly but surely, the continent proceeds toward savagery. And then one fine day the bourgeoisie is awakened by a terrific reverse shock: the gestapos are busy, the prisons fill up, the torturers around the racks invent, refine, discuss.
>
> (Cesaire, 1955, pp.13–14)

The connections that Cesaire mentions have been developed more systematically by subsequent writers, most trenchantly by Paul Gilroy.

In *Between Camps*, Gilroy explores the filiations between the definition of the nation in the age of the European colonial empires and the culture and politics of fascism. In the age of the European colonial empires, the nation was increasingly defined in racial terms, in terms of what Gilroy calls a 'camp': 'The camp mentalities constituted by appeals to "race", nation, and ethnic difference ... work through appeals to the value of national or ethnic purity' (2000, p.83). The life and welfare of the population within the camp became identified in terms of biological notions of racial purity and, in an imperial context, this was associated with ideas of a natural hierarchy of races. Politics was 'reconceptualized and reconstituted as a dualistic conflict between friends and enemies. At its worst, citizenship degenerate[d] into soldiery and the political imagination [was] entirely militarized' (Gilroy, 2000, p.82).

Camps are also political technologies, or forms of organization – 'refugee camps, labour camps, punishment camps, concentration camps, even death camps', places where the surveillance and coercion of the state are exercised over bodies and peoples. Understood in the first sense as imperial nation states based on 'militaristic, camp-style nationality, and encamped ethnicity,' says Gilroy, camps 'have been implicated in the institution of camps of the second variety' (2000, p.85). Colonialism, according to Cesaire and Gilroy, represented the application of camp thinking and camp technology to the non-European world; fascism, especially German fascism, represented their instantiation within Europe. The 'easy racialization of the European ideal,' writes Gilroy, should remind us that, alongside the universal, secular humanism to be found in Enlightenment thought, 'we should acknowledge the stubborn presence of Nordicism and Aryanism' (2000, p.63). Cesaire expressed a similar point more bluntly: '*Christianity = civilization, paganism = savagery*, from which there could not but ensue abominable colonialist and racist consequences' (1955, p.11).

Indeed, it was the impact of Nazism within Europe (as well as the impact of this on the Black population within the USA), its racial jurisprudence and abandonment of the principles of international law, that provided the necessary impetus for the Western powers to subscribe to notions of racial equality after the Second World War. Thus the refusal to recognize racial equality in the Covenant of the League of Nations (signed immediately after the First World War) stands in sharp contrast to the UN Charter (written immediately after the Second World War), which recognizes racial equality and the right to self-determination. John Vincent pointed out that: 'What stood behind this change was not a recognition on the part of the white world that they had been racialist long enough in their relations with the non-white world, but the abhorrence felt at the working-out of a noxious doctrine of racial superiority within the Western world' (1984, p.252).

Activity 3.3

This section has covered a great deal in a short space of time.

1   Outline the evolution of European ideologies in dealing with non-European peoples.

2   Does this history mean that the claims of universalism of international norms in the post-Second World War era are always tainted by their origins?

---

4   Universalism and particularism in international society

By the nineteenth century, European international society had evolved to the point where its major powers sometimes spoke of Europe as a distinct diplomatic entity, and of the European 'family of nations' which others might aspire to join provided they passed the requisite tests. In the first half of the twentieth century, this system was torn apart by what many international historians refer to as a European civil war, an eruption of barbarism in the very centre of 'civilized' Europe; in the second half, the states-system was rebuilt on new foundations on the basis of two sets of universal principles – those of sovereign equality in international law, based in a universal right to national self-determination, and those encompassed by the Universal Declaration of Human Rights of 1948.

The UN settlement no longer spoke the language of 'civilization'. Given the double standards associated with that term in the non-Western world, a different language – that of sovereign equality, universal human rights and the international community – prevailed. Nevertheless, this language was immediately subsumed beneath the Cold War conflict which meant that, for the next 40 years, debates in international politics were couched in terms of a contest between liberalism and communism. These ideas derived primarily from European and North Atlantic political thought with both ideologies claiming a universal applicability. The defeat of communism as an ideological rival to the liberal world at the end of the Cold War meant that the question of difference and its place in the international order was once again placed on the agenda, and it is to these debates in the contemporary era that I now turn. I shall first outline two contending views of the contemporary international system (in Section 4.1) before looking at the different ideas about what makes up a political community upon which these two views are based (in Section 4.2).

4.1   A new standard of civilization or a *modus vivendi* among plural civilizations?

Francis Fukuyama saw the end of the Cold War as the end of history, culminating in a worldwide liberal civilization that was equally accessible to and valid for all cultures (Fukuyama, 1992). This was, essentially, a latter-day statement of Hobbes. By contrast, Huntington maintained that: 'the intracivilizational clash of political ideas spawned by the West [that is, the Cold War] is being supplanted by an intercivilizational clash of culture and religion. ... Peoples and countries with similar cultures are coming together. Peoples and countries with different cultures are coming apart' (1996, pp.54, 125). We are presented here with two contrasting visions of world order.

On the one hand, there is the claim that, notwithstanding their European origins, the norms of post-colonial international society – sovereign equality, the balance of power, upholding international law (including universal human rights), the special rights and duties of the great powers (now formalized in the Security Council of the UN) – are part of the universal inheritance of humankind. From this perspective, there are widely shared values, and the claims of those without wealth and power are simply about getting more and seeing standards consistently applied. This is known as solidarism, or the cosmopolitan conception of international society, and it argues that, for good or ill, the encounters between civilizations as well as the many elements shared among them have produced a significant degree of convergence around values and norms. From this account, it is possible to speak, as the UN does, of a single civilized international community, or international society, in which states share certain values. Liberal theorists (as well as many of their radical critics) contend that different communities share enough to speak of a single international community, even if that community is marked by widespread inequalities of wealth and power and glaring gaps between principles and practice.

On the other hand, there is the idea that the society of states can at best encompass a *modus vivendi* among fundamentally different civilizations. Within each civilization, there may be shared principles of domestic politics and international relations, and each civilization may have its own, regional, dominant power; but between civilizations the rules of international society are confined to those necessary for peaceful co-existence. 'The world will be ordered on the basis of civilizations or not at all. In this world the core states of civilizations are sources of order within civilizations and, through negotiations with other core states, between civilizations' (Huntington, 1996, p.156). The 'avoidance of a global war of civilizations,' says Huntington, 'depends on world leaders accepting and cooperating to maintain the multicivilizational character of global politics' (1996, p.21). International order rests on a form of co-existence based on mutual concerns with survival.

There are several ambiguities in the term 'civilization', and this no doubt helps to account for its rhetorical force. 'Civilization' can be used in the singular in opposition to barbarism. This was its original sense in Greek and Roman thought: civilization was connected to the doings of citizens, with the law-governed, peaceable life of cities, the world of settled agriculture, literacy, technological innovation and the pursuit of reason. Other civilizations, such as the Chinese, have had similar terms for those beyond their frontiers. Evaluations of the costs and benefits of civilization, of what was gained and what was lost as a result of a civilizing process, varied, but nobody doubted that it was preferable to barbarism.

'Civilization' can also be used in the plural. At this point, vagueness tends to cloud discussion because there is considerable disagreement about how to identify the contours of one civilization in comparison with another. Are the distinguishing marks of civilizations material – pastoral, agricultural, industrial and so forth – or are they cultural and, if so, what is the basis of relatively enduring cultural differences – religion, ethnicity, history?

Huntington argues that it is possible to distinguish between modernization, or industrial civilization, on the one hand, and Western civilization, on the other. Modernization, Huntington avers, is indeed a universal process,

Solidarism
Solidarism (or cosmopolitanism) refers to the idea that, despite differences and the particular origins of international norms, these norms have become sufficiently widely shared to allow us to speak of a single international community based on 'universal values'.

involving economic and technological development, growing social differentiation and popular mobilization, state building and nation formation. Westernization – that is, individualism, secularism, notions of universal human rights, the rule of law and pluralist forms of representation – is only one way of becoming modern. Huntington's definition of civilization is that it is primarily based on religion. Since a 'universal civilization can only be the product of universal power', the identification of modernization with Westernization is an illusion, destined to fade with the passing of the European empires and the eventual decline of US hegemony. Rather, 'the world is becoming more modern and less Western' (Huntington, 1996, p.78).

Huntington's definition of civilization

According to Huntington, civilizations are comprehensive, long-lived cultures based on common descent, language, religion and way of life, in which the most important element is usually religion.

According to Huntington, 'the revolt against the West [that is, anti-colonialism] was originally legitimated by asserting the universality of Western values; it is now legitimated by asserting the superiority of non-Western values' (1996, p.93). Moreover, even those non-Western societies that originally (and earlier) modernized in the era of Western dominance are turning against the West:

> Initially, Westernization and modernization are closely linked, with the non-Western society absorbing substantial elements of Western culture and making slow progress towards modernization. As the pace of modernization increases, however, the rate of Westernization declines and the indigenous culture goes through a revival. Further modernization then alters the civilizational balance of power between the West and the non-Western society and strengthens commitment to the indigenous culture.

> (Huntington, 1996, pp.75–6)

At one level, as we have just seen, this is a debate about the nature of the similarities and differences between the politically organized peoples that make up the international system. Underlying this, however, it is a debate about whether the forms of political identification which go to make up any given political community or people are universal forms of identification, or particular to each separate community.

4.2 Living as friends or as strangers?

We can see this debate about political identification if we return to the autonomous, rights-bearing individuals we encountered in our discussion of Hobbes and later liberal thinking. On a liberal understanding of sovereignty, particular states are, in Bull's words, 'local agents of the common good'. That is to say, states serve a purpose for individuals in providing a framework of order that makes legally and practically effective their assertions of rights and interests. In this way, the justification for state sovereignty is that it is necessary to define and protect the rights and interests of a given set of individuals. The state is seen as an instrument of the latter, its *raison d'être* is the rights and interests of individuals. Put differently, while the legal definition and practical protection of rights might require the establishment of particular political orders, the moral justification of those orders is offered in universal terms. Particular polities are to be judged against moral criteria that are applicable to all humanity. Understood in these terms, the members of international society are states but the legitimacy of those states, and thus the degree to which they should be accorded international recognition, is a function of how far they conform to criteria enshrined in international norms of universal human rights. On this account, international society constitutes essentially a single, cosmopolitan civilization, embodying a universal code of conduct.

Critics of this view have argued that, despite its apparently universal appeal, it in fact represents a very particular view of politics that has no obvious claim to universality. It is, Pagden contends, 'a constitutive element in European cultural and political thinking: the belief in the possibility of a universal human code of conduct' (1995, p.200). The solidarist account of international society is based on a highly moralized account of politics, in which 'politics becomes equated to a search for legitimacy in which all social arrangements are regarded as in need of rational justification' (Brown, 2002, p.184). And, one might add, a rational justification that appeals solely to the rights and interests of individuals. The solidarist view, its critics maintain, embodies a particular form of political thinking, a 'specifically *Anglo-American* form', in which the state is 'understood to be an institution designed to solve the problems of collective action rather than an institution which [is] central to the constitution of the collectivity itself, and to individual personality' (Brown, 2002, p.61). Its dominant idiom of expression is still that of a contract or covenant among autonomous, rights-bearing individuals, given to us by such thinkers as Hobbes and Locke in the political discourses of seventeenth-century Europe. Fukuyama represents a contemporary instance of this approach.

Criticism of this individualist, liberal tradition has developed in two rather different ways. In the first place, it is argued that even genuinely universal values (assuming that such exist) require a determinate embodiment if they are to be realized; as Hegel saw, all universals worth the name are concrete, not abstract. But this means that, as G.A. Cohen has said, 'there is no way of being human which is not *a* way of being human' (2000, p.354). This argument does not challenge the basic idea of universal human rights but it does suggest that there can always be legitimate disagreement about the actual embodiment of those rights in concrete social and political contexts. It also suggests that it is for particular political communities to make those judgements, not for others to seek to impose their conception of what it is to be human as *the* conception.

The 'we' of the peoples of the world can be authentically human in different ways. There might be a family of legitimate and reasonable conceptions of universal human rights, realized in different ways in different contexts. After all, one of the principal arguments for sovereignty is that it allows different political communities to express and realize their particular aspirations in co-existence with other such communities. It allows different political communities to have a voice in the international system. If a political community has nothing particular to express, then the value or purpose of sovereignty is correspondingly diminished.

The second line of attack constitutes a much more radical challenge to the solidarist understanding of international society, since it takes issue with the underlying conception of politics at work in that approach. Rather than seeing politics as a search for legitimacy and a terrain of rational justification among autonomous, rights-bearing individuals, many have argued that politics is always a contest and that political outcomes always reflect or embody a set of power relations. The conservative political theorist, Michael Oakeshott, makes this point in his critique of 'rationalism' in politics when he argues that politics is the activity of making collective choices in 'political situations', these being defined as 'a condition of things recognized to have sprung, not from natural necessity, but from human choices or actions, and to which more than one response is possible' (1991, p.70). Oakeshott is certainly not an advocate of irrationality in political life; rather, he is critical of the idea that political reality can or should be made to conform to principles derived from necessarily abstract and universal (because general) reasoning.

The source of political obligation, for Oakeshott, is not to be understood on the model of a social contract among bearers of pre-existing rights and interests, but is better seen as the outcome of a conversation among friends, often defining themselves against 'enemies', that depends on traditions and allegiances that have affective as well as rational components. Political authority may rest primarily upon upholding certain collective practices and identities, embodied in a particular set of cultural traditions. Moreover, there may be no schedule of rights or set of interests against which these different cultures can be compared and evaluated, as it were, from the outside. Terry Nardin (1983) has used this alternative understanding of politics to develop a 'particularist' account of the underlying purposes of international society. Nardin understands international society as a 'practical association' whose primary purpose is to facilitate the co-existence of states in which *different* and inherently *particular* conceptions of a legitimate political order can flourish. The norms of a practical association are inherently limited to those that are required to sustain peaceful co-existence, they constitute a *modus vivendi* among peoples. This is precisely Huntington's view of what is now required for international order.

5   Conclusion

At the beginning of this chapter, I posed three sets of questions prompted by reflections on the implications of 11 September 2001. One was about the existence or otherwise of an international community and the shared norms on which it is based; the second was about the origins of universal claims in the spread of European international society; and the third was about how different ideas about political communities lead to different views about the contemporary international system.

Question

How might we present different ways of constructing answers across these three questions?

On one reading, the UN settlement represents the fulfilment of a global political project, which, though originating in Europe, has contributed to the common heritage of humankind a set of values and principles of international order that, if not the last word, are the best yet on what a universal, cosmopolitan, international community should look like. This development has extended liberal principles which were initially restricted to propertied, male Europeans, but now embrace all of humanity. Indeed, the liberal project proclaims itself as, if not universal, at least universalizable. This reading argues that criticisms of liberalism represent demands for inclusion on equal terms and for a consistent application of its principles to others and that even radical critics of liberalism share this view of universal international norms. For liberals, the (universal) liberal basis of identification within political communities provides the basis for shared norms at the international level. I have used the figure of Thomas Hobbes, arguably the most insightful theorist of the domestic and international politics of this world, to characterize some of these key ideas but he is but one part of a much wider liberal tradition of thought.

A different reading, represented in rather different ways by Osama Bin Laden and Samuel Huntington, sees the present international community as an ideological fiction, as the dominance of the West and characterized by a clash of civilizations. Universal norms are the expression not of a common heritage, but of the power of Western civilization. From this position, liberalism, like all political ideologies, is but one particular way of ordering human collective life, with no special claims on the attention of those who wish to live differently. Furthermore, while liberalism argues that its prescriptions for political life can be grounded in a general process of rational assent, others see politics as always involving forms of power that cannot finally be legitimated by an appeal to a 'universal' reason.

Between these two positions stand a range of thinkers who argue that both liberalism and other traditions, such as Islam, are themselves internally contested and mutually entangled.

Whereas Enlightenment liberalism suggests that the future of international order depends on an extension and deepening of the liberal project, some of its critics call instead for an honest recognition of that project's particularity and for it to learn to live in peace with other, equally valid, ways of being human. In the terms I used at the outset, this is ultimately a question of the extent to which we have a choice to live together as friends or strangers, and how we exercise the choices we have.

Further reading

An important collection of essays on the expansion of European international society and the impact of this on world politics is Bull, H. and Watson, A. (eds) (1984) *The Expansion of International Society*, Oxford, Clarendon Press.

For a powerful challenge to the universal claims of (European) international society and a statement of his view that 'Peoples and countries with similar cultures are coming together. Peoples and countries with different cultures are coming apart', see Huntington, S.P. (1996) *The Clash of Civilizations and the Remaking of World Order*, New York, Simon and Schuster.

For an excellent introduction to contemporary debates in international political thought, see Brown, C. (2002) *Sovereignty, Rights and Justice: International Political Theory Today*, Cambridge, Polity Press. A collection of many of the key texts can be found in Brown, C., Nardin T. and Rengger, N. (eds) (2002) *International Relations in Political Thought*, Cambridge, Cambridge University Press.

Some interesting and difficult questions about the universality or otherwise of European Enlightenment thought and its impact in the colonial and post-colonial world are raised in Chakrabarty, D. (2000) *Provincializing Europe: Postcolonial Thought and Historical Difference*, New Jersey, NJ, Princeton University Press.

Chapter 4 A liberal international order?

William Brown

1   Introduction

> ... let your thoughts and your imaginations run abroad throughout the whole world, and with the inspiration of the thought that you are Americans and are meant to carry liberty and justice and the principles of humanity wherever you go, go out and sell goods that will make the world more comfortable and more happy, and convert them to the principles of America.

US President Woodrow Wilson, Speech to Salesmanship Conference, Detroit (cited in Levin, 1973, p.18)

> I reasoned that if we could get a freer flow of trade ... so that one country would not be deadly jealous of another and the living standards of all countries might rise, thereby eliminating the economic dissatisfaction that breeds war, we might have a reasonable chance of lasting peace.

Cordell Hull, US Secretary of State 1933–44 (cited in Gardner, 1956, p.9)

> In a new era of peril and opportunity, our overriding purpose must be to expand and strengthen the world's community of market-based democracies. During the cold war we sought to contain a threat to the survival of free institutions. Now we seek to enlarge the circle of nations that live under those free institutions. For our dream is a day when the opinions and energies of every person in the world will be given full expression, in a world of thriving democracies that cooperate with each other and live in peace.

US President William J. Clinton, Remarks to the 48th Session of the United Nations General Assembly, 27 September 1993 (Clinton, 1993, p.1614)

For world leaders like US President Clinton in the 1990s, the liberal view of the international system presents us with the possibility of achieving progress and transformation in international affairs. Not only can ideals of democracy and freedom be a goal of foreign policy, but the world in which we live, and the principles by which states interact with each other, can be fundamentally altered. In place of insecurity and a struggle for power, international relations can become a realm of co-operation and peace. By the end of the twentieth century many commentators and politicians thought that the creation of just such a liberal international order – a goal which had animated US President Woodrow Wilson at the end of the First World War as much as President Clinton at the end of the Cold War – was finally within reach.

For many, the end of the Cold War, with the collapse of communist regimes in Eastern Europe, the fall of the Berlin Wall, and the break-up of the Soviet Union, removed the only remaining alternative system of international order to liberal capitalism. Other competing forms of international order from the European empires to the international dictatorship of Nazi Germany had already been defeated. The evolution of relations between the Western capitalist powers during the Cold War had laid the basis for a new kind of international order. The triumphalist tones of Francis Fukuyama, that 'history' – defined as the struggle over how to organize society – was at an end, were echoed by the likes of President Clinton. All that remained was to enlarge the circle of market-based democracies.

This chapter will investigate the claim that the modern states-system is now a liberal order. I shall ask whether the liberal narrative of the history of the modern states-system is credible, and whether the liberal analysis of international relations is convincing. In order to do this I shall first provide an overview of the liberal tradition and the founding assumptions on which liberalism is based. Liberal claims are both present in 'real life' politics, as a political ideology acting in the world, and as academic approaches to interpreting and analysing the world. In Section 2, therefore, I shall provide a working definition of liberalism as well as briefly review the historical background of liberalism and some of the key concerns in studying the international system with which it is associated. I shall then look at the historical record of liberalism, focusing on the ways in which the USA has pursued liberal aims in the international system in the twentieth century. However, lying underneath many of the specific, substantive claims that liberals make about aspects of international relations, is a distinctive view of the nature of relations between states which differs in crucial respects from the traditional 'power politics' view associated with realism. In Section 3, therefore, I shall unpick some of the key analytical debates that liberal claims draw our attention to. In Section 4 I look at some of the ways in which this case is contested – by claims that power politics remain dominant, or by arguments that deeper processes of change within capitalism have shaped the modern states-system. I shall conclude by considering the importance of the end of the Cold War for the future of a liberal international order.

2   Making a liberal international order

Liberalism is both a political ideology informing some of the most important attempts to intervene in, and re-shape, the international system and an analytical tradition seeking to interpret, understand and theorize about the international system. In this section I shall provide some preliminary comments about liberalism in these two senses and, in particular, outline a working definition of liberalism as a theory of international order.

2.1   The liberal tradition

The roots of liberalism as a political ideology can be traced back to the late seventeenth century and thinkers such as John Locke. The core characteristics of developed liberalism are a concern with individual liberties, said to be universally applicable to all, a view of society as basically a co-operative endeavour for mutual advantage, and a doctrine of the possibility of progressive change in social relationships. Liberalism is an individualistic doctrine in two senses. It is individualist about the form that values must take: something is of value only if it is capable of being enjoyed by a distinct person. Also it is individualistic as to the content of values: 'a social situation where human individuals have scope for self-development and self-realization through autonomous decisions and choices, taken either individually or in free collaboration with others, is of value both to the self-realizing individuals and to others' (MacCormick, 1999, p.175). It is a universalist doctrine in the sense that it holds that all human beings, by virtue of a common capacity for autonomous rational action, are capable of enjoying similar liberties. For the same reason, liberalism is a doctrine of equality: it postulates a *common humanity* in virtue of a shared rational capacity' and it aims to universalize liberties among all (Freeden, 1996, p.159). Liberalism therefore advocates an equality of liberties. Politically, liberalism focuses on the relationship between the individual and the state: it aims to limit both the power and the functions of the state by upholding individual rights and the rule of law and by leaving large areas of 'private' life – family life, religious matters, the economy, civil association and so forth – outside the direct control of state agencies. Economically, liberalism focuses on the freedom of agents to own property, to make contracts and to trade under a common framework of law and regulation. In both spheres, liberalism views social arrangements as forms of mutual advantage: by co-ordinating on a set of individual rights, a law-based political order and the institutions of a market economy, liberals contend that people are able to pursue their own individual interests while also serving the mutual interests of all (Hardin, 1999). Liberalism is also associated with notions of individual and collective progress, the idea that individual self-development and

Liberalism as a political ideology
Liberalism as a political ideology is associated with the attempt to achieve individual rights and liberties (including freedom in the private sphere and in economic matters), on a basis of universality and equality and to promote mutual gain through co-operation, including co-operation among nations.

collectively shared institutions are capable of moving from a less to a more desirable state.

Most importantly for our present concerns, liberalism, at least since Kant, has a proposal for international affairs as well as a set of prescriptions for how domestic political and economic arrangements should be ordered. The external policy of liberal states should allow individuals to trade and to travel freely across their borders, and this right should be extended to the citizens of the state and to foreigners. Any given state is thus a 'local guardian of the world republic of commerce' (Hirst, 2001, p.64). Moreover, liberal states should develop international institutions and forms of international law to ease commercial transactions across their borders, thereby advancing the benefits of the division of labour and specialization and political co-operation on an international scale.

Liberalism as a model of international order
Liberalism as a model of international order is based on three assumptions: that basic actors are individuals and private groups; that state preferences represent the interests of some subset of these individuals and groups; and that state behaviour is determined by the interdependence of state preferences across the international system.

As an analytical tradition, liberalism as a model of international order builds on these philosophical and political foundations. Andrew Moravcsik, a leading international relations scholar, has defined three core analytical assumptions of liberalism (Moravcsik, 1997). First, Moravcsik claims that the fundamental actors of international relations are individuals, and private groups of individuals. It is assumed that they will act rationally in pursuit of their interests which might be defined in material terms (economic interests, for example) or ideal terms (fundamental beliefs, for example). This pursuit of interests is inherently competitive given that not all interests can be realized at the same time, and thus at any one time some will be more dominant than others. Converging interests will produce a more co-operative society than where interests are deeply and irreconcilably opposed.

Second, a liberal model of international order argues that states 'represent' the dominant subset (or sets) of the individuals and groups within society. Quite how states represent the dominant interests within a state will depend on the nature and institutions of the state; a sub-group might be dominant through an electoral system in democratic polities, or the state might 'represent' the interests of a very small clique, or single dictator in tyrannical systems, or a state may exist somewhere on a continuum in between. These institutions are thus a 'transmission belt' between social actors and state policy. But whatever the nature of the state's institutions, what the state seeks to do and achieve in the international system – what are called the state's preferences – are socially defined. Such social definition may not simply be a 'domestic' process as interests can be formed, and social actors operate, across borders on a transnational as well as national basis.

Finally, states' behaviour internationally, how they do in fact act, is determined by the international configuration of state preferences. What do I mean by that? Simply that while states will seek to pursue their preferences they do this in the context of, and amid the constraints of, what other states are seeking to do. Another way of saying this is to say that state preferences are interdependent. As with the first assumption about domestic interests, a more co-operative and harmonious world will be achieved when states' preferences are similar, than when they are deeply divided.

Question

Think about the realist approach to world politics. What are the chief contrasts between realist and liberal assumptions?

Moravcsik argues that these liberal assumptions build a 'bottom-up' view of world politics – proceeding from individuals within states to the international system – in contrast to realism's 'top-down' approach which says that it is the distribution of power across the international system, and the existence of anarchy in the international system, which determines what states seek to do and how they behave.

One of the important implications of these 'founding assumptions' as Moravcsik calls them, is that the nature of international order can change. This is because state behaviour ultimately rests on what individuals seek, together with the way in which these interests are translated into state preferences. Given social and political change, state preferences are likely to vary between states and to change over time. In principle, states may seek to achieve a wide variety of aims (preferences), and states or sub-groups of states might have very similar preferences, or widely diverging preferences, making for very different kinds of international system. In contrast to realism, which argues that states operate within the inescapable reality of international anarchy in which they must always seek similar things (to achieve their own security against other states), liberalism therefore holds out the possibility of change in the states-system. Given that state preferences might develop in what liberals would consider a progressive direction it also allows for the possibility of the progressive transformation of the states-system itself. (I shall return to this idea in Section 3.) Indeed, it is in discussions about transforming international order that the liberal analytical tradition (which posits the possibility of, and assesses the extent of, transformation) and the political ideology of liberalism (which actively seeks that transformation) become closely associated with one another.

Within the liberal tradition, these founding assumptions have produced a number of different substantive claims about international order.

Activity 4.1

Identify the general claims about the international system and the imperatives for political action that are contained in the quotations at the beginning of this chapter.

The answer to Activity 4.1 makes it clear that the quotations, particularly those of Hull and Clinton, encapsulate two important liberal claims. The first of these, sometimes referred to as 'commercial liberalism', is a claim about the economic relations between states, namely that a freer international economy is desirable both because it increases overall welfare and because it helps to create peaceful relations between states. You can see this idea in the quote from Hull. Cordell Hull was Secretary of State to President Roosevelt at a time when barriers to international trade had been increased by most of the industrialized countries. It was, in the minds of people like Hull, associated both with the poor economic performance of the time (these were the 1930s depression years) and with increasingly antagonistic relations between states (an idea I come back to in Section 3.2). Hull was centrally involved in the initial moves by the USA away from protectionism and negotiated a series of bilateral trade agreements which contributed to a gradual liberalization of trade.

As such, Hull was following in a long liberal tradition in making such arguments. In the nineteenth century, Richard Cobden, a British Member of Parliament and vociferous campaigner against barriers to international trade, argued that breaking down barriers to trade would increase international peace. He was successful in removing Britain's restrictions on imports of corn in 1846 (the 'Corn Laws') and brokered international trade agreements between Britain and France in 1860 (the Cobden–Chavalier Treaty). Cobden justified his free trade stance thus: 'I see in the Free Trade Principle that which shall act on the moral world as the principle of gravitation on the universe, drawing men together, thrusting aside antagonism of race and creed and language, and uniting us in bonds of eternal peace' (Cobden, quoted in Calleo and Rowland, 1973, p.261). In fact, Cobden's legacy was that Britain held to the free trade principle until the 1930s, even while other countries re-established barriers to trade in the late nineteenth century.

As you will be aware, such claims in favour of a more liberalized international economy are hotly contested and the sanguine view of the benign effects of international trade is deeply questionable. In particular, many critics claim that the benefits of such liberalization are often highly unevenly distributed (see for example Mackintosh, 2004). This is a position supported by the realist critics of liberalism who argue that free trade has been promoted by the richer countries for their own, rather than universal,

Cordell Hull, US Secretary of State 1934–44. Hull was a major actor in the creation of the United Nations and a key liberal figure in US politics, promoting freer international trade in the 1930s

benefit as we see in Section 4. The historical record, particularly the way in which a high level of trade between the major capitalist countries at the start of the twentieth century was blown asunder by the First World War, should give us pause for thought. However, liberals argue that in the latter half of the twentieth century an unprecedented level of economic integration between liberal capitalist economies was created and furthermore, that this process of integration has been buttressed by a highly institutionalized rule-based system of international economic governance. Thus, the advantages (as liberals see it) of moving towards freer exchange of goods, services, finance and money have become consolidated in a profoundly new way.

The second liberal claim is reflected in President Clinton's expressed desire to 'expand the circle of market-based democracies'. In what is sometimes referred to as 'republican liberalism', this policy aim reflects the normative belief in constitutional democracy and liberty which is at the heart of the liberal heritage. However, it is linked to a more substantive thesis made by some liberal analysts and politicians, namely that democratic countries have never gone to war with one another. This 'democratic peace thesis' traces its roots to the work of Immanuel Kant, who argued that what he called 'a perpetual peace' could be achieved if states had 'republican constitutions' (broadly liberal–democratic regimes in today's parlance); if there was a 'universal association of states' (treaties of mutual respect and non-aggression between parties); and 'universal conditions of hospitality' (that is, commercialized interactions between states). In such a circumstance states would share common values and cease to feel threatened by each other, eliminating the causes of war. Whether or not one accepts the empirical accuracy of the modern democratic peace thesis put forward by writers such as Michael Doyle and Bruce Russet (Doyle, 1986; Russett, 1993), the reasoning behind this is that democracy either acts as a brake on the war-making tendencies of leaders, or that democracies share similar goals and values and seek peaceful, rational solutions to common problems. Thus even if there are inequalities of power and conflicting interests, these will be solved peacefully and not by recourse to war. This has been an important strand in the foreign policies of some of the most powerful capitalist states in the late twentieth century. It also reflects the liberal version of many other ideologies, namely the claim that if a political system is universalized, harmony and peace can be achieved (for example, communism made similar claims about a future socialist international system eradicating war; and both the British and the French empires claimed that the community of shared values within the empire made for order and peace among its constituent parts).

You will notice that both of these arguments – that freer trade and democracy will both help to cement peaceful, co-operative relations between states – also contain, implicitly or explicitly, imperatives for action: that policies and practices which support freer trade and democracy can help to transform the world in which we live. President Clinton's invocation to 'enlarge the circle of countries living under free institutions' implies an ongoing process of action to expand the scope of liberal international order. It is to the purposive making of a liberal international order, led by the USA in the twentieth century, that I shall move on to now.

2.2 The USA and the making of a liberal order

No state is so associated with the liberal project of remaking international order as the USA, and in many ways the ebb and flow of the US promotion of a liberal international order in the twentieth century has shaped the world in which we now live. In this section I shall relate some of the history of this project largely from a liberal standpoint. In the sections that follow I shall take a more detailed look at the analytical debate over how to explain this history, how we understand the USA's role in the states-system and the debate over the international order which it bequeathed to the twenty-first century.

It is often the convention to portray twentieth-century international history through the punctuation marks which scar it: the First and Second World Wars, the beginning and end of the Cold War. This is understandable given that these were indeed events which changed the shape of the international system. Each great international conflict has been followed by active attempts to remake international order (the remaking of international order after the end of the Cold War is discussed further in Chapter 5). However, in doing this it is often easy to miss the longer histories and trends and to focus only on the

Bill Clinton, US President 1992–2000, addressing the United Nations

outcomes which, while they may seem clear with hindsight, were much more messy and uncertain in reality. Thus, one telling of the liberal project would have it that the USA engaged in an attempt to create a liberal order at the end of the First World War which failed, resulting in an era of economic stagnation, protectionism and conflict, and this only ended with the conclusion of the Second World War in which a liberal order was brought into being among the Western powers. The demise of communism after the long Cold War then allowed the possibility for this order to expand outwards.

Such a view captures some of the important features of the century but I want to tell a less well-defined story. Certainly it is true that the emergence of the USA as a world power was encapsulated in the entry of the USA into the First World War in 1917. However, American foreign policy had for some time been the site of an ongoing struggle between unilateralist and multilateralist tendencies (that is, whether the USA should decide independently when and how to intervene internationally or to commit to systems of international rules shared with other states), and between isolationist and interventionist pressures (Ruggie, 1998, pp.207–10). President Woodrow Wilson's gradual acceptance of the need to enter the European war then left the USA, at its conclusion, confronting a dual problem. On the one hand, the USA wished to establish an order among the European states in the aftermath of the war which would help to prevent further conflicts and, importantly for the USA, thus to prevent the prospect of the USA being drawn into future conflagrations. However, this mission to reshape the European states-system was undertaken also in the context of the Russian Revolution of 1917. The two aims – of a refashioned European states-system and a campaign against the spread of Bolshevism – lay behind Wilson's proposals for a League of Nations.

It is worth noting here, given the debate we shall come to over explanations of liberal international order, that the USA's attempts to make a liberal *international* order were fused with a definition of the USA's *national* interest. As Levin summarized, 'the Wilson Administration first defined the American national interest in liberal internationalist terms in response to war and revolution' (Levin, 1973, p.2). By liberal internationalism Levin means: 'the Wilsonian vision of a global situation beyond power politics to be characterized by open world trade and by great power co-operation within a framework of world law and international capitalist commercial relationships' (Levin, 1973, p.3). Indeed, Wilson's international view was informed by his analysis of domestic politics. Domestically, Wilson was a staunch advocate of the need for separation between the branches of government in order to prevent the build-up of concentrations of power. Internationally, Wilson thought that competition between great powers within a system of international law would prevent aggregations of power to any one state while keeping such competition peaceful. This idea of peaceful competition (particularly economic competition) between capitalist states is one I shall return to in Section 3.2 below.

Lying behind Wilson's liberal offensive was thus a fusion of American commercial interests (particularly for open trade); a desire to refashion great power relationships in the context of an international organization to serve the peaceful settlement of disputes; and the need to rebuild, or create anew, liberal democratic (and capitalist) nation states to forestall the spread of Bolshevik revolution.

The core of Wilson's efforts was the creation of the League of Nations, the forerunner of the United Nations (UN). Like the UN it had a Council (with permanent membership for Britain, France and the Soviet Union) and an Assembly. Its main purpose was to prevent international conflict and the central instrument was an ability to impose economic and military sanctions under Article 16. However, none of the major powers was fully committed to supporting the League and the USA never joined. In the 1930s the League proved incapable of preventing Italy's invasion of Abyssinia, or Japan's invasion of Manchuria and was effectively dead by the time of Nazi Germany's expansion.

Ultimately, Wilson's vision was undermined by the domestic unilateralist tendencies in US politics. As Ruggie has argued, by seeking to keep America free of any binding commitments (which the League of Nations would have necessitated) and able to decide for itself when and how it would intervene in world affairs, the 'door was left open' to isolationism and a withdrawal from the activism of Wilson's internationalist stance (Ruggie, 1998, pp.209–10). The refusal of the US Congress to agree to join the League of Nations effectively crippled the organization from the start.

The subsequent turmoil of the inter-war years had a profound effect on many political actors, not least liberals within the US political system, and served as a constant reference point to those who sought to re-create a new role for the USA. Some of the earliest attempts to do this were led by Cordell Hull, who as we have seen, began to turn the tide against the protectionism of US economic policy in the 1930s. Hull's strategy prior to the Second World War was motivated by a belief in both the economic and political advantages of freer movement of international trade and he negotiated a series of bilateral trade agreements which helped to reduce international barriers to trade. Indeed, in many respects, liberals like Hull in the Roosevelt administrations (others included Harry Dexter White, one of the architects of the Bretton Woods Institutions) were crucial in fashioning not just the principles on which the USA entered the Second World War, but also the vision for a post-war order.

Such planning focused on two key areas: creating a more open international economy and creating some mechanism for dealing with security issues between states. In both fields, there were strong universalist, liberal tendencies. These included proposals for a more or less total and rapid dismantling of discriminatory practices of the European states in trade and finance and the idea of a re-vamped League of Nations – an international organization based on equal status of all member states (the latter also involved the dismantling of the European empires and independence for the constituent colonies). These ideas informed the US position over the negotiation of the Atlantic Charter – the 1941 declaration of war aims agreed between US President Roosevelt and British Prime Minister Churchill – as well as subsequent plans for what were to become the Bretton Woods Institutions and the United Nations. However, in both fields, such universalism was substantially watered down in practice.

In the security field, two aspects are worthy of note here. First, as Ruggie has argued, US wariness of the League of Nations and wartime negotiations between the major powers meant that Roosevelt 'grafted a collective security regime onto a concert of power' (1998, p.212). That is, while the UN was created to prevent threats to international peace and security, the organization was a combination of a universalist body (the General Assembly) with the preservation of the rights of great powers (the Security Council), as seen in Chapter 3. In particular, the five permanent members of the Security Council (the USA, Britain, USSR, France and China) reserved the right to veto actions by the UN and thus to remain free of binding sanctions on their own actions. In addition, the idea that all nations would enjoy self-determination and thus take their place at the UN was only gradually realized in the post-war world. The initial obdurate defence of empire by France and Britain meant that the transfer of sovereignty to the colonies was for many nations delayed until the end of the 1950s and after.

However, the second factor in the security field was the rise of the Cold War which, for the Western powers, meant that it was the regional body, the North Atlantic Treaty Organization (NATO), not the UN which was at the centre of Western states' security policy. NATO was created in 1949 during the first intense confrontation of the Cold War in the context of a worsening of relations between the Soviet Union and Western Europe. Western countries were particularly antagonistic to the Soviet Union consolidating its control of the areas of Eastern Europe which the Red Army had occupied at the end of the war. The North Atlantic Treaty was signed between a group of West European states (Britain, France, the Netherlands, Luxembourg and Belgium) and the USA and Canada.

The core of NATO is a collective defence regime outlined in Article 5 of the North Atlantic Treaty: 'The Parties agree that an armed attack against one or more of them in Europe or North America shall be considered an attack against them all' and that they will take 'such action as it deems necessary, including the use of armed force, to restore and maintain the security of the North Atlantic area.' The Treaty explicitly places this arrangement for collective defence within the ambit of the UN Charter, Article 51, which allows for the creation of regional security arrangements designed to maintain international peace and security. The Treaty also provides for the Parties to 'separately and jointly' to 'maintain and develop their individual and collective capacity to resist armed attack' (Article 3). Furthermore, the Treaty commits the Parties to seek peaceful solutions to international conflicts (Article 1) and to promote co-operation on economic matters between the Parties (Article 2).

As such, NATO became the dominant security organization for Western states. The UN Security Council represented a substantial concession to great power politics through the veto powers accorded to the permanent five and it was paralysed by Cold War rivalries, with both the USA and USSR making recurrent use of the veto until the 1990s. However, among Western states, NATO represented for liberals a remarkable development. Here, among some of the most powerful states in the world, extensive co-operation was developed on the core issue of security, including joint planning in the military field which penetrated deep into these states' core purposes. Furthermore, the period after the Second World War saw the elimination of armed conflict between Western powers in sharp contrast to the repeated wars of the previous 150 years and more.

In the economic field, liberal post-war plans also came up against international obstacles. A key US concern had been to eradicate the discriminatory trade and monetary systems which had dominated the inter-war period. However, this entailed the dismantling of the British and French systems of imperial preference and the creation of some new means of governing international trade and monetary matters. At first it seemed that the USA's plans for liberal institutions had been successful with the creation of the International Monetary Fund (IMF) and the International Bank for Reconstruction and Development (the World Bank) at the 1944 Bretton Woods conference in New Hampshire in the USA. Here, US planners, led by Harry Dexter White, in conjunction with Britain's chief negotiator, John Maynard Keynes, forged the new institutions. While US proposals for an International Trade Organization (ITO) foundered, the fall-back option of the 1947 General Agreement on Tariffs and Trade (GATT, which in 1995 was subsumed within the new World Trade Organization) proved capable of achieving the liberalization of trade that the USA sought.

However, none of this was straightforward. Neither the move to allow currencies to be converted (an essential requirement for international trade) under IMF guidance, nor the liberalization of trade under the GATT were achieved quickly. In particular, the parlous state of the European economies after the war, and the continuing adherence to imperial preference delayed currency convertability until the late 1950s. In addition, the funding of European reconstruction by the World Bank, which was (on paper if not in practice) supposed to be devoid of political interests and interference, was in fact largely achieved by Marshall Plan aid from the USA. Marshall Plan aid was explicitly politically motivated and was granted in order to shore up the capitalist European states. This was done, in 1947, in response to severe economic problems in Europe, the prospect of communist parties winning greater political power in the elections of that year in France and Italy, and in response to the Soviet Union strengthening its grip on Eastern Europe.

Nevertheless, it was from these foundations that a gradual but substantial liberalization of the world economy was achieved. And even though the IMF system for managing exchange rates was brought to an end in the early 1970s, there was no recourse to the thoroughgoing protectionism of the inter-war period. Furthermore, some of the considerable limitations on this liberal order – such as the rise of protectionist policies among the newer developing countries, and the consolidation and expansion of the communist block – were by the 1980s also being eroded. Pressure from the IMF and World Bank and from Western states contributed to some far-reaching processes of liberalization in the developing world in the 1980s and 1990s, even while important areas of protection (such as trade in textiles and agriculture)

The architects of the Bretton Woods Institutions – Harry Dexter White (left) and John Maynard Keynes (right)

remained in the developed countries. The demise of the Cold War set states in Eastern and Central Europe on a problematic path of transition to capitalism, economic and political liberalization and incorporation into the Atlantic security apparatuses created in the post-war period. As Ruggie has claimed, for liberals, the triumph of the US vision, albeit messy, was nevertheless 'an achievement of historic proportions' (1998, p.73). This liberal narrative thus sees the end of the Cold War as the end of over 70 years of competing attempts to define the principles of international order. As Bruce Cummings argued in 1991: 'The 70 years' crisis of the world system is over, and we now have before us the potential to realize a prolonged period of peace and co-operation among the industrialized countries – a new world order.' (Cummings, 1991, p.199).

In this section I have presented to you a narrative of the creation of a liberal international order in the twentieth century. Although, in many respects, this is a 'liberal story', much of the broad sweep and central claims are widely accepted. Namely, that by the end of the Cold War the states-system was characterized by a high degree of economic openness (even if this is uneven) consolidated in rule-based systems of international governance and an unprecedented level of co-operation and peace between the major powers.

However, when it comes to the explanations for these features of the modern states-system, and assessing the importance of them for our understanding of international order, the liberal case is open to more far-reaching challenges. It is to the debate over how to account for liberal international order that we now turn.

3   Accounting for a liberal order

As I hope Section 2 has shown, liberal ideas about international order are politically and historically important and have motivated some of the most significant attempts to re-shape the modern states-system. However, I also noted that they are analytically distinct from other approaches in their understanding of the states-system.

In this respect, as I outlined above, the liberal analytical tradition operates with three core assumptions about international order – that it claims to build a 'bottom-up' view, moving from the interests of individuals and groups, to states' preferences, to the interaction among states in the international system. I also noted that this implied the possibility of change in the states-system as both state preferences and the configuration of preferences could change. I now present some of the substantive historical analyses of how the post Second World War era saw a transformation of relations among liberal capitalist states. There are perhaps three elements to the liberal analytical case that I wish to cover here: the claims about the nature of relations between the advanced capitalist countries after the Second World War; the basis on which co-operation, particularly over economic matters, has arisen; and the institutional form of multilateralism which underpins both of these. (In Section 4 I shall present alternatives to these arguments.)

However, I first want to note that liberal analyses vary in the extent to which they see the states-system as being transformed. In fact, liberal claims about transformation can be placed in an 'ascending order' as to how far-reaching they are.

- The first and least controversial claim is that liberal states will share a harmony of interests (such as increased welfare through trade and investment in liberalized markets; or shared values of liberal democracy).

- The second is that co-operation based on these shared interests can replace the balance of power (discussed in Chapter 3) as the dominant principle of international relations. This implies a substantial move away from the realist view of international politics being ultimately a realm of 'power politics'.

- The third idea is that if the balance of power is displaced, states can begin to share their sovereignty in forms of collective decision making, even in matters of security. This means that states may be willing to relinquish some aspects of their independent exercise of sovereignty in supra-national institutions.

- The fourth, and most far-reaching claim, is that these transformations can, in principle, apply to all states in the international system, not just a subset of them. Short of this fourth claim, while a subset of states might co-operate together for common aims, they would still exist in a balance of power world with non-liberal states. If all states can be brought within the liberal order, then the international system as a whole might be transformed.

3.1   Relations among the powerful states

Against the traditional realist idea that relations among states are anarchic and that security and survival dominate the purposes of all states, leading to a pursuit of power in an essentially zero-sum interaction, liberals claim that relations among the developed capitalist countries after the Second World War evolved in new and novel ways. Daniel Deudney and John Ikenberry – two North American liberal international studies scholars – have argued that relations between the developed capitalist countries included three interlocking principles: 'penetrated hegemony', 'semi-sovereignty' and 'co-binding'. Let us take each of these in turn.

A common argument to many explanations of the liberal international order is that the USA had a hegemonic position in the system. The term hegemony is used in different ways but, as was noted in Chapter 3, at the most general level it refers to something exercising influence over something else, in this case a particular state over the international system. From this there are a number of ways of being more specific, by identifying the particular ways that leading states have exercised influence over the states-system. As we shall see, the two critiques of the liberal position dealt with below (Sections 4.1 and 4.2) both analyse US hegemony very differently. Deudney and Ikenberry's position focuses on two aspects: that the USA was the most powerful state (defined in terms of military capability, size of economy, geo-strategic position and so on); but also that, because of the internal nature of its political and economic system, it exercised hegemony in a particular way.

Deudney and Ikenberry argue that rather than leadership implying a relationship of dominance and coercion, in fact, US hegemony has been based more on consent and reciprocity. The nature of the political system in the USA means that there are a variety of channels through which other states can influence US policy and access information about US policy formation which helps build a strong consensus between liberal powers. In their terms, penetrated hegemony builds a robust relationship between the leading liberal state and the other states.

As Deudney and Ikenberry put it:

> When a liberal state is hegemonic, the subordinate actors in a system have a variety of channels and mechanisms for registering their interests with the hegemon. Transnational relations are the vehicles by which subordinate actors in the system represent their interests to the hegemonic power and the vehicle through which consensus between the hegemon and the lesser powers is achieved. Taken together, liberal state openness and transnational relations create an ongoing political process within the hegemonic system without which the system would be undermined by balancing or become coercive.

(Deudney and Ikenberry, 1999, p.185)

In particular, they argue, the US policy process is both open to inspection by foreign states, and thus is transparent, and is open to influence – to lobby groups and representation by allies of their concerns and wishes about American policy. The result of this liberal system is that it makes US policy and hence the use of US power more predictable and safe to other liberal states, it allows for some level of consensus to be formed between the USA and other states through their involvement in the policy process, and it

Hegemony
Hegemony in its general meaning is that a political actor (in this case a state) exercises de facto influence over other states, despite the *de jure* independence of those states.

Penetrated hegemony
Penetrated hegemony refers to the way in which the dominant power (the USA) allows access to and representation within its own political system to other liberal states.

increases the density of transnational linkages between the USA and other countries at both the state and sub-state level.

> The system provides transparency, access, representation, and communication and consensus-building mechanisms. Because of the receptiveness of the liberal state and the existence of transnational relations, subordinate states achieve effective representation. ... In hegemonic systems infused with transnational relations, the legitimacy of the asymmetrical relationship is enhanced. Such processes endow the relations with a degree of acceptability in the eyes of subordinate powers.

(Deudney and Ikenberry, 1999, p.186)

From this perspective, while the USA certainly led the post-Second World War reconstruction, it did so to a large extent in partnership with the other liberal powers.

The ability of the USA to perform this role was also enhanced by the second interlocking principle, 'semi-sovereignty'. Semi-sovereignty refers to the settlement at the end of the Second World War and the way in which the defeated powers – Germany and Japan – were re-incorporated into the states-system. Following the Second World War, both Germany and Japan were accorded sovereign recognition despite their defeat and occupation by the Allied Powers. However, 'They were able to gain juridical sovereignty only because they were willing to eschew the full range of great power roles and responsibilities.' (Deudney and Ikenberry, 1999, p.188). Most notably, they were characterized by self-imposed constitutional constraints ('peace constitutions') which greatly limited the nature of, and ability to use, their military force. In particular, neither state can use offensive military force and neither possesses nuclear weapons. The post Second World War reconstruction of the defeated states therefore helped to preclude the re-emergence of great power rivalries by making their sovereignty conditional. However, this reconstruction of Germany and Japan was possible partly because of the penetrated nature of US hegemony in providing a channel by which reassurance could be gained as to the future actions and intentions of the USA.

Co-binding

Co-binding is the novel institutional form by which liberal states have sought to mutually constrain one another's actions.

These two aspects – penetrated hegemony and semi-sovereignty – were reinforced by a third dimension, that Deudney and Ikenberry call co-binding. Co-binding, 'is a practice that aims to tie potential threatening states down into predictable and restrained patterns of behaviour ... that is, they attempt to tie one another down by locking each other into institutions that mutually constrain one another' (1999, pp.182–3). Deudney has argued that binding represents an alternative foreign policy practice to the more traditional tactics of 'hiding' or 'balancing' (Deudney, 1996). By hiding he means the ability of states either to maintain a neutral stance internationally or to maintain non-involvement in international disputes and competition. The former is exemplified, for example, by Switzerland and the Republic of Ireland maintaining a position of neutrality, the latter in the USA's isolationist posture prior to and between the two World Wars which was itself based on its geographical distance from the main arena of Great Power competition. By balancing is meant the active pursuit of power in order to offset threats from potential aggressor states in an anarchic system. By contrast, 'binding is a foreign policy practice of establishing institutional links between the units that reduce their autonomy vis-à-vis one another.' (Deudney, 1996, p.214). Co-binding thus helped to consolidate the penetrated hegemony of the USA and the semi-sovereignty of Germany and Japan in a single interlocking international order. The way this worked is perhaps best illustrated by the case of NATO.

As we have seen, NATO became the key security institution for Western states and was created in a three-way context: as a means of confronting and deterring the Soviet Union; as a means of preventing the resurgence of a threat from Germany after the War; and as a means by which the Western European states could ensure that the USA would maintain a commitment to the defence and security of Western Europe. In the words of Lord Ismay, the organization's first Secretary General, NATO was created to keep the 'Russians out, the Germans down and the Americans in.' (quoted in Deudney and Ikenberry, 1999, p.183). While the first aim constituted traditional 'balancing' behaviour, the other two were more to do with binding (Deudney, 1996, p.226). As Deudney and Ikenberry go on to note: 'these aims were all interrelated: in order to counter-balance the Soviet Union it was necessary to mobilize German power in a way that the other European states did not find threatening and to tie the USA into a firm commitment to the continent' (Deudney and Ikenberry, 1999, p.183). As a consequence, Western Germany was eventually rearmed, within the limits of semi-sovereignty, and joined NATO in 1955. But this rearmament was made 'safe' for other Western European powers by West Germany's membership of NATO. The USA's role in Europe, and the recreation of a German military force, were thus achieved in ways that did not pose the kind of security dilemmas which would have been expected under a purely anarchic system characterized by balancing: co-binding security through NATO, combined with the limitations on Germany and the penetrated nature of US hegemony, transformed the nature of relations among the major powers. The anarchy of the states-system was mitigated by the creation of a novel, interlocking form of liberal international relations among those powers.

Activity 4.2

1   In terms of the four kinds of liberal claims about transformation listed at the start of Section 3, where would you place Deudney and Ikenberry's analysis of the relations among liberal capitalist states?

2   Which of Moravcsik's three assumptions of a liberal model does their explanation focus on?

3.2   The pursuit of absolute gains

The second dimension of the liberal case relates to interactions in the economic realm. One of the politically important claims liberals have often made is that states pursuing shared aims in a co-operative endeavour can increase the welfare of all. That is, states can pursue absolute gains rather than worry about relative gains. The pursuit of absolute gains has been defined as a situation where states can evaluate their gains from co-operation independently of the gains or losses of other states. States pursuing relative gains are acutely aware of the potential of other states to gain more than they do. It is widely recognized that, given that gains from economic co-operation – such as engaging in international trade, or co-operating to liberalize international trade – are often unevenly distributed, states pursuing relative gains are likely to be more cautious about international economic co-operation than states pursuing absolute gains. In the latter case, the uneven distribution of these gains will be less important than the fact that a state can gain something from co-operation. It is one of the core liberal contentions that in the post Second World War era the liberal capitalist states pursued, and achieved, large absolute gains from economic co-operation. This was achieved through the liberalization of trade, investment and international monetary payments associated with the Bretton Woods Institutions mentioned in Section 2.2.

How might this have become possible? One answer to this is that the pursuit of absolute economic gains was made possible once the security threat between these states had been solved. This is certainly how Deudney and Ikenberry present things: co-binding, semi-sovereignty and penetrated hegemony effectively removed the security threat among liberal powers. In this circumstance, the possibility of one state using economic gains for a military advantage no longer represented a threat. Indeed, they argue that the possibility of the large absolute gains from a liberalized international economy was in fact an incentive for liberal states to tackle the security dilemma between them by abridging the anarchic nature of relations between them: 'In a world of advanced industrial capitalist states, the absolute gains to be derived from economic openness are so substantial that

Absolute gains
Absolute gains are gains measured independently of the gains (or losses) of others.

Relative gains
Relative gains are gains evaluated in relation to those of others. This can be done in various ways. Here we assume that states are concerned with their share of the total income or total military capability, or both.

states have the strong incentive to abridge anarchy so that they do not have to be preoccupied with relative gains considerations at the expense of absolute gains' (Deudney and Ikenberry, 1999, p.191).

However, it may be more historically accurate to see things the other way around (see Pollard, 1985). Part of the analysis of, for example, Cordell Hull was that the key problem of the 1930s was that international economic competition had become 'politicized'. That is, in the inter-war years, states sought to direct and intervene in international economic exchanges (and in many cases national ones too). Because ploughshares could be turned into swords, states sought to gain relative to other states in the economic realm. As Hull put it in the quote at the start of this chapter, each became 'deadly jealous of the other'. The 'beggar-thy-neighbour' rises in protective tariffs and devaluations of currency in the 1930s exemplified this. This inevitably turned economic competition into political conflict, ultimately sowing the seeds of military conflict. The answer, so it seemed to some liberals, was to take economic competition out of the inter-state equation, that is, to make economic competition what it 'should be' according to liberals – a matter for private individuals and companies operating in the market. This involved two linked developments. First, the reconstruction of capitalist states as *liberal* capitalist states (in place of the 'politicized capitalism' of fascism, for example) which thus did not seek to intervene in such a directive way in economic exchanges. Second, the international order should be reconstructed as a rule-based system which would restrict states' autonomy to politically interfere in international economic exchanges. The gains from this were therefore not just the welfare gains enjoyed by individuals and firms from increased economic activity, but also the removal of what seemed to liberals to be one of the underlying causes of war. Thus, rather than a solution to the security issue paving the way for economic co-operation, it was a restructuring of the nature of economic relations along liberal lines that removed the cause of security threats.

Whichever way round the explanation is given, liberals agree that the economic gains which were realized were substantial and one of the major claims that liberalism makes is that in the post Second World War era an unprecedented acceleration of economic growth took place. However, we should note, finally, that the form in which greater economic openness was achieved – within a rule-based structure of governance – was characterized by multilateralism.

3.3   Multilateralism

Liberals claim that the international order has developed within, and been underpinned by, the particular institutional form of multilateralism. In contrast to earlier periods, the USA's plans for the post Second World War era were avowedly multilateralist and this view has been strengthened since. But what is multilateralism? John Gerard Ruggie has argued that multilateralism is a 'generic' form of international relations and defines it as:

> ... an institutional form which coordinates relations among three or more states on the basis of 'generalized' principles of conduct – that is principles which specify appropriate conduct for classes of actions, without regard for the particularistic interests of the parties or the strategic exigencies that may exist in any specific occurrence.

(Ruggie, 1998, p.109)

Multilateralism
Multilateralism is a generic form of international relations which co-ordinates relations among three or more states on the basis of generalized principles of conduct.

To explain this definition, multilateralism is here presented as one characteristic way in which relations among states may be organized. There are others, as discussed below. Multilateralism co-ordinates relations among three or more states, which distinguishes it from bilateralism (between two actors – see below) and may potentially cover the whole globe (the UN system comes close to this) but need not do so (NATO and the European Union (EU) are multilateral but fall short of covering the entire society of states), although the rules apply equally to the members of the collectivity of states concerned. Multilateralism establishes 'generalized principles of conduct' (all states will reduce tariffs on manufactured products, for example) which apply regardless of whether or not they may be in the interests of any particular state or actor. Finally, these generalized principles cover a 'class' of action. How a particular product is treated in trade rules, modalities for international communication, navigation rights on water, land and air, conduct in warfare, how certain human rights are defined, are all different classes of action.

In some respects, it might be useful to think of multilateral systems as similar to systems of domestic law in liberal states. Just as such a system might specify that it is illegal for a member of the system (an individual citizen) to steal (a class of action governed by a rule framed in a general way), so a multilateral international system might say that all member states will manage their currencies according to certain rules (as the IMF system did). Of course there are very important differences too, not least that there is an authority 'above' the individual citizen, up-holding the law, namely the state itself. There is no 'higher' authority at the international level; instead rules are agreed between states who then subject themselves to those rules and, according to Deudney and Ikenberry, seek to co-bind each other to those rules. At times, as with the IMF system, states create an authority at the international level to which they agree to subordinate their policy, that is, they collectively share sovereignty over aspects of decision making in order to achieve a common aim.

You might find it easier to see what is distinctive about multilateral international relations if you contrast multilateralism with alternative institutional forms of international relations such as bilateralism, colonialism and some forms of hegemony – all also present in the twentieth century (Table 4.1).

Table 4.1   Institutional forms of international relations (twentieth century)

	Number of states involved	Rules/principles of conduct	Twentieth-century examples
Multilateralism	Three or more	Generalized for all members of the collectivity for particular classes of action	Bretton Woods Institutions; WTO; United Nations; Law of the Sea; international communications agreements; conventions on human rights, etc.
Bilateralism	Two, or multiple two-way relationships	Specific as to the two states in question and as to the kinds of behaviour	Nazi Germany's international relations
Empire/ colonialism	One central power and one or more subject territories	Authority and property rights claimed over subject territories/ peoples	British Empire; French Union
Hegemony	One predominant power	Variable and historically specific, depending on the hegemon and its strategic interests	USA post Second World War

Source: based on the discussion in Ruggie, 1998, pp.102–30

First, as has been discussed in Chapter 3 (Section 2.6), there is a formal distinction to be made between empire and colonialism, as it is used here to mean the formal political control of another territory, and the other three, which are all in some senses systems based on sovereign independence. However, note that for hegemony, formal independence may still allow informal influence by one state or states over another. How this influence is exercised and on what power resources it is based, will vary from one historical instance to another. Note also that the term empire, or imperialism, can be used in a more general sense of 'influence or dominance over' another territory which blurs the distinction with hegemony (Lundestad, 1990, pp.37–8). Indeed, as Chapter 5 discusses, some see imperialism as present in sovereign international systems.

These qualifications aside, bilateralism is distinct from multilateralism in that the rules are specific to the two-way relationship concerned (rather than generalized) and will not necessarily be extended to other bilateral relations. For example, Nazi Germany had a system of multiple bilateral economic relations with subordinate states, but the nature of each relationship varied on a case-by-case basis. Furthermore, especially given the unequal nature of the relationships, the rights and duties on each side were unbalanced so that the rules were specific both to the states and the actions involved. A bilateralist system is thus made up of a series of compartmentalized 'dyads' (two-way relationships) so that the rules of one dyad may be completely different from another.

In some ways empire or colonialism – defined in a formal sense above – has some similarities with bilateralism. Relations were often a two-way affair between the imperial power and the subject territory and the imperial power might have a series of different arrangements with different colonies (as the British state did). A hierarchical arrangement is also present in some forms of hegemony, in that hegemony implies leadership by one state of other independent sovereign states. Quite what form the specific relations between hegemon and subordinate take will vary according to the historical and strategic context and the specific interests of the hegemonic power.

Historically, multilateralism has become an ever more important institutional form in the international system. Ruggie argues that multilateral arrangements have developed in response to three kinds of problem. First, the need for states to define rules governing property rights of states (such as territorial rights over the sea and rules governing diplomatic representation). Second, the need for states to co-ordinate on the practicalities of international interactions, particularly international commerce from the nineteenth century onwards. Examples are arrangements governing the technology of international commerce: navigation on waterways, telegraph and electrical communications, postal services and so on. Here, the vast bulk of multilateral arrangements are to be found (Ruggie, 1998, p.115). Third, multilateralism has been used as a means to govern collaboration problems between states. These include some of the classic collective action problems faced by states – most famously regimes for free trade and currency arrangements – as well as the kind of collective security regimes discussed above. Finally, the twentieth century has seen both the expansion of multilateral arrangements based on international organizations (for example, GATT), as well as multi-purpose multilateral organizations such as the League of Nations and the UN

(Ruggie, 1998). Alongside these, multilateral principles have come to form a basis for the actual mechanisms by which much international negotiation and decision making is conducted. This is true of many international conferences, the rules of the UN General Assembly and so on.

You should also note that the analytical distinction in Table 4.1 is, in reality, less clear cut as different kinds of system have overlapped and co-existed at different times. In addition, you should note that the advance of multilateralism has been promoted by hegemonic powers in different ways: Britain in the nineteenth century and the USA in the twentieth and twenty-first centuries. Hegemony has at times been used to further the creation of the multilateral form of international relations.

Finally, a multilateral order is not the same thing as a liberal international order; multilateralism is an institutional form of international relations which could in principle have varying political 'content' (rules to raise tariffs, or to imprison religious minorities could be multilateral but not liberal). However, historically, this expansion of multilateral arrangements between states has accompanied the rise of modern liberal capitalist states. This is particularly evident in the growth from the nineteenth century onwards of the 'co-ordination' solutions mentioned above, which was driven above all by the expansion in international trade and commerce and the development of technologies of communication and transport which accompanied this. Here, multilateral solutions have reduced transaction costs and facilitated the expansion of cross-border economic exchanges and communication. Indeed, in principle, while it is possible to have non-liberal multilateralism – for some the nineteenth-century 'Concert of Europe' was one – nevertheless a liberal order is likely to involve increasing multilateralism. This is because the increasing dominance of liberal capitalist states, which themselves are rule-based forms of authority, means that that form – a generalized, rule-based form – characterizes the relations between such states as well.

This latter point should also remind us of the claimed 'bottom-up' nature of liberal analysis. For, as Moravcsik claims, it is above all the nature of states and the interests that they represent which determine what states seek to achieve internationally. The point is made historically by Ruggie when he argues that it was the characteristics of the USA itself which explain the international order which emerged after the Second World War, not simply the fact that one state (any state) emerged dominant. Thus, for Ruggie, the extension of multilateralism was due less to the fact that the USA had overwhelming power than to the fact that it was the USA, and not some other less liberal power, which exercised such hegemony: 'When we look more closely at the post Second World War situation, then, this implies that it was less the fact of American *hegemony* that accounts for the explosion of multilateral arrangements than it was the fact of *American* hegemony' (Ruggie, 1998, p.107). Furthermore, he goes on to say that, 'had Nazi

Germany or the Soviet Union ended up as the world's leading power after World War II, there is no indication whatsoever that the intentions of either country included creating anything remotely like the international institutional order that came to prevail' (Ruggie, 1998, p.121).

However, both this, and the consequent liberal arguments that this indicates some degree of transformation of the states-system, is vigorously contested by other analytical standpoints. It is to those contesting the liberal analytical case that I now turn.

4   Contesting the liberal case

There are perhaps two main rivals to the liberal analysis of the post Second World War international order. One, the realist position, argues that these claimed novel features of international order in fact can be better explained by reference to the more traditional issue of the distribution of power across the international system. The second, from a Marxist standpoint, argues that while liberals are right to emphasize the role of social forces in shaping international order, the explanation of these should instead be focused on the ways in which the development of capitalism, both within the USA and internationally, has helped to forge the 'Atlantic order' among the leading capitalist states. Both positions focus on different understandings of the nature of US hegemony.

4.1   The power politics response

Within the realist tradition there are in fact two main ways in which it is argued that power politics lie at the heart of the creation of the liberal international order. The first of these rests on a different interpretation of US hegemony than that offered by the liberal analyses reviewed above.

Hegemonic stability theory
Hegemonic stability theory holds that a stable international order and, in particular, an open international economy are most likely if there is a hegemonic state holding a preponderance of power.

In what is known as hegemonic stability theory it is argued that:

> ... the distribution of power among states is the primary determinant of the character of the international economic system. A hegemonic distribution of power, defined as one in which a single state has a predominance of power, is most conducive to the establishment of a stable, open international economic system.

(Webb and Krasner, 1989, p.183)

As this quote implies, the focus of much hegemonic stability theory is on the creation of an open international *economy*. However, there is a more general assertion also being made that, 'order in world politics is typically created by a single dominant power' (Keohane, 1984, p.31). Historically it is argued that there have been two hegemonic powers in the modern states-system: Britain in the nineteenth century and the USA since the Second World War.

Since the Industrial Revolution, the two successive hegemonic powers in the global system (Great Britain and the United States) have sought to organize political, territorial and especially economic relations in terms of their respective security and economic interests. They have succeeded in this role partially because they have imposed their will on lesser states and partially because other states have benefited from and accepted their leadership. ...

The Pax Britannica and the Pax Americana, like the Pax Romana, ensured an international system of relative peace and security. Great Britain and the United States created and enforced the rules of a liberal international order.

(Gilpin, 1983, pp.144–5)

The primary target, therefore, of hegemonic stability theory is the liberal explanation for economic openness. Instead of openness being achieved by a combination of attenuated anarchy and the pursuit of absolute gains, in fact, this critique argues, economic openness is achieved because a dominant power is able and willing to bring it into being. The collective benefit of an open international economy would not normally be realizable in an anarchic system because each state, looking to its own gains relative to others, would not be willing to open its economy for fear that other states will 'cheat' by not opening their own economies and gain relative to the first state. As such, achieving an open international economy can be represented as a Prisoners' Dilemma kind of problem. A Prisoners' Dilemma is a game-theoretic representation of a collective action problem in which all 'players' have a preference for the co-operative outcome (all open their economies) but the equilibrium outcome is that all players cheat (close their economies) (see Mehta and Roy, 2004). A crucial aspect of a Prisoners' Dilemma is that there is no overarching authority which can impose the optimal solution on the players. However, it is argued that in the period after the Second World War, the USA was so dominant militarily and economically, that it was able to enforce co-operation among the lesser powers. The role of the hegemon in this circumstance is both to enforce a regime of economic openness internationally by disciplining non-co-operators, and to take on board some of the costs of providing the public good themselves. 'Only the Hegemon has sufficient power and motivation to provide the public good of international economic stability by its own actions' (Webb and Krasner, 1989, p.184). The role of the hegemon is thus coercive in the sense of disciplining those who cheat through the imposition of sanctions and by offering incentives for others to comply. In this way the hegemonic power can get what it wants – an open international economy – through the exercise of its power internationally.

However, such stability as is achieved is ultimately at the mercy of the distribution of relative gains. That is, the hegemon may allow other states to gain relatively to it in order to induce co-operation and maintain the system overall. But if other states' relative gains begin to imperil its own security, its commitment to the open economy will wane. As Webb and Krasner put it:

> Even though an open system may raise the absolute level of welfare of all participants, some states will gain relative to others. If the pattern of relative gains threatens the security of powerful states, international economic liberalization will be restricted even though those states could have increased their absolute welfare by participating in a more open system.

> (Webb and Krasner, 1989, p.184)

Activity 4.3

In what ways does the hegemonic stability case differ from the liberal account discussed above?

1   In its analysis of what ultimately shapes international order.

2   In terms of the degree of transformation in the states-system.

The second line of critique focuses on the power balance between the USA and the Soviet Union in the Cold War. Remember that part of the liberal explanation for why liberal states were able to pursue absolute gains in the economic field was that the security threat between them had been reduced to such an extent that relative gains were no longer seen as threatening. However, realists have argued that this 'long peace' following the Second World War was itself largely the product of the worldwide distribution of power characterized by bipolarity. Thus Waltz has claimed that, 'The longest peace yet known rested on two pillars: bipolarity and nuclear weapons' (Waltz, 1993, p.44). Importantly it is this, rather than some fundamental change in the nature of the international system, which creates the apparent liberal cohesiveness among Western powers.

The argument is based on two assertions. First, it is claimed that bipolarity is an inherently stable international system.

> A bipolar system is more peaceful for three main reasons. First, the number of conflict dyads is fewer, leaving fewer possibilities for war. Second, deterrence is easier, because imbalances of power are fewer and more easily averted. Third, the prospects for deterrence are greater because miscalculations of relative power and of opponents' resolve are fewer and less likely.

> (Mearsheimer, 1990, p.14)

In such a system more minor powers are likely to line up behind one of the major powers, especially in the core geographical region (in this case Europe). This has the effect of inducing cohesion among the two groups of states. Thus, it is the worldwide bipolar conflict which generates the apparent unity of purpose among the liberal states.

Second, such cohesion is reinforced by the existence of nuclear weapons which submerge war-making propensities within the two sides to an overarching bipolar structure of nuclear deterrence. To explain why this is so, particularly among the Western powers, we need to consider the nature of the nuclear stand-off. Nuclear weapons offer a greater destructive potential than any other weapon yet created. Moreover, once a certain level of nuclear capability has been reached, an all-out nuclear exchange would mean the total destruction of both parties. Such a situation, perhaps accurately known as MAD (Mutually Assured Destruction), not only creates great caution in the use of force, it also means that the only rational purpose for such armaments is to deter an attack on one's interests. For realists, deterrence based on the threat of nuclear retaliation became the bedrock of the bipolar power balance between East and West in the post-1945 era. As Waltz put it:

> Nuclear weapons bend strategic forces to one end: deterring attacks on a country's vital interests. Partly because strategic nuclear weapons serve that end and no other, peace has held at the centre of the international system through five postwar decades, while wars have often raged at the periphery. Nuclear weapons have at once secured the vital interests of those possessing them and upheld the international order.

(Waltz, 1993, p.53)

Deterrence can be defined as the possession of force sufficient so that a potential aggressor will not attack if it is persuaded that it will suffer unacceptable punishment from a defender as a result of an attack. For deterrence to work it is necessary that both sides have the capability to retaliate. If a 'knock-out' first strike could be delivered by one side which eliminated enough of the other's nuclear force so that it could not retaliate, then the temptation would always be present to take that chance of a winning blow. The maintenance of a 'second strike' capability thus became a justification for both sides to build up a large stockpile of nuclear weapons and for devising ways of making them hard to destroy (putting them on submarines, for example). The Soviet Union and the USA both pursued the development of 'counter-force weapons' – weapons designed to destroy the other's weapons systems – which was for this reason a destabilizing action. Deterrence also requires that both sides are convinced of the willingness of the other to retaliate. This is less obvious than might first appear. MAD is based on the belief that each side would rather cease to exist than to be defeated by the enemy. It means

Deterrence
Deterrence is the possession of force sufficient so that a potential aggressor will not attack if it is persuaded that it will suffer unacceptable punishment from a defender as a result of an attack.

for example that, for the USA, it really was 'better to be dead than red'. It is far from clear that this is a rational position to hold, although threatening this in the hope that it will prevent an attack may be a rational, if inherently high risk, posture.

In principle, a stable and relatively equal balance of nuclear force provides for a stable relationship between adversarial powers. In practice, these conditions and the particular circumstances of the Cold War made deterrence a more complicated problem for politicians and military planners generally (see Mandelbaum, 1991). This was particularly so for the Western side. The USA not only threatened retaliation for an attack on itself but deployed 'extended deterrence' to prevent an attack on Western Europe. The cohesion among the Western powers that liberals highlight, was, from this perspective, partly a result of this 'nuclear umbrella'. But the question arose as to whether the USA would really carry out 'massive retaliation' to defend Western Europe from a conventional Soviet attack: would the USA sacrifice itself to keep Europe safe? France's President De Gaulle certainly came to doubt this and prompted the development of France's own nuclear force in the early 1960s. And US and NATO planners also recognized the limitations of such a posture and increased both the level of conventional forces and the variety of nuclear weapons at its disposal so that it could adopt a posture of 'flexible response', that is, a graduated range of forceful reactions to Soviet aggression which meant all-out nuclear exchange was not the first and only option. Anti-nuclear protesters in Europe in the 1980s pointed out that this made a limited nuclear war in Europe more, rather than less, likely.

The impact of bipolarity in general and extended deterrence in particular, was therefore to increase the cohesiveness of the Western side. However, like hegemonic stability, such order is subject to disruption caused by shifts in the global power balance, and to tensions within the Western alliance based on the uncertainty that extended deterrence would in fact be implemented. Thus, both of these realist perspectives on post-war order emphasize the distribution of power, and the military and economic dominance of the USA among the Western powers, to explain the apparent closeness in their relationships. Both are based on the kind of power and security conflict in a context of international anarchy which the liberal case claims has been, or can be transcended. As discussed in Section 5, this approach holds out a very different prognosis for the development of international order after the end of the Cold War.

4.2   A liberal *capitalist* order?

Before assessing the above question, I want to examine one other critique of the liberal case. Coming from the Marxist tradition in international political economy it gives a very different understanding of hegemony from both the liberal and realist positions, and a different understanding of the role and importance of social forces in explaining the rise of a liberal international order.

As seen in Chapter 2, Marxist accounts of international order emphasize the nature of social property relations in explaining different kinds of international relations. As such, they share some of the *structure* of liberal accounts in so far as Marxists allow state–society factors a determinate role in shaping the international purposes of states. However, within this broad approach a number of different accounts are put forward to explain the evolution of the states-system. One claim to be a Marxist analysis of the post Second World War liberal order comes from 'neo-Gramscian' accounts of the nature of US hegemony and it is on this particular set of writings that I concentrate here.

You have seen already that hegemony at a general level refers to influence over others, but that different specific arguments are made (by liberals and realists) as to exactly how that influence is constructed and on what it is based. Hegemony is a term also used by Marxists, following the Italian Marxist Antonio Gramsci, to explain how an essentially conflictual social system like capitalism can be (at least temporarily) stabilized. For Gramsci, hegemony referred to the way in which dominant social classes could maintain their leadership through consent as much as coercion. What Gramsci called a ruling hegemonic 'historic bloc' was a combination of social classes (including elements of subordinate classes), organized around particular interests and ideology, which provided a basis for the general acceptance of capitalist order in society. Gramsci's approach focused a Marxist analysis of class domination on both ideological as well as 'material' (economic and political) factors.

In the study of the liberal international order, the neo-Gramscian approach transferred this use of the term hegemony (neo-Gramscian) to the international level in its interpretation of US leadership of the Western capitalist world. For writers such as Robert Cox (1987), a hegemonic order comprises a congruence between three levels: the dominant elements in production in the economy, the form of state–society relations, and the form of world order. In the post Second World War era, US dominance combined all three. In the realm of production, the leading sectors of the US economy were characterized by 'Fordism', interpreted as mass, assembly line-based production for a mass market. This was in turn supported by a state–society complex which involved both political incorporation of elements of subordinate classes (particularly organized labour) and interventionist economic regulation to support economic growth and mass consumption. Internationally, US hegemony therefore exists in both of these spheres: in military power in the states-system and in the mode of governance of an

Hegemony (neo-Gramscian) Hegemony in this more specific, neo-Gramscian sense refers to the way in which the USA exercises political, ideological and economic leadership over the capitalist world, based on its possession of the most advanced sectors of production, the generalization of these and its state–society relations to other capitalist societies, and its relative military and economic dominance.

international capitalist economy in which the US economy (or leading sectors of it) is the most advanced element.

The liberal international order is thus both an order comprised of relations between states as liberals and realists contend, and also an order involving a transnational dimension. This latter includes classes, ideology, structures of production (for example in multinational firms) and markets. As Cox has argued:

> World hegemony is describable as a social structure, an economic structure, and a political structure; and it cannot be simply one of these things but must be all three. World hegemony, furthermore, is expressed in universal norms, institutions and mechanisms, which lay down general rules for the behaviour of states, and for those forces of civil society that act across state boundaries – rules which support the dominant mode of production.
>
> (Cox, quoted in Gill, 1990, p.48)

Here, the multilateral principles highlighted by liberals are both an expression of the particular interests of the dominant state and the dominant sectors and classes within the USA, and the general requirements necessary for capitalism to expand internationally. Integration at the level of international governance which liberals highlight and attribute to the pursuit of absolute gains is, for Marxists, an expression of the collective activity of capitalist states in maintaining the global conditions for capital accumulation. In the post-war period this was achieved under the leadership of the USA.

The idea of a transnational dimension to the liberal order has been elaborated in great detail from a Marxist standpoint by Kees van der Pijl in his analysis of *The Making of an Atlantic Ruling Class* (1984). He argued that we can interpret successive attempts to create a liberal international order as a series of 'liberal offensives' in which particular groups within the USA sought to establish the structures within which capitalist unity across the Atlantic could be created. Most importantly, this would allow the free circulation of capital in the form of trade, investment and currency. The economic fragmentation of the world economy in the 1930s had disrupted this circulation, and the creation of structures to govern a more open international economy dominated US policy from the late 1930s on, as we have seen. He characterizes the 'domestic' class interest in the USA as 'corporate liberalism', combining the open circulation of money in the Atlantic area, the generalization of Fordist methods of production and the development of state intervention. He argues that the creation of the liberal order after the Second World War generalized these features to other capitalist states, particularly through the revitalization of the European economies in the

Marshall Plan. Importantly, the Marshall Plan was not only a means to spur on economic growth in Europe but a means by which European systems of production, and the class relations entailed in them, even the relations between state and economy, could be reconstructed along American lines. This expansion of American 'corporate liberalism' to the other capitalist states created the basis for a capitalist Atlantic unity.

Question

How fundamentally does this neo-Gramscian account differ from the liberal analysis presented above?

While sharing much of the liberal description of the post-war order, both van der Pijl and Cox are concerned to identify the class interests which are served by this order and argue that such interests operate both domestically and transnationally. Second, US hegemony, and international order more generally, consists of both a pattern of inter-state relations focused on the military–security arena and as transnational capitalist social relations. Furthermore, by emphasizing the way in which a liberal international order also helps to strengthen the position of particular social forces, both argue that the lines of causation go from the domestic to the international (as liberals do) and from the international to the domestic. That is, an interaction exists whereby the dominant forms of state and of production help to shape world order (the impact of Fordism on US post-war plans, for example) and particular world orders in turn help to shape the dominant forms of state and production in the constituent states (open international economy strengthening the position of dominant sectors of the economy, for example).

However, for Marxists, such hegemonic projects are always ongoing. The inherent instability in capitalism, its uneven development internationally and the class struggles which it entails mean that hegemonic orders are subject to disruption from within. The delineation of change in international order is thus identified rather differently from liberals (who emphasize the expanding number of liberal states after the Cold War) and realists (who emphasize the changing distribution of power – the rise or decline of US economic power or the demise of bipolar military conflict and rise of US unipolar dominance). Indeed, one of the implications of this approach is a reading of post Second World War history that highlights rather different 'punctuation marks'. Perhaps most notably, the neo-Gramscian approach points to the disruption of the USA-led hegemonic order by the recessions and economic crises of the mid 1970s and early 1980s. These prompted changes at all three of Cox's levels: in production (with the decline of mass industries and the rise of new kinds of production and new sectors of the economy), in state–society complexes (with the fiscal crises of the welfare state, privatization, deregulation and re-regulation of the economy), and at the level of world order. The relative decline of US economic leadership, particularly in the light of the resurgence of capitalism in Europe, and especially in East Asia, is particularly important in this latter respect. However, the economic and political crises of post-war capitalism in the 1970s and early 1980s led not to a resurgence of protectionism but a re-invigorated liberal offensive to recreate world order.

It is to the different implications for the post Cold War order of these three analytical accounts that I now turn.

5   The Cold War and after

As noted at the start of this chapter, the claims about a liberal international order were given added emphasis with the end of the Cold War. However, the significance of this change, and the implications that it holds for the future of the liberal international order is contested. Among the issues at stake are whether the liberal international order is robust – can it survive such momentous international upheaval? – and what are the implications of the existence of a liberal order among the liberal capitalist states for the rest of the world?

In large part, these issues go back to how one characterizes the Cold War itself. At the most general level, the term Cold War refers to the antagonistic relationship which existed between the Western states and the Soviet Union and its Communist allies. As such, its origins lie in the creation of the Soviet state after the Bolshevik revolution in 1917 and Western states' antagonistic reaction to it. More usually, however, the term is used to refer to the period between the end of the Second World War – when the Soviet Union and the USA emerged as two 'superpowers' – and the collapse of Communism in Eastern Europe and Russia between 1989 and 1991. Within this era one can identify periods of more and less intense confrontation and crisis between East and West. Thus the 'first Cold War' is generally dated between the Soviet blockade of West Berlin in 1948 through the communist revolution in China in 1949, the Korean War and nuclear arms race of the 1950s, to the resolution of the Cuban Missile Crisis of 1962, after which a more stable stand-off between East and West began to emerge. The 'second Cold War' saw a renewal of crisis from the late 1970s, with a resumption of nuclear arms build-up in Europe, the Soviet invasion of Afghanistan and a series of confrontations in the developing world in Central America and southern Africa (Halliday, 1990).

The end of the Cold War came with the rise, after 1985, of a reformist leadership in the Soviet Union under Michael Gorbachev, who sought to revitalize the Soviet economy through internal economic and political reforms, and by establishing a more co-operative relationship with the West internationally. Part of this involved East–West negotiations in the security field: limitations and reductions in nuclear armaments, the negotiated end to protracted regional conflicts in the developing world and the withdrawal of Soviet forces from Afghanistan. However, it also involved a revision of the Soviet Union's relations with the communist states in Eastern Europe and a declaration that the Soviet Union would allow the central and Eastern European states to follow their own political paths (hitherto the Soviet Union had reserved the right to intervene to maintain the communist character of these states). The rapid and short-term response was the collapse, under pressure from mass, popular demonstrations, of all the communist regimes in Eastern Europe. Ultimately the reform of communism led to the break up of the Soviet Union under nationalist pressure from its constituent republics, and in Russia itself the embarkation on a long and difficult road of transition to a capitalist market economy.

As Halliday has argued, specifying the beginning and end of the Cold War depends a great deal on what one thinks the Cold War was 'about' (Halliday, 1990). For those who understand international order primarily in terms of the distribution of power, the Cold War reflected the bipolar division of the world between two superpowers after the Second World War. The fact that one was capitalist and one communist was of secondary importance to the fact that the two sides were far ahead, in terms of their capabilities (particularly nuclear arsenals but also conventional weapons, economic size and population), of all other powers in the system. Nuclear confrontation and deterrence thus formed a central axis in the Cold War confrontation. If, however, one sees the Cold War as a contest between two different social systems, communism and capitalism, then the antagonistic relationship between East and West can be traced back to the Bolshevik revolution in Russia in 1917. From a power-based standpoint, the end of the Cold War was simply the triumph of the more powerful state. From the 'systemic conflict' perspective it was the triumph of one social system over another and the beginning of the incorporation of the formerly communist states into the liberal capitalist orbit.

Activity 4.4

Think about the different explanations for the rise of a liberal order in the post Second World War era reviewed in the previous section.

1   Identify the key variable each is using to explain that order.

2   What would you expect to be their prognosis for the survival of a liberal order after the end of the Cold War?

One way to think about these questions is in respect of the cohesion among the Western powers. As we have seen, for liberals this was something which developed at least semi-independently of the Cold War confrontation. The variables which the liberal case focuses on – the character of the state–society relations involved and the existence of institutional factors which transcend pure anarchy – allowed the pursuit of common purposes in both security and economic fields. While the Cold War certainly shaped these, and constrained their geographical scope, it was not fundamentally deterministic. The end of the Cold War would not necessarily undermine this cohesive order. Indeed, Deudney and Ikenberry are adamant that the liberal order created during the Cold War is robust. While for them it does rely on the USA exercising its hegemony in a particular way, the gains to be had from this mean that any fundamental change from within is unlikely. Indeed, the strengthening of some of the features of the liberal international order would tend to support this view. The GATT, which as we have seen was a product of the failure to establish a proper international organization on a par with the IMF and World Bank, was subsumed within a new World Trade Organization in 1995 which involved a marked strengthening of its rule-based nature. NATO, far from disappearing from view after the Cold War, expanded to incorporate – in a manner consistent with the liberal view of co-binding – the former communist countries. Indeed, their inclusion in NATO and application to join the EU, were seen as one of the means by which their membership of the liberal world would be consolidated.

For the bipolarity thesis, the Cold War was clearly a conflict caused by the distribution of power after the Second World War. Such cohesiveness as existed among the Western powers was 'forced' in the sense that it was the product of an alliance determined by the distribution of capabilities and the pursuit of the balance of power. The emergence of the USA as a single dominant military power is for many such theorists a transient phenomenon. Counter-balancing by other leading states – Russia and China as well as Germany and Japan – will, we are assured, emerge sooner or later (Waltz, 1993, 2000; Mearsheimer, 1990). It is worth noting that if calculations of power capabilities are limited to military power, the hegemonic stability thesis would posit a very different view, seeing dominance as renewing the ability of the USA to maintain stability and order. However, if economic considerations are included then the prior rebalancing of power relations among Western countries – with a demise of US dominance in the economic field – would similarly predict a period of instability and disruption in relations between the liberal states.

It is this restructuring of the international economic landscape which neo-Gramscians most focus on. They argue that shifts within economies (from the Fordist, Atlanticist Eastern USA to the post-Fordist, high-tech Western, Pacific USA) and between them (the rise of East Asia and stagnation in

Eastern USA and Western Europe) undermined the post Second World War liberal world order. However, the response to economic crisis was not a resort to protectionism but, if anything, a renewed collective effort to reassert the conditions for the profitable expansion of capitalist accumulation. This, as liberals would agree, has seen a renewal of liberalization efforts internationally and a strengthening of the commitment to international economic governance which ensures the operation of an open international economy, thus allowing the free circulation of trade and capital. This revitalized commitment to global accumulation has gone hand in hand with 'internal' restructuring of class relations, the decline of influence of organized labour and the re-organization of state–economy relations under 'neo-liberal' economic policies adopted in most advanced industrial countries.

6   Conclusion

A second way to answer the questions posed in Activity 4.4 is to ask what the implications for the rest of the world are of the liberal international order after the Cold War. There are perhaps two ways of answering this. One is to argue, like Clinton, that the liberal order can in principle simply expand to cover the entire states-system. For liberals, the end of the Cold War opened up this possibility and the expansion of NATO, the creation of the WTO and the increasing membership of this and the other major international institutions committed to economic openness, seem to support this idea. Marxists too might emphasize the expansion of capitalist social property relations into new areas, 'breaking down Chinese walls', as Marx put it. Indeed, such factors could be cited in support of the idea that a universal, liberal international society (as discussed in Chapter 3) could be brought into being. However, another way of answering this question is to recognize that the expansion of liberalism beyond this core is likely to face some substantial barriers. In this circumstance, the liberal order among the Western powers will need to confront other new and less liberal states.

Finally, all of the analyses in this chapter recognize, in different ways, the central position of the USA in shaping the twentieth and twenty-first century worlds. Speculation on the future development of the international order, and whether or not the liberal elements of it survive and prosper will also depend, to a great extent, on the role of the USA and the nature of its power in the international system. This task is discussed in Chapter 5.

Further reading

The liberal thesis is well set out in Deudney, D. and Ikenberry, J. (1999) 'The nature and sources of a liberal international order', *Review of International Studies*, vol.25, no.2, pp.179–96.

A review of some of the key arguments made by hegemonic stability theorists can be found in Webb, M.C. and Krasner, S.D. (1989) 'Hegemonic stability theory: an empirical assessment', *Review of International Studies*, no.15, pp.183–98.

For a trenchant neo-realist counter to some liberal claims, see Waltz, K. (2000) 'Structural realism after the Cold War', *International Security*, vol.25, no.1, pp.5–41.

Perhaps the best-known of the neo-Gramscian works is Cox, R.W. (1987) *Production, Power and World Order: Social Forces in the Making of History*, New York, Columbia University Press.

Chapter 5 American power and the future of international order

Simon Bromley

1 Introduction

This chapter was written around the time of the US-led war against Iraq that began on 20 March 2003 and during the early stages of the subsequent occupation. At the time of writing, a stunning, and for some shocking, military victory has been achieved by the US-led coalition, while the wider political and geopolitical consequences in Iraq, in the Middle East and beyond are uncertain. The conflict between the USA and Iraq had its own specific causes and issues (and I shall comment on these in Section 7), but for many commentators it marked a basic shift in the nature of US foreign policy occasioned by the reshaping of the international order that followed the end of the Cold War in 1991. The end of major geopolitical conflicts such as the First and Second World Wars tends to produce post-war settlements that reflect the new dispensations of international power as well as the constitutional, economic and even cultural characteristics of the winning states and societies. The Cold War competition between the USA and the Soviet Union, and between the social systems that each claimed to represent – liberal capitalism and state socialism, respectively – had been won by the USA and by the liberal capitalist world.

Now that the USA confronted the rest of the world as the sole superpower, what some French commentators called a 'hyperpower', the settlement crafted after 1945 was due to be rewritten. The world after the Cold War was a unipolar world, at least militarily speaking, and many commentators argued that the USA would be in a position to reshape the world in its own image. To some extent, that had been the case after the Second World War, but then US power had been balanced by the power of the Soviet Union and by the force of nationalist, anti-colonial mobilization in the South. After the Cold War, the economic power of the USA vis-à-vis its leading capitalist allies was much diminished compared to the situation after the Second World War, but its military pre-eminence was historically unparalleled. Outside the USA (and in some cases inside as well), and across the political spectrum, analysts turned to the language of 'empire' and of 'imperialism' to describe its role within the international order.

In this chapter I shall consider the shaping of the future of international order through an analysis of the role of the USA in the contemporary world. I begin in Section 2 by looking at the nature of the USA and the self-image with which it has sought to reshape the world. Then, in Section 3, I look at the idea of imperialism, which has come to the fore in many contemporary debates, and I present contrasting Marxist views of imperialism. In Section 4 I turn to an analysis of the nature of US hegemony from this perspective. In the second half of the chapter I turn to different aspects of the US role – its relationship with other liberal states (Section 5), with non-liberal states (Section 6), and in policing other areas and dealing with the threat of terrorism (Section 7). Finally, I reconsider the overall shape of US power in the international order.

2   Where in the world is America?

As you have seen in Chapter 4, the USA claims an exceptional role in world affairs, uniquely defining its national interest as more or less synonymous with that of the international community *tout ensemble*. Its liberal advocates concur: 'America's national interest ... offers the closest match there is to a world interest' (Emmott, 2002, p.10).

Question

Why does the USA claim such an exceptional international role?

To answer this, I need to go back to the historical development of the USA itself. The formation of the USA was a result of the networks of trade, people, settlement and ideas that circulated in the Atlantic economy, linking northwest Europe, the Americas and Africa during the seventeenth and eighteenth centuries. After the independence of 13 colonies from Britain in the American Revolution of 1776, the subsequent development of the USA was in part an indirect continuation of that process of European expansion into the non-European world – both globalizing and imperial.

At the same time, however, US expansion was defined as anti-colonial rather than colonial, republican rather than monarchical, the New World rather than the old European order. Unlike the major European states, the USA became a major power more or less without a formal empire. Rather, independence cleared the way for westward expansion and settlement and 'the whole *internal* history of US imperialism was one vast process of territorial seizure and occupation' (Stedman Jones, 1972, p.217). As John Adams, the second president of the new Republic (1797–1801), expressed it in 1774, the purpose of American independence was to pursue the formation of an 'independent American empire' (quoted in Stedman Jones, 1972, p.214).

It was only by presenting this 'internal colonialism' as an expansion into uninhabited or freely alienated lands that the American ideology of 'exceptionalism' could take root. Yet among the overwhelmingly European majority of the population such an idea did strike a deep chord. The ideology of exceptionalism encompasses two sets of ideas: first, that the USA is uniquely fortunate in having escaped the patterns of historical development characteristic of the old order in Europe and in being able to create anew a society based on security, liberty and justice; second, that it is an exemplary power, representing a model that is universally applicable to the rest of humankind. In this way, the USA has been able to present its national interest as simultaneously unique and universal, as entirely consistent with a form of cosmopolitan internationalism.

The consolidation of the sovereignty of the Union after the Civil War of 1861–65 and the development of the national market, based on federal transfers of land to private ownership, laid the basis for the later development of a mass society: the USA pioneered the culture of mass consumption as well as the consumption of mass culture, both of which were based in mass production, or what foreigners simply called Americanism. The age of mass destruction followed shortly after as the USA led the combination of the mass production of high-explosive weapons and massive increases in the mobility of their means of delivery. This is what a 'superpower' originally meant, defined by William Fox (1944) as 'great power plus great mobility of power'.

Americanism
Americanism refers to the combination of mass production, a culture of mass consumption and the mass consumption of culture pioneered by American capitalist society.

2.1 Americanism outside America

Substantial elements of Americanism proved to be transferable to other capitalist countries. This meant that the leading economy in the world became a pole of attraction for others. It was this generalization of the US model, its partial replication outside the USA, that gave the unique ideology of exceptionalism – the only national interest that presents itself as a universal, cosmopolitan interest – such a powerful grip.

In a highly prescient analysis of 'Americanism and Fordism' in his *Prison Notebooks*, the Italian communist Antonio Gramsci, asked 'whether America, through the implacable weight of its economic production (and therefore indirectly), will compel or is already compelling Europe to overturn its excessively antiquated economic and social basis' (1971, p.317). Gramsci's conclusion was that this was indeed the case, but that it represented 'an organic extension and an intensification of European civilization, which has simply acquired a new coating in the American climate' (1971, p.318). That is to say that just as the USA itself was partly a product of European capitalist expansion overseas, so European capitalism was now being reshaped by the more advanced economic order in the USA.

Gramsci also saw clearly that Americanism was not simply a new mode of economic organization, mass production, and a new kind of cultural system, mass communication and consumption, but also a new form of ideology, social structure and state:

> Americanism requires a particular environment, a particular social structure (or at least a determined intention to create it) and a certain type of State. The State is the liberal State, not in the sense of free-trade liberalism or of effective political liberty, but in the more fundamental sense of free initiative and of economic individualism which, with its own means, on the level of "civil society", through historical development, itself arrives at a regime of industrial concentration and monopoly.

(Gramsci, 1971, p.293)

At the time that he was writing (in the 1920s and 1930s), Gramsci observed the beginnings of Americanism in Europe – in Berlin and Milan, less so in Paris, he thought – but this was to become a much more important development after the Second World War. Thus, Americanism was reproduced outside the territory of the USA. In an essay seeking to place US history in a wider world context, Charles Bright and Michael Meyer describe the consequences after 1945 as follows:

> The postwar American sovereign, built on territories of production, had created vectors along which elements of the US state and American civil society could move off into the world and benefit from the permanent projections of American power overseas. ... The tools of control – military (the alliance systems and violence), economic (dollar aid and investments), political (the leverage and sanctions of a superpower), and ideological (the image of the United States as leader of the free world) – were tremendously powerful, and the ideological imaginary of the territories of production, with its emphasis on material progress and democracy, proved extraordinarily attractive.

(Bright and Meyer, 2002, p.86)

Hence, Bright and Meyer's question 'Where in the World is America?' has two parts: first, what is the position of the (territorial) USA in the international system; and second, where – and with what effect – is Americanism in the rest of the world? The idea I want to explore by asking these questions is that US power in the round is based on both these Americas. Or rather, that the key to US power is the *relation* between these two senses of American power.

3   The meanings of 'empire'

As I mentioned in Section 1, many commentators now talk about the USA as an imperial power.

Question

What does the term 'imperialism' or 'empire' mean?

In Chapters 3 and 4 you have seen that empire can be used in the 'narrow' sense of the formal political subordination of one polity to another, the clearest example being the discussion of colonialism (see Chapter 3, Section 2.6). However, it was also noted that if we look at the international system not only as a states-system, if we include other actors and dimensions of international order, then it is possible to speak of empire and imperialism in a somewhat broader sense, in a way which is closer to the discussions of hegemony that you have already come across. Bearing this in mind, I want to build on the preceding chapters by developing further the discussion of what is meant by empire and imperialism.

One way in which the term empire has been used is an idea, originally derived from the Roman Empire and from the impact of Greek and Christian cultures, of empire as a hierarchy of polities that produces a universal order based on shared identities, values and interests, in which one power, the imperial or hegemonic power, is raised above the others. This is a notion of empire as 'first and foremost, a very great power that has left its mark on the international relations of its era' (Lieven, 2003, p.xiv). It is empire as a form of rule (not necessarily direct rule) over many territories and peoples, usually associated with an economic and cultural order that proclaims itself the basis for a universal civilization. No such empire has ever been truly universal since there have always been rival claims to universality from without and because different groups within interpret the shared identities, values and interests in their own particular ways. Nevertheless, this is one way of thinking about the American empire at the beginning of the twenty-first century. A key question for this idea of an American empire is how does the USA leave 'its mark on the international relations of its era'.

Another sense of empire is more modern, informed by the radical liberal and Marxist traditions, and derives from attempts to understand the character of the European capitalist empires in which imperialism represents the 'political and cultural domination, and the economic exploitation, of the colonial periphery by the metropolitan state and nation' (Lieven, 2003, p.xiv). A key question for these modern theories of imperialism, formulated during the climax of European colonialism in the 1890s and early 1900s, was about the nature of the competitive relationship between the rival national imperialisms that, in combination, dominated the non-European world until the era of decolonization. In this respect, the radical liberal critic and analyst of the British Empire, John Hobson, drew a distinction between what he called 'Imperialism' and 'Informal Empire'.

Giovanni Arrighi explains this distinction as follows:

> At least in principle ... two quite distinct types of rivalry were involved. In the case of Imperialism, rivalry affected *political relations among states* and was expressed in the arms race and the drive to territorial expansion; whereas in the case of Informal Empire, it concerned *economic relations among individuals of different nationality* and was expressed in the international division of labour. Thus Imperialism signified *political conflict* among nations, Informal Empire *economic interdependence* between them.

> (Arrighi, 1983, p.41)

Note the distinction drawn between the political and economic aspects of empire in Hobson's formulation. The narrow view of empire as formal political control (see Chapter 3, Section 2.6) could only encompass Hobson's Imperialism, while some of the discussion of the economic dimensions of hegemony discussed in Chapter 4 could here be interpreted as Informal Empire.

3.1   Marxist theories of imperialism

Marxist analyses have long been an important part of debates about imperialism, and much of my subsequent discussion will draw on the Marxist tradition. I, therefore, want to take a little time to outline contending Marxist views of imperialism before going on to look at the nature of US power in the twenty-first century.

In the debate among Marxists prior to the First World War, a similar distinction to that drawn by Hobson emerged. At a general level, in classical Marxism 'imperialism' referred to aspects of international capitalist development – its forcible expansion into pre-capitalist regions and the economically exploitative relations between differentially empowered regions within the capitalist world. Capitalist imperialism, then, was understood as a set of coercive power relations established between different parts of the world economy, such that one region benefited at the expense of another. While metropolitan control over the periphery often involved the use of force and direct (colonial) political rule, the central mechanisms of imperialism were economic and involved the ability of the dominant capitalist powers to manipulate market imperatives to their advantage. The central question in these debates was how rival imperialisms related to one another and here the lines of the distinction between Imperialism and Informal Empire can be seen.

Hobson's notion of Imperialism became the basis for the most influential statement of the classical Marxist theory of imperialism, namely Lenin's idea of inter-imperialist rivalry leading to war and revolution. Inter-capitalist competition operating internationally has, in Perry Anderson's formulation, 'an inherent tendency to escalate to the level of states' and, left unchecked, 'the logic of such anarchy can only be internecine war' (2002, p.20). This view accorded priority to the division of the world economy into national states. While competing capitalist firms have a common interest in political arrangements which ensure the subordination of labour to capitalist command and in the guarantee of the overall preconditions for capital accumulation, these political functions are divided between multiple states. For Lenin, national states became tied to nationally organized blocs of capital, which are compelled to compete against one another, as rival imperialisms, when competition among firms becomes increasingly international. The key link for Lenin was between a given state and its 'national' capital; the end result was an increasing militarization of inter-imperialist rivalries.

> The epoch of the latest stage of capitalism shows us that certain relations between capitalist combines grow up, based on the economic division of the world; while parallel and in connection with it, certain relations grow up between political combines, between states, on the basis of the territorial division of the world, of the struggle for colonies, of the 'struggle for economic territory'.

(Lenin, 1916, p.89)

The central idea here is that competition between capitalist enterprises of differing nationalities is translated into competition among states that seek to defend the interests of 'their' firms by means of the 'struggle for economic territory'. In turn, this territorial competition between states becomes mutually destructive, leading to wars and revolutions.

This argument was questioned by Karl Kautsky, the German Marxist and contemporary of Lenin. His untimely claim, published on the eve of the First World War, was that the survival of capitalism depended on the emergence of a mechanism for co-ordinating competing states – ultra-imperialism – in order to ensure that the general preconditions for accumulation were met (Kautsky, 1970). Kautsky's notion of ultra-imperialism is similar to Hobson's concept of an Informal Empire, and Kautsky reckoned that an international division of labour structured along corporate lines, rather than national ones, would provide the basis for such an order. Capitalist firms as well as 'their' national

Inter-imperialist rivalry
Inter-imperialist rivalry refers to the tendency of international economic competition among capitalists to escalate to political competition among states as a result of the links between national blocs of capital and nation states. It is usually seen as a zero- or even negative-sum phenomenon.

Ultra-imperialism
Ultra-imperialism refers to forms of co-operation among imperialist powers aimed at securing the mutual interests of internationally operating capitalist firms and the leading capitalist states. It is usually seen as a positive-sum phenomenon for the states and firms concerned.

151

states would recognize the mutually destructive nature of inter-imperialist rivalry and fashion forms of co-operation to secure the mutual interests of the leading capitalist countries. Lenin recognized the force of Kautsky's argument but argued that it was nonetheless utopian, since there was no agency in the international system that could effect the requisite co-ordination.

Debating imperialism: Karl Kautsky (left) and Vladimir Ilyich Lenin (right)

The outbreak of the First World War and the rivalries between the leading capitalist states in the inter-war depression and the Second World War seemed to support Lenin over Kautsky. But after the Second World War, relations among the leading capitalist states stabilized and, under US leadership, deep and extensive forms of co-operation were fashioned.

Super-imperialism
Super-imperialism refers to a situation in which one imperialist power – the USA after the Second World War – is sufficiently powerful to perform general political and geopolitical functions for all the leading capitalist states and in which subordinate states defer to that leadership. It is usually seen as a positive-sum phenomenon.

Theories of US super-imperialism, in effect, argued that Kautsky's world had been achieved by Leninist means. US imperialism had established such overwhelming dominance, by virtue of the defeat and exhaustion of rivals during the war, that it was able to monopolize the stabilization of capitalism in the periphery as well as the defence of world capitalism against the challenges now posed by the Soviet Union and the rest of the communist world. This argument suggested that because the USA was so powerful in relation to its allies, and because it performed the general functions for all the major capitalist power centres of controlling the periphery and defending the capitalist world from the communist, it was able to play a decisive role in directing a wide range of co-ordinating actions among the leading capitalist powers. Paul Baran and Paul Sweezy, for example, argued that, given the economic weakening of Europe and Japan, the new challenge of 'the rise of a world socialist system as a rival and alternative to the world capitalist system', combined with the emergence of social and national revolution in the colonial regions, meant that 'policing the [US] empire and fighting socialism are rapidly becoming, if they are not already, one and the same' (1966, p.204).

Activity 5.1

1   Make sure that you can identify the differences between Lenin's imperialism, Kautsky's ultra-imperialism and the idea of super-imperialism.

2   If you think back to Chapter 4, can you spot any echoes of the debates about US hegemony discussed there?

Thus, during the Cold War, two different objectives of the USA reinforced one another: first, 'making the world safe' for capitalism; and second, ensuring its hegemony within the capitalist world. The first ambition involved containing the power of Russia in Europe and Asia, and of China in Asia, including the ability of these communist states to support revolution outside their borders among the anti-colonial struggles in the developing world. In pursuit of this aim, US capitalist allies were generally willing to follow its political leadership. Since the collapse of communism, the project of making the world safe for capitalism has gone global, with China and Russia as the biggest potential prizes. What does 'making the world safe' for capitalism now involve? As to the second ambition, the economies of Western Europe and Japan grew more rapidly than that of the USA during most of the Cold War, thereby eroding some of the latter's economic leadership. What, then, might become of the ambition to ensure hegemony within the now much expanded capitalist world?

After the end of the Cold War, Peter Gowan (1999) described Washington's pursuit of a super-imperialist role as a 'global gamble' for world dominance, a Faustian bid to utilize the unipolar moment following the end of the Cold War to restructure the international political economy in ways that serve the particular interests of the USA. While the advent of military strategic parity between the Soviet Union and the USA in the 1970s had checked the US super-imperialism exercised after the Second World War, Gowan argued, in effect, that the end of the Cold War restored the USA to the status of a super-imperialist power. Western Europe and Japan had caught up somewhat *economically*, but Gowan highlighted what he saw as 'the central fact of contemporary international relations: one single member ... has acquired absolute military dominance over every other state or combination of states on the entire planet' (2001, p.81). This military dominance imposed political unity on the capitalist world, a world 'whose empire is guarded not by any supra-state authority, but by a single hegemon' (2001, p.89).

Others contended that this not only overstated the continuing degree of US super-imperialism but also, thereby, displaced the analysis away from the economic character of contemporary capitalism. This alternative argument suggested that capitalism is no longer configured into national blocs of capital. Rather, most internationally competitive firms are oriented to international markets and seek to break down national and regional barriers to trade and investment, such that all the leading capitalist states have an interest in a relatively open and liberal world economy. The upshot of this, says Peter Green, is that 'the G7 states, and most of the states of the second tier, are now almost inextricably locked into structures that they themselves have created, which do not simply serve the interests of US capitalism, or any other particular capitalism' (2002, p.50).

4   The nature of US hegemony

In Section 2, I asked where in the world is America. And we have just reviewed some different ways of thinking about imperialism and empire.

Question

How do the different senses of American power relate to theories of imperialism?

Section 2 distinguished between the power of the territorial USA – that is, the power of America as one state–society complex in a system of others – and the ways in which America acted as a target of imitation, or pole of attraction, as Americanism became a model that others sought to replicate or emulate. I concluded that US power to shape international order depended on both the power of the territorial USA and that of the place and effects of Americanism in the rest of the world. Section 3 began by defining empire as a universalizing economic and cultural order in which one power is raised above others and leaves its mark on the international relations of its era. We can begin, then, by saying that the first sense of American power is that it has shaped (and continues to shape) the international order by virtue of the territorial power of the USA being raised above others and by means of Americanism being something that others wish to emulate (as Gramsci stressed). It is the combination that is key: not all superordinate powers have been targets of imitation.

Section 3 also argued that imperialism could be seen as involving relations of domination between a centre and a periphery, and relations of competition among (national) empires. In turn, the relations of competition among national empires could either be seen as involving political conflicts between states and national blocs of capital (what Hobson called *Imperialism* and Lenin referred to as *inter-imperialist rivalry*) or in terms of a division of labour and economic interdependence among competing firms of different nationalities (what Hobson called *Informal Empire* and Kautsky referred to as the basis for *ultra-imperialism*). And finally, I introduced the notion of super-imperialism: that is, where one state is so powerful vis-à-vis others that the latter dare not pursue policies of inter-imperialist rivalry, even though the relations among them are more Leninist than Kautskian.

This means that, secondly, we can see the world as a series of rival imperialisms, potentially configured in postures of (Leninist) inter-imperialist rivalry, but pacified by the overwhelming military power of US super-imperialism. Or, thirdly, we can see relations among the leading capitalist states as altogether more co-operative, as a form of (Kautskian) ultra-imperialist co-ordination based on the mutual interests of internationally organized capitalist firms and markets.

However, these are not mutually exclusive and elements of all three may be present in different parts of the world and in different circumstances.

Question

How might we make sense of US power by seeing the way in which these three different elements relate to one another?

Perry Anderson has proposed an interpretation of US power that draws on both the classical Marxist heritage and Gramsci's observations on hegemony. Anderson begins with the Leninist story of inter-imperialist rivalry akin to Hobson's notion of rival national Imperialisms: 'once it becomes international, the Darwinian struggle between firms has an inherent tendency to escalate to the level of states. There, nevertheless, as the history of the first half of the twentieth century repeatedly showed, it can have disastrous consequences for the system itself' (2002, p.20). These were the consequences that led Kautsky to envisage an ultra-imperialism, which Lenin decried as utopian.

> The second half of the century produced a solution envisaged by neither thinker, but glimpsed intuitively by Gramsci. For in due course it became clear that the coordination problem can be satisfactorily resolved only by the existence of a superordinate power, capable of imposing discipline on the system as a whole, in the common interests of all parties. Such 'imposition' cannot be a product of brute force. It must also correspond to a genuine capacity of persuasion – ideally, a form of leadership that can offer the most advanced model of production and culture of its day, as target of imitation for all others. That is the definition of hegemony, as a *general* unification of the field of capital.

(Anderson, 2002, pp.20–1)

This formulation goes a long way to explaining the unique role played by US capitalism – its economy, culture and legal order – in shaping the direction of capitalist development beyond its shores.

Anderson stresses the first sense of US power identified above – that US hegemony offered the most advanced model of production and culture of its day, as a target of imitation for all others. By Anderson's account, this is what explains the *consensual* nature of the USA's ability to direct the co-ordination of the capitalist world as a whole. Anderson also stresses the role of US military power in providing the coercive moment of hegemony, the element of domination. These are surely important parts of the story.

4.1 The power of co-ordination

However, there is another element of the consensual nature of US leadership of the capitalist world. In addition to the US being a target of imitation, a model that others seek to emulate, it also performs the role of co-ordinating co-operation among the capitalist powers. The fundamental point about co-ordination is that it is, in the parlance of game theory, a positive-sum process in which all parties are better off afterwards than in the pre-cooperative status quo. That is to say, all prefer co-ordination to an absence of co-ordination, even if some would have preferred to co-ordinate differently. Co-ordination on unfavourable terms is still better than no co-ordination at all. For liberal capitalist states, the gains from co-ordination relate especially to the maintenance of an open international economy and the political arrangements within states (upholding contracts and rights to private property, and the subordination of labour to capital) necessary for increased accumulation, and to security arrangements protecting the liberal states from challenges from without. Anderson appears to recognize this, since he says that co-ordination is 'in the common interests of all parties'. Perhaps the reason Anderson does not stress this is because he believes that only a hegemonic power can effect such co-ordination, only a target of imitation can act as a pole of attraction and overcome the obstacles to co-operation. This is, however, a debateable proposition.

Writing in the 1970s, when the military power of the USA was checked to a substantial degree by that of the Soviet Union, and when the long boom had seen Western Europe and Japan grow more rapidly than North America, theories of hegemonic stability (see Chapter 4, Section 4.1) considered that hegemony was destined to be a temporary phase. The very stability and openness that resulted from a hegemonic order allowed competitors to pursue catch-up growth and to free ride on the security services of the hegemon, thereby undermining its original preponderance (Gilpin, 1983). These theses gave rise to an extensive debate, triggered by Robert Keohane (1984), about the degree of inter-capitalist co-operation that might survive 'after hegemony'.

Before this debate could really be tested, the end of the Cold War suddenly changed the geopolitical landscape. As Anderson says, 'if the consensual structure of American dominion now lacked the same external girders [making the *world* safe for capitalism during the Cold War], its coercive superiority was, at a single stroke, abruptly and massively enhanced' (2002, p.7). With military, if not economic, hegemony unambiguously restored, a clear test between the prognoses of Lenin and Kautsky looked unlikely since the USA was once again a super-imperialist power, at least in regard to military power.

Anderson's argument for the necessity of a hegemonic co-ordinator is basically Lenin's, and this, as I pointed out in Section 3.1, comprises two separate claims. The first is that there is an inherent tendency for competition between capitalist firms for profit to escalate to the level of states, once capital is internationally mobile. This is surely true in some respects, but Leninist conclusions do not necessarily follow without the addition of the second element of the thesis: namely, that competition between states tends to rivalry which is ruinous for the system as a whole. Clearly, this is a standing possibility, but it is by no means the only one. It may not even be the general case.

Competition between states – for market shares and for access to internationally mobile capital – is not a zero-sum phenomenon in the way that competition between firms in any given market is, because the overall process of competition, capital accumulation and technological innovation is constantly expanding the size of the market from which all can gain. In these circumstances, the only way in which interstate competition becomes strictly zero-sum is if states evaluate the gains they make relative to those of others, that is, if they measure their success in terms of their share of world output, or if there are no gains to share, for example, if capital accumulation and innovation are stagnant. In all other circumstances, there is some scope for positive-sum interactions, even if some states are able to garner more of the gains than others. In a world where states are only concerned about their absolute gains – where they evaluate their positions in relation to their own starting point, independently of the position of others – economic competition among states can be a purely positive-sum process. In reality, most interactions are mixes of positive- and zero-sum interactions. Co-ordination between dynamic centres of capitalism is, in general, a positive-sum process. (Inter-imperialist rivalry in the Leninist sense is, of course, a negative-sum game in which all parties are worse off.)

In short, states that are able to uphold broadly liberal forms of economic and political regulation are able to compete with one another to mutual advantage and, because of this, they have strong incentives to co-ordinate with one another in order to govern this competition. This was the logic correctly anticipated by Kautsky. Anderson assumes that only a *superordinate*

Co-ordination
As it is used here, co-ordination refers to a form of co-operation among leading capitalist states over questions of policy about international economic management, in which all states benefit over the pre-cooperative status quo, even if some would have preferred to co-ordinate differently. It is usually seen as a positive-sum phenomenon.

157

power is 'capable of imposing discipline on the system as a whole, in the common interests of all parties'. In order to be co-ordinated, there must be a co-ordinator. This is simply a restatement of hegemonic stability theory as found in the work of Charles Kindleberger and Robert Gilpin, the theory criticized by Robert Keohane. In his account of *The World in Depression*, Kindleberger wrote: 'For the world economy to be stabilised, there has to be a stabiliser, one stabiliser' (1973, p.305). In one form or another, this has become the conventional wisdom in much realist writing about the international economy.

This is a literature that stresses the need for a coercive power to impose co-operation, even when common interests are served. There are, indeed, many forms of co-operation where a superordinate power is required to achieve mutually beneficial outcomes because parties cannot come to binding agreements in the absence of some form of sanctions. The structure of incentives facing the parties in a co-ordination situation is, however, different. There is no reason why a multipolar system of capitalist power centres cannot co-ordinate on common policies and institutions to realize a range of mutual gains. In the absence of a superordinate power able to impose discipline on the system as a whole, the co-ordinated outcome is a function of the bargaining power of the parties concerned, measured by the degree of their preference for the pre-cooperative status quo. It may be easier to establish co-ordination if there is a superordinate power than if there is not, but the logic of co-ordination does not presuppose such an agency.

This is not, in any sense, to deny the fact that in the contemporary world 'domination' or force, especially military force, is concentrated as never before in the hegemonic power, the USA. Nonetheless, the question is whether this is either necessary or sufficient for inter-capitalist co-ordination among liberal capitalist states (liberal in the sense defined by Gramsci). It is not necessary because if there is scope for co-ordination, that is, if there are common interests in which being co-ordinated is better than not being co-ordinated, multiple centres can effect the necessary agreements. And it is not sufficient because unless there is scope for co-ordination, in the sense just defined, then domination need not serve the common interest. Co-operation after hegemony is perfectly intelligible in a liberal capitalist order, even in the absence of an overwhelming military power. Contra Lenin, there is in general nothing utopian about Kautsky's logic.

The historic core of the contemporary capitalist world – Western Europe, North America and Japan – today operates on the basis of a system of states that are partly co-ordinated with one another to their mutual advantage, organized in networks of international governance whose principal purpose is to enhance the openness of their territories and peoples to the competitive dynamics of capital. This represents a partial consolidation of a liberal capitalist order within and among the leading capitalist states. It is, of course, a highly asymmetric order, in which there are marked disparities of power, despite the more or less universal maintenance of *de jure* sovereignty. There is, in short, a hierarchy of economic and military power between the constituent states of that co-ordinated international order. Undoubtedly, US hegemony has played, and continues to play, a key role in bringing this order into being.

4.2 Different kinds of US power

However, the very success of the USA in fashioning this order and, hence, the steady expansion of its membership – as measured by the numbers of states that have joined its key institutions, the World Trade Organization (WTO) and the International Monetary Fund (IMF), or by the share of world output and trade accounted for by its members – is undermining the economic dominance of the USA in the world economy. Its latest entrants – China, India, South Korea, Mexico and Brazil (and perhaps before long Russia) – are reshaping it in new ways, further eroding US economic dominance over the system as a whole.

Question

Is US economic hegemony declining, and what does that imply? Or can US military hegemony compensate for, or even restore, its loss of economic dominance?

Underlying this issue is the question of the relationship between the co-ordinated liberal capitalist order on the one hand, and the hierarchy of power among its constituent states on the other. Now that the communist challenge to capitalism has folded, the relationship between the collective empowerment of states and capital, which is a product of a co-ordinated liberal international order, and the patterns of economic domination and subordination among states is, arguably, the central question of inter-capitalist relations.

In order to address these questions, we need to recognize explicitly something that has been implicit in what has been said thus far: namely, that the uneven distribution of economic and military resources underpins relations of power of two fundamentally different kinds between and among states.

In the first place, there is what I shall call distributive or coercive power. This is the notion of power implicit in realist balance of power (and hegemonic stability) thinking and in much of the Marxist literature on imperialism, including especially notions of inter-imperialist rivalry and super-imperialism. What I call distributive power is the capacity of one party to get another to comply with its goals; power relations are hierarchical relations of super- and sub-ordination – there is a given distribution of power in which

Distributive power
Distributive power is the capacity of one party to get another to comply with its goals by imposing costs.

some have more at the expense of others having less; and power operates by imposing costs on others (or by means of a credible threat to do so).

Collective power
Collective power is the increase in the total ability of a group of co-operating actors to effect favourable outcomes over and above that which could be achieved by each acting independently.

Secondly, there is what I shall call collective power. This is the notion of power implicit in the idea that states have common interests that can be advanced by forms of co-operation. Collective power is a property of a group of co-operating actors in which the total ability to effect favourable outcomes is increased over and above that which could be achieved by each acting independently. Collective power works, not by imposing costs on some, but by producing gains for all.

4.3 Economic multipolarity and military unipolarity

Although the world economy is multipolar and will become more so in the future, one economy – the USA – has a privileged position because of its technological lead, the scope and depth of its financial markets, the global role of its currency, and the size of its domestic market and the asymmetric integration of the latter with the world market. Yet the unchallenged position that the US economy enjoyed after the Second World War has gone for good. No single state, not even the USA, is in a position to exercise significant macroeconomic and regulatory control over the world economy without the co-operation of others. Of course, the abilities of different states to manage and take advantage of this vast system of interconnected markets and centres of growth vary enormously, as do their capacities to work with, or against, one another. The USA retains a privileged role in this regard. However, on many key matters – opening foreign markets to trade and investment, managing major currency crises, governing international finance, for example – the USA can only achieve its own objectives by working with others. Consequently, the governance of the world economy is increasingly something that has to be accomplished collectively, if it is to be accomplished at all.

The states-system is effectively unipolar in terms of military power. The only sense in which the world is unipolar, the meaning of the epithet 'hyperpower', is in the military sphere. How far the USA can sustain the unipolar moment is much debated, but it is certainly with us for the foreseeable future. Nevertheless, the implications of unipolarity for political struggles to shape the future of the international order are far less clear. Unipolarity undoubtedly confers advantages on the USA that it did not possess during the Cold War, at least not after the Soviet Union attained a rough strategic parity in the early 1970s, but the collapse of bipolarity and, perhaps more importantly, the absence of a clear ideological division defining the fault lines of international politics, renders the purpose of military power more opaque and makes the cost-benefit calculus involved in its exercise immeasurably more complicated. Who is to be deterred from doing what? Who is to be compelled to do what? Moreover, how can deterrence and compellance reassure allies when there is no longer a single axis of strategic political competition?

In the following sections, I want to use the analysis of US hegemony developed in Sections 3 and 4 to interrogate different aspects of the position of the USA in the international order: its relationships within the liberal capitalist order (Section 5); its relationship with the non-liberal powers of China and Russia (Section 6); and its response to challenges from without the liberal order (Section 7).

5   Relations within the liberal capitalist order: the transatlantic alliance

The boundaries of the liberal capitalist world are hard to define but its historic core has been the transatlantic alliance forged after the Second World War, and this is what I now focus on. Among the European states of the alliance as it now stands – that is, roughly speaking, the expanded membership of the European Union – and those of North America, the generation of collective power plays an important role. (Japan is, of course, strongly integrated into the Atlantic order by virtue of its economic links with the West and its security arrangements with the USA.) Among the developed capitalist countries, the power of the USA in the international system and that of Americanism can be thought of in largely positive-sum terms. Most of the power generated in this arena depends on co-operation, mutually advancing the interests of all, even if there is hard bargaining to determine the distribution of the gains from that co-operation. Overall, the collective production of power generated through acting as a pole of attraction and co-ordinating US military and economic policies with those of its capitalist allies overrides distributive conflicts. Gramsci and Kautsky rather than Lenin are the better guides to inter-capitalist relations here.

Perhaps the central question facing US policy towards this region is how, if at all, to develop further the forms and levels of co-operation achieved thus far. At the core of this is the issue of American attitudes towards the European Union (EU) and the North Atlantic Treaty Organization (NATO). Although the reproduction of Americanism in Europe provided an economic basis for transatlantic co-operation, there can be little doubt that the Cold War rivalry between the superpowers and the competition for global influence between capitalism and communism also served to cement political and military relations across the Atlantic. It was NATO's guarantee of the post-war division of Europe, defining the westward limit of Soviet power and settling decisively the German problem, which stabilized the states-system in Western Europe. The US military presence in Western Europe, as well as the extension of the US nuclear guarantee to its NATO allies – that is, extended deterrence – may have been a form of informal empire, or hegemony, but it was also an 'empire by invitation' and it provided the framework within which the EU could develop as a 'civilian' power (Lundestad, 1986, 1998; Milward, 1992). European integration has, in effect, been the enemy of European military power on a wider international stage.

Under NATO's security umbrella, extensive and deep forms of economic and political co-operation prospered. Post-war recovery saw the economies of Western Europe (and Japan) rapidly catching up with the USA, at least until the 1970s, and the Atlantic powers appeared to consider their (collective) position vis-à-vis the Soviet Union as far more important than the relative position of each within the alliance. However, at no stage was US military preponderance within NATO ever in doubt. In fact, the continuing imbalance in military power within NATO, even as the two sides of the Atlantic became more equal economically, was and remains a major source of tension.

5.1 Breaking with NATO?

With the end of the Cold War, the dissolution of the Soviet Union and the reunification of Germany, many concluded that NATO's original purpose had largely evaporated. NATO began a process of enlargement to include states that had formerly fallen under Soviet control in Eastern Europe, while the EU also began accession talks with many of the same countries. At the same time, the EU began to develop a Common Foreign and Security Policy (CFSP). On the European side, membership of NATO and the EU increasingly overlapped. This posed the question of the division of labour between NATO and the CFSP of the EU, in turn raising the question of the definition and purpose of NATO.

Established in order to commit US military power to preventing the re-emergence of a hegemonic power in Europe, from an American point of view NATO was a military alliance with a clear rationale. Enlargement ran the danger of turning it into a strategically neutral organization for collective defence, with no defined mission. Increasingly, the USA bypasses NATO for its 'out of area' operations, preferring ad hoc arrangements with those of its members (as well as other non-NATO states such as Australia) that join a 'coalition of the willing'. Simultaneously, some advocates of the EU's CFSP have wanted to develop procedures by which the European members of NATO might act independently of the USA. Underlying all this uncertainty has been the overwhelming military fact that the already marked imbalance between European and US military capabilities widened after the end of the Cold War. Not surprisingly, some in Washington began to ask whether the USA needed NATO.

Considered in these terms, there are several possible futures. First and most likely, the CFSP will amount to little and fail to develop a serious military capability that can act independently of the USA, in which case the European members of NATO will have little option but to seek ultimate military security through the alliance. Second, the EU might become serious about military matters such that the expansions of the EU and of NATO go hand in hand. The obvious way of accommodating this change would be for the EU to declare an interest in safeguarding its territorial integrity and for NATO to affirm that this is one of its vital interests. NATO would then become a more equal partnership between the USA on the one side, and the EU on the other. While this has been the declared policy of successive US administrations, Washington's enthusiasm for this might diminish if it challenged US dominance of the alliance. Third, the EU (or some of its members) might develop a serious military capability outside of NATO, prompting the USA to disengage militarily from Europe, both in the sense of removing the forward deployment of personnel and *matériel* and, by implication if not declared policy, ending the nuclear guarantee provided by extended deterrence. While the Republican right in the USA might welcome this in favour of alliances with perimeter states such as Poland and Spain as well as new alliances out of area such as India, it is anathema to most of the foreign policy elite in the USA who view the transatlantic alliance as the core of US security.

French policy has long favoured a policy pointing towards the second option noted above. The UK has always favoured the first. Prior to reunification, (West) Germany defined its foreign policy primarily in the context of limited rearmament under NATO auspices, and secondarily, through Franco–German co-operation in the EU. Whenever it had to choose between its NATO and EU commitments, NATO came first. Now that reunification has been achieved, whether Germany will continue to give priority to its transatlantic ties over its leadership ambitions in Europe is one of the most important questions facing European geopolitics. (It remains to be seen if Germany's decision to side with France (and Russia) over Iraq is a portent of things to come.) Many of the new members of NATO and the EU from former Eastern Europe regard the transatlantic commitment as especially important, as a safeguard against potential future Russian, and even German, domination.

5.2 Transatlantic tensions

A final complication is that the importance attached to global questions of military security differs markedly on the two sides of the Atlantic. This is, as Robert Kagan (2002) has pointed out, partly a consequence of the massive disparity in military power. It is also because the EU is more a regional than a global power, whereas the converse is the case for the USA. Moreover, the EU has developed as a civilian power. Indeed, European integration has, thus far, gone together with a decline in Europe's relative military power, while that of the USA has increased. This leaves the EU no option, for the present, but to conduct its foreign policy through diplomacy and economic statecraft. Simply put, it has no serious military options. Yet, it aspires to a global role in a world that is far from dispensing with military power. 'Today's transatlantic problem', writes Kagan, '... is a [military] power problem. America's power, and its willingness to exercise that power – unilaterally if necessary – represents a threat to Europe's new sense of mission. ... American [military] power made it possible for Europeans to believe that power was no longer important' (2002, pp.23, 25, 26).

This is an oversimplification, since much of the transatlantic debate – as in the dispute over how to deal with Iraq – turns on different assessments of the long-term costs and benefits of using military power, but it does capture one reason why politicians across the Atlantic often appear to talk past one another. (It also overlooks the fierce divisions within both Europe and the USA, as evidenced by the run-up to the war in Iraq in 2003.) Nevertheless, the only distributive power possessed by the EU is economic. The USA, by contrast, has military power as well. Consequently, the assessment of how far to pursue goals collectively is bound to differ from one side of the Atlantic to the other.

6   Expanding the liberal capitalist order: the USA–Russia–China triangle

Question

What is the nature of relations between the USA and powers outside the liberal core?

In contrast to the partial transcendence of inter-imperialist rivalries and balance of power considerations within the Atlantic order, the other potential great powers – Russia and Japan, and potentially China and India – consider one another, or at least potential coalitions of others, as possible future threats to their security. As noted above, Japan is also integrated into the Atlantic order. Yet in other respects these states treat one another as military–strategic rivals, even as they engage in forms of economic co-operation. Notwithstanding growing economic integration between and among these (and other) countries, each is either tempted, or threatened, by competition for regional dominance; all are currently increasing their military capabilities against one another as well as their smaller neighbours, and there are no regional or continental forms of co-operation durable enough to encompass and contain these differences. Questions of distributive power assume a much greater salience among these powers and the USA.

This is a complex area for US policy since its Cold War alignments, directed at containment towards the Soviet Union, no longer make sense; important legacies of the Cold War – most notably the division of Korea and the problem of the North – remain to be dealt with; and the underlying balance of power in the region is being rapidly reshaped by the knock-on effects of the collapse of Soviet power and the dynamics of Asian and especially, most recently, Chinese capitalist development. The operative principle for maintaining international order in this region is likely to remain the strategic management of the balance of power. What remains to be seen is whether (Leninist) inter-imperialist rivalries will develop in this region; whether the US model can act as a target of imitation for these rising powers (Gramsci); or whether they can be incorporated into an ultra-imperialist world. I shall explore this by considering the strategic triangle between the USA, China and Russia.

6.1   Chinese and Russian strategies

In the era of the Cold War, China's external strategy focused on maintaining its political and territorial integrity in the bipolar, superpower system. Initially, China pursued an alliance with the Soviet Union against the USA; this was followed in the 1960s by an abortive attempt to unite revolutionary forces in the less developed world against both superpowers; and finally, once China concluded that the Soviet Union was less interested in the cause of international communism than it was in achieving a traditional great power status, it made a limited rapprochement with the USA directed against the Soviet Union.

The collapse of Soviet power, together with the rapid and increasingly market-oriented industrialization of the Chinese economy, brought about a new orientation in China's foreign policy based on an attempt, first, to maintain the international preconditions for its internal development and, second, to reduce the ability of the USA (or others) to frustrate its international ambitions. (The domestic legitimacy of the Chinese government now rests squarely on national unity and economic performance – communist ideology no longer plays a significant role.) Accordingly, China has embraced multilateralism as a means of countering US primacy, seeking to dissuade Japan and Australia from developing strengthened bilateral ties with the USA, ties which would be, in effect, directed against China. This is, however, a conditional and partial embrace of multilateralism since 'Beijing still views national military power as the primary guarantee of "comprehensive security"' (Goldstein, 2001, p.844). China's pursuit of multilateralism is intended to forestall others balancing against it, with or without the USA.

As the successor state to the Soviet Union, Russia has had to make the most dramatic adjustment to the post-Cold War world. Russian foreign policy is still in a state of considerable flux and one can only hazard an interpretation of its long-term national strategic priorities. These are, I tentatively suggest, as follows: first, to manage the military, especially nuclear, balance with the USA in a way that ensures the continuing viability of Russia's deterrent forces; second, to stabilize its 'near abroad' by making independence among the former republics of the Soviet Union so painful that returning to the Russian embrace becomes the least costly option; third, to seek external assistance for its economic reconstruction, especially foreign investment in key sectors such as oil and membership of the WTO; and fourth, to co-operate with the other permanent members of the Security Council – the USA, China, France and the UK – in selectively containing the proliferation of weapons of mass destruction and in the campaign against 'international terrorism'. For similar reasons to China, Russia has an interest in working multilaterally on many issues.

One critical, unresolved question for both China and Russia concerns nuclear proliferation. Whereas the USA has a clear interest in attempting to prolong its military dominance by preventing the emergence of new, regional nuclear powers, the logic for China and Russia is less clear. They cannot aspire to a unipolar moment of their own; rather, the best they can achieve is regional dominance and international recognition – essentially US recognition – of great power status in a multipolar world. Accordingly, the prospect of a series of secondary, nuclear powers poses a quite different kind of challenge to their future power than it does to the USA. And without their co-operation, it is unlikely that the USA will be able to prevent further proliferation, save at the expense of risky pre-emptive strikes.

In short, both China and Russia, perhaps like France and Germany in Europe, envisage a long and complicated struggle between US efforts to preserve its unipolar moment and their desire to hasten the transition to a multipolar world, in which the major powers fashion some kind of agreed regional division of labour among themselves, while working in concert on truly global issues. Nonetheless, until such a situation evolves, neither has anything to gain from directly antagonizing the USA. Nor are they likely to forge an alliance hostile to US interests. China and Russia share a long border that constitutes a zone of potential instability and there is scant prospect that either will trust the other to guarantee its security. Moreover, it is far from clear how they could gain from establishing closer links with one another than they have with Washington.

It is true that both China and Russia can make life difficult for the USA in several respects: both have a veto on the Security Council; both can export nuclear and missile technology, effectively undermining the non-proliferation regime concerning nuclear weapons; both can limit their support for the 'war on terrorism' to areas of direct mutual concern; and both can be uncooperative on the settlement of various regional issues – for example, Iraq and North Korea. However, aside from frustrating unilateral US efforts, they have no interests in staging a direct confrontation with the USA.

6.2 Strategic 'partners' or 'competitors'?

What is the logical course of action for the USA faced with this strategic environment? As yet, forms of capitalism organized along broadly liberal lines, let alone liberal democratic norms of politics, have not sunk deep roots in China and Russia – they may never do so. Correspondingly, the level and depth of economic co-operation and co-ordination between the USA, China and Russia do not match those found in the transatlantic arena, although China has now joined the WTO and Russia has expressed an ambition to do likewise. Assuming, however, that China and Russia integrate smoothly into the existing institutional framework of the capitalist world, hegemony cannot rest on the kinds of economic preponderance that the USA enjoyed in respect of its European and Japanese allies on the eve of the Second World War. US distributive economic power can only continue to decline in this scenario.

As with Western Europe and Japan after the Second World War, US policy must aim at the maximum reproduction of the economic aspects of Americanism outside the USA, and at keeping the US economy at the leading edge of productivity and technological development (even as its share of world income declines). Its economic power in relation to these other centres of capital accumulation and innovation will increasingly come from the co-ordination of the US economy with these economic competitors. Economically speaking, the USA has no option but to follow the logic of Gramsci and Kautsky rather than Lenin.

Militarily speaking though, the unipolar moment offers a temptation to attempt to freeze the current position of US superiority for the foreseeable future, to maintain its distributive military edge over all other powers. The central question for the USA is, therefore, how to combine its economic and military ambitions. One way in which the choices have been debated is in terms of whether to treat China and Russia as 'strategic partners' in the project of managing a universal capitalist order, that is, to enlist them as partners in the production of collective power, or to deal with them as 'strategic competitors' that threaten that order, as potential adversaries in clashes of distributive power. Until now, and for a while yet, the obvious answer is to do both. Nonetheless, the important point to understand is that at some stage this will involve a choice in which the decisions of the USA, China and Russia are interdependent.

Treating China only as a strategic competitor would be tantamount to a new policy of containment. This makes little sense. On the one hand, it is not obvious that the USA possesses the distributive power to stall Chinese industrialization to any significant degree. And on the other hand, there is no evidence that Western Europe, Japan and Russia could be brought into a collective alliance directed to such an end. If anything, US hostility to China's emerging great power status would be likely to drive China and Russia closer together because its attempted dominance would look increasingly threatening to both. Briefly, the USA really has no option but to accommodate the rise of China's power.

In playing this game, the USA does have some considerable support since neither Russia nor Japan can regard an unchecked rise of Chinese power in the region with equanimity. The USA already maintains a close defence and security arrangement with Japan. Furthermore, the prospects for common ground with Russia are substantial on two important issues: Russian ambitions for future membership of the WTO and its more general economic trajectory; and prosecuting the 'war against terrorism', especially as it pertains to Central Asia. Yet there is a factor limiting closer US–Russian relations. For the USA, at least, Russian membership of NATO would undermine its sole remaining strategic purpose as an insurance against any single power bidding for hegemony in Europe. As long as Russia maintains an interest in dominating its 'near abroad', including the resource-rich and strategically crucial regions of Central Asia, the USA is unlikely to welcome Russia fully into a collective security arrangement.

Moreover, Russian membership of NATO would have destabilizing consequences elsewhere. It would either dilute the military character of the alliance to such an extent that it would become, in effect, a mini-Security Council or, if it remained a coherent alliance, what would it be directed against? It would become a mini-Security Council minus China. As Henry Kissinger has pointed out, this would amount to an 'anti-Asian – especially anti-Chinese – alliance of the Western industrial democracies', assuming that Russia becomes a democracy (2002, p.79). Who, apart perhaps from Russia, could gain from this?

The obvious role for the USA, therefore, is as the global power that acts as an external balancer to these essentially regional powers. It is possible that the current readjustment of the balance of power in Asia, as well as the armament of many major states in the region against one another, can be peacefully managed by the USA using its forward military deployments around the edges of the region as a sign of its intentions and as a means of deterring local attempts to disrupt the regional balance. For this strategy to be successful, however, the USA will need the co-operation of the major states in the region if faced with a serious attempt to disrupt the status quo. This policy might founder if several states within the region began to balance against the USA, but this looks very unlikely any time soon. It also presupposes the continued ability of the USA to forward base its armed forces – something that is increasingly being questioned in, for example, South Korea and Japan.

In the longer term, both economic integration within the region and changing assessments of the costs and benefits of seeking security through a finely balanced and nuclear-armed balance of power, might bring about greater political co-operation, mutual security guarantees and a diminishing concern with the military–strategic balance of power. If stably managed, this might allow China and Russia to join Japan alongside the 'West' as members of a global Concert of powers – Russia is already a member of the G-8 – for the international economy. (Other important regional powers, India in the sub-continent, Indonesia in southeast Asia, Brazil in Latin America, etc. might also eventually join the club.) This is the distant future envisaged by the liberal theorists of international order – the Pacific Union anticipated by Kant (1991a; first published 1795).

Alternatively, the delicate balancing act might break down. The removal of US forces currently guaranteeing the security of the South against the North on the Korean peninsula, for example as a result of genuine steps towards peaceful reunification, would almost certainly raise serious questions about the future of US bases in Japan. More generally, a widespread withdrawal of the forward deployment of US forces from the Pacific Rim, while not threatening the homeland security of the USA, would dramatically change the strategic and political calculus among the remaining major powers. The USA would no longer be able to play the role of an external balancer in these circumstances. This would open up the prospect of major geopolitical alignments as the regional powers sought to balance against one another – perhaps Russia and India balancing against China, Pakistan and Iran. What would this imply for Japan and hence South Korea and Taiwan, and so on? This would be uncharted territory.

For the present, however, the USA is a global power operating to sustain the regional balance and this suits the regional powers well, since all fear each other more than they do the USA. The strategic imperative for the USA is to continue to manage this regional balance and forestall the emergence of a threatening regional hegemon. Thus, the military and increasingly nuclear balance of power remains a fundamental basis of international order as the domain of the liberal capitalist world expands.

Activity 5.2

At the beginning of Section 4 I noted three senses of American power in relation to the debates about imperialism: first, US power as the territorial power of America raised above that of others and Americanism as something others wish to emulate; second, US power as a form of super-imperialism that pacifies potential inter-imperial rivalries; and third, US power as one state among others in patterns of co-ordinated, collective power in which America seeks to focus the direction of co-ordination. In terms of these senses of power, note down some of the contrasts between US relations with liberal states and its relations with China and Russia, as discussed in Sections 5 and 6.

---

7   The boundaries of, and challenges to, the liberal capitalist order

The 'war on terrorism', declared by President George W. Bush in the aftermath of the attacks on the USA of 11 September 2001, is shorthand for a complex set of problems that defy easy summary. Many analysts took issue with the use of the word 'war' because the perpetrators of the acts were not states but part of a transnational network, a cellular structure that crossed a number of territories on a clandestine basis, and because there were no obvious ways in which the war aims could be specified and measured. Like many other critics, the British military historian, Sir Michael Howard, argued that the attacks should be treated as a criminal matter and that the appropriate response was one of international policing and judicial process. Other commentators saw the actions of al-Qaeda as an example of an 'asymmetrical conflict', that is, a conflict whose nature is determined by the marked lack of symmetry in the power of the contending forces. President Bush's response seemed determined, if anything, to increase this asymmetry, thereby prompting the fear that it would only serve to generate yet more conflict in the future. What could be gained, these various critics asked, by a military campaign by the most powerful state in the world against one of the very weakest? This was not so much the clash of civilizations predicted by Samuel Huntington (1996) as a clash of barbarisms (Achcar, 2002).

The immediate background to the rise of al-Qaeda was the civil war in Afghanistan. The rise to power of the pro-Soviet People's Democratic Party of Afghanistan (PDPA) in 1978 provoked a civil war as significant elements of the Muslim society resisted its secularizing and socialist measures. The decision of the USA to arm the mujahidin (those engaged in a jihad or struggle) was taken, according to President Carter's National Security Adviser, Zbigniew Brzezinski, in the summer of 1979 to 'induce a Soviet military intervention'. Brzezinski later said that: 'The day that the Soviets officially crossed the border [24 December 1979], I wrote to President Carter, saying: "We now have the opportunity of giving to the USSR its Vietnam War"' (quoted from an interview with *Nouvel Observateur*, 15–21 January 1998 in Johnson, 2002, p.xiii). Moreover, when the USSR finally withdrew from Afghanistan in 1988, on condition that the West and Pakistan stop supporting the mujahidin, the Reagan administration illegally continued such support. After years of more civil war, Pakistan and Saudi Arabia created and financed the Taliban and supported their conquest of power between 1994 and 1996.

Al-Qaeda was created during this Western, Saudi and Pakistani backed operation to finance and organize the mujahidin's resistance to communism in Afghanistan and to recruit (mainly Arab) Muslims from abroad to fight in that cause. Once the Taliban came to power in Kabul (1996), they formed a close alliance with Osama Bin Laden's al-Qaeda organization, indeed in some respects al-Qaeda was the military arm of the Taliban (Rashid, 2001). However, while the Saudis had been willing to provide support for the fight against the PDPA, they were not prepared to accede to demands for a strictly 'Islamic' Saudi state and, in particular, the demand that the 'infidel' and 'crusader' armies – that is, the USA – withdraw from the Arabian peninsula. This would have amounted to a transfer of control of the Saudi state from the monarchy to Islamist forces. And so, after helping to evict the Soviets from Afghanistan, al-Qaeda turned their attention to their erstwhile Western backers who were also engaged in the military support of the monarchical regime in Saudi Arabia. The result was explosive, as Fred Halliday explains:

> Three elements therefore came together: a reassertion of the most traditional strands in Islamic thinking, a brutalization and militarization of the Islamic groups themselves, and a free-floating transnational army of fighters drawing support from Pakistan, the Arab world, south-east Asia and Chechnya with its base in Afghanistan. In the context of the greater west Asian crisis, and the revolt against the states of the region, as well as their western backers, there now emerged an organized and militant challenge.

(Halliday, 2002, p.45)

7.1   Asymmetric conflict

The term 'asymmetric conflict' was widely used during the Vietnam War to refer to the way in which the militarily weaker party seeks to take the conflict to public opinion in the enemy's homeland, as an attempt to undermine the enemy's will to prosecute the war. In this context it was an adjunct to the theory of guerrilla war, which also relied on an asymmetry between forces able to move and mix among the rural population and urban-based combatants (local and foreign). As such, it is one plausible reason why the USA, the dominant military party to that conflict, lost. The most likely rationale of the 11 September attacks is that they too were an attempt to undermine the adversary's will, only this time the will of the USA to support the monarchy in Saudi Arabia and, perhaps, Israel in its dispute with the Palestinians. Whereas the Vietnamese appealed to international and American public opinion in the name of a universally acknowledged value – that of a national right to self-determination – al-Qaeda's strategy was essentially negative, to instil fear, and its positive appeal extended to only a minority of the world's Muslims. For the Vietnamese, an appeal to norms of justice embodied in international public reason was a weapon of the weak; for al-Qaeda, terrorism was the weapon.

By its very nature, asymmetric conflict is extremely hard to deter. In particular, violent asymmetric conflict carried out by clandestine adversaries is almost impossible to deter. The operation of the balance of power and the logic of deterrence presuppose conflicts of interest as well as a common recognition of certain shared objectives – namely, survival. The logic of deterrence is, says Thomas Schelling, 'as inapplicable to a situation of pure and complete antagonism of interest as it is to the case of pure and complete common interest' (1960, p.11). Faced with an adversary that has an absolute hostility, that is prepared to risk all, deterrence is largely irrelevant. As Gilbert Achcar has argued, in this situation 'the causes of "absolute hostility" must be reduced or eliminated, in such a way that a "common interest" emerges as a possibility' (2002, p.69).

One way to reduce the hostility of al-Qaeda would have been to address the issues that provoked its hostility in the first place, broadly US foreign policy in the Middle East and, in particular, its military support to the regime in Saudi Arabia. Another response was to try to eliminate al-Qaeda. If the asymmetry of US power was producing absolute antagonists that could not be deterred, then why not use that power to destroy the adversary, even before it attacked, and engineer a new situation capable of producing some minimal common interests? This is the doctrine of pre-emption: rather than wait for a recognized *casus belli* (as in the case of Afghanistan), the USA would act to remove potential threats before they materialized.

Since al-Qaeda was, in effect, the military arm of the Taliban government in Afghanistan, the latter was directly implicated in the attacks of 11 September. The precondition for treating the attacks as a criminal matter – that the state from which the attackers operated was prepared to uphold international law – did not obtain. Nor were the war aims of the USA unlimited. Indeed, the aim of destroying al-Qaeda's ability to operate inside a state that itself repudiated all international responsibilities was fairly clear, even if other aims were less so. Although the war against al-Qaeda was not fully successful, there is little doubt that its capacity for organized activity was dramatically curtailed by its eviction from most of Afghanistan; the Taliban government that had existed in symbiosis with al-Qaeda and allowed its territory to be a haven for transnational terrorism was routed; a new administration was established in Kabul that had some chance of ending the long-running Afghan civil war; and the USA was able to establish a (perhaps temporary) military presence in resource-rich Central Asia. There are no guarantees that any of this will prove durable, but from the point of view of the USA it is hard to see that it is a worse situation than that which existed prior to 11 September 2001. In that sense, those who questioned whether it was a war that could be won were on shaky ground: it was a war, and a major battle was won.

7.2   The doctrine of pre-emption

In fact, what caused most concern among the USA's allies, in relation to the 'war on terrorism', was not the war in Afghanistan, despite the bypassing of NATO that this involved, but the subsequent mobilization against Iraq and the new doctrine of pre-emption at work in US foreign policy. Moreover, the doctrine appeared to receive a more or less open-ended remit because it was to apply not just to terrorist networks and those who harboured them, but also to 'rogue' states, that is, states that the USA deemed unfit to possess weapons of mass destruction. In his State of the Union address in January 2002, President Bush pulled these originally distinct ideas – that of 'international terrorism' and 'rogue states' – together and spoke of an 'axis of evil' formed by Iraq, Iran and North Korea, a symbiotic alliance of transnational networks of terror and states with access to, or aspirations for, weapons of mass destruction.

Many argued that the USA was, in intention and effect, embarking on exactly what the historian Charles Beard had cautioned against when he spoke of a 'perpetual war for perpetual peace', a charge resurrected by Gore Vidal (2002). Ellen Meiksins Wood offered a Marxist gloss on this, suggesting that the purpose of such a response was to declare war on all states that dared to challenge the US-dominated international order, a declaration of 'infinite war', in which US military super-imperialism would discipline other states in the system: 'It is this endless possibility of war that imperial capital needs in order to sustain its hegemony over the global system of multiple states' (2002, p.25). The idea is that as the economic components of US super-imperialism, or US hegemony, decline, so the balance of rule shifts in a more coercive direction.

At the centre of this analysis of US policy is the claim that the war against Iraq represented a general shift from containment and deterrence to a doctrine of pre-emption, and that pre-emption was aimed at producing a general disciplinary effect over rival powers tempted to challenge the

Doctrine of pre-emption
The doctrine of pre-emption describes the policy adopted by the Bush administration in the USA after 11 September 2001, in which the USA reserved the right to strike militarily at adversaries abroad before they could launch attacks against the US homeland or US national interests abroad.

imperial order. Along with the war in Afghanistan, this seemed to open an entirely new chapter in post-war international relations. Such accusations have been a standard criticism of the interventionist strand of liberal imperialism in US foreign policy. The realist thinker Kenneth Waltz, for example, argued that interventionist liberals do not reject the balance of power, 'they think it can be superseded', and cautioned that these policies must 'if implemented, lead to unlimited war for unlimited ends' (1959, pp.110,113). Waltz pointed out that, 'The state that would act on the interventionist theory must set itself up as both judge and executor in the affairs of nations'(1959, p.113).

Now it is certainly true that after 11 September 2001, the question debated in Washington was whether continued deterrence of Iraq made better sense than pre-emption. (However, 'regime change' in Iraq had been Washington's policy since 1998.) And no doubt, the war against Iraq was also intended to signal a message to others, especially to Iran and Syria. Yet it is perhaps not surprising that the USA believed that what was done in Afghanistan could also be done in Iraq, for all the differences between the two cases. Strategically, the only real difference was that the action in Afghanistan could be presented as a defensive response, whereas that in Iraq was clearly pre-emptive. Important though this difference may be, the underlying rationale was, I believe, broadly similar: namely, state or nation building.

7.3 Nation building

Between the end of the Gulf War of 1991 and 11 September 2001, US policy towards Iraq had been one of containment and deterrence. This was based on two principles: UN monitored disarmament and economic sanctions. By the late 1990s, these had stalled and demonstrably failed to achieve their objectives. (The Russians and Serbs, for example, had been active in rebuilding Iraq's air defences; the French and Russian governments were more concerned with commercial links to Baghdad than completing the disarmament process; and there was growing international criticism of the disastrous effects of sanctions, as implemented by Saddam Hussein, on the civilian population of Iraq.) In order to see why pre-emption was in some ways an attractive alternative from Washington's point of view, it is necessary to situate Iraq in relation to the broader role of the USA in the Middle East.

Ever since the Iranian Revolution of 1979, US policy in the Middle East had been based on a series of contradictory commitments that increasingly undermined its ability to play a directive role. Its hegemony has increasingly relied on its military power. Nonetheless, the lesson of the Iranian Revolution was that this was an unsustainable strategy in the long run. Prior to the second USA-led war against Iraq (March–April 2003), its policy in the Middle

East comprised hostile relations with Iran, a failed attempt to disarm Iraq (because of a collapse of support from Russia and France on the Security Council), and support for Saudi Arabia and the smaller Gulf states which was generating considerable opposition among many Arab Muslims, to say nothing of its support for the hard-line policies of Israel in its conflict with the Palestinians. There was, in short, precious little basis on which the USA could construct even a minimal set of common interests with the region.

A new start in Iraq, however, might provide the beginnings of a strategy for dealing with what Halliday has called the 'west Asian crisis', a series of crises affecting the region that encompasses the Arab states of the Middle East, Iran, Afghanistan and Pakistan (Halliday, 2002). The new logic of US policy thus became pre-emption in order to establish common interests by means of 'nation building'. The USA was extremely reluctant to admit this, and made strenuous efforts to garner multilateral support for it, but its overwhelming military power gave it the confidence to regard pre-emption as favourable to a messy combination of containment and deterrence. Reconstituting states that are able to operate successfully within, rather than against, the prevailing capitalist order of co-ordinated sovereignty was the prize.

The alternative, as viewed from Washington, was a continuation of hit and run guerrilla tactics against terrorist cells as and when they could be found; economically ruinous and otherwise ineffective sanctions; and a policy of dual containment – of Iraq and Iran – that had already lost the determined support of key Security Council members. In this context, Iraq presented a golden opportunity to set down a new set of parameters on how to contend with those parts of the international system that either would not, or could not, conform to the norms of co-ordinated competition and the balance of power. What made this particular region of crisis a candidate for this approach was, of course, its strategic and resource significance: the oil and gas resources of the Middle East and Central Asia are a vital economic interest for the dominant capitalist powers and, increasingly, for powers such as China and India too. (By 2020, over half and perhaps as much as two-thirds of the world's oil is predicted to come from the Persian Gulf region.) What made the new approach something more than a reckless gamble was the overwhelming military preponderance of the USA after the end of the Cold War.

In the west Asian region of crisis, 'Americanism' is established hardly at all – there is no basis for the common interest required for co-ordination. It is an aspiration among some elites, a yearning among many impoverished and powerless, but not a substantial reality. Even worse, from an American point of view, many of the states in the region were in danger of becoming too unstable to be deterred from attempting to disrupt the regional and, by extension, international order. Both co-ordination based on mutually beneficial economic interactions, and the predictable management of the balance of power based on deterrence, presuppose the existence of states with sufficient domestic legitimacy and stability to negotiate and uphold the requisite compromises.

In the absence of such states, the USA had no operating principles to guide its interventions, save the obvious attempt to control or protect strategically important sources of raw materials and, by extension, the regimes that facilitated access to them. This was an expensive and risky policy of crisis management based on regimes that were liable, at best, to generate more opposition to US interests, and at worst, to be overthrown by even less palatable forces. It was not a realistic basis for a durable international order that guaranteed US economic interests. Pre-emption, followed by nation building, appeared to offer the possibility of constructing the requisite stability and common interests.

That was the theory. What this might mean in practice and how it could be implemented was not at all clear. Many, especially in Europe but also in America, doubted that it could be implemented at all. In particular, it was far from clear that the domestic constraints on US policy would allow the long-term commitment of resources and political will necessary to make it succeed. It was, of course, an explicitly imperial policy, aiming to engineer from the outside a new form of rule – however much it sought to involve the directly affected populations. It is an attempt to impose a new dispensation of power, such that the resulting states and economies can be successfully co-ordinated with the rest of the capitalist world, rather than a prize to be won by the USA at the expense of rival core imperialisms. It was imperialism aimed at strengthening the brittle points of the international capitalist order, but it was not, primarily, inter-imperialist rivalry. At least since the post-war occupations of Germany and Japan, no US administration had given any thought to how it might be done. And notwithstanding its experience in Cambodia and the Balkans, it is something of which the UN – which above all has been a machine for effecting decolonization – has precious little authority, experience or expertise.

It was, in brief, a policy in search of an advocate and an agency. Thus far, its bearers have been the military forces of the USA and the UK. The aftermath in Afghanistan involved both the UN and other members of NATO, and (at the time of writing – March/April, 2003) this looks likely to be the case in Iraq as well. Even if Afghanistan and Iraq remain effectively a one-off enterprise (future targets in the Middle East might include Syria and Iran), a composite response made possible by the events of 11 September 2001 and the corresponding (yet probably temporary) shifts of public opinion in the USA itself, it represents a significant departure from the norms of international order that stabilized once the post-war settlement was completed. Yet we should not over-emphasize its innovative character. The USA's definition of self-defence to include, in certain circumstances, pre-emptive attacks may have shocked the pieties of the UN, but if this is an innovation at all, it is one in the politics of military strategy consonant with a strand of US thinking that has existed since considerations of pre-emptive nuclear strikes against the Soviet Union in the early 1950s and a string of interventions in the South throughout the Cold War.

Nation building? A US soldier in Baghdad, 4 October 2003

8 US power and the future of the international liberal capitalist order

The modern international system has witnessed two routes to international order. In the first, the dominant military and economic powers use their oligopoly of distributive power to compete and balance against one another and to manage the rest of the system, either on the basis of conceding spheres of more or less imperial influence to one another or through more concerted forms of global diplomacy. Understood in these terms, the USA is now in a unique position because of the unparalleled asymmetry of its military power. Nevertheless, as I have suggested above, we need to be careful about the conclusions we draw from this. The second route to international order is more co-operative and involves both acting as a pole of attraction for others and the generation of forms of positive-sum power by means of collective action in a partly co-ordinated liberal capitalist world, the hegemonic and ultra-imperialist order theorized by Gramsci and Kautsky.

8.1 The ambiguous role of military power

Given the nuclear revolution and the end of colonial rule, the direct utility of military dominance to compel adversaries is much diminished compared with the widespread use of great power military force in inter-imperial conflicts prior to the Second World War, though the wars in Afghanistan and Iraq demonstrate its continuing importance in some settings. But are wars against China, India and Brazil, for example, feasible, even for the USA? Ellen Meiksins Wood's 'infinite war' (2002) is not, in my view, directed at them.

What about the indirect uses of military power to deter enemies and reassure allies? A comparison with the position of the USA during the Cold War is instructive in this regard. The USA's NATO allies (and Japan) were willing to defer to its political leadership of the capitalist world on many issues because they thought that its military containment of the Soviet Union served their collective interests. For the same reason, if the USA's military power was to be enlisted in purposes that are not recognized as based on a collective interest, if it was seen as serving the self-interest of the USA alone, then it would cease to generate the consensual leadership that has served it so well in the past. The collapse of the Soviet Union and with it the advent of the unipolar moment, massively frees the hand for the use of US military power, as many commentators have rightly insisted but, for the same reason, it correspondingly reduces the role of that power as a lever of integration within the capitalist world.

For example, if the revolution in military affairs (see Chapter 13) and a successful national missile defence programme, that is, a means of destroying intercontinental missiles before they entered US airspace, were effectively to decouple the security of the USA from the balance of power in Europe and Asia so that the USA were able to retreat from its continental commitments and seek security in more unilateral ways, then it would be unable to command the political leadership of the capitalist world that it has treasured since 1945. Therefore, the price of that leadership is a forward commitment to maintaining stability in Europe and Asia. However, that stability has to be one that genuinely accommodates the interests of Europe and Asia, not one that merely serves the self-interest of the USA.

Within the Atlantic order, the prospects for a coercively imposed US hegemonic order are, in my judgement, non-existent. US leadership in this part of the world is based much more on the positive-sum interactions of an essentially economic kind among the leading capitalist economies than it is on the ability of the USA to use its distributive power, economic and military, to impose a hegemonic form of rule. Military power remains important to US leadership in this region but largely as something that must be used on its collective account, to protect and secure the transatlantic order's interests against other parts of the world.

Among the other major powers – Russia and Japan; China and India – US military power continues to play a fundamental role, this time in stabilizing the regional balance of power during a period of radical change. In this theatre, the USA is likely to play the role of an external balancer, that is, a power that does not have direct regional interests of a territorial kind save the general ones of peace and stability, growing economic openness, and access for the forward basing of military forces, but which aims to prevent regional powers disrupting the status quo. This provides the best chance of integrating these powers into the broadly collective capitalist order already fashioned in the North Atlantic arena. The temptation (and danger) for the USA is to use the unipolar moment to impose its interests unilaterally, thereby at best undermining the prospects for multilateralism and at worse provoking some powers to balance against it.

8.2   Keeping the world 'off-balance'

Putting these two sets of considerations together – that is, the need to manage the Atlantic order and respond to the rise of new powers in Asia – means that the USA, as Stephen Walt has argued, needs to keep the rest of the world 'off-balance', to stop other powers (individually or collectively) balancing against it, to co-ordinate so as to prevent inter-imperialist rivalries from developing. As Walt points out, 'the ability of the USA to achieve its foreign policy objectives at relatively low cost will depend in large part on whether other powers are inclined to support or oppose U.S. policies, and whether others find it easy or difficult to co-ordinate joint opposition to U.S. initiatives' (2000, p.30).

Some realist analysts, such as William Wohlforth (1999), argue that unipolarity means that the USA has no need to act strategically. Some Marxist analysts of super-imperialism, such as Peter Gowan (1999, 2001), seem to agree. Using Walt's summary, these arguments say that:

> So long as the United States maintains a healthy economic advantage and a global military presence that is second to none, other states will not dare to balance against it. Potential rivals will be unwilling to invite the "focused enmity" of the United States and key U.S. allies like Japan and Germany will prefer to free-ride on U.S. protection rather than trying to create stronger military forces of their own.
>
> (Walt, 2000, pp.11–12)

This is a prescription of perpetual dominance for perpetual leadership but is it realistic? Or, rather, given that it is realistic militarily speaking, how is the distributive power based on military primacy to be turned to economic advantage? Seeking primacy vis-à-vis an adversary that threatened your potential allies – as the Soviet Union did during the Cold War, even posing a threat to China after the early 1960s – made eminent sense, as leadership over those allies followed as a by-product. Yet seeking primacy over a range of powers – Western Europe, Japan, Russia, China, India and so on – when the strategic alignments among them are varied and changeable is far from straightforward.

8.3 Economic power: co-ordination in a multipolar world

Economic power, at least in relation to the major centres of accumulation, has to be exercised collectively. US distributive economic power persists but it is a wasting asset. In this field, the key to US power has included both the specific economic assets of the territorial USA and the reproduction of what Gramsci called 'Americanism' outside the rest of the capitalist world (the USA as a target of imitation), and the co-ordination of these replicas with the original. This system has naturally been designed to secure US interests, but it has equally served the interests of the other leading capitalist powers. Increasingly, the USA will lose the ability to determine the shape of this co-ordination on a unilateral basis. Just as other centres of capital have needed to co-ordinate with the USA, so the US market will increasingly need to co-ordinate with the most dynamic poles in the rest of the world.

The collective interest in the reproduction of a (albeit selective and asymmetrical) liberal capitalist world order has formed the basis for an extensive network of economic and political co-ordination between the main capitalist powers, a form of co-ordination from which they all benefit. (Some may prefer to co-ordinate differently and undoubtedly the USA has the largest single say in this, but nearly all prefer some such co-ordination to none. Co-ordination is a positive-sum, not a zero-sum, process.) It is this economic basis for political co-ordination that, after the Cold War, forms the core of US hegemony among the majority of capitalist states. The fact that the USA has a greater ability to determine the nature of the co-ordination – its specifically directive role within the hierarchy of capitalist powers – presupposes collective benefits to all deriving from that co-ordination.

In this context, US military power only assists in integrating its core capitalist competitors when it is used in pursuit of what are widely recognized to be common interests. The question of who to deter, compel and reassure is now far more complicated than it was during the Cold War. Mutual deterrence among a number of major powers is a perfectly credible strategy but it does not require primacy by one against the rest, though the USA will no doubt seek to maintain such a position. This may yet provoke attempts by the others to reduce its effects. Compellance – that is, the use of military power to forcibly change political circumstances – can work against some (as long as they do not have nuclear weapons), but it is not a general recipe for international order or a mechanism for disciplining all states. It is, rather, an imperial project – as in Afghanistan and Iraq – for constructing some minimal common interests on which deterrence and co-ordination can subsequently operate. Where there are common interests in compellance, US military power can serve to buttress its directive role in an ultra-imperialist order. Compellance is not, however, a strategy of inter-imperialist manoeuvre in the Leninist sense. Reassurance – that is, the use of either deterrence or compellance to reassure allies – presupposes a clear definition of allies and adversaries as well as means. (Iraq was a clear case of allies – France and Germany – failing to be reassured by a unilateral switch from deterrence to compellance.)

If and when China and Russia (and then perhaps India and others) join the club of core capitalist powers, similar considerations will continue to apply. Until such time military power will continue to play its traditional distributive role under the rubric of deterrence and reassurance, though the game is becoming increasingly complex and the USA is unlikely to gain the advantages it reaped from the simpler Cold War alignments because no systemic, ideological challenge to capitalism is involved.

9 Conclusion

I have argued that the core of the liberal capitalist international order is an increasingly co-ordinated set of territorial centres of political power, in which the power of the USA plays a complex and ambiguous role: sometimes acting as a target of imitation or pole of attraction to others; sometimes directing collective forms of empowerment; sometimes using its distributive power to deter adversaries; and sometimes using military and economic coercion to engineer an imperialist creation of new forms of capitalism. This is a form of liberal capitalism and liberal imperialism with deep roots, and a more or less continuous presence, in the history of capitalist development since the late seventeenth century (see Chapter 3). Now that the Cold War has ended, the USA is making determined efforts to spread this model on a wider and deeper basis.

The extent of its success in this regard will depend on its ability to continue as a model that others seek to emulate and to co-ordinate power in an ultra-imperialist order, since a return to Leninist inter-imperialist rivalries would damage the interests of all concerned. For powerful states that are both partly within and partly outside this order – such as China and Russia – a mixed strategy of deterrence and co-operation is likely for the near future, and US interests will be best served by co-ordinating to prevent mutually damaging forms of economic competition and, still worse, active balancing against US power and an outbreak of negative-sum, inter-imperialist rivalries. Direct imperial interventions are only likely to work against weak and recalcitrant regimes which are poorly integrated into the co-operatively organized world of economic competition, and which are too unstable to be credibly deterred. North Korea and Iran will probably be critical cases in this context. Short of a marked deterioration in relations among the major powers, from which the USA – like others – cannot benefit, the role of US military power in a co-ordinated liberal capitalist international order is far more ambiguous than the simple balance of power of super-imperialist considerations suggest. Economic multipolarity, rather than military unipolarity, may be the real key to the future of the capitalist international system.

Further reading

For an interesting attempt to relate Marxist theories of imperialism to the politics of the territorial state in the context of a discussion of American power, see Harvey, D. (2003) *The New Imperialism*, Oxford, Oxford University Press.

A sophisticated, well-informed and provocative liberal reading of US power, which argues that America gains more by working collectively with others rather than by pursuing unilateral initiatives, can be found in Nye, J.S. (2002) *The Paradox of American Power: Why the World's Only Superpower Can't Go It Alone*, Oxford, Oxford University Press.

A useful survey of Marxist theories of imperialism can be found in Brewer, A. (1980) *Marxist Theories of Imperialism*, London, Routledge & Kegan Paul.

Part 2 Culture, rights and justice

Flags are powerful, and usually colourful, symbols of our political identity. Every state has one. Together with other reminders, such as passports, postage stamps and currencies, flags proudly proclaim a state's authority and confirm that its citizens belong to one place rather than to another.

National flags adorn public buildings, state ceremonies, coffins at military funerals, prize ceremonies at sporting events, and national monuments. All frontier posts, whether located on roads, airports or harbours, fly the flag. Sometimes the flag is aggressively visible, as in periods of national mourning, independence ceremonies, coronations or celebrations of victory in war. At other times they are just there, subconscious reminders of where we slot in. The flag symbolizes the cultural and political identity of the nation. It is designed to embody and portray the commonality and collectivity of the political unit. It also marks territorial limits. For as soon as somebody crosses from one state to another, old flags are left behind and new ones are displayed.

National flags deliberately symbolize a nation's wholeness through their carefully chosen designs. Flags invite or reinforce an attachment to just one political community – in this case, the nation state. However, they celebrate only selected phases or aspects of national life. They are by definition the emblem of a single, sovereign community, the nation state, and by inference they proclaim that particularity over rival claims. The pattern of every flag is unique and each pattern encapsulates a story. That story can be historical or mythological but in all events it is designed to consolidate national loyalty and to be a focus of allegiance. Needless to say, the 'message' of any flag does not always sit comfortably with all the inhabitants bounded by the frontiers of that state. Some will maintain that it expresses only a dominant political identity and that it spells insecurity and can be threatening for minorities. These critics may contend that flags stand for agendas that flout the fundamental rights of sections of the population. In the international arena, certain states will share that sense of threat and challenge the values, stories and interests represented by the simple icon. In both cases the flag is seen as a potent symbol of power and, importantly for our story, unjust power.

The Australian flag serves as an excellent example of how nations try to identify themselves. Its design is deliberate, but that very deliberateness raises questions about the meaning of Australian national identity. The flag itself was adopted after a public competition, held in 1901 at independence, for the best design. It portrays a series of interlocking narratives. The Union Jack depicts Australia's ties with Great Britain. (The British flag was first raised over Australia by Captain James Cook in 1770 when he sailed its eastern coast, and again in 1788 when he staked a claim to Sydney Cove on behalf of the British government.) The five stars on the right of the flag are the Southern Cross, a constellation that appears only in the night skies of the southern hemisphere. Finally, the Federation Star, the large star under the Union Jack, symbolizes the federation of the six Australian states and the Northern Territories.

The Australian flag

However, the flag is a contentious issue in contemporary Australia. It serves to rally, but it also hits some raw nerves. It all depends on who you are and where you stand. The Australian flag's dominant motif still underscores the British connection. It narrates Australia's colonial origin and its continuing ties with the English-speaking world. It does not recall Australia's longer history with an indigenous, or Aboriginal, population whose numbers were decimated by the settlers in the late eighteenth and nineteenth centuries. The natural world is depicted by unreachable stars, not by the land desecrated by early settlers. The political history embodied in the representation of the states through the large Federation Star does not recognize a history before the Europeans arrived. The flag tells a story, but from one standpoint. It defines the nation, but in one particular way. So when Australians are faced with their flag at airports, sports events or on the battlefield they are confronted with a carefully constructed notion of what constitutes Australia's political and cultural identity.

There is nothing unique about the selectivity of Australia's chosen identity. All states adopt particular stories and identities which are jealously guarded. As we shall see, the principal vehicle for protecting identity is the doctrine of self-determination. The right of a political community to determine its own institutions, rules and folkways is enshrined in both intellectual tradition and international law. States defend that right, sometimes even through violence and war.

However, the inclination of states to insist on the right to do what they want within their frontiers comes up against another principle. This is the principle that there are certain rights that transcend the right of governments to determine how people should live their lives. Justice in particular is often held to be the highest form of political endeavour. Cultural identity and habits may be revered, but if they flout the principle of a just political order the respect they claim may be contested. In short, much of the disputation about rival claims is conducted in moral terms. Flags symbolize the oneness and integrity of the sovereign state. The language of rights and justice, as well as the claims of minority cultural groups, can challenge that integrity.

So let me come back to the example of Australia. A number of Australians insist that the symbols of nationhood emblazoned on the flag are constructed symbols, which underscore the exclusion felt by some citizens: their flag identifies only certain aspects of their national history and culture. Republicans, who wish to end the association with the British monarchy, claim that Australia's form of government is a holdover from colonialism. Aborigines point out that the flag ignores the indigenous presence and call for special group rights that will end their disadvantages and give them specific protection. Recent immigrants and other assorted communities sympathize with the Aborigines and point out that a national flag should represent the current cultural and political identity of the populace, not an imagined or repudiated past. The current flag, they insist, represents a particular ancestry, particular political ties and a particular political culture that is now outdated. Such accusations of cultural exclusivity and arrogance may also be endorsed by other nations that find themselves at odds with Australia. For example, when Japanese troops fought Australian soldiers in the Second World War, they made it quite clear that they were not simply fighting Australian military power but also the Anglo-Saxon culture that Australia claimed to share with its British and American allies.

These debates about the meaning of flags raise issues that point to the very foundations of international politics. States claim that they embody the identities of the peoples living within their territorial boundaries. These identities are a powerful force, even if they are sometimes contrived or imagined. The principle of state sovereignty is often upheld not just as a fundamental political and legal tool but also as the means of protecting the culture or cultures operating within the state's boundaries. Over the last century or so, challenges to the legitimacy of the state from other states have increasingly been couched in the language of rights. Subordinated or marginalized groups within a state can also use the language of rights to claim recognition and equality within the state. Rights and justice as abstract principles have, perhaps, even greater moral resonance than the notion of culture. They can also be threatening. An insistence on certain specific rights can serve to erode local cultural practices and even lead to a negation of cultural identity. They can ultimately undermine the integrity of another sovereign state. To put the argument in its most polarized form, cultures indicate that we are all different while rights tend to emphasize that we are all fundamentally the same. It is a minefield.

The chapters that follow will explore the tensions between these powerful agendas. They will try to unravel the meanings, motives and vocabulary of these varying standpoints. In Chapter 6, Robert Garson examines how culture and identity drive the international system. He asks why culture is so highly prized and how the concern for cultural integrity influences the interactions between states. In Chapter 7, Raia Prokhovnik considers the tension between the belief in the value of preserving particular cultures and the parallel belief in universal human rights and justice. She shows that the language of rights and justice is particularly powerful in articulating political disputes and negotiating rival claims. In Chapter 8, Sami Zubaida analyses the interplay between rights and culture and examines the political struggles within cultures about these issues. The chapter is written from the perspective of the Middle East and argues that the politics of Islam does not stem from some religious essence but from social, economic and political processes within and between the states of the region. The final chapter in Part 2, Chapter 9 by Jef Huysmans, builds on this idea but moves to the global level in analysing how a 'global rights culture' interacts with struggles over power relations in local cultural contexts. By the end of this part of the book you will see that, while those seemingly innocent flags make proud and bold statements, they also pose some of the most difficult and divisive questions about the contemporary international order.

Chapter 6 Culture, identity and international relations

Robert Garson

1   Introduction

The language of international politics is often the language of the familiar. It also tends to expose some of our most cherished aspirations. Its phrases are redolent with allusions to survival, respect, autonomy and justice. Despite the complex, strategic calculations about military and economic power and the diplomatic horse trading, the men and women who are in the limelight of the international system use words that tend to reflect the urgency and immediacy of the issues confronting them. The discourse of international politics is often articulated with references to safety, anxieties, lifestyle and visions, all expressed in the belief that carefully chosen words will make a difference. Politicians, business leaders, lobbyists for human rights organizations and other actors who shape the international map spend their time deliberating and persuading. Persuasion is the stuff of politics. It serves to define issues and to make those issues clear to those who matter. Speeches, public statements and symbols, such as flags, coins or statues, are used to cajole. They embody and convey the ideas and conceptions that resonate in the international system. This chapter will examine the idiom that drives the system in certain directions and will show why some ideas are so jealously guarded. In particular, it will argue that the fundamental stakes of international politics are essentially cultural because culture strikes at the very heart of social cohesion.

Certain concepts and beliefs recur time and again in the vocabulary of international relations. Ideas that affirm the essential dignity of humankind tend to capture the imagination and provide the emotive armoury of global affairs. They are frequently wrapped in the language of national, ethnic and social identity, nationalism, self-determination and those aspects of political life that reinforce our tendency to define issues in terms of values and local loyalties. This chapter will consider the power and force of these ideas and show how they interrelate. It will discuss the circumstances in which these ideas tend to atomize the world into discrete, self-defined national or cultural groupings. It will also show that they can sometimes serve to blur local affiliations and nurture a sense of the cosmopolitan.

The idiom of international politics emanates from a complex web of interests and values. Yet it is generally the case that the intricate tapestry is normally expressed in simple language. Read any speech by most political leaders and the issues are reduced to bare essentials. The language employed normally strikes familiar chords among the targeted audiences. When states articulate their interests, they tend to express those interests as embodiments of the core values of the inhabitants. Those values, the 'way of life', are at the centre of political dialogue. They encapsulate the elements of social existence that give meaning to people's lives. I shall use the term *culture* as a descriptor of those meanings. Culture provides an explanation, however imperfect, of why people think and behave as they do. States, like families, companies, or clubs, want to preserve the best of what they have. They define themselves by their links and traditions. It is culture that informs and guides the direction and rhythm of life. Culture acts as the leaven that enables communities to carry on. For better or for worse, states, nations and other communities use culture to evaluate themselves and others. Culture is everywhere.

1.1   The social basis of cultural identity and loyalty

Question

What exactly is culture and why does it matter so much?

Culture, of course, means different things to different people. A Frankfurt stockbroker, an Inuit fisherman from the Canadian Arctic, or a tribal leader from Afghanistan would doubtless produce diverse definitions. For the purposes of the current discussion, culture consists of the body of value preferences, customs and perspectives that enables a society to function. (In Chapters 8 and 9 you will encounter a different understanding of culture and other ways of analysing it.) This society can be a tribe, a nation, a lifestyle enclave, a religious group or any other group that gives itself (or is given by others) a definable identity. Culture incorporates those meanings and understandings that give rise to a sense of collective identity and enables communities to make sense of the world they inhabit. It serves as the grammar that sustains a community's bond.

> **Culture**
> Culture, for the purposes of the current discussion, refers to the body of values, customs and perspectives shared within a society that enables it to function.

Modern nation states contain within their boundaries a variety of cultures. However, they invariably claim to represent certain core values that bind these diverse cultures. All states make this claim, irrespective of whether they are liberal democracies or one-party dictatorships. Even repressive states that marginalize and stigmatize particular religious or ethnic groups justify their actions in the name of collective identity. For example, the People's Republic of China proscribed the religious sect, the Falun Gong, on the grounds that it is a cult directed from abroad which challenges the country's cohesion. Most states identify and cultivate a system of values emanating from preferred cultures within their frontiers. They mobilize to ensure preservation of those values to enable them to survive as entities. Political leaders and their regimes will generally command the loyalty of citizens if they are perceived to protect the culture cherished by those citizens.

Cultural loyalty sometimes exacts the highest price and extends to the willing sacrifice of life. There are poems and monuments all over the world dedicated to people who have died for country or tribe. Psychological attachment to the state or nation is often great enough to impel people to go to war, engage in revolutionary or guerrilla activity, or, as in the case of Japanese *kamikaze* pilots in the Second World War or Palestinian insurgents in the *intifada*, to send themselves to certain death. In most cultures soldiers killed in battle are revered. The centrality of this ultimate cultural loyalty suggests that culture is more than just a series of social traits that define a communal enterprise. A culture stems from humankind's inner desire to belong and identify. When it is under threat, people will mobilize to protect the framework that makes sense of their preferences and values.

The tapestry of meaning that I call a culture finds expression through various elements. It can be language, religion, a special association with landscape or a narrower enclave such as sexual lifestyle or a social movement. It is reinforced by signs and symbols such as flags, national or religious holidays, arts, folklore and rituals, as well as the social conventions that enable individuals to live within a community. It is woven into the fabric of everyday life and coalesces to provide social identity. I cannot consider culture in all its constituent elements here. For the current purpose I shall concentrate on those aspects of life that give communities a sense of their uniqueness which then has an impact on the international order. In this scenario, culture serves as the arena in which different causes expose themselves and contend with each other. The language and tone of these contestations will vary, according to the focus of allegiance. Strong religious or ethnic identity will have a different impact on the international system than, say, national identity. In divided societies, ethnic and religious divisions can pose challenges to the cohesion of states and often, as a result, to relations between states. Whatever their concerns, groups usually distinguish themselves from another group by pointing to differences in their respective cultures. That distinctiveness is cherished and jealously guarded. The Tamils of Sri Lanka want to separate from the Sinhalese because they believe they are different. In Canada, French-speaking Quebecois seek special protection for French institutions because they believe that their points of political and personal reference are distinctive and worthy of preservation. Those claims have a profound impact on the politics and policing of those states. Where cultural claims are rooted in a sub-state region or even transcend a given territory, they call into question the legitimacy of existing state boundaries and thus challenge the international order.

Identity
Identity is a form of identification with a given community. Shared or collective identities are social in that they are 'acknowledged by others, and acknowledged by others because they play a part in politics' (Hawthorn and Lund, 1998, p.39).

A people can be regarded as distinct either because they say they are distinct or because others say they are. As a result, the political arrangements that are put into place in the name of cultural protection can be fair or oppressive. It depends, of course, on one's standpoint. The cultural identity from which these arrangements flow may be embraced or they may be imputed by others. Some cultural identities, particularly those based on race, tend to be imputed. Apartheid in South Africa was justified by the ruling white minority on the grounds that black Africans and 'Coloureds' were a separate 'race' and therefore carried a separate cultural baggage. Religious identity usually tends to be claimed by the religious group itself, although such claims can be used to insist on political differentiation. Northern Ireland and Kashmir provide vivid examples of this. National identity is both claimed and imputed, usually in that sequence. These identities can be benevolent in what they include and oppressive in what they exclude. They want to protect themselves and in the course of that self-protection often tend to encroach on others. In the case of national identity, it is this tendency to look beyond politically defined frontiers that produces conflict and contestation within the international system. Issues of culture and identity can touch on raw nerves; their potentially volatile roles remind us that in many respects the international system rests upon some quite ordinary human drives.

It is important to recognize that identity has a deep-rooted psychological basis. Whether psychology is the final determinant of identity is a matter of debate. Suffice to say, students of international relations have drawn heavily on the work of social psychologists in explaining the power of identity and making the connection between the personal and the international. In this view, attachment to a political unit, be it the nation, the state or the region, is a fundamental desire, almost akin to a biological imperative. Human beings form personal relationships and cherish them. Most forms of attachment give humankind a sense of well-being. They generally give comfort – but not always. Some identities are encouraged to exclude individuals from certain territories, to deprive them of their property or to isolate them from social networks. Social attachments, for whatever purpose, need to be fostered in the first place. In the political world, a people will identify with their state if it provides that sense of personal safety and comfort, and if it is able to interpret the world in a satisfactory way. According to this view, the state fulfils fundamental human needs but in turn depends on continuing loyalty to continue functioning. This requires a steady output of stimuli to confirm the experience of community. These vehicles of solidarity will include language, political organization and mundane reminders of the values that hold the community together. Those reminders will comprise anthems, banknotes and coins, flags, education, commemorations, monuments and so on, which become part of the conversation of politics. These artefacts form the material culture of the community and flag the special characteristics that distinguish it from others (the pun is intended).

Identity then is an integral part of our communal lives. We are reminded of it in our schools, our newspapers, our songs, our money, our tax bills, our surnames and in the stories we hear from our families and friends. But it is not always fixed. Identities shift according to circumstances and motives. In the international system, particular identities are brought to the fore in particular circumstances. After all, individuals experience a number of identities simultaneously. A Jewish woman from New York could identify herself with a number of different groups: as a woman, as a Jew, as an American. The list can be expanded. In the delicatessen shop, she can pose as housewife or upholder of the Jewish home. At times of national crisis, she will probably identify with her country. If she had been a witness to the aerial attacks on the World Trade Center on 11 September 2001, she would react as an American and as a citizen of New York. If Israel were threatened, she might identify with Israel, even if she were not a Zionist. The point is that within the parameters of where they live, individuals can make choices about their identity and culture. A nation state can make similar choices. It can claim to pose as the voice of the multiple cultures within its national boundaries, as the champion of one particular cultural group, be it ethnic or social, as the defender of a minority culture, or as the advocate of an internationalism espoused by the community of nations. Circumstances will dictate. In short, sectarian, ethnic, national or international claims reflect not only the social and cultural values of the claimant, but are mediated and shaped by the interests of the political actor(s) at any one time. Identities surface or change in accordance with the shape of the political moment.

I have established the centrality of cultural identity in political life. In Section 2 I shall explore further how identity is formed and the role it plays in shaping the behaviour of nation states before going on to look at the impact of interactions between different cultures. However, before proceeding, complete this short activity to help to illustrate the point about the seamless nature of identity.

Activity 6.1

List three or four loyalties or identities with which you associate yourself (occupation, ethnicity, gender, nationality, region and so on). In which circumstances do particular identities become more salient? Consider how they might affect your political judgements and behaviour.

---

2 Culture, identity and states

2.1 States and nations as cultural embodiments

You have already seen in Part 1 that the modern international system is based on the primacy and sovereignty of the nation state. The state claims exclusive and supreme political authority within a defined territorial area and tolerates no rivals to that authority. States also add a moral dimension to that authority by claiming legitimacy. That is to say, they give an account of the justice of their political arrangements and thereby insist that citizens are morally required to obey their rules and to owe loyalty to the state. States further consolidate this claim to legitimacy when other states recognize them. (Legitimacy is discussed in more detail in Chapter 9.)

One of the important claims that states use in order to justify their rule and engender consent, at least since the middle of the nineteenth century, is that they are the representatives and guardians of the culture or cultures found within their boundaries. This claim is special; it gets to the heart of the most fundamental aspects of human identity and the layers of values, traditions and beliefs that make up that identity. States have insisted that they are indispensable for sustaining the entire fabric of life within their boundaries. They warn that if the machinery of state is weakened, culture is weakened. Thus, the nation state generates a gigantic apparatus through schools, military service, the legal system, and iconic symbols such as flags and national holidays to ensure its strength and vigour. Within its boundaries, people are mobilized to uphold the enterprise of state. In the international arena, the state strives to create an environment that will preserve and invigorate that culture and to protect it from powers that might seek, or be thought to seek, its erosion or extinction. In the labyrinth that makes up the layers of culture, nationhood stands out as the most important expression and protector of culture. Nationhood claims to embody the essence of culture and, therefore, claims special status within the international system.

2.2 Nations and nationalism

In Chapter 3, you saw that nationalism was 'the principle that each nation should have a state of its own' (Section 3.3). Yet Simon Bromley also noted that definitions of the nation have always been contested. Indeed, there are many instances where national entities are claimed to exist but do not have a state. Palestinians, Kurds, Basques and Aboriginal Australians are just a few that fall into this category. They say they are nations but do not have the statehood to go with it. If these groups are nations and there is international consensus that nations can only be made safe through independent statehood, then how does the international system adjust to the fact that the territorial maps of the world do not always conform to national boundaries?

The definition of nationhood is not just an abstract, metaphysical question that continues to challenge the wits of anthropologists, historians and political scientists. It is a crucial issue. Since the end of the eighteenth century and, more particularly, since the end of the Second World War, national groups have called for a sovereign state to protect their integrity and the free development of their cultures. Conflict between Palestinians and Israelis or between Kurds and Turks has been premised on the notion that these groups are separate nations and that the basic protection that should be afforded is not forthcoming. Nevertheless, invocations of nationhood are not always protective devices; they can be aggressive. Nationalism, which involves the integration of the perceived cultural bonds into a perceptual framework that defines a group as different from its neighbours and welds that difference into an ideology, usually tends to militate against anybody not included in the category. In brief, it categorizes people as insiders or outsiders. When nationalism espouses an ideology of exclusion, it anchors culture to the national state and manipulates its definition to suit the preferred political goals. These goals can vary; they can consist of anti-colonial struggles against foreign domination, assertions of political autonomy within regional or supranational organizations such as the European Union (EU) or narrower invocations of patriotism. This last category will have an equal impact on a country's domestic politics. Anti-immigration sentiment, for example, often masquerades as nationalism.

Nationalism, in both its mild and more virulent forms, has played a vital role in shaping the structure and development of the international system. As you will see, that system has had to accommodate the nationalist phenomenon through developing a process that recognizes the plurality of cultures. It has done so because strong national sentiment is inherently unstable and tends to challenge the existing order. Before examining this further, however, it would be useful to pause by dwelling on what precisely nationhood is.

Question

What makes a cultural group a nation, and what is the basis on which it makes claims to statehood?

There are different ways to approach this question. In fact, you have already encountered one interpretation. Namely, nations are expressions of our psychological make-up and reflect the force of emotional attachments and the value we place upon them. Nations in this version resemble families in their structure and emotional life. The wish to be associated with a larger group is instinctive or 'primordial'. Human beings want to belong, and that fundamental urge is as natural as smell or speech. Human groups, whether

Ethnicity

Ethnicity is what defines an 'ethnos', that is, a human group. It covers, and sometimes covers up, a range of different things that might define an ethnos: language, faith, descent or culture in the general sense of a particular set of collective identities. Ethnicity can be claimed by a group for itself, or at least by its leaders, or it can be attributed to a group by others.

defined by nation or ethnicity, are best understood by the emotion they generate. This primordialist approach to explaining nationalism argues that national attachments spring from the basic elements of human existence. They include family ties and kinship, language, sense of locality and an instinctive desire to be involved with one group or another. Individuals attach huge importance to these ties and so try to create states that will enable these subjective emotions to flourish. By definition, the primordialists insist that a sense of nationhood is not manipulated or invented. It lies at the very core of our social existence.

The sense that nationhood – or at least a sense of belonging to a defined political community – verges on the natural is affirmed by some historical sociologists who argue that national identity evolves from an enveloping cultural environment that has historic roots that go back for centuries. This environment includes religion, reverence for sacred and canonical texts and monuments, language and folk memory. They coalesce to reinforce the tendency for national affinity. The sense of solidarity stems from this shared experience and is repeated and refined through the generations; the nation is the product of a complex past. It combines the instinct for belonging with the most potent signs of our cultural heritage. In short, to understand what it is to be Greek, Persian or Jewish, an archaeological eye needs to be applied to the respective histories and ethnographies of those peoples (Smith, 1999, p.163).

An alternative explanation of nationhood, which can be called modernist, argues that nations are not the products of time-tested language, custom or instinct, but are essentially the products of developments stemming from the rise of modernity, originating largely in Europe. In contrast to the primordialist, the first version of the modernist approach sees the nation as an act of will, a creation by powerful interests. The historian Eric Hobsbawm maintains that nations were the products of nineteenth-century ideologues who wanted to create independent territorial states that would provide the most effective mechanism for ensuring that large-scale market economies could flourish (Hobsbawm, 1991). Hobsbawm does not dismiss outright the social and cultural traditions that bind communities together. Instead they are a social and political resource, available and amenable to political mobilization. The nation is then an actively created entity, serving other political and economic purposes.

A second, and different, modernist account also traces the emergence of nationalism to wider social and political changes in Europe. However, rather than Hobsbawm's active, political process of creation, in which the members of the nation are somewhat arbitrarily defined, the second view sees nations as a new form of social imaginary made possible by social and technological change and the dissolution of religious cosmologies. According to Benedict Anderson in his suggestively titled *Imagined Communities* (1991), national identity only emerged with the decline of religious identity and the rise of secularization. The revolution brought about by the printing press enabled a national identity to emerge whereby a people could relate to each other over long distances via print media. Anderson claims that we do not experience the national community in the way we experience, say, the family. Modern nations are large entities where most people do not meet each other. Their existence requires a leap of imagination, and they need special mechanisms to hold them together. Books, art and newspapers are the vehicles that create and bind these imagined communities (Anderson, 1991, pp.6–7, 44–6). Thus, national cultural artefacts such as literature, flags, monuments and anthems are devices that serve to construct a national community that otherwise has no natural basis. For Anderson and others influenced by his approach, national communities can hang by a thread. If the cultural artefacts do not bind, the community can break asunder and fragment into tiny ethnic enclaves.

Whichever theory of nationalism is followed (and you will encounter these as tools to interpret the history of nationalism in Section 3), nationhood matters. References to nationhood abound in international dialogue. Each nation state (or aspiring nation state) values these cultural icons and guards its identity through the mechanism of territorial boundaries. Nation states couch their case for recognition by reference to these cultural meanings. For example, the state of Israel justifies its creation and survival in terms of a common Jewish history and ancestry. The state is still seen as the most effective device for protecting and nurturing the components that give rise to this group loyalty. It provides the connectedness that is the prerequisite of any flourishing community. All nation states claim their own special destiny and crave perpetuity. They realize this by venerating the past and ensuring that safe frontiers are in place that will enable cultural survival. If the governments of states cannot provide security, they will endanger the continuity of the culture they acclaim. Governments accordingly dedicate considerable energy and resources to generating loyalty to the state (Smith, 1999). When territorial claims beyond existing boundaries are made or when there is a perceived threat to the fabric of the political community, governments invariably appeal to the solidity of the perceived national culture in justifying and legitimizing their actions.

Consequently, territory and national identity are congruent in people's consciousness – and this also applies to instances where nations do not enjoy sovereign statehood. Identity is based on membership of a particular political community and that community defines itself through territorial spaces. Yet there is nothing fixed or inevitable about any of these boundaries; they simply define who belongs and who does not. The world's political map does not satisfy everybody, and international life has been marked by numerous attempts to change it. Kashmir, the Balkans, Ethiopia and Taiwan are just

Imagined communities
According to Benedict Anderson, 'all communities larger than primordial villages of face-to-face contact (and perhaps even these) are imagined' (1991, p.15). The national is imagined as 'limited' (because it has finite boundaries), 'sovereign' (because it replaced religious authority) and as a 'community' (because it connects all the people of a given territory regardless of the social divisions among them).

some of the areas where there are continuing challenges to the territorial status quo. Despite these disputes, the nation state remains the centrepiece of political and international organization. The contention lies in the location of territorial boundaries, not in their very existence.

Indeed, rival claims for territorially bounded nations lie at the root of much international conflict. Claims are made and denied. The contestation often revolves around the meaning of nationhood. If claims to territory or political authority are based on the raw need for political stability or economic security – as was often the case with the Soviet Union during the Cold War years – those claims may be disputed by communities that place high value on cultural self-determination. If, on the other hand, they stem from an understanding that the nation has a special claim as a result of common ancestry, shared history and a common cultural experience, the terms and language of the controversy will be cultural in tone. Cultural vocabulary is often more intractable, partly because it does not lend itself to compromise and partly because disputing parties will bring different versions of history to bear. Serb claims in Bosnia, or Jewish claims to land in Israel and Palestinian territory may have strong economic undercurrents with a clear political purpose. Rhetorically, nonetheless, they are forged in largely cultural, historic and ethnic terms. In short, nationalism has a strong ideological dimension in which claimants insist on autonomy to protect their unique identity and unity.

However, the stories that cultural communities tell to reinforce their identity are contested. There is no single cultural experience in most communities; experiences are varied. There is diversity and heterogeneity as a result of centuries of migration, and so different groups have different national claims. Thus, the modern nation state has generally insisted on the renegotiation or even transfer of certain cultural loyalties in order to achieve national effectiveness. A naturalized Korean in the USA or a Bengali in the UK may preserve his or her cultural identity, but is required to surrender citizenship of the state of origin. Individuals may keep their cultural associations, but only as part of their individuality. The motto on the Great Seal of the United States, *E pluribus unum* (from many, one), sums up modern nationalism. It may have diverse origins but from that diversity a new sense of national unity emerges.

National identity, therefore, combines ancient lore with modern necessity. Its components are constructed, but only in the sense that they are selected to suit particular purposes. National identity is still one of the most potent forces in the international system – embodied in the nation state, it has served as a rallying call in the development of national projects. In this capacity, which we call national*ism*, national identity becomes a tool. It defines and shapes what we value and in turn becomes a value itself. In this context, nation is not just a place or a community; it is a call. Each state generally develops its own identity by distinguishing itself from other states. At the most basic level, flags, postage stamps and national holidays serve to confirm those distinctions. When people celebrate national symbols, they do so because the celebrations fulfil a fundamental psychological drive and because the nation is seen as the wrapper and guardian of other forms of cultural identification. If the national fabric is weak, other forms of cultural identity (class, gender, religion and so forth) may also be fragile. The modern cultural nation can serve as a midwife to other aspects of human identity and provides the yeast of international discourse. In essence, whatever their foundations, culture and identity form much of the psychological and emotional basis of relations between states. More of this will be discussed in Section 4.2 where it will be seen that security is often defined as security of society and the culture on which it rests.

2.3   The projection of culture and ideas on international life

Until now, national identity has been discussed as the product of specific historical, sociological or psychological forces which are internal to a particular community. Territorial boundaries protect the identity of the political community which claims to embody those cultural values. Still, the world is not hermetically sealed. Cultures are exposed to other cultures through trade, communications, migration, consumerism and participation in international life in general. When different cultures encounter each other, they give an account of themselves in a variety of direct and indirect ways. In publicizing their distinctiveness, they strive not only to secure protection for their identities but also to influence the rules and conventions of the world in which they find themselves. When states claim to speak on behalf of the cultures within their borders, they tend to invoke the beliefs and values of those cultures.

Question

What effect does this international realm of cultural interaction have on our understanding of international politics?

One answer is that while power and interests determine what states do and try to achieve, the language in which their actions are pursued, justified and explained hides this underlying reality. In fact, nation states often avoid the political vocabulary of power and interest that is normally associated with realism. International politics may boil down to a struggle for power, but leaders of states often insist otherwise. They ascribe a character to their communities and try to wield the authority of that character on the world stage. It is the character that drives the dialogue.

Others go further. According to one school of theorists, the constructivists, ideas are the very motor of national and international life. Constructivism is a school of thought that argues that states' identities and interests are not fixed but are constructed intersubjectively by interaction in the international system. Different identities and interests can produce very different kinds of international system. Constructivists argue that the cultural environment is crucial to understanding why states behave as they do. As discussed above, the domestic culture has a crucial role in shaping the formation of interests 'within' a state. Of course, belief systems adapt and change. Nevertheless, states are quite painstaking in cultivating and transmitting the meanings which inform their actions. States value the corps of beliefs that they claim constitute their identity.

However, some constructivists, such as Alexander Wendt, also argue that ideas at the international level help to construct states' identity and interests (1992, 1999). That is, the ways that states behave towards each other at the international level, the ideas they form about other states and the ways in which they interpret other states' actions and beliefs feed back into their own definitions of their national identity and their interests. States' identities and interests are, in the term used by constructivists, 'intersubjective', that is they are formed through the interactions between subjects (states). In this view, the sinews and even the very kinds of international system created are a social construction. They are made up of the ideas and cultures that exist within and between states. Ideas are not just icing on an economic or military cake nor are they mere subterfuge for baser motives; they have a vitality of their own and stand in their own right.

Social construction
Social construction refers to the fact that the shared concepts of the social world play a key role in creating and sustaining social institutions and practices, wherever those institutions and practices operate by virtue of collective agreement or acceptance (Searle, 1995).

Constructivist theorists do not deny the importance of material calculation; they concede that calculations of material capabilities will influence whether a state takes this course or that (Wendt, 1999, Chapter 3). Yet they also maintain that material capabilities cannot be understood in isolation from the ideas that states have. As Wendt put it, 'Five hundred British nuclear weapons are less threatening to the USA than five North Korean ones because of the shared understandings that underpin them' (Wendt, 1999, p.255). In other words, understanding the material capabilities of states involves understanding the ideas that states have about each other and themselves: for the USA, the UK is a 'friend', North Korea an 'enemy'.

Ideas are also a *source* of power. Wendt argues that states may observe rules or be made to act in a certain way, either by the use or threat of force, appeals to self-interest including the use of incentives, imposing costs and offering bribes, or by appeals to shared norms and ideals (1999, p.250). If, as I argued in the Introduction, persuasion is the stuff of politics, then in the international arena appeals to shared norms become a source of power in themselves.

This in turn leads to two outcomes. On the one hand, constructivists point out that states are more likely to exert influence on the international system if they employ ideas and a vocabulary that are generally shared by the community of states. In the modern world, states are socialized into an international community, as individuals are in society, by adopting and conveying selected common values. States and nations can best preserve their particular identities through constructive association with other states and nations. It is through such interaction that we become conscious of our similarities and differences. This may ultimately mean the international system itself is converted into a discrete system with its own special rules and procedures. On the other hand, international alignments are often formed along ideological lines, which are shaped by the respective cultures from which ideas emanate. In their attempts to exercise power and to influence the structure of the international system, states will invariably seek the support of other states with similar values. The UK has identified with the USA since the First World War not just because it believes that its trading and military interests point in that direction. It aligns with the USA because both nations share common political values and traditions and it is those traditions that inform their strategic interests.

The idea which you came across in Chapter 3, of an international society of states with its shared rules, institutions and conventions, can now be refined a little further. States subscribe to the principle of mutual recognition not only to allow different political communities to survive and flourish; they also understand that mutual recognition equates authority over particular territory with the notion that the state also embodies a national culture, however contested that culture might be. Membership of the society of states enables individual states to protect and consolidate their discrete national cultures. However, as the constructivists suggest, those cultures have the potential to become part of the common idiom that is so crucial to an international society. Nation states claim to represent their own unique cultures, but at the same time are directed through the necessity for communication and interaction to adopt common codes and may, thus, be changed by this process themselves. For example, nearly all states claim to be 'fair', 'democratic' or 'peaceful', even though many are not.

Question

If you think back to Chapter 3, can you spot any tension which might arise between states using mutual recognition as a means of strengthening and protecting their 'own' culture, and the idea of an international society of shared norms and institutions?

The tension arises if states represent very different systems of values. Mutual recognition (a principle claiming universality) empowers states to protect their difference from others. This creates the potential for the emergence of clusters of states with claims of commonness of purpose. When cultures are able to align or identify with others sharing similar values, they may claim to belong to a 'civilization'. Networks of national communities have emerged with familiar if slightly misleading labels: the 'West', the 'Middle East',

'Pacific Asia' or 'the Islamic world'. These are not mere geographical descriptions but cultural constructs. While these clusters might be stepping stones to a wider world community, they might also be a sign that the world is breaking up into irreconcilable blocs – the antithesis of an international society. Samuel Huntington (1996) has argued that these clusters of civilization are becoming rigid and so represent a new and unstable vortex in the international system (see Chapters 3 and 15).

Before we can understand how preoccupation with identity has driven the foreign policy of the nation state and how notions of shared culture have tended to direct the states into blocs, it is necessary to take a historical perspective. Ultimately, historical forces have shaped the frontiers of states and determined which aspects of their culture would inform policies on the world stage. In Section 3 I shall attempt, therefore, to trace the unfolding of the historical story. In particular I shall show how the protectiveness of culture moved to the forefront of international dialogue and how some major players developed a code of practice tailored to provide order and justice in the international system. You will also see that the created system was essentially a European and Christian model which came to be challenged and partly refined with the decline of European empires and the emergence of a new order in the non-European world.

3 Culture and identity in historical perspective

3.1 The Westphalian system: the state and Christianity

Culture has many meanings. Nevertheless, the definition that has suited us so far is the framework of values and practices that enables people to give and extract meaning in their lives. In Christian Europe until the eighteenth century, Christianity provided that framework. Christianity informed law, economic regulation, social rhythms and, above all, the authority of rulers and sovereigns. The Protestant Reformation in the sixteenth century posed penetrating questions that went to the root of the Church's authority over all aspects of life. It did not, though, challenge the notion that the political order existed to protect and further religious concepts. Quite the opposite. Its main theologians, such as Martin Luther and John Calvin, argued that reformed religion should wrest authority from papal power and redirect it. Rulers and laws would change, but the purpose of the political order was still to protect religious values. Their ideas unleashed forces that for over a century brought in its wake civil strife and warfare. The bloodiest of the religious wars, the Thirty Years' War, ended with the Peace of Westphalia of 1648 which was discussed in Chapter 2.

As noted by Benno Teschke in Chapter 2, Westphalia is something of an icon for students of the international system, representing for many the origins of the modern states-system. Teschke's argument challenges this view, and the interpretation of Westphalia he develops is based on a study of the social property relations and class structures of the societies concerned. I want to present an alternative interpretation which looks instead at religious identities and the religious dimensions of the conflict. From this perspective, Westphalia established a system by which the sovereign, territorial state became the nucleus of a new order in Christian Europe. It was designed to end religious wars between states once and for all by recognizing the right of each ruler to determine which Christian church should operate within his or her authority. The signatories to the treaties recognized each other as a series of independent entities in which individual rulers had jurisdiction within their own territories. The rulers were supreme in their own realm and could determine the state religion. It established the principle of the monopoly of authority and the principle of non-interference in the affairs of other states. However, this settlement also entailed an agreement between states not to interfere in the affairs of other states in support of 'their' co-religionists abroad. Catholic minorities in Protestant states or Protestant minorities in Catholic states were the subject of loose provisions for religious tolerance. Yet such provisions only extended to Catholicism and Protestantism, and outside states agreed not to act in defence of minorities sharing the same religious affiliation. Essentially, the rulers of mid-sixteenth-century Europe acknowledged that the purpose of authority was the protection and furtherance of religious practice.

Seen from this perspective, Westphalia demonstrates the notion that the purpose of the state is to uphold and reflect the cultural values to be found within its boundaries. In the seventeenth-century context, culture had a narrower definition. While it embraced the arts, philosophy and ordinary lifestyles, it was informed by religion – in the case of non-Ottoman Europe, it was the Christian religion. The architects of the peace employed these narrower definitions of culture in their design. They would not have used the term *culture*. Language patterns, local tradition and ethnic descent would not have crossed their minds. Nonetheless, they did try to devise a system where political authority and religious practice reinforced each other. Thus, while the Westphalian settlement established a political order that entertained only Christianity, it did recognize that sectarian violence could only be ended if there was an understanding that culture – and in this instance religious culture – was crucial to the legitimacy and efficacy of the state. While the small print of the Peace of Westphalia in 1648 did not make sovereignty watertight, it did encapsulate the idea that political entities could only survive if they upheld those aspects of life that assured a particular value system.

However, while the supremacy of Christianity remained, the political geography established by Westphalia was redrawn many times. For the next century and a half in Europe, monarchs looked to the preservation of their dynasties by forging strategic alliances with other kingdoms and principalities and by marrying into other royal families. In terms of foreign affairs, each state was supposed to possess a set of strategic, territorial and commercial interests which the sovereign would pursue. Territories were exchanged or conquered to preserve the balance of power and secure the future of the various dynasties (see Chapters 2 and 3). Little regard was paid to the wishes of the inhabitants or other considerations. Poland was partitioned, fragmented territories in Germany and Italy were swapped around between the great powers irrespective of religious preference, and empires were acquired in India and North America. Large numbers of the indigenous populations of North America and, later, Australasia were exterminated by settlers without serious concern or pangs of Christian conscience. Good and effective statesmanship was equated with the ability to preserve the balance of power and advance the economic interest of the state. The individual rights of citizens or the protection of cultures in the broader sense scarcely entered the equation.

3.2   Order and its challenges: the Concert of Europe and the rise of nationalism

The end of the eighteenth century witnessed some fundamental reassessments of the nature of the state and, concomitantly, the role of the international system in protecting the state structure. The intellectual ferment known as the European Enlightenment served as the catalyst. Political thinkers of the Enlightenment inverted the notion that security and stability were the principal purposes of government. They argued that society served the individual and that the function of government was the fostering of the individual's rights. Rights, according to the new wisdom, were universal (at least for European males), not privileges held at the whim of the ruler. These ideas fell on fertile ground in some societies. In Britain's North American colonies, the colonists argued that a people should determine its own government and that the primary duty of the state was to protect the political values of the local population. Those values could only be protected by independent statehood. In Revolutionary France, the middle classes called for wider participation in government and dismissed the notion that the state was little more than territory assigned to a monarch by war, treaty or marriage. The democratic vanguard insisted that the only legitimate state was one based on the collective will of the people encapsulated in the idea of the nation. New forms of cultural identity emerged, forms that transcended religion. Political leaders in the newly created USA as well as in France, Norway, Finland, the Netherlands and Ireland, redefined the state as a national state, containing a distinctive cultural and linguistic community.

The nineteenth century marked the turning point for nationalism as an informing ideology in the conduct of international relations, at least in Europe and the USA. The Napoleonic wars (1798–1815), which saw the attempt by France to establish hegemony over Europe through military conquest and occupation, served to develop an intensified awareness of national difference. However, the victors recognized that nationalism was a hornet's nest which could upset political arrangements throughout Europe. Consequently, the settlement established after 1815 in the wake of the Napoleonic wars sought to create a network of great powers, the so-called Concert of Europe, which would hopefully stem the tide. The Concert, consisting of Great Britain, Austria, France, Prussia and Russia, was conceived as a kind of club, in which members agreed to preserve peace and order by recognizing each others' authority in designated geographical areas and preserving the balance of power by leaving frontiers alone. The Concert's code cared little for the idea of national self-determination. Early nineteenth-century rulers were preoccupied with equilibrium and order, not with redrawing the map to take into account cultural sensitivities. Prince von Metternich of Austria, the principal architect of the Concert, sought to create a diplomatic community that would stem the tides of liberalism and nationalism. Thus, in one respect the Concert reaffirmed the Westphalian principle that sovereignty was best guarded by cultivating international co-operation in sustaining a stable political order (Kissinger, 1957).

The architects of the Concert of Europe: the great powers meet at the Congress of Vienna at the end of the Napoleonic War, 1815

The heads of state in the post-Napoleonic order believed that responsibility for foreign affairs and public order lay with the patrician class. They recognized that the Enlightenment and the French Revolution had unleashed social forces which challenged the restrictions on political rights throughout Europe. They hoped that if their aristocratic principles could deliver a peaceful order, they could nip these new forces in the bud. In Britain and France there were calls to extend the franchise, while in other parts of Europe the tide of nationalism began to rear its head. European nationalists echoed the views of the successful revolutionaries in the USA – namely, that the self-governing nation was the only just political form. The Concert began to strain at the edges. As old allegiances declined, intellectuals and other opinion makers began to identify specific cultural communities tied by descent, history, language and religion as the basis of political order. Movements emerged in Italy, Germany and parts of the Hapsburg and Ottoman Empires that championed the right of communities based on common language and historical experience to determine their own fates. The political state, nationalists argued, should mirror the cultural state. States were legitimate only if they reflected the cultural character of the population and if they fostered a sense of identity that would bind inhabitants. Nineteenth-century nationalists accordingly cultivated an instrumental meaning of history and culture. That is, they selected aspects of their culture that suited their case. If they were going to invent nations, they had to invent histories that went with them.

The nationalists' remedy was not that straightforward. Their claim that specific territorial space accorded with specific cultural identity was conveniently tidy, but generally untrue. They invoked the primordialist ideal, yet on closer look it was more complicated. There simply were no areas populated exclusively by one ethnic or national group. In the Balkans, the population was ethnically mixed. In Italy, the populace of the various states may have spoken Italian but they did not feel any allegiance to an Italian entity. Nevertheless, Italian speaking Lombards or Orthodox Christian Greeks believed that it was no longer tenable to be ruled by Austrians or Turks. Even more importantly, they believed that if the institutions of government reflected the cultural claims of the community, this would enable their culture to thrive. Nation-building did not cease with the creation of the nation state. National and cultural consciousness in all its dimensions could be promoted through the institutions of the state. After the unification of Italy in 1861, Massimo d'Azeglio summed it up well: 'We have made Italy and now we have to make Italians' (quoted in Hobsbawm, 1991, p.44).

3.3 International harmony or a mapmaker's nightmare? Self-determination in the twentieth century

There was one glaring irony in European nationalism – the system coincided with the push of the great powers to establish empires in other continents (see Chapter 3), regardless of local cultures prevailing in colonized areas. This tension came to a head in the aftermath of the First World War. The most eloquent spokesman for the principle of self-determination was Woodrow Wilson, President of the USA from 1913 to 1921. Wilson's ideas sprang from the principles of the French and American Revolutions. He believed that a peaceful and just world order could only be secured if nations were self-governing. For Wilson, territoriality was entwined with the exercise of authority over people as well as space. Self-determination became his universal panacea. It was just. It was also a necessary ingredient in the attainment of a new world order, marked by the establishment of an international security organization (the League of Nations, discussed in Chapter 4). It would provide a common principle for settling disputes over national boundaries and the legitimacy of governments. It would dissolve oppressive political empires and also serve as a check on Bolshevism, which had taken root in Russia after 1917. For it was the Bolsheviks, under the leadership of Lenin, who claimed that capitalism, not culture, was at the root of nationalism and that a new order, based on justice for the working class, could only come about through revolutionary socialism.

Whatever the merits of their analysis, the Bolsheviks raised a question that has plagued the principle of self-determination ever since. Namely, if a community is to determine its own government in accordance with the dominant culture of the particular area, how can the rights of those who do not feel part of that community be protected? Similarly, if a community determines its own destiny, but that destiny is held by neighbouring communities to be unjust or simply destabilizing, what are the principles on which the international community can intervene and negate the self-determined wishes of the nation?

The Paris settlement of 1919 that ended the First World War provided sharp examples of this conundrum. President Wilson had stated that national groups in Europe should, wherever possible, be given their independence and that frontiers should demarcate areas of spoken language. The principle was clear, but the detail was confused. Europe's map did not consist of defined spaces neatly separated by language, religion or ethnicity. In central and Eastern Europe there was a plethora of smaller nationalities intermingled with larger, majority nationalities. The various peace treaties imposed by the victorious powers after the war resulted in new boundaries that deliberately placed ethnic and national groups under the jurisdiction of other nationals. German-speaking Alsace was assigned to France. The German-speaking

Sudeten area was transferred to the newly created state of Czechoslovakia. A large Polish minority ended up in the new truncated Germany. Turkish islands in the Aegean Sea were assigned to Greece. New states were forged out of the former Hapsburg and Ottoman Empires. Most of them contained more than one ethnic or linguistic group who thought of themselves as separate nations. The problem was simple, the solution impossible. Namely, which group or minority was to be given the right of self-determination? Yugoslavia had within its assigned frontier Orthodox Serbs, Muslim Bosnians and Kosovars and Catholic Slovenes. Populations were very mixed throughout Eastern and Southern Europe, and the new political map did little more than identify ethnographic clusters. The final settlement left some 30 million people living as national minorities. The ethnographers and cartographers who came to Paris did their best. No matter how imaginatively they drew their maps, some groups were going to be left out and disgruntled. Deliberately constructed nation states tend to gloss over ethnic and national rivalries.

Wilson and his associates recognized that their grand scheme could only work in a symmetrically ethnographic world. Self-determination held out little promise to minorities whose status was now confirmed by geographical boundaries. The victorious Allies knew that the whole edifice could collapse unless these minorities believed there were safeguards in place. Therefore, they required the signatories to the various peace treaties to sign special treaties to protect minority rights. They believed that internationally guaranteed minority treaties would prevent those minorities from opposing the new framework and convert them into loyal citizens. The Polish Treaty, signed in June 1919, set the principles. It stated that 'Poland undertakes to assure full protection of life and liberty to all inhabitants of Poland without distinction of birth, nationality, language, race or religion ... Polish nationals who belong to racial, religious or linguistic minorities shall enjoy the same treatment in law and in fact as the other Polish nationals' (The Polish Treaty, 1919, Articles 2 and 8). The treaty served as a model for similar minority treaties with other nations such as Czechoslovakia, Greece, Lithuania and Turkey. This attempt to marry self-determination with the principle of minority rights confirmed the inherent tension between the two and the difficulties of resolving that tension. The contradictions would unravel cruelly over the next 20 years and came to a head with the conquests and annexations of the Soviet Union and Nazi Germany under Stalin and Hitler. Political reality and power decided who lived where and under what government. Maps, historical charts and statistical tables did not clarify matters in 1918 and the minority rights treaties did not herald a new dawn. The architects of the Versailles Treaty paid lip service to the principle of self-determination but they could not deliver in any consistent way.

Activity 6.2

In Section 2.3 I drew your attention to a tension between states' adherence to international principles and their claim to defend and represent a particular culture. Briefly note how this was manifested in the reconstruction of Europe after the First World War. (You might also find it useful to refer back to Chapter 3, Section 3.3.)

The principle of self-determination, as enunciated by Wilson, was applied only to selective communities. There were no agreements about the treatment of the Irish by the British government, nor of Asians living under the jurisdiction of the USA. Indeed, the non-European world revealed an even greater contradiction raised by the right to self-determination. The right of the victorious powers to rule over their colonies was not challenged (also see Chapter 3, Section 2.6). Moreover, as if to reinforce the legitimacy of colonialism, former German colonies in Africa were ceded to South Africa, Britain and Belgium. Some support was given to the eventual right of selected territories to determine their destiny, but only at some future date. Article 22 of the Treaty of Versailles identified 'mandate' territories 'which are inhabited by peoples not yet able to stand by themselves under the strenuous conditions of the modern world', but which would under the tutelage of the major powers eventually form their own nation states (Treaty of Versailles, 1919). For example, Palestine was assigned to British tutelage, but Britain revealed the ambiguous and muddled notion of self-determination by grooming the area for the Arabs while promising a homeland for the Jews who were scattered throughout the world.

The selectivity of the major colonial powers in their campaigns for national self-determination began to unravel after the Second World War. In Asia, Africa and the Caribbean, nationalists confronted the imperial powers with their own contradictions. National self-determination could not be right for Europe but wrong elsewhere. Drawing on the rhetoric of the war against Nazism and fascism, political leaders called for independence and an end to empire. The colonies resented being sources of cheap labour and raw materials, and believed that they could prosper better through self-government. More importantly, they argued that the domination by an imperial power deprived the inhabitants of the very dignity that European nationalists argued was only possible under conditions of self-determination.

Non-European nationalist leaders tended to avoid emphasis on overtly cultural differences such as religion, language or traditions. Instead, they inveighed against political repression and economic exploitation. In many instances, their reluctance to highlight differences between their own and European societies was occasioned by an awareness that there was no single national culture within their own political boundaries, which were in many cases the creations of the imperial powers. They were conscious of the broad mosaic of different religious and linguistic traditions within their territories, and that these would be intensified or even redefined by changes in regime. Furthermore, many nationalist leaders harboured a residual identification with the imperial country. Most French West African leaders, for example, applied a political and cultural self-definition within a broader assumption of remaining part of Francophone culture. Leopold Senghor, president of Senegal from 1960 to 1981 and a distinguished poet, wrote in French and was himself a Christian in an overwhelmingly Muslim country.

The nationalists' challenge was formidable. They recognized the need to carve out a meaningful national identity that would enable independence to hold (Young, 2001). Certain cultural manifestations such as, for instance, Islam in Algeria were mobilized as vehicles of political protest. That is to say, Algerian independence was not sought to protect one religion. Rather religion in this instance served as a political tool. States could not survive unless there was a clearly delineated sense of national identity; heightened senses of religious identity or ethnicity were nurtured in the service of a political cause. The emerging leadership in the colonies employed the rhetoric of identity in mobilizing the population against the imperial powers. Cultural difference may not have been the spark for the various liberation movements but over the years it came to be groomed as an essential point of departure. Whether cultural difference was an afterthought or a catalyst, nationalists soon came to insist that indigenous cultures could not flourish under conditions of imperial dominance. It was time for a transfer of power.

But transfer to whom? India, for example, remained a pluralist, fragmented society divided between Hindus and Muslims. Nigeria was divided between Ibo, Hausa and Yoruba. Belgian Congo was a territory of 2.5 million square kilometres inhabited by many different tribal federations. The frontiers of India and Nigeria were convenient constructions and scarcely conformed to the idealized model of the primordialists. Similarly in Palestine, Arab and Jew vied for authority. In the end, power was generally transferred to the most dominant and influential group and its leaders. More often than not, independence was followed by ethnic, religious and regional violence. Claims that nationalists had closed rank were often wafer thin. Although most of the remnants of colonial rule had been shed by the mid 1960s, they were replaced by ethnic and sectarian divisions that were to plague the political landscape for years to come. Rearrangements of power did not resolve cultural differences and the strong attachments to those cultural matrices.

The movement for national independence received great encouragement from the United Nations (UN), which was formed in 1945 to provide effective machinery to prevent further war. The UN was designed as an association of sovereign states and it banned interference in the domestic affairs of its members. However, this proscription was qualified. For while the Charter recognized that each community possessed unfettered sovereignty and, implicitly, its own cultural norms and values, it also acclaimed the universal principle of human rights. To clarify matters, in December 1948 it adopted the Universal Declaration of Human Rights, thus reaffirming and updating the universalism of the Enlightenment. Human rights were now placed at the centre of global politics. The problem was that some cultures contested the version of rights that came to be expounded over the years. The story of that contestation, and the problems of the friction between state sovereignty (with its presumed protection of a national culture) and the idea of universal rights, was raised in Chapter 3 and will be discussed in Chapters 7 and 9. Yet one thing stands out: culture, identity and loyalty to nation and ethnic group was one of the most potent, if not the most potent, instruments of debate. While the agendas and configurations of global politics had changed over the centuries, some fundamental concerns remained. People still wanted protection for their national and ethnic groups, and they still identified themselves by their culture. Despite the creep of global norms and values, culture and, very specifically, national culture remain at or near the surface of contemporary life. Moreover, cultural identity has continued to permeate the vocabulary of international politics. In Section 4, I turn to how identity is manifested in international politics.

Activity 6.3

This historical section provides several examples of nation-building. Refer back to Section 2.2 and ask yourself whether the references to newly created nation states in Section 3 reinforce the primordialist explanation of nationhood, or whether they substantiate Hobsbawm's modernist view that nations are essentially political creations with political purposes.

---

4   Culture and identity in the international system

4.1   Mobilizing identity: the role of ideology and nationalism

We can begin to think about the ways in which cultural identity manifests itself in international politics in terms of the public identity of states. That is, the ways in which states present themselves and identify themselves as representing the populations and cultures of their communities. States develop public identities in a variety of ways. Those identities are an amalgam of different aspects of their culture. Public identity can be based on any combination of ethnicity (or multi-ethnicity), religion, legend or political

Public identity
Public identity is the amalgam of ethnicity, religion, political ideology and dominant values which states claim to embody and represent.

ideology. The weighting given to each of these factors will vary from state to state. The process is complicated because many have communities with sub-national loyalties such as the Catalans in Spain or the Zulus in South Africa, and all of them have different enclaves and interest groups that vie for a voice in the exercise of power. One of the greatest challenges of statecraft is to combine these different voices into one credible, single voice. As you have already seen, the fostering of nationalism is a particularly effective device for this. One obvious way to highlight national identity is to distinguish it from other identities. Nationalism can take a variety of forms. It can be creative by binding communities that might otherwise founder, and it can also be aggressive and violent. Militant nationalists make it quite clear that there are boundaries of belonging. Their moral community ends at the appointed frontier. In this scenario, there are obligations to those inside the community but none towards those that lie outside. In the world of the nationalist zealot, people located outside those boundaries do not belong and can serve to threaten. Militant nationalism can be turned against communities living within a nation's frontiers – for example, Jean-Marie Le Pen's National Front in France at the turn of the twenty-first century. Alternatively, it can be turned against other nation states which are deemed to be inimical to stability or survival.

Modern nation states will often seek to generate a sense of belonging if they are diverse in ethnic or religious composition in order to provide an overarching identity. A state's public identity can serve to transcend these other loyalties and to tighten political bonds; in this sense it can discipline cultural diversity. It has been estimated that only 10 per cent of the world's existing states are ethnically homogeneous and so solidarity has to be cultivated. The ability to cultivate national identity reinforces the arguments of the modernists, referred to in Section 2.2. Therefore, when political leaders call for a strengthening of national bonds, they may do so because national unity is brittle. Some nation states are more effective than others in mobilizing this sense of loyalty. Identity is, after all, a moveable feast; individuals can weave between a multiplicity of overlapping identities. Globalization, multinational production, migration and alternative cosmopolitan ideologies such as feminism, environmentalism or cosmopolitanism itself can break up the terrain on which loyalties once rested. Some multicultural nations succeed rather well in reaffirming basic political values. For instance, the USA and Israel, both highly pluralistic states with a mosaic of immigrant communities, appear able to mobilize identity quite easily (this should not be confused with political unity), while Belgium, divided between the French-speaking Walloons and the Flemish, finds it difficult and generally appeals to one of the two communities and even to a supranational European identity.

The reasons for the ability of some states to invoke national identity effectively are complex. Generally, the best clues are to be found in the historical experience of individual nations. The USA, for example, is overwhelmingly multicultural but has tended to display an extraordinary sense of national solidarity in times of difficulty. Although it grew as a nation of immigrants, it has developed a parallel and unique national identity of its own. Nearly all immigrants came to the USA voluntarily in search of a better life: for economic opportunity, for religious toleration or for values associated with these. The USA is strong, with a wide sense of legitimacy and a military ability to defend itself. If a state appears to be efficacious, the chances are that a people will identify with it more strongly. As shown earlier, the nature of the national identity may be fabricated or highly selective. Not all ethnic, religious, sub-national or interest groups will agree on the dominant version of that identity. Nevertheless, a sense of cultural solidarity, wrapped in the language of national values, is a potent and vitally adhesive force in both national and international politics.

An important part of a state's public identity is the political ideology that informs its political and social system. Ideology consists of a set of political assumptions which inform and shape attitudes to a common enterprise. It provides the code to why a political community behaves as it does. Unlike culture, which has largely historical and anthropological underpinnings, ideology flags the purpose of a political project. Ideology accordingly serves as both a prism and a vehicle through which policy makers and opinion makers evaluate the world they inhabit. It also acts to sustain the culture or cultures that form the basis from which the political system flows. States often claim to represent a particular ideology within the international system and so provide a code for understanding a set of policies or attitudes. Consequently, many explications of state action are couched in ideological terms because they remind citizens at home of the values which are supposed to bind them and inform other states of the fundamental intellectual assumptions that serve as a vein for all national interests. In international politics, the ability to induce identification with a particular political ideology, however contested or fabricated, strengthens the state both internally and externally. Shared political values hold the state together, and if governments believe that other governments or rivals endanger the very threads that bind the state, they will act accordingly.

Political ideology
A system of ideas, beliefs and values aimed at supporting or contesting political arrangements and serving to mobilize people for political action.

In many instances, international conflicts are couched in terms which combine particular ideological confrontations with broader claims about clashes between, or threats to, the culture of the contending states. The most enveloping and certainly the most extensive example was the Cold War. In both the USA and the USSR, the stakes of the Cold War were presented as a fundamental clash between two ideological systems *and* between two 'ways of life'. The rhetoric of the Cold War was designed to consolidate loyalty and heighten solidarity for both rivals. The elevation of ideology and the association of that ideology with the identity of the state enunciating it was not just a political ruse. It demonstrated an awareness that societies need to be able to understand the world in finite and comprehensible terms. The evocation of a value system gave US and Soviet citizens a stake in the issues. One of the most articulate and influential statements of the ideological and cultural differences between nations can be found in the words of Harry S. Truman, President of the USA from 1945 to 1953. In 1947, he placed the Cold War on an ideological *and* cultural footing when he spelled out to Congress what he saw as the essential differences between the USA and the USSR. Truman said:

> At the present moment in world history nearly every nation must choose between alternative ways of life ... One way of life is based on the will of the majority, and is distinguished by free institutions, representative government, free elections, guarantees of individual liberty, freedom of speech and religion, and freedom from political oppression. The second way of life is based upon the will of a minority forcibly imposed on the majority. It relies upon terror and oppression, a controlled press and radio, fixed elections, and the suppression of personal freedoms.

(Truman, 1963, pp.178–9)

Truman recognized that invoking US ideological foundations, linking those to the US 'way of life', and contrasting them with what he perceived to be those of the Soviet Union, would sharpen the USA's sense of national cohesion, and prepare it for an unfamiliar political crusade against communism. The Soviets employed similar tools and those tools became the hallmark of the Cold War.

This kind of reductionism was also to be found in the Falklands crisis of 1982. In this instance the rallying cry invoked country and nation rather than political ideology. Argentina under General Leopoldo Galtieri had tried to recapture the Falklands islands from the UK on the 150th anniversary of their occupation. The decision was prompted in large part by Galtieri's domestic political difficulties. He faced high inflation and determined opposition to his regime which witnessed the killing or torture of some 30,000 dissidents. Galtieri saw the Falklands issue as a way out of his difficulties and presented the Falklands, or Malvinas, as an integral part of Argentina's national heritage. The UK's possession was an affront to that heritage. Similarly, the UK could not make a convincing case that these tiny and remote islands constituted a vital part of its national security or that they contributed to its economic fortunes. Instead, Margaret Thatcher, Prime Minister of the UK, interpreted Argentina's stance as a challenge to the fabric of its national values and used a rhetoric that kept those values to the forefront. The strategy worked; public opinion swung in support of the war in the South Atlantic. Stories that stir treasured historical memory or remind citizens of the essence of their social existence carry special weight in most societies.

4.2   Culture and security

The mobilization of identity is based on the premise that there is one over-riding political community which meshes into a common cultural denomination. Under the states-system, every individual belongs to one, and only one, legal political community. Through its rules of membership, that community shapes its identity. Its methods include the school curriculum, property laws, enlistment in the army and, perhaps most important of all, official language. However, communities are seldom culturally monolithic. Most are multi-ethnic or multinational. In such societies, imposed cultural values will often be contested, perhaps even to the point of challenging the authority of the state itself (Horowitz, 2000). At the international level, fear of ethnic or national domination or oppression is a constant concern. Woodrow Wilson's notion of self-determination continues to serve as a benchmark, but it raises further questions about who should take part in the determining process and how outcomes can be implemented. In Ivor Jennings' famous phrase: 'The people cannot decide until someone decides who are the people' (Jennings, 1956, p.56). This paradox was born out in the western Sahara when the UN scheduled a referendum in 1992 to allow the indigenous Sahrawis to decide between integration with Morocco or independence. The referendum had to be postponed because the parties were unable to agree on who was eligible to vote.

One consequence of this has been a freezing of the political map. The UN has elevated self-determination as a fundamental principle of international equity. Yet the claims of groups without a state are blocked by a reluctance to revise state boundaries. To put it simply, international law subscribes to the idea of leaving nations to determine their own fates, but baulks at the idea of putting territory up for grabs.

The effects of movements for self-determination since the end of the Second World War have been devastating. In Biafra (Nigeria) and Eritrea (Ethiopia), secessionist wars produced bloodshed and starvation. New states were successfully carved out of Yugoslavia and the former states of the Soviet Union in the 1990s, but again only at shocking human cost and international instability. Territorial revision since the era of decolonization is rare. The odds for changing the political map of the world are very long. After all, there are fewer than 200 independent states in a world that is estimated to contain some 8000 separate national cultures. The great waves of state creation came in the wake of collapses of empire, for example, in nineteenth-century Latin America, in Europe after 1918, in Africa and Asia after 1945, and in Europe and Central Asia since 1991. These collapses unleashed new and seemingly unstoppable nationalist forces, but there was generally little enthusiasm for redrawing maps and facilitating territorial revision (Mayall, 1990). States recognize that once the apple cart is upset, any territorial boundary is open to dispute. Thus, while there is a general consensus that ethnic and cultural groupings should line up with political ones, it is power and economic stability that drive our cartography.

If culture does not always steer the positioning of national boundaries, it still remains an axis around which international dialogue revolves. The state is at the heart of world order. However, the state is not merely the government, the population, the territory or the units of production within its boundaries; it is also, as you have seen, an idea. Without the idea – it may be nationalist, religious or ideological – the state will not hold together. Therefore, the idea becomes in itself an object of defence.

Some states claim to represent particular ideas. These can be ideological or religious. Saudi Arabia and Iran claim to incorporate Islam, Israel speaks for Judaism, and the USA sees itself as the embodiment of liberal pluralism. These states entwine their chosen idea with their very existence. If Israel ceased to be a Jewish state or the USA ceased to be a liberal democracy, they would lose the essence of their statehood. Accordingly, when states protect their security, they are not merely looking after their borders or economic viability. National security is defined in ideological and cultural terms because it is culture and ideology that give the state meaning. Barry Buzan, a scholar concerned with security issues, has argued that political threats and what he calls 'societal' threats are often more destabilizing than military threats. States are political entities. If the cultural, ideological and historical threads that weave them together are threatened, then their foundations can be undermined. Political threats call into question the fundamental identity of the state and are directed at the states' organizational stability, and they have taken various forms. Republicanism has challenged monarchism, communism has opposed liberalism, and fundamentalist Islam has confronted the modernity of the West. 'Because the contradictions in these ideologies are basic,' Buzan writes, 'states of one persuasion may well feel threatened by the ideas represented by others' (Buzan, 1991, p.119). Other threats to national security can come from within, where there are separate cultural and ethnic identities that do not accept the authority or sovereignty of the dominant group. If minority cultures do not believe they have a stake in the common national enterprise and that national, ethnic or cultural differences cannot be accommodated, there will be a temptation to rearrange or even dissolve the current arrangements. The Bosnians and Croats in the former Yugoslavia, the Chechens in Russia, and the Tibetans in China are just some examples of this tension.

Thus, culture is not just the voice of the nation state; it is also its raw nerve. Where it calls into question the *raison d'être* of state formation, it is rapidly converted into a vital security issue in its own right and an existential threat to the survival of the community. The resurrection of culture also raises problems for conflict resolution. By and large it does not lend itself to compromise in the way, for example, trade disputes do. Emotive concerns tend to generate emotive ways of dealing with them. Some have claimed that cultural divisions are becoming the central axes on which international politics turn.

4.3 The clash of cultures and civilizations

You have come across Samuel Huntington in Chapter 3, and earlier in this chapter. His best seller, *The Clash of Civilizations and the Remaking of the World Order* (1996), fuelled the controversy over culture in international politics. Huntington had always believed that the Cold War, with its division of the world into power blocs, had provided a framework within which rational decision making could operate. Yet with the ending of the Cold War and the dissolution of the Soviet Empire, the international configuration had changed. He perceived a world composed of nine major civilizations: Western, Confucian, Sinic, Japanese, Islamic, Buddhist, Slavic-Orthodox, Latin American, and African. He insisted that culture, not class, wealth or even nationality, differentiates the power blocs. Most importantly, he has argued that cultural differences are so deep that they lead to civilizational strife. While nation states, according to Huntington, are still the primary actors in the international system, they increasingly define themselves in pan-national terms. He rejected the view, examined below, that the world is moving towards a common, global order. The world, according to Huntington, is a world of diffusion, riven by the cultural imperative. He wrote:

> Spurred by modernization, global politics is being reconfigured along cultural lines. Peoples and countries with similar cultures are coming together. Peoples and countries with different cultures are coming apart ... Political boundaries are increasingly redrawn to coincide with cultural ones: ethnic, religious and civilizational ... Almost everywhere one looks, people have been asking, "Who are we?" "Where do we belong?" and "Who is not us?" ... what counts for people are blood and belief, faith and family. People rally to those with similar ancestry, religion, language, values, and institutions and distance themselves from those with different ones.

(Huntington, 1996, pp.125–6)

Huntington's arguments should not be taken at face value and are flawed in many respects. Even if the world is divided between differing concepts of civilization, there is nothing to say that they will necessarily conflict with one another. His thinking remains bounded by the assumptions of political realism. The blocs still vie for power, even if their framework is a little different. Huntington also simplified the map and conflated ethnicity, culture and civilization. Muslim nations are not all alike and neither are Western ones. Most interesting of all, Huntington brings us back to where this discussion began. He does not ask whether his cultures and civilizations are constructed or whether they are primordial and inalienable. If cultures are modern and mere constructs, they can be changed. If they are primordial, there is nothing new in his thesis for, by definition, it was ever thus. Culture is a political concept and politics knows no fixed formulae. Its permutations come and go. You have seen that culture is a potent driving force and can be the basis of political mobilization. However, culture changes and culture varies. Islam in Turkey is not the same as Islam under the Taliban regime in Afghanistan. Huntington also does not take into account that there is as much conflict within his civilizations as there is between them. (These issues are taken up in detail in Chapter 8.) The bloody tribal struggles in Rwanda, Ethiopia, Sierra Leone and Burma, not to mention the ethnic and religious divisions in Iraq, Afghanistan, and Lebanon at the end of the twentieth century, do not point to civilizational solidarity.

Notwithstanding the flaws, Huntington evokes a world that you may recognize. Culture still serves as a rallying point in the international system. Identity is a fundamental sinew of the political community. Historically, communities feel most threatened when that identity is called into question. Culture also provides an accessible shorthand for understanding one's society. Cultural clash does happen, but it generally happens when conditions persuade one group that it is endangered by the other. There is a profound cultural difference between the USA and Iran, and between Muslim and Hindu in India. Yet hostility does not arise from the fact that fashions differ in Iran and the USA, or that Muslims eat cows while Hindus revere them. Differences only really count when instrumentalities for reconciling the differences fail to materialize.

5 Culture and international society: *E pluribus unum?*

5.1 Popular culture and a shrinking world

So far my discussion has centred on cultural difference and the impact such difference has on the stability of the nation state and the international system as a whole. If I were to end at this point, you might assume that the world was divided by different cultures, with each one striving to ensure survival and continuity, sometimes at the expense of its neighbour. The jealous vigilance exhibited by all cultures tends to point to an anarchic order. Nonetheless, this is only part of the picture. Ever since the age of exploration, cultures have intermingled with and influenced each other. The world is fluid and it is hardly surprising that cultures borrow from one another. Cultural patterns in other societies are not necessarily alien or threatening; they can be attractive and enriching. Therefore, there are features of the cultural environment that reinforce the idea of international society.

The earliest and probably the most influential transnational culture is religion. The world's major religions stretch to all continents and bring with them ethical codes and ritual patterns that are embraced and celebrated in diverse parts of the world. Similarly, language, technology, communications and popular culture cross most frontiers with relative ease, and introduce new cultural alternatives to communities that earlier were more insulated. A Roman Catholic mass in Rome will resemble that in Manila. A student in Los Angeles may wear the same clothes and listen to the same music as a student in Seoul. An English-speaking Indian may listen to a news bulletin on CNN at the same time as an English-speaking person in the Netherlands.

Question

What implications might this idea of transnational aspects of culture have for our understanding of the international?

In themselves, these common manifestations of cultural access do not make much difference to the configurations of international politics, but in generating images, lifestyles and forms of information they enable different societies to know more about each other – even if that knowledge is not always accurate. They also produce some common aspects of cultural expression and, more significant for our purposes, a convergence in the codes and interests that drive state behaviour.

However, some critics argue that the availability of other forms of cultural expression is producing cultural homogenization and that the authorship of this homogenous culture largely originates in the West. If English is the lingua franca of the major news organizations, soccer is the most popular spectator sport, and US jeans and T-shirts the most popular fashion for young people, then it is true that in many respects the globalization of certain aspects of culture can and does erode traditional local cultural patterns. In one sense, this perspective of cultural universalism as based on an expansion of Western culture mirrors the arguments in Chapter 3 about universal norms and institutions in the society of states representing the norms of the Western states in international society. However, it should also be remembered that the very availability of TV news, tourism, the Internet and ethnic foods results in an interchange between cultures in all directions. Communications and technology make us more aware of other cultures and different lifestyles. The worldwide availability and fondness for McDonalds, Levi jeans or the latest in sound systems may reflect the power of companies producing these products and their ability to shape tastes. They may even be foisted upon people by those companies. One critic, Naomi Klein, has accused the brand manufacturers of exploitation and oppression (Klein, 2000). Nevertheless, the prevalence of brands does not necessarily mean that each culture becomes like the other. Big Macs may be available and popular in Nairobi, Jakarta and Rio de Janeiro, but that does not mean that the social and cultural experiences of the inhabitants of those cities converge. One commentator has remarked: 'The assertion of global homogenization of culture is a little like arriving by plane but never leaving the terminal, spending all one's time browsing amongst the global brands of the duty-free shops' (Tomlinson, 1999, p.6).

5.2 A shrinking world of whose making? The idea of cultural imperialism

Some cultural critics maintain that the power of the West, specifically the USA and Western Europe, stifles the ability to understand other cultures in their own terms. The late Edward Said, a prominent cultural theorist, argued that culture is the main 'battleground on which causes expose themselves to the light of day and contend with one another' (Said, 1993, p.xiv). While his indictment embraces all cultural manifestations, Said confined most of his specific examples to cultural expression. He argued that in literature, music and the arts, the West has never cast off its imperial past. It has treated the 'outlying regions of the world [as if they] have no life, history, or culture to speak of, no independence worth representing without the West'. He believed that studies by outsiders distort the subject of inquiry by turning persons into objects. Said had no illusions – the West is not unique: all cultures want to dominate. However, the West has manipulated its position since the seventeenth century through the dispossession wrought in the wake of colonialism. Asia or the 'Orient' provided Said's most developed example. According to Said, the 'Orient' is a Western construction, fabricated to legitimize Western domination. He stated that it is never understood; it is merely 'watched' (Said, 1978, p.103). Intercultural 'understanding', in his scenario, is not a process engaged in by equal participants; it emanates from fundamental inequalities and mindsets that stem from differences in wealth and power. (Said is discussed in more detail in Chapter 15.)

The contention that being an outsider disqualifies good, insightful scholarship is questionable. Yet it should be conceded that globalization and, in particular, the influence of the USA on that process undoubtedly has an impact on cultural consumption and taste. A visit to a modern shopping mall in any capital city will confirm that. Nonetheless, the ubiquity of casual

Cultural globalization: women queue at the 'Women Only' counter at a branch of McDonald's in Dhahran, Saudi Arabia

clothing or popular music may just reflect the globalization of taste rather than of ethical values and standards. Despite the universality of the paraphernalia of popular consumption, the cultural differences that distinguish one society from another remain. Demonstrators on the West Bank of the River Jordan may sport US clothes, but they also burn the US flag in protest against US domination of the cultural discourse on the Arab–Israeli conflict. The Inuit in Arctic Canada may possess the gadgetry of modern households, but many aspects of their cultural heritage, practices and lifestyles are different to the majority of Canadians. Some of them feel that difference sufficiently to advocate the division of the Northwest Territories into separate units so that they can form a majority and become self-governing. If anything, the turn of the twentieth-first century has witnessed an increase in national fragmentation. In Eastern Europe, Central Asia, the Indian subcontinent, and multi-ethnic USA and Canada, there has been a growing concern that cultural diversity is not protected by existing state institutions.

5.3 Global culture and global dialogue

Although cultures retain their distinctiveness and continue to foster a sense of belonging, there are indications that some preferences are increasingly international. While Said may be right in insisting that the globalization of ideas is a manifestation of cultural imperialism, there is nevertheless a growing cosmopolitanism that poses a moral alternative to the way the world has developed over the centuries. This internationalism does not replace local or national cultures nor does it hold up the idea of global belonging. It cannot, because the world has no single shared history or memory. But it exists in parallel. It is not new: for example, the crusade against slavery in the eighteenth and nineteenth centuries was a worldwide movement and flourished in part as a result of interconnecting networks. Internationalism is also not universal. It is more likely to infiltrate urban cultures than rural ones, and more likely to have an impact in a society with an effective communications system. An international consciousness will develop more easily in societies where there is ethnic and political pluralism and where there is wider exposure to international financial institutions and trade.

An alternative view to that presented in Section 5.2 perceives these shared tastes in fashion and leisure as a prelude and symptom of an emerging global society. In contrast to the idea of an international society of states which you encountered in Chapter 3, in this version of an international society, transnational culture becomes the midwife of a new internationalism. In this account, people value the material culture that is increasingly available worldwide because it serves as a vehicle for interpreting other cultures and reconciling differences. The availability of experiences and products from other cultures carries with it information about how life is or may be lived elsewhere and suggests the possibility of transferring it home. Cultural goods can be seen as types of hearing aid that enable a more cosmopolitan and universal perspective on the world. Proponents of cultural globalization value the trend to uniformity as they believe that, ultimately, uniformity will help remove the sources of friction between different cultural communities. They argue, with the constructivists, that the world is not just an order of discrete states with separate interests. Rather it is an area of socio-cultural interaction that informs and shapes all aspects of international behaviour. The connections and links between government organizations, corporations, tourists, exchange students, migrating populations and so forth generate their own norms and culture that defy categorization by state, nationality or ethnic group. This connectivity releases culture from its tie to a fixed locality and has the potential to create new identities that are transnational.

The question of whether the global permeation of different cultures will result in the development of an independent global culture will be examined further in Chapter 9. You should notice though that the changes outlined above mark a substantive modification to the cultural contours already discussed. I noted that individual cultures are generally tied to a particular space or territory and are shaped by shared memory. Global culture, by contrast, transcends territory and knows no frontier. It also has no collective memory. One can recount, even if it is contested, a Jewish or an Uzbek or a Zulu experience. That experience stems from a history with parameters defined by the narrator, but what is the global narrative? And how is a global identity constructed? There is no convincing answer because there is no meaningful global history.

The emergence of cosmopolitan culture also implies some sort of transformation in the consciousness of individuals and the communities in which they live. While total transformation seems a far-off possibility, there has developed, particularly since 1945, an ethical discourse in the society of states. That ethical discourse strives to communicate with the world's cultures and thus transcends cultural difference. This dialogue is encapsulated in the UN and its many agencies and especially its Commission on Human Rights. The 'global covenant' acknowledges the existence of an international moral code. Essentially it requires states and their governments to obey international law and respect fundamental human rights (Jackson, 2000). The nature of these rights and the tensions between rights and self-determination will be examined in Chapters 7, 8, 9 and 15. For now I shall note that the existence of a rights regime rests upon the admission of a normative global understanding. It recognizes that every state has its own interests, its own history and its own culture, but it also recognizes that there is a commonality and a connectivity by which each culture submits to specific standards. While there is no common culture or civilization, there is a common vocabulary. The meanings of the words and terms employed in international transactions continue to form the basis of international dialogue, even if it is disputatious. (Such cross-fertilization has been already encountered in the discussion of the English School of international relations in Chapter 3.) This international grammar has ethical underpinnings which are enshrined in international institutions. The architects of the foreign policy of individual states have to guard the interests of their constituents, but at the same time they perceive international responsibility. Of course, the perception of what constitutes that responsibility will vary and will be challenged, as will the execution of that responsibility. However, nearly all states acknowledge that they cannot and do not operate unilaterally. By participating in international society, they subscribe to its vocabulary.

Despite the plurality and continuing robustness of cultures, there are points of convergence. These points stem in part from common humanity. At a simple level, respect for one's elders and ancestors, the fear of death, protective and affectionate feelings for one's children, and the desire for safety and security are universal traits and are not specific to any one culture. These traits, of course, have done nothing to prevent wars and civil conflict in the past. Nevertheless, they form a starting point in the growing subscription to the notion of global rights. Martin Shaw has commented that despite the tenacity of particularist identities, 'the growth of a common culture is still very striking ... People are coming to see their lives in terms of common expectations, values and goals. These cultural norms include ideas of standard of living, lifestyle, entitlements to welfare, citizenship rights, nationhood, gender equality, and environmental quality' (Shaw, 1994, pp.21–2). How much this will tamper with cherished notions of ethnic or national identity remains to be seen. Cultural values remain relative and contested. While the state remains at the centre of the international system, its citizens identify with aspects of culture beyond the bounded frontier. The kernels of cosmopolitan citizenship may be in place, but to date there are no monuments to the dead who died for the world.

6 Conclusion

The international system may still be driven by states, yet states consist of people and their leaders. The men and women who make foreign policy bring with them an intellectual and psychological baggage which informs their views, their decisions and the way those decisions are articulated. Napoleon Bonaparte, Nelson Mandela, Mao Zedong and Margaret Thatcher cannot be understood without reference to their reading of what it means to be French, South African, Chinese or British. At the same time, we cannot understand these concepts of nationality and the culture they underwrite without some appreciation of their respective histories and the way those histories are publicly interpreted. When states and the spokespersons claiming to represent those states articulate their interests, fears and aspirations, they employ a grammar that stems from a cultural experience. The claims and counterclaims that are the stuff of international politics cannot be separated from their cultural contexts. Simple tales of power and interests do not tell the whole story. Nor do they capture the whole tone of international politics. Of course, politics is about interests but emotion, memory, values and even ideals play their part too. Our world is a human construct and explanations about those who build it must take into account what makes those humans tick.

Further reading

A book which draws on social psychology to examine the relationship between identity and the nation, and its impact on the international system, is Bloom, W. (1990) *Personal Identity, National Identity, and International Relations*, Cambridge, Cambridge University Press.

Mayall, J. (1990) *Nationalism and International Society*, Cambridge, Cambridge University Press, discusses the consequences of national self-determination for territorial boundaries and the effect on international order.

A work which argues that nations and nationalism are neither primordial nor nationalist but instead proposes that national identity stems from cultural and symbolic components that go back centuries is Smith, A.D. (1995) *Nations and Nationalism in a Global Era*, Cambridge, Polity Press.

A study of globalization and culture which argues that cultural globalization is beneficial because it stimulates local customs to resist the erosion of cultural boundaries is Tomlinson, J. (1999) *Globalization and Culture*, Cambridge, Polity Press.

Chapter 7 Rights and justice in international relations

Raia Prokhovnik

1 Introduction

There are many examples of claims for rights in the international sphere.

One example was reported in September 2002. The British government was asked to make efforts to have a British man held by the Americans at Guantanamo Bay deported to Britain to face charges of terrorism there in connection with the attacks on 11 September 2001. Concerns were expressed about the denial of this man's human rights at Guantanamo Bay. Are alleged terrorists entitled to human rights? Can the denial of their human rights be justified on any grounds?

Another example, from around the same time, concerned a woman in Nigeria who faced death by stoning, once she had weaned her baby, after being convicted of adultery. In another case a teenage single mother was given 100 lashes for adultery, even though she claimed that she had been raped by three men. The court ruling in this case said that the woman 'could not prove that the men forced her to have sex' (*The Guardian*, 20 August 2002).

We can hardly imagine the novelty of the idea of universal human rights embodied in the Charter of the United Nations and subsequently codified in the United Nations' (UN) Universal Declaration of Human Rights of 1948. A radical change occurred in the vocabulary of international politics with the adoption of the Charter, the 1948 Declaration, and later conventions clarifying and extending the notion of human rights. The UN Charter (including the 1948 Declaration) was an important part of the international post-war settlement and it established the UN as an organization devoted to peace and security alongside human rights and the rule of law. So many states have joined the UN, and signed its Declaration and later conventions, that this has had the effect of consolidating the concept of rights, both the right of peoples to national self-determination and individual human rights.

The 1948 Declaration, in particular, establishes a powerful moral claim for individual rights. It asserts that each individual matters, deserves to be heard, and must not be silenced. Each individual deserves respect and is entitled to be treated with dignity, regardless of their race, gender, creed, colour or mental capacity. The Declaration utilizes a common, universal

A new idea: Eleanor Roosevelt, chair of the UN Human Rights Commission 1946–51, holding a copy of the Universal Declaration of Human Rights

moral language to specify its principles and norms, and signatory countries have come under pressure to implement those rights. Once codified and interpreted, rights become normative.

At the same time, the Charter expresses the intention to recognize the right to national self-determination and the corresponding principle of sovereign equality among the different peoples of the world. Indeed, the ideas of 'rights' and 'culture' are closely linked in that the advocacy of individual human rights is tied to the notion of the right to 'self-determination' for peoples and to statehood for national cultures. In Chapter 6, Robert Garson discusses the powerful cultural ties that bind a community together. The political identity of a national community is an important part of its culture, but different groups in society perceive it differently, depending on their wealth, social position, cultural background, gender, geographical position and age. Furthermore, different national cultures have different political identities. The language of rights and justice is one of the commonest ways of articulating political disputes, and of negotiating rival claims. In short, claims and counterclaims to rights (and justice) take place within national and now international cultural communities.

This chapter is about rights and rights claims. It is also about the idea of implementing justice in the international sphere based on the concept of rights. It is agreed by most people that 'rights are a good thing' and in many respects they are. However, this chapter deliberately takes a critical view. It seeks to examine closely why rights are a good thing and highlights some of the problems associated with rights. In this way, I hope that the sense in which rights are still, ultimately, 'a good thing' can be clarified and sharpened, and the valid reasons for rights thereby strengthened. The belief in rights based on a moral assertion of a common humanity that we all share is not self-justifying, and it needs to be located within the complex political field of international relations. In Section 2, I look briefly at some aspects of the development of internationally recognized human rights as expressed in the UN Charter and 1948 Declaration. Sections 3 and 4, respectively, will consider rights and justice by elucidating the meaning of the terms and some of the debates about how best to conceptualize them. In Sections 5 and 6, the working definitions just outlined are used to think about the impact that notions of rights and justice can have on international relations. In the concluding section, I shall consider the future of rights and justice in the international realm.

2   The United Nations settlement

The UN Charter and the Declaration form part of a post-Second World War international settlement which established, on the one side, the formal legitimating ideology of the international system, national self-determination and sovereign equality and, on the other, the ideology of universal human rights (see Chapter 3 for a discussion of this liberal legitimating ideology of the modern international system). The appeal of this set of claims was the hope that different peoples could live together in peace and security. It was an attempt to accommodate difference (through the idea of national self-determination) within a common framework (of the sovereign equality of states and universal human rights). The UN Declaration also helped to foster a new understanding of the international order, that is, of the power politics of nation states tempered by a rights agenda. One of the things that lay behind this development was the distinctive view of an international order governed by justice. Rather than being based on competing national self-interests or another moral value such as charity, rights advocates contended that international relations should be conducted on the basis of principles of justice.

Question

Where did the attempt to define notions of rights internationally come from?

To some extent, this ideology of rights was new because it was expressed at the international level with new vigour, with the horrors of the Second World War and the calculated extermination of Jews, gypsies and others in mind. The discourse of individual rights had a stronger impact on international politics than at any time previously, as did the notion of a right to national self-determination. Yet this new departure for international politics also built upon ideas about rights that had been around for a long time in thinking about the relation between individuals and the state. Since the idea of a national right to self-determination has been discussed in Chapter 3, I shall concentrate on human rights applied to individuals. The Congress of Vienna of 1815 had contained an obligation on states to abolish the slave trade, which represented a major attempt at international humanitarianism and standard setting. The 1907 Hague Conventions and 1926 Geneva Conventions attempted to regulate the humanitarian conduct of war. Nonetheless, at that time such measures were understood as framed by the principle and norm of state sovereignty, and were tempered by exclusionary Western beliefs about 'standards of civilization'. After the horrors of the First World War, there was a move to institutionalize international co-operation in the League of Nations. Although the League of Nations, inspired by UK and US liberal internationalists, had 'no explicit human rights provision, the underlying assumption was that its members would be states governed by the rule of law and respecting individual rights' (Brown, 2001, p.606).

After the Second World War, the Universal Declaration was adopted by the General Assembly of the United Nations (10 December 1948 – now known as World Human Rights Day), with no votes against and seven abstentions (the Soviet Union and its allies, South Africa and Saudi Arabia). Subsequently, all but Saudi Arabia have adopted the Declaration.

2.1   The origins of a rights discourse

In some form, the ideas of 'rights' and 'justice' could probably be found in all societies and cultures. They are moral concepts because they are concerned with moral ideals; with how things *should be* rather than describing how things *are*. However, the notion of rights now has a prominence in political debate in a way it has not had in other times and places. In the political thought of the ancient world, for example, a key question was how individuals could best contribute to the sound running of the political community, with the accent on their obligations rather than their rights. In medieval Europe, a person's place in the social hierarchy was of key importance, and different sets of specific rights and responsibilities were assigned to each level on the scale.

Nevertheless, the medieval concept of natural law from which the modern, international human rights culture derives, specified that in principle all persons were subject to natural law and could understand its content and standards (you have seen the idea of natural law in Chapter 3). The conception of rights which grew up in the modern period is concerned with *equal* rights. This is a very important point. By equal rights, I mean those that specify equality between persons, rights which say that no person should be treated as inferior, or excluded, marginalized, discriminated against, or made 'other' or abject. A society upholding equality of rights implies a sense of reciprocity in social relations and interaction, of 'do unto others as you would have done unto you'. Moreover, the modern notion of rights, based on claims to equality of rights and treatment, contain potentially emancipatory appeals to progressive political campaigning and action, which can imply the disruption of settled social relations within a community.

The modern rights movement has its origins in two separate sources – the tradition of ideas and political theory of the late eighteenth century, and the social reform movements of the nineteenth and twentieth centuries. Milestones of the first source include the development of the modern view of rights established with the popularity of the American Bill of Rights in 1791 and the French Declaration of the Rights of Man and of the Citizen in 1789. Works like Thomas Paine's *Rights of Man* (first published in 1791) were also important in spreading Enlightenment notions of human rights and freedom from hierarchical forms of authority such as the church. Through such means, that is, the juridical codification of rights in state law, the nation state became the body authorized to enact and protect rights.

The move from constitutionally protected rights within a few states to the establishment of the modern notion of rights as articulated in the UN's Declaration was crucially significant. This move has increased the visibility and legitimacy of rights claims within any particular state. It has also had a powerful effect on international politics and law by setting standards or norms of conduct and treatment. In both ways, it has fostered the momentum for social change.

In addition to legal charters and political theory, the modern rights movement is also grounded in a second source – modern social movements. For instance, the anti-slavery campaigns of the nineteenth century argued that the customary pattern of human relationships was unacceptable on the basis of a religious argument about the divine origin of the human body. Subsequent campaigns for the equal rights of women, civil rights (anti-segregation, anti-apartheid) movements, and non-government organizations (NGOs) like Amnesty International have employed arguments about self-possession and self-ownership as well as an argument for communal relational responsibility and interdependence as part of freedom. These groups have also used the liberal argument for the autonomy of the rational individual to pursue their rights claims. They have, in the words of an anti-colonial discourse, 'used the master's tools to dismantle the master's house'. In this way, such campaigning groups use the language of the powerful to demand access to those same rights, and call the powerful to account for their easy statements of equal rights.

3 Defining rights

As this history might suggest, defining and conceptualizing rights is not straightforward. This section aims to provide a working definition of 'rights' and introduce some important debates about rights. It aims to supply some conceptual tools to use when the discussion moves to the sphere of international politics.

3.1 What are rights?

Rights
A right is a justifiable entitlement to something (the object of the right), by virtue of the possession of a relevant attribute, against an agent or agents with the corresponding obligation to meet that entitlement.

The modern discourse of universal human rights has a number of features. The idea that everyone, everywhere has rights refers to the concept that there are certain entitlements justifiably owed to all individuals by virtue of certain features that all human beings have in common. As the nineteenth-century French politician and historian, Alexis de Tocqueville, put it, the idea of rights 'removes from any request its supplicant character, and places the one who claims it on the same level as the one who grants it'. The justification for (universal) human rights is essentially twofold. First, the ground for a basic moral equality among people is identified. This may differ from one formulation to another, but all refer to some notion of a shared human capacity for moral agency, and to the idea that such agents should not be treated merely as ends. Second, human rights specify the general preconditions for exercising moral agency over a lifetime. These preconditions have been variously described – physical security, material means of subsistence, development of capacities, enjoyment of liberties, and so forth. These necessary preconditions for the exercise of moral agency form the basis of human rights. The idea of human rights is designed to advance core values associated with basic needs, interests and liberties relating to what it is to be human and live a human life.

Rights are claims to something, say, 'to life, liberty and security of person' (Article 3 of the UN's Universal Declaration of Human Rights), and as such presuppose corresponding duties or obligations on the part of others if they are to be effectively realized. Henry Shue (1980) has argued that there are, in fact, different kinds of duties which are needed to make rights claims effective. There is a duty of avoidance, to avoid depriving people of some necessary precondition for exercising moral agency; a duty of protection, to protect people from such deprivation; and a duty of aid, to assist people who have been so deprived. Individuals and states can owe such duties, and they can be assigned in more or less general or specific terms. Thus, individuals may have a general duty to avoid depriving others, specific duties to some (parents to children, for example), while the state may have a general duty to protect and to aid.

Therefore, universal rights do not presuppose universal duties; there can be a division of labour on the side of duties. For instance, the International Covenant on Economic, Social and Cultural Rights recognizes that 'it is governments that have the overarching duty to ensure a division of labour in the matter of positive duties, and one that is appropriate to their own societies and sufficient to ensure that the rights are effectively secured' (Beetham, 1999, p.128).

In the modern world, rights claims are most often made against other individuals and against the political community comprising those individuals, that is, against the state. Now, while the state can be seen as a powerfully benign institution in acting to protect, enable and indeed to foster rights claims, the idea of moral rights also defines the fundamental inviolability of persons who need to be protected *against* state interference. So, the state can be seen in two, contradictory, guises – as both the protector of rights and as the body claiming to override individual rights.

Many things have been claimed as rights as can be seen in the text of the Universal Declaration of Human Rights in Table 7.1 (overleaf). One set of rights is citizenship rights. Primarily concerned with basic constitutional issues, these rights should, in Dworkin's phrase, 'trump' other considerations such as political expediency and policy-making imperatives (Dworkin, 1984). They are often categorized into legal, civil and political rights. Legal rights include such things as: due process of law; equal treatment under the law; and the right to a fair trial. The right to own property (individually or in association) and the right to enter into binding contracts are also important legal rights. Examples of civil rights are free speech, free association and free movement. Political rights concern the right to participate in the community's self-government, and in democracies might include the right to vote, to stand as a political candidate, to fair elections, and to a secret ballot. Related to citizenship rights are things like employment rights, for instance, the right to join a union or to go on strike. If rights presuppose duties, and if moral rights presuppose the legal order of a state for their protection, a citizenship right such as the right to a fair trial may express the basic right to life. Likewise, freedom from torture can be defined as a basic moral right (to life, security of person) and as a civil right in a given legal system.

Table 7.1   The 1948 United Nations' Universal Declaration of Human Rights

Of the 30 Articles in the Declaration, the first two set out that '[a]ll human beings are born free and equal in dignity and rights' and are 'endowed with reason and conscience', and that '[e]veryone is entitled to all the rights and freedoms' set out, 'without distinction of any kind, such as race, colour, sex, language, religion, political or other opinion, national or social origin, property, birth or other status'.

Articles 3–5 set out the rights to life and liberty, and against slavery or servitude, torture or cruel, inhuman or degrading treatment.

Articles 6–12 lay down legal rights, to be recognized 'as a person before the law' and equality before the law, against arbitrary arrest, to be presumed innocent until proven guilty, privacy and protection against attack.

Articles 13–15 concern the right to freedom of movement within one's country and freedom to leave it, the right to seek asylum, and the right to a nationality.

Articles 16 and 17 establish the right to marry and have a family, and to own property.

Articles 18 and 19 enjoin the right to freedom of thought, conscience and religion, and to freedom of opinion and expression.

Articles 20 and 21 establish a right to peaceful assembly, and the right to take part in the government of his [sic] country, such that the 'will of the people shall be the basis of the authority of government'.

Articles 22 and 23 prescribe a right to social security, the right to work, equal pay for equal work, and the right to join a trade union.

Articles 24–27 dictate rights to rest and leisure, to a 'standard of living adequate for the health and well-being of himself and of his family' [sic], to education, and to participate freely in cultural life.

Article 28 specifies a right to a social and international order in which these rights and freedoms can be fully realized, while Article 29 commands a duty on the part of the rights holder to the community in which the development of his [sic] personality is possible.

Source: United Nations, 1948

As you can see, these rights cover a broad range of what we described earlier as basic, citizenship, and social and economic rights.

3.2   Debates about rights

There are at least four big debates about modern individual rights. The aim in putting these before you is to introduce these hotly contested issues to which there are no conclusive answers, but which help frame discussions about human rights. Considering these debates is designed to help you weigh up the different arguments and form your own opinions about the meaning and effectiveness of rights claims.

The first debate concerns how our rights are grounded. One view is that our rights as individuals are natural, that is, basic and human rights which transcend any country or culture we live in, accord with our moral intuitions, and are 'inalienable' or cannot be legitimately taken away. The outline of the thinking behind modern human rights discourse discussed in Section 3.1 is often presented in these terms. The opposing view holds that our rights are always cultural – whether they come from a religious source, from an explicit or tacit social contract, or simply from the social practices and traditions that have evolved in a specific community. In other words, do rights reflect a natural order that lies behind the shifting appearance of all contemporary societies, somehow prior to any particular social and political organization, or do they depend only upon their meaningfulness within a culture? Do rights claims provide their own transcultural justification or do they only make sense in terms of the justification given in the particular society we live in and as established in its legal norms?

The second debate centres on whether legal, civil and political rights need to be underpinned by social and economic rights in order to be effective. This is the belief that we can only fully enjoy our legal, civil and political rights if we have equal opportunity on the basis of a right to education, a right to work, a right to decent housing, a right to health care, and a right to welfare. Those against accepting social and economic rights as having the same status as 'basic' rights, make the case that rights are principles which do not involve costs. So-called social and economic rights are not rights at all, they say, for such things involve huge costs by governments, while legal, civil and political rights are cost-free. An example of this view is that it costs nothing to have a right to free speech.

Question

How might Henry Shue reply to this argument (see Section 3.1)?

Those in favour of social and economic rights (sometimes called positive rights) as the basis of legal, civil and political rights (sometimes called negative rights because they are freedoms *from* various kinds of unwarranted intervention) argue that no such sharp distinction between the two types of rights can be maintained. They claim that even negative rights involve costs to protect and enforce them, such as a police force, a prison service and a judicial system. At this level, the key distinction would appear to be 'not between different categories of *right*, but between different types of *duty* necessary for their protection' (Beetham, 1999, p.126). On this basis, writers like Amartya Sen (1999) and Martha Nussbaum argue that a certain minimum quality of life is required in order for individuals to be able to exercise their human capabilities (Nussbaum and Sen, 1993).

The third debate centres upon whether it is sensible to talk about group rights as well as individual rights. Some rights, such as the right to marry and the right to have children, can only be exercised collaboratively, and some rights are relational, for example, the right of a child to be parented. Yet these are still, essentially, rights held by individuals. The argument for group-specific rights, developed by writers like Iris Marion Young (1990), is that the rights of minorities and other self-identified groups on the basis of a shared characteristic need to be explicitly protected. In one sense, of course, this is not a new idea, since the right to national self-determination – that is, a group right for a people to govern itself – is widely and generally accepted. Group-differentiated rights, however, typically refer to groups within or sometimes across a political community, and are advocated so that the interests of the majority do not override those of the minority. Furthermore, without the right (for instance, to exemption from a dress code associated with a particular profession, or to the slaughter of animals for food in a certain manner), it is held that a form of injustice important to group members would occur. The hard cases arise when the claims of the group (for example, to educate its children in a particular language) conflict with the freely chosen claims of some of its individual members.

Group rights claims might involve important practical issues such as special forms of political representation (to empower participation in democratic politics), education rights or language rights. For instance, James Tully's important discussion of group rights in Canada analyses the claims of English and French-speaking Canadians as well as first-nation Canadians. Another example is land rights claims in the post-colonial period, promoting the status and rights of groups such as native Americans, Australian Aborigines, and the New Zealand Maoris.

The fourth debate concerns how far the stretching of rights claims can go. Can they be expanded indefinitely? To illustrate, there is a current move in the USA to assert the rights of those allergic to deodorants, shampoos and perfumes to a public world in which these substances are banned for us all. A further instance is whether sales of military arms could be challenged on the grounds that arms sales will result in human rights violations. Does an infinite expansion devalue the currency of rights? Possible areas for the growth of rights claims in the current climate include the rights of future generations, the environment, animals and cyborgs.

Question

Are we likely to take these new kinds of rights more seriously in the future?

Relevant to this question is whether, in order to qualify for a right, one needs to have not only an interest, but also the potential for articulating and claiming that interest, and for ordering conflicting desires. On these grounds, future generations, the environment, animals and cyborgs would not qualify. Moreover, as we noted above, it is said that only a moral agent (defined as someone capable of recognizing a moral duty) can have a moral right. If this is so, might it be that future generations have a narrow legal right rather than a fundamental human moral right? And what about the rights of children and those with severe mental disorders?

This line of thought leads to the argument against the arbitrary and endless proliferation of rights claims. Such endless proliferation, critics maintain, reduces all moral talk to rights claims, which takes away the specialness of rights claims and the impact they can have. Furthermore, according to this view, we all have our own definitions of what is valuable to us and this 'value pluralism', a central principle of liberalism, should be encouraged. However, these values should not be translated into rights and imposed by the state on everyone; the state should not be in the business of promoting particular goals for its citizens. We should accept that value pluralism is inevitably going to lead to conflicts, and that if all values are translated into rights, rights will conflict as well. We have a right to hold different values as important, a right to value pluralism. In addition, critics argue, the language of rights creates a social atmosphere of grievances and victims. 'Rights talk' polarizes disagreement within national contexts. For instance, the right to life in the USA is claimed both by those in favour of abortion rights in terms of women's rights to choose and women's health, and by those in favour of foetal rights and against abortion. This perspective maintains that 'rights talk' also encourages a legalistic view. It transforms moral, social, cultural and political matters into legal ones, and misdirects people to the courts to seek redress.

4   Defining justice

Justice is commonly thought to have two applications which Aristotle distinguished as 'distributive' and 'commutative' justice. The first, distributive justice, is concerned with the distributions of things (rights, goods, services and so on) among a class of individuals. Its root idea according to Aristotle is that of 'treating equals equally'. Nevertheless, it is far from simple to specify what this means. Who are the relevant equals? The members of this class might be the individuals of a given political community, the many political

Distributive justice
A principle of distributive justice specifies how things such as rights, goods and well-being should be distributed among a class of people.

communities that make up the world, or even all the individuals in the world. And what is involved in treating people equally? That they all have the same rights, that they all achieve a minimum standard of living?

Commutative justice
A principle of commutative justice specifies how individuals should be treated in a given class of actions and transactions.

The second form of justice, commutative justice, is about the treatment of an individual in a particular transaction – it is about giving someone what he or she deserves or has a right to. According to Plato, it is about giving each person their due. An example, often referred to as retributive justice, might be the redress someone is due for a wrong suffered, or the punishment due for an offence committed. Notions of desert and of what people have a right to are also complicated.

Thus, like 'rights', the term 'justice' is a 'contested concept', one whose meaning is never completely fixed or finally closed and agreed upon. This contestability and flexibility of outcome is what Aristotle referred to when he said that 'justice is the mean (middle) point between conflicting claims'. This view believes that each society (or group within it) will have its own definition of justice and rights, and those definitions cannot (and perhaps should not) be reconciled. Each society (or group) will have its own ideas about justice and rights, and its own practices for implementing them. Such concepts are inevitably conflictual, contestable and politically charged.

Consequently, as a matter of retributive justice, for example, the legal system in the UK no longer upholds capital punishment, but it is an important part of the legal codes of a range of US states. Another instance from the sphere of distributive justice is that liberal societies (which hold that, in principle, maximizing the scope of individual freedom takes priority over developing and politically implementing a shared view of the good life of the community) take the view that justice involves allowing individuals to have the largest possible amount of freedom so that they have the widest scope for their own choices. By contrast, some societies with different cultural and political traditions see distributive justice in terms of the needs of the collective body of members, thereby tempering individual rights. For instance, free speech is a valued right in the American Constitution, but the prohibition to deny the Holocaust in Germany is important to the political identity of that country.

It is part of the contestability of concepts such as justice and rights that the definitions of these terms shift over time, and the process by which this change occurs involves a debate between different normative (value-laden) positions. Therefore, capital punishment used to be practised in the UK as an important form of retribution, and although a majority of UK citizens still support capital punishment, it is no longer held by Parliament to be morally justifiable and does not form part of the legal code. A further example of reforms in rights and justice under the impact of changing social values is a much stronger emphasis on the idea of children's rights than there was even 20 years ago.

'Justice', then, is a term that refers to society and its political arrangements as a whole. One way of describing the relation between rights and justice is to say that rights recognize everyone as, in a fundamental sense, the same, whereas justice accommodates the fact that we, while living together, are all different.

Question

What is a 'just society'?

A 'just society' is one that deals fairly with all its members. This does not necessarily have to indicate that it treats them all in exactly the same way. This is what Plato meant when he argued that 'justice is giving each person their due', and what Aristotle implied by saying that distributive justice involves 'treating equals equally' and commutative justice involves giving people what they deserve. Plato had in mind a hierarchical society in which the benefits and responsibilities were distributed depending on one's position. Bentham's utilitarian model is another influential idea about justice. Bentham, considering that justice refers to society as a whole, argued that it was the function of government to maximize the interests of all (adding up those of each person) by promoting the general good or utility of all.

Like rights, any particular idea of justice (even the idea of 'natural justice') needs to be entrenched in a society's codes in order to be effective. I have already noted that ideas about the proper content of retributive justice differ from society to society. Moreover, within any given society ideas about what is just change over time. Equal access to justice means not dealing with people in an arbitrary fashion but fairly, giving them a fair trial and dealing with them impartially and neutrally, without prejudice.

A particularly important set of debates arises in relation to different notions of distributive justice. Do notions of distributive justice apply to the rights of individuals and the acts that they commit, or do they also apply to states of affairs, to the pattern of the results arising from those actions? In the former case, an outcome is just or unjust if it arises from just or unjust actions; whereas in the latter, the principles of justice apply to the pattern of outcomes. This latter notion is often described as social justice and is concerned with the fair distribution of goods and resources between and among the members of a society. This leads to the idea that social welfare should be provided (by the state in many countries) for those who need it, at a level defined differently in different places. Social justice is based on the concept that a state has responsibilities to its citizens, and can fund those responsibilities by levying taxation at a level acceptable to the members of that society, which again varies from country to country. 'Fair distribution' is, of course, inherently contestable.

Social justice
A theory of social justice involves applying the principles of justice to the economic and social opportunities or outcomes in a given society.

Political justice
A theory of political justice involves applying the principles of justice to the basic political institutions, the constitutional order, of society.

Ideas of social justice aim to be in the interests of the community as a whole, and in the interests of social cohesion. This is also the basis of political justice – the notion that fixing the level of social justice and the rules of legal justice is something that does not happen 'naturally', but is established within a political order. The state is responsible for the level of social justice and the rules of legal justices, usually based on the dominant political culture and identity. In many countries, establishing or reforming political justice involves healthy debate between conflicting views. This concept of social justice relates closely to what was said earlier about social and economic, and citizenship rights. As maintained by this view, equal citizenship involves social and economic rights so that everyone has the same access to justice. Critics of social justice argue that it often operates at the expense of individual rights, that in order for a particular pattern of outcomes to be achieved certain individual freedoms have to be curtailed.

5 Rights in the international arena

Question

What happens to notions of rights and justice when we move the discussion to the level of international politics?

In fact, three crucial things happen. First, the meaning of rights takes its bearings from the rights discourse developed from the UN Declaration. We will investigate the effects of this, both on rights and on international politics. Second, we find that it is not always easy to establish who the right can be claimed against. In consequence, there can be a tension between the rights of individuals and the rights and authority of states. Third, the discussion of justice centres on the effectiveness of international organizations. The question becomes whether, and if so how, to strengthen the rights of NGOs, international institutions and international law to implement international justice.

A further dimension is added when we consider whether the development of the international human rights agenda now amounts to a form of globalization. As Chris Brown notes:

> [while] it was once the case that rights were almost always associated with domestic legal and political systems, in the last half century a complex network of international law and practice (the 'international human rights regime') has grown up around the idea that individuals possess rights simply by virtue of being human, of sharing in a common humanity.

(Brown, 2001, p.599)

As you have seen, this is the core idea behind the concept of universal human rights.

In this section, I shall first look again at the international codifications of human rights and then discuss some of the problems associated with them.

5.1   Human rights in the international arena

The UN's 1948 Universal Declaration of Human Rights asserted that the 'recognition of the inherent dignity and of the equal and inalienable rights of all members of the human family is the foundation of freedom, justice and peace in the world'. It further affirmed that human rights should be protected by the rule of law, that they were 'essential to promote the development of friendly relations between nations', that these fundamental human rights include the equal rights between men and women, and that these rights represented 'a common standard of achievement'. The Declaration also reminded member states of the UN that they had pledged themselves to promoting the observance of these rights.

The second half of the twentieth century saw an enormous growth of the rights discourse, whereby norms for universal domestic standards were elaborated. For instance, in 1966 the UN supplemented its 1948 Declaration with the International Covenant on Civil and Political Rights, and the International Covenant on Economic, Social and Cultural Rights. Moreover, the Convention on the Prevention and Punishment of the Crime of Genocide was signed in 1948, and further UN human rights treaties include the International Convention on the Elimination of All Forms of Racial Discrimination of 1965, and the International Convention on the Elimination of Discrimination Against Women of 1979. The UN's 1992 Declaration on the Rights of Persons Belonging to National or Ethnic, Religious and Linguistic Minorities also supplements its earlier Declaration; it amplifies the entitlements owing to members of minorities but does not contain prescriptions about the consequent duties of states.

Regional charters have also been made in Europe, Africa and America. The European Council set out the European Convention on Human Rights in 1950 under the headings of dignity, freedoms, equality, solidarity, citizens' rights and justice. The European Commission on Human Rights and the European Court of Human Rights provide the machinery to enforce these instruments. The European Union (EU) included an article asserting respect for human rights in the Treaty of Amsterdam, which came into force for member states in 1999, and the EU Charter on Fundamental Rights was proclaimed at the Nice Summit in 2000. The EU also includes human rights clauses in its agreements with other countries. The African Charter on Human and Peoples' Rights was adopted by the Organization of African Unity in 1981 and has 51 state signatories. The American Convention on

Human Rights was adopted by the Organization of American States in 1969 and has been ratified by 25 countries.

The extension of rights since the 1960s has also been made to many forms of 'group' rights, including women's rights, gay rights, the rights of the child, and post-colonial group claims. Furthermore, there has been an increased focus in the rights discourse on social, economic and cultural rights, as well as on civil, legal and political rights. Most recently, UN agencies have talked of 'mainstreaming' rights in development work, peace and security operations, humanitarian relief and social programmes.

The primary practical benefits claimed for the rights discourse include enfranchisement, the extension of rights to groups which were previously socially excluded, and the recognition of an entitlement to complain about inhuman treatment. According to rights advocates, other benefits include the acknowledgement that hitherto silenced groups and oppressed minorities also have a voice, and facilitating socially inclusive policies. For its proponents, while the rights discourse may make a community unstable by legitimating social conflict, it forces institutions to justify themselves. More broadly, advocates of universal human rights argue that the introduction of rights has led to the legalization of a normative order, whose intentions are to advantage the disadvantaged and lead to a lessening of civil and international conflict. However, I want to draw attention to the fact that there are costs and problems associated with rights and the progressive legalization of the international order as well as benefits.

5.2 Problems with international rights

The international human rights discourse claims that the value of its conception of rights lies in it being universal, empowering and human-centred. The idea of universality asserts the relevance of human rights to anyone, anywhere. Empowerment is the concept of human rights as a defence against inequality and the domination of the powerful over the weak. The human-centred feature of international rights seeks to provide a perspective on global questions, 'putting the value of human dignity above the search for economic gain or the narrow interests of particular national governments' (Chandler, 2002, p.1).

I want to identify four specific sets of problems and a wider concern for this discourse. First, the rights discourse is not universal but is deeply informed by a Western perspective. Second, feminist critiques dispute the universalism of rights and argue that they have a masculine bias. Third is the question of who can claim what rights against whom. The fourth problem is a specific instance of the third, relating to the way that individual rights may trump state sovereignty, and it challenges the human-centred feature of the international rights discourse. As you will note, some of the criticisms I am about to develop are objections to rights in principle; others are objections that rights are not realized, or are hard to realize, in practice.

With regard to the first set of problems, it is striking that many actors and commentators on the international stage now frame their arguments and assertions in terms of the language of rights and justice. Yet we need to ask to what extent this language of rights and justice really underpins shared understandings and values. There is a strong case for saying that if there are shared understandings of rights and justice, they are a result of the power of the West by force or example, rather than common responses to similar sets of circumstances.

The cultural specificity of the current rights agenda cannot easily be overcome, because it derives directly from an Enlightenment and modern, rational, Western tradition and its accompanying context of emancipatory, progressive, liberationist politics. Rights in this sense cannot simply be applied to other places and times. This partially refers to the distinctively Eurocentric and liberal elements in the construction of 'rights' and 'justice'. These elements include the particular liberal idea of tolerance and impartiality between different standpoints and between different normative evaluations in international relations, resulting in a healthy pluralism. A further element concerns the characteristically abstract, universal, foundational and individualized notions of autonomy, equality and freedom found in the Western liberal tradition of rights and justice. A distinctively Western-inspired element informing the discourse is the ideal of social democratic egalitarianism. The critique of the Western currency for the dominant meaning of, and agenda for, rights and justice notes the specificity of the Western rights discourse. That discourse is linked not only to liberal principles but also coincides with a democratic political agenda, and the growth of a democratic culture of egalitarian citizenship.

Reading international rights through the lens of Western concepts can lead to distorting effects. For instance, some critics have argued that there is an unwarranted tendency in both Europe and North America to see human rights as problems for other countries but not for themselves, and to be complacent about poverty and institutionalized racism in Western countries. Critiques of rights notions in the West are often disregarded yet deserve to be taken seriously. The criticisms from some Muslim groups, for instance, of the objectification of women's bodies and the power of the pornography industry in the West, are well-placed. Another example is that the conditions often tied to humanitarian aid for developing countries have the effect of politicizing aid from Western governments and increasing their control, instead of simply universalizing the right to aid. This analysis also extends to questioning the limits of the Western emancipatory agenda in the light of the power of market capitalist multinational corporations. This view believes that the Western rights agenda simply masks another form of hegemonic power, domination and subjection.

Critics of the Eurocentric and liberal nature of the dominant meaning of rights point to other definitions of rights and justice in non-Western countries and to non-Western conceptions of human rights. Such alternative definitions of rights draw upon religious or community identities rather than those of citizens within the territorial nation state. For instance, human rights in some Muslim societies contain the idea of separate and equal spheres for men and women rather than universal egalitarian rights (see Chapter 8). Traditionalist conceptions of human rights exist in China and different African societies, and in cultural values informing the caste system in India. 'Asian values' is a prominent alternative form of human rights conception which is less individualistic than the Western-derived notion, and places greater value on religion, family and elders.

Since the end of the Cold War divisions between the West and the Soviet bloc, the human rights discourse and agenda have become even stronger guides to policy making. The dominant human rights discourse can appear universal since the decline of Cold War barriers to international regulation. The move to a world dominated by a single superpower has given the illusion that a particular definition of human rights as a policy instrument is universal. Nonetheless, a strong case can be made that the meaning of international human rights should be derived from theoretical analysis and debate and not, by default, from geo-political shifts in international relations alignments.

Problems with the universalization of a Western rights agenda are closely linked to problems with the idea of international rights as empowering. The assumption that the human rights culture will empower those who have been marginalized or excluded from the political process can be questioned. To illustrate, consider the UK Department for International Development (DFID) view that the 'human rights approach to development means empowering people to take their own decisions, rather than being the passive objects of choices made on their behalf' (2000, p.7). In practice, instead of granting new rights, it is sometimes the case that good intentions are not fulfilled. Chandler notes that the 'rights of advocacy claimed by international bodies provide little accountability for those they claim to act on behalf of, while potentially undermining existing rights of democracy and self-government' (Chandler, 2002, pp.14–15). There is evidence that the human rights framework can have the effect of empowering international institutions rather than those they claim to represent.

There is also a strong argument that the meaning of international human rights is not widely shared but has been driven by particular contingent crisis situations. Debate has tended to centre on specific ad hoc cases and not on the broader consequences of the prioritization of a human rights agenda.

Debate has also focused narrowly on how to make institutions effective in implementing their new role, rather than on the broader implications of the shift they are bringing about in international organizations and policy making. Likewise, there has been very little discussion of the theoretical basis of the central justification for this understanding of human rights. As Chandler observes, for 'many commentators, the human rights framework appears to be justified as a *fait accompli* because governments and international institutions have already accepted it' (Chandler, 2002, p.12). The international human rights culture is so well established that it has deterred the kind of sustained theoretical debate that developed in previous centuries over rights which were understood within a nation state context.

Activity 7.1

How do these views about the Eurocentric and Western nature of internationally recognized universal human rights compare with those discussed in Chapter 3?

The second source of criticisms that I want to explore comes from feminist critiques. Some feminists argue that the universal notion of rights makes invisible the special problems faced by women as a group, and that, thereby, specific articles of the various human rights declarations and conventions reinforce traditional gender roles in the family and the workplace. This criticism comes in at least two forms. The first is that rights for women (as for other disadvantaged groups) may be particularly difficult to enforce against the claims of the powerful and the dominant. An example is the poor pay and conditions, and isolation faced by women 'home-workers' in developing countries. Catharine MacKinnon (1993) documents forms of gendered ill-treatment and harm to women, including sexual and reproductive abuses, rape as a weapon of warfare, forced motherhood in Ireland, domestic violence against women as part of the honour code in Brazil and Italy, and suttee in India. Such human rights abuses are not prevented by universalistic human rights conventions. Further examples concern the sexualization of women's and children's bodies in international prostitution. Examples include the market for sex workers for tourists in the Philippines or Barbados, sex workers to service American bases, and the influx into Western Europe of prostitutes from Eastern Europe by mafia gangs.

The second form of this feminist criticism is more far-reaching, arguing that making effective a given right, say, the right to employment, may have different implications for men and women. In a context of pre-given unequal distribution of domestic and reproductive labour, equal employment rights for men and women may involve a transformation in childcare arrangements, for example. Without such a transformation, equal rights may perpetuate inequalities. The rights regime needs to recognize the impact of rights in structuring and maintaining inequalities.

The third set of problems relates to whom the rights claims are made against, and what kinds of claims can be made. In the case of individual human rights, a rights claim is usually addressed to or claimed against the legal order of the state. However, it is often one of the problems at the international level that either the state claimed against does not recognize the claim, or that the body claimed against is not a state (that is, a political entity that is in some sense morally accountable) but, say, a corporation. An example is the fight of Nigerians against the Shell oil company. The international sphere of politics in its own right is made up not just of states but also of other powerful organizations and institutions, including regional political and economic organizations such as the EU and North American Free Trade Agreement (NAFTA), and transnational economic organizations such as the International Monetary Fund (IMF) and the World Bank. Non-state actors also include multinational corporations, paramilitary forces and radical religious groups. It is often difficult to bring non-state actors who are responsible for human rights violations to account.

Another group of actors on the world stage is international NGOs such as Amnesty International, and aid-giving and development charities such as Oxfam. The diversity of international actors makes the picture of the international sphere more complex. International NGOs are playing a greater and greater role in international politics. For instance, at the 1993 UN World Conference on Human Rights in Vienna, over 500 NGOs were represented, almost equalling the number of state representatives, and at the 1995 UN World Conference on Women's Rights in Beijing, most of the 35 000 participants were from NGOs. Some commentators see these developments as demonstrating the increasing influence of ordinary people, generating a 'people's politics' which is campaigning to hold governments to account. Yet at the same time international NGOs are largely unregulated and unaccountable to a wider public.

Due to the fact that the link between rights claims and responsibility is more opaque at the international level than at the national level, human rights are more difficult to claim than might be envisaged from a simple focus on the individual and the state. The language of rights is often not effective in promoting egalitarian remedies for ill-treated and discriminated groups, and can raise expectations among the disadvantaged that it cannot meet. It comes as a shock to hear that, 50 years after the UN Declaration, it has been estimated that there are 27 million slaves in the world. Slavery is defined as the complete control of a person through violence or the threat of violence in order to exploit them economically. Slavery has changed its face since its traditional forms and now predominantly involves, for instance, the sale of 14-year-old girls into brothels in Thailand, and the sale of girls from Mali to work for families in Paris. The tripling of the world's population since 1945 and the prices of slaves being at an all-time low help to account for the current high number of slaves. Slavery is just one category of human rights violation that carries on and even increases, despite 'rights' talk.

The UK DFID document, *Realising Human Rights for Poor People* (2000), accepts that there is a 'large gap between the aspirations contained in the principles of the Universal Declaration of Human Rights and the experiences of people living in poverty'. The report notes that there are 'problems with relying solely upon legal measures for the protection of human rights', since 'poor people are rarely able to use formal legal systems to pursue their claims' (DFID, 2000, p.16). For example, the on-going murder of street children in cities across Latin America leads to the question of whether the interests of those street children are best advanced through international action based on human rights.

Another aspect of this issue concerns which rights states say they can and cannot respond to. There is a question about whether legal, civil and political rights, economic and social rights, and group rights are all compatible with each other. Commentators sometimes refer to the history of the development of the rights culture over the second half of the twentieth century in terms of: 'first generation rights', which focused on individual broadly political rights; 'second generation rights', which targeted individual economic, social and cultural rights; and 'third generation rights', which were concerned with group rights. Indeed, Brown raises the question of whether second and third generation 'rights' are 'rights at all?' (Brown, 2001, p.601), although it is clear from Table 7.1 (Section 3.1) that even the original UN Declaration went far beyond 'first generation' rights. Nevertheless, social and economic rights might be impossible to meet for a cash-strapped state. Furthermore, governments have been known to argue that the development of social and economic rights through the promotion of economic growth must take priority over and preclude the possibility of the early granting of political rights.

The fourth set of problems is really a specific example of the third set and relates to the ways in which individual rights relate to state sovereignty. The Millennium Conference of the UN in 2000 endorsed the need for people-centred changes to the institution and renounced its previous 'state-centred' structure. The human-centred logic of rights regards human rights as a value which places legitimate constraints upon the politics of national self-interest and interstate competition. Chandler notes that at the 1993 'UN World Conference on Human Rights' in Vienna, 'the UN Charter was widely construed to mean that human rights should take precedence over sovereignty'. Moreover, he argues that, 'by the end of the 1990s, with UN protectorates established in Kosovo and East Timor and the indictment of former Yugoslav president Slobodan Milosevic for war crimes, international relations were no longer seen to be dominated by the need for inter-state consensus' (Chandler, 2002, p.8).

Do human rights provide a universal principle on which to justify intervention that 'trumps' state sovereignty? There is no current consensus about what constitutes sound arguments to justify forms of legitimate intervention. Besides, the line between humanitarian and military intervention can be a very blurred one. The current human-centred approach to rights can also lead to unwanted consequences. Understanding human rights conflicts on the model of victim and abuser can lead to a moralized discourse where the underlying grounds of the conflict are neglected, the victim is regarded as incapable of remedy without international assistance, and the abuser is considered as incapable of adopting right over wrong. There is some proof that this model, applied to the Rwandan genocide for instance, has neglected the wider political and social framework in which mass killing took place. There is also evidence that in media coverage of Bosnia and Rwanda, 'public understanding of these conflicts has been distorted by advocacy journalists calling for military intervention against demonized human rights abusers'. Analysis of the Kosovo crisis also suggests that 'human rights intervention can easily become a dehumanizing project of bombing and sanctions in the cause of great power interests' (Chandler, 2002, p.15).

Activity 7.2

Review the four criticisms of rights at the international level discussed above.

1   Identify which of these criticisms are objections in principle to the discourse of universal human rights and which are objections in practice.

2   Identify which of these criticisms relate particularly to implementing rights internationally and which might apply to rights more generally.

These criticisms sharpen the idea that there is a gap between principle and practice. The human-centred approach refers to the view that moral and ethical considerations should be central, rather than policies being mediated either by profit or by the grand ideological designs of left-wing and right-wing politics. Nonetheless, the disjunction between the pure, principled character of rights and the real world of conflicting interests, compromise and power politics throws this feature into question. In part, this is due to the problem that abstract human rights (as propounded in the UN definition) are only or 'merely' rhetorical unless they are backed up by the capacity to implement and operationalize them, and unless they are recognized by the country in which one lives. Rights may belong only to 'discourse' and not be 'real'. In support of this view, some critics maintain that the evidence shows that rights have not, in practice, impinged much upon states' national interests or the interests of international financial and trade organizations, let alone on national and international violence and intervention.

6 International justice – communitarian and cosmopolitan perspectives

The international level can be viewed as an arena of politics in its own right and not just as a context for states and other actors. If we think of the international world in this way, how should relations between states, and other actors on the international stage, be constructed? To what extent should those relations be regulated? We can ask whether relations between states, and states' policy making, should be dictated by allegedly universally shared human rights principles, or by other objectives such as national political or economic interest, regional interest, international peace or serving alliances with other like-minded states. A related consideration is whether relations between states should be driven by moral principles such as rights and justice, or by other legitimate interests?

In Chapter 3, Simon Bromley introduced a distinction between two different ways of understanding the role of states in international society: first, as 'local agents of the common good' in an order of (increasingly universally) shared notions of human rights; and second, as the embodiments and protectors of different cultures or civilizations in an inherently plural *modus vivendi*. The question is of more than academic interest, since how we think about the international sphere affects how real world actors operate in it. The debate between the communitarian position and the cosmopolitan position has developed as the primary way of structuring this issue and I want to consider it further now. The communitarian/cosmopolitan debate takes a theoretical and normative approach to the role of rights and justice in different conceptions of the international realm.

I shall begin by outlining and comparing the communitarian and cosmopolitan positions, and then introduce the understanding of rights found in each case, leading onto a discussion of two contrasting forms of international justice and intervention in the light of the two perspectives. While there are differences between advocates of communitarianism and among proponents of cosmopolitanism, the two viewpoints can be characterized as broad umbrella positions championing a particularist and state-centric perspective, and a universalist and global perspective respectively. Section 6.1 will discuss theoretical and normative issues, while Sections 6.2, 6.3 and 6.4 will consider how the two positions inform highly charged political debates on international distributive and retributive justice and the question of intervention. It should be clear that, in line with the critical view of rights adopted in this chapter, I think the communitarian case is the stronger one. However, I hope this sympathy will not lead me to be unjust to the cosmopolitan viewpoint.

6.1   Some general features of communitarianism and cosmopolitanism

There are two very different and sharply contrasting views about how the international arena can be theorized, should be organized and can be described. One side sees the international sphere as made up of a plurality of interacting cultures with incommensurable values, while the other side deploys general concepts of rights and applies these to humanity as a whole. These two constructions rest upon very different views of what human beings are, and how they do and should interact together. Communitarians understand human beings firstly in terms of their cultural identity, while according to cosmopolitans reason should be, though perhaps is not always, the governing principle of human interaction. The cosmopolitan belief in the emancipatory power of the human capacity for reasoning derives from the idea that reasoning is a shared capacity capable of providing the basis for moral principles which aim to deliver humankind from the mire of ignorance and superstition. Cultural identity and the human capacity for reasoning are strongly divergent principles on which to base the construction of international politics.

For communitarianism, the international arena is dominated by states but this does not discount the role played by other, subordinate actors to help co-ordinate interstate activity. International NGOs, international regulatory organizations like the World Bank and IMF, the UN as a forum for states, and global civil society campaigns such as the campaign to end apartheid in South Africa or anti-globalization protests can all play a role, provided that states are still regarded as central. However, public debate on the role and basis of legitimacy and accountability of organizations such as the IMF, World Bank, World Trade Organization (WTO), and International Labour Organization (ILO) remains to be conducted.

As stated by cosmopolitans, the international arena is a public sphere and potentially an arena of governance in its own right. Some cosmopolitans look forward to a global order with a stronger set of institutions above states. Areas identified as requiring faster reform include the composition of the UN Security Council and the power of veto by its permanent members, and the restrictions on international intervention arising from the UN Charter and from state sovereignty. The form of accountability that supranational institutions would have, how that accountability would be delivered, and to whom, remain in question.

Communitarians distrust claims made for proposals of cosmopolitan democracy, advanced for instance by David Held (1995), on the grounds that it can be questioned whether the proposed frameworks to extend democracy at the international level will bring about the empowerment of the 'global citizen'. There are fears that the mechanisms of regulation envisaged by cosmopolitans, based on ideas such as international civil society, cosmopolitan governance and cosmopolitan citizenship, do not involve sufficient means of political accountability, and instead provide more opportunities for freedom of action by leading world powers.

Communitarians argue that rights and justice are culturally specific and cannot be applied across borders. They consider that what we have in the world, and what should be valued in a positive sense, are different, plural, political communities with divergent and incompatible interests. They hold that the diversity and heterogeneity among a plurality of communities and their values is as important to sustain as is a diversity of species among animals and plants. Communitarians contend that while moral principles should have a place in the conduct of interstate relations, there are no overarching principles sufficiently widely endorsed to form the basis for a strong legal authority that would limit the claims of the sovereign state. The UN and other international organizations are valid if they help to co-ordinate communication and action within the complex society of states, but such organizations should not seek to supplant the sovereign state as the highest law-making body for its domestic population. The key principles to uphold are those of the self-determination of peoples, and the legitimate rights of a state to manage its own affairs and to defend itself from interference. States should respect one another's independence.

Communitarians claim that the separate communities (most often nation states) remain the basic building blocks of international relations, and that reasonable states have political institutions, governments, electoral systems, the rule of law, and constitutions, all of which should together be the focus of political activity for citizens. Although some issues, such as global environmental problems and morally-motivated aid to developing peoples need to be regulated globally, this is best achieved through interstate co-ordination. We should value an international society of sovereign states whose interaction is based on the principle of non-interference.

As maintained by the communitarian position, human rights cannot be defined universally because they only have meaning in terms of the social fabric of the particular societies and cultures that proclaim them. 'Human rights', it is argued, mean something different in Somalia from what they mean in the context of, say, Japan. 'Human rights' is a term that only has meaning when anchored in particular political allegiances and an explicit historical development. Communitarians hold that rights are grounded in specific cultural understandings and have no universal fundamental basis, and that they should instead be recognized as radically socially constructed. They question the usefulness of universal definitions of rights and justice, arguing that such definitions are so abstract that it is difficult to apply them and to match them to any specific situation. They are so universal that they do not take account of different social and cultural contexts and histories. These definitions also narrow the range of acceptable action. As Brown notes, the 'very idea of human rights implies limits to the range of variation in domestic regimes that is acceptable internationally' (Brown, 2001, p.610).

The communitarian critique of the international human rights culture extolled by cosmopolitans also argues that, in this reading, rights are so fixed that they do not allow any challenge. In order to be useful in the real world of politics, definitions of rights and justice, like other political concepts, need to be interpreted. The concept of rights is clear but thin, and too far removed from real life. What we need, according to communitarians, is different, thick interpretations of the concept, that is, diverse conceptions. Yet as soon as we start talking about different conceptions of rights and justice, we begin to realize how complex and contested those conceptions are. Do they then lose their universality? The price of having conceptions that fit real situations is that there are no agreed fixed meanings to refer to in order to referee disputes. There is no neutral language with which to discuss international human rights, and all perspectives carry an ideological charge. There is no objective 'God's-eye' view from which to arbitrate.

Moreover, some communitarians also believe that 'rights' talk individualizes and fragments social bonds. It is necessary, in contrast, to think about values for society as a whole. In addition, the communitarian perspective might argue that 'relationality' (the idea that our relations with others are as important to our well-being and individual identity as our sense of individual freedom and rights) is profoundly important to us. A standpoint which does not recognize that our needs are usually interdependent with those of others, and so does not take relationality into account, can lead to damaging consequences for all concerned.

The communitarian position is strengthened by the argument that many human rights conflict with each other, for instance, potentially between a mother and her unborn child. Its appeal is also fortified by pointing out that because the meaning of rights is contextual, many interpretations will conflict, and there is no obvious principle to appeal to for resolving disputes of interpretation. This view holds that the answer to the dilemma lies in the need to compromise absolutely-held political positions and convictions. Compromise and consensus can only be achieved politically, on a case by case basis. This quandary occurs at the international level as well as at the domestic level, and can only be settled by a process of negotiation between the particular set of actors involved, not by reference to some overarching 'global institution' or principle.

Activity 7.3

Rather than seeking a single set of human rights upheld by all states, communitarians argue that we should value a diversity of 'reasonable' ways of living together and, therefore, different conceptions of the political good in international society. What, if any, are the limits to what is 'reasonable'? On what grounds should we accord respect to other cultures?

Table 7.2 (overleaf) summarizes the difference between the communitarian and cosmopolitan perspectives.

In the remainder of this section, I consider how the differences between the cosmopolitan and communitarian views on how to describe and organize international interaction lead to divergent political positions on three key debates on international justice – distributive and retributive forms of justice, and interventionism.

6.2   International distributive justice

While communitarians strongly support an interpretation of the UN post-war settlement based on the principle of national self-determination, many cosmopolitans seek to go beyond that settlement. Those who endorse cosmopolitanism look forward to a further development and structuring of global relations, governed by the principle of universal rights, in which the exercise of national sovereignty is conditional on respect for human rights. Some, but not all, cosmopolitans wish to institutionalize this development in an international framework that would over-ride the authority of nation states. Cosmopolitans argue that international relations need to reach beyond power politics and each state acting in its own interests, and instead institutionalize the principles of rights and justice as the basis of order between states. They argue that distributive justice is not just at issue within a state or even between states, but also at a global level among individuals. The contention is that international inequalities are not only the unplanned outcome of competition and differently positioned access to resources, but they raise a broader moral issue about the unacceptability of large differences in welfare, resources, income, and life chances within an 'international community'.

Table 7.2 The communitarian/cosmopolitan distinction

	Communitarianism	Cosmopolitanism
Principle of human interaction	Cultural identity	Reason
Basis of interaction	Plurality of intersecting cultures with incommensurable values	Single humanity with everyone having equal moral worth because all human beings share capacity for reason
View of international system	System dominated by sovereign nation states that co-operate and conflict with one another	Suprastate public sphere and an arena of governance in its own right
Preferred form of international authority	Sovereign state and interstate institutions, no strong legal and political authority above the state	Community of states upholding universal human rights and international law
Basis for addressing common problems	Common problems are best addressed through co-ordination between states	Common problems governed by principle of universal rights and the related principle of universal international justice
Concept of rights	Only have meaning in terms of the social fabric of the particular societies and cultures that proclaim them, they do not have universal meaning	Rights can have universal meaning when they are based upon human reason
Values versus rights	Values for a society as a whole prevail over rights talk because the latter individualizes and fragments social bonds	Universal rights prevail over particular values because they express universal reason
Concept of international justice	Justice can at most be international, that is express co-operation between states and justice between states	Universal justice valid for every individual, justice as expression of universal human reason for humanity as a whole

Consequently, a key tenet of the cosmopolitan position is that global relations should be governed by the principle of rights which informs the principle of international distributive justice. For instance, only at this level can redress for inequalities between the North and the South, from the affluent to the impoverished, be sought. Furthermore, cosmopolitans mostly hold that the transferred resources should be distributed to individuals rather than to states. Some cosmopolitans argue that resources should be targeted at those who are least well-off, while others believe that all persons are entitled to an equal share of the earth's resources.

Communitarians focus on the argument that the claims of one's own fellow citizens for a redistribution of resources must take priority over the claims of those residing in other countries. Radical cosmopolitans assert that people and states have just as strong an obligation to distributive justice anywhere in the world as they do to their co-nationals or fellow citizens, or within their state boundaries. Whereas communitarians subscribe to a notion of needs-based distributive justice, cosmopolitans are committed to rights-based justice. The logic of the argument for cosmopolitans is that if one agrees that '(a) individuals have moral worth' and '(b) they have this equally', it follows that '(c) people's equal moral worth generates moral reasons that are binding on everyone' (Caney, 2001, p.977). The argument is that 'a person's nationality or citizenship should not determine their entitlements' (Caney, 2001, p.979). If it is agreed that all persons have equal moral worth, how can the country you happen to live in compromise this universal principle?

Indeed, many cosmopolitans argue for strong and interventionist versions of international distributive justice aimed at measures associated with subsistence, economic and welfare rights. Such measures include international development efforts, humanitarian aid, debt relief, immigration policy and regulating the environment. Thomas Pogge (2002), for example, considers that the need for cosmopolitan international justice follows as a consequence of the development of economic globalization. For cosmopolitans, international distributive justice can and should be premised on universal principles and not simply conducted at the level of relations between nation states.

6.3 International retributive justice

A further difference between communitarians and cosmopolitans arises over the question of retributive justice. Communitarians think that it is the responsibility of each state to uphold justice. Collectively, states can pursue international justice through the auspices of the UN, and are answerable to each other, to public opinion and to NGOs. However, there is no basis for claims to universal jurisdiction, and to deal with matters not found in specific states (such as piracy), or that cross borders (for example, global ecological damage), states should sign conventions with each other.

By contrast, some cosmopolitans hold a more radical model of international retributive justice in which a supranational international court plays a key role. A model of universal, rather than national, jurisdiction is envisaged in areas of retribution. This notion of international retributive justice is concerned with international bodies that have jurisdiction everywhere in the world and are able to bring to trial and punish those accused of crimes such as genocide and ethnic cleansing. An international court along these lines could supersede the authority and jurisdiction of courts within a state. Formerly, high courts in national arenas were the only places where extra-territorial claims, involving the prosecution of nationals in other countries, and disputed claims to rights in the international sphere could be assessed and adjudicated.

For cosmopolitans, the idea of universal retributive justice follows logically from the notion of the universal human rights-carrying citizen. Partly as a result of cosmopolitan ideas, the period since the Second World War, and particularly from the 1990s, has seen significant moves to develop international law, international policy making and practice in order to put some muscle into delivering international retributive justice. The aim of these developments is to enforce claims to rights and to progress efforts to codify limitations on state immunity. International justice in this sense has developed as one of the extensions of the meaning of rights.

Thus the 1990s saw the UN Security Council establishing ad hoc tribunals for war crimes in the former Yugoslavia and Rwanda, and UN and North Atlantic Treaty Organization (NATO) actions in Somalia, Bosnia, Kosovo and East Timor. These developments are proof of new extensions to international law and enhanced powers of intervention granted to international institutions and states in the name of human rights. New legal safeguards to protect minorities from oppression and persecution, in both international and national courts, are also becoming institutionalized. In the early 1990s, the Hague and Arusha tribunals for war crimes were welcomed by many cosmopolitans as building on the legacy of the post-war Nuremberg trials. Subsequently, in 1998, the Rwandan tribunal sentenced the former prime minister and head of the Rwandan government, Jean Kambanda, to life imprisonment for crimes against humanity. The following year, this precedent was employed to create a milestone in international justice when the UK House of Lords directly raised the issue of who has jurisdiction. Breaking with the previous norms of national jurisdiction (supplemented by international treaties of extradition), the House of Lords ruled that the Chilean General Augusto Pinochet did not have sovereign immunity and could be extradited from the UK to Spain, to be tried for crimes against humanity allegedly committed in Chile while he was head of state. A few months later, Chandler notes, 'the indictment of a sitting head of state, Slobodan Milosevic, for crimes against humanity was greeted as confirming that there had been "a revolution in international law"' (Chandler, 2002, p.7).

Of more import is the establishment of the International Criminal Court (ICC). In 1998, important steps were taken towards setting up a permanent ICC with jurisdiction over individuals accused of serious war crimes, crimes against humanity, and genocide. Compared with the UN settlement, the ICC is a radical institution with overarching global competence, expressing the cosmopolitan commitment to the principle of reason in an 'international public sphere'. One aspect of this radicalism is that the only body with the authority to over-ride an ICC decision is the UN Security Council, by a unanimous vote.

Question

Can you think of some problems with the communitarian and cosmopolitan positions outlined above?

Cosmopolitans, in the name of universal human rights, pursue both distributive and retributive justice at an international level in ways that compromise the independent sovereign rights of states to national self-determination. Nevertheless, sovereignty remains a key principle of international order. How to recognize both human rights and state sovereignty, given that states can be both protectors of, and threats to, individual rights, is a key question for cosmopolitans. Its critics argue that too often cosmopolitan justifications for superseding sovereignty represent the interests of the wealthy and the powerful. The communitarian approach stresses the social shaping of rights claims, the needs of communities and the role of states in upholding a political order that can define and protect these claims and needs. Where do other actors, most especially the individuals that comprise any given community, fit into this picture? How do their rights relate to the rights of the state? These are pressing issues for communitarian positions.

6.4 Military and humanitarian interventionism

While the ICC may be the most radical cosmopolitan effort at global justice institution-building so far, it is not the only one. The move towards cosmopolitan global institutions that extend beyond the UN's original goals and values has speeded up during the 1990s. Cosmopolitans would contend that international institution-building does not necessarily lead to more interventionism. Communitarians such as Chandler see as significant that in the field of international human rights interventionism, 'the shift in policy practices has been institutionalized on an ad hoc manner through the UN Security Council, which since 1990 has empowered itself to consider humanitarian emergencies as a threat to international peace and security' (Chandler, 2002, p.5). The Gulf War to 'liberate' Kuwait in 1991 was followed by the international community's attempt to set up a 'safe haven' policy to protect the human rights of the Kurds and Marsh Arabs. The international regulation of Iraq, through the establishment of 'no fly' zones and UN provisions to prevent Iraq from developing weapons of mass destruction and limiting trade with other states, represented a crucially significant legal precedent whereby a state's sovereignty was subordinated to human rights concerns. This legal precedent for universal human rights-based intervention was invoked in 1992 with the UN authorization of unilateral US intervention to protect humanitarian food conveys in Somalia.

The precedent was also used in 1993 when the UN authorized a multilateral military intervention in Bosnia to protect humanitarian aid, and again two years later when a NATO force was mandated to impose a peace settlement. In 1999, international military action against Yugoslavia over the Kosovo crisis was widely regarded as the first international military intervention against a sovereign state for purely human rights reasons. The language of human rights was also used by the USA and the UK as a framework for the 'war on terrorism' after the events of 11 September 2001.

Cosmopolitan advocates of universal human rights applaud what they see as the radical extension of the competence of the UN. From being charged with standard setting, monitoring and exerting pressure on states to comply, the UN is now very much in the game of intervention. Chandler is critical of the enhanced role of the UN Security Council and argues that it 'has been fundamentally transformed from being a policeman of international security, concerned with the welfare of states, to a supranational "government and administration body" supporting the human rights of citizens in situations of complex political emergencies'. A primary example is that of 'a number of international institutions acquiring powers of long-term administration over Bosnia in the Dayton peace settlement'. Those administrative powers 'were later extended on an indefinite basis and, in 1999, the UN acquired further powers of administrative regulation in Kosovo and East Timor' (Chandler, 2002, p.8).

Activity 7.4

Can these tensions between the claims of sovereign states to national self-determination and the claims of universal human rights be reconciled? If not, how can they best be managed?

---

7 Conclusion

One might think of the different interpretations of internationally recognized notions of rights and justice as running along a spectrum, from which I shall now identify four different positions.

■ The first interpretation would argue that, overall, the extension of rights to the international sphere has been benign and effective. It has led and will lead to further successful claims for justice.

Evidence for the development of a globalized rights agenda is found, for instance, in the 1995a UN Report of the Commission on Global Governance, *Our Global Neighbourhood*. The report recommended that international policy making should increase its focus on global concerns such as war, poverty, the rights of children, women and minorities, and the environment. The emphasis given to universal concerns over national ones is sustained by the claim of the globalized nature of key issues. Examples include the spread of HIV/AIDS, international terrorism, ozone depletion and international drug trafficking. According to this viewpoint, a cosmopolitan approach to rights need not necessarily lead to intervention.

- The second interpretation might say that the UN Charter and other declarations are successful in employing and promoting a common universal language, but a gap between theory and practice persists. Problems remain with developing effective mechanisms to translate those universal principles into concrete practices.

One concern is that there is no guarantee that the development of a structure of international institutions designed to implement human rights and international justice would always be driven by moral values, free from the intervention of power politics and national self-interest. It is hard to see how a structure of international institutions based on moral norms could protect itself from reinterpretation in terms of power politics under pressure of blandishments and threats. Some of the interventions in the international society of states initiated by President George W. Bush, for instance, raise concerns for a rights-based international framework remaining independent, rather than being interpreted to coincide with the national interest of the remaining world superpower.

Chris Brown also raises the problem of compliance. He argues that, over the last 50 years, 'the growth of an international human rights regime based on the idea that human rights should be internationally protected has been striking, and seems a prime example of globalization'. However, he notes, 'the record of compliance with human rights law is patchy, and states seem unwilling to give international action in support of human rights a high priority'. The problem of 'compliance' is that of translating the legal obligations of states into actions and policy changes that implement the rights. Brown concludes that, in the current century 'only a limited notion of human rights will be defensible – or perhaps human rights will have to be defended in explicitly cultural terms' (Brown, 2001, p.599).

- The third position might argue that the notions of 'rights' and 'justice' are too slippery and context-specific to constitute a meaningful form of communication.

The idea of the intractability of incommensurable difference (apples cannot be measured in terms of oranges) leads to the view that rights and justice are culturally-specific and cannot, and should not, be applied across borders. This is, to some extent, the burden of the communitarian position discussed above.

Moreover, we saw at the beginning of Section 5 that things change as we move from the national to the international level as the focus for realizing universal human rights. Rights and justice, when applied to the international sphere which is considered as an arena of politics in its own right, can refer both to international actors such as states and economic organizations, and to individuals and groups. There is likely to remain a tension between the rights of individuals and the rights and sense of justice of international actors.

■ Finally, the fourth interpretation might say that the notion of universal rights and justice is untenable, its grandiose claims bankrupt, and its recent strengthening dangerous.

This interpretation forefronts the idea that establishing the levels of international social justice and legal retributive instruments is a matter for debate between conflicting perspectives in the public domain. A range of different states, NGOs, social movements and other international actors will all have views which deserve a proper hearing. The application of abstract and universal standards of rights and justice always needs to be mediated by interpretation, and interpretations can be widely divergent.

Yet in addition to this spectrum of the interpretations of rights and justice, and in the light of novel and radical developments in international politics like the ICC, the question we arrive at is whether the rights project is now unstoppable or whether it will, in time, be tempered by communitarian concerns. If the shape of the future does indicate a move from an international rights advocacy to a full-blown global rights culture and project, this is likely to remain deeply contested in the short term. How best to analyse international relations as a whole also remains a matter of debate. Jef Huysmans explores these issues further in Chapter 9.

On the basis of the argument advanced in this chapter, what is likely to happen and what should happen may be quite different. It would seem, on the available evidence, that a deeply interventionist global order driven by a rights ideology and culture may well emerge above the nation states, structured either by accountable or non-accountable international institutions of global governance. This outcome is all the more probable if international relations continue to be framed by a single superpower. However, if the development of a rights agenda and culture is unstoppable, then we do not have a choice *not* to use rights. Egalitarian rights institutionalizing a right to intervene are becoming a common currency both inside particular countries and in international politics. Putting aside what is liable to happen, what should happen? I have suggested, in line with the communitarian position, that there is a strong normative argument for an international system that is less than a full-blown global society, in which nation states should remain crucial players.

Further reading

For a wide-ranging, accessible and powerful defence of the idea of universal human rights and their role in the international system, see Chapters 1, 5, 6 and 7 of Beetham, D. (1999) *Democracy and Human Rights*, Cambridge, Polity Press.

For a brilliant, feminist discussion of the claims of culture and the claims of universal rights, set in a context of a range of concrete, contemporary examples, see Benhabib, S. (2002) *The Claims of Culture: Equality and Diversity in the Global Era*, Oxford and New Jersey, NJ, Princeton University Press.

A highly informative and detailed discussion of conceptions of human rights in political theory, the role of human rights in a global context and different regional perspectives on human rights can be found in Beetham, D. (ed.) (1995) *Politics and Human Rights*, Oxford, Blackwell.

Chapter 8 Culture, international politics and Islam: debating continuity and change

Sami Zubaida

1 Introduction

In the last three decades of the twentieth century, Islam came to prominence as a political ideology animating many diverse movements in different parts of the world. This growing pre-eminence increasingly served as a focal point in some of the debates about culture and rights that you studied in Chapters 6 and 7. The Iranian Revolution of 1979, which installed the Islamic Republic in Iran, was seen as a spectacular demonstration of the mobilizing power of religion in that part of the world. The Iranian Revolution, together with other Islamic movements, was considered radical, opposed to the prevailing 'secular' regimes, such as that of the Shah of Iran, and was also 'anti-Western' and especially anti-American. These turbulent decades culminated in the spectacular attacks on the USA on 11 September 2001, which seemed to demonstrate further the potent and hostile power of Islam. To some, these events appeared to justify the 'Clash of Civilizations' thesis advanced by Samuel Huntington. As you have seen (in Chapters 3 and 6), Huntington insists that the world is dividing into fundamentally different and separate civilizational blocs, and that these are largely defined in religious terms. The Western bloc, in his argument, stands distinct from the others, which include Islamic and Buddhist civilizations. The West, in Huntington's model, is distinguished by the culture of democracy, citizenship, individualism and rights, as against the collectivist and authority-centred cultures of the Islamic (and other Asian and African) blocs.

Huntington's thesis has been subjected to cogent critiques (see Chapters 3, 6 and 15, and Halliday, 1996). Yet, its suppositions retain a surface plausibility in public discourses and sentiments, particularly in the media of the West and the Islamic world. The mutually reinforcing stereotypes that lie at the centre of Huntington's argument see a totalized Islam opposed to an equally totalized West. Each is regarded as historically and culturally separate and antagonistic. Huntington assigns the language and institutions of democracy and rights to Western culture. Other cultures, at least in these respects, are marginalized. In so far as democracy and rights regimes are adopted in other regions, they remain superficial and alien grafts, vulnerable to being displaced.

How, then, should we understand the relationship between culture, rights and political change? Sometimes, as Chapters 6 and 7 have shown, discussion of culture and rights focuses on a purported 'clash' between particular cultures and the putatively universal claims of rights. The claims of one may come up against the resistance of the other. Yet things are rarely so clear-cut. Not only can the notion of 'culture' and the notion of 'rights' be unpacked in various ways, as the previous two chapters have shown, but the inter-relationship of rights and culture is more mixed, complex and changing than the image of a clash implies. Furthermore, presenting these dimensions of international order in this way often actually misses the politics of debates about rights and culture. Approaching these issues from the perspective of Muslim countries (I mostly focus on the historical core of the Islamic world, the Middle Eastern countries, in this chapter) helps to reveal the different ways in which debates over rights and culture interact with, and are shaped by, processes of political change at both the national and international level.

The first of the main arguments of this chapter, developed in the rest of this section and in Section 2, is that 'Islam' and the 'West' are not unitary categories of homogeneous societies and cultures, but that each comprises a diversity of such entities, historically and at present. The politics and cultures of these diverse entities are not emanations from some religious essence, but are shaped and transformed historically by social processes. This applies equally to the question of human rights and democracy.

The second main argument, developed in Sections 3 and 4, is that the different strands of Islamic politics and religion are best understood in terms of processes of social and political change. In particular, I shall draw attention to the rise of notions and practices of constitutionalism, democracy and citizenship in the emergence of political modernity in the region, and the contests and struggles over these issues between different political, religious and ideological interests. I contend that these social and political processes need to be understood in the context of the international relations of the region, including the impact of the Cold War, regional wars and wars involving the USA and others in Afghanistan and Iraq. Sections 5 and 6 take a closer look at the politics of law and human rights in Muslim societies and at contemporary debates over Islam and human rights. Throughout, I show that constructions of human rights and the tensions between religion and secularism are expressed in the region's debates about its own identity and role in the world. They are inseparable from the political and social developments that are integral to everyday experience in the region.

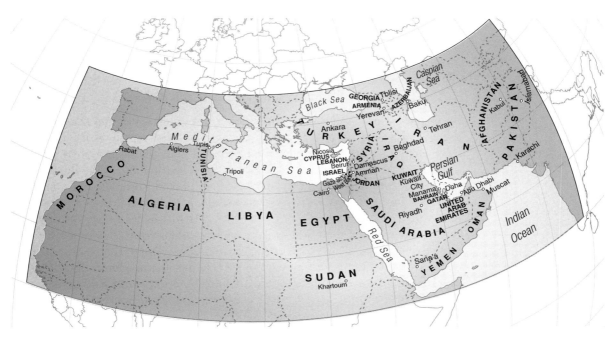

Figure 8.1   The Middle East

1.1   The role of religion

Question

What are the alternatives to Huntington's totalizing and essentialist conception of religious civilizations?

Instead of this totalizing approach, which sees religion as some fixed determinant of culture and therefore a fixed marker in attitudes to rights, I shall try to understand religion (and culture more generally) as an arena of change, contestation and struggle. Elements of Western and Muslim societies have mixed and intermingled throughout their diverse historical trajectories. Europe and the Middle East, for instance, shared a common heritage of philosophy, science and medicine through the Middle Ages and into early modern times. They only started to diverge in the seventeenth century with the Scientific Revolution and the beginnings of capitalism in parts of Western Europe. I shall try to show how the spread of capitalist-led modernity in parts of the Ottoman Empire started processes of transformation parallel to those that earlier changed Europe, then later other parts of the world. These changes included the formation of new types of state and politics, the individualization of labour, the break-up of 'primordial' communities, and the emergence of ideas of citizenship and rights. These ideas and their institutions are at the centre of contests and struggles which are moved by social and political interests, but which are often expressed in terms of religious idioms. Religion, then, rather than forming an unvarying essence of a culture, becomes an arena of struggle. Religion, in this approach, becomes just one element amongst many that shapes the ways and functioning of society, including how far a society recognizes and upholds rights.

Islam, like Christianity, is a world religion, with a history extending over many centuries in diverse countries and regions. Historically, world religions have entered into the shaping of all societies and civilizations, yet in very different ways. Consider Italy and Ethiopia, both Christian, with Christianity playing a crucial part in their historical formation. Despite the common religion, they are totally different societies and cultures, with very distinct forms of Christianity, both in doctrine and institutions. Even countries in closer geographical and political proximity, such as Italy and Greece, or France and England, have diverse churches and doctrines. Christianity may be clearly identifiable as a religion, yet it has diverse manifestations in different historical and geographical contexts. Religion may enter into the shaping of cultures, but it itself acquires distinct character in different contexts.

Islam, too, takes distinct cultural forms, even between different classes and groups within the same country. It has, of course, recognizable common elements, such as its sacred book, the Quran, belief in the prophethood of Muhammad and rituals of worship and purity. It is also marked by an emphasis on religious law, the *Shari'a*, derived from the sacred sources. But these elements acquire different significances and values under different conditions. While all Muslims believe in the centrality and sanctity of the Quran, many in some sufi (mystic) traditions make little reference to it, favouring the teachings of their founders and chiefs, or read it as an esoteric text with hidden meanings. Others select particular chapters and interpret them in accordance with certain traditions and ideologies. Vastly different cultural forms exist in Egypt, Iran, Indonesia or Nigeria. Even within a given country, Egypt for example, there are diverse religious observances between rural and urban groups, between the lettered and the illiterate, 'high' and 'low' cultures, mystics and strict adherents to the holy texts. Religion at the present time in many Muslim countries and communities is a field of contest and disputation, more so than other elements of culture, not some unchanging unitary category.

This diversity of Muslim societies therefore makes it unrealistic to try to encompass the whole of what is called 'the Islamic World' in the deliberations of this chapter. I shall, therefore, concentrate on the Middle East, a region central to the historical formation of Islam, and prominent in the current 'Islamic revival'. The insights gained from a study of this region will have implications for other parts of the Muslim world and for the politics of other religions, such as Christianity in the USA or Hinduism in India.

2   The diversity of modern Islamic politics

In this section I elaborate on a point I have already made, namely, that Islam as a political ideology comes in very different forms with varying attitudes towards ideas about rights, democracy, the law and the like. However, let me make an important clarification at the outset. The categories of 'Arab' and 'Muslim' are often wrongly identified together. 'Arab' is an ethnic or national and linguistic category, which includes many non-Muslims, such as the Christian and Jewish communities of the Arab world. 'Muslim' is a religious identification that covers large non-Arab populations in Iran, Turkey, Asia and Africa, as well as the now large Muslim populations of Europe and the USA.

There is a tendency in public and media discourses in the West and elsewhere to assume Islamic politics to be unitary, all subsumed under the label of 'fundamentalism'. If any distinctions are to be made then it is between 'moderates' and 'extremists'. These labels hide a wide diversity of ideas and movements. They mask rather than reveal. Indeed, it should be noted that for the majority of Muslims in the world Islam is not about politics but about faith and observance. Politics may come into it when religious identity comes to define social groups or forces in conflict, in much the same way as 'Catholic' and 'Protestant' religions do in Northern Ireland. What we see in the 'Islamic revival' of the late twentieth century is the rise of political movements drawing on Islam for identities and ideologies. This ideologization of Islam is not new, but has been a feature of politics since the inception of modernity in the Middle East in the nineteenth century. For most of the twentieth century, however, with the secularization of society and politics, Islamic politics as such constituted only one element among other secular ideologies. This observation will be borne out in the historical survey that follows (Sections 3 and 4).

For the present, I want to note that contemporary Islamic movements and ideologies are diverse. Islam can be seen as an *idiom* – the terms in which many social groups and political interests express their aspirations and frustrations, and ruling elites claim legitimacy. This can be seen in a number of types of orientations in the Islamic politics of recent decades.

There are three broad and overlapping types of Islamic political orientations across the countries in the region. First, conservative or *salafi* Islam (*salaf* means 'ancestors', so for its adherents it is the correct religion of the first Muslims), is the dominant orientation in the Saudi Arabian establishment, but has a strong presence throughout the Muslim world. Its main emphasis is on authority, hierarchy, property, meticulous observance of ritual and correct conduct, including segregation of the sexes and the covering up of women, and other strictures on family morality and propriety. Its position with respect to rights is repressive, with a strong tendency to censorship of opinions and expressions. This orientation is political in that it seeks to influence government policy towards the application and enforcement of religious law and morality, and the regulation and censorship of the media, art, and other cultural products. These attitudes are typical of the 'pious bourgeoisie' of businessmen, professionals and many clerics. There are some interesting parallels between this leaning and that of the Christian Evangelical right in the USA, which is also concerned to pressure government into the enforcement of religious observance and moral conduct. They share the desire to censor intellectual and cultural products judged contrary to religious teaching. They are both, for instance, opposed to the teaching of Darwinian evolution in schools. We see here an instance of affinities across supposed civilizational boundaries: *it is a clash within, not between, civilizations.*

The second type of orientation is radical and militant, typically pursued by young students and other sectors of alienated youth. It differs from the conservatives not so much in its objectives, but in its methods. While the conservatives seek to promote their interpretation of Islam through influencing government and controlling levers of power and communication, the radicals tend to favour direct (often violent) action. They take the religious injunction, taken from the Quran, to enjoin the good and forbid evil-doing as a mandate to every Muslim to intervene forcefully in implementing religious precepts. This direct action applies especially to government and authority, which is often seen as neglectful of religious law, and therefore corrupt. The leading ideologue of this trend was Sayid Qutb, a militant member of the Muslim Brotherhood in Egypt, executed in 1966 for armed sedition. He argued that any state that ruled by man-made law, and not by what God had decreed, is an infidel authority, however much it may pretend to Islam. A society governed by laws other than those of God is equally errant. As such the governments and societies of the Muslim world were not truly Muslim, but lived in a *jahiliya*, a term used to describe the state of ignorance and barbarism that preceded Islam. It is the duty of true Muslims, then, to insulate themselves from this barbarism, recruit followers, entrench their strength in faith and in military training, and, in time, come out to wage Jihad against the infidel government and the non-believers. This would lead to the re-conquest of the world for Islam, in imitation of the Prophet and his generation. These goals have been the dominant creed of the militants throughout the region.

The third type of orientation is reformist and modernist. Intellectuals, professionals and modern businessmen typically advocate it. It seeks to Islamize government and society, but in the context of economic development, social reform and political democratization. That is to say, it espouses a politics that goes beyond the moral and ritual agenda of the others. In some respects its cadres seek to continue the national projects of the previous nationalists and leftists, with an emphasis on economic and social programmes. This reformist trend is the one most concerned with questions of rights and democracy, and comes to the fore wherever Islamism becomes part of a genuine pluralist electoral politics, primarily in Turkey, and in another form in Iran.

The violent militants dominated the headlines in the 1980s in Egypt and the 1990s in Algeria with their outrages and massacres. In Egypt, a wide-ranging and intensely repressive campaign by the authorities decimated the militants who were killed, imprisoned and tortured – many of them alongside members of their families and neighbours. By the mid 1990s their leadership declared an end to hostilities from their prisons. In Algeria the militants waged a civil war. Their tactics entailed massacres of whole villages and other similar outrages, rivalled only by the violence of state security forces. They, too, were suppressed in the end. It should be noted that the decline or demise of the militants, while directly effected by government repression, was also aided by the fear and loathing of most sectors of the population, which experienced these atrocities first hand, together with the disruption wrought in their wake. In Egypt, for instance, in attacking foreign tourists they threatened the livelihoods of the many Egyptians dependent on tourism. The conservative pious bourgeoisie and their clerics supported the militants in their attacks and assassinations of secular intellectuals and artists, but drew the line at the disruption of social order.

We have seen, then, that in its political dimensions Islam is not a unified force, but is diverse in both its goals and tactics. This brings us then to the place of 'human rights' in the orientations of Islamic politics. Rights, and particularly universal rights, have no intrinsic connection with any religious tradition. They are modern political and legal constructs, which emerged in the process of political liberationist struggles, first in Europe and the USA with the American and French Revolutions, then in other parts of the world. Religious authorities in Europe tended to be pitted against the kind of human rights that emerged in the European Enlightenment. Indeed, they were often part of the conservative establishments that resisted these liberationist movements with their doctrinal baggage of constitutionalism, democracy and rights. (Consider, for example, Thomas Hobbes's views on the Catholic Church discussed in Chapter 3.) Where they became established, rights and liberties were based on the rule of law, as part of the constitutional regimes that emerged with the reordering of political life in the late eighteenth and nineteenth centuries.

Law, then, is integral to any discussion of rights. This brings us to the question of legal ideas and institutions in relation to Islam. A common element central to all Islamic political movements is the call for the application of the *shari'a*, the religious law of Islam, believed to spring from divine commandments. The *shari'a*, like other religious and traditional legal systems, emphasizes obligations to God and to authority, as well as to family and community, rather than rights. Conservative Muslims hold on to these doctrines of obligations and dismiss the call for human rights as alien and hostile. Reformist and modernist trends, however, have tried to accommodate the issues of human rights into the *shari'a* in two contrasting ways. Liberals have re-interpreted the sacred sources to accommodate a universalist notion of human rights, akin to natural rights doctrines in political philosophy (see Chapters 3 and 7 for the idea of natural rights). Apologists, by contrast, have argued that the traditional Islamic notions of rights are superior to the universalist declarations and that Muslims should continue to follow these traditional beliefs.

I shall consider these formulations and debates about rights in more detail in Sections 5 and 6. However, they will make more sense after a consideration of the historical development of these issues. In particular I shall examine them in the framework of the politics of modernity since the nineteenth century (in Section 3), followed by an account of the development of modern Islamic movements in the broader international context (in Section 4).

Activity 8.1

Before reading on, make sure that you have grasped the main arguments that have been put forward so far.

1   List the main dimensions of unity and diversity within Islam.

2   Identify the role of social and political processes in accounting for the differences.

3   Islam, modernity and rights: the impact of Europe and Islamic reform

Notions of citizenship, constitutionalism, and, implicitly, individual rights were first contemplated in the Ottoman world in the nineteenth century, and in Iran later in that century and at the turn of the twentieth. These were the two major Muslim polities to maintain formal independence until the twentieth century, and to give rise subsequently to modern states. They thus serve as a useful starting point in our discussion of the surfacing of human rights agendas in the Islamic world.

Table 8.1   Key events in modern Middle Eastern history

1882	British occupation of Egypt.
1918	End of First World War; defeat of the Ottoman Empire, British and French occupation of Arab lands.
1922	Egyptian independence.
1923	Turkish Republic established.
1932	Iraqi independence.
1947	Independence of Syria and Lebanon.
1947	United Nations partition of Palestine.
1948	Declaration of the state of Israel; the first Arab–Israeli war.
1952	Free Officers *coup d'état* in Egypt; end of the monarchy.
1955	The Bandung Conference of non-aligned nations in Indonesia.
1956	The Suez crisis; UK–French–Israeli attack on Egypt, then withdrawal.
1958	The Iraqi Revolution displaces the monarchy.
1967	The 'Six-Day War' between Israel and the Arabs.
1970	Death of Nasir, accession of Sadat to the presidency of Egypt.
1973	'Yom Kippur' Arab–Israeli war.
1979	Camp David accord: peace agreement between Egypt and Israel.
1979	The Iranian Revolution.
1976–91	The Lebanese civil war.
1979	Soviet invasion of Afghanistan.
1981	Assassination of President Sadat of Egypt; accession of Husni Mubarak to presidency.
1980–88	Iran–Iraq war.
1990–91	Iraqi occupation of Kuwait, followed by Gulf War.
2001	Terrorist attack on New York and Washington, known as 9/11, followed by US invasion of Afghanistan and the end of the Taliban regime.
2003	US and UK war on Iraq.

Caliphate
The Caliphate was the institution of the Caliph, a successor of the Prophet and head of the Muslim community.

The Ottoman Empire was the most durable Muslim Empire, lasting from 1389 to 1922. At the height of their power from the fourteenth to the sixteenth centuries, the Ottomans ruled over vast territories extending from Arabia to the Balkans and west to North Africa. They embraced many ethnicities and religions, with considerable Christian domains in the Middle East and Europe. Though cosmopolitan, the Ottoman Empire was formally Sunni Muslim, and had appropriated the title of the Caliphate, connecting itself to the earliest Islamic dynasties. Religious legitimacy and its trappings were as important for the Ottomans as for their European counterparts: monarchs were anointed by clerics and assumed the titles of defenders of the faith. Being a Muslim dynasty the Ottomans enshrined the *shari'a*, the divine law, as the law of the state, and instituted its courts, tribunals and scribes as part of that state. In practice, however, the *shari'a* was applied largely to the private affairs of the subjects and not to matters of state. Public affairs were regulated by royal statutes, issued on the accession of each sultan, as well as by traditions and by the bureaucracies of state. Senior clerics, largely employed in state bureaucracies, some attaining positions of power and wealth, acquiesced in this division, and sanctioned it by conceptualizing state practices in *shari'a* terms. Formally, all law and regulation originated from divine commands or royal authority. In practice, a multitude of customary regulations and practices prevailed. Rights and obligations were theoretically specified in law, although in practice flowed from the contingencies of power and custom.

The rise of the European powers, primarily Britain, France and Russia, but also Austro-Hungary from the seventeenth century onwards, began to encroach on Ottoman power and territory. The advantage of these powers, especially Britain and France, rested on the wealth, technology and social organization generated by capitalism, industrialization and the general processes of modernity, including measures of constitutionalism and citizenship (Russia was an exception). The confidence of the old Ottoman ruling classes in the superiority of their empire and of the Islamic religion and its traditions was shaken. The military and economic dominance of the European powers allowed them to dictate terms to the Ottomans, including commercial, fiscal and administrative reforms. These developments opened markets and commercial opportunities to European merchants. New elites of politicians, high functionaries and intellectuals realized that reforms could not be just military and fiscal, but must relate to state and society, including the forms and processes of rule and administration. At the same time, commercial and financial penetration by European capitalism brought about transformations and dislocation, benefiting some classes and regions, but impoverishing many others.

These changes, allied to modernity and reform, generated discontent, which ultimately pitted Christians against Muslims. The telegraph, the railways, new legal institutions, modern education and crucially the press, as well as all the administrative bodies created to cope with these developments, led from the nineteenth century to the formation of a new middle class with modern outlooks. Science, art, literature and inventions fascinated and preoccupied this middle class.

Question

What were the political legacies of this encounter between Islam and European modernity?

The nineteenth century also witnessed the generation of many of the outlooks and ideological conflicts between conservatives and reformers that characterized the twentieth century. Conservatives and reactionaries fought reforms with appeals to Islam and its eternal verities, and their stance was to be exploited by politicians and rulers resisting democratic and legal constraints on their power. This was typically the case with the sultan Abdul-Hamid II (reigned 1875–1909), who bypassed the recently enacted constitution and parliament with religious rhetoric. But the reformers did not leave Islam to their opponents. They engaged in new interpretations that justified their demands for a constitution, representation and political participation in Islamic terms. The group of intellectuals known as Young Ottomans in the middle decades of the nineteenth century was educated in European languages and familiar with modern political theories and ideas. The Young Ottomans were in favour of reforms and a constitution, but insisted that these were original to Islam and not just European products. This was not the Islam of their contemporary clerics and shaykhs, corrupted, as they saw it, by centuries of foreign accretions and political misrule, but the original Islam of the Prophet himself and the community of believers he inaugurated in Medina in the seventh century. This community was, in their reading, an egalitarian community, ruled by divine command in consultation (*shura*) between its members. Successors to the Prophet could only rule with the consent of the community to their leadership in a ceremony of allegiance (*bay'a*). Uncertainty over policy and interpretation was to be decided by consensus (*ijma'*). These arguments and their vocabularies are repeated by the present-day Muslim thinkers of different hues, who assert the originality of political modernity to the pure Islam of the ancestors. This view discounts or dismisses the centuries of Muslim dynastic rule, which was uniformly authoritarian and repressive, like all historical empires, but does celebrate the past when it comes to military triumphs and civilizational brilliance.

The question of citizenship and individual rights, then, became an issue of contest between the different sides in this process of casting Islam as a political ideology. Conservative clerics rejected any notion of 'rights', such as the right of free expression, which challenged religious authority. Their interests coincided with those of despotic rulers who insisted on the authority and discretion given to them in traditional Islamic teaching as Muslim rulers. Theoretically, they had absolute power within the limits of the *shari'a*, and these limits were malleable on matters of state. In the nineteenth and early twentieth centuries, these arguments were used to reject constitutional and democratic rights, and they still are in Saudi Arabia.

Elsewhere, the development of the modern nation state, together with nationalist ideologies with varying relations to Islam, has largely been accompanied by the ideas of a constitution enshrining basic rights of citizenship and of political representation. However, in the Middle East, in most countries, these constitutions became largely redundant due to the manipulations of the ruling elites. The abrogation and suspension of constitutions has largely been carried out in the name of national independence and state security, backed by nationalist and sometimes socialist legitimation, and not in the name of religion. Religion, however, was also invoked to justify dictatorships after military coups in Pakistan (1977–85) and then in Sudan (1977–85 and again after 1988). The Islamic Republic of Iran, as we shall see, also claims divine sanction for its despotism.

We should note an important conceptual shift with regard to the sources of law which emerged in the nineteenth century reforms, and which had deep implications for the issue of rights and liberties. Traditional notions ascribed law to two sources: divine commandments contained in canonical texts and the sovereign will manifested in royal decrees. The conceptual shift, which emerged in the nineteenth century, was for the law to be seen as a component of an impersonal state, legislated in its institutions, and in relation to public utility.

Much of the advocacy of constitutionalism, democracy and human rights in the twentieth century has been 'secular', in the sense that religious questions were absent or marginal to its concerns. However, some religious reformers and liberals in the nineteenth century and also in the twentieth century, joined the movement for democratic rights by giving it religious legitimation. As we have seen, the kernel of their arguments was a return to the 'original' and 'pure' Islam of the first ancestors, into which they read liberal political modernity. In addition, religious reformers, starting with Muhammad Abduh, the prominent Egyptian shaykh, rector of al-Azhar in Cairo (the foremost Sunni Muslim university) and Mufti of Egypt (d. 1905), embarked on a process of reinterpreting and recasting Islamic law and education to make them compatible with social and political modernity. Abduh and his associates were concerned at what they saw as the emerging duality of their contemporary society and government, including law, between a religious sphere increasingly confined to worship and personal faith, and a public sphere dominated by European models of law, education and general culture. Their proposed remedy was to reform religion so that it could encompass those modern spheres. The categories of citizenship and rights were to be encompassed within this reformed religion. Under Abduh's formulation, for instance, all Egyptians, including Christians and Jews, were to be equal before the law, with full citizenship rights. This was a crucial departure from classic Islamic law, which relegated non-Muslims to the inferior status of protected tributaries, with many regulations and restrictions on their status and entitlement.

Islamic politics in the twentieth century, then, was divided between many different orientations: conservative, reformist, liberal and radical. These developed different relationships with the secular ideologies that dominated much of twentieth century politics. Outright secularism in the Turkish Republic subordinated religion to a nationalist state and created unique combinations of religion and nationalism. Egypt, where religion was much more prominent in public life, saw a variety of tendencies and patterns. These included an alliance between the Muslim Brothers (the first modern Islamist movement, emerging in Egypt in 1928, oriented to mass recruitment and mobilization from below) and the fascists in the 1930s. The 1950s and 1960s saw the emergence of 'Islamic socialism'. Islamic radicalism continued to thrive throughout the century, with a militant spurt from the 1970s, but culminated in a more 'civil' Islam of the last decade of the old century and the turn of the new. Iran's history presents yet another totally different articulation of religion to politics and the state.

Essentially, then, each society had its own unique experience of the connection between religion and politics. This again illustrates my argument that there is no such thing as a single Islamic politics. An understanding of the role and position of rights and citizenship in the region can be achieved only through an appreciation of the political contexts in which they operated. And these contexts were all different.

4   International relations and the shifting contexts of Islamic politics

The social and political processes shaping Islamic politics must themselves be seen in the context of the international political environment. From the nineteenth century, the casting of Islam as political ideology proceeded from the reforms that were implemented under the pressure of European dominance. International relations in the twentieth century continued to shape the political field in different countries, and the place of Islamic politics and ideology within them. As in other parts of the world, conceptions of rights and justice emanated not only from internal conditions but also from encounters with other societies and states.

While Turkey and Iran did not undergo direct colonial rule, their histories were shaped by European expansion and their inclusion in the capitalist world. Most Arab countries did experience direct colonial rule at various periods. The British ruled Egypt from 1882 until formal independence in 1922. It continued, however, to be under British dominance until 1952. Iraq and Palestine were under British mandates for various periods after the First World War, and Syria and Lebanon were under French mandates. Algeria, Morocco and Tunisia were under French colonial rule until the 1950s and 1960s. Nationalist anti-colonial struggles, then, played an important role in shaping politics, ideology and sentiment in all these countries, and Islam played various roles in these fields of political contestation.

The populations of North African countries (the Maghreb) were predominantly Muslim, ethnically divided between Arabs and Berbers. Small Jewish communities were soon absorbed into the French colonial sphere, some enjoying French citizenship. It was in this context that Islam merged with national identity and nationalist struggles against the French. Secular nationalist ideologies continued to identify Arab with Muslim. This identity could not be maintained in many countries in the Middle East, such as Syria, Lebanon, Egypt and Iraq, where native Christians and Jews constituted part of the Arab population, and were often prominently engaged in public life, including nationalist politics. Pan-Arab and regional nationalisms in these countries had a more ambiguous relation to Islamic identity, and were the source of a recurring tension.

The nation states, which followed independence, were mostly constituted as modern states with formal constitutions and some form of parliamentary life. In the first half of the twentieth century, these democratic forms survived, more or less, under the dominance and interference of the former colonial power, which tried to maintain a balance between local political forces to favour its own interests. In Egypt, for instance, this led to a plurality of power centres, including the royal court, the British High Commission, and the parliament and government, mostly dominated by the constitutionalist Wafd party. Islamic politics, in the form of the Muslim Brotherhood, played a fluctuating role in this set-up, often opposed to the liberals and the left (predominantly secular, with representation of non-Muslims), sometimes allied to the king, and frequently involved in anti-colonial activity.

In the 1950s and 1960s there occurred a series of military *coup d'états* undertaken by nationalist officers in these countries. These coups ended the dominance of the former colonial powers, as well as the formal democracies, in favour of authoritarian one-party rule on the pattern of many Third World countries of that era. These developments took place in the broader context of the Cold War and were coloured by its ideologies.

4.1   The Cold War and Middle East politics

A crucial transformation in Middle East politics occurred in 1956. Following the military coup in Egypt in 1952, Gamal Abdul-Nasir emerged as the leader of the Free Officers, the junta which dominated the country. His ambitions for Egyptian independence and economic development were frustrated by the Western powers, which denied him the finance he sought for an ambitious dam. In 1956 Nasir embarked on the dramatic gesture of nationalizing the Suez Canal, thus challenging and jeopardizing the interests of the old colonial powers of Britain and France. He also turned to the Soviet Union for financial and technical aid, and ultimately for military supplies. Britain and France plotted with Israel to attack the Canal Zone and occupy it. This plan was carried out without the agreement of the US government, which denounced the invasion and demanded a withdrawal. The USA's reaction came as a rude shock to the old European powers. They had been slow to realize the changed balance of power following the Second World War. This episode marked a clear break for Egypt from the old sphere of Western influence into the emerging constellation of the 'non-aligned' nations. Like many others in this bloc, Egypt moved closer to the Soviet Union, which became its military supplier and aid provider. This change estranged it from the 'Free World' bloc of the Cold War. Syria and Iraq, followed later by Algeria, Libya and South Yemen (the former British colony of Aden), followed in similar directions.

The ideology of these 'revolutionary' regimes was pan-Arab nationalism and statist socialism. They were all one-party states, which declared their ruling party as the vehicle of national unity and independence, threatened by imperialism and Israel. The prominence given to these outside forces demonstrated that national security and foreign affairs were to be given priority over other considerations. In line with prevalent ideologies of the Marxist and 'Third Worldist' left at that time, parliamentary democracy and political pluralism were declared to be 'bourgeois' frauds. True independence, economic development and national security came before any other consideration. 'True' democracy was the will of the people, which coincided with the objectives of the national leaders. These regimes broached no opposition and suppressed or incorporated all political forces and organizations, including unions and syndicates, which were often affiliated to the state and the single, ruling party on the Soviet model. While 'citizenship' was loudly proclaimed, it did not entail the individual rights associated with this term elsewhere, and which were discussed in the last chapter.

In the international alignments of the Cold War, the West's allies in the region were mainly the monarchies, which had not been overthrown by nationalist coups, and, of course, Israel. Saudi Arabia and the Gulf states, Jordan and

Iran, were the main bastions of the Western alliance in the Middle East, and, to a varying extent, Morocco and Tunisia. Turkey, by then a member of NATO, was in a different category and occupied a different political orbit. These Cold War alignments also marked deep political and ideological divisions among the states of the region, and these played an important part in the genesis of more recent politics and especially of political Islam.

Nasir's Egypt raised the banner of pan-Arab nationalism and 'Arab socialism'. After the Suez episode Nasir became the idol of the Arab people (as well as Third World sentiments elsewhere). Egypt emerged as the main bastion against Israel and its Western backers, and the champion of the Palestinians. This nationalist and populist appeal posed a challenge to the monarchies allied to the West, especially in Saudi Arabia and the Gulf, and the antagonism included a bloody war between Egypt and Saudi-supported forces in Yemen during the early 1960s. Despite the fact that the divisions in the Middle East were overtly political, Islam became an important tool in the counter propaganda from Saudi Arabia, which harboured the Egyptian Islamic opposition.

The Muslim Brotherhood, the main Islamic political movement, initially supported the Free Officers coup, some of whose members (including Anwar Sadat, Nasir's successor as president) harboured Islamic sympathies. However, the Brotherhood's ambitions for an Islamic regime in which they exerted influence were dashed by Nasir's clear intolerance of any rival political forces. In 1954, after an assassination attempt, Nasir turned to ban and persecute the Muslim Brotherhood alongside other independent political forces. Nasir's turn to the Soviet Union and to Arab socialism secured the support of some leftist forces, which were incorporated into the regime and its single party (most, however, were suppressed and many imprisoned), while alienating the Islamists. Some Muslim Brotherhood personalities escaped persecution and prison by taking refuge in Saudi Arabia where they were welcomed. Some of them were businessmen who prospered in the oil kingdom, others were professionals, teachers and clerics who found lucrative employment. These exiles were to have considerable influence in the subsequent growth of political Islam in Egypt and elsewhere, in which their financial resources and Saudi institutional connections played important parts.

It is important to note that during the Nasirist period and right up to the 1980s the dominant ideologies in the Middle Eastern political fields were nationalist and leftist, and mostly secular. Islamism was one strand of politics amongst many, and often a minor one, until, that is, the cataclysmic events of 1967. That was the year of the Arab–Israeli war, the so-called 'Six-Day War', in which the Arab armies, notably the Egyptian, suffered swift defeat. This had a profound effect on the Arab psyche, and is known to this day as *al-nakba*, the catastrophe. While the charismatic Nasir himself retained much of his popularity with the Egyptian public, Nasirism as such suffered from a credibility deficit, as did the other nationalist regimes. Their *raison d'être* of national power and independence backed by extensive military expenditure and drastic repression in the name of security seemed to come to nothing in the first confrontation with Israel. On the economic front, incompetence and corruption had grossly impeded and distorted economic development. Many of these countries, especially those such as Egypt which lacked oil resources, were suffering increasing poverty and youth unemployment fed by the growth of the population. Nationalism and socialism became discredited, as they were associated with failed and corrupt regimes. Leftist revolution, on the Guevarist and Maoist guerrilla models, enjoyed a vogue in some quarters, particularly in support of the incipient Palestinian resistance movements, but not for long. From the 1970s, Islamism of various hues was on the rise in most countries of the region, and local as well as international forces and processes backed its growth.

The perceived failure of nationalist–socialist regimes in the region to deliver on their most basic promises of national power and shared prosperity led to disillusionment with these ideologies. A political vacuum was created which organized political opposition could not fill because any such forces had been ruthlessly suppressed. Islamic organizations had an advantage in this setting because they could draw on forms of organization and networks that were not easily eliminated: mosques, religious associations and charities. While the Muslim Brotherhood as such was suppressed, its clandestine apparatus could still draw on these networks, supported by financial resources from private and official sources in Saudi Arabia and the Gulf.

Islamic forces also benefited from the growth and diversity of the urban populations, fuelled by natural increase as well as accelerated rates of rural–urban and provincial–metropolitan migrations. At the same time, the commercially-based middle classes and professionals in the provinces were more inclined to a conservative outlook. This outlook found its expression in religious idioms, especially in their antagonism and antipathy to the older Westernized urban elites. These constituted what Gilles Kepel (2002) called the 'pious bourgeoisie'. These processes also led to exponential growth of the urban poor, with disproportionate representation in the younger age groups. Contrary to common perceptions, these were not the main cadres of the Islamic movements. The poor tended to be apolitical and, while frustrated and oppressed, were also preoccupied with the urgent pursuits of daily bread and shelter. They did and still do provide a reservoir of volatile rage which can be mobilized for organized protest.

The most important cadres for militant political action, Islamic or other, are the students and young graduates. Most countries in the region have seen a great expansion in this age group. Mass higher education with paltry resources cannot maintain high standards, and many of the graduates are poorly educated. The economies and occupational structures of most countries could not expand to absorb the large numbers of graduates, so graduate unemployment and under-employment became chronic. Frustrated youth represents a potent reserve for political dissidence, and in many countries they have been directed since the 1970s into Islamic dissidence. Prominent figures in the Islamic movement in Egypt and elsewhere were drawn from graduates, especially in technical fields like medicine, engineering and agriculture. Many of the student militant leaders of the 1970s in Egypt went on to leading roles in the professional syndicates of medicine and law, which tended to be dominated by Islamists in the 1980s and 1990s.

Question

How did the Cold War impact upon the political role and character of Islam in the Middle East?

For the early Cold War period, secular and nationalist ideologies dominated much of the Middle East and drew support from allies in the global confrontation. However, secular nationalism declined after 1967 and Islam began to become more prominent as a political force. Note that the success of political Islamism was buttressed by changing Cold War alignments. You have seen how the conservative monarchies in the Western camp, and especially Saudi Arabia, fostered Islam in the region as an antidote to secular nationalism and the left. Political change in Egypt also exemplified this interaction of Cold War alignments and 'internal' political contests. Egypt was drawn into the Western camp in the 1970s. Nasir died in 1970 and was succeeded by Anwar Sadat who embarked on a different route, opening up the statist 'socialist' economy to capitalism, the so-called *infitah*, or opening up. This was accompanied by international realignment, ending the linkage to the Soviet Union in favour of closer ties with the USA. Within the region Egypt drew closer to Saudi Arabia and the Gulf states, in the hope of acquiring some of the wealth generated by oil. Nasirists and leftists, still prominent in government and public life, were strongly opposed to these steps, and so Sadat turned to Islamic elements for support. In the universities, for instance, Islamic students were encouraged by the government to take on and defeat the then dominant leftist students. The success of the Islamists led to their attempts to impose religious norms on the students, in terms of segregation of the sexes, the 'encouragement' to women to wear the veil and the institution of prayers and rituals. That is to say, the social liberties and individual rights gained in the previous decades, amidst the suppression of political liberties, were being eroded.

Sadat's alignment with the USA culminated in the momentous Egyptian peace with Israel and the Camp David agreement in 1977–79. The accords traumatized Egyptians and Arabs of all political colours, including, of course, the Islamists. The latter responded in various ways. The official state clerics issued *fatwas* (religious rulings) justifying the move in terms of Prophetic precedent and injunctions to peace. The conservative leaders of the Muslim Brotherhood were reserved in their opposition. They were mindful of the compact they had with the president, giving them a range of liberties of organization and publication, though no license to operate openly as a political grouping. Islamic militants, however, both from the Brotherhood and the more radical groups, were forthright in their denunciation of the president's policies and accused him of treachery. The radical groups of Jihad and Jama'at al-Muslimun were inspired by the ideas of Sayid Qutb (discussed above), whose accusation of apostasy against the supposedly Muslim rulers seemed vindicated by Sadat's actions. Militants from these groups eventually assassinated Sadat in 1981.

Before his assassination, Sadat sought to counter Islamic and other opposition by playing the familiar game of 'more-Islamic-than-thou'. To counter the press photos of himself socializing with Kissinger and the Israeli leaders, Sadat cultivated an image of *al-ra'is al-mu'min*, the believing president, appearing in native cloths and pious attire performing prayers and rituals. He also insisted on the supremacy of the *shari'a*, the holy law. He wrote amendments into the Egyptian Constitution to the effect that the *shari'a* was the primary source of legislation. This change clearly contradicted the actual content of Egyptian positive law, which had evolved since the nineteenth century on European models, except for the provisions on family law and personal status. Sadat's manoeuvres opened the way for subsequent Islamist moves to push law and legislation in even more religious directions.

During the Cold War, international relations combined with internal developments to shape the political fields of the main countries and the place of Islam within them. The changing profiles and roles of Islam directly affected the prominence and function that human rights and law would play within society. This intertwining of international and regional developments continued to mould political Islam in the 1980s and 1990s as the Cold War came to its end.

4.2 The Iranian Revolution and the two Gulf Wars

The Iranian Revolution of 1979 transformed the regional and international scene. The dramatic overthrow of the monarchy was achieved through popular revolution, not a military coup. There was one special aspect, however. The Revolution displaced a seemingly powerful and despotic state, in the name of religion. In fact the Iranian Revolution had much more complex causes and was effected by a coalition of social forces, only a part of which was religious. But it occurred under clerical leadership and culminated in clerical hegemony under the Islamic Republic. This development gave a boost to Islamists everywhere. It reoriented the thinking of many nationalists and leftists into believing that the only impetus that would move the 'masses' of nationalist and leftist mythology, was 'authenticity', and that meant religion. The new Islamic Republic transformed the regional, Islamic and international alignments.

Before proceeding further in the discussion of Iran I should explain the difference between Sunni Islam and Shi'i Islam. The split refers to disputes in the early years of Islam, in the seventh century, over the legitimate succession to the Prophet Muhammad. The Shi'a follow from those who supported the succession of Ali, cousin and son-in-law of the Prophet, and subsequently of his descendants. They formed a community distinct from the 'mainstream' Sunni Muslims, who accepted the Caliphs and Sultans who actually ruled. There are some doctrinal and ritual differences between the two, but their religious and legal practices are, for the most part, similar. The differences between them are mostly attributable to communal and historical antagonisms. A new ruling dynasty, the Safavids, conquered and unified Iran in the fifteenth and early sixteenth centuries, and established Shi'i Islam as the official faith. The majority (around 60 per cent) of the population of Iraq is Shi'a, although the political rulers since independence (at least until the fall of Saddam Hussein in 2003) have always been Sunni. There are considerable Shi'a populations also in Lebanon, Bahrain and Saudi Arabia, in an otherwise predominantly Sunni Middle East.

The Iranian Revolution deprived the Americans of a close and powerful ally in the region, but the US loss was not a Soviet gain. The change gave birth to a new source of anti-American dissidence. The Shah and his policies had been secular, modernizing, pro-American and despotic. The Revolution, which overturned his regime, reversed all these trends except its despotic character. The revolutionaries argued that Western political and cultural dominance was corrupting, invasive and weakening of national and Islamic virtues. They restored national and religious authenticity and the rule of God through the leading cleric, Ayatollah Khomeini.

The Islam of the Iranian Revolution was unmistakably Shi'i Islam, and its ideology in the early days was unmistakably populist, borrowing many terms and policies from the left. It championed the *mustazifin*, the oppressed, against the *mustakbirin*, the oppressors. Although this is Quranic vocabulary, it was also used in the rhetoric of other Third World revolutionaries inspired by Frantz Fanon and Che Guevara. As such it posed a powerful challenge to Saudi Islam, which is militantly Sunni and regards the Shi'a as heretics. Saudi Islam is also conservative, authoritarian, hierarchical and pro-American. These two camps competed for the allegiance of Islamic groups and movements in the region, many of which were ambivalent about the new developments. Iran had the glamour of popular revolution and a reputation for what was perceived as a spectacular revolt against the West. Yet it was

Sunni Islam
Sunni Islam is mainstream Islam, which has accepted the actual succession of Caliphs after the Prophet; they are the majority of the Muslim community.

Shi'i Islam
Shi'i Islam has contested the succession, insisting that the legitimate heir to the Prophet should have been Ali, his cousin and son-in-law, to be succeeded, in turn, by his descendants, being in the line of the Prophet and inheriting his charisma.

The Iranian Revolution: demonstrators burn the US flag on top of the US Embassy in Teheran, 9 November 1979

Shi'i Islam, which jarred with the militant Sunnism of the Muslim Brotherhood and most other movements in the region. The Saudis also had the advantage of vast wealth channelled through established institutions and networks, aided by the ranks of the 'pious bourgeoisie', with connections and interests to Saudi institutions and finance. Each camp acquired its clients. The Iranians had their supporters in Shi'a communities, primarily among the Shi'a of Iraq and Lebanon. In Lebanon they established their foremost Arab ally in the form of Hizbullah, a militia which played an important part in the Lebanese civil war (1976–91). Hizbullah also joined the fight against Israel, while later transforming itself into a political party in Lebanon. It acquired allies in the Palestinian struggle in the form of the Jihad organization.

The Iranian Revolution was just one step in the shaping of alignments and ideas in the region. The Iran–Iraq war of 1980–88, the first Gulf War, was also crucial. The Iraqi Ba'thist regime, one of the bloodiest and most tyrannical in the region, had much to fear from the Iranian Revolution. The majority of the Iraqi population is Shi'a, and the regime is narrowly based on the minority Arab Sunni sectors. (The Kurds, mostly Sunni but not Arab, constituting about one-fifth of the population, were another oppressed and dissident minority.) The appeal of the Islamic Republic to the Iraqi Shi'a was a threat to the regime. In this respect, the interests of this regime coincided with US interests in overthrowing or at least weakening the Islamic Republic. Until then, Iraq had been closer to the Soviets who supplied most of its weaponry. The war with Iran led to a reorientation towards the USA. Iraq's attack on Iran in 1980 was predicated on the expectation of post-revolutionary military weakness caused by purges and defections in the military, as well as the interruption of US military supplies and spare parts. The attack was robustly repulsed. Over the course of the war, the Iraqi forces could only maintain advantage with US and sometimes Soviet help. Both superpowers had reason to fear an Iranian victory. In the end the US navy intervened openly in Gulf waters against the Iranians. In the face of such determined US force, and after the Iraqi regime resorted to the use of chemical weapons against the military and civilians (and against its own Kurdish citizens), Khomeini reluctantly ended the war in 1988.

Question

What were the effects of this war on regional and Islamic alignments?

Saudi Arabia and the Gulf states, as we have seen, had every reason to fear Iran and its revolution. They firmly supported Iraq in the war, and provided hefty financial aid. All Arab states except Syria sided with Iraq, under the rhetoric of pan-Arab solidarity. The Syrian regime, still close to the Soviet Union, its main arms and credits supplier, was a strong antagonist of its fellow Ba'thist neighbour, and sided firmly with Iran. Syria was also the major player and arbiter in the Lebanese civil war (1976–91), and facilitated Iranian access to that country to supply and organize the Hizbullah forces. Contingents of Iranian Pasdaran, revolutionary guards, were stationed in the Beqa' valley, one of the main centres of Lebanese Shi'ism. Sympathy and support for Iran in that war came mainly from Shi'a quarters, but also from some Arab intellectuals and activists inspired by the populist and anti-imperialist stances of the Islamic Republic. The Muslim Brotherhood and other Sunni Islamists continued, for the most part, to be tributaries of the Saudis, and consequently were guarded about Iran. Their ideological credit was enhanced at the very time of the Iranian challenge by the Jihad against the Soviets in Afghanistan. Thus you can see that what are often presented from the outside as exemplars of a unitary, anti-Western Islam – namely Iran and Saudi Arabia – have been involved in major political, ideological and geostrategic confrontations with one another across the region.

4.3   The Afghan War and the Islamic Jihad

Soviet forces entered Afghanistan in 1979 to shore up the communist regime there under threat from multiple insurrections, many in the name of Islamic Jihad against the infidels. The USA supplied these mujahidin (the term they applied to themselves, with connotations of fighters for the faith) with funds, arms and training, mostly channelled through Pakistan, but with the active support of Saudi Arabia and Gulf allies. The Saudis and Pakistanis set up organizations and channels for the recruitment of volunteers to wage the Jihad (holy war) in support of the Afghani factions against the communist regime and the Soviets. This met with great success. Arab Islamists from all over the region, but particularly from Saudi Arabia, the Gulf, Egypt and North Africa, volunteered in large numbers. Peshawar, a border city in Pakistan, became a base for the Arab mujahidin.

These events had far-reaching consequences for subsequent movements and events in the region. First, the Jihad in Afghanistan gave Saudi Islam a badly needed legitimacy in terms of international activism, to counter Iranian revolutionary appeal. The conservative and repressive Wahhabi Islam (the puritanical and disciplinarian creed of the Saudis) now had an activist, Jihadist arm. It recruited radical militants to its cause. Osama Bin Laden came to active prominence at this time, as the leading Saudi link in the operation of recruitment, finance and military operations. In 1989, the Soviet forces withdrew from Afghanistan and two years later, in December 1991, the Soviet regime itself collapsed. The Americans lost interest and left Afghanistan to warring mujahidin factions which inflicted further havoc and destruction on the country. This process culminated in the rise of the Taliban, creations of Pakistani Islamic schools, trained and supplied by Pakistani military intelligence and supported by the Saudis, with affiliations to some of the Pushtun tribal forces in the country. The Taliban then proceeded to defeat rival factions and impose their notorious regime. Most of the Arab mujahidin were now redundant, but some remained in Peshawar or elsewhere in the region. Most, however, returned to their own countries where their ideology and military training were employed in armed action. Their most spectacular activities were in the Algerian civil war starting in 1992. They were also prominent in Egypt in the violent actions against opponents, politicians and tourists, until stopped in the later 1990s by intense government repression. Bin Laden and his organization were also products of that war, but soon their attentions turned to the Saudis who found themselves involved in the second Gulf War of 1991.

Wahhabi Islam
Muhammad ibn 'Abd al-Wahhab (born 1703) was a preacher who taught that the Quran and the Prophet were the only valid religious authorities. His cause was adopted by Saudi tribal principality in 1745. This alliance was later to become the basis of the state of Saudi Arabia in the 1920s.

4.4   The second Gulf War

Saddam Hussein's invasion of Kuwait in August 1990 was greeted with great joy by the Arab 'street'. To the disaffected, Kuwait typified all that was wrong with the Gulf states – rich, small enclaves ruled by autocratic tribal dynasties, endowed with huge wealth, which many thought should rightfully be invested in the development and strength of the Arab nation. Saddam became a hero, vowing to proceed from Kuwait to Jerusalem, to regain the lost Palestine for the Arabs. His regime had been largely secular and had persecuted the Islamists, not to mention all other opponents. Saddam adopted popular religious symbols and slogans, declaring himself a descendant from the Prophet and adding the words '*Allahu Akbar*', God is the Almighty, to the Iraqi flag. He was a military threat beyond Kuwait's borders to Saudi Arabia. The Saudis welcomed US and allied forces, and it was from Saudi lands that the attack on the Iraqi forces proceeded. In 1991, Iraq's forces were defeated and expelled from Kuwait.

These events divided Islamists in the region. Many of them were tributaries of the Saudis, but nevertheless took a pro-Saddam stance, condemning their paymasters as stooges of US imperialism. The USA was denounced as the enemy of Islam and the Arabs, and the patron of Israel. Significantly, the erstwhile Saudi commander of the Arab mujahidin forces in Afghanistan, Osama Bin Laden, turned against the rulers of his country. The Saudi rulers' control over the rigour of Wahhabi Islam was broken: the dissidents turned that rigour against them. They denounced the presence of infidels and enemies of Islam on the sacred soil of Arabia. Scriptures, traditions and sacred authorities were cited against the Saudi rulers and their hosting of US forces, and Jihad was declared against them. These calls found a ready response amongst Islamists, including many sectors of Saudi society and their ulama. They were already disenchanted with the high living and Western lifestyles of their rulers. In the 1970s and 1980s these religious elements had been bought off by generous funding of their institutions, schools and charities, and the well-paid jobs their graduates could take in these spheres. The decline of oil revenues and the rapid growth of the Saudi population made this generous funding more difficult. The large number of graduates from religious seminaries faced unemployment and they comprised the main cadres for religious and political dissidence and were receptive to Bin Laden's mission. This setting became the source of supply of recruits for the suicide attacks of 11 September 2001 in the USA.

Ulama
Ulama is the collective term for the scholars or learned men of Islam.

We have seen that international relations played an important part in shaping the region's politics. It led and continues to mould national and international configurations and the networks that link them. However, Islamic movements are, for the most part, creatures of the societies and politics of the particular nation states, and their fates are shaped within them. They look at regional and international issues through the politics of their governments. The Egyptian Muslim Brotherhood, for instance, while concerned about international patterns of Western dominance, and passionate in the cause of the Palestinians and their antagonism to Israel, nevertheless pursues these issues alongside domestic concerns in relation to Egyptian government and politics. Its policies and programmes relate to issues of the Islamization of law and education in Egypt, and alignments with politicians, clerics and institutions in the country. Egyptian radical Islamists supplied cadres for the Afghan Jihad, and received some of them back in Egypt, but the two spheres remain separate. Ayman al-Zawahiri was a leader of the Jihad movement in Egypt. In Afghanistan he became a prominent leader of the Arab mujahidin and second in command to Bin Laden. At the same time he lost most of his connections and influence over the radical movements in Egypt itself.

By the turn of the twenty-first century, most Islamists had given up on the installation of an Islamic state by force or revolution. Faced with repression and persecution by authoritarian governments, they have increasingly opted for campaigns for democracy and political participation. The Egyptian Muslim Brotherhood, for instance, is now calling for political liberalization and pluralism, apparently accepting other, non-Islamic political parties and forces as legitimate. The Turkish Islamic parties have long participated in elections and entered into coalition governments with other parties. They base their tactics on political realism rather than on ideological affinity. Their opponents, however, have questioned their democratic credentials, accusing them of using democracy to gain power, in order then to subvert that democracy. The fact of the matter is that although many people in the region now speak the language of democracy, including presidents, kings and shaykhs, there are few democrats in action.

Activity 8.2

Having read this section, reconsider one of the main points made in Chapter 6. There, Robert Garson argued that culture served as a primary key for understanding the policies and rhetoric of states and their governments. How does this study of the Islamic politics in the Middle East challenge that contention?

5 Politics, law and rights

As you have seen, some commentators seek to present the Islamic world as a unified (anti-Western) whole. Yet in the preceding section I have shown that divisions within the Islamic world extend to major international confrontations among the states of the Middle East. As I shall show in this section, divisions also exist when we move to the more specific question of the relationship between Islam and individual rights. As we shall see, rights are integral to Islam but are not always in harmony with the kinds of human rights contained in universalist and liberal conceptions. In Islam, as elsewhere, rights are enshrined in law and legal practice, and law and its operation are subject to politics and authority. Yet within Islam there are competing agendas for the nature and place of law in society and these lead to significant differences over the attitude to rights. We saw that the primary demand of the various Islamic movements is the application of the Shari'a.

Shari'a
Shari'a, 'the path', is Muslim religious law.

How does the *Shari'a* relate to positive law as developed in the West?

5.1   The *Shari'a* and the law

The *Shari'a*, in Muslim doctrine, is of divine origin. Theoretically, it is derived from the Quran, the word of God, and Prophetic tradition and example, believed to be inspired or approved by God. In practice most Muslims recognize that this sacred law was developed and elaborated by men practising the discipline of *fiqh* or jurisprudence, which is an elaborate rational methodology of derivation and construction. In effect, this body of law, while in theory derived from sacred sources, is in practice a human construction referring to the sacred sources, which are too scant to encompass the complex range of human affairs. In modern times, the *Shari'a* has become a source of contention for both reformists and radicals. The reformists argue that the sacred law had always been shaped in accordance with the affairs and interests of successive generations of Muslims. It is appropriate, therefore, to follow their example and reshape the law in accordance with modern needs and sensibilities. Their arguments are the most congruent with a doctrine of rights. The radicals reject the historical constructions of the *Shari'a* precisely because they are man-made. They seek to apply the injunctions of the Quran and the Sunna directly to human affairs without the mediation of *fiqh* and its human constructions. Their quest, as a result, tends to be mostly rhetorical, and when practised totally antithetical to any notion of rights.

In the history of Muslim societies and polities, the *Shari'a* was applied primarily in the field of private and family law, and in commercial and contractual transactions. The affairs of state, public law and taxation largely bypassed the *Shari'a* in favour of statutes promulgated by the ruler. Government tribunals also dealt with penal law and 'crimes against the state'. This was partly because the *Shari'a* required high standards of evidence to convict people accused of criminal offences, while the tribunals dispensed with such niceties. In fact, religious courts were reluctant to impose corporal punishments of amputation of limbs, and required strict conditions for such verdicts. This is at variance with the eagerness of modern dictators ruling in the name of Islam to inflict these punishments as a sign of their devotion. The irony is that these punishments are often described in the West as medieval barbarism, when in fact they are much more a product of modern tyrannies.

The Ottoman reforms of the nineteenth and twentieth centuries, noted earlier, and the development of modern nation states after the collapse of the Empire, featured the development of unified codes of law administered by the state. This is in contrast to the historical multiplicity of laws between the *Shari'a*, customary law and royal decrees. The codification of law in modern times, whether the content was drawn from the *Shari'a* or from European models, instituted it as state law, subject to state legislation. This is a radical step, for it took the law out of the hands of the jurists and their schools and put it into institutions of state. It also altered legal and court procedures, in conformity with modern European models. *Shari'a* court procedures empowered the judge to conduct the process single handed, hearing the case of each party, then calling and interrogating witnesses. Oral testimony was privileged over documents and material indicators. The value of the testimony depended on the status of the witness, with Muslim males accorded the highest and with a devalued status for women and non-Muslims. Cases were brought by private parties, with little or no scope for state prosecution, except on matters of public order and state security, which were, in any case, dealt with by police and government tribunals. There was also no provision for lawyers.

These developments in legal institutions and procedures had important implications for regimes of rights. Modern constitutions and legal systems have rested on the notion of common citizenship, with equality before the law. A unified legal system would ensure uniformity of rule and procedure, thus furthering this equality. Women and non-Muslims would be fully enfranchised as equal legal subjects. The one exception was in family law, which continued to be based on the *Shari'a* in most countries (though codified and conducted in accordance with modern procedures for the most part). In this instance women continued to be disadvantaged, as we shall see presently. Modern court procedures, with prosecutors and lawyers, considering a wide range of evidence, provided better conditions for fair trials. It should be kept in mind, however, that authoritarian states throughout the region do not always respect the law and its procedures, but entrust many issues which affect state security and powerful interests to the police and to exceptional, often military, courts with wide powers to dispense with the law.

5.2   The *Shari'a* and rights

There are elements of *Shari'a* provisions which conflict with modern doctrines of rights. This is particularly true in the case of family law. The *Shari'a* conceives of marriage as a contract in which a woman gives her sexual and reproductive functions to a man in return for an initial *mahr* or dower, and the provision of shelter and upkeep. The man has many prerogatives in this relationship, including the right to terminate the contract at a moment of his choosing. He can end the marriage with or without financial compensation and with no obligation for maintenance beyond the first few months after divorce, while the woman is prevented from re-marrying.

A divorced wife has no rights in the matrimonial home. Typically, she would take refuge in her father's household or that of other relations. The husband also has the right to take four wives and as many slave concubines as he can afford (a largely redundant provision because slavery is outlawed in modern contexts). A wife is entitled to her own property, which she can invest or endow. Her movements outside the home and contact with others, however, are subject to the husband's permission, which can make economic activity, including work outside the home, impossible to undertake. Custody of children after divorce or widowhood is, in principle, the prerogative of the father or his family (at least after the early years of maternal care, variously defined).

All these provisions are at variance with modern notions of equal rights. As such, they have been the subject of much conflict and controversy. Modern family laws, derived from the *Shari'a*, have been under pressure to make concessions to contemporary needs and sensibilities. These are resisted, in turn, by patriarchal conservatives who insist on the traditional provisions, and by Islamists seeking religious rule and legal authenticity. Liberals, including religious reformers, argue that these provisions were appropriate in the historical contexts of the *Shari'a*. They insist that successive generations of Muslims have had to adapt the rules to new circumstances, and that modern conditions demand radical reforms. The conservatives and Islamists insist that these are God-given rules for all time.

These conflicting views on the place of *Shari'a* surfaced in most Muslim states. In Egypt, for instance, pressures from liberals and feminists, particularly from elite women, have led to measures of liberalization, in turn vociferously resisted by the Islamists. In 1979, President Sadat promulgated a family code which gave women more rights in marriage and divorce. It limited the husband's right to unilateral divorce, and empowered a first wife to demand divorce upon her husband's second marriage. It also gave divorced wives a share of the matrimonial home. These reforms became known as 'Jihan's law' after the president's wife, believed to have been behind the initiative. They were widely denounced by Islamists as an oppression of the man's rights, as given by divine law. Agitation against these laws after Sadat's assassination in 1981 culminated in a challenge in the Supreme Constitutional Court in 1985 which ruled that the law was unconstitutional because it was promulgated by presidential decree and not ratified by parliament. Soon after, the Egyptian parliament passed similar but watered down provisions. Finally, in 2000, new measures were enacted, allowing a wife the right to demand divorce, exploiting an obscure *Shari'a* provision called *khul'*. The condition for this procedure, however, is that the wife renounces any financial claim on the husband and any entitlement to the matrimonial home. This step has also led to controversy and denunciation by the Islamists, and the debate still continues.

In Iran, before the Revolution of 1979, reforms of family law were introduced by the Shah's regime. They gave the wife more rights and powers in marriage, divorce, custody, and the matrimonial home. After the Revolution, Iran's leader, Ayatollah Khomeini, nullified the reforms. He proclaimed that divorces obtained under its provision were null and void, and parties to such divorces who subsequently remarried to be adulterers (though, fortunately for them, he did not act on that ruling). The Revolution, however, contained many populist and radical components, including a wide range of women's groups. 'Islamic feminism' is one element, often discordant, in current Islamic agitations and it was well represented among elite women in Islamic Iran, including Khomeini's own daughter and others in revolutionary families. Islamic feminists argued that Islam was a liberating force, favourable to women's participation in public life, and empowering women within the family. It banished Western capitalist exploitation, which made women into passive sex objects, and instead emphasized their family and public roles. They cited sacred texts and precedents to reinforce their interpretation. Indeed, right from the beginning, women were enfranchised as voters and candidates for a restricted range of public offices (they cannot be president, or, at first, judges, though the latter is in dispute and subject to change at present). At the same time, they had to be veiled when they appeared in public. The wearing of the *hejab* became compulsory by law and was fiercely enforced. Women's public rights contrasted with their subordination within the family, a common feature of modern Islamic polities.

Women's public presence and voice in Iran, though subordinated and veiled, is able to exert pressure in favour of reform of family law and practice. Their successes owe much to the exigencies of modern society. Crucially, the Iranian economy requires the participation of female labour. Efforts in the early days of the Islamic Republic to confine women to the domestic sphere were unrealistic, especially after the start of the Iran–Iraq war (1980–88) which sent large numbers of young men to the front. During the 1980s and 1990s a number of reforms alleviated the disabilities of women. For instance, many of the measures regarding divorce and property were incorporated into the standard marriage contract. Formally, this in not in breach of *Shari'a* rules, because it did not alter the law but allowed the parties to stipulate conditions for the marriage, which is allowed in some legal schools. Subsequent laws enacted by parliament granted a wife who had been divorced not through her own fault the right to claim 'wages' for the housework she performed during the marriage. These reforms, however, should not obscure the fact of the continuing and considerable disadvantages suffered by Iranian women, from the imposition of the *hejab* to subordination to the husband's rights within the family, which include unilateral divorce, polygamy and rights to custody of children.

It should be noted that family law is one of the few areas of modern life in which the *Shari'a* has definite rules. The bulk of legislation under the Islamic Republic has been concerned with aspects of administration and social and economic policy which are irrelevant to the *Shari'a*, a fact which prompted one divine to proclaim that all legislation enacted by the Islamic Republic is by definition Islamic. In relation to a modern society, the application of the *Shari'a* is indeterminate and, as such, an area of contestation. The advocates of Islamization put forward its few specific aspects: family law, penal exactions (always controversial), banning alcohol and gambling, and prohibiting dealing in interest (which entails disguising it). Their adoption became markers of Islamic authenticity.

The diversity of Islamic law is also borne out in a comparison of the rules regarding family and women in Iran and Saudi Arabia. The latter maintains a much stricter regime regarding female visibility in public life. Saudi Arabia is a dynastic monarchy with no parliamentary system, so the question of voting does not arise. Women are strictly excluded from public office. They are not allowed to drive a car. They cannot travel without being accompanied by a male relative. They are subject to the marriage and divorce rules, noted above. Husbands can also restrict the movements of their wives. Once again the application of *Shari'a* is determined by local political and economic conditions.

5.3   The politics of rights

Rights are inextricably linked with law and religion in many Islamic societies. Indeed, their relation to each other is central to their politics. The Egyptian example is instructive. Egypt's legal system developed from the nineteenth century along the lines of modern European models both in content and procedure. Yet, first in 1971, then in 1980, President Sadat, in an effort to establish religious legitimacy against Islamist challenges, wrote amendments into the constitution declaring that the *Shari'a* is the principal source of legislation in Egypt. These changes were clearly at variance with the positive, secular nature of Egyptian law. The situation became confused. It still left the positive law intact, and courts had to rule in accordance with the actual law, which was not *Shari'a*. At the same time it empowered Islamic agitation in favour of Islamizing law through the parliamentary process. The government, which controlled parliament (through creative electoral procedures), stalled without openly opposing the project. It recognized that actual enactment of *Shari'a* provisions would be disruptive to social and economic arrangements, and that the application of the penal measures of amputations and stoning would offend international public opinion, as well as local sensibilities.

Islamist lawyers and judges, however, endeavoured to introduce Islamic principles and measures into gaps in Egyptian law. The most notorious case was in the 1990s and it concerned Nasr Hamid Abu Zayd, a critical theologian and professor at Cairo University. In his writings he argued that the Quran had to be understood in its historical perspective and was critical of literal interpretations. Like many Christian commentators on the Bible, he considered many of the stories of the Quran to be allegorical, and many of the injunctions to be specific to the time and place of revelation. Islamist opponents contended that Abu Zayd's pronouncements were apostasy because he had questioned the literal and eternal truth of the word of God. There is no charge of apostasy in Egyptian law (though in the *Shari'a* it is a capital offence), so Islamist lawyers resorted to personal status law that forbids the marriage of a Muslim woman to a non-Muslim. They brought a case petitioning the court to nullify the marriage of Abu Zayd to his Muslim wife. After a prolonged legal battle in the courts, the Islamist lawyers succeeded in getting a ruling from a sympathetic judge who granted the petition on the grounds that Abu Zayd was clearly an apostate for denying the truth of revelation. This verdict made Abu Zayd a target for any militant who took upon himself the enforcement of the Islamic rule that an apostate must be killed. So Abu Zayd, with his wife, took refuge in a European university, where they remain.

More spectacular applications of the *Shari'a* were introduced in some countries after military *coup d'états*, in an effort by new dictators to shore up their legitimacy by appeal to Islamic authenticity. Once again, ostensibly religious changes had essentially political motives. The overt application of the holy law, especially with public displays of Quranic punishments, also served to intimidate dissidents and opponents. Two primary examples in this category are Pakistan under the military dictatorship of Zia-ul-Haq (1977–88) and the Sudan under Nimeyri (Islamic phase 1977–85), and again under the present military Islamic regime which started with a coup in 1988.

In Pakistan the Islamist parties had only marginal leverage in elections, and concentrated their efforts in the religious schools and mosques of particular regions. Zia overturned the elected government and eventually hanged the popular Prime Minister, Zulfiqar Ali Bhutto. He proceeded to institute the *Shari'a* as the law of the country, which, as we have seen, has little significance in the main affairs of a modern country. But it does have a definite and unique impact on social disciplines of family and morality, most demonstrably in the notorious corporal punishments of beheadings, amputations, stoning and flogging. Traditionally, jurists and judges had been reserved about the application of these punishments and imposed strict conditions on their use. Modern dictators had no such compunction. They used the public display of these punishments as a means of demonstrating their Islamicity and at the same time intimidating a largely unsympathetic population.

After Zia's assassination, Pakistan went through a period of political uncertainty, with restorations and suspensions of democracy. Some successor governments tried discreetly to modify the rule of the *Shari'a* but never abolished it for fear of Islamist reactions. One ruler, Nawaz Sharif, reintroduced the rigours of the *Shari'a* to buttress his Islamic credentials during corruption scandals. The most notable and publicized victims of the rule of the *Shari'a* in recent years have been women accused of adultery and subject to death by stoning. Many of these women had been raped and become pregnant. The male perpetrator(s) can deny the offence, but the woman's pregnancy is taken as evidence of her guilt. These cases are currently subject to legal and political campaigns for justice within Pakistan and from international human rights quarters. The campaigns underscore that contestations about practices that are ostensibly cultural come from within as well as outside states.

Nimeyri's and al-Bashir's rule in the Sudan have similar features, complicated by the constant war the government is fighting in the south of the country against separatists who are predominantly Christian and animist. Islamicity, then, becomes an important counter to non-Muslim challenges. The application of the *Shari'a* is especially contentious with non-Muslim subjects.

The application of the *Shari'a*, and its implications for rights regimes, is political. Rulers who fear a deficit of legitimacy use Islamic virtues to remedy this, and the shelter of Islam also serves as a means of social control and intimidation. Conservative patriarchs use it to seek a restoration of hierarchy and authority in the application of the holy law. Cultural nationalists use it to affirm their roots in history and to defend people against imported imperialist products. These positions, however, are subject to challenges, not only from secularists but also from liberal Muslims. We now turn to these contestations and their link to the wider debates on human rights.

6   Debates over Islam and human rights

There are many sides to this debate. First, there is the straightforward (and honest) rejection of the notion of human rights on the part of Islamic conservatives who argue that the notion is of Western provenance, alien or even hostile to Islam. Equally, there are straight secularist positions, which argue that human rights must be sustained regardless of religious beliefs and commitments. Before we explore these further, let me make an important, perhaps obvious, point: not all secular ideologies respect human rights. The worst fascist and authoritarian regimes of the twentieth century have been secular, and in the case of Stalinism militantly so. In the Middle East, the self-declared secularism of the Kemalist Turkish Republic has included periods of intense repression and instances of gross violation of human rights. Equally the secularizing nationalist regimes of Nasir in Egypt and the Ba'th parties in Iraq and Syria have been among the most repressive and bloody of the twentieth century. So secularism does not guarantee respect for human rights. Many Muslims are aware of this. It may be argued, however, that while secularism is no guarantee of respect for human rights it constitutes a necessary condition for them. This view is widely contested by Muslim liberals, as well as by independent commentators. Not all Muslims who espouse human rights, however, are liberal. Islamic apologists who are not liberal seek to appropriate the notion of human rights without reforming the elements of their violation in religious law.

The position of Islamic apologists is best illustrated in the example of the 'Universal Islamic Declaration of Human Rights', issued by the Islamic Council in 1981, intended by leaders and ulama as a counter to the United Nations Universal Declaration. It starts with the assertion that Islam was the first to promulgate a universal doctrine of human rights fourteen centuries ago (a common discursive strategy whenever a dominant idea comes from elsewhere and has to be accommodated, such as 'democracy'). It then proceeds to specify these rights, but always qualified as 'within the Law', meaning the *Shari'a*. Article 1 states that human life is sacred and inviolable and that 'no one shall be exposed to injury or death except under the authority of the Law' – a typical fudge on the question of Quranic penal prescriptions. Freedom of worship is assured for minorities, but no mention is made of the *Shari'a* prescription of death for a Muslim apostate. On the question of women and the family, the Declaration reproduces the conventional *Shari'a* positions but in the guise of rights language such as 'every spouse is entitled to such rights and privileges and carries such obligations as are stipulated by Law'. Like many Islamic apologias it presents the inequalities in rights between men and women as a reflection of God's natural order. Overall, the Declaration insists that duties and obligations to God have priority over rights. This is typical of many proclamations claiming the priority and superiority of Islam in the specification and protection of human rights. It reproduces Islamic moral principles and rules in rights language, but glosses over all the internal incompatibilities. Western statements of rights are often denounced as permissive license, while the moral restrictions of religion are presented as a virtue.

Islamic liberals normally start from a position of full support for a universal understanding of human rights then proceed to readings and interpretations of sacred sources to show their compatibility with their position. Typically, they make a distinction between religion as revelation and religious knowledge and religious law as human extrapolations, products of time and place. Liberals reject the idea of an unalterable, historic jurisprudence which has produced the *Shari'a* as we know it, in favour of *ijtihad*, a conscientious effort to derive rules and principles from novel readings of the sources. These efforts, however, come up against explicit statements and injunctions in the Quran which clearly contradict their notions of rights. For example, the penal specifications of executions and amputations are clearly stated in the holy book, as are the justifications for inequality between men and women. There are, of course, contradictory and ambiguous statements in different parts of the book, and interpretations can draw on these uncertainties for favourable conclusions. But still there is a bedrock of text which does not permit such latitude. A typical discursive strategy of the liberals is to argue for the historicity of the Quran. God spoke to people in terms that they could understand, and rules that were appropriate for the seventh century are not appropriate now. They salvage the theology by applying the spirit and the intent of the holy sources to contemporary concerns. For example, they maintain that rules regarding women and the family were highly progressive at the time of the Prophet. They were steps towards emancipation and equality of women. We must now follow in that spirit, it is argued, and fully establish that equality. Abu Zayd (discussed above) represents this trend of Islamic liberal intellectuals in Egypt, Iran and elsewhere in the Muslim world engaged in a campaign to reform religion in the direction of democracy, tolerance and human rights.

A prominent advocate of human rights in Islam is the Sudanese academic and activist, Abdullahi An-Na'im. Like Abu Zayd of Egypt, An-Na'im works in exile in the USA and Europe. His friend and mentor, Mahmoud Muhammad Taha, was hanged by President Nimeyri in the Sudan in 1985 for apostasy. Taha and An-Na'im adopt a novel approach to the Quran. They argue that the holy book is divided into two parts, the early Meccan and the later Medinan. The first, in the period when Muhammad proclaimed his Prophethood, is concerned with the moral and divine foundations of the faith, and as such should have priority over the later chapters, which were concerned with the practical and political issues of the day. Their application was historical, not contemporary. Many of the rules and injunctions that pose a problem for the Islamic espousal of human rights occur in the Medinan verses. For orthodox (and most) Muslims who believe the Quran to be the direct word of God and as such eternally valid, this is indeed heresy.

An-Na'im illustrates the dilemma of the liberal Muslim who wants to combine personal faith and cultural authenticity with an active pursuit of democracy and human rights, and is then faced by the hostility of vociferous voices from his fellow Muslims. He justifies his adherence to the *Shari'a* despite these problems, in the following terms:

I find the first option [abandonment of the *shari'a*] objectionable as a matter of principle and unlikely to be realistically available for much longer in practice. It is objectionable as a matter of principle because it violates the religious obligation of Muslims to conduct every aspect of their public as well as private lives in accordance with the precepts of Islam. Moreover, in view of the mounting Islamic resurgence [in the 1980s – the book was published in 1990], this option is unlikely to continue to be available for much longer in practice. I also find the second option [of full application of the historic *shari'a*] morally repugnant and politically untenable. It is morally repugnant, in my view, to subject women and non-Muslims to the indignities and humiliations of the application of *shari'a* today. ...given the concrete realities of the modern nation-state and present international order, these aspects of the public law of the *shari'a* are no longer politically tenable.

(An-Na'im, 1990, pp.58–9)

Personal faith and cultural authenticity make the *Shari'a* essential in the life of Muslims, yet the historical *Shari'a* includes elements repugnant to a liberal. So the liberal proceeds to fashion a favourable version of the *Shari'a* in terms that are objectionable to many of his fellow religionists.

Many Muslim liberals, including An-Na'im, believe that the indifference if not hostility of many Muslims to universal notions of human rights is, at least in part, the result of their Western provenance. They are seen as a doctrine pushed by the West and imposed on others. They are especially cynical when they recall the poor human rights record of Western powers in their colonies and client states. This view rests on a totalization and unification of 'the West' as one agency and is oblivious to the divisions and conflicts between its different components and parties. Authoritarian governments denounce human rights in similar terms, as hypocritical imposition of Western imperialist values against authentic native principles, such as the slogan of 'Asian values' advanced by the Malaysian premier, Mahathir Mohamad (discussed in Chapter 9). So, the project for the Islamic liberals becomes one of showing how human rights are compatible and even intrinsic to Islam. As a political strategy, however, this approach is of doubtful merit.

The fact of the matter is that the great majority of Muslims are indifferent to questions of human rights until aspects of them touch them directly. It is something of a contrivance to show that human rights, at least in the 'Western' sense, are compatible with Islam. At the time of writing, government and Islamic opposition in Egypt converge on the suppression of rights of association and expression. The Muslim Brotherhood advocates democracy and rights but belies this advocacy in its actions. Enforced morality in public life and censorship by government and religious authority are now common. In addition to repressing dissent, the police have targeted homosexuals in a campaign widely supported by both Islamists and nationalists. They have been helped by human rights associations, which have shied away from the issue, some even declaring that homosexual rights are outside the scope of human rights. Thus the impact of liberal readings of Islam is limited in this situation.

The current situation in Iran, on the other hand, offers a different prospect. The Islamic government more than twenty years after the Revolution has spent its revolutionary and Islamic charisma. An increasingly young population, which did not experience the Revolution or the ancient regime, is alienated from a ruling clique perceived to be corrupt, hypocritical and incompetent. And that clique rules in the name of Islamic authority. Large sectors of the Iranian population, especially women and the young, are frustrated and discontented with the moral rigour and social restrictions of the regime, especially in the context of worsening economic hardships. The more educated are receptive to doctrines of human rights, the rule of law and civil society, despite the opposition of the ruling mullahs. Their receptiveness is nothing to do with the Islamicity of the doctrine of rights. It is the consequence of changing social developments.

7   Conclusion

Respect for human rights is tied to democracy and the rule of law. In the Middle East and most of the Muslim world these commodities are in short supply. Repressive and corrupt regimes are common. Islamic political advocacy, whether in government or opposition, is often no better than the regimes. In countries such as Egypt, freedom of expression and association, as well as women's rights, suffer from assaults by both a repressive regime and Islamic forces imposing morality and religious observance. In Iran a vigorous opposition, aided by a limited measure of political representation, has challenged an authoritarian regime imposing considerable restrictions on the liberties of its citizens and especially its women in the name of religious righteousness.

The end of the Cold War may have generated a sense of celebration in the West. There were triumphal declarations of confidence in the future of liberal democracy and market capitalism expressed in Fukuyama's thesis of the 'end of history' (see Chapter 3). However, it did not ring in the changes in the Middle East. The USA, with its unrivalled power, continued to shore up authoritarian and corrupt regimes, such as Saudi Arabia and Egypt. The shock of 11 September 2001 may have forced some rethinking of these commitments. Certainly the war against Iraq in 2003 that toppled Saddam's rule may have been an initial step in such an evaluation (for one reading of the thinking behind this war, see Chapter 5). But in the end it is national and political interests that continue to drive foreign policy in the Middle East, not a preoccupation with human rights. It is the unfriendly regimes – Iraq and Iran – that are opposed.

Many people in the Middle East now speak the language of democracy and rights, including presidents and kings, as well as many Islamists. Yet their 'democracy' is always heavily qualified, and the language of cultural difference and authenticity often used to subvert the common understanding of democracy, liberty and rights. We saw this sleight in the example of the Universal Islamic Declaration of Human Rights. In practice, it is not ideological or religious commitment to liberties and rights that makes a difference, but actual political processes and the realization of sections of the population of the relevance of these issues to their own lives and interests. Arguments about Islam and human rights may be interesting from an intellectual or doctrinal point of view, but they do not convert people to the cause of human rights and democracy. It is only by making these issues of relevance to people's lives and interests, that they will take a firm place in the consciousness and agendas of the region.

Further reading

For a comprehensive, scholarly discussion of political Islam based on detailed knowledge and research, see Kepel, G. (2003) *Jihad: The Trail of Political Islam*, London, I.B. Tauris.

The foreign policies of the Middle Eastern states and the politics of the region in relation to wider currents of international politics are surveyed in Hinnebusch, R. and Ehteshami, A. (eds) (2002) *The Foreign Policies of Middle East States*, Boulder, Col., Lynne Rienner.

The approach taken towards the study of Middle Eastern societies in this chapter is set out by the present author in more detail in Zubaida, S. (1993) *Islam, the People and the State*, London, I.B. Tauris. And for a more detailed discussion of the issues surrounding rights and democracy, law and politics, see Zubaida, S. (2003) *Law and Power in Islam*, London, I.B. Tauris.

Chapter 9 Culture, rights and justice in a globalizing world

Jef Huysmans

1   Introduction

In Chapter 7 Raia Prokhovnik observed that discussions about rights, ranging from the right of states to intervene in another state to the right to be protected against persecution by one's own state, have taken on a global dimension in the twentieth century. Political struggles for and against the global propagation of rights will most likely continue to retain a prominent place in global politics. In other words, they will play a role in the formation and transformation of global order in the twenty-first century.

In Chapter 6 Bob Garson introduced another important development in contemporary international relations: the globalization of culture. He asked whether the globalization of culture will lead to a common global culture or to global conflict between civilizations. Contemporary international relations comprise indications supporting both developments. The tension between these two developments is, and most likely will remain for some time, another significant factor shaping global international politics (see also Chapter 3).

One of the political issues around which these two developments – globalization of rights and globalization of culture – meet is the question whether human rights are truly universal. On the one hand, the Universal Declaration of Human Rights is proof that they are indeed (almost) globally accepted. On the other hand, the universal scope of human rights remains contested. One of the issues of debate is that human rights represent a particular cultural tradition. According to the latter view, they are very much an outcome of European and North American historical struggles. They favour individual rights above social or group rights, for example. They also propagate a secularized culture – which is nevertheless not necessarily incompatible with religious traditions (see Chapter 8). In this interpretation human rights are not a universal good but propagate, or even impose, a particular cultural tradition.

In Chapter 8 Sami Zubaida discussed the tension between rights and culture. He focused on the interplay between culture, religion, international rights and politics in the Middle East. I shall continue his discussion of the relation between culture and rights. But instead of focusing on a particular geographical area and cultural location, I shall deal more explicitly with its global dimensions. The lead question of the chapter is: 'How do global rights relate to local or regional cultural traditions?' I shall discuss various political aspects of the tension between rights and culture in the context of the global propagation of sets of rights. More specifically, I shall develop a few instruments for critically engaging in political and academic debates about the tension between rights and culture in a globalizing world.

The discussion is organized around four puzzles:

1   How are rights cultural?

2   How serious a stake is culture in human rights debates?

3   How are rights powerful?

4   Are cultures homogenous or internally contested blocs of values and meanings?

By working through these four questions, I shall also develop a number of insights into one of the interesting political tensions that shape the contemporary transformation of global (and local) order.

2   Culture, rights and globalization

In this section I develop the idea that a global propagation of rights is a cultural process. More specifically, I make three points:

■   The global propagation of sets of rights is part of cultural globalization.

■   Globally institutionalized rights are cultural because they express particular values.

■   Global rights do not only express particular values but also support the development of a rights culture.

2.1   Cultural globalization

In Chapter 6, Section 5 it was argued that, with economic globalization, Western lifestyles and consumption preferences are spreading across the world. One of the popular versions of this cultural fall-out of economic globalization is 'McDonaldization' and 'CocaCola-ization' of the world. These concepts suggest that economic globalization produces *a global homogenous consumer culture* in which Western models increasingly displace alternative cultural traditions.

But this is only one way of understanding cultural globalization. As Jocelyne Cesari rightly remarks:

> [Cultural] homogenization contains several aspects. The propagation of lifestyles, clothing, music, and consumer products from the West is the most visible and striking. But aside from the McDonald's and Coca Cola effects, uniformization also progresses ... through the propagation of a set of norms and values such as human rights, democracy, market economy, and protection of the environment, which are imposed in all corners of the earth.

(Cesari, 2002, p.5)

The latter aspect – that is, *the global propagation of sets of norms and values* – introduces an important element in the discussion of cultural globalization. It implies that cultural globalization cannot be reduced to consumption patterns and lifestyles. But more importantly, it indicates that cultural globalization cannot be reduced to a side effect of economic globalization. It is a development in its own right that is (partly) independent of economic processes. The Universal Declaration of Human Rights, for example, has to be understood against the background of the catastrophic experience of totalitarianism in the first half of the twentieth century in Europe (Ignatieff, 2001).

The globalization of rights, especially of human rights but increasingly also of property rights, has provoked a debate about the cultural content of rights. Do they impose Western value systems upon other value systems in the world? As seen in Chapters 3 and 7, it is often argued that universal human rights mainly incorporate Western traditions that prioritize individual freedom rights and individual property rights above family rights, rights of the community and social rights.

The underlying assumption is that global rights have a specific cultural content. They are not natural rights that everyone has by nature. Instead, the debate about rights versus culture assumes that universal rights originate from particular cultural histories that prioritize particular values such as individual freedoms, market interaction, individual property, and so on. By imposing rights globally one can indeed argue that one is not simply favouring particular rights but enforcing a cultural tradition and its values upon other traditions that may not wish to prioritize the right of free speech and movement above equal distribution of wealth.

Rights as expressions of cultural values are the first and most obvious way in which rights relate to culture. However, rights are also cultural in a slightly different – though not unrelated – sense. They express a rights culture.

Rights culture
Rights culture refers to the idea that rights express a particular kind of society in which people relate to each other in a particular way. People define themselves and are defined by others as individual holders of rights and relate to others on the basis of the rights that they hold.

Question

What does it mean to talk of a 'rights culture'?

The concept 'rights culture' refers to the idea that rights systems are a culture in another sense of the word. They do not just express values but they also 'entail certain constructions of self and sociality, and specific modes of agency' (Cowan *et al.*, 2001, pp.11–12). Let us try to unpack this statement.

At the heart of the concept of rights culture is the idea that claiming rights requires a specific way of understanding how one relates to oneself, other people and to the wider community. Individuals are first of all understood as rights holders. They define themselves and are defined by others on the basis of rights they hold. For example, refugees under the Geneva Convention are defined as persons who 'owing to a well-founded fear of being persecuted for reasons of race, religion, nationality, or membership of a particular social group or political opinion' (United Nations, 1951, art. 1) have a right of not being sent back to the country where they were persecuted. This is a 'specific construction of self'. They are defined on the basis of rights they hold and their capacity to claim them. They are not identified on the basis of their skills to play football or to tell fairy-tales.

It is worth noting here that a rights culture in this sense has strong links with the liberal philosophical and political tradition discussed in Chapter 4. There, it was argued that liberalism was an individualistic and universalistic doctrine with a particular concern to uphold individual liberties vis-à-vis the state and with individuals' rights to own property. To a great extent, supporters of a rights culture are operating in a close relationship to the liberal political tradition.

In a rights culture people relate to one another and to the community as a whole on the basis of rights they hold and duties they are expected to deliver. This is a specific construction of sociality, that is, a specific way of relating to other human beings. For example, citizens relate to one another and to the state by exercising their rights to vote and by claiming welfare entitlements. As citizens they do not relate to one another and the state on the grounds of religious beliefs or financial status or by exchanging pints of beer.

In a rights culture one expresses and pursues values and desires in a socially acceptable way through claiming and contesting rights. In that sense rights cultures also imply a particular mode of agency. In a rights culture I would not try to defend freedom of speech on the basis of the argument that I am authorized by God to speak freely. That would be seen as an awkward claim and most likely would not be taken seriously. In other words it is not the accepted mode of agency. I would rather say that I can speak freely because the right to speak freely is written into the constitution of my country or into a global convention signed and/or ratified by my country. To be taken seriously in a rights culture one has to talk a particular kind of language.

Let me take up this differentiation between rights and religion to further clarify what is meant by saying that a rights culture is a specific kind of culture. In a rights culture a forest can be protected by delimiting the right of its exploitation and use. For example, a state can declare that the forest is a nature reserve, which entitles the state to prevent unrestricted access. People then have a duty to respect the 'right' of the forest to be left alone. People trespassing can be subjected to particular sanctioning procedures – for example, court procedures.

In Malshegu in Northern Ghana a small forest has been preserved in a different way. Let us follow Katrina Brown's description.

> ... for nearly three centuries, the community of Malshegu in the northern region of Ghana have preserved a small forest they believe houses a local spirit, the *Kpalevorgu* god. Access to and utilisation of plants and other resources in the grove are strictly controlled ... When it was first demarcated, unwritten regulations were put in place by the fetish priest and other village leaders regarding land use in and around the grove, and over time these rules have been amended to ensure their continued relevance and affectiveness. ...
>
> The religious leader, the *Kpalna*, is shown to play an important role in the preservation of Malshegu's sacred grove. This is a result of the complex roles that these figures play, and the linking of the spirit and natural worlds.
>
> (Brown, 1995, pp.220–1)

In the example, relations to the sacred grove are not based on respect for or fear of institutionalized rights and duties but on respect for or fear of a local spirit. In other words, respect for and preservation of the grove does not rely on an institutionalized relation of rights and duties but on a sacral relation – that is, a relation to a spirit. The relation with the spirit, and therefore with the forest, is mediated by a religious figure – the *Kpalna* – rather than by a judge. The *Kpalna*'s power or agency seems to be based on a religious status and the knowledge of rituals. It does not derive from constitutions, conventions or treaties assigning to the religious figure the capacity to uphold rights. This suggests that the preservation of the grove does not depend on a rights culture but on alternative, in this case, sacral constructions of self, sociality and agency.

Activity 9.1

In this section I have argued that the global propagation of rights is an important element of cultural globalization. That means that rights must be cultural. In what two ways is the propagation of rights a cultural process?

---

3   Politics of cultural relativism

Cultural relativism
Cultural relativism is the belief that the world consists of different and incompatible cultures and that global rights are merely the expression of one particular culture and therefore lack universal validity.

If the universal propagation of rights is a cultural process it is not surprising that it is contested on cultural grounds. In Chapter 3 you have come across the idea that rights are universally valid, but also that this notion is hotly debated. On cultural grounds it is particularly challenged by those who hold a position of cultural relativism. Cultural relativism refers to the belief that the world consists of different and incompatible cultures (as does communitarianism, which is discussed in Chapter 7). In the latter view, global rights represent a particular cultural tradition, and therefore they do not have universal validity. In this section I illustrate how cultural relativist arguments have been used and questioned in political debates about human rights. First, I show how cultural relativism relates human rights to questions of cultural identity. Then I illustrate that the cultural argument can also be related to more traditional power political arguments. I conclude with an example of how a counter-argument in support of the universal value of human rights can be constructed. The purpose of this section is to illustrate how contests of the universal value of human rights in a globalizing world involve a variety of political arguments.

3.1   Human rights and cultural relativism

A cultural relativist understanding of the global propagation of rights sees it as a global propagation of one set of values that challenge other entrenched cultural traditions. Arguing for universal respect for rights such as freedom of speech, freedom of organization, patenting of inventions and gender equality in fact represents support for imposing an alien cultural tradition upon another society that may wish to prioritize other values such as respect for family and duty towards the community.

Question

What do you think happens to the debate on human rights in this case?

In a human rights culture the discussion is usually about whether human rights are respected or violated in particular cases. Are prisoners tortured in country X? Does country Y respect the right of free speech? Are people persecuted because of their religion or political opinion in country Z? However, when cultural relativist arguments make their way into this debate the focus shifts from a question of how well universally-valid rights are protected in different places, to the protection of particular cultures against globalizing processes.

An interesting example to illustrate this is the assertion of Asian values in the 1990s. After the end of the Cold War, Western states started asserting more radically than before a respect for human rights and democracy in their foreign policy. For example, the member states of the European Union introduced respect for human rights and the introduction of democracy as a condition of aid policy. Also, international organizations such as the IMF and the World Bank regularly asserted the need of good governance which included references to human rights.

In Asia, Singapore and Malaysia took the lead in opposing Western human rights agendas by affirming Asian values. For example, the *Financial Times* reported in March 1994 that:

> Dr Mahathir Mohamad has asked Malaysians not to accept western-style democracy as it could result in negative effects. The prime minister said such an extreme principle had caused moral decay, homosexual activities, single parents and economic slowdown because of poor work ethics (Voice of Malaysia radio, 29 May 1993). A resurgent Asia is spurning the dogma of western liberalism and forging for itself a new and improved set of political and social beliefs, if we are to believe east Asian leaders such as Dr Mahathir, the Malaysian Prime Minister. Trumpeted across the region as 'The Asian Way', this emerging ideology is loosely based on the teachings of Confucius, who championed family values and respect for authority ... Not all supporters of the Asian way claim that democracy makes you decadent and gay, but they reject many of the western liberal democratic ideas that seemed poised to dominate the world after the collapse of European Communism in the 1980s.

(Mallet, 1994)

The 'Asian Way' thus rests on an explicit distinction between Asian and Western values. They affirm the priority of the nation over the community and of society over the individual. The family is seen as the basis of society and respect for the individual is related to the contributions of the individual to the community. They emphasize the importance of consensus over conflict (Cassen, 1995, p.2). The focus on collective rights, consensus and the family are opposed to Western individualism, to the belief that conflict and competition are progressive forces, and, in more extreme discourses, to Western decadence.

Asian values: the Malaysian Prime Minister Mahathir Mohamad

I do not wish to make a judgement about the validity of opposing individualistic Western cultures to collectivist Asian cultures here. Instead, the key issue I want to focus on, is that the cultural relativist argument changes the debate on human rights. The focus moves from the question of the universal implementation of human rights to the protection of cultural identity. The global propagation of human rights turns from a universal good that should benefit everyone into a problematic cultural strategy that risks undermining a variety of other cultural traditions. By shifting the focus from universal rights to particular cultures, cultural relativism emerges as a political strategy that makes the cosmopolitan project of developing an international community organized around a universal rights culture problematic. (Note that there are close links between this discussion and the discussion in Chapter 3, Section 4 on solidarism and in Chapter 7 on communitarian and cosmopolitan views.)

3.2   From culture to economics and back to human rights

The political affirmation of Asian values is not simply a cultural discourse opposing the globalization of human rights, however. Let us return to another of the statements made by the Malaysian prime minister, Mahathir Mohamad:

> Believe me ... if it was Africa that was rising economically, we would be having a discussion on African values, not Asian values. The West fears that Asian success will lead to Asian self assertion.

> (quoted in Ibison, 1996, p.12)

This is an interesting statement for two reasons. First, it suggests that the fascination with Asian values does not simply originate from within Asia. The discourse on Asian values also results from a Western fascination with Asian values. Second, the quotation suggests that the Malaysian prime minister believes that the West's fascination with Asian values results from a fear of Asia's self-assertion. In his opinion the West fears the economic success of the Asian Tigers and the rise in Asian self-confidence that results from it.

Let us focus on the second point. What does this add to our discussion of cultural relativism so far? It suggests that the issue is not simply Asian cultural identity and the universal validity of human rights but also changing power relations between Western and Asian states. Mahathir Mohamad seems to suggest that what is at stake for the West is that the Asian economies pose a threat to the dominant power position of Western states in the international system. (At least, that is one way of reading his claim that the West fears Asian self-assertion.) This is a realist interpretation which turns the Asian values debate into a story about the international competition for power.

Is that all there is to the Asian values debate? Is the assertion of human rights and of cultural values just a cover for power politics? Let us attempt a slightly more complex interpretation; one which does not subordinate cultural dimensions, and therefore cultural relativist arguments, to power politics but which demonstrates that both are equally important elements of the debate.

In building this alternative reading I want to start from the first element that the quotation from Mahathir Mohamad introduced: the Western fascination with Asian values. The militant cultural discourse on Asian values mirrored to some extent Western cultural explanations of the success of some Asian economies – the Asian Tigers as they were called – in the 1980s and 1990s. Before the Asian financial crisis of 1997–98, the economic success of the Asian Tigers contrasted sharply with the economic sclerosis that struck Europe and the USA. Many Western analysts explained the difference as a result of the economic significance of Asian values.

> Dozens of books were written describing the unstoppable nature of Asia's rise. While Europe was stuck in a sclerotic mire of overgenerous welfare and inflexible labour markets, and America had become chronically dependent on foreign, particularly Japanese, capital to fund its twin budget and trade deficits, Asia was fresh, innovative and increasingly wealthy. And behind this success, indeed the only logical explanation for it, were Asian values. While individual countries differed in their precise application of the model, the broad characteristics were similar.

(Smith, 1998)

In these explanations, challenges to Asian cultural identity directly challenge the economic capacity and thus the global power position of the Asian Tigers. If enforcing the global protection of human rights undermines Asian cultural identity, it weakens one of the key resources of economic success, and thus of the global power position, of these Asian states. (Note that this constructivist interpretation turns some orthodox Marxist accounts on their head. In constructivism, changes in identity in international politics determine economic outcomes. In some orthodox Marxist accounts, cultural politics are the product of underlying economic interests. For constructivists, culture is not simply an ideological justification of economic power but it is also an important source of economic power.)

In this rendering of the Asian values debate, cultural identity is not simply something that is worth fighting for in its own right. It also needs to be protected because it is an important resource in the global economic power struggle. As a result, cultural relativist strategies are more than cultural strategies. They are also strategies in the struggle for economic and political power in the international system. The Asian values debate is thus part of a political contest in which cultural identity, human rights protection and a struggle for economic power are closely tied together. According to this reading it would be a mistake to ignore the contest of cultural identity and human rights protection in favour of more traditional power politics – and vice versa.

In some sense the above is simply an illustration of, and an exercise in, constructing an interpretation that allows cultural understandings of international relations to co-exist with power–political explanations. However, the exercise also implies a more general point. Both proponents of the universal value of human rights and their cultural relativist opponents operate within political arenas in which states, regions and other international actors compete over a variety of issues and resources. These include cultural identity and relative economic power. By implication, political analysis of the tension between culture and rights cannot limit itself to philosophical or normative differences between cosmopolitan and communitarian positions. It needs to focus on the specific stakes that define the political struggle between cultural relativists and supporters of universal rights.

In addition, the exercise illustrated that cultural and power political arguments are not necessarily contradictory in international politics. In other words, realist interpretations emphasizing economic and military power and constructivist interpretations emphasizing cultural identity to explain international politics are not necessarily mutually exclusive. In the exercise I developed an interpretation in which the question of economic power and cultural identity are complementary rather than contradictory. I read the political game as containing contests over cultural and economic power which were closely connected to one another.

3.3   What about the universal value of human rights?

I am not satisfied with where we have ended up in our discussion so far. I cannot find anything that would help me to support the universal value of human rights against a cultural relativist onslaught. It seems that I am stuck with reading the globalization of human rights as a matter of power politics, a clash of cultures, or a combination of both. It is time to introduce a few elements that could help those who would like to argue in favour of the universal value of human rights.

Question

If you believe that the global propagation of human rights is worth fighting for, how would you try to counter Mahathir Mohamad's discourse and the general argument that human rights impose a Western culture? How would you try to cut the ground from under the feet of cultural relativists in defence of a belief that everyone's human rights should be equally respected?

By way of illustration, let us discuss one line of argument that has been used in defence of the global propagation of human rights. I shall develop the argument again in the context of the debate on Asian values. A possible starting point is that the Asian values discourse is not first of all about culture but about legitimating authoritarian political regimes. Anwar Ibrahim's argument is a good example:

> Before the currency turmoil, the dazzling performance of the Asian economies led some observers to conclude that sound policies alone could not explain what was then called a 'miracle'. Western countries had experimented with various sound policies yet were then suffering a prolonged economic downturn. Observers and scholars competed to discover the deep secret of the Asian success: thus were 'Asian values', the chemistry behind the Asian success, born. Asians, especially some political leaders, rapidly seized on this, at first tentative, explanation as the secret of their own particular 'miracle', trumpeting to the world that 'Asian values' was the single vital and distinguishing factor behind their success. *Their interpretation of what constituted Asian values* was largely self-serving. Leaders who leapt on the convenient doctrine happened to be those who ruled in an authoritarian manner; naturally they singled out the strong state and respect for authority as the soul of Asian culture, closing their eyes to the humanistic aspects of the culture, its tradition of dissent and reform and the struggle for justice and freedom.

(Ibrahim, 1999, p.26, my emphasis)

In the heat of a debate with a cultural relativist one could indeed provocatively ask: Is it not strange that those political leaders who most strongly assert the primacy of society and collective rights above the individual, and who support the primacy of consensus over conflict, rule in an authoritarian way? Emphasizing these values seems to support such a political regime much better than human rights that emphasize the right of free speech or the prohibition to persecute people because of political opinion. In a similar way, some Western investors in economies ruled by dictatorial or authoritarian regimes, defend their actions on similar grounds – they stress that the countries concerned have their own values and traditions and it would be offensive and culturally imperialist to impose Western views.

This kind of argument emphasizes the opportunistic motives of those opposing universal rights. They are either protecting positions of power by denying rights to the population, or they are protecting lucrative investments under the guise of respecting other countries' cultures.

Raising the issue of political opportunism is only a first step in the argument. It is a negative argument that makes the Asian values discourse more vulnerable to assertions of universal human rights. It tries to discredit the cultural relativist argument by demonstrating that it is being used for selfish reasons: to shield investment decisions and/or a political regime from criticism.

To be effective a more positive assertion of the universal value of human rights needs to be added. So the next step is to construct an argument based on the understanding that human rights are valuable for everyone irrespective of their cultural identity. Dworkin's assertion of the universal value of free speech is a good example of such an argument.

> We must insist on that point, and repeat it whenever 'Asian' values of collective obligation and social responsibility are cited as justification for censorship. Freedom of speech has nothing to do with selfishness. It is, however, indispensable to the most basic, organic, social responsibility a people can have: the responsibility together to decide, in civic response if not in formal elections, what their collective political values are.

(Dworkin, 1997, p.19)

Dworkin's argument asserts two elements. First, he makes the point that freedom of speech is not a selfish right that undermines social responsibility. It is precisely the contrary. Freedom of speech is a vital condition for developing social responsibility. It allows people to be responsible for deciding upon which values they wish to build their community. The second element follows implicitly from the first. The right of free speech is a universal right because it is implied by 'the most basic, organic, social responsibility a people can have.' Only when people have a right to speak freely, can they assert that they indeed cherish Asian values more than the values expressed in the Universal Declaration of Human Rights.

Rhetorically, this is a clever argument. One of the arguments against human rights was that their individualist nature supports a selfish culture. Asian culture avoids this by valuing responsibility towards the group or political community above individual freedom rights. Dworkin's counter-argument turns this on its head. He first asserts that Asian values serve selfish individual political and/or economic motives. Then he emphasizes that one can only know that people cherish Asian values by allowing them free speech. At this point, those who criticize the right of free speech turn into selfish individuals who do not allow people to exercise their most basic responsibility. The proponents of the universal right of freedom of speech turn themselves into the ultimate supporters of social responsibility.

This argument in support of free speech, and the universal value of human rights more generally, is interesting for more than its rhetorical value. It tells us something about a liberal rights culture too. Although Dworkin focuses on free speech, the more important underlying assumption is that in a liberal rights culture rights holders are equal before the 'law'. In other words, the universal propagation of human rights also propagates a principle of equality of rights holders. In so far as rights are universal – that is, everyone is a rights holder – there is a fundamental democratic element to the liberal rights culture. The principle of equality in rights does not imply that this equality is always practically realized or that it leads to a redistribution of wealth. But it does imply that ordinary people can call upon these rights to assert themselves against political authorities or other agencies that deny them these rights. The equality principle also implies that the authorities who have subscribed to human rights are themselves, in principle, bound by it. Rights and prohibitions also apply to the powerful and therefore have a capacity for restraining the arbitrary exercise of political power.

Another important principle of a liberal rights culture, but one that is less visible in Dworkin's statement, is that a rights holder whose rights are abused can ask other rights holders to support their cause. If human rights are universal it implies that the community of rights holders has a duty to uphold the rights universally, that is not just for the selective few but for all rights holders. In that sense one can argue that a liberal rights culture facilitates the global propagation of rights by the people themselves. In principle everyone can call for support by others if their human rights are violated.

These different dimensions of a liberal rights culture – that it allows the expression of support to local values; that it has a democratic and anti-authoritarian aspect and that it has a universalizing dynamic – have important implications for cultural relativist arguments. Rather than a clash between rights and culture, a liberal rights culture would now seem to facilitate the creation of a universal rights culture that *promotes* the ability of people to articulate cultural difference: if people do not have the freedom to say whether they support local cultural values how can we know that such values are authentic? That is, instead of imposing a culture, the global propagation of rights aims at the creation of a global context for the free assertion of cultural identity. Furthermore, the call for applying human rights does not necessarily come from Western liberals but also from members of other cultures, including victims of abuse of human rights (as was argued in Chapter 8).

Of course, these observations do not end the debate. It remains the case that human rights are steeped within a liberal and democratic tradition which has its historical roots in Europe and the USA. They also articulate a particular mode of organizing social relations that not everyone supports. For example, liberal rights cultures are secularized cultures in which the sacral aspects of life are moved to the background. They are also cultures that favour conflict above consensual or ritualized expressions of traditions. Claiming rights often implies a conflict of rights or an abuse of rights by others against whom one can legitimately claim that they should respect these rights.

The purpose of this section was not to end the debate in favour of the superiority of a liberal human rights culture or to uncritically endorse the universal value of human rights, however. The objective was more limited. I wanted to introduce a few elements that could be useful for those among you who prefer defending the universal value of human rights against the cultural relativist critique. In the previous section I introduced the idea that global rights are cultural. In this section I focused on the contested nature of global human rights and on how the protection of culture and power politics are key elements in debates about the value of human rights in world politics.

Activity 9.2

1   Summarize two arguments against governments who pressure other governments to protect human rights.

2   Construct an argument against cultural relativist positions in favour of the universal validity of human rights.

---

4   The power of global rights

Both the Asian values discourse and Dworkin's reaction to it assume that human rights can be powerful. Opposing human rights in the name of the protection or superiority of Asian values suggests that rights are significant in world politics. If Dworkin says that dictators are afraid of assertions of the right of free speech, he must assume that dictators consider these rights a significant political tool for dissidents. Indeed, why discuss or resist the globalization of human rights in the name of cultural identity, if human rights are insignificant?

Michael Ignatieff eloquently generalizes this observation.

> Since 1945, human rights language has become a source of power and authority. Inevitably, power invites challenge. Human rights doctrine is now so powerful, but also so unthinkingly imperialist in its claim to universality, that it has exposed itself to serious intellectual attack. These challenges have raised important questions about whether human rights norms deserve the authority they have acquired: whether their claims to universality are justified, or whether they are just another cunning exercise in Western moral imperialism.

(Ignatieff, 2001, p.102)

Ignatieff's observation that the debate about the cultural dimensions of human rights is closely related to the power of these rights is an important one. It helps to explain why the global propagation of human rights stirs up a number of tense debates in world politics. However, it does not explain how global rights are powerful.

Question

Can you think of ways in which global rights might be powerful?

There are two ways of approaching this question that I want to focus on. The first takes an institutional and legal position. From this position it becomes easy to see why many people in international relations disagree with Ignatieff's observation and see rights and international law as playing at most a minor role in international politics. I shall deal with this view in Section 4.1. The second way of approaching this issue is from a more political–discursive standpoint. In Section 4.2 I introduce an alternative understanding of the power of rights which emphasizes that global rights are a source of political rather than legal practice. These two models are not mutually exclusive or contradictory but they do have a different conception of how the global propagation of rights can be powerful.

4.1   Powerful rights in world politics? You must be joking!

Let us leave human rights for a short while and briefly revisit a war in the early 1990s. On 2 August 1990 Iraq invaded Kuwait. Five months later the USA and allied forces attacked Iraq to restore Kuwait's sovereignty. The second Gulf War of the late twentieth century had started. (The first Gulf War was the eight-year war between Iran and Iraq in 1980–88.)

US President George Bush Senior justified the military intervention of Iraq in name of international rule of law.

> This is an historic moment. We have in this past year made great progress in ending the long era of conflict and cold war. We have before us the opportunity to forge for ourselves and for future generations a new world order, *a world where the rule of law, not the law of the jungle governs the conduct of nations* ...

(US President George Bush quoted in *USA Today*, 1991, p.1, my emphasis)

The official reason for the international intervention was indeed that Iraq had violated one of the most sacred international rights: the right of territorial integrity of the state and the principle of non-intervention (Chapter 3).

Not everyone agreed, however. Critical observers quickly criticized the language of a new world order and the rule of law in world politics as window dressing. For them it justified the intervention but it was not the real reason for going to war. The reference to international law veiled more important interests such as access to oil, the global oil price, and the affirmation of the hegemonic position of the USA in world politics. These were seen as the more 'serious' reasons for spending huge amounts of money and for risking lives to reinstate Kuwait's sovereignty.

Underlying this critique of an international rule of law is the realist assumption that international relations was, is and, possibly, will always be a realm of the law of the jungle in which states maximize their own interests, irrespective of global declarations of rights and new world orders. States are not motivated by defending international or universal rights but by pursuing national interests, such as wealth and security, and possibly prestige (that is, the affirmation of one's power position). International law will only be observed and endorsed if it does not work against political and economic interests of major powers.

If in a case in which the hard-core of international law – that is, the principle of national sovereignty – is at stake, many analysts do not seem to consider law an important factor, you may wonder how seriously they would take the importance of individual human rights in world politics. Despite the prevalence of human rights language in international politics, human rights remain for most observers a marginal element of international politics.

That sounds plausible at first sight. But why does one assume this is the case for international rights and not for the domestic application of law? Not many people would argue that the law of the jungle, that is the survival of the fittest, rules domestic politics. Could it be that domestic law differs from international law and global rights declarations?

> The problem with international law is that it is not law. While a theory of international law has existed since the seventeenth century – initially in the writings of Hugo Grotius – Thomas Hobbes and others have since argued that there is no true international law, since there is no sovereign international authority to proclaim or enforce it.

(Pfaff, 2000, p.48)

This quotation reiterates one of the main reasons why the endorsement of international law and assertions of rights in world politics by liberal theorists and commentators are not taken seriously by realists: there is no independent international authority that can enforce them. This view relies on a legal–institutionalist understanding of law. Rights derive their power from being translated into law that can be sanctioned by a sovereign authority (mostly in the form of judicial institutions). Respect for law and fear of sanctions should assure that rights will be observed. According to this view, the power of global rights depends on the creation of an independent international judiciary that has the power to enforce obedience to the law. (You have already come across a debate on the extent to which international law is in fact law, in Chapter 3, Section 2.3.)

An independent judicial authority is also important for a repeated and consistent application of the law. In other words, the USA and its allies may declare that international law should rule in the case of Iraq's invasion of Kuwait, but why would the same law not apply when the USA invades Afghanistan ten years later? Selective application of international law sustains the suspicion that it is a veil for self-interested state practice. The consistent application of law is important because it socializes people into accepting the law as a norm – that is, a rule defining proper practice. '[It] intensifies social expectations and thereby reinforces compliance' (Bassioumi, 1999, p.805). So, besides the need to enforce global rights their power also depends on the degree to which people respect international law and rights as norms defining proper international practice.

There are limited instances of international judicial or quasi-judicial authorities. But if the power of global rights depends to a large extent on an independent judicial institution and its power to enforce compliance with global rights, I shall have to concede that their power is limited indeed. International legal institutions are generally weak unless they are consistently backed by major powers. From this legal–institutionalist point of view, therefore, the power of global rights will in practice depend to a large extent on whether or not they support interests of powerful states. The power of rights depends on the power of states supporting these rights because the independent judicial institutions are not powerful and/or not respected enough.

4.2 Rights, language and power

Too bad! Let us delete this chapter. After all, it seems that the global propagation of rights is simply window dressing. The liberal endorsement of the importance of international rules is misleading. It hides the reality of politics. International politics is ultimately conducted on the basis of state interests and relative power between states – as the realists have said all along.

Wait a minute! If that is the case, why then bother at all about using rights language to justify state action? Why do states then not simply declare 'let us go to war because it is in our interest'? Why were the frequent references to international law in the case of the Gulf War of 1991 often seen as being important for holding the coalition of states together? Could they not all just claim: well it is in our interest to support the intervention, either because we are afraid of the USA or because we will benefit from the intervention?

States do often justify a variety of political choices – including intervention and embargo – by referring to law or to rights not codified in law in the strict sense. In other words, rights language is being used in world politics, sometimes simultaneously with the language of national interest. Let us return to the example of the second Gulf War. If the cohesion of the coalition of states against Iraq does, to an extent, depend on the proper use of rights language, then it seems that rights language is more than just window dressing, or that window dressing is an important source for binding allies together. If that is correct then rights can make a difference. In that sense one can say that rights can be powerful without having to rely on an independent judicial authority that is backed up by a sovereign authority capable of enforcing the law. The coalition in the Gulf War was not held together by an independent institution forcing them to endorse the law. To understand what is going on here I need to develop a more political and less juridical reading that brings out the political power of rights language.

How does one interpret such a power that does not follow from the capacity of a legal institution to enforce rights? Let us return to human rights and see if we can come up with a satisfactory interpretation of the power of rights in non-legalistic terms. There is no global human rights court where individuals can claim their human rights and that can enforce its judgements. Neither is there a global police force and prison system to enforce these rights. So, how can human rights be of importance in world politics? Why are some regimes afraid of human rights declarations?

One of the possible answers is to return to a traditional understanding of power politics combined with the idea that rights are only powerful when they can be enforced. Since we do not have a world government, human rights will only be significant when backed by a powerful state or coalition of states that is prepared to sanction (economically or military) these rights. Although it is a plausible explanation, this interpretation places the source of power outside of the rights discourse. The power of global rights does not really reside with the rights themselves but with the relative economic and military power of the states trying to enforce respect for human rights. Resistance to the global propagation of human rights then depends on the relative power of the states opposing human rights. According to this line of thought, the Asian Tigers could resist the propagation of human rights as long as they maintained their economic power. When their economies were badly hit after the financial crises of 1997 and 1998, Asian values were no longer that readily endorsed in opposition to human rights pressure.

However, this is not the only possible political interpretation of rights. There is an alternative political reading possible that endorses the political importance of rights language itself. Let me return to Michael Ignatieff with whom I started this section. Ignatieff goes on to provide an interesting example of how rights can become a source of power in political contexts.

> Human rights do not, and should not, delegitimize traditional culture as a whole. The women in Kabul who come to human rights agencies seeking protection from the Taliban do not want to cease being Muslim wives and mothers; they want to combine their traditions with education and professional health care provided by a woman. And they hope the agencies will defend them against being beaten and persecuted for claiming such rights.
>
> The legitimacy of such claims is reinforced by the fact that the people who make them are not *foreign* human rights activists or employees of international organizations but the victims themselves. ... *Human rights* have gone global by going local, *empowering the powerless, giving voice to the voiceless.*

(Ignatieff, 2001, pp.110–11, my emphasis)

Ignatieff makes two important points. First, he states that claiming human rights does not necessarily imply giving up one's traditions. This is a critique of the cultural relativist argument against the universal validity of human rights discussed in Section 3. I shall not develop this point here. It is the topic of the next section. The second point he makes is that human rights are powerful for giving voice to the voiceless. How does that work? How can a particular language and certain international conventions and declarations empower the subordinated?

The core element of this view is that human rights are an instrument for expressing a desire to change the conditions of everyday life for themselves. Women in Kabul might have wanted to change things independently of whether they had heard about global rights or not. But they might not have been able to articulate this desire publicly with the same level of legitimacy without the global human rights framework.

Ignatieff also suggests that the discourse or idea of human rights has a capacity to mobilize subordinated groups (for example, Afghan women) in struggles to change their conditions of life (for example, access to education and health care). That means that rights language is an instrument that can bring people together to make claims for certain provisions or changes in status. In doing so it makes the desire for change political. Collective mobilization can make issues that were kept off the public agenda into publicly contested issues. In other words, by facilitating the mobilization of these women they can become a political factor in local struggles for changing or maintaining structures of domination and subordination.

In this interpretation the power of rights does not depend on the existence of legal institutions through which they can be enforced. The language or the idea of rights itself is powerful because it allows people to translate private desires or interests into public claims around which collective support can be mobilized. The emphasis is on the power of the discourse of rights for mobilizing subordinated people. In this social constructivist reading, which emphasizes the power of discourse and ideas, the political power of rights does not follow from court procedures or the presence of a major power supporting the cause of Afghan women, but from the very availability and legitimacy of the discourse of human rights (see also Frost, 2002).

The power of human rights discourse does not just depend on the discourse being available or on individuals believing in the idea of human rights, however. The local mobilization in the name of human rights – and thus the power of rights discourse – also depends on the global propagation of human rights and the political legitimacy that claims in the name of human rights have acquired over the past decades. In other words, the global human rights culture provides a structure of legitimacy which makes rights claims recognizable and, at least to some extent, acceptable in political struggles. Global human rights culture is thus a source of global political legitimacy. It remains a *contested* legitimacy – as we have seen in the previous section – but it does provide claims with a seriousness that they otherwise might not have had. Human rights language has successfully set particular norms which one can to a certain extent legitimately invoke, that is, without being immediately ridiculed and with a chance of drawing in support from other people. And as Ignatieff remarks, every time that they are used, their legitimacy – that is, the acceptance of human rights as the norm – is confirmed.

Legitimacy
'Where power is acquired and exercised according to justifiable rules, and with evidence of consent, we call it rightful or legitimate' (Beetham, 1991, pp.3, 16–18). Beetham adds that rules must be justified in terms of the values and beliefs in the society or societies concerned. In this instance, rights discourse has power because it accords with the norms of a rights culture that is widely accepted.

Of course the political use and power of rights does not follow from the global availability of the discourse as such. Local human rights groups and international governmental and non-governmental actors propagating global human rights play a very important role in bringing the rights discourse into local situations and struggles. They also often play a significant role in mobilizing people in the name of rights claims. Giving voice to the voiceless is not simply a magic act of declaring rights globally. It requires a lot of political work and mobilization. The political power of rights language thus depends to an extent also on the organizational and financial capacity and the political credibility of organizations supporting human rights claims in both global institutions and in more local political contests.

In the previous sections I looked at the contested nature of the globalization of liberal rights cultures. If global rights are contested in world politics it implies that rights are considered important enough to be contested. This observation led to the question of the power of rights in world politics.

The power of global rights? Afghan women protesting in Islamabad against the Taliban regime, 12 October 2000

Activity 9.3

How are global rights powerful in world politics?

---

5   Changing cultures

Why do I wish to introduce this peculiar political interpretation of the power of rights in a chapter on cultural dimensions of global rights? The political–discursive interpretation introduces a new idea. Challenges to a culture do not come exclusively from the outside, that is, from another cultural tradition. People who belong to a cultural field may want to change it. The change in the power concept, thus, allows me to relocate the confrontation between global rights and local cultural traditions from a global clash of cultural blocs to more local political and social contests for improving conditions of life. This move in the argumentation is one of the two steps I need for my re-conceptualization of the cultural encounter between global rights and cultural traditions. The second step is a change in the understanding of culture.

If human rights are not simply imposed but are also willingly appropriated by people – in Ignatieff's example above, Muslim wives and mothers – the idea that cultures are homogenous blocs, which underlies the clash of cultures thesis (see also discussion of Huntington in Chapters 3, 6 and 8), is no longer sustainable. Instead of being tectonic plates that move as a whole, cultures are more like fields containing many participants affirming and contesting values among themselves. Then culture does not refer to a bloc of shared values but to a field containing different opinions about the important values and a contest between these opinions. (Note: the term 'culture' is used rather differently here from how it was used in Chapter 6. Here it refers to a field of *contestation* over values rather than an arena of *shared* values. It is a field in which participants examine, explore, contest and confirm values and cultural patterns.)

This observation leads me to the key question of this section.

Question

If a global propagation of rights triggers encounters between different sets of values within a culture, what do these cultural encounters within a culture look like in practice? How can they be conceptualized?

I shall use the case of violence against women to develop the concept of culture as a field of contest (see also Chapter 8). First, I briefly illustrate how the discussion on women's rights is related to the rights versus culture debate. Then I argue that this debate is overlaid by a question of the subordination of women and that cultural justifications of the subordination of women are contested from within a culture. Finally, I develop the idea that cultures are a field of contestation.

5.1   An example: women's rights

In the 1990s violence against women was codified as a violation of human rights.

> ... by 1992 the Committee on the Elimination of Discrimination Against Women (CEDAW) had formulated a broad recommendation that defined gender-based violence as a form of discrimination, placing it squarely within the rubric of human rights and fundamental freedoms and making clear that states are obliged to eliminate violence perpetrated by public authorities and by private persons.

(Merry, 2001, p.36)

Typical examples of gender-based violence are wife-beating, killing female babies, honour killings and female genital mutilation. Having to assert that violence against women should not be tolerated indicates that these forms of violence do not fall in the same category as murder or assault. Why does beating one's wife or killing a female baby differ from beating up someone in general or killing a human being? Why do states often treat gender-based violence differently, while generally speaking they consider murder, assault and mutilation of people to be crimes? Why is gender-based violence defined as a separate category of violence? Why does it require a specific legal framework?

One of the answers to these questions is that some forms of violence against women are tolerated because 'it has always been like that. It is part of the traditional way of life.' Let us take the example of female circumcision. In certain parts of Africa, women have had their daughters circumcised for centuries. Circumcision refers to 'an array of practices which range from – rarely – the removal of the prepuce (circumcision in the proper sense of the term), to the ablation of the clitoris (excision), to the cutting of the labia, which are left to heal through scarring while a small hole is maintained for the passage of urine and menstruation (infibulation)' (Dembour, 2001, p.60). When Marie-Bénédicte Dembour asked women why they practice circumcision they said that it has always been done. In addition they used reasons of health, religion and sexuality. At the kernel of most of the arguments, however, was something else. Circumcision is what makes a woman a woman. That means that if a female subject wished to be recognized as a woman she would have to be circumcised. By implication, those who refuse to circumcise their daughters make them vulnerable to an array of exclusionary practices (for example, that their daughter could not be married) (Dembour, 2001, p.60).

From this perspective it is not surprising that the abolition of female circumcision on the basis of a human rights framework will be opposed on cultural grounds – by men and women. The violence of circumcision is a highly symbolic practice through which women partly gain their identity and social position within this culture. Upsetting this framework requires that women redefine themselves and their respective positions within society. This is not a simple act of waking up one morning and saying well now I am going to do something different with my life. It will meet resistance. One also needs alternative concepts of what it means to be a woman and of ways of organizing one's life and the life of the community. For example, a society can support the idea that the main goal for women is not to be married and have children but that women can chose to remain single, build up a career, and have different sexual partners.

I have to be careful at this point in the argument. So far, it seems I have not offered you anything but what seems like a justification for the continuation of circumcision. The argument ultimately reproduces a stark opposition between rights (in this case a prohibition of circumcision) and culture (circumcision as a traditional method for defining womanhood). But this does not necessarily have to be the conclusion. It is a conservative conclusion that assumes that 'what always has been done' is preferable to 'creating new ways of life'. It remains the case that introducing global prohibitions against certain forms of gender-based violence indeed may challenge some of the fundamental patterns of life in particular communities. However, the normative – or political – question is whether one prefers the way of life as it exists or whether one risks the path of change. The latter position is the one underlying the Declaration on the Elimination of Violence Against Women issued by the CEDAW. The declaration explicitly stated that 'States should condemn violence against women, and should not invoke any custom, tradition, or religion or other consideration to avoid their obligation with respect to its elimination' (United Nations, 1992). In other words, cultural reasons cannot justify a passive attitude of the state in the case of violence against women. The declaration has encountered a lot of resistance. Although 160 states ratified the declaration by 1997 many only did after having added substantive reservations (Merry, 2001, p.37).

5.2   Culture: power relations and internal challenges

Introducing the normative question of whether one opts for change or the *status quo* does not in itself redress the fact that I am still stuck with broadly speaking a clash between the global propagation of women's rights on the one hand and the identity of local cultures on the other. The normative choice is still very much a choice between a communitarian and a cosmopolitan position (Chapter 7). Either I resist the global human rights culture that favours women's rights in the name of tradition and cultural identity or I embrace this global culture at the cost of local cultural patterns. I will try to provide a few elements that may help to break down this dyadic way of thinking about cultural encounters.

I start by showing how focusing on the tension between global rights cultures and local cultural patterns tends to silence the fact that the political struggle is not limited to cultural identity but also concerns the preservation and transformation of existing relations of domination that are sanctioned within a local cultural tradition. This element is nicely formulated in the 'Platform for Action' agreed at the UN's Beijing Fourth World Conference on Women in 1995:

> Violence against women throughout the life cycle derives essentially from cultural patterns, in particular harmful effects of certain traditional or customary practices and all acts of extremism linked to race, sex, language or religion *that perpetuate the lower status accorded to women* in the family, the workplace, the community and society.

(United Nations, 1995b, quoted in Merry, 2001, p.37, my emphasis)

This quotation highlights that the justification of certain forms of gender-based violence is related to the subordination of women in the private sphere of the family, in economic structures and in society at large. In other words, the relative lack of protection that women enjoy against certain forms of violence is an aspect of the wider issue of the domination of men over women in most societies. By implication, gender-based violence such as female circumcision is not just a question of identity – of how to become a woman and what it means to be a woman in particular cultures. It is also a question of power relations. Being defined as a woman through circumcision often locates one firmly in a subordinated position. The justification for this subordination is done in cultural terms – along the lines of 'it has always been like that' or 'God has given everyone their place and it is not up to "men" to change it'. In that sense, cultural patterns that perpetuate the subordination of women are a factor that helps to explain gender-based violence.

For example, in Western societies women were located primarily in the private sphere of the household. Their presence in the public sphere was limited as much as possible for a long time. The diplomat's wife may have organized receptions and run the household but she usually could not seriously aspire to the position of ambassador. Her task was defined within the private sphere while her husband wielded state power in the public sphere of diplomacy (Enloe, 1989, pp.93–123). In Western societies, the private sphere is subordinated to the public sphere. It is not the domain where the common good or the definition of the proper way of life is debated and transformed in a community. In the private sphere one defines what matters for the family but not what counts for the community as a whole. This cultural structuring of family life may help to explain why gender-based violence has been relatively invisible to the state. Not only women but also the violence done against them is kept relatively hidden within the private sphere of the family.

When drawing too stark an opposition between the global propagation of rights and the protection of local cultural traditions one risks squeezing this key element of gender-based violence out of the picture. Gender relations are indeed highly cultural but they are also about the subordination of women and the domination of men. The global propagation of women's rights then turns out to be not simply a cultural intervention into a local culture. It is also a possible tool for contesting the particular way in which women are subordinated *within* a society. Women can appropriate globally declared women's rights and play them off against men and the traditional cultural patterns that support male domination for the purpose of improving the social position of women. By implication, the political contest is not dyadic but triangular. Its stakes are not just rights and culture but rights, culture and power asymmetries. As a result the question of the global propagation of rights can no longer be limited to a question of cultural change – of a choice between two value systems. Both are part of a struggle for the transformation or conservation of power asymmetries in particular communities.

The important point is that the power asymmetry that is at stake is not one along the lines of the West against the rest, as in the second section of this chapter in which I discussed cultural relativism in relation to the Asian values debate. The asymmetry consists of relations of domination and subordination that exist *within* particular communities between the men and women who both share a cultural tradition. In so far that the global propagation of women's rights triggers a clash between cultural values, this clash is relocated from an external incursion of global values to an internal struggle over hierarchies of values and relations of domination and subordination that they sanction.

5.3   Cultural field

This interpretation takes issue with arguments that conceptualize cultures as blocs of values. The latter often ignore that dissenting voices usually do already exist within cultures. Cultural challenges are not necessarily created by the propagation of rights itself. In a cultural community people usually have different opinions about which values and practices are preferable and what the shared cultural tradition consists off. Recognizing that circumcision is a cultural practice does not imply that all women are happy with circumcision, for example. Similarly, recognizing that wife-beating in Hawaii or the UK exists within a particular cultural framework that may sanction this form of gender-based violence differs from assuming that the wives being beaten therefore support this practice and that no one has tried to change it (Merry, 2001, pp.43–50).

Question

How can we conceptualize culture in a way that recognizes rather than hides the conflicts within cultures?

Let us start with a long but interesting quotation from Sally Engle Merry.

> I became acutely aware of the limitations of conventional thinking about the nature of culture and rights while listening to a panel discussion on violence against women at a 1998 conference in the Solomon Islands. The panelists, from the Solomon Islands, Australia and Samoa, insisted that they were not interested in importing a Western, rights-based model for understanding women's rights and protection from violence. They wanted *to develop an indigenous conception of rights.* One man told the panel that there in the Solomon Islands men valued women, paid a high bride price for them and protected them. He did not understand what else the women wanted. The panelists replied that this was not what they had in mind, *struggling to describe an indigenous concept that was different from the one the man had proposed.* One Solomon Islands woman *resorted to the conception of women's rights to equality developed at the Beijing Conference* in 1995 to make clear how their views differed from those of the male speaker.
>
> (Merry, 2001, pp.31–2, my emphasis)

The quotation raises a few important elements that will help to introduce a concept of culture that emphasizes the internally contested nature of cultural traditions. Note that this is different in emphasis from some of the earlier discussions – for example, Chapter 6 – where cultures have been presented as arenas of shared values and understandings binding communities together. It is, however, an elaboration of the idea of a cultural field that you met in Sami

Zubaida's discussion of the politics of Islam in Chapter 8. First, the quotation confirms the point I already made above. Cultural communities are not harmonious. The discussion between the women on the panel and the man indicates that different and conflicting points of view do exist within a cultural community. As a result it is difficult to maintain that cultures are simply a constellation of values shared by all participants in the culture. The discussion between the panellists suggests that culture exists more like *a field in which participants examine, explore, contest and confirm values and cultural patterns*. As a field a culture is very much alive and kicking. Instead of static and pre-given sets of values, cultures exist within and are continuously transformed through the interaction between members of a cultural community who have different views on whether and how dominant cultural patterns need to be changed or maintained. The panel discussion between the women and the man is a concrete manifestation of a cultural field in which some are seeking a particular transformation of the hierarchy of values and the patterns of life of women while others are resisting this change.

The second issue that the quotation raises is that the local appropriation of rights by women does not function like a typical clash in which one group of values is externally imposed upon another group of values. Women's rights are not simply an external given. Particular groups within the cultural field use these rights to articulate and support their attempt to change the position of women in society. In the example, one of the women resorted to the language of the Beijing Conference to try to explain to the man how her point of view differed from his. The language of women's rights thus helped her to articulate her understanding of what requires changing. It helped to formulate the position she wished to take in the cultural field and to demonstrate that this position is quite different from the position of the man (see also the political–discursive approach to power in the previous section).

A third issue that the quotation raises is that rights are not just repeated but are themselves reformulated in a process in which these women try to make sense of these rights from within their own cultural context. The quotation highlights how women wish to use and strengthen the rights framework but without uncritically taking on board all cultural values that are written into the framework. The panellists are looking for a way of introducing women's rights within their cultural community without being completely alienated from their own traditions and values, which do not value individualism higher than responsibility towards the family, for example. It remains a question whether this is indeed possible. However, the important issue for the discussion here is that the example suggests that the concept of a cultural clash is not adequate for understanding what is going on in the encounter between global sets of rights and local cultural traditions. Instead of being a global clash the cultural encounter seems to work on the basis of a local appropriation of rights. It is a process of negotiating both one's cultural tradition and the meaning of universal rights in a political struggle for improving conditions of life.

As a concluding point I would like to introduce one further layer of complexity. Renegotiating values through appropriating global human rights in local political struggles does not only import values expressed by global human rights (for example, equality of men and women). It also introduces or reiterates a rights culture, that is, a particular mode of agency, self and sociality (see Section 1). It imports the idea that one can aim for change through claiming rights against others or that one can use court-like procedures to frame and settle disputes. In other words, by relying on rights language to renegotiate values the participants do import a liberal, legalistic understanding of society, rule and self. In other words, they mediate cultural traditions and human rights through a rights language.

This observation opens a number of questions. One of them is that even if we accept that the concept of appropriation of rights within a contested cultural field is a better concept than a clash of cultures for understanding how the global propagation of rights relates to regional or local cultural traditions, does there not remain a different kind of imposition of Western liberal culture in the form of imposing a liberal rights culture? I do not have the space to go into this question but it should be possible to explore how a liberal rights culture itself is tweaked and twisted in the process of appropriation. The process of re-negotiation of cultural tradition most likely does not only concern the substantive values but also concerns questions such as what are legitimate forms for expressing opposition to existing relations of domination and what are acceptable ways for making claims upon other people?

In the previous section I introduced two different ways of understanding how global rights can be powerful – as an international legal order made powerful either by powerful states or by international authority; or as a mode of political practice. In this section I looked at how this second concept of power – the political–discursive model of the power of global rights – makes it possible to reinterpret the confrontation between global rights culture and local cultural traditions.

Activity 9.4

Can you summarize how I reinterpreted the idea that cultural globalization instigates a clash between cultures, which is the interpretation with which I started the chapter?

---

6   Conclusion

The key question of the chapter was 'How does the global propagation of rights and values relate to local and regional cultural traditions?' In dealing with this question the chapter introduced a number of aids to interpret and discuss cultural dimensions of globalization. More specifically, the chapter critically discussed two arguments. The first argument states that the global propagation of rights and values leads to cultural homogenization. The second argument states that the international order after the Cold War is characterized by a clash of cultures (or, in terms of its more popularized version: a clash of civilizations) which is partly played out in the area of the propagation of sets of rights (Chapters 6 and 7). My key argument is that the encounter between global rights and national or regional cultures should not be exclusively understood as a process of imposing one culture upon another or as a clash of different cultural systems. Instead I presented a third way of interpreting this encounter. Tensions between global rights and local cultural traditions are also negotiated in contests of values between members of a cultural tradition.

This view rests on a particular concept of culture. It replaces the idea that cultures are blocs of shared values (as in Chapter 6) with the notion that cultures are fields in which values are contested (as in Chapter 8). In other words, I displaced the understanding of culture as a unity of shared values with the understanding of culture as a contest of values among people who claim to belong to the same cultural tradition.

One of the key elements of this view is that the power of rights does not only follow from the power of legal institutions or powerful states to impose their protection. Rights are also powerful as a political discourse which can help people to mobilize in specific political struggles for improving conditions of life (for example, women seeking to reduce gender-based violence in their community) and which can help to legitimize their position in the political contest of values.

An important implication of this view is that the study of cultural globalization can be limited neither to the study of global cultural contests between the West and Islam or the West and Asian values, for example, nor to the contest of global rights in international institutions such as the UN and the WTO. Globalization is also intensively practised in issue-specific local political contests for the preservation or transformation of ways of life (see also Chapter 8 for a discussion of similar issues in relation to politics and power in the Middle East). Personally, I think that these more micro-political manifestations of the contest between global rights and cultural traditions ultimately give us a better understanding of how cultural globalization, including the global propagation of rights, feeds into politics and everyday life.

If you would like to revisit the flow of the argument – that is, how I built up my argument in this chapter – I would recommend you do the four activities. They summarize the conceptual building blocks of the argument. A final, summary activity is given below.

Activity 9.5

In Chapter 7 you learned about the difference between communitarian and cosmopolitan interpretations of rights. Is the view developed in this chapter communitarian or cosmopolitan? Or, does the chapter present a third approach in the interpretation of rights?

Hint: To answer this question you will need to:

1   Revisit the distinction between communitarian and cosmopolitan views described in Chapter 7.

2   Consider what has been said in this chapter about the origins of global rights.

3   Consider what has been said in this chapter about the relationship of global rights to local cultures.

Further reading

For an interesting and accessible introduction, see Frost, M. (2002) *Constituting Human Rights*, London, Routledge. It strongly supports a particular view of human rights culture and many of the ideas are very close to the argument developed in the first part of this chapter.

The book that relates most explicitly to the position defended in this chapter (especially in the latter sections) is Cowan, J.K., Dembour, M.B. and Wilson, R.A. (eds) (2001) *Culture and Rights: Anthropological Perspectives*, Cambridge, Cambridge University Press. It contains a wide variety of case studies that illustrate the theoretical arguments presented here.

Part 3 Technology, inequality and the network society

We are living through one of those rare intervals in history. An interval characterized by the transformation of our 'material culture' by the works of a new technological paradigm organized around information technologies.

(Castells, 1996, p.29)

[New technologies] are shrinking the world [and] offer considerable potential as a source of democracy to the extent wiring for such technologies is available. More accurately, by facilitating the continued proliferation of networks that know no boundaries, these technologies have introduced a horizontal dimension to the politics of globalized space. They enable like-minded people in distant places to converge, share perspectives, protest abuses, provide information, and mobilise resources – dynamics that seem bound to constrain the vertical structures that sustain governments, corporations and any other hierarchical organisations.

(Rosenau, 2000, p.194)

Technology networks are transforming the traditional map of development, expanding people's horizons and creating the potential to realize in a decade progress that required generations in the past.

(quotation from the cover of United Nations Development Programme, 2001, *Human Development Report*)

The idea of a 'global network society' has become influential, both in academic analyses of the international system and in the policy recommendations of governments and international institutions of economic governance. But what is this 'global network society', and what questions does it raise for our understanding of international order?

The term 'global network society' is most closely associated with the sociologist Manuel Castells, who argued – in a major, three volume work entitled *The Information Age* (1996–98) – that new technologies are driving a fundamental shift in social organization which is reshaping the world in which we live. The information and communication technology (ICT) revolution, the rise of social movements, and what Castells calls the crises of forms of capitalism (and state socialism) based on the nation state have contributed to a 'network society' in which power is shifting from national states to global networks.

Castells' analysis is sophisticated and far reaching, and we cannot hope to do justice to it here. Nor is this part of the book intended as an elaboration of Castells' theses. Rather, we present Castells' image of a global network society, an image that is shared by many other analysts, to open up a series of related but distinct inquiries into the international order. Before detailing what these inquiries are, let us sketch a few of the key arguments that have been made about the global network society.

There are perhaps three key ideas related to the thesis that a transition to the global network society is underway. The first of these is a claim about the influence of technology on the shape of the international system. Castells' case is based on the idea that society is moving to a new information age. He suggests that there have been two main modes of historical development and that we are witnessing the advent of a third, that is, the information age. The two earlier modes were an 'agrarian mode', in which economic growth came about by increasing the amount of labour devoted to production based on the land, and an 'industrial mode', in which economic growth stemmed from the wider and more efficient use of inanimate energy sources to foster the mechanization of production and technological innovation. Both these earlier modes carried with them particular ways of organizing society. The new era, Castells argues, is one in which economic growth stems from 'the generation of new knowledge as the key source of productivity' (1989, p.10). Furthermore, the development of ICTs both creates a continuous 'feedback loop' between innovation and production, so driving economic change, and enables the (electronic and digital) dissemination of knowledge throughout society, so creating the possibility of a single integrated network. New ICTs, therefore, not only change the way in which the economy develops but also influence social organization as a whole. In this respect, Castells' thesis gives a new twist to an older idea: namely that we can understand social order in terms of the kinds of technology on which society is based.

Globalization
Globalization, understood as a process of social change, refers to a movement towards ever more extensive and intensive social relations of global scope, operating at increasing speed and with greater effect.

This brings us to the second key idea behind the global network society thesis. The rise of networks based on ICTs, Castells claims, also means that we have to rethink what is meant by international order. The network form of organization sits between the anonymous, impersonal competitive world of markets and the kind of authoritative hierarchy associated with political orders. Furthermore, the kinds of innovation made possible in the information age by ICTs are not confined to national boundaries. International order, therefore, should be understood neither as a system of interacting national markets nor as a system of interacting national states but as a global and networked order. One might say that, for Castells, if industrial capitalism gave rise to national economies and the nation state, then informational capitalism gives rise to networks and globalization.

The third claim linked to the global network society thesis is that the information age and the global network society create new opportunities for participation for those at the margins of the international order, and new means by which inequalities within the international order can be overcome. This claim does not come from Castells himself. Indeed, he is rather sceptical about it, because networks also create new sources of technological and social exclusion. But others have developed his notion of a global network society in this direction. The quote from UNDP at the beginning of this introduction is indicative of the ways in which important international institutions have appropriated the notion of the global network society to put forward a case that the world may become less unequal as networks and information technologies come to dominate the international order. (The World Bank has developed similar claims.) Access to ICTs and the development of networks across state borders will, it is argued, act as equalizers between individuals and nations.

Let us be clear. This part of the book is not concerned to argue the case either for or against the network society thesis as a whole. Rather we shall use three ideas about the global network society – that new technologies are changing the nature of (global) society, that global networks are transforming the international system away from a state-based order, and that patterns of inequality in the world are changing – to open up some new ways of understanding international order.

The chapters in this part of the book do not try to deal with all aspects of this thesis at once but attempt to develop deeper inquiries into particular aspects of the thesis in turn. In Chapter 10, Suma Athreye and Roberto Simonetti focus on the relationship between technological innovation and economic growth. They look at how innovation has happened in the past and at how it has helped to shape patterns of growth. They also point out that the idea of technological revolutions has a long history, and contrast some earlier revolutions with the ICT revolution at the centre of the global network society argument. The chapter investigates both the international diffusion of technology and the extent to which systems of innovation have broken free from national boundaries.

In Chapter 11, Grahame Thompson takes up the question of patterns of inequality and focuses on the debate about whether the world has become more or less unequal. The key dimensions of what is a complex and heated debate are teased out and the different aspects and mechanisms of global inequality are investigated. Thompson also considers the extent to which network forms of organization are likely to change the character of international trade and investment.

In Chapter 12, Helen Yanacopulos and Giles Mohan look at the idea of networks as new forms of social organization. They focus on 'networks of

knowledge, the economic drivers of technological change, and organizational and institutional factors. One of the main aims of this chapter is to equip you with the tools needed to think about these questions. We also want to make these general considerations concrete by looking at some countries that have used the opportunities provided by new technologies to increase their economic growth and achieve positions of industrial leadership (such as the USA, Germany and Japan). Finally, we want to consider the factors that influence technological diffusion across the world, and the possibilities open to countries that want to catch up with the technological leaders.

The chapter is organized as follows. In Section 2 we introduce Freeman and Louçã's 'long waves' of technological change and briefly review some of the changes associated with the industrial revolution. This will give you an idea of the complexity of technological change and its relationship to economic growth. Section 3 considers the nature of technology, its relation to knowledge and the economic character of technological innovation. Section 4 examines the ways in which waves of technological innovation can shuffle the pack of world economic leaders by looking at how Germany and the USA forged ahead of Britain in the late nineteenth century and early twentieth century. Section 5 then returns to the analysis of technological innovation that was started in Section 3 and develops the notion of a 'system of innovation', a much broader concept than technological innovation itself. Sections 6 and 7 look at the opportunities for catch-up growth during the post-war, USA-led Fordist wave and the ways in which the diffusion of ICTs was in part a response to the crisis of Fordism. Section 8 then asks whether ICTs, and the networked forms of activity that they facilitate, make it any easier for developing countries to pursue catch-up growth. The concluding section, Section 9, reviews the implications of what we have learned for our understanding of the impact of ICTs and the global network society thesis.

2 The historical experience of technological change: the textile industry and UK industrial leadership

Since the advent of industrial production in particular, technological changes have been intimately related to economic growth and industrial leadership. Following Freeman and Louçã (2001), we can identify five economic cycles (or waves) of approximately 50 years duration, starting from the industrial revolution that took place in England in the late eighteenth century. The five long cycles are listed in Table 10.1 which summarizes the main features of each of the 'techno-economic paradigms' linked to each cycle.

Let us consider the first two of the long economic cycles in Table 10.1 which correspond to the industrial revolution and the emergence of Britain as a

Table 10.1 Summary of the long business cycles: a condensed summary of the Kondratiev waves

(1) Constellation of technical and organizational innovations	(2) Examples of highly visible, technically successful and profitable innovations	(3) 'Carrier' branch and other leading branches of the economy	(4) Core input and other key inputs	(5) Transport and communication infrastructure	(6) Managerial and organizational changes	(7) Approximate timings of the: 'upswing' (boom) / 'downswing' (crisis of adjustment)
1 Water-powered mechanization of industry	Arkwright's Cromford mill (1771) Henry Cort's 'puddling' process (1784)	Cotton spinning Iron products Water wheels Bleach	Iron Raw cotton Coal	Canals Turnpike roads Sailing ships	Factory systems Entrepreneurs Partnerships	1780s–1815 1815–1848
2 Steam-powered mechanization of industry and transport	Liverpool–Manchester railway (1831) Brunel's 'Great Western' Atlantic steamship (1838)	Railways and railway equipment Steam engines Machine tools Alkali industry	Iron Coal	Railways Telegraph Steam ships	Joint stock companies Subcontracting to responsible craft workers	1848–1873 1873–1895
3 Electrification of industry, transport, and the home	Carnegie's Bessemer steel rail plant (1875) Edison's Pearl St New York Electric Power Station (1882)	Electrical equipment Heavy engineering Heavy chemicals Steel products	Steel Copper Metal alloys	Steel railways Steel ships Telephone	Specialized professional management systems: 'Taylorism' Giant firms	1895–1918 1918–1940
4 Motorization of transport, civil economy and war	Ford's Highland Park assembly line (1913) Burton process for cracking heavy oil (1913)	Automobiles Trucks Tractors, tanks Diesel engines Aircraft Refineries	Oil Gas Synthetic materials	Radio Motorways Airports Airlines	Mass production and consumption 'Fordism' Hierarchies	1941–1973 1973–
5 Computerization of entire economy	IBM 1401 and 360 series (1960s) Intel microprocessor (1972)	Computers Software Telecommunication equipment Biotechnology	'Chips' (integrated circuits)	'Information Highways' (Internet)	Networks; internal, local and global	?

Source: Freeman and Louçã, 2001, p.141

world leader in manufacturing. The industrial revolution heralded the growth of modern industry and modern economic growth, and followed a period of expanded international trade due to the opening up of sea routes and a revolution in agricultural productivity. Towards the end of the eighteenth century, England experienced high rates of growth in the cotton textile industry which, in turn, resulted in high overall rates of growth relative to previous periods. Estimates suggest that, starting in the 1780s, the rate of growth of investment, output and trade in industry were nearly three times as high as in the preceding decades.

This phenomenal growth coincided with innovations in machinery and the mechanization of textile production. Rising wages and the need for control over workers created incentives for widespread adoption of mechanized practices within the factory system, which gradually replaced the system of putting out piecework. In addition, as David Landes (1969) has forcefully argued, innovation in one sector, say, faster spinning machines, created imbalances in others, say, weaving. This then spurred inventions which increased the output of weaving machines.

Christine Macleod (1999) has also shown that, by the mid nineteenth century, several innovations came from the shop floor. Supervisors patented their productivity-enhancing innovations and sold them, often to the owners of the firm or rival firms, for royalties based on discounted future incomes or a share of equity. England developed the patent system to protect new inventions based on an extension of copyright law which had been used to protect works of literature and science. Once patented, the inventor could sell an invention to other firms in England or abroad. Infringement of patents, that is, the use of the invention without payment to the patent holder, became an offence in law.

As these innovations diffused, they resulted in a growing mechanization of the cotton textile industry, first based on water power and then on steam power. All this was possible thanks to the availability of cheap inputs: cotton from colonies such as India (and later the USA) and, perhaps more crucially, iron, which was needed for the construction of the machines. The rate of growth in the iron and cotton industries soared compared to other industries, and the efficiency of the new machines grew rapidly. Innovations also became common in related industries such as chemicals, whose outputs (for example, dyes) were used in the textile industry, and in building houses and factories for the expanding urban sector.

Two factors contributed to the fast growth and rapid transformation of British industry. First, radical changes in the organization of industrial production were introduced as factory production became widespread and replaced the putting out system not only in textiles but also in other lines of manufacture. This change in organization enabled large productivity savings both because of technical advantages and because workers could be controlled more effectively. Second, the diffusion of the new technology throughout the country and in regions far from the industrial centre at Lancashire was speeded up by the existence and development of a good transportation network (through well-maintained waterways) and the availability of water power.

The economic leadership gained by Britain during the first industrial revolution persisted for many decades, surviving what Freeman and Louçã (2001) call the first crisis of adjustment in the first half of the nineteenth century when steam replaced water as the main source of power. Nevertheless, the emergence of steam technologies and the mechanization of transport with the rise of the railways was a window of opportunity for new countries wishing to industrialize such as Germany and the USA. Both adopted the railways relatively early and utilized the resulting large domestic markets to imitate British industrial achievements. However, in order to understand how Germany and the USA were able to make such technological and economic advances, we need to consider in rather more depth the nature of technological change and its relationship to economic change. To do this, we need to think about what we mean by technological change, or innovation. We shall do that in the next section before returning to the historical narrative in Section 4.

3   Conceptualizing technological change and innovation

Question

Based on the discussion in Section 2 (including Table 10.1), what do the words 'technological change' make you think about? How would you define the term 'technology'?

One answer might be that technological change constituted the entire move from water-based to steam power-based mechanization of industry. Another would point to particular inventions that affected production such as the Arkwright mill or the emergence of new industries like the railways. Even without the historical examples, we all have an intuitive idea of what technology is. Technology is often associated with physical objects such as computers or rockets. Certainly, machines are part of technology's definition. Yet you might have associated technology with science. Indeed, technology is often applied science, that is, the application of scientific principles for practical use, and it is difficult to deny that science and technology are closely related. Thus, we can speak about genetic technology or information technology, and they too would have definite meanings for us.

3.1 Defining technology and technological change

It is perhaps not surprising that many scholars of technology still think about technology in different ways since the term 'technology' is used in very different contexts and includes a great variety of things. We are primarily interested in technological change as a source of industrial growth and leadership in the world economy. Therefore, our definition of technology will be closely connected to economic production and markets. From an economic viewpoint, rather than defining what technology is, we can infer the salient characteristics of technology by focusing on what constitutes technological change. In the context of the production function, economists think of technological change as something that allows a firm to use an existing technique more efficiently, or the firm may introduce a new technique of production altogether. However, technological change has done more than influence production processes. As you have seen above, it has also provided new products for consumption, that is, it has created new sources of demand for industrial goods. Consequently, a broader definition of technological change is the introduction in the economy (usually on the market) of a new product or process of production.

Technological change
Technological change is the introduction in the economy of a new product or process of production.

Our next step is to characterize technology. We have already associated technology both with objects such as machines, that is, artefacts, and with scientific principles, that is, knowledge. So, we begin by drawing a distinction between technology as an *artefact* and technology as *knowledge*. In fact, these two aspects of technology are linked because an artefact embodies the knowledge needed to produce it. For this reason, the terms 'embodied' and 'disembodied' technology are often used. Embodied technologies refer to the objects of new technology: machinery, tools and plant. Disembodied technology refers to the non-material aspects of technology: for example, ideas that can be patented and licensed, that is, technological knowledge. Although artefacts are important, the knowledge necessary to produce them is more important, and it is the component most likely to change. In order to understand technology, therefore, we have to understand the nature of the knowledge required to produce artefacts.

3.2 Technological knowledge: codified information and tacit knowledge

It is conventional to distinguish between two types of technological knowledge: codified information and tacit knowledge. One part of technological knowledge consists of ideas that can be articulated and therefore codified. Equally, large amounts of technological knowledge cannot be codified but are learnt through experience and practice. Such knowledge is vital for innovative activity in firms and is sometimes termed tacit knowledge. Codification, however, involves more than articulation. As a category of scientific problems is better understood, new abstractions emerge to explain the encompassing nature of those problems. Indeed, this is the function of a large part of basic scientific research and, for example, this is how the different engineering disciplines emerged as did the subject of management. One implication of this aspect of codification is that, as science is increasingly applied to production, the stock of codified knowledge and the possible re-combinations of it also increase. In other words, technologies become more science based than before. In general, ICTs are said to be intensive in their use of knowledge and knowledge workers.

Another way to think about technological knowledge is to ask if it is privately owned or publicly available. A patent, for example, is privately owned technological knowledge, until the patent expires and it then becomes publicly available. Almost all tacit knowledge is both private and non-tradable. However, some kinds of technological knowledge have the characteristics of a public good.

Codified information that can be articulated and is publicly available has an important characteristic which makes it important for the welfare of society. Paul Romer, an economist at the forefront of the research on the impact of technology on growth, explains:

> If you find a valuable object like a piece of fruit, it does me no good because you and I cannot both eat the fruit. But if you find a valuable idea about how to do something, you and I can both enjoy its benefits. An idea can be used again and again by everyone, provided that it can be communicated.

(Romer, 1993, p.87)

Nonetheless, this benefit has a social cost. To the extent that, once discovered, a valuable idea becomes a public good, it makes sense for individual producers to free ride on the efforts of others. This problem is intensified because the discovery is not assured, and one cannot know in advance what exactly will be discovered. If many individuals or firms act on this premise, society as a whole may under-invest in the costs of generating new ideas. Historically, this has been one of the main reasons for the public funding (subsidy) of basic research institutions and the development of the patent system, since the latter attaches a private good to the public one.

In Section 2 we noted that supervisors of textile factories could, and did, devise new ways and designs for machinery to increase productivity. More generally, we can think about each run of production as being an experiment for the firm. Over many runs the firm has many sources of information on the production processes it is using and, though these may not be articulated in public papers, the firm may develop superior working practices on the basis of this knowledge. Sometimes this knowledge can result in innovations that can be codified and placed in the public sphere (through the use of patents);

more often this technological knowledge cannot be fully articulated and codified. For this reason, such knowledge is often referred to as tacit knowledge. Tacit knowledge is specific to a firm's history of production and its ability to learn; different firms have different histories and varying abilities to learn.

3.3   Sources of new technologies: the 'technology-push' model

We turn now to the process by which technological change happens. Even if a brilliant university sector generates ideas which are valuable to society, their translation into technological innovation in the form of a product or process innovation can be an expensive undertaking. After an initial creative idea – the invention – a long, risky and costly process is needed before the new product or process is introduced in the economy. Many firms spend millions of pounds on research and development (R&D), and the bulk of that expenditure goes towards industrial development, in which initial ideas are made to work effectively and profitably or, ultimately, discarded. Only at that stage, when the new product or process is introduced in the economy, can we talk about innovation.

The transition from invention, the initial intuition or idea, to innovation – the commercial development of a new product or process of production – often requires substantial investment. The Austrian economist, Joseph Schumpeter (1934), argued that entrepreneurs played a central role in this process by investing in innovative activities in the process of economic development. Certainly, many current debates in innovation policy focus on the promotion of entrepreneurship in high technology fields such as biotechnology. Schumpeter also drew attention to the distinction between the introduction of a new product or process in the economy, the act of innovation (that is, technological change), and its diffusion throughout the economic and social system. The economic benefits of an innovation are small when it is initially introduced. The benefits for the economy occur when a new technology is widely used within society. For instance, a key factor in the first and second waves outlined in Table 10.1 (see Section 2) was the fast diffusion of new pervasive inputs of production (iron and coal) based on a new technology (mechanization) and a new form of organization (factories). Note that it is not the appearance but the *diffusion* of the new technology that mattered for economic growth. Similarly, the computer did not have a great impact on the economy when it was first produced in the 1950s as a calculating machine. However, when microprocessors became much cheaper and could be used to automate many kinds of mechanical and administrative tasks, its impact on the economy was felt. All this took many years to happen.

Thus, the diffusion of new technology is as important for economic growth as the discovery of a new innovation. Although these distinctions between invention, innovation and diffusion are important, and we shall meet them again later, they can be misleading to the extent that they suggest that invention, innovation and diffusion always occur in a simple linear fashion. This idea underpins the 'technology-push' model of innovation which has been influential in science and technology policy. This model sees the innovation process as a linear sequence of various stages that starts with the creation of new ideas from the application of scientific principles and ends with the introduction of an innovation on the market (see Figure 10.1).

In the technology-push model of innovation, the scientific and technological knowledge created in the activity of basic research is the engine of innovation and therefore the prime mover of economic growth. The output of basic research increases the publicly available stock of knowledge, on the basis of which some firms are able to innovate through a process of applied R&D. Many policies which advocate government support to scientific research and R&D are based on this model, and assume that the main way to increase the rate of innovation, and consequently economic efficiency, is to increase the pool of scientific knowledge available by carrying out publicly funded R&D projects and by subsidizing the R&D activities of private firms. Such policies assume that private firms in the market do not allocate enough resources to innovative activities because of the public nature of technology. Yet there are feedbacks that run from innovation to science, from production activities to the creation of new knowledge and ideas.

Question

Can you think of examples where technological developments have influenced scientific advance?

One such example is scientific instrumentation. Advances in scientific instrumentation are often necessary for new scientific discoveries. Galileo had to first build his telescope before he could revolutionize our understanding of the solar system. Other less intuitive examples come from the history of science and technology. It is sometimes the case that scientific explanations of successful innovations only come after new products have been introduced on the market. This happened with the steam engine. It was only after steam engines were commonly used in industry that the laws of thermodynamics were discovered. The same applies to the science of aerodynamics, which was only developed after it was shown that aeroplanes could indeed fly.

A more crucial criticism of the linear, technology-push model is that it fails to capture the rich web of two-way interactions between various types of institutions that contribute to the creation of new technology. One way to understand this is in terms of the institutions required for the successful

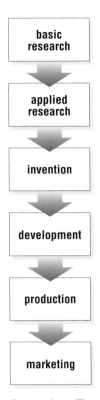

Figure 10.1   The 'technology-push' linear process of innovation
Source: Simonetti, 1998, p.304

diffusion of technologies. Once the value of an invention is understood, the key question is how rapidly it will be diffused. Financial institutions that supply credit or industry associations that share technological information among firms can become key players in determining the speed with which new technology is introduced. The tacit knowledge gained by such adoption can then stimulate new advances. In such cases, the linear sequence of the technology-push model is misleading.

A related criticism is that the linear model neglects the importance of complementary investments which raise the productivity of the original innovation. In Section 2, we suggested that well-developed transport networks were crucial to the increased growth rate of industry during the industrial revolution. This is an example of a complementary investment that raised the potential profits from the adoption of a technology. A new machine was capable of yielding much higher profits if, due to a well-developed waterway system, its output could be sold in neighbouring regions. Correspondingly, waterways enabled cheap coal to be transported to iron factories, reducing the costs of machinery production.

Complementary investment A and B are said to be complementary investments if an increase in the productivity of investment A causes an increase in the productivity of investment B.

These shortcomings have led researchers to formulate a different model of innovation which focuses on a system of institutions and actors whose co-ordinated activities give rise to new techno-economic paradigms. The third long cycle in Table 10.1 (see Section 2), which saw the emergence of electricity and the rise of the USA and Germany as challengers to British leadership, underlines the presence of diverse systems of innovation most dramatically. We now turn to this, before outlining the notion of a 'system of innovation' more formally in Section 5.

4 Changes in economic leadership and the rise of heavy industry: the age of electricity and steel

The third long cycle, which began in the 1890s, was associated with the diffusion of electricity. The discovery of electricity had already occurred in the eighteenth century in England and France, but it was not until the 1860s and 1870s that safe ways of using electricity were invented, and technological applications became viable in industry. The availability of electrical power brought about momentous change in the organization of industry, and provided countries such as the USA and Germany with opportunities for catching up with Britain.

Though electricity emerged as an alternative source of power for mechanization, it was a radically new technology in three ways. First, it was closely related to scientific activity, as no technology had been before. Indeed, many scientific advances were needed before the technology became economically viable. Scientific research was thus an important direct input to the development of the technology in a way that it had not been for the development of the textile industry. Britain was at the forefront of scientific research in electricity (the modern theory of electromagnetism is due to the Scottish physicist James Clerk Maxwell (1831–1879)). Nevertheless, firms in countries such as Germany that wanted to catch up began to set up their own R&D departments, often in collaboration with local universities. Thus began a new model of innovation: the institutionalization of R&D activity within large industrial firms such as Siemens and AEG.

The second characteristic of electrical technology was its generic nature. An example of this generic nature is the fact that electric power was used as an input for a range of industries, as well as playing an important role in the emergence of the chemicals industry which introduced completely new products and processes of production. Third, the generation of electricity used different inputs (steel and coal) from earlier technologies, thereby encouraging the growth of these sectors as well.

4.1   Diverse responses

At first glance, electricity seems to embody many characteristics of the linear model since it was clearly dependent on scientific advances for innovation. Britain was at the forefront of these advances, having secured important patents in electricity and in steel making (the Bessemer process). Many important innovations were made in Britain before, or contemporaneously with, their introduction in Germany and the USA. The technology-push model would lead us to expect that Britain would be one of the leaders in the use of this technology. Yet this was not the case and by the end of the third wave, Britain had lost its industrial leadership to Germany and to the USA. To understand what happened we need to study the diverse responses to the opportunities presented by electricity in Britain, Germany and the USA.

By the end of the nineteenth century, Britain had a well-developed educational system, a system of production based on family firms, a financial market developed around the financing of trade and large investments (joint stock companies), a strong patent system, and an empire of colonies that could serve as markets for its growing industry. The leading sectors of the economy consisted of a range of consumer goods industries, notably, textiles, metalware, paper, food, watches, and some producer good industries such as shipbuilding and textile machinery. Its industrialization and urbanization had begun before the emergence of the railroads, and the building of railways was a smaller scale activity than in the USA and Germany. Electricity was principally used as a new source of power in largely labour-intensive industries where more machines were employed with additional labour to generate more production.

However, the situation was quite different in the USA and Germany. Following the completion of the Union after the American Civil War (1861) and the unification of Germany (1871), both economies had large domestic markets. In both cases, railroad investments were made to connect the different parts of the country, and both economies enjoyed the benefits of a continent-wide system of transportation by the late nineteenth century. Moreover, large-scale investment in railways gave rise to new financial institutions and forms of corporate finance. In Germany, it led to the development of large financial banks (*Kreditbanken*) which sold government bills, collected household savings, and made investment loans on a national scale. After the railroad boom, these banks transferred their lending activities to the newly emerging industrial sectors and single banks were able to lend at scales unheard of in the UK. However, in the USA the same demand resulted in the centralization and institutionalization of the nation's money markets in New York, and the development in corporate finance of most of the modern instruments for underwriting investment risks.

Furthermore, investment in railways and machinery created a large demand for skilled labour (engineers) and for managerial expertise to run the large-scale operations. In both Germany and the USA, new institutions emerged in higher education which were designed to fulfil this need. In particular, the training and education of engineers was more widespread and deep than in Britain, despite the presence of world-class universities such as Oxford and Cambridge. In Germany, the state also played an important role in supporting the bureaucratization and management of industry.

The initial impetus for industrial development in Germany came from the demand for chemical dyes for the fast-growing textile industry, and from the demand for steel and machinery due to the large investments in the nationalized railways. Electricity was useful as a source of power in its metal and machinery industries that fed the railway industry. In addition, the range and control of temperatures permitted by electricity were crucial to German dye-making firms who saw the potential for producing many more chemicals on large industrial scales. The benefits of transportation ensured that firms could reach distant markets across the European continent. The absence of laws prohibiting cartelization meant that German producers were more inclined towards inter-firm collaboration and the abatement of (potentially ruinous) competition. By 1913, German firms had built up industrial specialization in metals, machinery and chemicals, and were undisputed world leaders in machinery as well as very close competitors to US firms in chemicals.

Germany's economic success led it to seek export markets in the Balkans, Central Asia, the Middle East and Africa, bringing it into competition with the existing European colonial powers, especially Britain and France. In contrast to Germany, the US impetus for development largely came from its own domestic market, which was vastly larger than that of Britain and growing quickly because of large-scale migration from the continent. Maddison (1982) estimates that the US population grew from 39.3 million in 1870 to 97.2 million in 1913, while in the same period Britain's population grew from 31.3 million to 45.7 million, and Germany's from 39.2 million to 67.0 million. Although ethnically diverse, the US population was socially more homogeneous (not subject to the same degree of class and income stratification as in Europe), and concentrated in the working age group.

A large domestic market enabled US industry to grow organically and in a broad-based fashion, moving from consumer goods to producer goods much in the way that British industry had grown in an earlier period, albeit on a much greater scale. The large scale of the US market also paved the way for significant inter-firm divisions of labour, and the emergence of specialized markets such as in machine tools where US firms soon became world leaders. In order to exploit the large scale of its markets, US producers co-ordinated on establishing standards in different components of production. For instance, various incompatible configurations of electricity technology emerged and standards had to be chosen – the best known and well documented example being the choice between direct and alternate current (David and Bunn, 1987). The US 'system of manufactures' based on standardized and interchangeable component parts became an important feature of US industrialization.

Activity 10.1

List the main differences in the responses of the USA and Germany to the economic potential of electricity.

The economic boom in the USA, based on engineering technologies, electricity and steel, continued until the famous stock market crash of 1929, which also coincided with the start of the 'great depression' of the 1930s. In the meantime, by historical accident, the USA had stumbled upon a cheaper source of power: petroleum. Rockefeller's giant firm, Standard Oil, formed through mergers, had achieved substantial cost reductions, with the unit cost per gallon dropping from 2.5 cents in 1879 to 0.4 cents in 1885. Cheap oil became a core input of production in many industries in the USA and was also used to produce electricity. Europe, in contrast, mainly used coal for electricity generation. A significant expansion of industries linked to oil took place in the USA and a new product, the automobile, based on the internal combustion engine, was developed.

4.2   The rise of the vertically integrated firm

The use of electricity in various industries also brought about radical changes in the way economic production and social life were organized. The fact that electricity could be generated in one place and transmitted to another drastically changed the attractiveness of some locations for industrial development. It was no longer necessary to generate and use energy in the same place, and plants were relocated according to new criteria. Moreover, even within plants, there was more flexibility in the way that machines were organized on the shop floor, and new styles of production appeared. In transportation, the use of electric trams and trains made it possible for commuters to travel longer distances; this gave rise to a rapid growth of suburbs. (Later, cars and petrol engines were to drive this process even further.) In communication, the appearance of the electric telephone represented a step change in the way that economic activity could be co-ordinated at a distance.

One major change in the organization of industrial production was the vastly larger size of firms. Although small firms derived benefits from the electrification of industry because it gave them more flexibility on the shop floor, in many key industries large amounts of capital were needed for production. The increase in the size of firms during the third cycle was phenomenal. These large companies had a multi-divisional structure and employed a large number of managers to supervise the operations of the various divisions; owners no longer directly controlled the firm.

The business historian, Alfred Chandler (1990), has argued that technological change was ultimately responsible for the birth of the large corporations that continue to dominate the contemporary industrial landscape. The development of faster means of transportation and new forms of communication meant that each company could serve a larger market and greatly expand its production. This, in turn, meant that firms could achieve economies of scale and economies of scope in their production and distribution activities, thereby increasing their productivity and cost advantage over other, smaller firms. The main economic consequence of the presence of economies of scale and scope is that it becomes much more efficient to produce goods in one or a few large firms rather than in many small firms. The structure of industry becomes concentrated as a few large companies begin to dominate some key industries.

Economies of scale exist when outputs increase at a higher proportion than the increase in inputs. Put differently, unit costs fall and productivity increases as output expands. Often this can be a feature of technology. To understand what this means, consider a steel firm that wants to heat pig iron and turn it into steel. Typically, a large running cost is heating the furnace. The cost of heating such a furnace generally rises more slowly than the volume of steel

Economies of scale
Economies of scale exist when the average cost of output (the cost of a unit of the good produced) falls when the number of units produced increases. For example, economies of scale exist when it is cheaper to produce twice the output in one firm than it is for two firms to produce the same output: that is, when cost of $(2X)$ < cost of (X) + cost of (X).

that the firm can extract. In such cases, large capacity furnaces will have a higher productivity, other things being equal. A further source of economies of scale (not unrelated to technology) is the structure of costs. Cost can be fixed or variable: fixed costs are incurred irrespective of the quantity of output produced, for example, rent and cost of machinery; variable costs are incurred as output increases, for example, cost of raw material and labour. When a large proportion of the costs of production are due to fixed costs, economies of scale almost inevitably arise. This is due to the fact that as the unchanging fixed costs are spread over larger and larger quantities of output, the per unit cost falls.

The concept of economies of scope is similar to that of economies of scale, the difference being that the high fixed costs are spread over many products instead of many units of the same products. For instance, the R&D activities of firms give rise to economies of scope because the knowledge gained in R&D is often applied to different products. The investment incurred to set up distribution and marketing networks is also an example of economies of scope because those networks can be used for selling different products.

Economies of scope
Economies of scope exist when the sum of the costs per unit (average costs) of two or more goods is lower when they are produced jointly (for example, in the same firm) than when they are produced separately. For example, economies of scope exist when it is cheaper for a firm to produce $X + Y$ (two goods) together rather than for one firm to produce X and another Y: that is, when cost of $(X + Y)$ < cost of (X) + cost of (Y).

Activity 10.2

Does advertising investment in a brand name such as Virgin give rise to economies of scale and/or scope?

The existence of economies of scale and scope for a firm are closely related to a specific form of industrial organization, that is, the vertically integrated firm. A vertically integrated firm produces all of the inputs required for the production of its final product. Steel firms are a good example, as they would process the raw iron ore into pig iron, combine it with coal to melt the pig iron into steel and, lastly, cast the steel into ingots that could be sold to other firms. In such an organization, there were naturally economies of scale but also economies of scope from activities such as marketing and distribution. Once a distribution channel was established, firms could sell more than steel through it, and make money by trading other goods of scarce supply in the region, not necessarily produced by them.

While economies of scale and scope were important factors behind the increased productivity of leading firms in this third wave period, they also constituted an important barrier to the entry of new firms into these sectors. The scale of the investments and the accumulated technological learning of these large firms meant that industrial leadership was hard to challenge. New firms and countries seeking to industrialize would have to wait for a new window of opportunity, or find new markets.

4.3 Convergence and divergence in the Atlantic economy of the late nineteenth and early twentieth centuries

The third wave was also associated with the first big phase of internationalization in the world economy between 1880 and 1914, a period that saw a slow convergence in wage incomes between the leading economies and a number of countries in the European periphery. In order to measure this convergence, O'Rourke and Williamson (2000) looked at the gap between average wage incomes in the 'catch-up' countries (Sweden, Norway, Italy, Spain, Russia, and so forth) and average wage incomes in the leaders (the USA and Britain). They found that real wage convergence did take place over time as a consequence of economic growth: ferociously for the Scandinavian countries, more sedately for Ireland and Italy. However, Spain and Portugal never quite caught up in this period. O'Rourke and Williamson also investigated the sources of this convergence. They considered the role of five factors that might have raised productivity and hence incomes in the catch-up economies: schooling, mass migration, capital flows, trade and technological progress. Table 10.2 summarizes their findings. The figures in the table represent the share of convergence (or divergence) explained by the factor concerned. Notice that the figures for the technological progress column are a residual, that is, they are derived after the figures for the other columns have been estimated. In other words, convergence (or divergence) that is not explained by schooling, mass migration, capital flows and trade is attributed to technological progress. The wide range of figures in some cases results from the fact that these are statistical estimates.

Table 10.2   Sources of catch-up and fall-back around the European periphery (per cent), 1870–1910

	Real wage convergence (or divergence) on Britain explained by				
	Schooling	Mass migration	Capital flows	Trade	Residual (technological progress)
Denmark	5–8	3.9–5.7	30.0	<3.9	<52.4–57.2
Norway	5–6	8.9–20.0	35.1	4.4	<34.5–46.6
Sweden	4–5	2.9–8.4	43.0	3.1	40.5–47.0
Italy	0	64.8–67.8	Positive	Positive?	<32.3–35.2
Ireland	0	83.6–86.9	Small/ positive	0?	<13.1–39.7
Portugal	(58–all)	(16.7–29.6)	(0)	(0?)	(0–25.3)
Spain	(10–all)	(0–3.5)	(0)	(0?)	(0–90.0)

	Real wage convergence (or divergence) on the USA explained by				
	Schooling	Mass migration	Capital flows	Trade	Residual (technological progress)
Denmark	0–9	31.9–49.2	16.3	<12.1	<13.3–39.7
Norway	0–9	40.6–67.7	20.0	<13.9	<<0–25.5
Sweden	0–8	24.6–41.4	34.0	9.4	7.2–32.0
Italy	0	All	0?	0?	0
Ireland	0–5	All	0	0	0
Portugal	(94–all)	(0)	(0?)	(+?)	(0–6)
Spain	(51–all)	(0)	(0?)	(+?)	(0–49)

Source: O'Rourke and Williamson, 2000, Table 14.4

Activity 10.3

Look carefully at the data in Table 10.2 for Sweden, Italy and Ireland, Spain and Portugal. Then look carefully at the data in the columns for mass migration and capital flows compared with those for trade. What do these numbers indicate to you and what might you conclude from them?

Nevertheless, the inter-war years also saw the development of another form of catch-up which did not arise from trade and international movements of capital and labour: the surprise emergence of Russia, emulating aspects of the German response. Led by a strong state, the rapid transformation of the Soviet economy from an agricultural economy to a modern industrial one, through a mixture of import substitution and planning, was to powerfully appeal to and impact on anti-colonial movements, then and after the Second World War.

4.4   Challenges to economic leadership

As you have seen, the USA and Germany developed new organizations and institutions for the effective exploitation of economies of scale and scope which were offered by the new technologies and industries of the third wave. By contrast, the failure of Britain to take the lead in the development of the new technologies is surprising, especially given that many of the key inventions which underpinned the new technologies took place in Britain and that it remained the world's scientific leader. In fact, not only did scientific discoveries occur in Britain, but many innovations were introduced there either before or at the same time as in Germany or the USA.

Why was the UK slow in the take up of the new technology?

One important reason was that British institutions were largely suited to trade and the relatively small-scale entrepreneurship of the earlier long cycle. This was most clearly evident in the failure of its well-developed financial institutions. An effective financial system enables firms to raise the capital needed for investment in new technologies. Large sums of capital investment were required in the new industries, but the City of London was more preoccupied with the short-term return on the investments undertaken abroad than the more uncertain long-term prospects offered by the new technologies. Outward foreign direct investment (FDI) was favoured over domestic investment in new technology, and London was occupied with foreign and colonial issues rather than with the new technologies and entrepreneurial activity.

Britain was thus locked into an old system which made it difficult to support the diffusion and development of new technologies. It also failed to develop institutions that would support the two important complementary investments needed to realize the potential offered by electricity and steel-based technologies. The first was an educational system for engineering and managerial labour; the British system was still based on apprenticeship which was unsuited to the science-based nature of electricity and chemical technologies. The second was that firms failed to invest in market development activities which were crucial in order to realize the large-scale potential offered by the new technologies.

5   Changes in the techno-economic system

It is difficult to map what happened in the USA and Germany during the diffusion of electricity-based technologies on to the linear, technology-push model. This is primarily because in both countries new institutions emerged to facilitate the diffusion of technologies and, in this process, firms and the state behaved differently in each case. That is to say, particular configurations of actors and institutions evolved to produce a unique pattern of innovation and economic activity.

5.1   Systems of innovation

As an alternative to the technology-push model, we can understand innovation in terms of a 'system' of separate institutions which repeatedly interact with feedbacks throughout the innovation process. Indeed, technology itself is a system. Artefacts are usually made of components that are very different in terms of the knowledge and skills required to produce them. A firm that introduces an innovation needs to find and bring together the various components necessary to succeed. Sometimes, components of a new product can be bought on the market, and at other times the knowledge to produce them is publicly available. Firms may innovate themselves or draw on the innovations of others. In fact, many innovative firms buy important components from reliable suppliers. Often the role of suppliers in the introduction of innovations is crucial because they have the skills (tacit knowledge) necessary to produce important new components for new products. In many cases, customers also provide valuable inputs in the innovation process. For example, software companies release free 'beta-versions' of new software that are advance versions of the 'alpha' software, but not yet good enough to be sold. Users can then help them to find out how to improve the beta software through feedback.

The list of institutions involved in the introduction of new technology does not only include firms and their customers. Scientific institutions such as universities and government laboratories are the repository of knowledge about scientific disciplines; they provide essential training for scientists and engineers who work in firms, and play an important role in the development of scientific instrumentation. Since innovative investments are often substantial, uncertain, and usually pay off only after a long time, efficient financial institutions that support innovation are essential actors in the development of new technology. As the example of the development of the patent system shows, governments can do much to influence innovative activities besides funding R&D activities and ensuring a sufficient level of education by designing appropriate institutions. The institutions involved in the innovation process can also include trade associations, trade unions and so on. Figure 10.2 describes the structure of a 'system of innovation'.

Therefore, although often introduced by firms, successful innovation is ultimately the product of a system of institutions which are closely linked by economic and social relationships. The various institutions have different skills and make different contributions to the innovation process. The notion of a system of innovation recognizes that tacit knowledge has an important role in the innovation process. If technological knowledge was only public, a firm would be able to buy some new components on the market or to gather all the necessary knowledge to introduce an innovation without recourse to other organizations. Yet since technology is partly tacit and partly embodied in other organizations, any given organization usually has to interact with others in order to be able to use knowledge which it does not possess in-house.

System of innovation
A system of innovation is made up of economic agents (such as firms, universities and industry associations) and the institutional set-up in which they operate (such as regulations, customs and norms). It affects all the various processes, such as learning, searching, investing and marketing associated with the development of new technology.

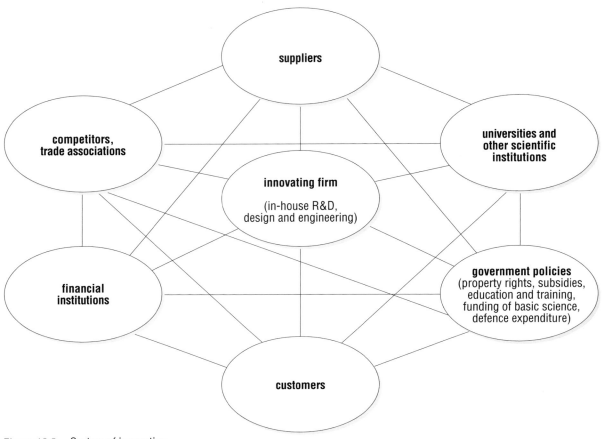

Figure 10.2   System of innovation

Source: Simonetti, 1998, p.317

Markets

The term used to define notional product spaces in which many buyers and sellers bid for the same product and so determine its price. It identifies a realm of exchange based on competitive price formation, usually involving private property and legally enforceable contracts. Markets may exist for goods, services, currencies, shares and so on.

The activities and relationships within systems of innovations are institutionalized in different ways, according to the nature of the organizations involved. First, innovation systems are located in market economies, where firms compete for customers in order to make profits. Many relationships between firms and their suppliers, customers and financial intermediaries occur through the price mechanism, shrouded in the anonymity of markets. For example, firms buy many of the standard parts and components that they need from suppliers on the market.

Second, systems are shaped indirectly by government regulations and by more direct intervention as well as by funding. For instance, some argue that systems located in an institutional context with a strong definition and enforcement of intellectual property rights (IPRs), such as penalties for patent infringement, are more effective at promoting innovation because of the public nature of technology. Hierarchies also play an important role *within* large firms, in the way that R&D projects are funded and choices are made about what technologies to develop.

Third, some of the relationships between the various elements of the system are based on trust or on shared values or interests, perhaps reinforced by a common cultural background. These network relationships are important in the innovation process because collaboration in innovation is usually a very delicate matter because one party has the potential to exploit its partner by taking advantage of the knowledge received during the collaboration, given its public good attributes.

The actors and institutions comprising a 'system of innovation', bound together by different combinations of markets, hierarchies and networks, can be organized nationally (national systems of innovation) or around given sets of technologies (technological systems). Technological systems are more narrowly defined than national systems of innovation because they refer to technologies rather than countries, but the inclusion of multinational companies gives them an international dimension. Finally, systems of innovation have also been considered at the local, or regional, level. This is useful, at least in some cases where many organizations that contribute to a system are concentrated in a geographical area, as happens in Silicon Valley in the USA for information technology, or in various industrial districts in the North of Italy and Germany.

5.2   The evolution of technology systems: incremental and discontinuous technical change

Once we focus on a system of innovation, the distinction between invention, innovation and diffusion emphasized in the technology-push model becomes blurred because of the complex ways in which the parts of the systems interact. It is more useful to think of the accumulation of technological knowledge in the system through learning, often along a technological paradigm. According to the economist Giovanni Dosi:

> ... both scientific and technological paradigms embody an outlook, a definition of the relevant problems, a pattern of enquiry. A 'technological paradigm' defines contextually the needs that are meant to be fulfilled, the scientific principles utilized for the task, the material technology to be used. In other words, a technological paradigm can be defined as a 'pattern' of solutions of selected techno-economic problems based on highly selected principles derived from the natural sciences, jointly with specific rules aimed to acquire new knowledge and safeguard it, whenever possible, against rapid diffusion to the competitors. Examples of such

Hierarchies
As used here, the term refers to forms of organization that involve purposively regulated design and direction oriented towards an objective or set of objectives. A hierarchy is based on authority, rules and administrative procedures. Hierarchies exist within firms as well as in the bureaucracies of states and non-governmental organizations.

Network
As used here, networks are forms of organization that are neither governed by purposeful authority nor ordered by competition, but operate on the basis of things such as trust and loyalty. They may or may not be linked to technological networks, that is, connected forms of distributed ICTs.

technological paradigms include the internal combustion engine, oil-based synthetic chemistry and semiconductors.

(Dosi, 1988, p.1127)

Thus, the evolution of technologies within a paradigm is strongly cumulative and does not involve discontinuous, radical changes. While small, incremental change, the search by trial and error, is cheaper in terms of time and resources because it reduces the possible alternatives to be considered, it also creates institutional and cultural rigidities which can hinder the creation and diffusion of radically new technologies. Systems can be locked into some technological paradigms, and some promising technologies may be developed with great delays or not at all. It is difficult to change technology when everything works well just because an emerging technology *could* be promising!

Indeed, when a new dominant paradigm emerges, some of the existing accumulated competencies become obsolete because the knowledge base is different, or different organizations and institutions are required, or the type of new machinery needed is different. This discontinuity can result in what Schumpeter (1942) called 'creative destruction', that is, incumbents (firms, people, regions and even countries) being replaced by new, innovative challengers.

5.3 Changes in the techno-economic paradigm

Christopher Freeman and Carlota Perez (1988) have developed the distinction between incremental and discontinuous technical change within and between technological paradigms to encompass the idea of a techno-economic paradigm, that is, the emergence of new *generic* technologies which have such a pervasive impact on the economy that they produce new markets and industries affecting almost every branch of the economy. It is precisely these generic technologies, alongside the organizations and institutions that co-evolve with them, that form the basis of the waves identified in Table 10.1 (see Section 2). An important part of this argument is that, at first, new technologies are locked out of the system by the inertia of the previous paradigm, which acts at different levels, both technical and institutional. The new paradigm emerges 'only when productivity along the old trajectories shows persistent limits to growth and future profits are seriously threatened [so] that the high risks and costs of trying the new technologies appear as clearly justified' (Freeman and Perez, 1988, p.49). As new generic and pervasive technologies affect the whole economy, changes in the techno-economic paradigm have an impact on national systems of innovation and therefore on the technological (and hence economic) performance of countries.

In turn, this may have consequences for the relations between states: as international economic leadership shifts from one to another, so political relations may alter. The rise of German economic power before the First World War and during the inter-war years, as with the rise of Japanese economic power, played an important role in precipitating the two world wars. The political leadership of the USA in the capitalist world (see Chapter 5) was, of course, closely related to its economic leadership which began to emerge in the third wave and was decisively consolidated during the fourth (see Section 2, Table 10.1).

6   Catching up: 1950 to 1980

Just as the earlier waves of industrialization under British leadership unleashed a phase of globalization, so the fourth wave of mass production and mass consumption pioneered in the USA (Chapter 5, following Gramsci, called this Americanism) was associated with another phase of globalization after the Second World War. The post-war globalization boom saw many European countries experience a process of catching up with the USA which was linked to the domestic development of mass production and mass consumption. The technological and economic aspects of these developments – oil (petrol), automobiles, motorization and mass production assembly lines servicing mass consumer markets and so forth – are often referred to simply as Fordism, after the pioneering developments of Henry Ford's Model T factories. In the inter-war years, in his writings on 'Americanism and Fordism', Gramsci wrote of 'an ultra-modern form of production and of working methods – such as is offered by the most advanced American variety, the industry of Henry Ford' (1971, pp.280–1). After the Second World War, significant elements of this model of economic development spread to Europe and Japan.

Technology transfer from the USA to Europe took place both through European missions to study US plants and through the establishment of US multinationals in Europe. Increasing regional integration in the European market, as barriers to trade and investment fell, provided an important factor in the stimulation of mass production. In the Far East, Japan renewed its process of catching up which had begun after the Meiji Restoration of 1868 but had been halted by defeat in the Second World War. The assimilation of foreign technology played an important role in this catch-up. Though it started with import substitution in steel, Japan soon started competing in export markets (especially in automobiles and then in consumer electronics). Later, Japanese investment spread to several East Asian economies, becoming an important source of technology transfer to these economies.

The degree to which technology transfer was associated with openness to trade and capital flows varied widely. As noted in Section 4.3, the development of the Soviet Union had shown that it was possible to industrialize without extensive integration into the world economy. In many countries in the post-colonial world, the success of the Soviet model combined with a general pessimism about exports and a determination to overcome a 'colonial' international division of labour, provided a rationale for a new model of growth based on state-led investment, import-substituting industrialization (that is, industrial policy that aims to replace imported goods with locally produced goods, usually through protectionism and incentives to local production), and tariffs. In an influential paper, Sachs and Warner (1995) argued that as many as 73 developing countries followed some kind of import-substituting strategy and only 17 developing economies pursued openness as a strategy to increase growth.

There is now a significant body of statistical evidence and analysis devoted to the post-war performance of nations and the issue of catch-up in the world economy. We want to highlight two main findings from this literature. The first shows the existence of a 'convergence club', that is, a group of countries, led by the USA and including the Organization for Economic Co-operation and Development (OECD) countries and some East Asian economies, where average incomes converged on those of the leaders. Taken as a whole, this group of countries showed average levels of income and productivity far ahead of the second 'club' made up of diverse developing countries, where incomes (and levels of productivity) did not show any evidence of catching up, or convergence, with the first club.

The second group of findings shows that openness to international trade and investment is associated with faster growth and catching up (Edwards, 1993). These kinds of findings have been challenged by other economists on methodological and empirical grounds. There is also some dispute about what these associations indicate, as there is sometimes an ambiguity about the meaning of openness. It can refer to an outcome (that is, a high share of trade to GDP) or to a policy variable (that is, a low level of tariff and non-tariff barriers to trade and FDI). In particular, there is considerable disagreement about the impact of low trade barriers on growth. Qualitative evidence from case studies supports the idea that export orientation offers more opportunities for learning through contacts with foreign technology. In many ways, the experience of East Asian countries seems to support the link between openness and catching up. East Asian newly industrializing countries (NICs) carried out massive imports of technology through FDI (often joint ventures), sub-contracting and original equipment manufacturers, and licensing and other contracts. However, trade openness is not the same as free trade. The East Asian NICs also practised import substitution but they avoided the bias against exports characteristic of many models, and they actively sought out foreign technology and investment in key sectors (see Section 8).

This second group of findings suggests that globalization was important as a means to access new technologies, a point that emerged in O'Rourke and Williamson's findings for the period from 1880 to 1914 discussed in Section 4.3. The disturbing aspect of the catch-up in the post-war period is how little it changed the ranking of economic power in the world economy, which remained concentrated largely in the North, despite generating new challengers to US leadership in Western Europe and Japan (Chapter 11 explores some of these issues in more detail).

Increasingly, US firms faced competition from Europe and, in particular, from Germany, which had experienced a significant period of catching up due to the successful assimilation of Fordism. Notably, the Japanese challenge was based upon a new form of production organization which paid attention to process control and the minimization of inventory stocks by developing a network of supplier firms that would deliver key inputs to production 'just-in-time'. This marked a move towards outsourcing which enabled Japanese firms to reduce the extent of their fixed costs, and to keep capacity flexible to meet changing demand conditions. In addition, both German and Japanese firms placed utmost importance upon design and quality control, made possible by their better methods of process control. Not surprisingly these countries won large market shares on international markets. A second wave of challengers emerged with the progress of ICT technologies. In order to explore this, we now turn to the crisis of Fordism and the emergence of ICTs.

7   The crisis of Fordism and the emergence of ICTs

From the late 1960s, growing international competition and excess capacity plagued most sectors of mass production. The resulting fall in profitability exacerbated disputes with labour over wages, and poor industrial relations characterized a number of sectors. Meantime, ICT technologies continued to make scientific progress. Trends in data storage, processing power and networking were all on the increase. What is known as Moore's Law stated that the number of transistors on a chip would double every 12 to 18 months, implying that a chip containing just over 1000 transistors at the beginning of the 1970s would contain around 100 million by the turn of the century. At the same time, the cost of information stored per gigabyte plummeted from around US$10 000 in 1988 to less than US$10 in 2002.

In addition, important progress was made in connecting memory chips to other chips (giving rise to networked computers and the Internet), and to switching devices (making possible the emergence of numerically controlled devices and machines). The costs of telecommunications fell

importance of the *strategic choice* of technologies and related economic activities which are potentially available to developing countries. One clear message that emerges from the East Asian experience is the importance at any given time of what a country produces, and of what technologies it has mastered for subsequent economic growth. These countries were able to use trade and protection in a strategic way to acquire specialization (dynamic comparative advantage) in new technologies which were to have considerable economies of scale and of scope. Specifically, East Asian economies were strategic about protecting and promoting their ICT industries long before these were established as the dominant paradigm.

To what extent can others emulate this success? In order to address this, we shall now review two special features that are important for all developing economies: the importance of technological learning, including technology transfer and the accumulation of technological capabilities; and the role of trade and FDI.

8.1   Technology transfer and technological capabilities

The dominant model of technology transfer to developing countries in the 1950s and 1960s was based upon the linear model of technology push. Typically, technology transfer took the form of a project (for example, setting up a steel plant), using a developed country firm together with a developing country firm. By these means, it was assumed that technology would be transferred from one country to another. The view that technology was either publicly available knowledge, or that it could be purchased on markets, and the neglect of tacit knowledge embodied in the skills and routines of people, organizations and institutions, led many researchers and policy makers to a false assumption. They believed that developing countries had an advantage in the process of industrialization because they could simply access the available technological information and copy the advanced technology already produced by the leading countries, while incurring little innovative expenditure. If this were true, technology transfer would be easy and relatively cheap.

Question

Why do you think the linear, technology-push model of innovation might be misleading in the case of technology transfer to developing countries?

As you might expect, there were several problems with this model of technology transfer. The technology transferred was often developed in a US or European context and not fully suited to the individual needs of the developing country. Furthermore, while it was easy enough for developing countries to buy a piece of machinery (the artefacts) and the blueprints for a plant, the knowledge and skills necessary to build and operate the machinery efficiently were harder to acquire. Tacit knowledge embodied in skills, routines, organizations and institutions could not be easily copied. Successful technology transfer, therefore, involved much more than acquiring information and buying machinery; it required a process of learning that was neither costless, nor easy.

Moreover, since technologies require systems of innovation to support them, successful transfer of technology to developing countries often requires the creation of one or more new systems of institutions where people, firms and other organizations interact effectively in some technological areas. If some key elements of systems are missing, the transfer of technology often fails. In fact, viewed from a systems perspective, technology transfer is only part of a larger process of accumulation of technological capabilities.

In this context, Bell and Pavitt (1997) have drawn a distinction between *technological* and *productive* capabilities. Productive capabilities are the skills necessary to operate given production systems, while technological capabilities refer to the ability to successfully introduce changes in the technology acquired. The latter requires the accumulation of a stock of resources, both physical and disembodied, to generate and manage technological change. Technological capabilities also include a broad range of knowledge and skills which go beyond the purely technological sphere. Expressly, management skills are necessary for the successful acquisition of technology, and bargaining skills are important to obtain the technology at a fair price and with advantageous conditions.

Technology transfer involves a diverse set of activities which includes: the definition of technology wanted; identification of potential suppliers; negotiations; ensuring that the core technology is transferred (and not only part of it) with local subcontracting for the rest; the participation of local human capital from the beginning of the project; and investment in systems for future innovation. Many of these skills are only acquired by a process of learning through experience. The key element in this stock of resources is the tacit knowledge embodied in people, firms and other institutions – namely, an innovation system – through a process of learning. This is costly, takes time and requires an explicit investment in acquiring and accumulating knowledge and skill.

Although there are various channels through which knowledge can be accumulated in a system, it is important that explicit investment in learning takes place within firms so that their 'absorptive capacity', that is, their ability to acquire external knowledge, increases. Thus, private firms have a central role in innovation systems and are the main locus of technological learning and change. These firms can ultimately introduce the innovation on the market, but technologically advanced suppliers and competent customers are also an important part of the innovation system. In industrialized countries the suppliers and users of diffusing technology typically already possess the knowledge and skill needed to support the development of new technology, but in developing countries stocks of these capabilities usually have to be accumulated before the full benefit from technology diffusion can be realized.

A further important source of learning for East Asian countries was postgraduate education in developed countries which not only accessed technological knowledge but also gained access to international networks. Movements of personnel are also useful between firms within the same country in order to facilitate the diffusion of new technology in the economy. For example, experience is crucial to managerial learning, and managerial skills learnt in a specific area may be generic skills which can be used to promote technology transfer in related areas. For instance, in South Korea the use of knowledge developed in the petrochemical industry was used to manage technology transfer in the refinery industry; project management skills in electric power utilities were used in the development of power engineering and equipment industries (Enos and Park, 1988; Westphal *et al.*, 1985).

Government policy can favour learning in firms in various ways. A key area for government intervention is education. Although general education has little direct impact on technological knowledge because much of it is abstract in nature, various studies have stressed the indirect importance of universal education in development because it teaches people how to learn, and improves the effectiveness of on-the-job training. In addition, government can provide financial help for risky activities which are aimed at learning. One example is on-the-job training because firms traditionally tend to under-invest in training as skilled employees may then be poached from rival companies. Another illustration is risk-sharing in particularly new and risky technologies.

More generally, government policy has a crucial role to play in the design of the institutional environment in which the various parts of the innovation systems operate. A well-designed legal system which protects property rights generally and, especially, intellectual property rights such as patents, is conducive to more investment in innovation because it provides private firms with the incentive to learn and innovate. Other policies can also offer incentives to learn; for example, in Japan the Ministry for Trade and Industry (MITI) introduced a requirement for companies to demonstrate a minimum level of skills in order to tender for government contracts.

The investment made by the East Asian states and firms in technological learning of ICT technologies is clear when we look at Table 10.6. It compares technological specialization in ICTs between Brazil and South Korea (the former was also successful in the development and diffusion of ICTs). It shows distinctly that South Korea undertook a significant investment in the creation of knowledge and skill compared to Brazil.

Table 10.6   National systems of innovation in Brazil and South Korea: some quantitative indicators

Indicators of technological capability and national institutions	Brazil	South Korea
Percentage of age group in higher education (1985)	11	32
Engineering students as a percentage of the population (1985)	0.13	0.54
R&D as a percentage of GNP (1987)	0.7	2.1
Industry R&D as a percentage of total R&D (1988)	30	65
Robots per million employed (1987)	52	1060
Telephone lines per 100 persons (1989)	6	25
Technological specialization in ICTs (1990–96): laser technology	0.00	1.15
Technological specialization in ICTs (1990–96): telecom equipment	0.24	1.43
Technological specialization in ICTs (1990–96): machine controls	0.78	1.03
Technological specialization in ICTs (1990–96): semiconductors	0.10	4.79
Technological specialization in ICTs (1990–96): electrical and electronic instruments	0.41	0.67
Technological specialization in ICTs (1990–96): calculators, computers, data processing systems	0.05	1.59

Note: The indicator of technological specialization, which is based on US patent data, indicates a strength (positive specialization) in the technology if the value is above 1, and a weakness if the value is below 1.

Source: adapted from Freeman, 1997, and elaboration of US Patent and Trademark Office (USPTO) patent data by Roberto Simonetti

8.2   Trade, FDI and the accumulation of technological capabilities

The relationship between trade and investment policy, and development is a long-standing source of controversy. Supporters of protection stress the need for sheltering infant industries from foreign competition so that a domestic industrial base can be built up. However, supporters of free trade emphasize both the static advantages of trade, illustrated by the theory of comparative advantage, and the dynamic opportunities for learning offered by contact with foreign technology. Similarly, inward FDI has often been viewed with suspicion by those who argue that screwdriver assembly plants only exploit the existing cheap labour without transferring any skills or technology, but they are considered to be a key vehicle of learning by others. We commented earlier that a significant body of statistical evidence shows that openness to international trade and investment is associated with faster growth and catching up. Furthermore, we noted that qualitative evidence from case studies (especially from the experience of Japan and East Asia) supports the idea that export orientation offers more opportunities for learning through contacts with foreign technology. Nevertheless, a conclusion that free trade is always good across the board for the accumulation of technological capabilities and catching up would be too simplistic for two main reasons.

First, even East Asian countries such as Taiwan and South Korea went through initial stages of import substitution, which were important to start the accumulation of technological capabilities. Correspondingly, MITI in Japan engaged in some infant industry protectionism, although mostly temporary and retaining appropriate elements of competition, both domestically and externally. More recently, a similar argument has been made with regard to the rise of the Indian software industry (Athreye, 2004). More generally, it can be seen from a historical perspective that an initial period of import substitution is usually necessary for the creation of an industrial base with domestic technological capabilities (Reinert, 1995). This initial period sees the creation of dynamic comparative advantage, rather than reliance on static comparative advantage. In other words, relative costs are not treated as a given from the start, as they are in the model of static comparative advantage, but as variables which can be changed through investment in learning. Once strength is established in key products and technologies, freer trade and investment become more attractive options.

Second, while contact with foreign technology offers opportunities for learning, the absorption of foreign technology only occurs in particular conditions. For example, the research of Westphal *et al.* (1985) on the development of South Korean technological capabilities emphasized the importance of the early involvement of Koreans in inward FDI projects, as this enabled them to learn valuable skills from the experience. In addition, the training and learning components of technology transfer agreements with foreign companies covered much more than the acquisition of competences for operating and maintaining new facilities. They explicitly focused on acquiring various combinations of design, engineering and project management.

Given the right conditions, foreign investment can be a positive sum game for both the host and home country firms. Carlota Perez (2000) argues that in the 1950s and 1960s, import-substitution policies tended to work because of the characteristics of the mature and capital intensive paradigm of the time. Multinationals from industrialized countries faced saturated domestic markets, and expanded their markets by exporting parts to their subsidiaries in developing countries where the final products were assembled. Those subsidiaries, in turn, provided some learning opportunities for local workers and managers, and stimulated the demand for infrastructure required for industrialization such as roads, ports, transport, electricity, water and communications. Mature technologies could also be transferred relatively easily to developing countries and, in the 1960s, the production of many goods was moved from industrialized countries to 'export processing zones', which were attractive because of their low wage costs.

Perez stresses that these arrangements were successful because they were beneficial for both multinationals and consumers in industrialized countries which gained from low labour costs, and for developing countries which received both physical investment and transfer of technology. This situation changed with the crisis of adjustment during the 1970s which marked the decline of the mass production paradigm. With the advanced countries facing recessions or slow growth, export markets for developing countries shrunk. At this time, East Asian countries were able to exploit the potential of ICTs both by entering some new markets and, crucially, by capturing market share in mature industries that were rejuvenated through the application of the new technologies. They did so by keeping an outward orientation and by joining networks of multinationals as original equipment manufacturers, suppliers of parts and components. The participation in global networks was achieved thanks to the earlier phase of explicit investment in learning and the active absorption of technology. Moreover, being part of those networks offered excellent opportunities for further learning and catching up.

To return to the question of the implications of ICTs for enabling developing countries, our conclusions are ambiguous. The emergence of global networks of production and distribution create opportunities for firms in developing countries to access the technologies, capital and markets of the developed world. However, the ability of developing countries to assimilate these technologies in an effective manner presupposes a host of complementary economic, organizational and institutional developments. Indeed, the latter may be more important in the case of ICTs precisely because of their complexity and pervasiveness across modern economies. While the former set of considerations might suggest that ICTs *lower* the barriers to developing countries participating in world trade and investment, the latter might suggest that ICTs *raise* these barriers. The balance between these forces is likely to differ from country to country and the overall impact remains to be seen.

9 Conclusion

The aim of this chapter has been to give you some tools with which to think about the economic components of the global network society thesis. The first claim was one about the novelty of ICTs and their dependence on knowledge. We have seen that there have been earlier 'waves' of basic technological change that have had major impacts on economic developments. The alleged novelty of ICTs has to be evaluated against these other changes. We have also seen that the relation between knowledge, learning and innovation is complex. In particular, we have seen that it can be more useful to focus on systems of innovation as whole, rather than a simple idea of knowledge and technology as the linear drivers of economic change. This suggests that ICTs are one element of a complex picture of change.

ICTs emerged as pervasive and important because they enabled economic leaders in the 1970s (the USA, Japan and Germany) to tackle problems of overcapacity arising in Fordist mass production industries. And although technological change has been part of the solution to the crisis of the economic leaders, the organizational and institutional changes that enabled new technologies to take root have been far more important. The successful diffusion of ICTs has involved new forms of production based on vertical disintegration; new sets of institutions (such as venture capital); and access to complementary investments (for example, in education and telecommunications). Some of these can be networked across borders and others are highly localized. For example, smaller, more flexible firms can be networked with one another, while the infrastructure of higher education remains predominantly national. There is no simple trend to more global, less local forms of organization.

This finding bears directly on the second claim – that ICTs are facilitating networks, specifically global networks. It may well be true, and Chapter 11 considers this topic in more detail. But international economic integration, especially through factor markets, and economic convergence operated in the Atlantic economy of the late nineteenth and early twentieth centuries, long before the advent of ICTs. Innovation, investment and growth can be configured by a mixture of markets, networks and hierarchies and, in any case, network forms of organization long pre-dated ICTs.

This also suggests, finally, that the ability of forces of globalization based on ICT networks to raise the incomes of the poor needs to be evaluated carefully. There are undoubtedly opportunities for developing countries arising from new technologies, but there is also the danger of exclusion given the range of complementary investments in people, organizations and institutions needed to realize those opportunities. These questions of international inequality form the central concern of Chapter 11.

Further reading

For a wide-ranging synthesis of a range of literatures on the sources and waves of industrial development, including a discussion of the perspective that informs this chapter, see von Tunzelmann, G.N. (1995) *Technology and Industrial Progress: The Foundations of Economic Growth*, Cheltenham, Edward Elgar.

Another very readable account of the role of technology in the economic growth of nations, covering ancient society, China and medieval Europe as well as the industrial revolution, is Mokyr, J. (1990) *The Lever of Riches: Technological Creativity and Economic Progress*, Oxford, Oxford University Press.

A more detailed exposition of the idea of long waves based on a succession of techno-economic paradigms is given in Freeman, C. and Louçã, F. (2001) *As Time Goes By*, Oxford, Oxford University Press.

Chapter 11 Global inequality, economic globalization and technological change

Grahame Thompson

1   Introduction

> Today technology deserves new attention. Why? Because digital, genetic and molecular breakthroughs are pushing forward the frontiers of how people can use technology to eradicate poverty. These breakthroughs are creating new possibilities for improving health and nutrition, expanding knowledge, stimulating economic growth and empowering people to participate in their communities. Today's technological transformations are intertwined with another transformation – globalization – and together they are creating a new paradigm: the network age.

(United Nations Development Programme, 2001, *Human Development Report*, p.27)

> Between 1988 and 1998, the incidence of global poverty fell by the derisory rate of 0.2 per cent a year. Already obscene global income inequalities are widening. ... The world economy ended the 1980s more unequal than any national economy, and since then it has become even more unequal.

(Watkins, 2002)

> The anti-globalization movement is not simply a network, it is an electronic network, it is an Internet-based movement. And because the Internet is its home it cannot be disorganized or captured. It swims like fish in the net.

(Castells, 2001, p.142)

> In the talk in America and Europe about the 'war on terrorism', little has been said about tackling root causes. Somewhere along the line, the attacks on the World Trade Center and the Pentagon stemmed from tensions created by the widening gulf between the rich and poor nations.

(*International Herald Tribune*, 3 October 2001)

These four quotations neatly provide a snapshot of the interrelated issues that are raised and discussed in this and the following chapters. First, as discussed in Chapter 10, there is the issue of technology, particularly information and communication technologies (ICTs), which are argued by many to be heralding a new way of organizing society: the 'network age'. This technologically-driven network age is in turn linked to the advent of economic 'globalization' – the progressive extension of trade interdependence and investment integration across the globe. Second, there is the issue of economic inequality. Has this grown globally as the network age has matured and the process of globalization gathered pace? Moreover, there are two reactions to this. On the one hand, we have the anti-globalization movement which Castells, amongst many, has linked to these other developments. On the other hand, there is the issue of the possible larger consequences of growing global inequality and poverty, technological diffusion and globalization which some – the *International Herald Tribune* in this instance – have seen as one of the main causes for such acts as the 2001 destruction of the World Trade Center building in New York and the rise of the al-Qaeda movement. This movement is also often spoken of as a network – a loosely knit matrix of cells and groups, which operate relatively autonomously from one another, so that the network itself is very difficult to pin down.

Clearly, these issues are only loosely linked together and the connections are contentious. As we will see later, the claims made here are frequently disputed, but they do capture a flavour of the key international developments that emerged at the beginning of this century. This chapter is concerned with some of the international developments – growing global integration, income inequality, the uneven spread of technology, and network forms of organization – that lie behind these claims. We are concerned with global inequality and the relation of this to globalization, and to technological innovation. Chapter 12 considers the role of networks in relation to forms of protest and dissent, while Chapter 13 discusses some of the implications of inequality, networks and technology for the future of global conflict.

Section 2 of this chapter begins with the issue of international inequality because this is closely linked to technological inequalities. The inequality of incomes between countries is one of the reasons why the global distribution of technology is so unequal. At the same time, as you saw in Chapter 10, an unequal rate of technological innovation amongst countries is one factor behind the inequality of national incomes. The 'divergence, big time' (Pritchett, 1997) between the convergence club of the Organization for Economic Co-operation and Development (OECD) economies and the developing world is strongly associated with sustained, high rates of technological innovation in the former. One of the main contemporary manifestations of this divergence in the new network age is the so-called 'digital divide', that is, inequality in access to ICTs, as identified by Figure 11.1. The figure shows the users of the Internet relative to populations in various countries and regions. The rich countries of the USA and the rest of the high income OECD countries dominated Internet use in 2000, whereas they accounted for only 13 per cent of the world's population. It is also salutary to note that more than 80 per cent of people in the world have never heard a dial tone on the by now well-established telephone technology, let alone sent an e-mail message or downloaded information from the World Wide Web. Indeed, as shown in Chapter 10, the technological inequality illustrated by the digital divide is not new. The diffusion of inventions and technologies has always been slow and uneven between countries – only a few have caught up and joined the OECD – and the pace of diffusion may even have slowed further in recent years.

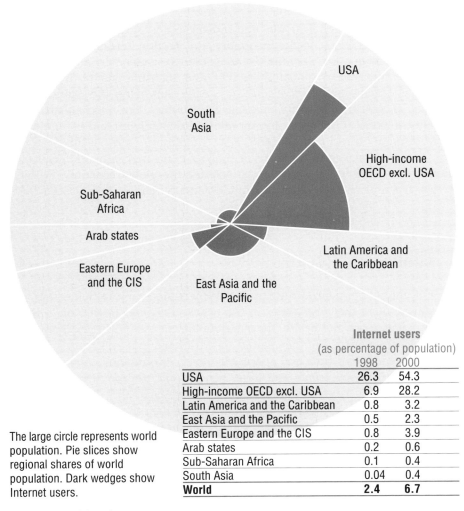

Internet users (as percentage of population)		
	1998	2000
USA	26.3	54.3
High-income OECD excl. USA	6.9	28.2
Latin America and the Caribbean	0.8	3.2
East Asia and the Pacific	0.5	2.3
Eastern Europe and the CIS	0.8	3.9
Arab states	0.2	0.6
Sub-Saharan Africa	0.1	0.4
South Asia	0.04	0.4
World	**2.4**	**6.7**

The large circle represents world population. Pie slices show regional shares of world population. Dark wedges show Internet users.

Figure 11.1   Internet users

Source: United Nations Development Programme, 2001, *Human Development Report*

Question

What might the data in Figure 11.1 tell us about the claims made by some commentators that the anti-globalization movement represents a global network?

The data in Figure 11.1 might lead us to become slightly more sceptical of bold claims about the scale of the networking involved. Note that only 6.7 per cent of the world's population was able to use the Internet in 2000. Thus, the Internet-based network of anti-globalization protesters was of necessity confined to a tiny percentage of the population, very much centred on protesters from the rich Northern countries. As yet, this 'global network' is highly uneven in its extent and coverage.

More generally, the digital divide, and indeed technological unevenness, is closely linked to global income inequality, and Section 2 opens the debate about global inequality. Sections 3 and 4 then consider, respectively, the problems of measuring global inequality and its component sources in inequalities *between* and *within* countries. After surveying the extent and character of global inequality, Section 5 examines the mechanisms of inequality, looking at the roles of economic interdependence and integration (trade, foreign direct investment and migration) and technological innovation. Section 6 shifts the focus of analysis to the new network forms of organization thought by many to characterize the global economy in the network age, and asks whether these fundamentally change the prospects for convergence in the world economy. A brief conclusion reviews what we have learned about inequality, economic globalization and technological change.

2   Global income inequality

Why concentrate upon income inequality? Why not look at wealth inequality, for instance, or at the inequalities in the use of fuels and power, or in the incidence of diseases and health, the length of life, and so on? In principle, all these could be covered, and they would show different patterns from income inequality trends over time and space. However, income inequality has the advantage that it represents the most general and thoroughly analysed aspect of inequality, largely because there is reasonable quality data available to do this with a wider coverage than for many of the other dimensions just mentioned. Evidently, international wealth inequality would complement income inequality since this also provides the means to gain access to other resources and services. Yet the coverage of wealth statistics is thin and difficult to interpret. Therefore, I shall stick with incomes. This is not to suggest that income inequality coverage or measurement is problem free, far from it (as you will see in Section 3).

2.1   Debating global inequality

The level and trends of global income inequality became much debated issues in the early years of the century. Governments in developed countries and the major institutions of international economic governance such as the International Monetary Fund (IMF) and the World Bank argued that economic globalization was an important part of the route to sustained growth for developing countries, and that such growth was the means to reducing both poverty and global inequality. However, many critics contended that globalization could just as readily increase inequalities both between and within countries. Some important aspects of this debate can be judged from the following opening exchanges between Robert Wade and Martin Wolf taken from a debate they conducted in the magazine *Prospect* in March 2002.

Are global poverty and inequality getting worse?

ROBERT WADE is Professor of Political Economy at the London School of Economics and MARTIN WOLF is Chief Economics Commentator of the *Financial Times*

Dear Martin,

[...] You make three main points. (1) Poverty and inequality on a world scale have both fallen over the past two decades for the first time in more than 150 years. (2) These falls are due to greater global economic integration. (3) The anti-globalisation movement encourages countries to adopt policies that will in fact only intensify their poverty and inequality.

[...] Let us take the first point about trends in poverty and inequality. On poverty, the World Bank is the main source of numbers. Bank researchers have found that the number of people in absolute poverty (with incomes less than about $1 per day) was roughly constant in 1987 and 1998, at around 1.2 billion. Since world population increased, the *proportion* of the world's population in absolute poverty fell sharply from around 28 per cent to 24 per cent in only 11 years. This is good news.

But recent research on where the Bank got the 1.2 billion suggests that the method for calculating the numbers is questionable. The effect is probably to understate the true numbers in poverty. How much higher than 1.2 billion we do not yet know.

---

for Western Europe and the USA, as Figure 11.4 shows. This plots the Gini coefficient (discussed in Section 3.2) for incomes in a range of countries for the period 1977–97. India and China also saw a rise in inequality during this period. Despite these increases of within country inequality, both countries also saw a big drop in the levels of poverty, as measured by the number of people living on less than a dollar (US) a day.

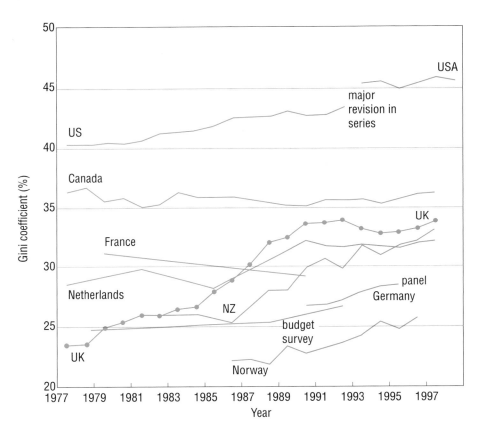

Figure 11.4   Changes in income inequality within selected high income countries, 1977–97

Source: adapted from Atkinson, 1999, p.4

Fischer's second point is that economic globalization is not to blame for global poverty. As Chapter 10 illustrates, there is considerable evidence that trade and investment integration *can* help rather than hurt the poor through a positive influence on economic growth, provided that other, complementary policies to acquire and develop technological capabilities are in place. The problem, according to Fischer, has not been too much globalization but that not all poor countries were able to take advantage of it. Fischer lays the blame for this on both rich and poor nations alike: rich nations did not open up their (agricultural and textile) markets enough to benefit the poorer countries; and the poor countries have not sufficiently explored the possibilities of increasing their trade with one another. Perhaps there is not much disagreement with Wade on this point, for Wade concludes that the 'engine of development' is not economic globalization as such but 'the advance of technology and the diffusion of technical capacities of people, firms and governments. Some forms of integration [globalization] may help this, others may hinder it, depending on a country's stage of development' (Wade, 2002). This is very much in line with the argument set out in Chapter 10.

3   Measuring global inequality

As you have seen in the Wade–Wolf debate, one of the great difficulties is that global inequality is a complex phenomenon that can be understood and described in different ways. To begin with, there is the question of how we acquire data on incomes. Do we ask a sample of people or households what their incomes or expenditures are (household expenditure surveys) and then use statistical inference to build up a picture of the total population? Do we use the country's national accounts, look up national income and then divide by the population to give us an average per capita income? Both are legitimate and both have their own strengths and weaknesses.

Next, if we want to study inequality worldwide, we must compare the incomes of people in one country with the incomes of people in another country. But countries have different currencies. To compare an income of US$20 000 with an income of £15 000 we must convert these incomes into a common currency. It is conventional to convert all incomes into US dollars and in Section 3.1 I shall explain some of the different ways in which this can be done and some of the issues that arise. We shall see that the different ways of converting one currency into another can have significant implications for measures of inequality.

Once we have a distribution of incomes, say, of average per capita income for all the countries in the world, there are different ways of expressing the inequality of that distribution. Standard techniques include ratio measures such as the quintile and decile ratios, and the Gini coefficient, which is a measure of the skew of a distribution. In Section 3.2 we shall consider another measure of the skew of a distribution, the Theil index, which is particularly useful for studying global inequality because it allows us to measure global inequality as a function of inequalities between countries and inequalities within countries.

All of these issues – different ways of gaining data on incomes, different ways of converting one currency into another, and different measures of inequality – mean that describing the pattern of global inequality is a complex task. That these differences exist should not be a surprise – it is precisely the point. Rather, it demonstrates that a complex phenomenon such as global inequality cannot be adequately described by a single measure. Finally, there is a potentially 'political' dimension to bear in mind, in so far as the World Bank has a near monopoly in the generation and supply of the raw data on inequality (especially in developing countries) but is one of the main protagonists in the debate.

3.1   Comparing incomes between countries

In order to make comparisons of incomes between one country and another, we must first convert the various national income estimates (GDP, per capita GDP and the like) into a single unit of currency. One way to accomplish this is to use market rates of currency exchange (say to the US dollar) to convert per capita GDP estimates in different currencies into US dollar measures. However, there are still a number of problems with this. First, market rates are highly variable and erratic, and they are heavily dependent upon rumour, expectations, speculation and other contingent events. Thus, at any one time, they may not very accurately reflect the underlying fundamental economic situation in a country in terms of the actual economic welfare of its inhabitants. A common way of overcoming this problem is to use a three-year moving average of exchange rates to smooth out the effects of transitory fluctuations.

Second, a further argument says that this does not satisfactorily deal with differences in fundamental purchasing power found in different national situations. The basic idea is that different national levels of economic welfare are better compared with one another after some adjustment to market exchange rates has been made which is designed to reflect different price levels from country to country. These different price levels affect what can actually be purchased from incomes and hence economic welfare. Such an adjustment is achieved by converting incomes on the basis of purchasing power parity (PPP) rates of exchange, that is, rates of exchange that equalize the purchasing power of a given amount of income. A simple example illustrates the point. *The Economist* publishes what it calls the 'Big Mac' index based on the ubiquitous fast food. Big Macs are sold in a large number of countries so their prices in domestic currencies are well known. If a Big Mac costs 100 Real in Brazil and US$2 in the USA, the PPP exchange rate between these two would be 100 Real to US$2, or 50 Real to US$1. Similar rates of exchange could be calculated for a range of other countries and these can then be used to compare incomes in one currency with those in another. When these rates are used, they are termed 'PPP equivalents'.

Purchasing power parity (PPP)
PPP currency conversions are a result of converting currencies into one another such that a given unit of currency has equivalent purchasing power in all countries.

Once converted along these lines, any PPP 'dollar', so constructed, has the same purchasing power over domestic goods and services as a US dollar has in the USA. Only for the USA are market GDP and PPP GDP exactly equal because the US dollar is taken as the base point against which every other currency is converted. Since, in general, the market prices of goods and services sold locally – that is, those not traded internationally – are significantly cheaper in poor countries than in rich ones, the PPP adjustment generally raises the PPP adjusted incomes in poorer countries. Consequently, the effect of PPP conversion is to lessen the income differences between poor and rich countries because it tends to boost the income of the poorer less developed economies. For example, in 2000 the gross national product (GNP) of Russia measured at market rates of exchange was US$241 billion, while at PPP rates it was US$1165 billion, a huge difference. This meant that GNP per capita in Russia was either US$1660 or US$8010 (nearly a fivefold difference) depending upon whether market or PPP rates of exchange were used. For Brazil, the equivalent per capita GNP was either US$3580 or US$7300 (a twofold difference). For Switzerland, the PPP conversion actually reduced the Swiss per capita income from US$38 140 at market rates to US$30 450 at PPP rates (all figures from the World Bank, 2002). The reason for the reduction in the Swiss figures is the relatively 'inflated' nature of domestic market prices compared to those in the USA.

In reality, PPP adjustments are not based on a comparison of the prices of a single commodity (the Big Mac or any other), but on price surveys of a basket of goods and services which is assumed to comprise a similar or comparable bundle of 'representative' goods and services. Yet when one looks around the globe at how variable a typical national consumption bundle might be, international comparisons become problematic. More importantly, the bundle is geared up to the needs of the 'average' person, not necessarily the poor, and the consumption bundles of the poor are often quite different to the average. They typically include a greater emphasis on the simple necessities of life like shelter and food, the importance of which can be underestimated in a representative bundle of consumption goods. If food and shelter are relatively expensive compared to, say, services like transport or haircuts, then distortions which make the poor seem better off than they really are can creep in. What is more, the comparison presumes that an apartment in Manhattan provides essentially the same housing services as a flat in, say, Mogadishu. All of these problems imply that, for the poorer countries in particular, PPP comparisons can produce some very uncertain results, and these are precisely the countries where changes in incomes are very important for establishing the overall trends in inequality.

Question

Leaving to one side the methodology of making PPP adjustments, what are the arguments for and against the use of PPP as opposed to market rates of conversion?

As I noted above, different measures attempt to represent different things. What PPP does best is to represent the purely domestic dimension of economic activity designed for the purposes of comparing total purchasing power, 'the standard of living' or overall 'welfare' of the inhabitants of a country (measured in monetary terms and with all the caveats mentioned above). Figures 11.2 and 11.3, for example, are based on PPP conversions. PPP does not represent so well the purchasing power that residents of different countries have over the goods and services produced in other countries. These have to be purchased at market rates of exchange. Thus, if we are interested in the capacity of developing countries to pay for the import of capital goods or to repay their foreign debts, or their ability to represent themselves in international diplomatic and negotiating arenas where key decisions about international economic management are made, market rates might give the best indication since these determine the actual resources available to meet the costs of these international obligations. Therefore, it becomes a matter of judgement, with both measures probably complementing each other. One measure should not be used to the total exclusion of the other.

3.2   Measures of inequality

Once we have a distribution of incomes expressed in a common currency, there is a range of measures that describe different aspects of that distribution. Perhaps the best known and simplest are ratio measures such as the quintile and decile ratios. To illustrate these, suppose we have countries ranked in order with the poorest (in terms of per capita income) on the left and the richest on the right. Start at the left, move one-tenth of the way along the line and look at the income of the country at that point – that is, the income at the first decile. Continue along the line, marking each tenth, until you reach the ninth decile, with just ten per cent of countries to the right. The decile ratio is, then, simply the income of the country at the ninth decile divided by the income of the country at the first decile. The quintile ratio does exactly the same but divides the distribution into fifths rather than tenths. So, to calculate the quintile ratio, you move one-fifth of the way along the line and look at the income of the country at that point, continue marking fifths until there are 20 per cent of countries left and look at the income of the country at that point. For example, suppose we have 100 countries and the annual income in country

Decile ratio
The ratio of the income at the ninth decile to the income at the first decile of an income distribution.

Quintile ratio
The ratio of the income at the fourth quintile to the income at the first quintile of an income distribution.

number 10, that is, the first decile, is US$400, in country number 20 (the first quintile) it is US$4000, in country number 80 it is US$16 000 and in country number 90 it is US$20 000. The quintile measure of inequality between these countries is 4 (16 000 divided by 4000) and the decile ratio is 50 (20 000 divided by 400).

The Gini coefficient is a little more complicated. It is a measure of the skew of an income distribution away from perfect equality (in the above example, each country having the same per capita annual income) to complete inequality (one country having all the world's income). It ranges from 0 to 1, 0 representing perfect equality and 1 representing complete inequality.

However, there is another, less well-known, index that is often used to measure global inequality: the Theil index. In some respects, the Theil index is similar to the Gini coefficient. It too varies between 0 and 1, with larger values indicating greater inequalities. Unfortunately, the derivation of the Theil index cannot be explained without some mathematics – and even with the maths, it is not an obvious measure. The eminent economist Amartya Sen, noted for his work on inequality, has remarked of the Theil index: 'the fact remains that [the Theil index] is an arbitrary formula, and the average of the logarithms of the reciprocals of income shares weighted by income shares is not a measure that is exactly overflowing with intuitive sense' (1997, p.36).

Nevertheless, the Theil index is widely used because it has two properties not possessed by the Gini coefficient that make it particularly useful for studying global inequality. In Section 2 I noted that *global* inequality could be thought of in terms of a compound of the inequalities *between countries* and the inequalities *within countries* and, following Fischer, that measures of global inequality should take account of the fact that countries differ in size. One of the key virtues of the Theil index is that it allows us to register both of these points. The Theil index for global inequality, that is, a measure of the skew in the distribution of incomes among all the people of the world, is the sum of the Theil index for the inequalities between countries plus a weighted sum of the Theil indices for the inequalities within countries, where the weights are proportional to each country's share of global income.

This is represented schematically in Figure 11.5. Starting with the distribution of incomes among people in countries 1, 2 and 3, we calculate Theil indices for the inequality *within* each country. Next we take the average income in each country and calculate the Theil index for *between* country inequality. Then, the Theil index for *global* inequality equals the Theil index for the inequality of incomes between countries plus the weighted sum of the Theil indices for the inequality of incomes within

Gini coefficient
The Gini coefficient is a measure of the skew of a distribution away from perfect equality (0) to complete inequality (1).

Theil index
The Theil index is a measure of the skew of a distribution away from perfect equality (0) to complete inequality (1). The Theil index for global inequality is the sum of the Theil index for 'between countries' inequality and a weighted sum of the Theil indices for 'within country' inequalities, with the weights proportional to each country's share of world income.

erratic for the group of African countries, but note that the sample size varied significantly. Without further information about which countries were included, it would be unwise to conclude anything general from these data. The Latin American experience is one of significant decreases in inequality from a high starting point, by either measure, though again the number of countries included in the sample varies substantially between the 1960s and the other decades. The Pacific Rim countries indicate no clear trend with either measure, even though both measures move in the same direction decade to decade.

Finally, notice that the trends in Table 11.1 do not help us to gain a picture of how *global* inequality has grown over time. To address this, we would have to compute a summary figure based on the data for each region and compare this over time. Let us look at how the Theil index enables us to do this.

4.1 Between and within country inequality

Figure 11.6 shows data drawn from a study of global income inequality during the period 1970–98 (Sala-i-Martin, 2002). The study is based upon household income and expenditure surveys carried out in 97 countries, collated by the World Bank. The vertical axis of Figure 11.6 measures values for the Theil index of inequality in incomes. Remember: a larger number for this index measures a greater inequality, and the index itself varies between 0 and 1. Time is plotted on the horizontal axis. The data are given so that you can read the actual value of the Theil index for each year more easily. Remember also that:

Theil (global) = Theil (between countries) + Theil (within countries)

Note that the numbers under the column headings 'Between countries' and 'Within countries' may not add precisely to those under 'Global' because of rounding to three decimal places.

There are three lines in Figure 11.6 which correspond to the three columns of data at the top. The top line represents the overall Theil index of the inequality of global income. It shows a slight fall in the 1980s and 1990s with a slight upward movement in the late 1980s. Global inequality as measured by the Theil index has fallen from about 0.78 in the late 1980s to 0.72 in 1998 (to two decimal places). The points on the middle line represent the values for the between countries index of inequality. This Theil index saw a sustained drop from 0.61 in 1974 to 0.51 in 1998. The bottom line illustrates the trends in 'within countries' inequality (also a Theil index), which showed a slow rise over the entire period.

Theil indices

Year	Global	Between countries	Within countries	Year	Global	Between countries	Within countries	Year	Global	Between countries	Within countries
1970	0.771	0.586	0.186	1980	0.786	0.593	0.193	1990	0.776	0.583	0.194
1971	0.775	0.588	0.186	1981	0.783	0.589	0.194	1991	0.763	0.568	0.194
1972	0.790	0.603	0.187	1982	0.767	0.574	0.193	1992	0.749	0.554	0.195
1973	0.800	0.613	0.188	1983	0.763	0.572	0.191	1993	0.729	0.533	0.196
1974	0.793	0.605	0.189	1984	0.765	0.573	0.191	1994	0.727	0.529	0.198
1975	0.780	0.591	0.189	1985	0.761	0.570	0.191	1995	0.719	0.520	0.199
1976	0.794	0.604	0.190	1986	0.759	0.568	0.192	1996	0.712	0.512	0.200
1977	0.791	0.601	0.190	1987	0.762	0.570	0.193	1997	0.712	0.511	0.201
1978	0.798	0.608	0.191	1988	0.767	0.574	0.193	1998	0.716	0.513	0.203
1979	0.796	0.605	0.191	1989	0.781	0.587	0.194				

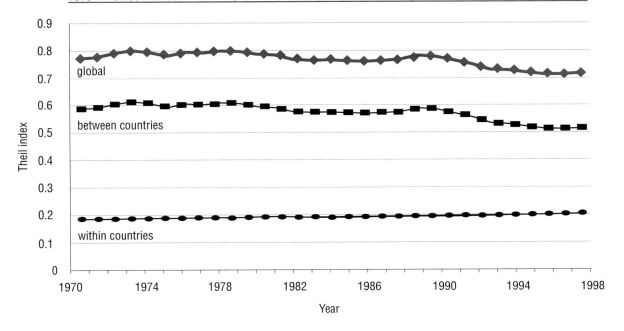

Figure 11.6   Comparison of global income inequality

Source: generated from Sala-i-Martin, 2002, Figure 12

Activity 11.2

1   Check that the Theil index satisfies the additive decomposition property.

2   Compute the percentage contribution of the between country and within country components of inequality to overall global inequality in 1998.

There are several noteworthy aspects to Figure 11.6. First, for the entire period of the study between country inequality explains in large part the trends in global inequality. The answer to Question 2 in Activity 11.2 demonstrates this: in 1998, for example, between country inequality accounted for 72 per cent of global inequality. This pattern holds true in periods of rising and falling global inequality. Between country inequality reflects the convergence or otherwise in productivity and incomes amongst the countries that you studied in Chapter 10. The absence of convergence amongst many developing countries and the rich countries is reflected in the large share of global inequality accounted for by between country inequality. By contrast, amongst economies where there has been substantial convergence, such as the OECD countries (also discussed in Chapter 10), studies suggest that within country inequality accounts for the greater part of overall inequality.

Second, for much of the period since the 1980s between and within country inequality have moved in opposite directions. Within country inequality has increased while between country inequality has fallen. You can see this in Figure 11.6 in the downward slope of the 'between countries' line (indicating a lower Theil index) and an upward slope to the 'within countries' line (a higher Theil index). Indeed, both movements are probably due in part to the rise of new economic powers such as China and India. It is interesting that this is quite different from the period of economic globalization in the late nineteenth century and early twentieth century that is considered in Chapter 10. At that time, both between country and within country inequality declined (at least for many economies experiencing convergence).

These results in global inequalities, presented on the basis of the Theil index, contrast strongly with the data presented in Table 11.2 which show the Gini coefficient and other measures of the global income distribution for 1988–93. Table 11.2 reveals a sharp increase in global inequality.

Table 11.2   More unequal: world income distribution, 1988–93

Inequality measure	1988	1993	Percentage change
Gini coefficient of world incomes	0.63	0.67	+6
Richest decile/median*	7.28	8.98	+23
Poorest decile/median*	0.31	0.28	−10

Note that the median is the middle point in a distribution.
Source: Wade, 2002, Table 3

Can you think of any reasons that might explain the difference between what these measures indicate and what you have just learned from the Theil indices? You might find it helpful to reread the Wade–Wolf debate and look again at Figures 11.2 and 11.3.

First, the data in Table 11.2 cover only a short period. Perhaps it is not typical of the longer term trends covered by the Theil index data. Second, the difference in the findings of the Theil index and the Gini coefficient is similar in nature to what we saw in Figures 11.2 and 11.3. Recall that Figure 11.3 weighted the data in Figure 11.2 by the share of population, and this produced a different trend in the overall scatter of points. The Gini coefficient measures the skew in a distribution. The Theil index in addition weights this skew, giving a larger weight to countries that have higher shares of total income. In short, measures of inequality that weight the data either by population (as in Figure 11.3), or by income shares (as in the Theil index in Figure 11.6) show a reduction in global inequality over the last several decades. This is not difficult to understand if we note that two of the most populous and poor countries have recently become somewhat richer, and thus increased their shares of global income. Yet China and India are only two of the many poor countries of the world. The Theil index is consequently still closer to 1 than to 0.

There are no simple answers to the question of whether the world is becoming more or less equal. As I noted above, different measures measure different things, and there is no single, correct way to measure global inequality. Rather, there are a number of different measures, each of which attempts to capture a different aspect of a complex phenomenon. It is useful to bear this complexity in mind as we now turn to some of the mechanisms that affect inequality.

5 Mechanisms of global inequality: economic integration and technological change

In Chapter 10 you saw that the economic integration was associated with the 'third' wave of innovation during the late nineteenth century and early twentieth century, and was related to the emergence of a 'convergence club' of economies that caught up with the industrial leaders of the age. You also saw that only a few countries have since joined that club. Many advocates of contemporary economic globalization maintain that the present wave of technological innovation associated with ICTs offers comparable opportunities for convergence for those countries willing to embrace globalization.

Not everyone agrees. Consider the following statement from the United Nations Development Programme, *Human Development Report* (HDR), of 1999:

> Poverty is everywhere. Gaps between the poorest and the richest people and countries have continued to widen. In 1960, the 20% of the world's people in the richest countries had 30 times the income of the poorest 20%. In 1977, 74 times as much. This continues the trend of nearly two centuries. Some have predicted convergence, but the past decade has shown increasing concentration of income among people, corporations and countries.

(United Nations Development Programme, 1999, p.29)

Alongside other research, and the kinds of popular dissent and protest discussed in Chapters 12 and 13, this report sparked a sharp and continuing controversy amongst the organizations of international economic governance, academics, journalists, policy analysts and politicians about what might have been the causes of global inequality. The debate particularly focused on the growing inequality within countries, and between the rich economies and those developing countries that were unable to take advantage of globalization. The HDR's own diagnosis was clear, putting the blame squarely at the door of 'globalization':

> National and international economic policies shifted sharply in the 1970s and 1980s towards more reliance on the market – diminishing the role of the state. ... Driven by technocrats, the changes were supported by the IMF and the World Bank as part of comprehensive economic reform and liberalization packages. ... Country after country undertook deep unilateral liberalization. Not just in trade but in foreign investment. These changes have sped the pace of globalization and deepened the interactions among people. The new rules of globalization focus on integrating global markets, neglecting the needs of people that markets cannot meet. The process is concentrating power and marginalizing the poor, both countries and people.

(United Nations Development Programme, 1999, p.36)

If this view reflects that of many in the developing world, there has also been a growing debate about the influence of economic globalization and technological change on income inequality in the OECD countries. In the rest of this section I shall address the mechanisms of inequality generation, treating these under the broad headings of economic globalization (including in this trade and foreign investment), technological innovation, and migration.

5.1   Economic globalization and inequality in relation to developing countries

The idea that globalization can cause inequality might be surprising given the argument of Chapter 10 that episodes of technological change, when linked with greater economic integration of trade and investment, offer opportunities for some countries to catch up. Surely, we should expect catch-up growth, or convergence, to reduce rather than increase global inequalities. However, you have seen in Section 4 that between country reductions in inequality can co-exist with increases in within country inequality. I have also emphasized the important role played in calculations of global inequality by just two, albeit very large, countries – namely, China and India – and the absence of any convergence between many developing countries and the OECD convergence club.

In fact, despite the growth of some developing countries, and although countries that trade more do generally grow more, only a small part of world trade involves developing countries. This can be seen clearly from Table 11.3 which reports on the direction of world merchandise trade for 1998. A little less than one-quarter of world merchandise exports originated in the developing countries, while just over three-quarters originated in high income countries. Since the ability to export ultimately determines the ability to import, we may safely conclude that these figures broadly represent the picture of world trade in general.

Table 11.3   World trading relations: direction of trade (percentages of merchandise trade), 1998

Origin	Destination		
	High income countries	Low and middle income countries	World
High income countries	58.5	17.3	75.8
Low and middle income countries	17.0	7.1	24.2
World	75.6	24.4	100.0

The numbers may not add to totals because of rounding of figures to one decimal place.

Trade is valued at export value f.o.b. (free on board, not including insurance and freight charges).

The figures are for trade in goods only; trade in services (which is less well recorded) is not included.

Source: World Bank, 2000

This uneven nature of globalization is also evident from data on foreign capital flows and investment. Easterly and Levine (2003) have summarized the global inequalities in respect to capital flows:

> In 1990, the richest 20 per cent of world population received 92 per cent of gross portfolio capital inflows, whereas the poorest 20 per cent received 0.1 per cent. The richest 20 per cent of the world population received 79 per cent of foreign direct investment, and the poorest 20 per cent received 0.7 per cent. Altogether, the richest 20 per cent of the world population received 88 per cent of gross private capital inflows, and the poorest 20 per cent received 1 per cent.
>
> (Easterly and Levine, 2003, p.205)

(Note: portfolio investment is the purchase of financial assets; foreign direct investment is the purchase of stocks and shares in already existing companies as well as 'greenfield' investment in the creation of new commercial activities.)

Tables 11.4 and 11.5 provide further evidence of the concentration in global capital flows. They show that an overwhelming proportion of foreign investment originates in and goes to high income countries. Further, a large amount of the increases in foreign inflows to developing countries in recent years has been on account of inflows into China.

Table 11.4   Distribution of foreign investment stocks, 1980–97

	1980	1985	1990	1995	1997
Total inward stock (US$ billions)	481.9	734.9	1716.9	2657.9	3455.5
Developed economies' share (%)	77.5	73.2	80.1	73.9	68.0
US share of developed stock (%)	22.2	34.3	28.8	29.2	30.7
Developing economies' share (%)	22.5	26.8	19.9	26.1	30.2
Chinese share in developing economies' stock (%)	0	1.7	4.1	18.6	20.8
Total outward stock (US$ billions)	513.7	685.6	1684.1	2730.2	3541.4
Developed economies' share (%)	98.8	96.9	95.9	92.1	90.1
US share of developed stock (%)	43.4	37.8	27.0	28.1	28.4
Developing economies' share (%)	1.2	3.1	4.1	7.9	9.6
Chinese share in developing economies' stock (%)	0.0	0.6	3.6	8.1	5.9

Source: Feenstra, 1999, pp.333–4; UNCTAD, 1998 (for 1997 figures)

Table 11.5   Distribution of foreign direct investment flows, 1983–97

	1983–88	1990	1991	1992	1993	1994	1995	1997
Total inward flows (US$ billions)	91.6	203.8	157.8	168.1	207.9	225.7	314.9	400.5
Developed economies' share (%)	78.4	83.4	73.8	70.0	64.8	61.4	68.4	58.2
of which US share (%)	47.9	28.2	19.3	15.4	31.8	37.5	29.7	38.9
Developing economies' share (%)	21.6	16.6	26.2	30.0	35.2	38.6	31.6	37.2
of which Chinese share (%)	9.2	10.3	10.6	22.2	37.6	38.8	37.6	30.4
Total outward flows (US$ billions)	93.7	240.3	210.8	203.1	225.5	230.0	317.9	423.7
Developed economies' share (%)	94.2	92.6	95.8	89.4	85.4	83.2	85.2	84.8
of which US share (%)	16.1	12.2	16.6	21.5	35.9	23.9	35.3	31.9
Developing economies' share (%)	5.8	7.4	4.2	10.6	14.6	16.8	14.8	14.4
of which Chinese share (%)	8.5	4.7	10.3	18.5	13.3	5.2	7.4	4.1

Source: Feenstra, 1999, pp.333–4; UNCTAD, 1998 (for 1997 figures)

Indeed, Tables 11.3, 11.4 and 11.5 are remarkable because only a few countries appear to account for the larger portion of the increases in world trade and international investment. This suggests that far from being a general process that has affected economies the world over, economic globalization has in fact been important in integrating only a few countries in the world economy. Other data support this point. The World Bank estimates that exports of manufactured goods rose from 25 per cent of poor country exports in 1980 to 80 per cent in 1998. This trade integration was concentrated in 24 developing countries (including China and India), which were home to 3 billion people. These countries doubled the ratio of trade to national income and their per capita incomes rose by an average 5 per cent a year. Yet for another 2 billion people in the developing world, including much of Africa, the ratio of trade to national output fell and income per head shrank. Similarly, more than half of the foreign investment inflows to developing economies are concentrated in just five countries.

Since a disproportionate amount of globalization originates in and integrates economies in the North, it is perhaps not surprising that much of developing country opposition is directed at the policies of Northern governments. This is despite the fact that many developing countries want to emulate the economic achievements of the North and join the relatively small number of developing countries that have been able to take advantage of globalization. Anti-globalization protests within the North have very often included vocal support on behalf of poorer, developing countries. However, this is not true of all the protestors. Could it be that there have also been large numbers of losers due to increased economic integration in the North? The evidence on increasing within country inequality, and the fact that in OECD countries a larger part of overall income inequality is due to within country inequality, raises the question of the link between globalization and within country inequality.

5.2   Trade, investment and income inequality within countries

In order to understand the fate of the losers from trade, we need to look more closely at what happens to economies when they start specializing, according to their comparative advantage, as a consequence of international trade. In recent decades, the UK has exhibited a comparative advantage in services and, following from this, the share of services in national income and employment has grown. The other side of the coin, however, is that UK manufacturers have faced strong import competition from countries such as China, South Korea and Taiwan. These manufacturing firms are in the UK's sectors of comparative disadvantage. In such circumstances, people working in a range of manufacturing industries may find that it is harder to find new work, and consumers discover that UK prices are higher than those of comparable imported goods. As comparative advantage and specialization progress, the share of manufacturing in national income and employment will fall. Thus, the structure of production and employment in the economy will have changed.

The general argument is that the UK economy went through a period of restructuring in the 1980s, in which its comparative disadvantage in manufacturing eroded the manufacturing basis of national production, while its comparative advantage in services boosted the share of the services sector in national income. Other industries such as steel and coal which depended upon the manufacturing sector for demand had to shut down as well, causing huge unemployment in these sectors. Such restructuring of the economy (as this process is sometimes referred to) is the consequence of trade when there is comparative advantage.

Of course, national income has increased so that the UK as a whole gains from this process. Yet consider what happens to the workers employed in a sector that loses out as the result of such restructuring such as the UK coal industry. Pit closures affected many families who lost their main source of income as a consequence. At the same time, few efforts were made to retrain the now unemployed labour in order to facilitate new employment in other growing sectors. While the economy as a whole gained as a consequence of trade and comparative advantage, particular groups lost out grievously. Trade may therefore have indirectly contributed to an increase in income inequality.

In fact, most economists believe that the growing inequality in the OECD countries cannot be attributed to trade alone (see Section 5.3). Many other changes took place in the 1980s and 1990s. In the UK, perhaps the most significant of all the changes in the 1980s was the loss of bargaining power by trade unions as unemployment rose and as some decisive tests of strength between the (Thatcher) government and unions were settled on government terms. This was also true of several other European countries, although less true for the USA where trade unions were historically weak. In contrast, French truckers and farmers, for example, still regularly exercise their rights to strike to defend and advance their terms and conditions. In many cases, changes in the strength of unions affected wages at the lower end of the pay scale.

The picture of within country inequality is all the more striking for developing countries, even the so-called 'globalizers' that benefited from huge increases in per capita incomes from 1980 to 1997. Prominent examples in this group are countries such as India and China. Even as growth rose and poverty fell, inequality increased. Systematic investigation into the influence of trade on inequality by Ravallion (2001) shows that, while on average (that is, taking all countries together) there is no relation between participation in trade and inequality within a country, in low-income countries increasing trade is always associated with greater within country inequality. Ravallion attributes this to a greater inequality in the distribution of skilled labour in poor countries compared with rich ones.

Foreign investment may also play a role in income inequalities. While foreign firms are notorious for shifting their production to lower cost locations in search of profits, and have questionable practices in their treatment of legal and environmental regimes in many countries, they almost always raise wages in the economies and sectors that they enter. This is a well-established empirical fact noted by Jenkins (1987) and confirmed in most studies on foreign investment and wage rates.

Question

Why would foreign firms raise incomes in the sectors they enter?

The entry of foreign firms adds to the demand for labour in the sector (for the same labour supply), thereby raising wages in the sector and so affecting wage dispersion. As an example of how potent that effect can be, software engineers working in India earn about 20 times the national average income for manufacturing employment. Much of this increase happened in the early 1990s when foreign multinationals set up software subsidiaries in India.

Foreign investment in developing countries often happens in selected regions called free trade zones or specialized export zones. Here, better infrastructure conditions prevail and investment is often subject to different tax and labour laws from the rest of the country. This means that the benefits of greater integration are often confined to these regions, increasing the disparity between regions of the entire economy. Thus, in China the inequality between the prosperous southeast coast and the rest of mainland China has increased. In India, the south and west of the country have prospered with the software boom while the rest of the country has not, so contributing to inter-regional inequalities.

5.3   Technological innovation and inequality

The emergence of new technologies in the 1980s and 1990s rewarded technological skills and training more than other work, causing an upward pressure on the incomes of skilled workers. A relative scarcity of such trained workers also meant that some could earn very high incomes and negotiate high salaries for their skills. There is evidence that suggests that the upward pressure on these incomes contributed more to the growth in UK income inequality than the downward pressure on the unskilled wage component.

This emphasis on labour skill intensity raises issues about the role of technology and its role in generating inequality within countries. The demand for different skill mixes is often the response to different technologies and to the changing nature of technological innovation. The overall effect on wages rather depends upon the effects of trade on the skill premium and the rate of technological innovation in different types of countries, which are difficult to predict a priori.

A lively debate started in the USA in the mid 1980s which argued that increased trade with low income countries was contributing to an increase in income inequality. As you have seen, many developed economies experienced a period of increasing income inequality during the 1980s and 1990s (see Figure 11.4). It is tempting to conclude that this was a result of increasing trade with low income countries, and that increasing inequality was due to factor price equalization as the wages of those in manufacturing fell due to competition from poorer economies. In the same period, however, Canada showed no great change in its inequality and France showed decreased inequality. Moreover, there is no evidence that they were participating less vigorously in the globalization of their economies.

In the 1980s and 1990s, the amount of trade relative to US output (the trade to GDP ratio) soared, even as a number of US industries were increasingly threatened by overseas competition. This happened at the same time that medium-skilled and unskilled wages fell, that is, the skill premium increased. This was also a period of rapid technological advance in the US economy (the widespread introduction of ICTs), leading to a sudden change in the demand for different skills, and significant relative wage changes. What was the relative importance of these various factors in the overall result of a sharp decline in the fortunes of less skilled US workers in particular? This remains a contentious question but the consensus opinion, after much empirical work, was that about 20 per cent of the increase in inequality in wage incomes was due to trade and 70 per cent due to technical innovation improving productivity and, hence, the premium paid to skilled labour (Cline, 1997). The remaining 10 per cent was explained by migration depressing the wages of unskilled labour (see Section 5.4).

In addition to increasing inequality among individuals within a country such as the USA, technological innovation may increase inequalities between countries. This proposition was considered in Chapter 10. Easterly and Levine (2003) also suggest that major external economies associated with technological spillovers concentrate economic activity around existing areas, and attract new activity to those existing locations. External economies are economies that make it cheaper for firms to produce their own output as a result of the increasing size of the whole industry or economy in which the firms operate. External economies can be contrasted with the internally generated economies of scale and scope discussed in Chapter 10. Internal economies of scale and scope apply to individual firms; external economies apply to groups of firms in a given industry or economy. Therefore, each firm can benefit from the existence and growth of certain other firms which help it to reduce its own costs. One source of these economies could be the development of specialized labour training facilities and a local skilled labour market that provides trained workers for a number of firms making similar products in an area. Another source could be organizational innovations (process technologies) that leak between firms so that all benefit from the innovations originally found in one firm. Comparable benefits can arise from product innovations which, as they are exploited by other firms, set in motion an escalation of further innovation that boosts output and productivity growth.

> **External economies**
> External economies are economies that make it cheaper for firms to produce their own output as a result of the increasing size of the whole industry or economy in which the firms operate.

The result is that a virtuous circle of growth and innovation can be sparked off so that the first, possibly lucky, innovation leads to a continuing cycle for the originating group of companies or countries who are propelled along a higher growth path, while the rest are left behind. The existence of external economies may make it difficult to break into this cycle since it feeds off those in the virtuous circle. This can reinforce the existing inequalities in the international system.

5.4   Migration and inequality

Thus far we have seen that trade, investment and technological innovation can be mechanisms for increasing global inequality, both within and between countries. What about the impact of labour migration on within country inequality? The main story of migration in the latter part of the twentieth century was one of intra-national migration, from rural to urban areas, not so much international migration, which in the nineteenth century helped to establish convergence in the Atlantic economy (see Chapter 10). Furthermore, much of the contemporary international labour migration that has taken place has been skilled migration from the developing world to the rich countries. Recent debates have tended to focus on the effects of migration on the relative distribution of incomes within the advanced countries, which suffered acute shortages of skilled labour when new technologies were being adopted in the late 1980s and 1990s. In order to study these debates, it is useful to distinguish between unskilled labour migration and skilled labour migration.

The effects of unskilled migration from the South to the North, which often capture the attention and the headlines, is to add to the supply of unskilled labour (for a given demand), thereby lowering the wages of the Northern unskilled workers. An alternative is that trade in low-skill goods takes place. As the Northern countries increase imports from the countries of the South, they increase the demand for the labour used in the South to make these imports. Consider the example of agricultural products which are the main exports of many poor countries. An increase in agricultural exports from these economies will increase the demand for the unskilled labour that goes into their production. As a consequence, over time the wages of such workers will increase making emigration to the North less attractive.

Therefore, trade and migration are to some extent substitutes in terms of the way within country and between country inequalities can emerge and evolve. Either labour can move to the Northern countries and produce low skill goods *in situ*, or the goods can be produced in the South and exported, with Southern low-skilled labour staying put. In either case, the wages of low skilled labour in the North are likely to fall. A good deal of low skilled manufacturing has been driven out of the advanced countries and relocated in developing countries, the output of which is then sold back to the developed countries. Instead of unskilled labour migrating to the Northern countries to produce low skilled goods there, labour is in effect 'imported' via the skill intensity of the products that are exported to the Northern countries from the South. In sum, to find out the outcomes of growing integration on the unskilled wages in the Northern countries requires not only an examination of the direct effects of migration but also an assessment of the indirect effects of the skill intensity of trade.

The effect of skilled labour migration from the South to the North (the South's 'brain drain') is somewhat more complex and its consequences are less well understood. Cheaper, skilled migrant labour 'dampened' the rise in high wage incomes that would have occurred in the North in response to technological change, but paradoxically increased the premium on skilled wages that firms in the South had to pay in order to use new technologies. In turn, this premium on skilled wages in the South may reduce the profitability of employing the new technologies, contributing to the growing inequality between countries. There is a real fear that this is a handicap for developing countries in their efforts to catch up. Some of the starkest examples of the disadvantage of this kind of phenomenon are evident in the health sector, where shortages of nurses and doctors in the UK, for example, have been met by skilled migration from countries such as the Philippines, thus exacerbating the problems of access to, and the costs of, health services in the labour exporting areas. On the other hand, India has benefited from the skilled labour that first moved to Silicon Valley, and then returned to play an important role in the development of the Indian software industry.

6   Networks of convergence?

As noted in Chapter 10, transnational corporations (TNCs) are important agents in the dissemination of technological innovation and the reconfiguration of dynamic comparative advantage between different countries. Moreover, ICTs are facilitating the configuration of the activities of TNCs in the form of networks. The technological transfers involved in the business strategies of TNCs are being transformed largely because of heightened international investment integration. And more and more this is taking advantage of ICTs like the Internet, the World Wide Web and internal intranets. Some analysts have argued that these developments will assist the transfer of technologies to developing countries as they are progressively integrated into the wider international economy, and that this in turn will have a profound impact on global inequalities. The optimistic case is that we are witnessing the advent of a period in which the ICT-aided integration of global investment will enable convergence mechanisms finally to 'kick in', undermining the external economies concentrated in the developed world and thereby reducing global inequality.

In this section, I shall examine networks as ways of organizing and integrating flows of trade and investment in the world economy. The latter is not simply made up of anonymous market forces operating through the competitive price mechanism; it also involves definite agencies that operate in those markets by means of collaboration and co-ordination – in networks.

6.1   The network enterprise and business networks

Increasingly, commentators are drawing attention to the rise of the 'network enterprise' as a new form of organization in the economy. What, then, is a network enterprise? One of the most forceful exponents of the idea that the global economy is being reconfigured by the rise of network enterprises is Manuel Castells, who sees them as a key component of a more general 'network age'. The network enterprise is:

> the organizational form built around business projects resulting from cooperation between different components of different firms, networking among themselves for the duration of a given business project, and reconfiguring their networks for the implementation of each project. The network enterprise evolved from the combination of various networking strategies. First, the internal decentralization of large corporations, which adopted lean, horizontal structures of cooperation and competition, coordinated around strategic goals for the firm as a whole. Secondly, the cooperation between small and medium sized businesses, pulling together the resources to reach critical mass. Thirdly, the linkage between these small and medium business networks, and the diversified components of large corporations. And, finally, the strategic alliances and partnership between large corporations and their ancillary networks. Taken together, these trends transform business management into a variable geometry of cooperation and competition depending upon time, space, process, and product. Thus, the network enterprise is neither a network of enterprises nor an intra-firm, networked organization. Rather, it is a lean agency of economic activity, built around specific business projects, which are enacted by networks of various composition and origin: *the network is the enterprise*. While the firm continues to be a unit of accumulation of capital, property rights (usually), and strategic management, business practice is performed by *ad hoc* networks. These networks have the flexibility and adaptability required by a global economy subject to relentless technological innovation and stimulated by rapidly changing demand.

(Castells, 2001, p.67)

The italicized phrase – 'the network is the enterprise' – is a deliberate paraphrase of Marshall McLuhan's famous assertion that 'the medium is the message'. This meant that the 'message', that is, the meaning or implication of any 'medium or technology is the change of scale or pace or pattern that it introduces into human affairs' (McLuhan, 1994, p.8; first published 1964). Thus, in saying that the network is the enterprise, Castells is making a strong claim to the effect that the conduct of economic activity ('the practice of business') is configured and accomplished through networks. Castells is not saying that markets or, for that matter, hierarchies are unimportant, but he is saying that network forms of co-ordination are central to economic activity in the new, global and informational economy.

TNCs, according to Castells, are subject to the impact of network forms of co-ordination just as much as domestic firms. It is estimated that TNCs conduct up to one-third of all international trade in the form of intra-firm trade, that is, trade within the boundaries of the firm but across national frontiers. These intra-firm trade networks have been built on the back of the primary activity of TNCs, the reorganization of production across borders via the deployment of foreign direct investment. In addition, TNCs are increasingly responsible for international financial investments of various kinds (for instance, merger and acquisition activity), for internal to the firm but 'across border' labour deployment (a form of international migration), and for various inter-firm partnerships and agreements. All of these can be considered in terms of cross-country networks operating within or between TNCs. According to Ietto-Gillies (2002), this is creating new 'fuzzy boundaries' around firms as organizational, locational and ownership relationships fragment and cross-fertilize between firms. The outcome is the creation of 'business networks' (not just production networks or inter-organizational networks) incorporating the three dimensions referred to above – organization, location and ownership – and welding these together into a strategically aligned but flexible whole. It may be that the ability to establish and manage complex international networks of this kind confers real competitive advantages on the firms involved.

As far as the empirical basis for these networks is concerned, data limitations prevent clear confirmation that there are robust business networks of this kind operating in any depth. However, there are signs that large TNCs are spreading their affiliation relationships globally, so there is evidence of some locational diversification. Nevertheless, there still seem to be significant advantages to single ownership, and the advantages of diversified organizations are as yet difficult to discern. Overall, Ietto-Gillies sees a process of international fragmentation amidst integration developing in this field, led by TNCs. Moreover, the role of ICTs is stressed as a force for transforming the whole nature of TNC operations and leading the new business networks.

6.2 Networks of trade and investment?

Another aspect of the growth of network forms of economic organization concerns 'outside the firm' trade networks. Following Rauch (1999), we can divide most international trade into three different categories. The first category is goods traded on 'organized markets', including such things as minerals and other raw materials, and primary agricultural products. The price of these goods is established according to classic market mechanisms. In this regard, one might think of markets like the Chicago grain markets, the London metal exchanges, and the Rotterdam spot market for oil. A second category is intermediate goods that are traded according to 'reference prices' quoted in specialist publications and the like (such as processed raw materials, chemicals and basic standardized components). For the prices of these goods, firms can consult a reference manual or trade price book. These are readily available in published form. The third type of trade is differentiated manufactured goods and services where there is no organized market or quoted reference prices. Here, there are no uniform, standard prices, but instead 'one-off' pricing, differentiated according to complex networks of supply.

Unlocking the determinants of trade with respect to each of these categories is not easy (see Rauch, 1999; Chen, 2002). The first and, to a lesser extent, second of these categories displays a high trade to production ratio; a high proportion of the output of firms in these sectors is exported. However, these types of trade are of declining importance as components of total international trade. What has expanded rapidly is the third category, particularly complex manufactured goods, but this kind of production has a relatively low trade to production ratio. That is, there is extensive production of these goods and services yet less of it is exported abroad than one would expect on the basis of rises in incomes and demand. Rather, other variables that affect trade (for example, the distance between the producer and the market, whether the countries are part of the same trading or currency bloc, whether they share a common colonial heritage or language, and so on) play a more important role in determining the levels of this kind of trade as compared with either the first or second category. It appears that institutional, legal, cultural and geographical influences serve to limit the growth of trade in the third category.

Consequently, those categories of goods (the first and second) where there is a strong link between income growth and the growth of international trade are declining in significance, while the third category, in which factors other than income growth play an important role in determining the growth of trade, is becoming more important.

 Question

Can you think of an explanation for the findings about the three categories of trade?

Where an organized market for exchange has developed in relatively standard commodities, as in the case of the first category, the conduct of trade is relatively easy and cheap. The costs of organizing and managing the trade are comparatively low. Correspondingly, the second category of trade is somewhat organized in stable and publicly accessible forms. However, with sophisticated manufactured goods and services there are no organized markets to facilitate exchanges. Instead, these are frequently traded in the context of one-off, lengthy and complex networks of supply and distribution. Manufacturers often have to set up singular and unique distribution systems for each category of good. This requires trading partners and securing a network of participants. Above all, these systems are costly to set up and maintain – transaction costs (the costs of doing business) are high. This is one of the reasons why migration has been found to be such a stimulant to international trade, since it can establish well-organized networks of trust that reduce transaction costs.

Similar considerations may also apply to foreign direct investment. Rauch (1999) has argued that portfolio and greenfield foreign direct investment share many of the characteristics of the first and third categories, respectively. Portfolio investment is organized through well-established stock markets, exhibiting low transaction costs, whereas greenfield investment requires the costly establishment of new sites, networks of suppliers, distribution systems and the like.

The implication of these considerations for the importance of networking for integrating trade and investment flows is that participation in these arrangements may become increasingly crucial for success in the global economy.

6.3   Value chains and commodity chains

A slightly different notion of network relationships is provided by value chains or commodity chains, many of which operate internationally. These combine trade and investment networks and can involve a single firm or a group of firms. While value chains and commodity chains are somewhat different concepts, they are often run together (Institute of Development Studies, 2001). Michael Porter's value (or value-adding) chain framework concentrates upon the role of individual firms in a chain of firms that produce goods and services and stresses the importance of the key value-adding firm in any such chain (Porter, 1985, 1990). Commodity chains, while not neglecting the value-added component, tend to stress the various activities as discrete stages in the chain, and look at the way they are co-ordinated or governed. Therefore, we can think of a move along, say, an agricultural chain from the farmer, to the broker, to the basic food processor, to the packaged goods producer, to the wholesale distributor, to the retailer and, finally, to the consumer. In this conception, the key aspect highlighted is the control and co-ordination of these activities. The discrete parts of a commodity chain may involve a single firm, or parts of several firms, and firms may be involved in more than one part of the chain.

The key point is that the value/commodity chain is seen as a whole rather than as an aggregation of its individual parts. If each player has a stake in the other's success, the entire chain is the competitive unit. Yet this poses a problem of securing co-operation between players; hence the emphasis on the co-ordination and governance of these chains. Who 'organizes' the chain?

Two responses have been forthcoming (Gereffi and Korzeniewicz, 1994). On the one hand, there are producer-driven chains, where the key lead agent is situated at the production end of the chain (a manufacturer, for example). On the other hand, there are buyer-driven chains, where the lead agent is nearer the consumption end (a retailer, for example). For each of these chains, particular agents are seen as taking responsibility for 'organizing' the governance of the chain, sometimes co-operatively, sometimes through more coercive means based on structured inequalities.

A visual image of a commodity chain is provided in Figure 11.7. This shows the schematic linkages in a buyer-driven chain stretching across the Pacific from the USA to Hong Kong, and how these are pushed further on into East Asia.

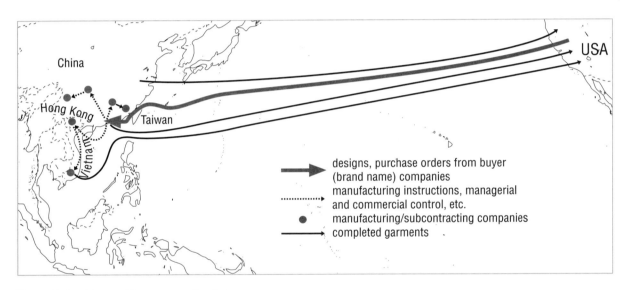

Figure 11.7   A buyer-driven commodity chain
Source: Henderson, 1998, p.371

These different conceptions of the network forms of organization which articulate global production and exchange offer pictures of a complex pattern of relationships that is being transformed by ICTs in particular. Whether these new forms – the network enterprise and business networks, networked forms of trade and investment and commodity or value chains – serve to promote convergence or further exclude many developing countries is as yet unclear. For all their potential to promote convergence by surmounting barriers to trade and investment integration, networks may increase global inequalities rather than reduce them. Networks tend to cluster into local production networks still largely centred in the developed countries. As you saw in Chapter 10, production networks are themselves embedded in wider systems of innovation, which has been one of the reasons for the relative lack of international transfer of technology. Furthermore, this might even imply that the diffusion of innovations is now slowing down. In short, while networks offer new ways of bridging old barriers or borders to trade and investment integration, and the diffusion of technology and technological capacity, they may equally serve to exclude those who are not inside the existing centres – and networks – of growth and innovation.

7 Conclusion

We began with the claims that technology and economic globalization are generating a network age and with the fact that the contemporary international economy is characterized by massive global inequality. Some have argued that, taken together, the forces of globalization and technology have the potential to reduce inequality as developing countries begin to converge with the developed world, just as many peripheral European economies did in the Atlantic economy of the late nineteenth and early twentieth centuries. Others fear that many countries and people will be excluded from the benefits of globalization and technological change, and that this will sow the seeds of future conflict and international disorder. This chapter has reviewed the debate on the nature of global inequality and explored some of the mechanisms at work and some of the new forms of organization in the world economy. While we have seen that patterns of inequality are changing in dramatic ways, and that networks create opportunities for some, it is too early to conclude that the 'divergence, big time' (Pritchett, 1997) that has characterized relations between the developed and developing world since the industrial revolution is a thing of the past. Our study of these issues has reinforced the finding of Chapter 10: whatever may be new and different in the network age, economic globalization and technological innovation do not offer any easy answers for those currently excluded from the mechanisms of convergence. Indeed, breaking into the virtuous circle of growth, innovation and a form of globalization that works for the poor may have become more difficult.

Further reading

For a wide-ranging review of the evidence and debates about global poverty and inequality, as well as a discussion of the relation of these to economic globalization, see Fischer, S. (2003) 'Globalisation and its challenges', *American Economic Review*, vol.93, no.2, pp.1–30.

The World Bank's policy journal *Finance and Development* regularly contains informative articles about international inequality and the prospects for developing countries in the international economy. It can be accessed online at http://www.imf.org/external/pubs/ft/fandd/2003/12/index.htm.

The ideas of the networked form and the network economy are discussed in Castells, M. (2001) *The Internet Galaxy: Reflections on the Internet, Business and Society*, Oxford, Oxford University Press.

Chapter 12 The global network society and transnational networks of dissent

Helen Yanacopulos and Giles Mohan

1 Introduction

One important element of the global network society thesis is that the growth of network forms of organization represent a challenge to the nation state in so far as they allow actors to create political communities operating within and across the territories of states, communities that can challenge the ability of states to order the international system. This chapter investigates that idea and looks at one particular form of network, what we call 'networks of dissent'. Dissent implies discontent, a disagreement with the way things are. Much current popular dissent manifests itself in the form of street demonstrations, social movements and civil disobedience. We use the phrase networks of dissent to describe the ways that individuals and organizations form and attempt to express their discontent and influence the governance of the international system. While dissent is not a new phenomenon, Information and Communication Technologies (ICTs) have enabled dissent to become what Bleiker calls a transversal phenomenon, that is, 'a political practice that not only transgresses national boundaries, but also questions the spatial logic through which these boundaries have come to constitute and frame the conduct of international relations' (Bleiker, 2000, p.2).

In this chapter, we shall be exploring these networks of dissent and how they link groups in civil society. Civil society, which encompasses networks of dissent, is one important arena where the existing social order is grounded and where a new social order can be forged: it is 'both shaper and shaped, an agent of stabilization and reproduction, and a potential agent of transformation' (Cox, 1999, p.5). We ask two related questions of these networks of dissent. First, do these networks represent a new kind of actor in the international system, one that is able to successfully influence the actions of states and other powerful institutions, thereby challenging their hegemony (the prevalence of a dominant world view) and transforming the international system in favour of the marginalized? And second, as a result, do these networks force us to rethink our understanding of the nature of international order? Specifically, how do these networks relate to the politics of states and the states-system? In order to explore these questions, we shall

Networks of dissent
We use this term to describe those networks that challenge existing social, political and economic arrangements and seek to influence the governance of the international system. Their transnational nature raises questions about how far they challenge received notions of international order as a state-based system.

consider two case studies: one on the transnational labour movement, and the other on a transnational debt cancellation network.

The aim of what follows is to help you to develop a critical understanding of the ways in which transnational networks and what has been frequently called 'global civil society' participate in shaping the international system. Transnational networks of dissent may generally be classified as part of 'civil society', although we shall see that civil society also contains other actors and relations of power. Such networks and the other forces that operate on the terrain of civil society are diverse. Networks oriented towards political violence, and human rights networks are both transnational: they are organized around their respective shared values; they are dissenting in that they express disagreement from established systems; and they could have (and arguably already have had) an influence on the international system. Our particular focus is on networks of dissent which are related to questions of global inequality – what are sometimes called economic or social justice issues – such as workers rights and cancellation of highly indebted poor countries' (HIPC) debts.

Thus far, you have studied the role of states and the states-system in international affairs (Part 1) as well as the importance of cultural struggles and the contested international agendas of rights and justice (in Part 2). In Chapters 10 and 11, we have explored the role of technological innovation and economic inequality in shaping the international and noted the importance of both technological and economic networks in thinking about the contemporary international system. This chapter seeks to develop your understanding of the role that networks play in international affairs. This is particularly relevant in the context of arguments which claim that advances in ICTs have made networks a more prevalent organizational form. It is, therefore, important to study the role of networks in order to assess the extent to which they are reshaping the international order. In Section 2 of this chapter, we review some general considerations about social networks, their role in relation to questions of global governance and the idea of a global civil society. Sections 3 and 4 present two case studies relating to the role of network forms of organization in co-ordinating international labour activism and in the debt cancellation campaigns around the millennium. Section 5 seeks to draw some general lessons from our case studies and discusses the ways in which network forms of organization are changing the nature of international order. Before we turn to some of the general theses associated with the idea of a global network society, let us consider briefly an example of a transnational network of dissent.

1.1 Transnational networks of dissent

The following story told by Jonah Peretti (2001) illustrates an instance of a transnational network of dissent that originated through one person dissenting against a multinational company. We shall consider the case of Nike and the international labour movement in more detail in Section 3, but the following is a taster of how ICTs enabled this protest to occur. In 2000, Jonah Peretti became embroiled in a private email exchange with Nike (the sportswear manufacturer) over their promotional offer to embroider customers' chosen words on their shoes. Nike refused to make a pair of shoes with the word 'sweatshop' on them. In January 2001, he emailed these messages to some friends, and a transnational network of dissent emerged. Jonah Peretti describes this process as follows:

> As a challenge to Nike, I ordered a pair of shoes customized with the word 'sweatshop'. Nike rejected my request, marking the beginning of a correspondence between me and the company. None of Nike's messages addressed the company's legendary labor abuses, and their avoidance of the issue created an impression even worse than an admission of guilt. In mid-January I forwarded the whole e-mail correspondence to a dozen friends, and since that time it has raced around the Internet, reaching millions of people, even though I did not participate at all in its further proliferation. The e-mail began to spread widely thanks to a collection of strangers, scattered around the world, who took up my battle with Nike. Nike's adversary was an amorphous group of disgruntled consumers connected by a decentralized network of e-mail addresses. Although the press has presented my battle with Nike as a David versus Goliath parable, the real story is the battle between a company like Nike, with access to the mass media, and a network of citizens on the Internet who have only micromedia at their disposal. ... Micromedia has the potential to reach just as many people as mass media, especially in the emerging networked economy. Most e-mail forwards die before they are widely distributed, but if critical mass is attained, it is possible to reach millions of people without spending any money at all. ... It takes so little effort for each person to pass the message to multiple recipients that an idea can almost seem to be spreading on its own, like a self-replicating virus. ... Nike has the advantage when it comes to mass media, but activists may have the advantage with micromedia. ... The only force propelling the message was the collective action of those who thought it was worth forwarding. Unions, church groups, activists, teachers, mothers, schoolchildren and members of the US armed forces sent me letters of support. This contradicts Nike's claim that only fringe groups identify with anti-Nike sentiment. Rather, an expansive group of people from all walks of life are concerned about sweatshop labor and are dismayed by Nike's brand hegemony. ... But the Nike e-mails did not reach these people all at once. Like all micromedia, the Nike e-mails jumped haphazardly around a network defined by personal relationships. The first people to get the message were friends or friends of friends who tended to be left-leaning and interested in technology ... Then, something

interesting happened. The micromedia message began to work its way into the mass media. This transformation was helped along by postings on media startups Plastic.com and Slashdot.org, two sites that use an innovative publishing technique somewhere between micro- and mass media. These democratic sites blur the line between editors and readers, so that Internet buzz can be transformed into a hotly debated news item seen by thousands of people. ... The dynamics of decentralized distribution systems and peer-to-peer networks are as counterintuitive as they are powerful. By understanding these dynamics, new forms of social protest become possible, with the potential to challenge some of the constellations of power traditionally supported by the mass media.

(Peretti, 2001)

Activity 12.1

Jonah Peretti sees 'micromedia' as having several advantages in terms of organizing for resistance. What are these advantages? What advantages does the mass media have over micromedia?

The Nike case demonstrates that globalization involves, in some manufacturing sectors at least, a restructuring of the division of labour which has thrown up various forms of resistance that are networked across national borders. However, do these forms of resistance have a lasting impact on the functioning of the international economic system and, if so, what role do new technologies play in this process? Before turning to our case studies on international labour organizing and anti-debt campaigns, Section 2 considers the general relationships between ICTs and social networks.

2   A global network society?

Technological innovations, especially in ICTs, have had an enabling role in transnational network formation, as you have seen in the case of economic networks in Chapters 10 and 11.

Question

What is new and different about ICTs and their influence on networks generally and networks of dissent specifically? Are ICT-based networks contributing to a global network society?

For the purposes of this analysis, there are three differences between old communication technologies (such as the printing press and the telegram) and new communication technologies (such as the Internet and telecommunications). First, ICTs make possible the instantaneous trans-mission of data, adding a 'live' element to communication. Second, ICTs have the ability to transmit vast quantities of data relatively inexpensively. Low cost means that information is available to anyone who is able to access it: as you saw in Chapter 11, this was only a small proportion of the world's population at the turn of the century. Third, as technologies, ICTs are already configured into network structures and complement existing personal and organizational networks, while also enabling individuals and organizations that were not previously connected to network with one another.

Let us examine these distinguishing elements of ICTs in more detail. The speed of information transfer of new technologies is dramatic – be it communicating in real time with someone in a different part of the world, accessing information instantly, or watching a moment in history as it occurs, for example, the events on 11 September 2001. While the ease of obtaining information and communicating instantaneously is one advantage attributed to 'new' technologies such as the Internet, it is also important to remember that 'old' technologies also had a dramatic impact. For example, Thompson notes that the effects of the telegram were in some ways more dramatic than the Internet, and that in the last 20 years of the nineteenth century the time taken to send a message from the USA to Europe was reduced from six weeks to 20 minutes (2003, p.224). Nevertheless, the immediate feature of ICTs has given them a 'live' aspect.

While the speed of communication has increased, access to information has also changed dramatically, and now the processing of information of all kinds is central to many forms of social interaction. Castells (1996), for instance, calls the new global network society an information age based on an informational mode of development. Some have seen in these developments the potential for radical change. Thus, John Fisher claims that ICTs make it:

> easier for individuals to find and follow what concerns them personally, and by lowering the cost of obtaining information, the influence of social status on political involvement may be reduced. Citizens and groups with few resources can undertake acts of communication and monitoring that previously were the domain mainly of resource rich organisations and individuals.

(Fisher, 2001, p.13)

The Nike 'sweatshop' case, in which networks of like-minded people soon built up a force to challenge that of a rich and powerful corporation, is one such example.

However, while access to flows of data has increased and the costs of many kinds of information have fallen, the ability to derive power from information is far from straightforward. As Joseph Nye has argued, 'power in information flows to those who can edit and authoritatively validate information. ... Among editors and cue givers, credibility is the crucial resource and an important source of ... power. Reputation becomes even more important than in the past, and political struggles occur over the creation and destruction of credibility' (2002, p.67).

ICTs also enable individuals and organizations to connect to each other in new ways. John Fisher describes this feature of networks as follows:

> The Internet certainly isn't a panacea, but it does have the potential to bring together large numbers of people in a form of civic dialogue. It can also provide immense stores of information for people to access and interact with. Importantly, if universal access is achieved, it allows those people with few resources to have equal opportunities for political debate and involvement.

> (Fisher, 2001, p.2)

An interesting aspect of these new technologies is that they are already configured as networks. They are structures of connectivity, connecting in some of the same ways that social agents do in social networks. It seems that technological networks (think of them as computer or satellite networks) work in the same way as social networks, which are comprised of a number of highly connected 'nodes' or 'hubs'. For instance, there are specific web sites which are focal points for individuals and groups – these might be search engines such as Google.com, or they might be hyper-linked web sites such as oneworld.net, where groups go to find information. These technological nodes are also social (between individuals and organizations) networks. It was originally thought that ICT networks, for example, the Internet, were scattered and unconnected (Cohen, 2002), but the relationship between technological and social networks needs further examination.

In fact, it would appear that technological networks can mirror and reinforce existing social networks, as we saw in the Nike case. The people engaged in the Nike email campaign were a loose social network of people and organizations with similar values ('left-leaning and interested in technology'). They were also individuals and organizations who had access to this technology and were all connected to the Internet. Thus, in this case, the technological connections facilitated the coming together of a social network (of individuals and organizations) around the issue of Nike production methods. Certainly, social networks of individuals and organizations have always existed. Technological changes such as the telegraph in the 1880s and 1890s and the diffusion of electrical products in the 1920s, affected the ways people communicated with each other and allowed the space of these networks to grow (from those within one's day-to-day contacts to people further afield). ICTs have allowed these social networks to grow even further. In some cases, an individual's or organization's location has become irrelevant in obtaining information and in linking with other actors.

Nevertheless, as we shall see in the case studies recounted in Sections 3 and 4, physical location is still important whether for mobilizing publics, lobbying, or expressing dissent in elections. Not everyone has access to these technologies because of the inequalities that exist both within and between countries. Moreover, some states have sought to restrict Internet and media access to their peoples. The global network society only encompassed a small minority of the planet at the turn of the century, as shown in Chapter 11. The disparities between continents were documented in a study by Brunn and Dodge (2001) that quantified Outgoing Linkages, that is, hyper-linked web sites originating in different countries. This study found that Europe alone accounted for half of the world's Outgoing Linkages, whereas Africa's share (with the exception of South Africa) was insignificant. What is sometimes called the 'digital divide' mirrors, in part, long-standing global inequalities of income as well as inequalities in access to education and other forms of social, institutional and technological infrastructure.

Despite these global inequalities, the diffusion of ICTs has enabled networks to develop and proliferate on certain issues, subtly changing the way many groups are engaging in the international system. Bleiker describes the relationship between dissent and ICTs:

> Processes of globalization, in particular the advent of new communicative capabilities, have fundamentally transformed the nature of dissent and its ability to shape socio political dynamics. In a world that is strongly influenced by global media networks, an act of dissent has the potential to reach a much wider audience than in previous époques. The dissemination of a dissident message no longer occurs gradually, but transgresses, almost instantaneously, various spatial and political boundaries.

(Bleiker, 2000, p.97)

Yet before we conclude that the growth of ICT-based networks, operating across national borders and empowering previously excluded groups, represents the advent of a global network society, we should pause to consider the fact that proponents of the latter are frequently promoting the idea of a 'stateless' capitalism. They emphasize how power is spread out throughout networks, how there are co-operative values when using the

Internet in particular, and how there is a sense of freedom in using this type of technology.

Nonetheless, to what extent is this sense of equality and freedom ideological, serving to conceal vast inequalities and processes of exclusion? One reason for the increasing emphasis on networks and analysis of (global) civil society is, of course, the changing empirical reality noted above. However, another important element behind the popularity of these forms of analysis is a particular ideological current of neo-liberal globalization.

Question

Is this sense of openness, equality and freedom real?

It could be argued that these claims are ideological in the sense that they obscure or conceal the continuing reality of vast inequalities and patterns of exclusion. In this context, the Marxist theorist Ellen Meiksins Wood (1995) has argued the need to recover a critical concept of civil society, as found in the writings of Antonio Gramsci (1971). Meiksins Wood observes that:

> Gramsci's conception of 'civil society' was unambiguously intended as a weapon against capitalism, not an accommodation to it. ... the concept [of civil society] in its current usage no longer has this unequivocally anti-capitalist intent. It has now acquired a whole new set of meanings and consequences, some very positive for the emancipatory projects of the left, others far less so. The two contrary impulses can be summed up in this way: the new concept of 'civil society' signals that the left has learned the lessons of liberalism about the dangers of state oppression, but we seem to be forgetting the lessons we once learned from the socialist tradition about the oppressions of civil society. On the one hand, the advocates of civil society are strengthening our defence of non-state institutions and relations against the power of the state; on the other hand, they are tending to weaken our resistance to the coercions of capitalism.

(Meiksins Wood, 1995, pp.241–2)

Gramsci's conception of civil society
For Gramsci, civil society is the terrain upon which dominant classes are able to legitimate their rule without the need for the direct use of coercion and repression. It is a contested terrain, however, where those seeking to transform society can use the freedoms associated with civil society to contest capitalist hegemony.

In the rest of this chapter, we examine the transformative potential of networks and how they fit into more established ways of thinking about the international system. We return to the relevance of Gramsci's conception of civil society in Section 5.

2.1 Transnational networks and global governance

While empirically difficult to quantify, many analysts contend that there has been a steep change in network activity as a result of ICTs. Chapters 10 and 11 have already noted the importance of networks in the process of technological innovation and in the global economy. Here we focus on the role of networks in the protests from below, from those outside the formal, hierarchical structures of state power, those often opposed to the dominant direction of change in the global economy. We are calling these networks of dissent: networks arising as organizational forms which are resisting and challenging power and inequality in the international system. These networks, we argue, have formed as a result of the combination of an opening of political space and the identification of shared values around a perceived sense of inequality or 'injustice'. In this framework, networks have become increasingly conducive forms for linking organizations of political protest both below and above the level of the state. The paradox is that while globalization and technological innovation are in some ways increasing global inequalities, they also provide means of resistance.

Question

Are transnational networks a new phenomenon in world politics?

Transnational networks are not new phenomena: Margaret Keck and Katherine Sikkink (1998) describe both the women's movement and the labour movements in the early part of the twentieth century, and the anti-slavery movement of the nineteenth century as forms of networks. The transnational, anti-slavery network, for instance, developed over the course of 50 years, and eventually put enough pressure on governments to abolish slavery in Europe and the USA. These examples are enough to demonstrate that new technologies are not an essential precondition for the existence of transnational networks of dissent. It remains the case that, as a result of numbers, size, speed and complexity, the density of cross-border connections in transnational networks has grown dramatically in the last several decades.

Keck and Sikkink argue that 'activists in advocacy networks are concerned with political effectiveness', defining effectiveness as policy change by 'target actors' such as governments, international financial institutions such as the World Bank, or private actors such as transnational corporations (TNCs) (1998, p.23). In order to bring about policy change, networks need to pressure and persuade powerful actors, which usually involves both the sharing of information and campaigning resources, and the mobilization of collective action. Networks are important because they serve several practical purposes for those who join them: they facilitate the sharing of information and other resources, and the co-ordination of collective action.

An important aspect of the global network society thesis is that ICTs enable co-ordinated action among actors who are physically separated from one another, that is, they are particularly important for those seeking to public sphere of the state, but more specifically a network of distinctively economic relations, the sphere of the market place, the arena of production, distribution and exchange.

(Meiksins Wood, 1995, p.239)

A vibrant and diverse civil society provides the opportunity for all people to participate actively in the decisions which affect their lives. Democracy requires more than periodic elections. It also requires freedom to form groups, develop ideas and speak for marginalised and oppressed people in society.

(Department for International Development, 1998, p.1)

Civil societies must view themselves in the framework of globalization, enabling each inhabitant to think about himself or herself as a member of the same planet earth. Above all, we members of civil societies must redefine ourselves as citizens of a globalised world.

(Grzybowski, 1995, p.1)

Question

What are the points of common ground in these extracts, and what are the main points of difference?

As you can see, there is some agreement over what constitutes civil society, and there are significant disagreements over how it operates and what it can achieve. Indeed, what it is deemed to be affects what it can potentially achieve. Most definitions see civil society as the political space between the privacy of the household and the public sphere of the state. It is a social category in so far as it refers not to individuals (or even families) in isolation but in their capacity either as collectives or in their ability to influence society at large. Some, like the World Bank, see civil society as a world of associations such as church groups, business organizations, religious bodies and NGOs. That is to say, civil society is a purely political space (or arena in their terms) in which groups participate in order to influence decision making, thereby, as the Department for International Development (DFID) suggests, producing a deeper form of democracy. By contrast, and crucial to our discussion, Meiksins Wood argues that civil society includes those relationships of property and markets that affect people's access to resources and ability to influence decision making, even though these are often not viewed as 'political'. Interestingly, all but the last quote are inexplicit about the territory over which civil society operates, although they all talk about the state and so perhaps presume that it is nationally bounded. The last extract is interesting because it talks of civil societies in the plural and argues that citizens (the members of a civil society and its associated state) need to see themselves as members of a single, globalized world. This highlights a tension that you encountered in Chapters 3, 6, 7 and 9 between the idea that people belong to and are embedded in national societies of distinct kinds, and the notion that the world in some sense constitutes a single community in which each society has certain universal obligations to all.

One reading of the state–civil society relationship is that civil society is not only institutionally and organizationally distinct from the state, but in conflict with it, serving as a means of resistance to encroachment by an overbearing state. Civil society is a means of channelling opinion to policy making in a co-ordinated fashion, and simultaneously increasing people's confidence in involving themselves in public affairs as well as building their institutional capacity to do so. This rather procedural view of civil society is very much that of the World Bank (2000) and DFID (1998) as expressed in the quotations above.

Yet by focusing too exclusively on the ability of civil society to limit state power, there is a danger of overlooking the dependence of civil society on a framework of law which is ultimately sanctioned by the coercive power of the state. In addition, this perspective can lead to a focus on only the 'good' elements of civil society and a neglect of the significance of class politics and other social divisions based on unequal access to resources of various kinds. It also leads to an obscuring of Gramsci's notion of civil society as a realm in which the ruling class seeks to legitimize its rule. Specifically, we must question the extent to which private economic interests are central to the constitution of civil society, thereby opening up questions about the degree of 'civility' involved as distinct from the importance of civil society's ideological role. We shall return to these issues in the context of a discussion of Gramsci's account of the importance of ideological and cultural hegemony in capitalist societies in Section 5. However, we first need to take a close look at networks of dissent in order to identify the issues around which they have arisen and their experiences of campaigning. We shall do this by focusing on two case studies from the labour and anti-globalization movements and debt cancellation campaigns. For each of these, we seek to address the following questions:

- What political circumstances precipitated the need and desire to form or activate these networks? We have termed this the opening up of new political spaces.

- How have the networks utilized ICTs to facilitate their campaigns and to what extent did the technology make a qualitative difference to their effectiveness?

Nike's initial response included a denial that working conditions were bad, the argument that a job with Nike was better than no job, and an appeal to corporate and national sovereignty. The latter argument was that Nike does not directly employ the workers and so it cannot be held responsible for what happens to them – it simply signs contracts with local firms for delivery of shoes and these firms operate in the context of the laws and policies of the countries concerned. However, in 1997 Nike made a public commitment to end sweatshop labour by contributing to the establishment of the Fair Labour Association (FLA) and by being the highest profile corporation to sign the United Nation's (UN's) Global Compact on labour. Although the FLA was a watchdog set up by the firms involved in the abuses of labour, prompting some campaigners to see it as a case of the fox guarding the hen-house, it can be argued that having such a high profile company on board is important for longer term reforms.

3.2 New political spaces?

An interesting point to note about the Nike case is not only that much of this high profile activity took place away from the locations where the shoes were being produced, but also that much of the campaigning was conducted by a coalition of religious, pro-democracy and developmental organizations, rather than the traditional organizations of labour – trade unions. These types of networks of dissent have campaigned on specific issues, for example, ending child and sweatshop labour, as well as all-encompassing crusades against globalization. Part of the explanation for the move away from union activity is the labour repression noted above, but it may also be that the labour movement has been 'slow to catch on to the advantages of a network form of organization' (O'Brien, 2000, p.523). Have labour movements simply been slow to realize the potential of network organization or are there other constraints which have rendered traditional forms of resistance difficult?

On the one hand, it is argued that the 'post-Fordist' economy, of which Nike has been a leader, is more competitive while labour is less secure, and competition for 'local' investment engenders a 'race to the bottom' for labour costs and standards. This places great pressures on the labour movement which has the invidious task of protecting its members while seeking various 'accommodations' with both the state and capital. On the other hand, ICTs are potentially making transnational labour activism easier and more viable.

In the 1980s, the relationship between labour unions, the state and capital were radically reshaped through a series of concerted attacks by neo-liberal governments. In the developed world, perhaps the best known example was the Thatcherite policies in the UK, which saw the end of many established union rights. Nonetheless, these struggles were relatively tame compared to those occurring in the newly industrializing countries of Latin America and Asia. In most of the developing world, the period from the early 1980s onwards has been the era of 'structural adjustment', notwithstanding trade union opposition. In Latin America, for instance, authoritarian governments bent on seeing through the adjustment agenda were especially harsh towards workers. The following describes an example of the violent and repressive forms this took:

> In Bolivia, the government attempted to defuse union opposition to the 1985 structural adjustment decree by declaring a state of siege and imprisoning 143 strike leaders in Amazonian internment camps. In Colombia, the government used anti-terrorist legislation in 1993 to try 15 trade union leaders opposing the privatization of the state telecommunications company.
>
> (Green, 1995, p.157)

In the face of these assaults on union power, some have argued that we are seeing the rise of new forms of labour organization structured around more inclusive and less class-based identities, similar to the type we saw in the anti-sweatshop campaigns against Nike. This so-called 'social movement unionism' (Waterman, 1999) is less hierarchical than 'older' forms of union activity and uses network forms of organization anchored in new technologies. The Nike campaigns are a good example of this since they brought together unions, pro-democracy movements, academics, development NGOs, religious bodies and human rights campaigners.

Question

How helpful is this contrast between the 'old' and 'new' forms of labour organization?

We would argue that while a distinction between old and new unionism is not without insight, it is highly schematic and represents an analytical distinction more than an accurate representation of actual processes and outcomes.

The rise of social movement unionism has seen alliances beyond 'class position' and the articulation of multiple identities and political concerns. It has also seen overlaps between class-based 'old' social movements and the 'new' social movements which focus on other social divisions such as race or gender, and supra-class issues such as the environment or peace. This form of political alliance tends to be more issue focused in the sense of mobilizing around a particular event, for example, a plant closure, or a more amorphous universal concern such as environmental degradation. Correspondingly, there is less of a unifying ideology to cement these struggles than in the case of the 'old' unionism. That said, common concerns tend to focus on the loss of economic and political control in the face of ever more powerful states, multilateral organizations and corporations. Thus, while it is this ability to forge alliances between seemingly disparate groups that gives these forms of political activism their strength, this is also the feature which renders them weak, since they lack a core and enduring set of values.

A stylized summary for this form of labour activism is given in Table 12.1. In terms of organizing dissent, Munck notes that 'whereas the worker's movement has usually stressed political mobilization, the new social movements often went for direct action and/or daring attempts at cultural innovations' (1999, p.12). Typically, these new movements have not been confined to the national level of organization. Indeed, as regional and global governance organizations have emerged (for example, the North American Free Trade Agreement (NAFTA) and the World Trade Organization (WTO)), so labour has responded at the same scale and, on occasion, used this as a springboard for more global forms of organization.

Table 12.1   The 'new social unionism'

1 Struggling within and around waged work, for better wages and conditions and greater worker and union control.
2 Struggling against hierarchical, authoritarian and technocratic working methods and relations.
3 Articulated with the movements of other non-unionized or non-unionizable workers and with other non- or multi-class democratic and pluralistic movements.
4 Working for the continuing transformation of all social relationships and structures and actively promoting education, culture and communication.
5 Favouring shopfloor democracy and encouraging direct horizontal relations both among workers and between workers and other democratic forces with a view to creating a global civil society and global solidarity culture.
6 Open to networking both within and between organizations, understanding the value of informal, horizontal, flexible coalitions.

Source: Waterman, 1999, pp.260–1

In terms of organization, 'old' labour movements were hierarchical and masculinist. They had complex committee structures, formal means of representation and a whole series of statutes relating to due process. The *model* of 'new' labour movements (for we believe it is still an idealization) is oriented around a network form of organization that allows the flexibility to respond to spatially and ideologically diverse concerns. As Waterman explains:

> The union form – participatory ideals notwithstanding – has always been affected by the 'iron law of oligarchy' ... meaning self-continuation of leadership and top-down control. The idea of national and international 'networking' ... which includes temporary coalitions and long-term alliances between groups, is of a horizontal coordination rather than a vertical one, something held together more by shared needs and values than by subordination, discipline, loyalty and faith. Thus the organizational/political model is increasingly being replaced by a networking/communication one.

(Waterman, 1999, p.250)

Harry Cleaver (1999) sees the *Zapatista* movement in Chiapas as the prototypical case for this form of activism. The movement forged national and international alliances with a range of activists and intellectuals, and used the Internet to communicate. Social movement unionism aspires to a similar global ethic but is rooted in the struggles around labour and the workplace. As such, its role is ambivalent since on the one hand it occupies a continuum between working with and accommodating the needs of international capital, and on the other seeking structural transformations. Therefore, activism may range from securing better maternity leave for women in South East Asian factories to curtailing the power of TNCs, or seeking 'non-capitalist' forms of economic activity through co-operatives. These political programmes reflect an enduring tension between securing a decent livelihood within a socially acceptable institutional framework for capitalism and seeking to change the fundamental conditions in which social and economic life is conducted. These tensions can be demonstrated with reference to recent women's struggles and their place in the labour movement.

A key feature of technological and corporate restructuring is that certain parts of the labour process have moved from the developed capitalist economies to the newly industrialized countries. With this has come, as the Nike case showed, an enhanced use of subcontractors who can deliver cheaply and flexibly. Central to this process has been the feminization of workforces (Elson, 1983). Women's wages and conditions are poor by developed country standards, but their participation in the workforce does mean that they have been forced to play a more overtly political role. In turn, this has meant a reconsideration of the nature of work and the structuring of society, especially the relations of separation between the 'public' and 'private' spheres of social life. Crudely put, for male labour unions the world of work was the public realm of the factory and the street since they were daily separated from the domestic sphere.

Much political theory and action on citizenship and rights cemented this divide, with politics being seen as the formal spaces of democracy and rights. Women's work and social worlds have generally been more closely tied to the domestic realm and, therefore, their political voice has been muted or deemed insignificant to the 'proper' realm of politics. However, as women entered paid labour from the nineteenth century onwards, the struggles over working conditions became inextricably linked to 'domestic' questions of reproductive rights, housing and so forth. With the enhanced feminization of the workforce, this tendency has been amplified. As Cynthia Enloe observed, 'any success in altering managerial and political policies will require taking up sensitive questions about home life, issues that male union leaders and nationalist intellectuals have dismissed as divisive or trivial' (1989, p.176).

Contemporary struggles have been for both immediate concerns of better conditions and wages to support children and family, and of broader agendas of transformation. In fact, immediate livelihood struggles are often the catalyst whereby women enter the public political space and from there develop this into more fundamental pressures for deeper democratization (Enloe, 1989). For example, following the 1985 Mexico City earthquake, women from a garment factory began a vigil for compensation for lost wages. Quite soon middle-class feminists became involved and urged the workers to form a union. The seamstresses were unsure what to do. Enloe comments, thus:

> If they did immediately form a union, especially one not affiliated to the PRI [the ruling party] federation, maybe they would risk government reprisal and so alienate their bosses that they would never receive the cash they so desperately needed. Women workers also had to figure out how to respond to the offers of support from suddenly attentive left-wing parties. And what about their *companeros*, their male partners: would they feel threatened if women began to take their working conditions so seriously?

(Enloe, 1989, p.171)

Eventually trust was developed, and the middle-class feminists proved valuable allies given their connections to other women's organizations, and their technical and legal experience. The key for the seamstresses was how to engage with the feminists and find meaningful solutions to their own problems. They did form a union, the September 19th Garment Workers Union, which by 1987 had formal recognition in 12 other factories and managed to remain independent of the Mexican ruling party which preferred only its own 'official' unions. This upset both the owners and government unions who sent thugs in to intimidate the women activists. More recently, the union has set up letter writing campaigns, formed solidarity networks with other garment workers organizations, and made a film about their struggles.

3.3   Using new technologies

In contrast to other transnational networks, the labour movement came late to the potential of new electronic communications technologies. The reasons for this are unclear although a possible hypothesis is that labour has always been 'threatened' by new technology because it has generally signalled a further decline in its autonomy. Even when the labour movement began to embrace this potential, it used the technology in 'old' ways. As Lee observes, 'trade unions have tended to use the Internet in the same limited, sectoral way they always worked' (1999, p.240). This may simply speed up the interactions between hierarchically organized tiers of the organization without exploiting the benefits of simultaneity and information sharing. Nonetheless, there has been a number of successes in using these technologies to bring about new and different forms of activism.

The first is in the area of information sharing. Kidder and McGinn (1995) analysed the Transnational Information Exchange (TIE) which was founded by European labour organizations in 1979 working in solidarity with labour movements in the South. Their focus was a new form of internationalism based on networking and information exchange through, for example, meetings and newsletters. TIE's strategy involved both short-term support for issues such as plant closures, and longer term goals of workers' power and democratization. The impetus for this came from the inadequacy of existing unions with their 'national optic', and the realization that the ability to share and compare information was vital for solidarity, consciousness-raising and activism. In an early meeting, the TIE announced that it would 'extend the scope of collective bargaining ... to include the aspirations and interests of other social groups, not just those working in industry' (quoted in Kidder and McGinn, 1995, p.18). Examples of such activity included pressing for fair deals for farmers in the South, lobbying the World Bank, and organizing environmental campaigns around transport. Since then various web-based networks have also emerged, for instance, Labournet, Labourstart, and the Global Solidarity Campaign.

The second case relates to the targeting of specific companies through ICTs. Herod (1998) describes how the United Steelworkers of America (USWA) and the International Federation of Chemical, Energy, Mine and General Workers' Unions (ICEM) used the Internet to change the policies of the Bridgestone tyre corporation. In 1994, the company illegally fired 2300 workers from five of its US subsidiaries and replaced them with cheaper, non-unionized labour. Despite this being illegal, Bridgestone refused the back pay due to the fired workers. At this point, the ICEM launched a 'cybercampaign' against the corporation, and the Internet enabled the campaigners to communicate throughout the globe and create an international solidarity network. In the *ICEM Update* the campaign group exclaimed, 'join the cybermarchers! As rogue employers go global, workers are responding with a creative new use of the World Wide Web' (cited in Herod, 1998, p.183). By accessing the Bridgestone web site they were able to inundate the company with protest material through its customer complaints facility as well as gain the addresses of its subcontractors and customers. From there, the campaigners could target the company's lifeline and effect changes. The result was a global boycott of the company and, by September 1996, the majority of the fired workers had been reinstated.

3.4 Tensions within networks

There are many tensions within this new form of labour activism. The first is between national and transnational interests. Competition between nations and regional blocs for investment and jobs tends to undermine labour solidarity across borders, with workers seeking national or local accommodations with governments and employers. While some activists argue that the target should be corporations, not governments, this ignores the close interaction between states and TNCs, which inevitably renders both as legitimate targets for action. A related issue in terms of organization and political strategy is the problem of fragmentation, in which some smaller, informal organizations may lack the legitimacy of older hierarchical organizations. The latter at least have structures of representation, even if these are rather ponderous and patrician.

A second tension concerns the relationship between 'Northern' and 'Southern' agendas. As Keck and Sikkink (1998) observe, some Northern actors tend to see the erosion of state sovereignty as a good thing, since states are seen as key obstacles to greater democratic participation. This kind of analysis spurred much of the post-communist, pro-civil society euphoria in the 1990s. Nevertheless, for Southern actors (and arguably all dissenting actors), the state is still an important defence against the forces of globalization, which erode autonomy and threaten national sovereignty. This suggests that decentralized, horizontal networks of dissent cannot afford to ignore the state. Yet they also need to be very careful not to be incorporated into the state if they wish to maintain an independent agenda and capacity for action.

A final tension common to most types of Internet-based action relates to language and censorship (Lee, 1999). While the existence of an extensive lingua franca facilitates cross-cultural exchanges, the use of the English language marginalizes non-English readers and writers. More intractable problems are associated with issues of inequality and the digital divide, with

Munck recounting the words of an African trade unionist who said that 'the Internet was of little use to those labour organizations still using typewriters' (1999, p.20).

Activity 12.3

Look back at the three questions we posed at the end of Section 2. Write a brief answer to each of them based on the discussion above.

---

4   Debt cancellation networks

Our second case study is typical of the 'new' issues that many see as displacing, or at least radically modifying, an older, class- and work-based politics. The end of the twentieth century witnessed the promise of the 'forgiving' of over US$100 billion of debt from highly indebted Southern countries. This was a result of the efforts of a number of essential players, including NGOs, civil society groups, governments, and the international financial institutions such as the World Bank and the International Monetary Fund (IMF), resulting in the G-7 governments competing over who could write off the most debt during the 1999 Cologne summit. Why did debt cancellation happen? Many claim that without the sustained efforts of certain groups within the 'debt cancellation network', it is questionable whether this debt cancellation would have occurred. Furthermore, much of the 'success' of the transnational debt cancellation network is attributed to its use of ICTs, which not only enabled networks to link with one another, get their message across, and communicate information to almost every part of the world, but also (arguably) to challenge power relations in international politics. As with the previous case study, we shall first outline some of the salient features of the campaign before addressing the three questions from the end of Section 2.

4.1   Jubilee 2000

The debt cancellation campaigns started in the mid 1980s, with the major breakthroughs occurring between 1995 and 2000. Most of the network building between groups and large debt cancellation campaigns took place during this time. Of the various groups working on debt cancellation during this five-year period, Jubilee 2000 (a broad transnational network of NGOs, trade unions, church groups and other civil society groups) was the most well known and extensive network. Jubilee 2000 existed on all continents and staged a very public campaign with a broad and vast level of public support. The UK coalition of Jubilee 2000, for example, had over 100 organizational members and there were 70 other national coalitions globally. The network operated at a global level and succeeded in placing the issue of debt cancellation on the international agenda, mobilizing the dissent of people around an issue that, in the case of its Northern supporters, actually had little impact on their daily livelihoods.

Regardless of how much one attributes debt cancellation to the Jubilee network, it is undeniable that the network brought a great deal of attention to the debt cancellation issue.

Question

Why was Jubilee 2000 so successful at raising the profile of the debt cancellation issue?

There are various responses to that question. Some would say that the timing of the Jubilee campaign was extremely important. The turn of the millennium was an opportunity to remind people of the Jubilee principle – the Judaeo-Christian ethic of freeing all slaves and forgiving all debts every 50 years. This was an effective campaigning tool to get churches and church groups involved (structures and networks already in existence) in order to work with existing development-focused debt cancellation networks. Shared values galvanized the broad support of varied groups throughout the course of the campaign and Jubilee 2000 helped to redefine debt cancellation in moral terms and made it an issue of social justice instead of a complex economic issue. Payne claims that 'the idea of social justice has great potential rhetorical appeal and could well lead to desired normative change' (2001, p.51). Jubilee 2000 utilized this in its reframing of 'debt'. The idea that poor people have to pay more on debt than they do on health or education struck a cord of injustice in many people, not only in the UK, but also internationally. The commonly-held view of this injustice brought people together on this issue, and organizations such as Jubilee 2000 helped in identifying this common value amongst people on all continents, amongst all age groups, and amongst all classes. The shared perception of this injustice and inequality was the catalyst which brought disparate groups under the debt cancellation transnational network umbrella. Jubilee 2000 generally refers to a transnational network of networks; national secretariats were set up in some countries, for example, Jubilee 2000 UK or Jubilee USA, which acted as national co-ordinating points as well as being part of the larger Jubilee 2000 global movement.

A turning point for the Jubilee 2000 campaign was the G-7 summit in Birmingham in 1998, where 70 000 supporters of debt cancellation formed a human chain around the summit meeting. Collins *et al.* state that this was the point when UK Prime Minister, Tony Blair, 'conceded Jubilee 2000's growing political influence when he reversed an earlier decision and met with British campaign leaders immediately after the rally' (2001, p.138). By April 1999, all G-7 governments had devised proposals for debt cancellation, and Canada and other countries pledged to cancel 100 per cent of debts owed to them (although the total amount of debt owed to some of these countries was negligible). Debt cancellation campaigns had been in existence since the early 1980s, but the dramatic cancellation of debt during the last five years of the twentieth century made it seem like an 'overnight success'. Twenty-four million signatures were garnered for a petition asking for the writing off of 'unsustainable debt'. The changed political climate surrounding this issue meant that lender governments now had to justify their positions if they took a stand *against* debt cancellation.

At the 1999 Cologne summit, it was promised that US$110 billion of debt from 42 countries would be 'forgiven' by the G-7 leaders. Of this, US$50 billion would be through the HIPC initiative (debt owed to the World Bank and the IMF), US$30 billion would be through the Paris Club, and US$20 billion would be cancelled by major industrialized countries (most provided 100 per cent debt cancellation of the bilateral debts owed to them by the poorest countries). While actual debt cancellation proved to be slower and more problematic than initially anticipated, figures showed that in those countries that benefited from cancellation there was an increase in education and health spending by governments. Debt activists used this evidence to argue that debt cancellation was not happening quickly enough but that, in the few cases where it had happened, it was working. However, different analysts use different criteria to gauge the success or failure of campaigns, and this is true for the debt campaign as well.

Debt cancellation networks have not changed the basic nature of the international economic system (although this point is disputed within various Jubilee groups). Additionally, debt cancellation, and specifically the HIPC initiatives of the World Bank and IMF, gave lender governments the opportunity to find new means of enforcing aid conditionality. Ironically, the critics of such World Bank and IMF programmes were also frequently the NGOs, trade unions and church groups who were campaigning for debt cancellation. Critics have said that debt cancellation is a means to offer 'Structural Adjustment lite' – a way to use debt cancellation to continue to impose conditionality on Southern countries. It can also be argued that cancellation of debt was an extremely convenient (and inexpensive) action for some lender governments. They could proclaim their benevolence in cancelling HIPC debt, yet the impact on the lender countries would be insignificant.

4.2 New political spaces – the formation of debt cancellation networks

Individual debt cancellation campaigns would not have been 'successful' had they not been part of a larger transnational network. What is striking about newly established transnational networks such as Jubilee 2000 is the role played by ICTs in enabling them to thrive. Their strength is that they work on a multitude of levels or across a range of scales, usually simultaneously (Yanacopulos, 2002). However, the dilemma for any organization joining a transnational network is that of co-ordination – everyone thinks co-ordination is a great idea, but each organization wants to be co-ordinated on terms set by itself.

Networks of dissent formed around the increase in the developing world's debt from the early 1980s, gaining momentum from the defaults of various Latin American countries on their debts. This debt was primarily owed to commercial banks, and the issue started to attract NGO and church attention. Increasingly, national debt crisis networks were forming to exchange information, and early efforts at international information exchange and policy co-ordination were made through conferences and mailings (Donnelly, 2002). During the early 1990s, various US faith-based groups formed around debt in response to their experiences in Latin America. In 1995, Oxfam International joined them to form the Multilateral Debt Coalition, and Oxfam International opened a Washington office in order to lobby on various issues, debt being at the top of their agenda. In Europe, other debt networks were formed, as well as regional networks in Latin America and Africa.

By the middle of the 1990s, attention had shifted from commercial banks to the World Bank and IMF, and to bilateral, that is, country-to-country, lending. Donnelly (2002) claims that this is because the most heavily indebted countries owed the vast majority of their external debt to bilateral and multilateral creditors. In 1996, UK NGOs and churches launched the Jubilee 2000 UK campaign, asking for a single cancellation of all unsustainable debt by the year 2000, with many other national Jubilee 2000 networks forming shortly thereafter. It soon became evident that to deal with an issue at the level of G-7 governments and multilateral institutions such as the World Bank and IMF, a global campaign was essential. Even though the will to form a transnational network around the debt issue existed in the 1980s, it can be argued that the technology to enable it to happen did not exist in the same way as some 15 years later.

The Jubilee networks were bound to go through a state of transition after the deadline date of the millennium. While many groups remained active at a national level and even at a regional level, there is no 'one' Jubilee network (and, arguably, there never was). Many groups remained active (the UK group had 75 members as of summer 2003), but there have been divisions about action at the global level.

4.3 Use of technology

Technological advances in new communication technologies made possible the multi-level tactics necessary for a global campaign. The instantaneous nature of the Internet enabled like-minded individuals and organizations (at least on the issue of debt cancellation) to collect and disseminate information, and to communicate and co-ordinate with each other. One Oxfam International official stated that 'there are lots of ingredients for successful advocacy, but one of them is undoubtedly in a modern communications world, in terms of how decisions are made, the ability to mobilize pressure in many places at once, and be able to move from one target to the next' (OXF-1, 1998). Technological advances in ICTs have particularly benefited non-state actors, in that they allow them to utilize information and communication sources to mobilize large numbers of people and organizations around reframed issues or norms, and thus to build a wide consensus amongst supporters.

Another contributor to the success of the debt cancellation campaign was the strategic use of the media, which allowed millions to hear the newly reframed ideas about debt cancellation. The mass media were used in various ways during the debt cancellation campaign and many media personalities also shared the same ideas about the perceived injustice of debt, and either joined the campaign or spoke out in a personal capacity. The most vocal media person involved in the debt cancellation campaign has been Bono, the lead singer of the rock band U2. And, at least in the UK, one of the most important media moments was in February 1999 at the annual Brit Awards, where pop musicians are awarded for their achievements. The Brit Awards, at which Bono spoke out about debt cancellation, are shown on mainstream television in many countries, so this message reached millions of people throughout the world, which gave the debt cancellation campaign a mainstream audience. During the course of the campaign, Bono, the Pope and Muhammad Ali – to name only a few – promoted the debt cancellation message.

The newspaper, *The Guardian*, describes this new genre of rock celebrity/ activist as follows:

> There is nothing new about rock activism, of course. Bob Geldof, a close friend of the U2 singer, epitomised the old approach: raise money, raise public anger, pile the pressure on the politicians. But Bono – working in collaboration with Geldof – has pioneered a new kind of celebrity activism: he is a lobbyist, not a fundraiser. 'Usually, famous faces are used to getting media attention,' says Lucy Matthew, one of two key behind-the-scenes players in Bono's campaigning (the other is Jamie Drummond, of the Drop the Debt campaign). 'But now Bono and Bob spend time on meetings,

> phone calls, how to get people on side, much more than on photo
> opportunities.'

(Bunting and Burkeman, 2002)

The transnational debt networks targeted international financial institutions and governments to cancel debt, but they did this through both targeted lobbying and public campaigns aimed at mobilizing public support. Thus, the media was used to capitalize on mass demonstrations and on famous supporters of the campaigns. Instant global media has enabled messages, whether targeted at specific audiences or targeted for general appeal, to reach their audiences.

An example of this targeted use of the media occurred during the negotiation and implementation of the HIPC initiative for Uganda, where there was a close relationship between the Ugandan government (the first country to receive debt cancellation) and Oxfam International. The Ugandan government worked both with debt networks in Uganda and with international NGOs, and the government utilized publications such as the *Financial Times* to present the case for earlier debt cancellation for Uganda. In its lobbying of other governments and governing bodies of the World Bank and the IMF, the Ugandan government made the connection between debt repayments and primary education. A member of Oxfam International outlines the Ugandan strategy:

> ... they said if you give us debt (cancellation) we'll use every penny to invest
> in poverty programmes and we'll particularly use it to get two million
> children into primary school. And we'll use every penny for that. Then you
> make the debate that you're stopping the Ugandan children from going to
> school!

(OXF-2, 1997)

This is just one instance of a broader media campaign used by Jubilee 2000 to expose publics to a reframed conceptualization of debt. The campaign was aimed at gaining mass support for this idea in order to exert political pressure, particularly in G-7 countries. Diverse advocates of debt cancellation, from the Pope to Bono, championed the immorality of debt, thus appealing to a larger audience who may not have been exposed to such ideas before. Through this kind of campaigning activity, Jubilee 2000 managed to reframe debt cancellation, make it accessible to the general public, and presented it as a question of morality.

4.4 Tensions within networks

The complex of debt networks has been phenomenally successful on a number of levels. For our purposes here, the most interesting aspect has been the ability to bring together a vast array of disparate groups around one issue. A key element was the presentation of technical and complicated economic issues in terms of a simple moral campaign against injustice. Together with the enabling information and communication technologies available at the end of the twentieth century, this generated a far more 'global campaign' than had previously been seen.

Nonetheless, these global networks have not been tension free. Ideological divisions became apparent, particularly over how various groups defined the issue of debt. For example, Jubilee South, which comprised a number of national debt networks, demanded that all debt, particularly to HIPC countries, should be cancelled rather than only unsustainable debt. Some debt networks boycotted the Poverty Reduction Strategy Paper (PRSP) process in their individual countries because this was seen as a mechanism for the World Bank and the IMF to co-opt and silence them. Other groups saw participation in the PRSP process as their first opportunity to influence policy at a formal level.

There have been tensions arising from 'Northern' debt networks speaking on behalf of 'Southern' debt networks. Additionally, the language used by different groups has also been divisive – debt 'relief' generally being seen as something used in the North, and debt 'cancellation' as something being used in the South. Tensions have also arisen around the idea that debt relief/ cancellation is a 'campaign' and that the campaign ended at the time of the millennium. Poverty still exists after the millennium, even in HIPC countries, so the argument from some Southern groups is that the 'campaign' has not ended. Finally, perceptions of the scope of legitimate dissent are a key divider: many groups see the injustice of the debt burden as part of a larger injustice, and advocate the cancellation of all debt, arguing that all of the debts owed are unsustainable. Other groups are pushing for more and deeper debt cancellation but not for the writing off of all debts.

Activity 12.4

Write brief answers to the three questions posed at the end of Section 2 based on the discussion above.

5   Evaluating global networks

Do our two case studies cast light on the more general theses associated with the emergence of a global network society: namely, the character and role of networked forms of organization and the scope for what Rosenau calls 'sovereignty-free' actors to reconfigure political space? To engage with these issues, we begin by considering some of the similarities and differences between labour and debt cancellation networks.

5.1 Comparing networks – the labour movement and debt cancellation networks

The two case studies present somewhat different and contrasting efforts by transnational civil society networks. In the case of debt cancellation, the issue was quite circumscribed with an identifiable outcome – the writing off of international debt. For the labour movement, the struggles are multiple and continuing with altogether less clarity about the criteria for success. The Jubilee 2000 campaign was (arguably) successful in meeting its aims and drew upon a range of different organizations, although the fact that debt cancellation came with a fresh set of policy conditions raised questions about the precise criteria for success. Its tactics were shrewd, and mixed 'virtual' campaigning and advocacy with well-planned street demonstrations that were very 'real'. Hence, it combined the place-based with the de-territorialized and virtual. The campaign's targets were also identifiable, that is, the international financial institutions and their member states. For labour campaigners, the targets are more diverse including international organizations like the WTO and IMF, specific national governments and, above all, firms and corporations ranging from small companies illegally employing child labourers to transnational corporations seeking single union deals.

Organizationally, the debt cancellation campaigns were built up from new alliances, even if the individual organizations had long histories of human rights, religious and social justice interests. By contrast, the labour movements have grown from largely male-dominated and hierarchical organizations which militate against the flexibility required of transnational campaigning. The 'new' movements have had to fight internal obstacles to change as well as the objects of their campaigns. We saw that this was particularly important for women campaigners who, following their enhanced social and political assertiveness, had to deal with the repercussions from male colleagues and family members.

The Jubilee 2000 coalitions made effective use of the media and technology. Not only did they use ICTs for information gathering and dissemination, they also managed to 'brand' their cause in moral terms. Labour movements have come late to such tactics although campaigns on child labour, for example, have taken a more moral tone. Both cases show that ICTs are increasingly important for information sharing, communication, and planning. However, the debt cancellation campaigns also stuck to more formal channels of representation, lobbying governments and key interstate organizations, while all the time spreading the message to the public. Labour activists have used such channels but have also, on occasion, resorted to innovative 'cyber-terrorist' tactics.

Within the networks a number of tensions, sometimes creative, emerged. The first concerned the pursuit of universal values, or transnational action, in a context of particular national or local conditions. Quite often the demands at local, national and global levels coincided, for instance, the case of debt reduction or labour standards. Yet at other times, the pursuit of supposedly global ideals, such as a particular version of 'feminism' or the anti-statism of some civil society groups, was at odds with the needs of local groups. This raises the issue of power relations within networks and whose agenda is ultimately served. For strategic reasons a network may present a united front which actually conceals certain differences in values and approaches.

This brings us to the second tension regarding unifying ideologies. The network form of transnational civil society is based on multi-level, flexible and shifting alliances. While this can be effective in resisting certain forms of governance, it has its weaknesses. Campaigns can fragment because they lack a single ideological focus. To illustrate, for some, debt reduction is a moral issue based on Christian values of forgiveness, whereas others see debt as a symptom of neo-imperialism and call for an overturning of global capitalist structures. We saw with the Mexican seamstresses how middle-class feminists viewed the labour issue as a problem of political organization, whereas the strikers seemed more concerned about immediate compensation. That is, the same issue can be interpreted and acted upon very differently.

The third tension leads from this and concerns the formal versus the informal routes of action and dissent. Some civil society campaigners pursue formal political channels which require engaging with state and interstate organizations, for example, as the debt campaign's lobbying of G-7 leaders. Others prefer informal channels which bring them closer to a form of civil disobedience, for instance, through cyber-hacking. Nevertheless, in reality most campaigns utilize both formal and informal political channels, depending upon strategy and circumstances. Therefore, for example, the debt campaigns used public demonstrations at the same time as lobbying members of parliament, while the Nike email campaign grew organically without a clear strategy. Moreover, when it comes to changing public opinion, it is difficult to say what is formal and informal since this involves subjective processes of awareness raising and action. How people become aware of issues and what they then decide to do about them is not an exact science, and consequently it is impossible to say precisely how a campaign worked. In this sense, the power of networked campaigns is subtle and may not result in an obvious or immediate change.

5.2 Transforming the international system?

This discussion raises broader questions about the effectiveness of transnational civil society networks and their ability to transform the international system. One way of addressing this issue is to consider the effectiveness of such networks. Measuring effectiveness can either be done by comparing the goals of a campaign with the outcomes, or by using externally generated criteria. In the case of debt reduction, large amounts of debt were written off, but this required the governments of the developing countries concerned to agree to new forms of policy conditionality. Many within the debt cancellation campaigns were critical of the reality of debt cancellation and argued that it was too little too late, and that many countries were not benefiting but, in fact, continued to become worse off. Furthermore, there was concern that the public may feel that it had 'done' debt and be unwilling to continue its participation in the campaign. Still others saw debt campaigns as a way in which dominant actors were able to co-opt networks of dissent. Thus, by one criterion they were effective, but by another they were not. Some aspects of the international system were changed, while others were maintained or even strengthened.

Our case studies certainly provide evidence that networks can be co-opted or marginalized. For example, the pressures for ending sweatshop labour resulted in key corporations setting up the Fair Labour Association, but this did little to alter working practices. Indeed, it is debatable whether the truly marginalized are represented by these organizations. Effective organizational networks generally evolve from successful pre-existing organizations, and we know little about forms of political mobilization that fail even to get to the level of an organization. This, in turn, raises questions about representation in network forms of organization. A common criticism is that the professional campaigners who tend to run the nodes of these networks are not those who have to live with the consequences of their actions, as seen in the divisions between North and South in the debt campaign for instance. For many, participation is a political commitment, but it is not directly related to their own livelihood struggles. Another illustration of this was the middle-class feminists who came to assist the Mexican seamstresses with their own, apparently different, agenda, although through dialogue a working and effective synergy did develop in this instance. Some of these problems are reinforced by the fact that technology is far from equally accessible. The optimistic advocates of the global network society thesis highlight the ease of access to technology and the ways this can permit broad-based participation, but this is clearly far from a reality given the present-day inequalities in global income and technology.

Thus far, we have dealt with problems of organization and strategy within networks, but in judging their effectiveness and capacity to transform social relations we also need to consider broader processes within the international system. A central issue is the relationship between these networks and the states-system that you studied in Part 1. In Section 2, we argued that civil society needed to be situated in relation to the state in order to assess the potential of non-state actors operating on the national terrain. Equally, transnational civil society both influences and is influenced by the interstate system. Within this context, some groups and forms of action seek new kinds of political and economic organization, while others simply seek modification of the existing state-based order. Our case studies are primarily examples of the success of civil society networks in seeking modifications to the existing order.

More generally, analysing the effectiveness of international NGOs and other transnational networks, Risse-Kappen found that 'differences in domestic structures determine the variation in the policy impact of transnational actors' and that success was also a function of the degree of institutionalization at the transnational level (1995, p.25). Clearly, states influence the degree to which civil society actors need to (or can) go transnational, and the states-system affects the degree to which these transnational networks become institutionalized. A number of analysts such as Ribeiro (1998), Keck and Sikkink (1998) and Rosenau (1997) paint a rosy picture of the changes possible through technologically networked organizations. Although it is important to recognize the existence and effects of transnational networks, it is also important to remember that states and the states-system remain potent forces in shaping the character of international politics. Networks need to be considered as just one of a number of actors in the governance process.

Certainly, our case studies support the argument that networks 'can amplify the demands of domestic groups, pry open space for new issues, and then echo these demands into the domestic arena' (Keck and Sikkink, 1998, p.13). Such processes are about the creative use of power amongst the relatively powerless. What we have found in the case studies, as have other writers, is that the speed of new technologies allows information to be passed more quickly and to more institutions than in the past. This can mean that the goals of transnational networks are achieved more rapidly. Simultaneous communication, afforded by ICTs, has meant that transnational networks can organize multiple activities, and access information about events that are occurring simultaneously in time but in different locations. This permits 'witnessing at a distance' and new forms of consciousness, thereby creating a greater threshold of awareness and allowing campaigners to forge solidarity across similar cases. The lower cost of electronic networking is important because it opens up the political process to more actors, although we have emphasized that this access is not unlimited. For organizations that only have limited time and resources, information retrieval and storage are greatly enhanced by participation in networks of like-minded organizations.

Finally, then, are we witnessing the emergence of a global network society? We have argued that transnational networks are worthy of consideration, that they have made a difference in international politics, but that it is important not to overemphasize their importance. Our evaluation of this issue depends partly on how we characterize international civil society and its place in the international order.

Question

In the light of the critical understandings of 'civil society' outlined in Section 2, how might we interpret the role of transnational networks and global civil society?

According to Gramsci, civil society in a capitalist order is the terrain upon which dominant classes and state elites are able to legitimate their rule, forging a consensual leadership of society so that their position is reproduced without the need for direct coercion and repression. Gramsci also raised the possibility that 'counter-hegemonic' forces within society, that is, forces seeking a general transformation of social relations based on class division, might use the freedoms and possibilities for action inherent in civil society against the hegemony of the ruling classes and the capitalist state. Many activists and analysts have drawn on these ideas to argue for the radical potential of the agency of transnational social movements. However, this has involved some rethinking of Gramsci's ideas.

On the one hand, where Gramsci saw the key target of counter-hegemonic mobilization as the capitalist nation state, the movements we have studied focus on a wider constellation of political agents including international organizations such as the WTO, IMF and World Bank. In a context of globalization, contemporary configurations of civil society 'look for political spaces other than those bounded by the parameters of the nation-state system' (Lipschutz, 1992, pp.392–3). This is because globalization is characterized by a paradoxical movement in which the state has been 'hollowed out' by multinational corporations and supranational organizations, for instance, the European Union, at the same time as the state has been internationalized, with powerful states projecting their power 'upwards' and 'outwards' into various institutions of 'global' governance. The IMF and the UN Security Council are examples of organizations in which powerful states, in the name of multilateralism, determine policy (and where this fails, they resort to unilateral action). This has meant that the 'target' for global civil society actors is no longer simply the nation state but interstate organizations as well as multinational corporations. This activism arises in response to and alongside both state and interstate forms of governance.

On the other hand, our case studies demonstrate that struggles taking place in global civil society are by no means straightforward vehicles for opposing capitalist hegemony. The issues addressed by these movements go beyond the inequalities generated by capitalism to multiple forms of marginalization and oppression. They include, for example, environmental degradation, peace movements and the exploitation of women – what are often called the 'new' social movements. We have seen some of the ways in which these organizations differ from the 'old' social movements such as trade unions, which were formed in the cauldron of patriarchal class antagonisms. Moreover, we have acknowledged how older forms of activism are merging with the new to form social movement unionism. The potential of these new developments for radical transformation remains a matter of fierce debate.

Some activists and theorists talk about the emergence of a 'global' or 'transnational' civil society, one that opens up the possibility of escaping the 'official' political structures of states and interstate organizations. To illustrate, the series of anti-capitalist demonstrations from the late 1990s onwards suggests that civil society action could produce counter-hegemonic momentum. Yet we must be wary of seeing all similar activity as tending towards radical transformation. The autonomy of many civil society organizations, such as development NGOs, has been severely compromised as increasing levels and proportions of official, that is, state, aid are channelled through them. Similarly, many civil society organizations, for instance, human rights organizations like Amnesty International, are not seeking a radical departure from state-based politics, but are looking to reform specific states and international institutions. In this sense, it becomes necessary to appreciate the mutually constitutive relationship between civil society and the states-system. Consequently, it becomes important to examine the tensions between state-based and civil society-based forms of politics. As Gramsci emphasized, civil society, and a fortiori global civil society, is an arena of contention – a place where power is both exerted and challenged.

6   Conclusion

We began this chapter by asking about the extent to which networks of dissent represent a new kind of actor in the international system and about whether they force us to rethink our understanding of international order. You have seen that straightforward answers to these questions are difficult. On the one hand, networks of dissent have achieved a highly visible public profile and have had some success in influencing the policies of states and other powerful institutions, as the debt cancellation case study illustrates. Their transnational growth has also been associated with and facilitated by the use of ICTs. On the other hand, we have also noted that such networks have some longer, historical antecedents, giving us cause to temper somewhat our evaluation of their 'newness'. In addition, the extent to which they can unproblematically challenge capitalist hegemony has been illustrated both by the varied nature of these movements and by the tensions that exist within and between them. Similarly, the issue of the extent to which networks of dissent force us to rethink our understanding of international order should be approached carefully. They are certainly significant actors and should not be ignored. But any simple image of a transnational civil society opposed to, and an alternative to, the states-system is, we think, misleading. International civil society is not separate from the states-system; the two are forged from, and transformed by, mutual collaboration and resistance.

Further reading

Among several studies that paint a rosy picture of the potentially emancipatory role of networks based on new technologies is Keck, M. and Sikkink, K. (1998) *Activists Beyond Borders: Advocacy Networks in International Politics*, Ithaca, NY, Cornell University Press.

Naomi Klein's *No Logo* (2000, London, Flamingo) has become a celebrated 'manifesto' for many anti-corporate activists.

More critical approaches to civil society that draw on Marxist understandings include Ellen Meiksins Wood's *Democracy Against Capitalism* (1995, Cambridge, Cambridge University Press), which is critical of the potential for new social movements to overcome capitalist domination. Robert Cox's 1999 essay 'Civil society at the turn of the millennium' gives a more mixed review, drawing on Gramsci's work (*Review of International Studies*, vol.25, no.1 pp.3–28).

A wide-ranging study of the nature and extent of networks as a distinct form of organization is Grahame Thompson's *Between Hierarchies and Markets* (2003, Oxford, Oxford University Press).

Chapter 13 Technologies, agency and the shape of the future

Helen Yanacopulos, Tim Jordan and Rafal Rohozinski

1 Introduction

In the previous chapter, we explored transnational networks of dissent and how ICTs (Information and Communication Technologies) have contributed to what many describe as a 'global civil society', a space that is neither market nor state, and in which political activity takes place within and across national borders, working with and against states, and challenging notions of governance in the international system. While these transnational networks are not new, ICTs have influenced the organizational forms they are taking. We argued that an examination of the role of networks allows us to explore different aspects of the international system to that of the states-system and international markets. In this chapter, we shall examine some specific actors in the international system who are likely to play a role in shaping the future. Writing about the future is always a risky undertaking and what follows is neither a prediction of future technologies nor of what the international system will look like. Rather, our aim is to examine the impact of ICTs on various agents or arenas in order to ask some questions about the changing dynamics of the international system.

We shall consider three agents or arenas of potential change – private financial institutions, social movements and the military. These are taken as exemplars of different social roles and orientations, that is, respectively, the merchant, the citizen and the prince. Broadly speaking, the merchant represents the power of economic agents, the citizen the social power of people and groups in civil society, and the prince the political power of the state. Clearly, private financial institutions, social movements and the military do not fully represent the power of merchants, citizens and princes, but they illustrate some of the tensions that emerge when these actors engage with networks and ICTs.

Specifically, we shall seek to explore three such tensions. The first of these is the tension between state and non-state actors. We shall concentrate on non-state actors as networks, and explore the tensions between the sovereign and territorial organization of state power and the challenges posed to this by network forms of organization. The second tension we shall consider is one of inequality and exclusion. Do the interactions between these agents and ICTs challenge or reinforce existing levels of inequality and patterns of exclusion? The third tension relates to questions of order and governance: to what extent is the use of ICTs by various actors contributing to an increased volatility and disorder in the international system, and to what degree is it providing new forms of stabilizing governance? There are many expectations placed on ICTs – that they will increase access to global markets and facilitate the development of a level playing field, that they will enable the voiceless to be heard, and that they will make warfare smarter. Against this, it can be argued that ICTs are increasing the volatility of markets, contributing to the development of an 'uncivil' society based on inequality and exclusion, and heightening the asymmetries of military power and the opportunities for coercive surveillance.

2 Private financial institutions

The first agent or arena we shall explore is that of private financial institutions, agencies of change that now play a prominent role in the international system. We will consider the political and economic ramifications of private financial institutions in so far as they form networks with other actors, as well as looking at their relation to governments and multilateral institutions. According to Filipovic (1997), the global financial market, which is primarily comprised of private financial institutions, has two main characteristics: first, private financial institutions are financial innovators driven by the pursuit of profits; and second, deregulation, liberalization and re-regulation during the last three decades of the twentieth century have created global markets, regulated by nation states.

Private financial institutions
Here the term private
financial institutions refers to
banks, investment firms or
companies that trade in
currencies and buy and sell
bonds, shares, derivatives.

For present purposes, we treat private financial institutions as private companies operating for profit, that is, they are banks, investment firms or companies that buy and sell bonds, shares, and derivatives, and that trade in currencies. Generally, these institutions fall under the umbrella of the financial sector; they are service industries whose main purpose is to mobilize capital while making profits for their shareholders. Historically, private financial institutions have served the purpose of facilitating the movement of savings into investments.

The financial industry has grown exponentially since the 1970s as it has become increasingly internationalized. This is not to say that finance has not always had an international focus, but that technological advances have meant that this focus has grown dramatically during this period. While many factors have aided this growth, two key factors are deregulation and technological innovation. To put the growth of the financial sector in perspective, at the turn of the twenty-first century, the volume of foreign exchange transactions totalled US$1.2 trillion per day, equal to the value of world trade in goods and service in an entire quarter. In the remainder of this section, we shall concentrate on this specific aspect – foreign exchange transactions or currency transactions.

2.1   Financial institutions, markets and states

Innovation has been a major factor in the growth of the private financial institutions. As Filipovic (1997) states, financial innovation is one of the two main characteristics of the growth of global capital markets. There are numerous reasons for this such as the international circulation of the dollar to finance US current account deficits in the 1960s and 1970s; the recycling of OPEC (Organization of the Petroleum Exporting Countries) oil revenues through the international financial system during the 1970s; the deregulation and liberalization of financial markets in the 1980s and 1990s; and finally, the prevalence of ICTs. All of these have made around-the-clock global financial markets possible.

Question

You have studied technological innovation in Chapter 10, but how is financial innovation different?

In this context, when we speak of innovation we are referring to the introduction of a new product or process on the market. So, financial innovation is the creation of a new financial product or process, and the innovations that have occurred during the latter part of the twentieth century cannot be separated from technological innovations in ICTs – without these, the financial innovations that have taken place would not have been possible. There have been three groups of financial innovations directly based on ICTs during this period (Strange, 1998). The first is the use of computers, which have allowed the settlement of financial transactions to be made electronically, resulting in electronic money. The second innovation is that of micro-chips and credit cards on the consumer end of the financial industry, making money plastic. Finally, the use of satellites and ICTs, where trading is carried out electronically and access to information is instant, has made markets global. Notwithstanding this technological facilitation of financial innovation, it is also a process driven by the need of private financial institutions to increase profits for their shareholders, and consequently try to reduce risk and maximize returns. As with any firm operating in a competitive environment, private financial institutions must innovate new processes and products in order to stay in business. Accelerating technological changes have obliged financial institutions to invest more capital in their business and to seek new markets.

As part of this competitive process, various new financial products have emerged, generally falling under the broad category of derivatives. Derivatives, which are financial products 'derived' from other financial products, allow private financial institutions and multinational corporations to hedge against potential losses, such as those resulting from fluctuating exchange rates. Since the Asian financial crises of 1997, one of the most criticized financial innovations has been the hedge fund. Hedge funds are highly leveraged investment funds, that is, the ratio of their liabilities to their assets is very high, they are usually based offshore (which means that they do not pay domestic taxes), and they have grown rapidly since the early 1990s (Temple, 2001). What all these different derivatives and financial products show us is that financial innovation originates from the basic tenet of the financial industry – to increase returns while minimizing risk.

Perhaps ironically, the highly innovative financial industry is also one of the most regulated through the actions of governmental bodies and central banks. Some argue that it is this very regulation that increases financial innovation: 'innovation of financial instruments and practices occurs in an effort to remove or lessen the financial constraints imposed on firms. Government regulations do indeed impose constraints and thereby induce innovation' (Silber, 1975, p.65). From another perspective, Susan Strange claims that recent financial innovations:

> take advantage of the cracks and chinks of the American regulatory system – but the consequences were not so much due to the innovations, as the failures of the regulators and of the legislatures that set the rules in the first place to respond to change with equal agility and quick thinking.

(Strange, 1998, p.39)

Either way, unlike innovation in most other sectors, permission for financial innovation is generally given or withheld by public authorities. Therefore, argues Strange, governments and regulators have a shared responsibility with the private financial institution for innovations.

Underlying the actions and effects of private financial institutions is a tension between the national and international, even global, forces. Stephen Korbin argues that the 'financial market is global in the sense that transactions are linked in an electronic network, and borders and territoriality are virtually irrelevant' (cited in Kapstein, 1994, p.4). In Strange's view, the 'problem in the [twenty-first] century is that the traditional authority of the nation state is not up to the job of managing mad international money' (1998, p.190). It is certainly true that a key aspect of financial innovation, and one that draws on the technological innovation of ICTs, is that many private financial institutions have looked beyond their national markets. And while the industry has gone global, the regulation of these markets remains primarily national, which leads us to the second of Filipovic's characteristics noted above – the regulation of private financial institutions.

The regulation of private financial institutions gained a great deal of international attention, particularly after the financial crises of the 1980s and 1990s. These crises exposed the volatility of the global capital markets and the consequences of actions by private financial institutions, leading many critics to warn of 'casino capitalism' or 'mad money'. These critics pointed to a tension between national regulation and an international or global marketplace. But the demarcation lines are actually not as clear as that. If one attempts to draw a diagram of the structure and relationship between private financial institutions (firm level), the cities they are based in (city level), the countries they are based in (national level), and the financial marketplace (global level), it is difficult to see these working in a linear way. Possibly the primary reason for this is that this type of illustration does not allow for networks, which can work between and within these levels.

Financial innovators: traders at the Pacific Stock Exchange in Los Angeles, 1999

Certainly, the empirical evidence indicating the increasing volume of trade in international finance is compelling. Yet to what extent are states able to regulate private financial institutions: is the national authority of the state defunct in this area, as argued by critics such as Susan Strange (1998)?

Does this activity need to be regulated and, if so, by whom? Typically, central banks have been states' traditional arm of financial regulation. These bodies are not just dealing with national pressures, but are frequently the main institutions for managing the intersection of national and global money markets. For many developing countries, financial deregulation (opening national commercial banking to greater competition) has been a condition of loans made to them by the IMF (International Monetary Fund) and bilateral donors. Saskia Sassen (2000) describes this as the engagement of states in the process of 'globalization', and terms such as privatization, liberalization, and deregulation are often used to describe the policies that states engage in. However, the problem with these terms is that they only 'capture the withdrawal of the state from regulating its economy. They do not register all the ways in which the state participates in setting up the new frameworks through which globalization is furthered ... nor do they capture the associated transformations inside the state' (Sassen, 2000, p.166).

Technological advances in ICTs have affected the time and space of communication and, therefore, that of financial transactions. Sassen claims that the importance of 'the social infrastructure for global connectivity points to the importance of location' (2002, p.25). Location is important, she argues, as social networks interact with technological ones – they work in tandem. Sassen looks at the relationship between 'global' cities, namely the 'big three' financial centres of London, New York, and Tokyo, and describes how these cities and the firms that are based within them work together on one level:

> Market participants often paint a picture of ruthless competition, which is only partly correct. In truth, the relationship is more complex. During the wave of deregulation in the 1980s, the big three already had some cooperative division of labour that continues today with increasing specialisation. Despite all the talk of bitter competition in the roaring 1980s, a truly global market was emerging that was circulating capital through the leading financial centres before selling it repackaged at home. Since this trend intensified in the 1990s, cross-border strategic alliances have been multiplying between both firms and markets. Competition coexists with strategic collaboration and hierarchy.

> (Sassen, 2002, p.26)

Therefore, financial markets are not simply comprised of private financial institutions, but are part of an intricate web of relationships between firms, national central banks, multilateral institutions and, using Sassen's language, global cities.

2.2   Agents of exclusion

Most people's direct experience of international financial institutions is the bank on the high street. Yet we are exposed to dramatic stories of 'rogue traders' controlling millions, and even more distant events such as the Asian financial crisis of 1997, or the devaluations and currency crises of pesos and rubles. While these may appear foreign and distant to many, these events have an impact not only on the lives of those who bank on the high street but more so on the lives of people in the countries concerned.

The private financial institutions that we have been considering are generally located in North America, Europe or East Asia, and the countries these institutions are situated in are by no means immune from financial crises. Nevertheless, in comparison, it is much more difficult for a developing country to exercise what is called 'adequate prudential regulation' over its liberalized financial sector than it is for richer countries. There has been a great deal of pressure (from bilateral donors and from international financial institutions such as the IMF) for developing countries to liberalize their financial sector – sometimes this has been done voluntarily, and sometimes through donor conditionality. The tension comes from the external pressure for countries to liberalize, while they are also told to exercise 'adequate prudential regulation'. This 'globalization' of financial markets has been a cause for concern, as expressed by the prominent US economist Paul Krugman's statement that: 'It's amazing how quickly the terrifying financial crises of the 1990s have faded from memory. The globalization of the financial markets created many new opportunities for things to go disastrously wrong, and they often did' (Krugman, 2000).

The extreme pressure on developing countries that have liberalized their financial markets is captured by Martin Khor:

> Given an international environment of big financial players with huge concentrations of money for speculation and investment, financially small countries are now subjected to great volatility and financial and economic danger. For instance, the Long Term Capital Management affair revealed that a hedge fund with $4–5 billion in equity could manage to raise so much credit that the banks were exposed to the tune of $200 billion. Few governments can withstand a determined bid by a few big hedge funds to speculate on their currencies and financial markets.

(Khor, 2000, p.157)

Although there has been pressure to liberalize financially, and to allow for the open trading of currencies, countries such as China and India have not allowed their currencies to be fully convertible, and therefore have not been subjected to volatile capital flows and currency instability. Malaysia is an example of a state that imposed regulations on the outflows of its currency. During the Asian Crisis of 1997, Prime Minister Mahathir Mohamad set tough measures on the outflow of capital from Malaysia, including the fixing of the exchange rate, withdrawing the rigit (the Malaysian currency) from international circulation, and a one-year lock-in period for capital already in the country. He has been a vocal critic of private financial institutions and speculation, stating that:

> We had asked the international agencies to regulate currency trading but they did not care, so we ourselves have to regulate our own currency. If the international community agrees to regulate currency trading and limit the range of currency fluctuations and enables countries to grow again, then we can return to the floating exchange rate system. But now we can see the damage this system has done throughout the world. It has destroyed the hard work of countries to cater to the interests of speculators as if their interests are so important that millions of people must suffer.

(Khor, 2000, p.142)

There has been growing pressure from various interested parties, such as non-government organizations (NGOs), some governments, and some international institutions to develop new methods of regulation for the actions of private financial institutions, even if these are confined to regulation by their home countries. Proposals for international financial reforms or international regulation of financial transactions (sometimes referred to as 'Tobin Tax' proposals after the economist James Tobin, one of the proponents of such a scheme) are being discussed in various forums. Free market advocates and many Northern governments generally oppose these kinds of proposals for the reform of the international financial regime. Most proposals for financial reforms involve a transaction tax on capital flows. Jetin and de Brunhoff describe the proposed process:

> Let's assume that a trader wants to convert francs into dollars. He or she would have to pay, for instance, a tax of 0.1 percent on this deal. If later that trader were to convert the dollars back into francs, the same tax of 0.1 percent would again have to be paid. If such 'in and out' trades were undertaken once a day, at the end of the year the trader would have paid up to 48 percent of the trade's face value in taxes. If such a trade occurred on a weekly basis, the annualised tax receipt would be ten percent while if it were to occur once a month, the figure would be 2.4 per cent.

(Jetin and de Brunhoff, 2000, p.199)

Proponents of such reforms argue that they are now feasible because of the development of the international infrastructure for making inter-bank foreign exchange payments. This system has been put in place because of the ever-increasing volume of trading, and because technological advances in ICTs have made it feasible (Schmidt, 2000). The advocates of international reforms are suggesting that this technological advancement should be used to counteract the adverse impact of increasing trading.

2.3   Shaping the international system – volatility and stability

The fundamental principle underpinning private financial institutions is the relationship between risk and return – the higher the risk, the higher the potential return. Conversely, the lower the risk, the lower the potential return. However, it is not always that simple. The very technology that has made global financial markets possible, mainly ICTs, has made the global financial markets increasingly volatile. Criticisms and warnings have come, not only from critics of 'global capitalism', but also from those who have promoted the globalization of financial markets. One such warning came from the former US Treasury Secretary, Robert Rubin, who admitted that part of the problem leading to financial crises all over the world 'stemmed from volatile capital movements that were exacerbated by modern technology, which increase the size and speed of the mistakes people can make' (quoted in Ignatius, 1999). Some of the crises include Mexico in 1995, South-East Asia in 1997–98, Russia in 1998, Brazil in 1999 and Argentina in 2001. It is evident that the crises are taking place in developing countries (or in the language of private financial institutions – 'emerging markets'). Bello *et al.* comment on this as follows:

> Since differences in exchange rates, interest rates and stock prices are much
> lower among the more integrated developed country markets, movements of
> capital from the North to the so-called 'Big Emerging Markets' of Asia, and
> other countries of the South, have been much more volatile. Thus while
> crises are endemic to the finance-driven global capitalist system, the crises
> of the last few years have been concentrated in the emerging markets.

(Bello *et al.*, 2000, p.6)

Private financial institutions are important agents in shaping the future of the international system for a number of reasons. The technological and financial innovations that have come out of this sector have enabled new forms of investments to be created. Additionally, electronic trading has meant that information and transactions, specifically on currencies, can be accessed from and performed anywhere in the world (there is always a market open) instantly. This has led to a staggering increase in currency trading. The novelty is that private financial institutions trade in such high volumes that they may (as a group) have a direct impact on a currency's value and stability. Some of these financial institutions go outside of the national regulatory systems and can arguably make the financial markets extremely volatile. Therefore, private financial institutions are part of a global financial regime, opening up international investment, but they are also international agents that are increasing volatility within the international system.

3 Social movements as agents of change

Public demonstrations and protests, such as the anti-globalization campaigns, have propelled social movements into the public consciousness. They have involved citizens both protesting and mobilizing around issues, and they problematize the ways in which we live our lives, and call for changes in our habits of thought, action and interpretation. Their existence, successes, failures and more generally their dynamics (though all incredibly difficult to read and interpret) allow us to gauge the workings of broader political international structures (Crossley, 2002). You studied what we called networks of dissent in Chapter 12. Social movements also encompass networks of dissent. However, in this section we shall be looking at social movements in a very broad way. When we examined the case studies of labour and debt cancellation movements in Chapter 12, these were specific social movements. Here we are interested in looking at social movements generally, as agents of change. The one specific movement we shall look at is the anti-globalization movement, which claims a broad support base and is generally seen as a number of social movements grouped together.

Question

Think back to the discussion of networks of dissent in Chapter 12, and try to identify the features of a social movement.

While there are many contending definitions of social movements, we shall use Della Porta and Diani's (1999) identification of four features that are typical of social movements.

Social movements
Della Porta and Diani (1999) define social movements as groups of people exhibiting shared beliefs and solidarity in seeking some form of social change. These movements are often informal and network-based and are involved in novel and unconventional, as well as more conventional, forms of activity and protest.

- Informal interaction networks: interaction between members of a movement is not formally defined, as it is in an office or, say, the army. It occurs as and when members initiate contact.

- Shared beliefs and solidarity: members of social movements generate shared meanings and identities. Solidarity between them may then result from the 'we' members generate.

- Collective action leading to conflicts: movements are involved in social conflict, usually because they seek some form of social change.

- Unconventional actions: movements generate novel and unusual forms of protest. Though movements may also use well-understood methods, such as petitions, they typically also develop new means of creating protests.

Social movements are generally understood as networked entities. They are made up of numerous elements – ideas, events, people and groups – that circulate around each other. The network may be thought of as a series of connections between different points, each point being some element of a movement. Sometimes these points become densely packed, as at the demonstrations in Prague during the World Bank and IMF meetings in 2000 (discussed below), where so many ideas, people and events connected in a short space of time. Alternatively, networks may spread out as activists develop community-based work. What makes a movement, rather than a mesh of connections, is the bonds of solidarity and shared beliefs out of which activists construct a collective identity. This identity is something activists share, a means of recognizing in each other a common belief, goal or purpose, and it provides a loose sense of unity. To complicate matters, this identity is not simply given but is constantly discussed and revised between activists. It is, in a sense, itself a networked entity.

ICT networks and social movement networks complement each other, and we can see that we are dealing with two different, yet related, types of agency. Social movements rely on the aggregation of the individual agency of people who join together to alter the conditions of their lives. ICT networks both constrain and enable agency and are informed by choices made by designers and builders of technologies in their agency. For example, it was striking how, during the anti-fuel tax protests in the UK in the early twenty-first century, a powerful blockade of fuel tankers was organized using mobile phones as a key technology. The mobility of the phone matched the fluid network creating and maintaining the fuel tanker blockade. Jenny Pickerill's work on environmental protest and ICTs develops a similar argument. Pickerill (2001, pp.142–3) argues that there were three aspects to the use of the Internet by green activist groups.

- New potential for organizing: e-mail and bulletin boards in particular offer new means of organizing.

- Fewer editorial constraints: there is no necessary hierarchy, people can say what they wish directly to each other.

- Using technologies innovatively and quickly: green groups have tended to adopt these new communications technologies quickly and to explore them innovatively.

Pickerill identifies some of the key ways in which communication via computer networks may affect social movements. First, she grasps that the different form of communication offered by computers fits well with some of the needs of social movements. These movements are often under-resourced and so a medium like the Internet, which is relatively cheap (compared to international phone calls for instance) and can be used globally, is very useful (see Chapter 12, Activity 12.1). The wide distribution of the medium also matches the decentralized nature of social movements. Communication that is more inclusive and works better with less hierarchical organization is well-matched to social movements.

Second, and related to the first point, the reduction in control by editors, or more generally those near the top of hierarchical organizations, also serves networked organizations well (or 'dis/organizations' as some activists call them). An essential component of social movements is the constant articulation of its collective identity; for this identity to command people's time and energy it must include and compel them. For most social movements, this results from the ability and willingness of people to contribute to shaping the collective identity so that they continue to see themselves and their concerns reflected in other people who are in the movement. Networked communication provides one avenue for this.

Finally, Pickerill suggests that movements have taken up innovative technologies and used these technologies more quickly than many others. Any organization interested both in innovation and in speedy use of innovation is highly likely to be involved in computer networking. This is simply because such networking is accessible and has been one of the quickest to develop.

Pickerill's work focuses on environmental groups, and we cannot easily extrapolate from her results to all social movements. Nevertheless, given that we have identified a general congruence between social movements and communications via computer networks, we might speculate that Pickerill has picked out one example of a general trend. This trend is the intensification of social movement activity mediated by ICTs. Perhaps we might even see a new wave of popular protest driven in part through computer communications. For example, since the late 1990s there has been a series of protests focused on processes of globalization. These protests are marked by major demonstrations and events – Seattle, Quebec, Melbourne, Genoa and more – and by some emerging international social movement groups – the annual people's summit in Porto Allegre, for example. This latter movement focuses on an international phenomenon and uses necessarily global communications. It is not that global communication did not exist before, but that global computer-networked communication offers new tools for social movements.

3.1   Movements as networks

The anti-globalization movement is a fluid network that spans many continents and can come together quickly around meetings of international stature. Many other social movements could be considered. Feminism, green, anti-racist, and the labour movements are all commonly mentioned but social movements also cover populist right-wing movements such as the Patriot movement in the USA. Furthermore, there are many movements which are hard to categorize as 'right' or 'left', such as the UK fuel protestors or the animal liberation movement.

To help us see network fluidity in action, we can take the example of the protests against the IMF and the World Bank in Prague in September 2000. The IMF/World Bank meeting was seen by protestors as a moment in the ongoing globalization of finance and capitalism that had been protested against in a series of events: the J18 demonstration in London, the WTO protests in Seattle, demonstrations against the G-7 in Genoa, and so on. Each of these was the site of a protest meant to force world leaders to either stop meeting or to take notice of 'world citizens'' complaints. In the Prague case, the aim was to stop the meeting from progressing by blocking the entries and exits to the conference hall. This would keep conference delegates inside the hall, both lengthening their day in order to prevent work being done on any future days and stopping attendance at dinners and entertainment. The demonstration was loud, prolonged and possibly successful, with the conference closing a day early (though the organizers claimed this was because all business had been completed early), and most evening events were disrupted.

These marches were made up of activists drawn mainly from across Europe, with some from further afield. We can see the elaborate manifestation of the four principles of social movements in the following quote from an activist on the day of the Prague march.

> Time and effort had been put into developing a complex communication and decision-making structure for the day. The idea was that in the centre of our marching column was a group of people with mobile phones and radios who were in contact with two central communication hubs Centrum and Traveller (one fixed and one mobile) – and also with a number of scouts, predominantly on bikes, who could go ahead and check out where the cops were and what route we should take etc. The communications team in the centre of the march then liaised with a route group who knew the area and had all the maps in order to decide where to go. This decision was then passed forward to the people at the front of the march and signalled to everyone by a big flag on a tall pole ... The whole march was made of affinity groups, each of which had a delegate. When a decision had to be made which the communications team and route group didn't feel they

between various agents in the international arena – social movements and governments.

3.2   Technology and exclusion

Discussions of social movements imply that they are inclusive, and their advocates claim that they are an emerging form of democracy, or a more direct form of democracy. Proponents see these movements as a reaction to globalization and capitalism, and to modernity. Alan Touraine, one of the primary theorists of social movements, makes this claim in the following statement:

> These really new movements certainly cannot be lumped together. We cannot say that the anti-globalisation movements – Seattle, Genoa and so on – are linked with the Taliban regime. Obviously not. However, the reference is the same. The reference is not to a certain type of civil society, but to a process of social transformation, to a process of globalisation. Referring to what is happening now, what is most visible at the world level is ... the predominance of a cultural fundamentalism against modernism and capitalism together.
>
> (Touraine, 2002, p.92)

Despite the fact that social movements are generally seen as part of a 'global civil society', there are also 'uncivil' society movements. What is seen as 'civil' in some contexts is 'uncivil' in others. The inclusive (or, as some would say, 'direct democratic') element of social movements is not just concerned with issues that are deemed 'good' or 'right' by Western societies, but also includes what is seen as reactionary and against the principles on which these societies are built. And, while these reactionary social movements are generally a reaction to modernism and capitalism, they too rely on the 'global' and technological aspects of the Internet to co-ordinate and to mobilize around issues.

Social movements can and did exist prior to ICT technologies; however, they are much more prevalent and successful because of ICTs. For example, the Zapatistas in Mexico were initially a very locally based movement. Their utilization of ICTs has been seen as the primary reason why they gained global attention for their cause. Additionally, there are a large number of social movements in India, but only some gain global attention such as the movement against the building of a series of dams along the Narmada River. Other movements remain localized, and do not activate the international pressure that the Narmada Dam movement has captured. The Narmada Dam movement has utilized ICTs, which is one element of its success in bringing attention to the issue and ultimately stopping the building of the dam. While there may be numerous factors contributing to the success of one movement and the lack of success of another, access and exclusion from technology is a key factor. This is outlined by Ron Diebert in the following terms:

> The current realities and future prospects are mixed. On the one hand, the Internet has provided a means through which citizens from around the globe can communicate and deliberate in a speedy and relatively open fashion. It has been the vehicle for a remarkable flourishing of citizen-to-citizen communications on a global scale and the proliferation of individual expression through web publication, all of which would be essential for the future of global democratic discourse. On the other hand, however, a confusing mix of private and public ownership structures criss-crossing several major international regimes presently governs the Internet. The vast majority of people on the globe have no access to it.

(Diebert, 2003, p.2)

3.3　Shaping the international system – agents of instability

We have now identified two different types of networks – ICT and social movements – both of which embody similar social relations. The intersection of these two networks may offer a trend to the future. It is feasible that computer networks and social movement networks will feed each other, promoting future protest. What we can see here is a particular dis/organizational form that matches a particular technological form.

Question

How would you characterize the relationship between ICTs and social movements?

We could describe the relationship as the 'use' of technology by social movements, but what is going on here is slightly more than that. Social movements are not simply using technology – their use is particularly powerful because the social or ethical imperatives behind the organizational form and behind the technological form somehow match each other. It is not so much a case of some social form 'using' technology, a difficult idea as technologies embody social values, but two different types of social form – one political and organizational, and the other technological – *amplifying* each others' effects. If this is indeed true, with the intersection of networked popular activism and ICTs we could be witnessing a trend reaching into the twenty-first century.

This intersection can have both 'good' and 'bad' effects when considering the efficacy of social movements. The sheer amount of information that can be processed and distributed via computer networks both facilitates and amplifies a social movement's abilities to act, but it can also clog up the works, overwhelming activists with too much information. The pressure to respond can introduce a problem of activists spending too much time organizing. The amplification effect of networked organization meeting networked computers might backfire on social movements. Nevertheless, even on this cautionary note, it can be recognized that the interaction between these networks could potentially produce a powerful amplification of social movements and their abilities to act.

4　The military as an agent of change

You have studied states and the states-system in Part 1. In this section, we shall be looking at one aspect of the state – the military. The reasons for focusing on the military are threefold: first, states claim a monopoly over the legitimate use of coercive power, and generally this is exercised through their militaries; second, the technological advancements made for military purposes have been both dramatic and immense; and third, the military is a key agent in international (or national) security, and its relationship to technology influences the international system as a whole.

During the twentieth century, technological advancement transformed the character of war. For the first time in history, humanity developed weapons capable of destruction on a planetary scale, and of genocidal proportions. Nuclear, chemical and biological weapons – so-called weapons of mass destruction – are now capable of destroying the very biological existence of the planet. At the same time, the greatly increased lethality of conventional weapons, ranging from small arms and landmines through to the new generation of 'smart weapons' guided by global positioning satellites (GPS), have made the application of force more precise while endowing the individual combatant with the ability to kill with industrial speed and efficiency.

The development of computers, telephony, television, satellites, and a whole genus of information and communications technologies has also endowed states with god-like powers of sight and hearing, reducing the fog of war and making the application of violence seem more predictable and controllable. In the Northern countries, and particularly the USA, that led and benefited most from this technological transformation, and which remain paramount in their capacity to wage war on planetary scale, the fusion of destructiveness, lethality, global surveillance and planetary reach has spawned a so-called Revolution in Military Affairs (RMA). Information is now considered a key resource which is fed through networks of sensors and processed onto weapons platforms capable of striking remote targets with increasing accuracy and effect. The apparent military success of these systems in, for example, the US-led war against Iraq in 2003, and the commensurate reduction in the number of allied military casualties, has made war seem less risky and less personal.

And yet, despite these huge and significant transformations, the military's apparent omnipotence is also matched by an unprecedented vulnerability. The success of the asymmetrical attacks of 11 September 2001 in the USA painfully demonstrated the poverty of Western war-fighting assumptions, grounded as they were in lessons of the past. In this respect, while technology has undoubtedly had a huge impact on the transformations of the war-fighting doctrine, especially the USA, these transformations have been premised on a conception of war and conflict that in itself may be changing as technologically-driven globalization reshapes and reorders power and agency on a global scale. In the rest of this section, we shall explore some of the ways in which technology is acting to change the global fabric of conflict, and the implications this has on the nature of military agency, and the ways in which power may be exercised and expressed through emerging forms of warfare.

4.1 The changing face of conflict – the 'New Wars'

For much of the twentieth century, the experience of warfare has been seen through the lens of modernity, which casts the nation state as the basic unit of political and military organization. The two cataclysmic world wars and the subsequent Cold War did much to reinforce this orthodoxy, as war and conflict were viewed as a stand-off between collections of states. Cold War ideologies therefore reinforced the state-centric opinions of the global order. While state socialism and market capitalism represented different paths to modernity, they agreed on the necessity of the nation state as the vessel. As a consequence, warfare was understood as an activity requiring the organizational and material resources of the state and, perhaps not surprisingly, warfare was seen and planned for as an activity primarily between states.

Throughout the twentieth century, these assumptions drove much of the discourse and practice of war (and more importantly, the preparations for war). Military structures were built around state capabilities, and oriented towards defeating state-based enemies. The vast nuclear stockpiles held by individual members of the North Atlantic Treaty Organization (NATO) and the Warsaw Pact (the two key belligerent blocs during the Cold War era) made the possibility of outright war unlikely given the fear of Mutually Assured Destruction (MAD) (see Chapter 4). Paradoxically, this 'balance of terror' also meant that the Cold War remained, to a large degree, a confrontation of posturing and so-called proxy wars, and never culminated in direct military action between the two sides.

However, the Cold War stand-off also served to occlude the reality that war and conflict were not just defined by the ideological divisions between state socialism and market capitalism, nor constrained by the state. While the two competing blocs fought a series of proxy wars in the developing world (that is, where both sides armed, trained, financed and, in many cases, instigated sub-state actors to rebel against existing state authorities), there was a general expectation, particularly after the collapse of the socialist bloc in 1989–91 and the withdrawal of outside support, that these sub-state conflicts would quickly fade away.

In fact, the opposite occurred. Throughout the 1990s, although interstate conflicts declined sharply, one-third of all countries were embroiled in violent conflict of one kind or another. Moreover, as vividly demonstrated by the 1994 genocide in Rwanda and protracted ethnic cleansing in the Balkans, the human tragedy incurred by these 'civil conflicts' was as destructive for the societies involved as the 'total war' of the First and Second World Wars was for Europe. Far from becoming an anachronism, war and conflict soon became a leitmotif for the post-Cold War era.

The reasons for the persistence of these post-Cold War conflicts are complex. Most scholars of these 'New Wars' agree that their root causes lie in an area between an axis of perceived historical grievances and an axis representing a structural weakening of the state. This allowed rival groups to see the pursuit of self-interest by force of arms as a viable and, in some cases profitable, course of action. Nevertheless, while these theories explain the 'what' of civil conflicts, they do not adequately illuminate the 'why'. The prevalence of conflict and the seeming ease with which it has continued, despite concerted amelioration attempts by bilateral and multilateral means, speaks of the degree to which conflict has become inexorably entwined with the complex set of processes collectively understood as globalization.

We tend to identify globalization with the global spread of institutions, markets and networks emanating from the core of the advanced market economies of Europe, North America and Asia, yet this view assumes that globalization is, in itself, bounded by a set of common rules and assumptions. In the absence of an ideologically definable, alternative path to modernity, globalization has become identified as the global expansion of 'liberalism', that is, the common set of assumptions pertaining to society, economy and politics which loosely defined the Western bloc of countries during the Cold War era that you studied in Chapter 4.

Question

How might we challenge this identification of globalization with liberalism?

One difficulty with this stance is that it assumes that the technological infrastructures created as a consequence of globalization – the increasingly densely interconnected networks of finance, transport and communication – are themselves governed by the rules of liberalism. New Wars are in fact a strong counterpoint to these assumptions. Their ability to survive the end of support from the competing Cold War superpowers is testament to their ability to leverage global networks, tap financial flows and become part of the global shadow economy of arms, drugs and diaspora politics that are essential to sustain the cycle of greed and grievance on which these conflicts thrive. As some scholars point out, New Wars are wars among networks of actors, some local, others global, that transcend state borders and are dependent on the very same technological infrastructure and global institutional order as those actors more conventionally associated with globalization (such as banks, multinational corporations and civil society actors). Rather than reflecting a rejection of modernity, these New Wars demonstrate its remarkable possibilities and the degree to which local actors have adapted, appropriated and embraced the technological means presented by globalization.

In this context, the attacks of 11 September 2001 can be interpreted as an escalation of New Wars from local conflicts perpetrated by global means, to a global war dependent on the globalization and networking of local conflicts themselves. While it is possibly premature to speculate whether this kind of mass terror becomes commonplace rather than the exception, it does point to a fundamental reordering of power wherein technology has transformed the agency of globally dispersed networks of agents, and endowed them with the ability to act with mass effect. At the same time, perhaps more so than any other single event, the attacks of 11 September 2001, where civilian airliners were used to attack public buildings, live on television, and before global audiences, exposed the limits of the prince's powers of sight and strength, and undermined the assumptions embedded in the discourse of the RMA regarding the predictability, manageability and containment of conflict.

4.2 Technology and the new spaces of war

The RMA thesis – the dominant discourse of war in the information age – posits that technology has transformed war in such a way that it enables the application of force where and when it is needed in the precise quantities required to produce a desired effect. The ultimate aim and intent is to make the actual fighting of wars a more manageable and predictable activity. Throughout the 1990s, the decade-long technology boom in computing, communication and software brought about substantial transformation in the structure and capabilities of modern military actors, at least for the few advanced economies that have been willing and able to meet the staggering costs required to maintain global military reach. For these countries, above all the USA, the traditional problems of command and control – how to deploy and manoeuvre forces to destroy the enemy's will to fight – have been transformed by the ability to collect, analyse, process, and act upon vast amounts of information and data. The battle space is now visualized as a three-dimensional information environment where 'sensors' (surveillance and reconnaissance assets) and 'shooters' (soldiers, aircrew and sailors) act as part of a unified and complex networked entity. This reliance on networks for organization as well as the tools by which force is applied in an interactive and measured fashion is at the core of the military's new doctrines of war fighting. These principles emphasize the network-centric structure of military operations in addition to effects-based measures in the application of force.

The significance of these doctrinal and material changes for military power is difficult to exaggerate – where the military has been unleashed against a conventional state-based opponent, the effects have been stunning. In five major military campaigns since 1991 – the second Gulf War (1991), the NATO interventions in Bosnia (1995) and Kosovo (1999), and the US-led campaigns in Afghanistan (2001–02) and Iraq (2003) – the full-spectrum dominance exhibited by the US and NATO forces was overwhelming. Opposing forces were eliminated or rendered unable to fight within days or weeks, while actual combat casualties suffered by US and NATO forces remained low.

And yet, despite the capacity to overwhelm and dominate conventional state-based opponents through the application of force made possible by the RMA, these kinds of set-piece military engagements are an exception rather than the rule. As war itself has transformed from a state-based, state-focused activity employing identifiable tactics and military formations to that of a globally dispersed activity carried out and supported by networks of actors, the effectiveness of the military as a guarantor of security may have commensurately become less effective. At issue is the extent to which the confluence of technology and agency has shifted the balance of initiative to actors best able to employ these technologies to bring about a desired political effect. If we accept von Clausewitz's dictum that war is a continuation of politics by other means, then the effectiveness of war is determined by whether a preferred political end state is achieved through the application of force or not (von Clausewitz, 1976; first published 1832).

Question

What happens if force cannot bring about the desired end state?

The effectiveness of force as a political tool may then be questioned. There have been many instances demonstrating the power and effectiveness of the military instrument, for example, in bringing about the end of the occupation of Kuwait, the withdrawal of Serb forces from Bosnia and Kosovo, the elimination of Taliban rule in Afghanistan, and the collapse of the Ba'athist state in Iraq. Yet there are also graphic instances of where the same military actors were unable to bring about the desired political outcome despite the ability to dominate in any force-on-force military engagement. In Somalia (1993) and Chechnya (1994–96), the use of force by the USA and Russia, respectively, failed to achieve a settlement of the conflict, and in both cases the actions of local actors (themselves leveraging information and communications technologies as a strategic and tactical force multiplier) precipitated a withdrawal of US and Russian military forces. Similarly, in the occupied Palestinian Territories (West Bank and Gaza), and despite an overwhelming military advantage and near total surveillance of the Palestinian populations, the Israeli military is unable to wholly eliminate the threat or political effectiveness of Palestinian suicide bombers and other militant groups. More dramatically, in 1994 in Chiapas in Mexico, the networking of local and global activists led to the end of offensive counter-insurgency operations by the Mexican military by effectively shaming the government into opting for the negotiation table as a means to achieve a desirable political end state. At the time of writing (2003), the apparent success (or threat) posed by what the military euphemistically has termed 'asymmetric' actors has shifted the field of battle into the realm of the political, at once rendering less effective the technology-heavy investment into network-centric warfare.

In recent years, states have had to consider two emerging forms of warfare that threaten to limit their agency and scope for action. Social Netwar, a term which was first coined in relation to the successful social networking employed by the Zapatistas in Chiapas to put pressure on the Mexican government, refers to a kind of political and information warfare that mobilizes globally distributed networks of social actors around a specific political cause. Describing this form of social networking as 'war' may be somewhat misleading because it blurs the distinction between legitimate political opposition (resistance) and the political decision of a state actor to label it as an 'illegitimate' form of conflict. The distinction is rendered even more difficult as the techniques used, which may include appeals to individuals, other networks of actors, the media, information/dis-information, and attempts to build or destroy trust, are common to both state and non-state actors, and part of normal political life in most democratic societies. However, the fact that it has been classified as a form of warfare and in need of attention from state security and military entities is an affirmation of the perceived power of this form of agency, as well as the degree to which it is seen as a threat by state actors.

Another new form of warfare that directly exploits the dependence on, and existence of, the global information infrastructure is limited to the virtual 'space and place' that this infrastructure has created. Interchangeably known as 'netwar', or 'cyberwar', this form of warfare is wholly contained in the networks themselves, and treats the channels and nodes, and the information they carry as the field of battle. While computer hacking has been around since personal computing became an accessible and affordable pastime for individuals, netwar implies a deliberate use of software code for the purpose of disrupting, destroying or tainting the information content of computer-based networks and the systems that depend on them. Like social netwar, sub-state actors in numerous conflicts throughout the late 1990s have used computer-based netwar, although its effectiveness has been largely at the level of drawing attention to the causes themselves rather than doing serious damage to critical computer infrastructures.

For example, during the early months of the second Palestinian intifadah (September to December 2000), pro-Palestinian hackers (although not Palestinian themselves) launched globally co-ordinated attacks against Israel's largest Internet Service Provider (ISP). The effect was to temporarily disable several key government web sites including those belonging to the Knesset, Ministry of Defence and Office of the Prime Minister. Some sources claim that the disruption to Israel's infrastructure caused an 8 per cent dip in the value of the Israeli stock market, but the evidence to substantiate these claims is absent. What is clear is that in response the Israeli Defence Forces did deliberately target Palestinian ISPs and Internet cafés in their subsequent reoccupation of West Bank towns and villages. Computers were destroyed and hard drives removed in an attempt to limit Palestinian ability to use and access the Internet, and as a means to gather intelligence on the activities of Palestinians (this despite the fact that, as noted above, most of the pro-Palestine hackers were neither Palestinian nor resident in the occupied territories).

Similar kinds of engagements have been documented between actors supporting differing pro-state and anti-state interests, or even in support of specific causes. In this respect, hackers have waged online conflicts consisting of defacement of web sites, denial of service attacks and spamming around such conflicts and issues as Kashmir (pro-Indian versus pro-Islam/Pakistan hackers), Taiwan (pro-independence versus anti-independence hackers), and Nagorno-Karabakh (Armenian versus Azeri hackers). Although in most cases these virtual conflicts have been fought across the global expanse of the Internet, and some hackers have come perilously close to being able to affect actual physical infrastructure, the spectre and threat of an 'Electronic Pearl Harbor' remains, for the moment, a possible rather than probable scenario.

There is also evidence suggesting that state actors are investing heavily in developing offensive netwar capabilities. In the USA, 'computer network attack' is classified as a form of warfare under the doctrine of information operations, and indeed, in the prelude to the March 2003 war against Iraq, the USA became the first state to openly use netwar techniques as part of its war fighting strategy. In this instance, e-mail spam was used as part of psychological operations targeting key Ba'athist leaders in an attempt to destroy their morale and willingness to oppose US and UK forces. By its nature, however, netwar will have influence and impact on those actors most heavily dependent on computers and communication infrastructures.

The danger of 'blowback' – that these weapons will be used intentionally or unintentionally against those state actors that employ them – holds the potential for catastrophic consequences for the ICT intensive and dependent societies of the USA, Europe and parts of Asia. The danger of netwar at an interstate level is therefore similar to, albeit less permanently destructive than, the use of nuclear or biological weapons. It is for this reason that protection of critical infrastructure is a key component of the USA's overall Homeland Defence strategy. Conversely, the potential of netwar also appears to be the motivation for states such as China, the Russian Federation, India and Pakistan to invest heavily in developing these weapons, as this form of warfare is the cheapest and perhaps most effective means by which to redress the advantage currently enjoyed by the network-centric US and NATO military machines. Nevertheless, as states are by far the most dependent entities, and hence most vulnerable, in the event of the collapse or failure of information infrastructures, the advent of netwar as both a technique and form of political resistance has created a means for expressing subordinate forms of agency.

4.3   Shaping the international system – shifting security landscapes

The attacks of 11 September 2001 serve as an important milestone signalling the end of a paradigm of security shaped by the experience of the Cold War where the threat was seen as emanating from state actors, and the peace was kept by the balance of terror between blocs of nuclear-armed states. The ability and willingness of a small and loosely allied network of actors to wreak co-ordinated death and destruction in the major cities of the world's leading superpower clearly revealed that the very same technology which had given rise to an interdependent global society was also the means by which its destruction could be wrought. Although the attackers of 11 September 2001 were relatively crude, using the mass and speed of hijacked aircraft as a weapon, arguably more sophisticated actors could employ weapons of greater lethality to much greater effect. Indeed, just such an attempt was planned by the Aum Shinrikyo cult and would have resulted in significantly higher casualties than those in New York and Washington had it not been for the prompt and decisive action of the Japanese government. However, it is still an article of faith rather than fact that non-state actors have either the capacity or the willingness to use weapons of mass destruction.

Undoubtedly, technology has changed the parameters and scope of the military domain, in some respects endowing military actors with new all-encompassing powers. While the future will bring further transformations, the trajectories and agencies it will enable remain open to question. For now, it seems the gaze of military agents has shifted firmly to new asymmetric actors, and previously unthinkable powers of surveillance and detention have been granted by governments to root out and eliminate the perceived threat posed by 'illegitimate' resistance and opposition. Nonetheless, the problem may be that the perceived threat is smaller and more ephemeral than portrayed thus far, its effect amplified by the distorted mirror and false intimacy of television and the global media. The potent mix of technology, agency and possibility of mass effect may now be in the realm of the possible, but the loss of liberties, mass violation of civil rights and freedoms is in the realm of the probable and real. The consequences of this eventuality should give us all something on which to ponder.

5   Conclusion

By looking at groups broadly categorized as merchants, citizens and princes, we hope to have illustrated the present relationship between technology, networks, and aspects of inequality, and their potential impact on influencing the changing nature of the international system as it shifts to and fro from order to disorder. In each case, we have noted that there are tensions between state and non-state (or network) actors, between the facilitation of inclusion and exclusion, and between tendencies towards order and disorder. We do not intend to offer an overall judgement about either the combined effect of merchants, citizens and princes on the international system or the balance of power and agency in each of the three tensions we have identified. We return to some of these issues in our review of the challenges to international order in Chapter 15. We hope that you now have a deeper understanding of some of the ways in which social and technological networks might reshape the international system and influence the future of international order and disorder.

Activity 13.1

To consolidate your understanding of this chapter try to complete Table 13.1. We have filled in some of the table to give you an idea of what we have in mind.

Table 13.1

	Relationship of non-state actors to states	Tendencies to inclusion and exclusion	Sources of order and disorder
Merchants			Mobilize flows of investment and finance in the international economy leading to economic integration, while precipitating severe economic crises in many emerging markets
Citizens			
Princes	Central element of the state, but military forces are increasingly networked among non-state, even anti-state, bodies		

Further reading

A good explanation of the idea of New Wars, which is especially helpful in understanding modern conflict, is provided in Duffield, M. (2001) *Global Governance and the New Wars*, London, Zed Books. For a discussion of the global context of New Wars and a challenge to existing conceptualizations of war, see Kaldor, M. (1999) *New Wars and Old Wars: Organised Violence in a Global Era*, Stanford, Calif., Stanford University Press.

A book that brings together activists, journalists and academics to examine what they see as the 'new politics' of social movements and resistance is Jordan, T. and Lent, T. (1999) *Storming the Millennium: The New Politics of Change*, London, Lawrence & Wishart.

An interesting work describing the role of networks and how they interact with places, such as cities, is Sassen, S. (ed.) (2002) *Global Networks, Linked Cities*, London, Routledge. The book not only discusses global cities such as Tokyo, London and New York but also examines other global cities that are usually ignored.

A good insight into global financial transactions and their impact is Strange, S. (1998) *Mad Money*, Manchester, Manchester University Press. Strange critically examines the way in which it has become increasingly difficult for nation states to control investment and currency transactions within and outside their borders.

Part 4 Models of international order

We began this book, in Chapter 1, by sketching out some general parameters as to how we were going to set about the task of analysing international order. We set ourselves three main overarching questions:

1   Is it possible to analyse the international system as a whole?

2   How can we best characterize, understand and explain the processes of international interaction and the kinds of order and disorder with which they are associated?

3   Is the contemporary international system changing and, if so, by whose agency?

We argued that understanding international systems involved being able to identify both the general features common to any international system – what we termed the 'general abstraction' of geopolitics – and the historically specific forms of geopolitics in any particular international system. In addition, it involves identifying the different ways in which the political aspects of inter-societal relations relate to the economic and technological dimensions and the socio-cultural dimensions.

Parts 1 to 3 of this book have explored these three sectors of the modern international system – the political world of the states-system; the socio-cultural sector; and the economic and technological sector – and have offered a variety of ways of characterizing international interactions and of understanding the extent and nature of contemporary changes.

In Part 4 we return to the three overarching questions to see what kinds of answers can be provided for the modern international system as a whole. In particular, we want to address some important general models of international order and examine claims about its contemporary transformation. Much of this will be familiar to you by now, although perhaps in somewhat different terms, because many of the substantive arguments discussed in the preceding chapters contain, implicitly or explicitly, models of international order as a whole. In this part of the book, however, we want to make these models explicit and discuss their relative merits.

First, in Chapter 14, William Brown takes four key approaches to theorizing international order – realism, liberalism, constructivism and Marxism – and sets out their main claims. These are all models that bring to the foreground the political aspects of the modern international system and define it (as we do) as a states-system. However, they all (with the possible exception of realism) argue that the political sector is not autonomous from the socio-cultural and the economic and technological sectors. Thus in *explaining* international order, they all have something to say about how the other sectors of the international relate to the political sector. The chapter introduces some ways in which the different models may be evaluated, offers some comparative comments about what each means by 'the state' and examines the different historical narratives about the evolution of international order that each puts forward.

In Chapter 15, Simon Bromley and Mark J. Smith address the issue of the transformation of international order in a number of different ways. On the one hand, they assess the ways in which the mainstream models discussed in Chapter 14 put forward particular theories of transformation. They argue that liberalism and Marxism in particular seek to identify and explain the agencies and processes of change. They also argue, however, that as theories of transformation both are instances of the ways in which social and political theory can serve critical purposes in relation to social reality. The chapter therefore also discusses what is meant by the term 'critical theory' as well as examining some other approaches to International Studies that claim a critical function, in particular post-colonial and feminist traditions. Finally, the authors discuss two of the most prominent claims that the contemporary world is undergoing a fundamental transformation, namely Huntington's thesis of a clash of civilizations and the notion of the rise of a global network society.

This part of the book serves as the conclusion to the book as a whole, returning to the general problematic of International Studies with which we began.

Chapter 14 Characterizing international order

William Brown

1   Introduction

In this chapter I am going to return to the first two of the big questions introduced in Chapter 1. That is, 'Is it possible to analyse the international system as a whole and, if so, how?' and 'How can we best characterize, understand and explain the processes of international interaction and the kinds of order and disorder with which they are associated?' In many ways you have been studying different ways to answer these questions in the preceding chapters. However, most of these chapters have sought to answer aspects of these questions in relation to particular substantive issues and themes pertaining to particular sectors of the international system – with regard to the states-system, rights and culture, or technology and inequality. The task of this chapter is to see how we might make some more general claims about international order in its entirety. How could we start to sketch out some general images of what we mean by the international system, what it is comprised of and how it operates? Fortunately, we do not have to start from scratch. The focus here is on some established ways in which writers in International Studies have constructed models of international order. That is, we shall examine some general attempts to specify the make-up of the international system as a whole, the key actors or units which comprise it, the structure of the relations between them, and the dominant processes and means of interaction. You have already been reading accounts and debates about international order that draw upon these established approaches. Therefore, much of what follows is not completely new, although it is presented in a slightly new way.

In this introduction, I first want to consider some of the reasons why specifying general models may be of use to you in analysing international order. I then want to discuss what the different 'component parts' of international order might be. In Sections 2 to 5, I shall take you through four contrasting approaches to understanding and analysing international order as a whole. In Section 6 I shall present two ways in which you might contemplate the contrasts between these approaches and develop your critical assessment of them.

1.1   Models of international order

Question

Why might models of international order be useful?

One might reasonably ask why we need to consider such grand intellectual enterprises as models of international order. Can we not simply focus on empirical reality 'out there' and build our understanding through better knowledge of more and more of this reality? A useful starting point to answer this is offered by Fred Halliday in his book *Rethinking International Relations*, where he states that 'facts are not, in [the academic discipline of International Relations] or anywhere else, enough ... there needs to be some preconception of which facts are significant and which are not. The facts are myriad and do not speak for themselves' (Halliday, 1994, p.25). Halliday goes on to argue that even if one can agree on which facts are important, several different interpretations can be imposed upon them. You saw this in the way that, for example, the different facts which make up an account of the construction of the international order among liberal states after the Second World War (discussed in Chapter 4) led to different explanations about what was really going on in that process. Similarly, there were the arguments about technological change and economic inequality in Part 3 and the debates about what they signify in terms of international order.

Models of international order enable us to look at things in a more generalized way. As with the use of models in the social sciences more generally, they allow us to paint in broader brush strokes or, rather, to produce a sketch or caricature that highlights a particular aspect of the subject matter at hand. By isolating some dimension or dimensions of what is being studied, and through abstraction and simplification, models reveal insights into that subject matter (see Bromley *et al.*, 2004, pp.501–3). Models are based on certain limiting assumptions that put some facts on one side and prioritize others. Then, through a logical argument about the relationships between the elements identified in the model, conclusions about specific aspects of the problem may be drawn. Models are, therefore, useful tools of analysis which help us to see certain aspects of a problem, and identify and explore certain key relationships. Such endeavours can help us to recognize the broad outlines of the phenomena we are studying.

Formulating general models allows us to begin to address our two framing questions: 'Is it possible to analyse the international system as a whole and, if so, how?' and 'How can we best characterize, understand and explain the processes of international interaction and the kinds of order and disorder with which they are associated?' Yet this begs the obvious question of why one would want to answer general questions of this sort. One response is that general questions direct our attention to real features of the world around us.

Categories like anarchy, capitalism, international culture or international inequality may be abstractions, but they are abstractions drawn from, and describing, real characteristics of the international system. Models are a way of focusing on one or more of these real features, and exploring their importance, dynamics and effects. Thus, one answer, a realist answer, to our two questions is that international order is an anarchy in which the units are states, as I shall show in Section 2. This approach prioritizes real features and looks at what this implies for, say, the prospects for international co-operation (another feature of international order).

A further way to address the issue of the usefulness of models is to note that this is one of the ways in which the actors and agencies involved in ordering the international in the 'real' world think about what they are doing. This is true whether we are talking about an anti-globalization protester who was angry at the effects of economic integration, or leaders of independence movements in the British colonies after the Second World War, or President Bush seeking to define the challenges facing the USA, or Lenin reasoning on the international impact of revolution in Russia, or President Woodrow Wilson seeking to reconstruct the states-system in response to that revolution. All of these actors, in different ways, will have formulated general ideas about the international as the basis for action. Consequently, theorizing at this general level often plays an important part in peoples' actions, whether they are history-changing interventions or much smaller, less noticed ones.

Of course, such grand ideas are not always couched in the form of theoretical models, and may be more or less clearly thought out, more or less clearly articulated. Nonetheless, within nearly any claim about the international there is some explicit or implicit notion about the key features of international order and how they fit together, followed by an idea of the implications for action.

This brings me to another benefit of seeking to identify and make explicit the core elements of some of the key models of international order. This is that it aids our understanding of international order by helping us to be precise about what is being argued. Elaborating a model involves clarifying some of the limiting assumptions on which it is based – which features are brought to the fore in the model and what 'messy details' are left out? Elaboration also explains exactly what is being argued about the relationships between the included features, and what conclusions are being drawn from them. This, in turn, allows us to use models not only as tools of analysis but also, at least sometimes, to generate hypotheses about our subject matter on which to base further research and enquiry. By identifying the importance of some components of international order and not others, by making claims about the relationships between these components, and by drawing conclusions from the model about international order, we can ask different kinds of questions and enquire about various aspects of international order. Moreover, we can ask whether what we have said at a general level does, broadly, fit the facts. In this way, empirical and historical enquiry can be brought together with general theoretical claims in our study of international order.

Question

What implications does this have for evaluating different approaches to international order?

I think that being able to clarify aspects of different models of international order makes the task of evaluating different traditions of thought in the field of International Studies easier. In this chapter, I would like you to think about three broad issues when assessing the use of different approaches: the empirical adequacy of the model; the coherence of the model; and how different models compare with each other in their presentation of a picture of international order. First, by empirical adequacy I mean how well the assertions on which the model is based fit the facts: are the limiting assumptions reasonable ones to make in terms of what they bring to the foreground and what they leave out? Are the claims about how different component parts of international order fit together (or don't fit together) a reasonable reflection of what is known? And are the conclusions that a model draws borne out? Second, is the model coherent in itself? Do the different parts of it fit together in a coherent way? Does one thing follow logically from another? And is the model consistent in terms of the things it claims about how actors behave and the relationships between them? Third, I shall highlight a comparative dimension for assessing different models of international order. In part this is one way to get to grips with what each model claims – a device to see where models differ. Nevertheless, comparison is also important for stressing some fundamental differences in both the assumptions and conclusions of the different approaches. I shall undertake this last task in Section 6 in particular, where I try to show how the models differ in what they mean by 'the state' and in what they emphasize in terms of the historical evolution of international order.

Finally, a word of caution. I have argued that understanding different models of international order can be useful. However, models are abstractions drawn from the messy reality of the international system, formulated in order to see some broad structures, patterns and processes. They are not reality itself. The messy reality might be very important and may prompt us to question the usefulness of models, or it might be interesting in and of itself. It is crucial to keep the tools of analysis in perspective, and not to try to cram reality into an ill-fitting mould.

1.2 Identifying the elements and sectors of international order

Before I go on to outline the four main approaches with which this chapter is concerned, take a moment to think about how you might construct a model of international order. In Chapter 1, Section 2.2, we introduced a framework for analysing international systems loosely based on Buzan and Little's work (2000). This framework is reproduced in Table 14.1. As you will recall, this framework specifies the 'elements' of an international system as the principal units, the structure of relations among those units, and the dominant means and processes of interaction. And it identifies the 'sectors' of the international system as the political, the socio-cultural, and the economic and technological. The chapters in Parts 1 to 3 of this book have had something to say about all the different elements of the international system and have discussed them through the different lenses provided by each of the three different sectors. Part of what I want to do in this chapter is to draw out models of international order as a whole in a somewhat more systematic way.

Table 14.1   A framework for analysing (changes in) the international system

Elements of the international system	Sectors of the international system		
	Political sector of authoritative rule	Socio-cultural sector of collective identities and conceptions of rights and justice	Economic and technological sector of production, trade and innovation
Principal units in the international system			
Structure of relations among units			
Interaction capacity			
Dominant processes of interaction			

Activity 14.1

As a start to thinking about models of international order, spend a few minutes jotting down some ideas about how you might fill in Table 14.1, drawing on Parts 1 to 3 of this book.

There has obviously been a great deal of ground covered, and my answer to Activity 14.1 is only a rough idea. Indeed, one could go on exhaustively listing different possible candidates for different parts of this framework. However, one of the purposes of formulating models of international order is to reduce the messy reality of the international system, to focus in on particular features of it and to make some claims about those features. There are several paths we could go down here. However, I shall limit the discussion in this chapter in the following way.

As we noted in Chapter 1 the political sector is the 'irreducible core' of International Studies as it is relations between politically organized societies that define the problematic of the international (see Chapter 1, Section 2). In this chapter I shall focus on those models which put the political sector – and specifically states and relations between states – at the centre of their attempts to analyse international order. That is not to say that approaches that do not prioritize the political sector in this way are ignored, or that other sectors of the international are left out, far from it. The ideas of an international order made up of cultures (whether 'clashing' or not) and of an international order made up of networks are two of the leading theses arguing that international order is undergoing some kind of transformation. In fact, they are often couched in terms of claims of a transition from a world of states to a world of cultures or networks. Discussion of these conceptions of international order will be left until Chapter 15, where Simon Bromley and Mark Smith assess the question of whether, and in what ways, the international order is undergoing some kind of fundamental transformation. In addition, all the models I shall discuss here have something to say about the other sectors of the international and how they relate to the political sector so these aspects will not be left out of what follows (and indeed will be discussed in Chapter 15 as well).

The approaches upon which I shall focus are four of the main theoretical traditions that have emerged in the academic field of International Studies: realism, liberalism, constructivism and Marxism. Try not to be too put off by this proliferation of 'isms'! Most of the key assertions that these theoretical traditions make have been raised in one way or another in Parts 1 to 3 of this book, although sometimes not explicitly. The purpose of this chapter is to stand back and make these general models explicit; to see how we can abstract from the more detailed debates and arguments which you have been reading and the particular issues that have been addressed in Parts 1 to 3, in order to determine what kinds of broader answers, compared to those already discussed, can be offered.

However, I ask you to note one further point. There exist, in the International Studies literature, clearly elaborated, representative models for three of our four approaches. Realism, liberalism and constructivism have all produced more or less explicit models of international order in the manner in which I shall discuss them. Marxism is the odd one out. The Marxist tradition has generally eschewed abstract modelling of international order of this type, and my discussion of Marxism will reflect this situation. In addition, for three of the approaches I shall concentrate my discussion upon a single author who can reasonably claim to have formulated a representative model for their tradition. Thus, instead of presenting a lengthy survey of the literature in each school of thought, I shall concentrate on specific 'exemplary' formulations: for realism, Kenneth Waltz; for liberalism, Andrew Moravcsik; and for constructivism, Alexander Wendt.

2   Realism

For a long time realism has occupied something of a special place in the academic field of International Studies. It is, to a large extent, the orthodoxy, indeed the 'common sense', in the field. Realist thinking has a long history, stretching back at least to Thomas Hobbes. In the contemporary era, realism came to dominate International Studies in the post-Second World War period. Particularly in the USA in the context of the Cold War confrontation with the Soviet Union, realist thinkers developed a tradition of analysis about the international system that sought to avoid what they characterized as utopian views about what the international system might be like and instead based analysis on a hard-headed assessment of what it was like. Leading figures in realism such as Hans Morganthau and Henry Kissinger were closely linked to US foreign policy debates and Kissinger served as Secretary of State from 1973 to 1977.

Part of realism's enduring strength lies in its apparent reflection of the common-sense way in which much international politics is discussed in everyday life and by the politicians, diplomats and activists in international politics (Halliday, 1994). However, as we noted in Chapter 1, by focusing almost exclusively on the political sector, realism also secures its centrality in International Studies by addressing its core – the ungoverned relations between politically organized societies.

Question

You have already come across various elements of realist analysis and realist claims in this book. Think back and note down some of the realist claims made in earlier chapters.

There are three places in particular where realism has been discussed explicitly. Chapter 2 began with a brief outline of the central tenets of realism: that international politics is an anarchical system in which the units are sovereign states and in which change is registered as shifts in the balance of power between states, determined by the distribution of capabilities.

These assumptions also form the basis for the discussion of hegemonic stability theory and the analysis of the Cold War as a bipolar conflict in Chapter 4 (Section 4.1). Finally, in Chapter 9, Jef Huysmans pointed out that realists argued that 'international law will only be observed and endorsed if it does not work against the political and economic interests of major powers' (Section 4). This claim points towards another aspect of realism: a sharp distinction between the domestic arena 'inside' states in which hierarchy and law operate, and the international arena in which anarchy and power determine outcomes.

These viewpoints cover some of the central ground of realism. Yet can we put them together in a more coherent way to illustrate what a realist model of international order consists of? In what follows, I shall focus on the work of Kenneth Waltz who can reasonably claim to have put forward one of the most coherent and influential re-statements of the realist case, commonly referred to as 'neo-realism', although Waltz himself calls it 'structural realism' (Waltz, 1979). Even for those who disagree with this approach, Waltz's neo-realism is a touchstone in debates about the character of international order and much writing in International Studies is in fact an ongoing debate with neo-realist claims, criticizing or analysing different aspects of the model. Note, for example, how Part 1 of this book started with a Marxist approach that defined its purpose as providing an alternative understanding of the origins of the European state system compared to that used by realists.

One of the express features of Waltz's formulation of a theory of international politics is that it explicitly sets out to build a model of the international system which mimics the kind of model building undertaken in economics. In particular, Waltz wanted to develop a 'parsimonious' theory: one which proceeded from a limited number of assumptions to a few important conclusions about the international system. Another detail to note is that Waltz's model is structural, that is, he argues that the structure of the international system (its units and the relations between them) determines international outcomes. This distinguishes Waltz's realism from the 'classical' realism of writers such as Morganthau who put greater emphasis on human nature, the lust for power, and the skills and attributes of state leaders in determining international outcomes (see Morganthau, 1978).

So what is Waltz's model? It can be stated quite succinctly. First, Waltz begins with a founding assumption that there is a rigid distinction to be drawn between domestic and international politics. Domestic politics is a world of hierarchy and authority presided over by the sovereign state; the international political system is one of interactions between sovereign states. The units of international order are, thus, states. Nevertheless, as sovereignty implies ultimate authority *within* a territory, it follows that there is no superior or higher authority *outside* states. There is, therefore, no international sovereign able to govern relations between these sovereign units. As a result, relations between states are anarchic.

The second major building block of Waltz's model is to argue that all states have to look out for their own security and survival. Indeed, survival is the basic requirement for states as it is the basis upon which all other things depend. Domestically, the survival and security of individuals is achieved by the authority of the state, but internationally there is no such authority to secure the survival of individual states. States must consequently rely on self-help to secure their own survival. The primary means of doing this is to depend on their own power, or to ally with other states, in order to counter the threat from potential adversaries.

Given these two assumptions, Waltz concludes that states, ultimately, will all be 'functionally equivalent'. This means that the basic structure of the system is such that states are compelled first and foremost to seek similar things: their own survival based on their own capabilities. Although internally states may vary in terms of their political make-up, culture, ideology and so forth, in the anarchic realm of the international they are compelled by threat of extinction to act in similar ways and pursue similar aims.

A number of other conclusions flow from this model, according to Waltz. First, in terms of international order, assuming the world remains one of independent states (rather than a world empire), change consists of shifts in the distribution of capabilities among the units. Different structures can be defined in terms of whether the world is bipolar, multipolar or unipolar (you will recall that Simon Bromley used these terms in Chapter 5 to analyse the position of the USA in the post-Cold War world). This also reveals why Westphalia is such a seminal moment for realist theorists. For them, Westphalia signified the emergence of a system of independent polities from the break-up of the Holy Roman Empire and the decline of the feudal era (see Chapter 2). From that point on, international order became one in which the units were independent states, and the dynamics of the system revolved around power balancing.

Waltz's second conclusion follows from this. If the structure of international order depends on the distribution of power, then the most powerful states have a particularly important role in the overall shape of the international system. This privileges the 'great powers' in any analysis of international order: their actions, alliances and power balancing are the key to the changing structure of the system as a whole. As Waltz put it, 'Concern with international politics as a system requires concentration on the states that make the most difference. A general theory of international politics is necessarily based on the great powers' (Waltz, 1979, p.73).

The third conclusion is that the constant search for security means that, for realists, the prospects for co-operation are inherently limited in international politics. You have seen already (in Chapter 4) that realists argue that the extensive co-operation among Western states was ultimately dependent on it serving the interests of the USA (hegemonic stability theory), or that it was simply a reflection of alliance-forming among Western states in order to balance the power of the Soviet Union. Yet more generally, co-operation is limited by the constant potential of a threat from other states and the fact that states ultimately have to rely on their own power capabilities to ensure survival. This means that alliances may be jettisoned if it is in the interests of a state to do so, and agreements can be reneged upon. Extending from this, international institutions such as international law and the adherence of states to codes of rights will always be dependent on how far they serve the interests of the powerful.

Finally, other sectors of international order are inherently secondary to the state system. Non-state actors of the kind discussed in Part 3 are not significant from a theoretical point of view and realists would reject the idea that sovereignty-free actors (see Chapter 12) have a determinant role in the structure of the system. Non-state actors such as multinational corporations and pressure groups may have some influence if they affect the capabilities of states (for example, as agents of economic growth that increase a state's capabilities). A similar line of reasoning is deployed towards the 'economic' issues discussed in Chapters 10 and 11. Realists take it as given that states will differ in their power resources, and leadership in technological development and wealth based on economic growth are among the factors that determine states' capabilities and, therefore, their power. The hegemonic stability theories discussed in Chapter 4 and the leading role of the USA discussed there and in Chapter 5 are both based on arguments about the distribution of economic gains and resources. However, for realists, given the priority of security, economic policy aims must ultimately be subordinate to the political–military aims of security.

Activity 14.2

In order to check your understanding of the realist model, outline in your own words the realist reasoning about why international law is effective only if it is in the interests of the powerful states (for extra help, see Chapter 9, Section 4).

The power and enduring influence of realism, especially Waltz's formulation, owes much to the apparent clarity of the model and the ways in which it can be deployed as a tool for developing analyses of international order. One of the benefits of a good model is that it allows us to paint with broad-brush strokes and to highlight some salient aspects of our subject matter. Realism does this by focusing almost exclusively on the political sector. Within that sector states are identified as the key units, relations between states are anarchic and structured by patterns of polarity, and the key process of interaction is the (changing) balance of power across the system as a whole.

Question

Think back to the discussions of the post-Second World War era in Chapters 4 and 5 of Part 1. What aspects of international order might the use of the realist model help to clarify?

The position of the USA and its relations with other major powers in the international system was central to the subject matter of those chapters. Realist assumptions would direct you towards trying to explain the behaviour of the most powerful states in terms of their search for security. The salient facts, which should be in the forefront of such an account, are the relative powers of the leading states. As discussed in Chapter 4, this leads realists to analyse the Cold War era as, above all, one in which international order was organized around a bipolar distribution of power. Similarly, analysis of the post-Cold War era would prompt you to prioritize power distributions when assessing the change that the decline of the Cold War brought. Some of the implications of these changes were discussed by Simon Bromley in Chapter 5 when he referred to the US role in a multipolar economic world and a unipolar military world. Thus, an argument based on realist claims allows you to make some fairly broad and sweeping statements about international order, its important features and the key changes. In so far as it does this well, the model is useful. Nevertheless, you can see that realism alerts you to a particular dimension of international order and not to others.

Question

How can you critically assess the usefulness of the realist model of world order?

As I argued in Section 1, we can begin to assess different theoretical models by questioning their empirical adequacy and coherence (I shall come to some comparative comments on realism in the sections that follow). From the more substantive and historical accounts discussed in earlier chapters, are too many important aspects moved to the background? Do the conclusions of the model (for example, about the structure of relations among the units being defined by a distribution of power) help us to make broad but reasonably accurate claims about international order? In addition, does the argument that justifies such a focus, stand up? Are the assumptions acceptable and is the argument that flows from those assumptions, sound?

There are a host of avenues to explore here, but perhaps one of the most appropriate is to think about the conditions necessary for realism to be a useful model. Andrew Moravcsik (1997) has argued that although under certain conditions realist assumptions may hold true and so give us an accurate sketch of international order, too often these conditions do not hold. This criticism raises issues about realism's empirical adequacy and its coherence. The inferences are that as a general model of international order, realism is at best inherently limited, at worst positively misleading. What does Moravcsik mean by saying that under certain conditions realist assumptions hold true?

Two aspects of the realist model are crucial for the conclusions that Waltz draws from it: first, the pre-eminence of security and, second, the reliance on self-help in states' behaviour. These twin concepts do much work in his argument and are crucial to its coherence. As you have seen, the belief is that states must secure their own survival, and that this is a priority over everything else because a state cannot pursue other aims if it has ceased to exist. Moreover, Waltz thinks that states ultimately assume the worst about each other and so must rely on self-help – by building up their own power to repel or deter an attack – to achieve security. Dependence on another state risks everything on the interests of that other state: promises can be broken, alliances shift and strategies change. Together, these two claims determine the focus on power relations as the chief factor structuring international order. But are they justifiable?

In fact, it is far from clear that these conditions dominate the actions of states to the extent that reliance on a realist model of international order would require. States may pursue a variety of goals and it is an assertion by realists that security goals always trump others. You might like to think about whether that is always the case. In the preceding chapters you have also seen that states pursue goals to do with wealth, ideology, religious belief, and cultural and national integrity. Besides, it is not always clear that states regard each other as actual or potential future enemies in the way that realism assumes. Some theorists such as constructivist writers like Alexander Wendt (1999) argue that states, in principle, can see each other as 'enemies', 'rivals' or 'friends'. The way that states view each other and themselves will be dependent on the history of interaction. In this situation, again, realist claims may hold true but only if states come to view each other as enemies; if they do not, then the coherence of the model starts to unravel.

An additional issue that arises (and to which I shall return in the next section) is that the realist assumptions portray interstate relations as though states are always locked in zero-sum conflicts with each other. Realists believe that given that every state could become an enemy and given that any increase in capabilities (for instance, economic growth) could ultimately be turned into military power, the scope for co-operation between states is highly limited. Even if states could gain mutually from co-operation, they will not do so because each will view the other as a potential adversary and will always be concerned that the other does not gain more than itself. That is another way of saying that, for the realist model, consideration of relative gains will always be more important to states than potential absolute gains (see Chapter 4 for a definition of relative and absolute gains).

A realist counter to these comments might acknowledge that of course other things go on and that state to state relations consist of more than security dilemmas. However, realists would say that these concerns will always trump others – it is the bedrock on which everything else is founded. If we were to cede this point, it still means that much goes on in ordering the international system about which realism can either only say fairly crude things (that everything else is ultimately determined by security issues) or is silent upon. The more far-reaching critiques are those that do not even allow this point – they consider that even on realism's home ground of security, the model fails to stand up. The approaches discussed in Sections 3 to 5 show how some alternative pictures of international order might be created.

3   Liberalism

In many ways, and despite realism's dominance of the discipline, liberalism has as long a tradition in studying the states-system as any, dating perhaps to Immanuel Kant's considerations on the conditions necessary for a perpetual peace. The liberal approach to international relations has been reviewed in some depth in this book already (see Chapter 4, especially Section 2.1). As noted there, liberalism covers plenty of philosophical, political and ideological ground. In terms of models of international order, there are a wide variety of approaches which claim to be liberal. As in Chapter 4, however, I am going to focus on the approach defined by Andrew Moravcsik (1997), a contemporary liberal scholar and author of a leading restatement of liberalism as a paradigm of International Studies.

It is perhaps worth noting here, as Moravcsik argues, that his definition of a liberal model varies considerably from that of other liberal writers. This is so in terms of the distance that he puts between the assumptions on which he bases his approach and realism. Moravcsik maintains, and this seems accurate, that some other approaches often referred to as 'liberal' – most notably what is known as '(neo)liberal institutionalism' developed by academics such as Robert Keohane – in fact share most of realism's core premises (for example, see Keohane, 1984). Indeed, Keohane's work accepts assumptions about states as the key units of the system and the anarchic nature of the international system. Where he departs from neo-realism is in the ability of states to pursue absolute gains. For Keohane, shared information about other states' intentions and the building of institutions that can clarify the gains of co-operation, mean that one of realism's strong conclusions – that of the limits of co-operation – is overly pessimistic. Not for nothing does Keohane term this approach 'modified structural realism', something Waltz has also acknowledged (Waltz, 2000, pp.24–5).

The disagreements between so-called neo-liberalism/liberal institutionalists and neo-realism occupy a vast amount of space in the International Studies journals, but in many ways amount to a very narrow debate. Moravcsik intends to set out a much broader agenda – and debate – by positioning a liberal approach further from realism's founding beliefs. Despite the importance of the institutionalist approach in the field, I am going to focus on Moravcsik's re-statement of liberalism. It is both a coherent and valid re-statement of a liberal position, and it opens up a much wider, and more interesting, contrast with realism, raising far-reaching questions for understanding international order.

Question

Look back at Chapter 4. What are the key assumptions of Andrew Moravcsik's liberal model of international politics?

The liberal approach to international order received extensive treatment in Chapter 4 and so I shall only recap the key elements here. Moravcsik builds his liberal theory on three founding assumptions:

1   The principal units are individuals and private groups of individuals who use states to further their interests.

2   State preferences represent some sub-set of the interests of these actors.

3   State behaviour in the international system and the structure of relations between states are determined by the configuration of state preferences across the system.

(If you need to refresh your memory of these assumptions, look again at Chapter 4, Section 2.1.)

As was remarked upon in Chapter 4, these claims provide a starkly contrasting idea of international order from the realist approach. First, unlike realism which takes states as the given actors of international order (determined by their possession of sovereignty), the liberal approach qualifies this with a focus on variations in state–society relations. Realism sees a world of sovereign states whose interactions with each other are dictated solely by the nature of international anarchy, but Moravcsik (1997) sees a world of individual and group interests organized within, and represented through, the institutions and agency of the state. Viewed at the level of international order, for liberals states remain key units, but their role, relations and actions are shaped, at least in part, from the bottom up. Second, in contrast to realism's assertion that states are functionally equivalent in being forced by the structure of relations between states always to seek security through self-help, for liberals states are 'functionally differentiated'. What they seek to do (their preferences) is determined by the nature of the social interests which they represent, and how those social interests are represented in the state. Third, whereas for realists the nature of the anarchic international order is characterized by the distribution of power between states, for liberals it is determined by the interdependent patterns of state preferences.

This last distinction leads to some very different conclusions about the character of international order and the nature of change within it. For Moravcsik, the important point about analysing international order is that it depends on the mix of different things that different states are pursuing, what he terms the 'configuration of state preferences'. State behaviour will be determined by the international context in which states try to realize their preferences and this is shaped by the preferences of other states: 'each state seeks to realize *its* distinctive preferences under varying conditions imposed by the preferences of *other states*' (Moravcsik, 1997, p.520). Another way of putting this is that states' policy preferences, and therefore the relations that exist between states, are interdependent; pursuit of a policy by one state may impose costs on other states (if they conflict with other states' preferences) or benefits (if they coincide with others' aims).

Moravcsik argues that in principle there are three broad categories of interdependence in terms of state preferences. First, where state preferences are coincident or the differences are insignificant to others; second, where state preferences are zero-sum or deadlocked, that is, where an attempt to realize preferences will impose costs on other states; or third, where there is a mixture of the two and bargaining can result in states exchanging policy concessions in return for realizing other aims. The importance of specifying these categories is that it then allows characterizations of international order to be made. These can identify the extent of conflict or co-operation and the substance of those conflictual and co-operative relations, in other words, what they are about.

Activity 14.3

Think of examples where relations between states are based on:

1 Conflicting preferences.

2 Coinciding preferences.

3 A mixture of 1 and 2.

As stated in Section 2, one criticism of realism is that its applications are limited to those circumstances in which its assumptions are present. Moravcsik makes a strong claim that his liberal model can, in theory, accommodate a wide range of different circumstances in which a highly variable set of relationships might be present. Realist conditions may be present (and therefore the realist model becomes useful), but it is necessary first to identify what states are hoping to achieve before you can say whether these conditions are present or not. Moravcsik asserts that this makes the liberal approach 'analytically prior' to realism. In terms of evaluating different models, we can attempt to improve the empirical adequacy of our model of international order by being more specific about what are the different kinds of relationships, defined in terms of patterns of interdependence, that exist between states. Moravcsik argues that identifying differing state preferences is the way to do this.

The implications for our own study of international order are important. From the liberal perspective, the first question we should ask in studying the international is not the realist question 'What is the balance of power?' but 'What are states seeking to achieve?' For liberals, as Moravcsik puts it, 'what states want is the primary determinant of what they do' (1997, p.529). Once we have identified the variations in state purposes and the patterns of interdependence they create, only then is it possible to paint a picture of international order that consists of varying degrees of co-operation and conflict, and to specify the subject matter of those interactions. This, Moravcsik alleges, lays the basis or sets the context within which realist assertions about self-help, security and zero-sum relations may or may not be important.

Question

How would a realist respond to this liberal model?

One of the key issues in dispute between realists and liberals concerns the role of social interests in international order. For liberals, social interests are the bedrock on which everything else is built. Yet realists would attack this founding assumption of liberalism. Waltz, in particular, argues strongly that if a theory of what happens between states is based on what happens within states, it is reductionist, that is, it reduces the international to the domestic. Indeed, he goes on to say that it would not really be an 'international' theory at all. As you have seen already, for realists the distinctiveness of the international sphere is one of the central elements in their understanding of world order.

Moravcsik's reply to this is twofold. First, he argues that in defining state–society relations as the basis determining what states do, he is not confining this to domestic society. That is, the liberal approach to understanding the underlying state–society relations encompasses both a state's representation of domestic social actors and the transnational social context in which they exist. For example, a state may form a preference, say for freer trade, in response to demands from specific economic interests such as owners of manufacturing firms. Nevertheless, these economic interests may themselves favour freer trade because of their particular location in international markets – they may benefit from a cheaper supply of component parts or gain greater access to overseas markets for their exports. US firms aiming to expand investment, production and sales into the European market have (as Chapter 4 pointed out) been cited as a reason for the USA acting as it did in reconstructing Western Europe after the Second World War. Such economic interests like large multinational corporations may indeed be transnational actors in themselves, operating in several different states. Consequently, the social interests underlying state preferences are never simply 'domestic' (Moravcsik, 1997, pp.522–4).

Second, Moravcsik claims that the liberal model is not reductionist because state behaviour will vary depending on the international constraints under which it pursues its preferences. As previously noted, international order is shaped by the interdependence of state preferences across the system as a whole. What states actually do internationally, the strategies they pursue to realize their preferences, is always done in the shadow of what other states in the system are seeking to do.

The second charge which is often levelled against liberal theories of international order is that they are theories of co-operation and cannot explain conflict in the international system. The focus of much liberal research on the potential for institution building, the role of international organizations, the possibilities of economic co-operation, and theories such as the democratic peace thesis (see Chapter 4) may give some credence to this. In Moravcsik's formulation, though, a focus on the configuration of state preferences allows for both conflictual and co-operative scenarios. While a realist might claim that this means that in a conflict situation it is realist assumptions that come to the fore, the liberal counter that the consideration of state preferences allows us to see whether these realist assumptions are relevant or not remains a powerful one.

Activity 14.4

Compare the liberal model as described here to Waltz's neo-realism using the following questions.

1   Which aspects of international order does liberalism bring to the fore that realism puts in the background?

2   What does the liberal model leave in the background that realism highlights?

3   Are there any ways in which the two accounts might be brought together in a single analysis?

4   Modifying anarchy: the English School and constructivism

If one were to draw a contrast between realist and liberal models of international order, two issues stand out. First, whereas the liberal approach sees co-operative relations that go beyond anarchy between states as a possibility (even an established fact) rooted in shared preferences, realism perceives conflicting relations based on a competitive search for security. Second, liberals see a world in which 'what states do' is at least partly determined by individuals and social groups, while the realist model is founded on a world where what states do is determined by the structure of the states-system. Existing somewhere between these two schools of thought is an approach which, like realism, largely bases its model of international order on relations between rather than within states but, like liberalism, allows for the possibility that these interstate relations may take a variety of different forms. There are in fact two related approaches in International Studies which fall broadly within this position: the English School and constructivism. In particular, both offer models of international order which purport to show that although the states-system is anarchic, it is capable of producing relations between states that go beyond the zero-sum interaction of Waltz. They do this by analysing the international system of states as, in one sense, a *social* system. In some ways, the English School represents a weak version of constructivism, and it is closer to realism. For this reason, I shall now briefly deal with the English School before providing a more extended discussion of constructivism in Section 4.2.

4.1   The English School

You have already studied the main principles of the English School in Chapter 3. Thus, here I shall give a short review before noting some of the distinctive aspects of the English School's approach to international order. In large measure, the English School accepts some of the key realist starting points. The English School interprets international order as an anarchic state system. The school also shares the realist concern for power and the balance of power in determining the character of international order and, as a result, the specific role of great powers in shaping international order.

However, here the English School departs from realism in both its classical and 'Waltzian' versions for, despite anarchy, the English School claims that the states-system is, in some senses, a social system. What is meant by that? As Chapter 3, Section 2 elaborated, the term 'society' when applied by the English School to the states-system, means that despite being an anarchy, states share some common norms and institutions and these shape both the structure of relations between them, and the dominant processes of interaction. This is a significant departure from realism in two ways. First, it means that contrary to realism there are certain norms, other than an individualistic concern to ensure their own survival, which have some purchase on the actions of states. For the English School, the shared values of international society are not mere window dressing but have an effect on the actions of states. The institutions of international society identified by the English School are: sovereignty and mutual recognition; the balance of power; international law; war; and the rights and duties of the great powers (Chapter 3 also argued that colonialism should be included in this list). This is a considerable challenge to the realist claim that states will ultimately first pursue survival based on self-help.

Second, some writers in the English School also assert that these norms and institutions do not just 'regulate' pre-existing units (states), but that they serve in part to 'constitute' those units. This is what Simon Bromley referred to in his discussion of regulative and constitutive rules (see Chapter 3, Section 2). For the English School, the norms and institutions of international society help to constitute the members of that society.

Question

Why does the assertion about the shared norms of international society 'constituting' the agents of that society mark such a contrast with Waltz's realism?

Perhaps the easiest way to answer this is to take one example of the constitutive rules identified by the English School: the mutual recognition of sovereignty. For realists, state sovereignty is primarily a domestic accomplishment. For writers like Waltz, domestic sovereignty is achieved in a manner suggested by Hobbes – individuals authorize a sovereign to rule over them in return for the security that such rule can bring. The system of states plays no part in this model; it is founded on a relationship between the sovereign and the individual. Nonetheless, as realists argue, the corollary of the establishment of domestic hierarchy is that there are multiple sovereigns in the world and none to rule over them. Therefore, the international system is anarchic and states have to look to themselves to secure their own survival.

In contrast, the English School presents the argument that establishing sovereignty involves both an external and internal dimension; it is implicit in sovereignty that the state asserts its authority both over domestic actors and in relation to outside actors, particularly other states. For realists, the recognition of any one state's sovereignty by other states is just a matter of power; sovereignty is respected in so far as a state is capable of maintaining itself against other states that threaten it. Yet for the English School, recognition of sovereignty is, or becomes, a norm shared by all states. States collectively recognize each other's right to rule their own populations within their territory. Indeed, for some states, especially some of the weaker states in the international system, the acknowledgement by other states of their right to rule is an essential part of the foundation of their sovereignty and the maintenance of themselves as independent states.

Thus, the English School introduces the notion that the actors in the international system do not simply exist prior to their interaction but are, at least in part, formed and sustained by their participation in international society. This idea is pursued in constructivist writing and used rather more strongly and systematically, and it is to that which I now turn.

4.2 Constructivism

The constructivist strand in International Studies takes the English School idea of the international system as a social system and of that society constituting the members of it further, and develops a more systematic attempt to show how this works.

Alexander Wendt is possibly the most influential contemporary constructivist, and his book *Social Theory of International Politics* (1999) was written explicitly as a constructivist response to Waltz's *Theory of International Politics* (1979). Constructivists begin from the premise that the international system is a social system. Unlike the English School they expand this idea by drawing on and developing an 'internationalized' version of sociological theory. Where sociological theories are concerned with human socialization, identity and the relationship between the individual and society, constructivists look at the relationship between states as if they were individuals in a society of states. Wendt uses this approach to try to analyse how, given the existence of anarchy between states, different kinds of international society can emerge.

Wendt's constructivist approach makes three key modifications to neo-realism (1999, pp.20–2). First, whereas for realism the structure of the international system is material, that is, determined by the distribution of material capabilities as the basis of power, for constructivists the structure is social. By social, Wendt means that states take each other into account in their actions. Yet in doing so they must form ideas about themselves and about other states. The system, for Wendt, is thus idealist rather than materialist. Second, states' identities (that is, how states define their own 'self' in relation to other states) and their interests (their preferences) are constructed through their interaction with other states to a much greater extent than is allowed for by realist approaches. While much of a state's identity and interests are formed domestically (as liberals argue, see Section 3), its interactions with other states also shape how it sees itself and others in the international 'social' system.

Here, I should note that Wendt is, by his own account and others', a 'weak constructivist'. For some 'strong' constructivists, the international system is all about ideas – objective material factors play no role in shaping international order independently of the socially-constructed ideas that states hold. For Wendt, 'rump material factors', by which he means things like military power, technological development and geography, do play some role in shaping international outcomes. According to Wendt, international order is ideas part, rather than all, the way down (1999, pp.110–11).

Third, Wendt believes that processes of interaction between states can vary to a considerable extent depending on how states view themselves and others. The structure of relations between states and the dominant processes of interaction that can arise in an anarchic international system, what Wendt calls the 'logics of anarchy', are not fixed but are constructed by the character of that interaction. As mentioned in Section 2, Wendt claims that at least three different 'subject identities' can emerge: states may see themselves and others as 'enemies', 'rivals', or 'friends'. These identities can, in turn, fashion three different 'logics' or 'cultures' of anarchy for the system as a whole – enmity, rivalry or friendship. At root Wendt asserts, contrary to realists, that even if one specifies the international order as made up of sovereign states in an anarchic environment, the pessimistic conclusions of realism do not necessarily hold. 'Anarchy,' Wendt says, 'is what states make of it' (1992, p.395).

That is a very brief identification of Wendt's argument so let me elaborate the key stages in his model and the contrasts the model presents to other approaches. One of the central assertions that Wendt makes, and the issue that marks out the constructivist position most clearly from realism, is that an anarchic states-system does not necessarily mean that states have to rely purely on self-help in order to survive. Realist logic is based on assuming the worst – other states must be treated as enemies and balanced against because they *may be* enemies. To do otherwise is to leave oneself open to attack – survival depends on playing safe. Given that all others act like this, self-help becomes a self-fulfilling prophecy. For constructivists like Wendt, states do not balance against other states *per se*, they balance against *threats*. And whether another state poses a threat depends on the ideas that each holds of the other. This may result in a realist end point if each perceives the other as an enemy, but it may not. It depends on how a state sees itself and others, and this is only formed through an experience of interaction: 'history matters' (Wendt, 1999, p.109). As Wendt summarizes, 'if we want to say a small number of big and important things about world politics we would do better to focus on states' ideas and the interests they constitute, and only then worry about who has how many guns' (Wendt, 1999, p.256).

Activity 14.5

In Chapter 6, Section 2.3, Robert Garson quoted Wendt: 'Five hundred British nuclear weapons are less threatening to the US than five North Korean ones' (Wendt, 1999, p.255). To check your understanding of the constructivist argument so far, explain why this is so.

Wendt then argues that because the logic of the system depends on ideas, the system can be seen as 'cultural' as well as social. It is social because it is an arena of interaction in which agents take each other into account. It is cultural in that it is an arena formed by shared knowledge. Note that here the term culture is being used in the sense discussed in Chapter 6: as an arena of shared beliefs and ideas. If these ideas are ones in which the agents see each other as enemies, this still forms an arena of shared knowledge. Wendt contrasts the modern states-system, where such basics of interaction as diplomacy, war, state and sovereignty have some shared, even if contested, meaning based on a long history of interaction, to the kind of 'first encounter' experienced for example by the Spanish Conquistadores and the Aztecs in the sixteenth century. Here, there were no such shared understandings (Wendt, 1999, pp.158–9). In the states-system, the history of interaction provides the basis on which extensive shared ideas can develop.

At this point, Wendt distinguishes his approach from that of the English School, specifically Bull's notion of international society (see Chapter 3). The English School emphasizes the shared norms of international society as an essentially co-operative endeavour towards common ends, but Wendt claims that the culture of the international system can be shared knowledge around either co-operative or conflictual relationships. To illustrate this, Wendt outlines the three cultures of anarchy already mentioned that can exist in the international system based on enmity, rivalry or friendship. (Wendt's terms for these are Hobbesian, Lockean and Kantian, but I shall stick to the more straightforward terms because they capture the essence of what Wendt is discussing.)

A 'culture of enmity' comes closest to the traditional realist picture: states view each other as adversaries whose relations with each other can be summed up as 'kill or be killed'. War, in this culture, is an ever-present possibility and states that fail to secure their own survival will be eliminated while power balancing governs the actions of the strong. The shared ideas are about what each state expects of the others' behaviour, and how to deal with other states through war, issuing threats, power balancing and so on.

A 'culture of rivalry', by contrast, reflects an acceptance of the continued existence of other states. In this culture, states view each other as rivals rather than enemies and, although there may be violence between them, warfare is no longer aimed at the elimination of enemies but is a more limited means of settling disputes, for instance, over territory. The key shared idea in this culture is the mutual recognition of sovereignty leading to a much lower 'death rate' among states and a more stable membership of the system. Such a culture may come about through brute material facts; each state has to accept the others' continued existence because it does not have the power to do otherwise but also because, in some circumstances, states come to accept the legitimacy of sovereignty. Correspondingly, this can have constitutive effects on the members of the system. It may allow states that are too weak to survive otherwise to continue to do so. Alternatively, it may lead members of the system to uphold the survival of some types of states and not others, and thus help to constitute the character of the 'internal' nature of the states in the system. A culture of rivalry may result in states forming 'collective identities' as members of a particular group of states (for example, 'Europe', 'the West', 'the developing world' and so on).

Finally, a 'culture of friendship' is one in which states not only accept each others' continued existence but also seek to settle disputes non-violently and come to each others' mutual aid if threatened from outside. The shared knowledge of each others' peaceful intentions and the idea that war is not a legitimate means of settling disputes leads to a qualitative change from a culture of rivalry. Military capability is no longer seen as a threat although other power resources (for example economic ones) may have greater salience in settling disputes. While a weak version of a culture of friendship might occur because of the rising costs of warfare as a means of settling disputes, in stronger versions states develop collective identities so that an attack on one from outside is literally seen as an attack on all.

Activity 14.6

Before reading on, think back to Parts 1 to 3 and note down some examples of a culture of enmity, a culture of rivalry and a culture of friendship.

Wendt's view, like the liberal approach, allows the constructivist model to be used to identify different kinds of international order among states and, consequently, to assess the historical evolution of international order. However, Wendt is not proposing any necessary tendency for movement from one culture of anarchy to another. Indeed, he argues that different cultures, once they become established, can exhibit tendencies militating against change. The very fact that shared ideas can help to constitute the members of the system means that cultures can become self-reinforcing. For instance, if states view each other as enemies and act accordingly, they will become and continue to act as enemies; if states view each other as friends and act accordingly, they can strengthen the tendency for others to act similarly.

Nevertheless, Wendt maintains that change can happen. It is possible that the high death rate among states characterizing a culture of enmity (as each tries to wipe out the other) may create incentives for states to move to a culture of rivalry. In seeking to secure their own survival, states may come to see a shared interest in the principles of sovereignty and mutual recognition – in this case, a collective norm can serve individual interests. Furthermore, characteristics of the relationships between states may increase the prospects for an evolution from one culture of anarchy to another. To illustrate, Wendt argues that a higher capacity for interaction between states creates both the possibility of, and incentives for, shared interests and identities. The development of issues of common fate, where survival and welfare depend on the group as a whole such as with some global environmental threats, may also create common identities.

Yet Wendt also argues that change within states may have causal effects on change in the international arena. In part, he has in mind the type of argument put forward by Kant's republicanism and echoed in the democratic peace thesis. If states become more similar to each other in certain, crucial ways, this will change their identities and how they see each other, changing the culture of anarchy as a result. It is these kinds of factors which lead Wendt to note that, while the focus of his analysis is on relations between states, the more the causes of historical change are located in change within states, the closer his model moves to the liberal approach reviewed in Section 3. Prior to examining the different ways that the different approaches understand historical change in Section 6, it is necessary to look at Marxism, the last of the four models of international order.

5 Marxism

Before I outline some of the key elements of the Marxist approach to international order, I need to note a number of features that distinguish Marxism from the other schools of thought already discussed. This is both a reflection of the peculiarities of Marxism as a body of social theory and, partly, of the slightly tangential relationship it has had with International Studies as it has developed as an academic discipline in the West.

First, as I mentioned in Section 1, unlike other traditions in International Studies, Marxism has mainly abstained from building abstract models and my presentation of the Marxist approach will reflect this. For Marxists, creating abstract models can often obscure more than it can reveal. In his writings, Marx was concerned to show the 'essential relations' that lay behind the 'phenomenal forms' in which social reality appears to us (Marx, 1970; first published 1867). What does he mean by that? Marx asserts that phenomena which appear to us as 'things' – commodities, states, property, markets, law and so forth – in fact embody real social relations between people. Moreover, these real social relations are historical – they form part of an ongoing process of social change and development. To create abstract models treating such phenomena as if they were solid and permanent is both to abstract from the social relationships which they embody and to blind us to the historicity of those forms. In short, this would treat social phenomena as if they were natural and unchanging things rather than the product of changing patterns of relationships between people. The sort of modelling found in economics and followed by Waltz's realism (and to a lesser extent liberalism) should, at best, be treated with a degree of caution. This may not necessitate rejecting modelling outright, but it does mean keeping in our accounts the historical specificity of what is being analysed and the character of the social relations which are present, instead of taking them for granted.

Second, the Marxist tradition has not produced a single account of international order that I can use in the way that I have for realism, liberalism and constructivism. Marxism is rooted in the writings of Karl Marx and Friedrich Engels, but developed as an analysis of the international from the 'classical Marxism' of Kautsky, Lenin and Luxemburg at the turn of the twentieth century through critiques of the position of developing countries in the post-Second World War era, to analyses of international political economy in the 1970s and after, with a particular focus on the role and position of the USA as the world's leading capitalist power. You will recall that some of this Marxist legacy – the theories of imperialism – was covered in Chapter 5 by Simon Bromley, and I shall return to those issues in this section. My account will, therefore, draw on a range of common themes shared by Marxist writers, rather than on a single author.

Third, in terms of International Studies, the object of study for Marxism has never been simply the international states-system, but rather the origins, spread and development of a specific social system, namely, capitalism. Capitalism is analysed as a single world process of development in which the specific problematic of International Studies (including the approaches previously outlined) – of relations between politically organized societies – is not the sole, or sometimes even central concern, for Marxism. According to Marxists, states and the states-system are constitutive parts of whole social orders and cannot be studied in isolation from them. As a body of theory and analysis, Marxism defines its concerns more broadly than some approaches in International Studies and certainly more broadly than the parsimony of neo-realism. Consequently, it is more difficult to extract the purely political sector of international order from the other sectors, notably socio-economic.

However, it would be a mistake to conclude that this list of distinctions means that Marxism does not deserve its place among the core approaches of International Studies. From the point of view of International Studies, Marxism puts at centre stage something which has arguably done more to shape the world in which we live than anything else: capitalist modernity. Remember that for approaches such as realism, the category of capitalism plays no role in the analysis of international order. For Marxists, capitalism always has to be problematized and historicized; we need to appreciate the distinctiveness of capitalism and its history and development if we are to understand international order. While liberal and constructivist accounts may devote much time to analysing aspects of capitalism (for example, the nature of the regulation of the world economy), these aspects need not be a central issue. Indeed, while both the liberal and constructivist models of the states-system contain historical accounts, the history being told is predominantly of relations between states. Marxists consider that any such account has to place this history in the broader context of the historical specificity of capitalism; it is the particular features of capitalism that are important for the kind of international order which can be created. Thus, Marxism offers a different and challenging perspective on international order. In addition, however, within the Marxist focus on the worldwide development of capitalism, distinctive and important things have been said about matters which are core to the problematic of International Studies. Marxist theorizing about the state, imperialism and US hegemony are possibly the three which stand out.

Question

What are the core building blocks of a Marxist account of capitalist international order?

As with the other models discussed in this chapter, you have already come across a substantial part of the Marxist approach to International Studies in the preceding chapters. Here, I shall pick out the main elements of a Marxist understanding of international order from those earlier discussions.

The starting point for Marxism is perhaps the nature of the societies, defined by their social property relations, making up the international system. This basic idea was most extensively dealt with in Chapter 2 and it would be useful to recap some elements of that account. Benno Teschke pointed out that Marxist accounts define different kinds of social property relations in terms of class relationships. Class is defined according to the ownership, part ownership or non-ownership of the means of production (which includes the material things used to produce and the labour power necessary for production) that different groups of people exercise (see Chapter 2, Section 2.1).

The Marxist argument is that different social property relations create different kinds of international system. The contrast presented in Chapter 2 was between feudal, absolutist and capitalist societies and the different geopolitics that they produced in Europe. Because of this, there cannot be a single, universally applicable 'model of international order'. Rather, a Marxist approach has to first identify the historical specificity of the social formations which constitute international order at any one time. The dominant form of social property relations of the modern international system is, of course, capitalist. And capitalism has forged an international order consisting of *both* a states-system and an international economy. To see why this is the case, we need to look at the particular way in which the realm of the political and that of the economic are constituted in capitalism.

While, as Benno Teschke argued, territorial states preceded the rise of capitalism in Europe, nevertheless, capitalism transformed those pre-existing states and the nature of relations between them. Accumulation in capitalism takes place in the economic realm – in the relationship between the bourgeois and the worker, based on the former's ownership of the means of production and the latter's sale of labour power. However, the market in which both operate is governed by the state which upholds contracts and rights, particularly property rights, through the law. Therefore, in a capitalist-dominated international order in which economies are relatively open (by allowing economic flows in the form of trade or investment to cross borders), the fixed territoriality of the state is in contrast to the fluidity of the world market. Economic exchanges are not tied to the territorial boundaries of the state but can and do cross state boundaries. Furthermore, what states seek to achieve internationally (state preferences) is no longer geared to accumulation by political and military means (the alliances, marriages, land acquisitions and so on of the absolutist era). Instead, the dominant concerns become the regulation of the domestic capitalist economy and, in conjunction with other states, of the international economy. The public, political arena of state-to-state relations exists alongside (and makes possible) the private sector of international economic exchanges in the world market. The two sectors – a states-system and international economy – are thus the twin constitutive elements of an international social whole.

For Marxism, an attempt to identify the units and sectors of international order would include not just states in an anarchic states-system (however one would define the dynamics of that), but also the classes, firms and other actors involved in economic accumulation. A characterization of international order from this approach would consequently have to specify the character of interstate relationships, especially in terms of the international governance of the world market, and the transnational dimension of class alliances and patterns of economic accumulation.

This task introduces a central theme of the Marxist approach: the uneven and combined nature of the development of capitalist international order. It would be easy to take the Marxist approach and draw from it an idealized image of international order consisting of homogeneous capitalist states and a unified world market of unrestricted flows of trade and investment. In fact, in a famous passage in *The Communist Manifesto*, Marx and Engels celebrated its creation:

> The need for a constantly expanding market for its products chases the bourgeoisie over the whole surface of the globe. It must nestle everywhere, settle everywhere. ... The bourgeoisie, by the rapid improvement of all instruments of production, by the immensely facilitated means of communication, draws all, even the most barbarian, nations into civilization. The cheap prices of its commodities are the heavy artillery with which it batters down all Chinese walls. ... It compels all nations, on pain of extinction, to adopt the bourgeois mode of production; it compels them to introduce what it calls civilization into their midst, i.e. to become bourgeois themselves. In one word, it creates a world in its own image.

(Marx and Engels, 2002; first published 1848)

Notwithstanding the quintessentially nineteenth-century way of referring to non-civilized, non-European societies (see Chapter 3), it would be hard to find a better statement of what is now referred to as 'globalization'. Nonetheless, the actual development of capitalism on a world scale has proceeded in a far more contradictory way than this implies. While Marx and Engels were surely right to draw attention to the transformatory impact of capitalism as it expanded outwards from its European origins to affect almost every society on the planet, it has not in any simple way fashioned 'a world in its own image'. Granted, the capitalist world has created, through colonialism and the convulsions of two World Wars, a world dominated by nation states (see Chapter 3). Yet the nature of the social formations of which these states form a part has not conformed in any simple way to the capitalist modernity established in Europe.

Instead, the uneven development of capitalism has proceeded in a combined way (in that the outward expansion of capitalism has connected all parts of the world with political and, especially, with economic threads). For most states, the development of capitalist modernity occurred in the context of an already existing world market and a world dominated by the leading capitalist states. Not only did these non-capitalist societies begin from very different starting points, leading to diverse historical trajectories, but the pressures created by attempting to catch up with the leading states meant that none would simply follow the path of the developed. Trotsky, who delineated this concept of uneven and combined development, pointed out that 'England in her day revealed the future of France, considerably less of Germany, but not in the least of Russia and not of India' (quoted in Rosenberg, 1996, p.8).

'Catching up' (see Chapter 10) has characteristically entailed a heavy role for the state. In terms of the domestic nature of the society, this has often led to combinations of elements of modern statehood and capitalist social relations on the one hand, with non-capitalist social relations and particular local cultural traditions on the other. In addition, most states have not managed to catch up. As Chapter 11 showed, global inequality, and specifically between-country inequality, has remained persistently high. Moreover, as Chapter 10 argued, few states have graduated to join the rich 'convergence club'. Authoritarian political forms, whether military dictatorships in the developing world, fascism, or the imperial despotism of Russia before the revolution, arose as a means of keeping the lid on these explosive mixes of modern capitalist and non-capitalist social relations. In many instances, this resulted in forms of society that differed considerably from the liberal capitalist states. While some of these were capitalist, they were hardly in the image of liberal capitalism. Indeed, some such as Germany and Japan developed into the highly politicized form of capitalism, fascism. Still others such as the Soviet Union challenged capitalism in seeking a non-capitalist path to modernity. The point, for the Marxist approach, is that 'the state' as an abstract idea reveals little when divorced from this socio-economic and historical context.

Activity 14.7

Consider the argument that Sami Zubaida put forward in Chapter 8 regarding the shaping of Islam in the states of the Middle East. Are there any parallels to the Marxist idea of uneven and combined development?

Accordingly, the Marxist account of international order has to combine specifying the nature of the societies (defined by their social property relations) which are interacting within that order with a historical account of the patterns of order and disorder created by uneven and combined development. Thus, Marxists view international order as a complex whole that involves:

> the actual interrelation of all these different societies by virtue of which they make up a larger dynamic whole, the contradictory but irreversible unity of human social development created by the spread of the world market – and

all the tensions and conflicts arising from this geo-politically combined but sociologically uneven development of the international system. *Within this totality, the states system is a crucial, but by no means a free-standing element.*

(Rosenberg, 1996, p.9; emphasis added)

This last point alerts us to a final aspect of the Marxist approach and that is the tendencies towards both co-operation and conflict that uneven and combined development creates at the level of international order. Co-operation can emerge between states, particularly the leading capitalist states in their efforts to manage the states-system and the international economy. Open conflict can arise between competing imperialist powers, between rival forms of society (as occurred in the conflict between liberal capitalism, fascism and communism in the Second World War or between capitalism and communism in the Cold War), and between more and less liberal capitalist states (for example, over the terms on which each is integrated into the world economy). In fact, Marxist accounts focusing on the political sector of relations between states have particularly focused on the nature of relations among the leading capitalist powers, and on relations between those leading states and the developing countries.

Chapter 5 noted three contending arguments about relations between the leading capitalist states. Lenin's theory argued that relations between the leading capitalist states were conflict-ridden and prone to war. Competition between capitalist firms, for Lenin, would turn into conflict between capitalist states. Against this, Kautsky claimed that the costs of warfare were so great that capitalist states had shared interests in jointly managing the international system as a whole in 'ultra-imperialism'. The theories of 'super-imperialism' argued that US dominance or hegemony regulated competition between capitalist states, primarily in response to the threat from the socialist block. Other writings from a Marxist standpoint have analysed the US-dominated world order as a combination of both state and class relations: the dominance of the US state as representative of the leading capitalist economy, combined with the interconnections created in the economic realm by the networks of trade and production which the international expansion of US capitalism has forged (for example, see the discussion of neo-Gramscian arguments in Chapter 4, Section 5).

To summarize this survey of the Marxist approach to international order, I would like to conclude with a comparative comment. Just as some of the Marxist debates on imperialism paralleled debates on US hegemony in other traditions (see Chapter 5, Activity 5.1), parallels can be drawn between the Marxist focus on state–society relationships and that of Moravcsik's liberalism. Moravcsik argues that state–society relationships determine what states seek to do internationally. Their actual behaviour will be determined by the preferences of other states. International order is thus shaped by the patterns of interdependence when the preferences of different states are combined globally. As Moravcsik has himself noted (1997, p.522, footnote 23), Marxism can develop a similar kind of argument. For Marxism, the nature and development of social property relations will determine the kind of geopolitics that different states will engage in. The place of different states within an unevenly developed international order will influence the types of international relationships different states have. When combined globally, these too can create different patterns of co-operation and conflict both between developed capitalist states, between capitalist and non-capitalist states, and between more and less developed states. Marxists consider that one of the main issues confronting the leading capitalist states like the USA is how to manage the ensuing international tensions (see Chapter 5).

However, there are crucial differences between Marxism and liberalism, and I shall now look at two dimensions of comparison between all of the four models.

6   Comparing approaches to international order

In Sections 2 to 5, I have outlined four of the mainstream approaches to answering our framing questions: 'Is it possible to analyse the international system as a whole and, if so, how?' and 'How can we best characterize, understand and explain the processes of international interaction and the kinds of order and disorder with which they are associated?' In this section, I shall not argue the case for following one approach above another, not least because different approaches may be more useful for some lines of enquiry than for others. This is not surprising given that in trying to characterize something as broad as international order, different models bring to the fore different aspects of international order and push others to the background. Nevertheless, I do want to ask you to begin to think about some of the differences between the approaches covered. To do this, I want briefly to raise two possible lines of comparison. First, what is meant by 'the state' and, second, how is history viewed?

Question

What do the different schools of thought mean by 'the state'?

In Section 1, I limited the scope of this chapter by concentrating only on theories of international order that placed the political sector as a central component part of their understandings of international order and within this prioritized the state as the key unit. The approaches which followed have all constructed their models of international order with states and relations between states as a primary aspect to be explained. For this reason, such mainstream models as these are sometimes criticized for being state-centric. However, the different approaches actually mean different things when they talk about a world of states. To this extent, 'The question is not whether we are or are not state-centric but what we mean by the state' (Halliday, 1994, p.77).

In fact, all four of the theoretical traditions see the state in very different ways. The simplest notion of the state is provided by realism. Waltz claims that a model of 'the international' has to remain at the level of relations between states and not relations that exist within them. In terms of his model, and the uses to which it can be put, it implies treating the state as a unitary actor (as if it were a single, rational individual), and actually rolls into one the various things to which the term 'state' is often taken to refer: a country, territory, population or political institution. Accordingly, realism is often referred to as a 'billiard-ball model' of international order: you do not have to look inside the balls, but merely observe their location and movements on the table to understand international order. This is one example of my earlier point of how realism echoes the everyday common sense language of international relations. In daily news reports, politicians' speeches and the slogans of protesters we hear that Germany believes this, or the USA is trying to do that. Yet we also know that politics goes on within states as well as between them. A key issue in assessing realism is whether trying to strip out all this messy detail leaves the model empirically inadequate. Does the most state-centric of approaches fail ultimately because it has no theory of the state?

In some ways, constructivism, at least in Wendt's formulation, is closer to realism than Marxism and liberalism. This may seem surprising given the fluidity that the constructivist approach brings to understandings of international order. But remember that Wendt, and the English School, both pitch their analysis primarily at the level of relations between states. The bulk of Wendt's model is an analysis based on interpreting states as if they were individuals and on how different patterns of relations between them, based on their identities and interests, can be constructed. This theory allows Wendt to pose his model as a direct counter to Waltz, and to show that even if some key aspects of realism are accepted (international order is anarchic and made up of states which can be treated as individuals), a variety of different orders can still emerge out of anarchy. Although it should be noted that when Wendt comes to discuss the establishment of the three different cultures of anarchy and the change between them, he begins to move away from the idea of the state as a single, unitary actor. Wendt argues that the variables which may lead to a movement from a culture of enmity to one of rivalry or friendship include domestic factors such as the internal political make-up of states and the type of economic system which they operate. These are the sort of things that are left out of realist approaches and are central to both liberalism and Marxism. Wendt acknowledges that, 'Explaining these considerations would take my theory in a liberal direction; in important ways my theory of international politics is a Liberal theory' (Wendt, 1999, p.365).

Liberalism and Marxism have a similar 'shape' as theoretical approaches – they place relations between the state and wider society at the centre of explanations of the state preferences, which in turn shape international order. For both, the term 'state' is not the all-encompassing notion used by realists, but a specific element of the societies which make up international order. However, liberalism and Marxism give very different accounts of this element and its relationship to wider society. Liberals view the state as primarily an institution of government for society. Historically, as Chapter 4 related, liberalism has been concerned with the respective powers and rights of the state and the individual citizen. Nonetheless, as Moravcsik's model acknowledges, the kinds of relationship between state and citizen, what he terms the form and institutions of representation, are highly variable. This has two important corollaries for Moravcsik. On the one hand, the form and institutions of representation are one of the determinants of state preferences (along with the character of the social interests that are represented). On the other hand, this means that state preferences will vary. For liberalism, states are functionally differentiated in part because there are different forms of state. The most obvious specific illustration of this from within the liberal tradition is the democratic peace thesis (that democratic states do not go to war with each other – see Chapter 4). Similar claims might be made about the propensity of different states to seek trade liberalization or human rights conventions and so on. The overall shape of international order here is, in a significant way, determined by the character of the state. Such an analysis is impossible if one were to operate with the realist 'billiard ball state'.

While Marxism shares some of these general points, it departs in how it accounts for differentiation among states in two key ways. First, there is a broad point that societies with different social property relations will have different forms of state. As you saw in Chapter 2, different social property relations entail not just the existence of different societal interests defined in class terms (lords, vassals, kings, worker and bourgeois), but different ways in which political and economic relationships are arranged. The clearest contrast is between the feudal and absolutist societies, where economic and political relationships (that is, social relationships in production and the social relationships involved in the exercise of political authority) were fused into one and the state was personalized, and in capitalism where the relations of political authority appear separate from economic relationships and are organized in terms of relations between an impersonal public power of the modern state and the citizen. The modern state for Marxists, therefore, is itself a product of the rise of capitalism as a system based on particular social property relations. Second, the Marxist approach claims that within this, our understanding of differentiation between states should also be informed by an account which seeks to explain the actions of states in terms of the influence of different classes and class fractions and the position of any particular society within the uneven international development of capitalism.

Consequently, in terms of assessing the usefulness of different models of international order, you need to be aware of the implicit or explicit ideas about the state that exist within these state-centric models of international order. You may conclude that the clarity gained from the realist suppression of the problem of explaining what is meant by the term 'the state' is reasonable, or you might argue that this over-simplifies, and too much of what happens in the international system cannot be explained with such a model. Alternatively, you might feel that insights from different approaches could be combined – the links between constructivism and liberalism which Wendt hints at is one example. Similar considerations are raised by the different ways that the four approaches view history.

Question

What kind of historical narrative does each approach tell?

One of the principal aspects of international order that you have been looking at in this book is the different ways in which the historical evolution of the international system might be viewed and approached. Indeed, a variety of historical trajectories have been sketched whether they be the evolution of the European states-system, the rise of the USA in the world, the development of cultural interaction, the evolution of attempts to define an international system of rights, the spread of different waves of technological innovation or the processes of convergence and divergence in incomes between countries. However, in line with the aim of this chapter to think in more general terms about international order, I want to finish this survey by considering some of the contrasts in terms of how our four models view historical change.

The odd one out of the four theories here is, quite clearly, realism. Realism makes the strongest claim to be a 'transhistorical' model, one which can be used to analyse and understand any political system consisting of several independent polities. The type of historical evolution that liberalism and constructivism allow for, that is, qualitative change in relations between states, is discounted by realists' insistence that state preferences are the same for all states and unchanging over time. This means that historical change in the international system cannot occur due to change within states, nor by the rise to dominance of a different kind of state. In this sense, as Martin Wight put it, 'international politics is the realm of recurrence and repetition' (Wight, 1966b, p.26). As a result, the only variance over time that realists do allow for is changing patterns in the distribution of power across the system as a whole. The fluctuations in the balance of power are thus at the heart of any historical narrative that a realist model develops. Most importantly, change is registered in changes in polarity (from bipolar to multipolar systems, for example) and in the relative positions of the great powers in the overall international pecking order.

Liberalism, constructivism and Marxism all have a more extensive view of what historical change means when applied to international order. As you have seen already, Marxism registers historical change 'internally' in the changing character of class relations and how they are manifested in certain types of economic relationship and particular forms of state. Marxists have specifically focused on the uneven and combined development of capitalism as an inherently international process, and on the attempts by the leading capitalist states to manage and respond to that unevenness. The contrast of Marxism with realism is profound when one considers the rise of capitalism in Europe:

> if the system is simply a set of external restraints given by the number and relative strength of the individual units comprising it, what could change *mean* beyond variation in the numbers involved and the distribution of weight among them? But of course this is not what we mean by historical change. The shift from weak, territorially disaggregated fiefdoms in which the monarchical state shared authority with the church and nobility to the modern bordered, sovereign nation-state cannot be registered in these terms.

(Rosenberg, 1990, p.295)

Marxism makes a claim to be able to account for aspects of change in international order that fall outside of the scope of realism.

You have also seen that constructivism and liberalism take historical change seriously within their respective models. Both accounts are predicated on the idea that the character of relations between states can and does vary. In fact, a feature of both approaches is to provide a framework within which qualitatively different types of international order can be accommodated. For Wendt, 'history matters' primarily because it is the particular histories of interaction between states which create, sustain and sometimes overturn different international cultures based on changes in states' identities and their views of other states (1999, p.109). Nevertheless, while at one level Wendt tries to account for difference in terms of relations between states via the historical production and reproduction of different subject positions, he ends up relying in large measure upon an analysis of changes in state–society relations as the basis of moving from one culture of anarchy to another. These ideas would be familiar to any liberal.

The liberal approach allows for an explanation of change at the international level founded on the changing configuration of what states are seeking to do. As a model, if we are to follow Moravcsik, the liberal approach can account for the rise or decline of co-operation or of conflict in the international system depending on whether different groups of states are seeking to act in conflict or harmony. Yet the liberal model is also tied to a series of more substantive claims about the historical evolution of international order. As you saw in Chapter 4, within liberalism different claims exist about the potential scale of change, from the development of relatively limited levels of co-operation among sub-sets of the international system, to more far-reaching claims about the transformation of world order based on the spread of liberal statehood across the world. The thesis of Francis Fukuyama (see Chapter 3) is one example of this and argues that the post-Cold War era has seen the triumph of liberal ideas about how societies can be organized and, in this sense, 'history' is at an end. Whether such bold liberal assertions can be supported; whether the process of historical change is more uneven and crisis-ridden as Marxists maintain; whether older themes of changes in the balance of power will continue to determine the shape of international order; or whether more profound changes away from a state-based international order are underway will be discussed in Chapter 15.

Activity 14.8

To consolidate and review your understanding of the different models, see if you can fill in the blanks in Table 14.2. Refer back to the relevant sections if you need to.

Table 14.2   Realism, liberalism, constructivism and Marxism compared

	What determines the actions of states?	What is the character of the relations between states?	What are the prospects for and bases of co-operation?	What parts do other sectors of the international play in shaping international order?
Realism	The nature of the anarchical international system and their position within the balance of power. State preferences are fixed by the search for power.		They are slim. States may co-operate in order to balance greater threats; or may co-operate if organized to do so in the interests of a dominant (hegemonic) power; but ultimately co-operation is subordinate to the requirements of self-help.	
Liberalism	What states want. State preferences are exogenous to state–state relations and are shaped by state–society relations. But how states will pursue these aims will also depend on, and be constrained by, the preferences of other states.	It depends on the configurations of preferences – whether they are in conflict, in harmony, or a mixture of the two.		(a) They help to shape state preferences (for example, economic actors). (b) They are the variety of arenas within which states pursue those interests (the world economy, an arena of co-operation or conflict over norms such as human rights, etc.).
Constructivism		It depends on the nature of the shared ideas which constitute international order. States can see themselves and each other as enemies, rivals or friends, and relationships will vary depending on this.		Wendt's theory is primarily based on relations between states. However, he acknowledges that a considerable part of a state's identity is formed domestically and non-state actors play a role in this respect in a manner similar to a liberal model.

(continued overleaf)

	What determines the actions of states?	What is the character of the relations between states?	What are the prospects for and bases of co-operation?	What parts do other sectors of the international play in shaping international order?
Marxism		This depends on the nature of the societies (defined by their social property relations). Capitalist states have historically had a conflictual and/or transformatory impact on non-capitalist polities. Among capitalist societies, relations can be conflicting or co-operative.	Among capitalist societies, co-operation is based on the shared class interests of the dominant elements (in a manner akin to liberalism). Where these coincide in the joint management of capitalism internationally, capitalist states may act in an ultra-imperialist manner. Where rivalries between nationally-based capitalisms come to the fore, conflict is likely.	

7   Conclusion

I began this survey of four different approaches to understanding international order by arguing that the usefulness of such general models lay in the ability to paint a broad canvas which captured something of the character of international order. Critical questions can then be asked of these approaches concerning what they bring to the foreground, what they exclude, and whether the simplifications on which they are based distort, rather than sharpen, our analysis of international order.

Perhaps the most simple and, in some ways, elegant theory reviewed is Waltz's neo-realism. Its simplicity may go a long way to explain its influence in the field of International Studies. But is too much lost through this simplicity? Would reliance on realist assumptions allow you to make enough important and broadly accurate claims about international order or would it distort or leave out too much from the picture? Liberalism and constructivism are both, in different ways, more complex models and arguably allow us to say a greater range of things about international order.

Marxism is possibly the least 'neat' of the approaches (I have noted already that Marxist writers have not attempted to build models of the kind used in other theories), and you need to consider whether this is a help or a hindrance in answering broad general questions about international order.

I have argued that different models can be evaluated in terms of their empirical adequacy and their coherence. As you give more consideration to these models and review the earlier chapters of this book in the light of them, you might bear these criteria in mind. Finally, I have reasoned that a comparison between models can help to sharpen our understanding of the differences between them and highlight potential weaknesses.

Further reading

To further your study of the different schools of thought I have covered in this chapter, it may be best to go to the key sources I have focused on.

For the classic statement of neo-realism, see Waltz, K. (1979) *Theory of International Politics*, New York, NY, Random House.

For a succinct statement of liberal theory, see Moravcsik, A. (1997) 'A liberal theory of international politics', *International Organization*, vol.51, no.4, pp.513–53.

For constructivism, see Wendt, A. (1999) *Social Theory of International Politics*, Cambridge, Cambridge University Press; and the earlier essay, Wendt, A. (1992) 'Anarchy is what states make of it: the social construction of power politics', *International Organization*, vol.42, no.2, pp.391–425.

On Marxism, an original reinterpretation of the history of the modern international order is given in Rosenberg, J. (1994) *The Empire of Civil Society*, London, Verso; but for a Marxist critique of realism, see Rosenberg, J. (1990) 'What's the matter with realism?', *Review of International Studies*, vol.16, no.3, pp.285–303.

Several overviews of the discipline as a whole are available, but for some good, accessible and critical commentary on theories of international order, see Halliday, F. (1994) *Rethinking International Relations*, Basingstoke, Macmillan.

Chapter 15 Transforming international order?

Simon Bromley and Mark J. Smith

1 Introduction

Is the contemporary international system changing and, if so, in what ways and by whose agency? These may seem like very ambitious questions but they are, in fact, ones that you have already studied several times in this book. Certainly, thus far you have studied particular sectors of the international system – the political realm of states and the states-system, the social and cultural aspects of national and religious identities and ideas of rights and justice, the economic and technological features of innovation and growth, trade, investment and migration, as well as the role of new technologies in facilitating network forms of organization. Yet each of these has provided a view of the international system as a whole – including how and by whose agency that order might be changing – albeit seen from the perspective of specific actors, relationships, forms of interaction, processes and institutions.

In this chapter we want to look at different approaches to the issue of whether, and how, the international system might be changing. In doing this we concentrate on three areas of inquiry. The first is to look at how the different mainstream models of international order address the issue of transformation and we shall review realism (in the remainder of this section), liberalism (in Section 2) and Marxism (in Section 4). In between our consideration of liberalism and Marxism, however, we pause to reflect on the fact that theories of transformation inevitably acknowledge that the existing state of affairs does not exhaust the possibilities of how our world is ordered. This critical dimension of theories of transformation forms our second area of inquiry. The idea of a critical theory is first introduced as part of our discussion of liberalism in Section 2.2. Section 3 then takes up the question of the 'standpoints' from which critiques are made and discusses this question in relation to post-colonial and feminist critiques of liberal claims to universality. Our third area of inquiry is concerned with those theories of transformation that take the cultural and technological sectors of the international system as their starting point. We review claims of theorists who focus on culture in Section 5 and on the technological basis of globalization in Section 6.

1.1   Identifying an international system

In Chapter 1 we argued that the international system encompasses different sectors. Indeed, different models of international order take different sectors of the international system – the political world of territorial states, the socio-cultural domain of collective identities and competing notions of rights and justice, and the economic and technological spheres of markets and networks – as their point of departure.

Question

Which sector of the international system forms the point of departure for the models of international order reviewed in Chapter 14?

The standard models encountered in the discipline of International Studies take as their starting point the idea that the modern international system is first and foremost a system of sovereign states; consequently their point of departure is the political sector. This was also our starting point in Chapter 1 where we introduced the idea of the 'problematic of the international' as the object of study in International Studies, and discussed the distinct characteristics of the modern international system.

One complication that arises immediately, however, is that while the models you reviewed in Chapter 14 do begin with states and the states-system, they do not agree upon what they mean by the state or upon how to analyse the basic units of the international system. In order to develop this argument, we need to remind you of some concepts we can use to define an international system which were first introduced in Chapter 1. There you saw that one way of defining an international system (or any given sector of a system) is in terms of four basic elements:

1   The basic *units* that comprise the international level.

2   The *structure* of relations among those units.

3   The technological and organizational *interaction capacity* within the system.

4   The *processes* of interaction that take place in the system.

You might find it helpful to re-read Chapter 1, Section 2.2 in order to refresh your understanding of this framework before moving on. In addition to giving us a framework for analysing international systems (and sectors of systems), this also provides a means of studying questions of transformation. Changes in a given international system can occur at the level of any of the above four elements.

We have already noted that different theories of international order as a whole start from different sectors of analysis; they also accord priority to different combinations of these elements (see Table 15.1).

Table 15.1   A framework for analysing (changes in) the international system

Elements of the international system	Sectors of the international system		
	Political sector of authoritative rule	Socio-cultural sector of collective identities and conceptions of rights and justice	Economic and technological sector of production, trade and innovation
Principal units in the international system			
Structure of relations among units			
Interaction capacity			
Dominant processes of interaction			

To see how to use this framework, we take a familiar example, realism, which analyses the international system from the perspective of the political sector and provides a structural theory of the system. As you have seen in Waltz's model (see Chapter 14, Section 2), the basic units of the international system are functionally equivalent sovereign states; the structure of relations among those states is one defined by anarchy and by the distribution of power capabilities across the units (that is, polarity); and the predominant process of interaction is the operation of the balance of power. (Interaction capacity plays no formal role in the theory, though its presence is tacitly assumed, and in practice attention is given to military capacities for interaction since these bear directly on questions of survival in a self-help system.) This theory is summarized in Table 15.2, which you can see is a reduced form of Table 15.1.

Table 15.2   Analysing international systems: realism

Elements of the international system	Sectors of the international system
	Political sector of authoritative rule
Principal units in the international system	Sovereign states
Structure of relations among units	Anarchy + polarity
Interaction capacity	
Dominant processes of interaction	Balance of power

However, specifying the international system in these terms also means that, for realism, as long as the more powerful states continue to uphold their sovereignty, there is no fundamental transformation of the international system. According to the realist view, even the emergence of a different kind of unit to the sovereign state capable of claiming effective political authority over human populations, possibly a new kind of territorial empire, would not really alter the character of the international system provided that there were several units, since anarchy would still impose a power-balancing logic on political actors. Only the worldwide replacement of anarchy by hierarchy would change the basic character of the system – and not even US power, discussed in Chapter 5, is sufficient for that! For the same reasons, changes in the socio-cultural or economic and technological sectors play no role because they do not change the basic condition of anarchy among the (politically defined) units, though such changes may be important indirectly if they affect polarity in the system.

In effect, realism is a transhistorical theory of the international that pays little attention to the specificity of the modern international system. It concentrates on aspects of geopolitics that bear most directly on the security of states, and it is confined to analysing changing balances of power *within* the international system rather than change from one international system to another. Still, such changes in polarity may be crucial. Chapter 5, for instance, argues that the international system effectively became unipolar in military terms with the end of the Cold War. In these circumstances, realism predicts that other powers would seek to balance against this development. Some analysts argue that moves to strengthen a European defence identity, especially French proposals for a Europe that can act as a counter or balance to the USA, are explicable in just these terms.

Nevertheless, the key point to emphasize is that, short of the replacement of anarchy by hierarchy, realism is confined to specifying changes to the balance of power *in* the international system. If politics continues to be territorially ordered and there is a plurality of powers, there is no change *of* system.

Perhaps for this reason, those who have claimed to identify a fundamental transformation of the international system have not usually started with realist theory. Other models of international order do put forward explicit theories of transformation. We shall begin with liberalism.

2   A liberal theory of international transformation

The primary task of liberal theories has been to identify as well as to advocate changes that might result in a transformation of the international system. Liberal theories of international order have always been concerned with the possibility of progressive transformation and with challenging the operation of the balance of power. Yet for the most part, liberals have sought neither to abolish sovereign states nor to replace the formal condition of anarchy with hierarchy.

Question

In what ways does liberalism differ from realism's focus on the political sector?

The key difference is that while liberalism characterizes the *political* sector of the international system as a states-system, it maintains that the international system as a whole cannot be understood by viewing it purely from the point of view of its political sector. In turn, the reason for this difference is that liberalism argues that politics to a large extent reflects and embodies interests and identities located in and shaped by economy and society. This means that liberals have based their analysis and recommendations for reform on a different understanding of the elements of the international system to that of realism.

Whereas realism is associated with the idea of the autonomy of the political – that is, the claim that states are able to pursue the national interest, defined as the pursuit of power in relation to other states, independently of the interests, values and identities of the social and economic groups that make up society – liberalism sees politics as something that is socially, culturally and economically constructed through the agency of individuals and private interests. Specifically, as you saw in Chapters 4 and 14, liberals have argued first, that the primary units in the international system are individuals and private groups who pursue their interests through states; second, that the structure of the system, the way in which relations among those units is ordered, is one of interdependence; and third, that processes of interaction depend upon how such interdependence among states is configured. Together, these claims lead to a radically different reading of the potential for transformation of the modern international system to that propounded by realists.

who can at all influence one another must adhere to some kind of civil constitution' otherwise their relations are those of a state of nature, and 'any legal constitution ... will conform to one of the following three types':

1   A constitution based on the *civil right* of individuals within a nation (*ius civitas*).

2   A constitution based on the *international right* of states in their relationships with one another (*ius gentium*).

3   A constitution based on *cosmopolitan right*, in so far as individuals and states, coexisting in an external relationship of mutual influences, may be regarded as citizens of a universal state of mankind (*ius cosmopoliticum*).

(Kant, 1991a, pp.98–9; first published 1795)

Kant was advocating a pacific federation of states based on the notion of cosmopolitan right, in which the 'federation does not aim to acquire any power like that of a state, but merely to preserve and secure the *freedom* of each state in itself', and he claimed that 'this idea of *federalism*, extending gradually to encompass all states and thus leading to perpetual peace, is practicable and has objective reality' (1991a, p.104; first published 1795). Towards this end, Kant proposed a number of specific recommendations for states – 'Articles of a Perpetual Peace' – such as the gradual abolition of standing armies, and a prohibition on intervention in the constitutional and governmental affairs of other states.

Question

Using material from Part 1, can you identify any developments that exemplify this liberal model of a transformed international order?

The idea of a liberal international order was discussed by William Brown in some detail in Chapter 4, where he identified novel forms of economic and political co-operation among the leading Western states (and Japan) after the Second World War. Perhaps the most developed model of a federated series of polities committed to conducting their international relations with one another founded on norms of right and legality is the European Union.

Although liberalism is rightly presented as a theory of the possibility of progress in human affairs, it has not minimized the fact that progress is often achieved as a result of difference and antagonism. After all, the European Union was built on the wreckage of devastated nation states and the legacies of the two World Wars. Indeed, Kant gave a leading role to antagonistic conflict in the eventual establishment of a realm of perpetual peace, for he argued that the principal motivation for such a political project is that in the absence of international right and law, domestic liberalism is under threat. In the 'Idea for a universal history with a cosmopolitan purpose' (1991b; first published 1784), Kant wrote:

> What is the use of working for a law-governed civil constitution among men, i.e. of planning a *commonwealth*? The same unsociability which forced men to do so gives rise in turn to a situation whereby each commonwealth, in its external relations (i.e. as a state in relation to other states), is in a position of unrestricted freedom. Each must accordingly expect from any other precisely the same evils which formerly oppressed individual men and forced them into a law-governed civil state. ... Wars, tense and unremitting military preparations, and the resultant distress which every state must eventually feel within itself, even in the midst of peace – these are the means by which nature drives nations to make initially imperfect attempts, but finally, after many devastations, upheavals and even complete inner exhaustion of their powers, to take the step which reason could have suggested to them even without so many sad experiences – that of abandoning a lawless state of savagery and entering a federation of peoples in which every state, even the smallest, could expect to derive its security and rights not from its own power or its own legal judgement, but solely from this great federation, from a united power and the law-governed decision of a united will.

(Kant, 1991b, p.47; first published 1784)

This kind of discourse is still a key part of the ideology of the dominant Western powers in the world today, a project that the USA presents as both distinctively American and universally relevant (see also Chapters 3 and 5). Indeed, Kant presented his proposal for a liberal international order as a universal theory. However, as a critique of an existing state of affairs, and a proposal of how to transform that state of affairs, it also has a strong claim to the title of the most ambitious, if not quite the first, critical theory of the modern international system. For Kant, the two were linked as the possibility of overcoming the balance of power was based on an appeal to what he saw as universal principles of reason. However, we want to take these two in turn. First, we want to use our discussion of liberal theories of transformation as a way of introducing the idea that models of international order can serve as critical theories before considering the notion of universalism more fully in Section 3.

2.2   Liberalism as a critical theory

Question

What is a critical theory?

Critical theory
A critical theory is one that is aware of its place in history and in a particular culture, is engaged in dialogue with other similarly located theories, and is oriented towards showing how, and by what means, the existing state of social affairs might be transformed.

There are many definitions of critical theory, but the basic idea is a theory that produces a critique. That is to say, knowledge and understanding that is self-conscious about its place in history and its location in a particular culture or cultures; that engages in dialogue with other theories similarly located in other histories and cultures; and that interrogates the social world 'recognizing that the existing state of affairs does not exhaust all possibilities, and offering positive implications for social action' (Calhoun, 1995, p.35). The aim of critique is to make a special effort to identify and question the often tacit, taken for granted assumptions at work in our knowledge and understanding. Consequently, our consideration of theories of transformation of world order inevitably demands a consideration of the critical dimensions of theories.

In order to explore the idea of a critical theory of international order more fully, it might help to begin by asking in what senses realism might serve as a critical theory. In some ways, it can make a convincing case for being considered a critical theory. Realism, as was noted in Chapter 14, has engaged in dialogue with other theoretical positions – notably as a self-styled critique of liberal idealism. It is also engaged in making claims about the role of norms in social life, and certain commitments about which values are important, just as liberalism does. Most obviously, realism attaches particular importance to questions of security because it holds that security, both for individuals and collectives, is a supreme value. Moreover, realism is perfectly capable of thinking critically about security. Indeed, one would be hard put to find a thinker who thought harder and more critically about security, both individual and collective, than Thomas Hobbes, often claimed, rightly, as a forerunner of realist as well as liberal thought.

However, realism is limited as a critical theory in respect of how far it sees the potential for the existing state of affairs to be transformed. Both liberals and realists (and others) share the idea that the existing state of affairs has, historically, consisted of co-existing politically organized societies. However, many, but not all, realists take a step further in claiming that this will always be so – that human political association is necessarily partial, always open to fragmentation and disagreements, which reason is powerless to resolve. This is a conservative, metaphysical picture of our place in the world, including a view of the place of human reason in the world, which is certainly different from that found in *most* strands of liberalism. From this viewpoint, political activity and identification always presuppose the possibility both of other, conflicting ways of doing things and of conflicting others who do things differently. 'The political world', wrote the influential conservative thinker Carl Schmitt, 'is a pluriverse, not a universe. ... The political entity cannot by its very nature be universal in the sense of embracing all humanity and the entire world' (1996, p.53; first published 1932). Schmitt's notion of politics underpins the idea that there will always be political differences among collections of people, or peoples. It reinforces the contention that polities will always confront one another as, at least potential, 'enemies' in which 'one fighting collectivity of people confronts a similar collectivity' (1996, p.28; first published 1932).

We might also note here that this is a very different claim to that which was advanced in Chapter 1 about the problematic of the international. There it was noted that politically organized societies have always co-existed with one another, thereby constituting the geopolitical as an irreducible dimension of inter-societal interaction. However, this does not mean that such division is an inevitable feature of our social existence as Schmitt contends. Nor, for that matter, does it mean that the co-existence of politically organized societies can be subsumed under an ahistorical concept of anarchy for the purposes of explanation, as Waltz (1979) seeks to do. Although realists concede that one power might come to dominate all others, establishing a universal empire – hierarchy might replace anarchy – this would not amount to the kind of transformation Kant envisaged but would merely be, in Kant's words, 'a soulless despotism' (1991a, p.113; first published 1795).

Still, if the conservative realist claim turns out to be true, it poses an outer limit to the kind of proposals advanced by Kant and the limits to how far realism can be 'critical'. Indeed, the contrast with Kant makes this clear. Kant's thinking was explicitly posed as an alternative to this idea because he believed that universal norms could be discovered by reason and could be shown to be operating in history. As a matter of historical and sociological development, Kant maintained:

> The peoples of the earth have ... entered in varying degrees into a universal community, and it has developed to the point where a violation of rights in *one* part of the world is felt *everywhere*. The idea of cosmopolitan right is therefore not fantastic and overstrained; it is a necessary complement to the unwritten code of political and international right, transforming it into a universal right of humanity.

(Kant, 1991a, pp.107–8; first published 1795)

Underlying the idea that perpetual peace might become a universal condition of humanity is a striking vision of historical progress in which apparently fundamental differences, say of morality and religion, are encompassed in a framework of cosmopolitan right guaranteed not by a single, overarching power, but by 'an equilibrium of forces and a most vigorous rivalry' (Kant, 1991a, p.114; first published 1795). This followed directly from Kant's characterization of enlightenment as individual freedom and critique established in a context of the public use of reason. The authority of public reason, for Kant, can only be established in dialogue among free citizens, it is not a fixed foundation on which political order can be built but rather an open-ended process of practical reasoning guided by the categorical imperative – that is, the injunction to act so that the maxim of one's action can be a universal principle – 'because reason is by definition that which could be accepted as authoritative by all free individuals within any possible community' (Garnham, 2000, p.180).

Kant's theory is critical because the universal character of reason creates the potential for relations of might (or power) among different – and hence particular – collectivities of people to be transformed into universal relations of right among individuals and states ordered by cosmopolitan right. Furthermore, it is a critical theory oriented towards at least a partial transcendence of the problematic of the international since, if fully realized, it would govern relations between states in the same way as relations between individuals within states, that is, according to norms of right and law; it would accord the same moral rights (if not the same legal entitlements) to those inside and outside a given community because the moral community would be the universal cosmopolitan citizens of the world; and it would, thereby, subsume the parts – both states and citizens – under a 'universal state of mankind'.

This is not the place for a detailed discussion of Kant's philosophy, but suffice to say that many critics, including many liberals, have doubted that Kant succeeded in defending his proposal for perpetual peace in these terms. Nevertheless, Kant's ideas remain important for us because they serve to question the appropriate standpoint of any critical theory, and we can now consider this in a little more detail. We shall see that even Kant came to doubt the idea that the progress of reason in history could ever attain a universal standpoint beyond all political differences. It is, therefore, a moot point just how far the divide between the metaphysical picture of the world held by liberals and conservatives reaches. Hobbes, for example, seems to straddle both sides – a universal appeal to natural law, on the one hand, and an unyielding insistence that the judgements of individuals and states are always partial, on the other – without too much discomfort, and Kant was never able to think himself beyond the dilemma presented by Hobbes: that is, that the creation of legal sovereignty *within* states resulted in an order *between* states lacking in legal, though not moral, authority.

3   Universalism and the standpoint of critique

As you have seen, Kant's critical liberalism was also based on claims of universality arising from the nature of reason. 'From Kant on', writes Craig Calhoun, 'most critical theory has claimed, or at least aimed at, a standpoint of universal validity' (1995, p.xix). However, it is important to see that for Kant the reach of reason remained an open question. For Kant the universality of reason is closer to an ideal that regulates reason from within, rather than a foundational claim about its contents or results. As the opening sentence to the 'Preface' to Kant's *Critique of Pure Reason* says: 'Human reason, in one sphere of its cognition, is called upon to consider questions, which it cannot decline, as they are presented by its own nature, but which it cannot answer, as they transcend every faculty of human reason' (1993, p.3; first published 1781).

In this section, we shall explore this idea of the reach or limits of reason in several ways. In Section 3.1, we begin by probing more deeply liberalism's claim to be universal. Conservative realists such as Schmitt deny that a universal standpoint is attainable and in Sections 3.2 and 3.3 we shall see that there are others who would not class themselves as conservatives who also reject the idea of a universal standpoint. Finally, in Section 3.4, we claim that buried within these debates are at least two senses of universalism that need to be distinguished. We argue for the retention of one of these – justificatory universalism – as a means of conducting dialogue among different standpoints on the basis of reason rather than coercion.

This question of standpoint is especially important for International Studies because the international system contains a number of different discourses about that system, arising from different historical experiences and different socio-cultural locations. These discourses of the international system function both as analyses or explanations of its workings and as narratives in and through which actors seek to evaluate its development and make sense of their and others' conduct. Like all knowledge of the social world, the discourses of the international system are themselves a part of the world, playing some role in shaping actors' orientations to that world.

In this context, the question of standpoint arises, first, because there is a multiplicity of such discourses speaking about a shared realm of interaction and, therefore, we cannot avoid comparing and evaluating them in relation to one another; and second, because it is always reasonable to ask of a given discourse how far it succeeds in articulating a position that is not tied to any particular standpoint as contrasted with being a partial view, based on a particular set of experiences, interests and values. To what extent does a given discourse rise above the partial and the particular, and offer a more general and universal viewpoint, that is, a standpoint that can be shared by others?

In an international system characterized by interaction between people with different standpoints, the alternatives to dialogue are either disengagement from one another or conflict, or both. Exclusion, subordination and conflict are all too present in the contemporary international system, so it is worth asking if dialogue is still possible on the basis of a shared and common human capacity for practical reasoning, that is to say, reasoning about what we should do and become. In short, the extent to which particular standpoints can be reconciled with one another, or learn to live with their differences without conflict, remains one of the most pressing questions of international politics.

Posing questions about the universality and particularity of any given standpoint is, therefore, a way of asking how different people can live together in a densely integrated international system. Framing the question of standpoint in this way does not assume that a fully universal standpoint is either available or desirable; it does not commit one to the idea that there is a 'god's eye view' of the world, that we can achieve a 'view from nowhere' (Nagel, 1986). Rather, it is a search for a regulative framework in which different standpoints can be brought into dialogue with one another.

3.1   The (false) universality of liberalism?

Question

What are the principal objections to the idea that liberal principles of national and international order are potentially universal? You might find it helpful to look at Chapters 3, 6 and 7 in particular.

Perhaps the main objection you have encountered thus far is the idea that what is represented as universal may in reality present a particular point of view as general: 'too often, the seemingly universal is the presentation of a partial view as though it were all encompassing', says Calhoun, so that concepts and arguments serve to constitute 'relations of inclusion and exclusion, of visibility and invisibility, particularity and generality even where it is most resolutely denied and the illusion of ... universality maintained' (Calhoun, 1995, p.187). A common way in which this happens is that a discourse talks in general, inclusive terms, for example, 'we', 'humanity', 'individuals', 'peoples' and the like, while the identities to which these refer are constructed on the basis of the experience or social location of, say, 'men', 'Westerners', 'property owners', 'nations that have achieved statehood' and so forth.

Figures 15.1 and 15.2 provide examples of how particular societies have viewed themselves as the centre of all things international. Artefacts such as these play a role in expressing and embodying the often taken for granted collective identity of a society.

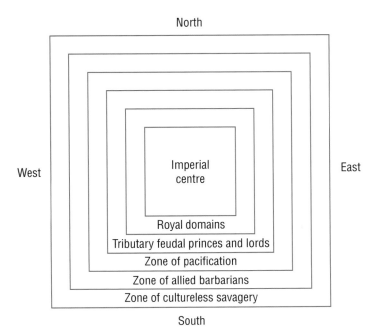

Figure 15.1   The traditional Chinese world view

Figure 15.2   A Eurocentric representation of the world

As you have seen, these kinds of issues are in contention in the post-colonial world. For instance, you have seen (Chapters 3 and 6) that some argue that the term 'universal' is one that the West has used in its confrontations with others; that what the West sees as universal, the non-West sees as Western; and that the claims of European and Western international society to represent an order equally binding on all cultures is a form of Eurocentrism. Dipesh Chakrabarty (2000) says that, notwithstanding its colonial imposition in many parts of the world, the heritage of enlightenment, secular, liberal thinking is now 'universal' (see Chapter 3). Yet he then asks whether this universalism represents 'genuinely universal' features of modernity or 'a forced globalization of a particular fragment of European history' (Chakrabarty, 2000, p.69). Similarly, Seyla Benhabib (2002) has noted that: 'The question Is universalism ethnocentric? betrays an anxiety that has haunted the West since the conquest of the Americas. It grows from beliefs that Western ways of life and systems of value are radically different from those of other civilizations' (2002, p.24).

A related example concerns the proto-liberal (but also imperial) thought of Hobbes and Locke, which considered those able to interpret and apply the natural law to be male, property-owning and European. However, nowadays liberalism proclaims its relevance to females, the property-less and non-European cultures.

In response to these kinds of consideration, Simon Bromley suggests in Chapter 3 that there is a need to distinguish principles that are established by reason of power from those that prosper by power of reason and that, while all human accomplishments from mathematics to political arrangements have origins in specific cultural and historical locations, this need not compromise their validity and potential cross-cultural relevance. Bromley suggests that much of the anxiety about the European (and hence Western) character of norms and institutions of international society rests on false generalizations about the essence of the West, and a failure to recognize that elements of other cultures or civilizations are equally compatible with these ideals.

By contrast, Raia Prokhovnik argues in Chapter 7 that the universal spread and adoption of given norms – say, of individual rights or notions of social justice – is not an indication that they are right or good for all, and that, although there may be some generally shared concepts of moral and political life, detailed and actual conceptions are always particular and culturally mediated. Prokhovnik's discussions of communitarianism and of the various critiques of 'universal' human rights indicate the diversity of authentic ways of being human. Unlike the ideal of universalism, communitarians argue for the relevance of the idea of a *modus vivendi* among plural civilizations or cultures.

Notice that even if you agree with Bromley, liberalism is still one tradition of thinking among others, one based on a belief in the fundamental moral equality of all human beings (so that inequalities have to be justified), a belief that doctrines should be open to critical scrutiny and only held if they withstand that test, and a belief that no religious doctrine can be held with certainty. 'There is no way that non-liberals can be sold the principle of neutrality [that is, the idea that liberal principles are impartial between competing conceptions of the good life],' says Brian Barry, 'without first injecting a large dose of liberalism into their outlook' (1989, p.35). If this is true, and we think it is, there is no reason to expect liberals to support neutrality when confronted with illiberal outlooks. The universal claims of liberalism might be better interpreted as a normative proposal and an empirical claim, such that the liberal tradition is in fact universalizable.

Should we conclude that all claims to universality are spurious, that all attempts to identify general principles by which the international can be ordered bear the mark of their historical and cultural locations, and that all such claims are unavoidably particular and exclusive? Or should we see universality as a valid ideal, something that is worth striving for, even if it is never reached in practice? Across the social sciences, including the field of International Studies, these questions have played an important role in feminist debates where the idea of standpoint has been explicitly addressed in a number of ways. Let us now turn to some of these contributions.

3.2   Feminism and the question of standpoint

Question

Consider the following extract about international development, conditions in the developing world and the role played by women in the everyday production and reproduction of society. What does it say about the question of standpoint?

> Gender and diversity are linked in many ways. The patriarchal world view sees man as the measure of all value, with no space for diversity, only for hierarchy. Commercial value reduces diversity to a problem, a deficiency. Destruction of diversity and the creation of monocultures becomes an imperative for capitalist patriarchy. The marginalization of women and the destruction of biodiversity go hand in hand. Loss of diversity is the price paid in the patriarchal model of progress which pushes inexorably towards monocultures, uniformity and homogeneity. Diversity is, in many ways, the basis of women's politics and the politics of ecology; gender politics is largely the politics of difference. These two politics of diversity converge when women and biodiversity meet in fields and forest, in arid regions and wetlands.

Diversity is the principle of women's work and knowledge; an alternative calculus of 'productivity' and 'skills' can be built that respects, not destroys diversity. The economies of many Third World communities depend on biological resources for their sustenance and well being. In these societies, biodiversity is simultaneously a means of production and an object of consumption. The survival and sustainability of livelihoods is ultimately connected to the conservation and sustainable use of biological resources in all their diversity. Tribal and peasant societies' biodiversity-based technologies, however, are seen as backward and primitive and are, therefore, displaced by 'progressive' technologies that destroy both biodiversity and people's livelihoods. Crop uniformity undermines work associated with diverse and multiple use systems of forestry, agriculture and animal husbandry. ... Women's work and knowledge is central to biodiversity conservation and utilization both because they work between sectors and because they perform multiple tasks. Women as farmers have remained invisible despite their contribution ... too many women do too much work of too many different kinds, concentrated outside market related or remunerated work.

Women's work and knowledge is uniquely found in the spaces 'in between' the interstices of 'sectors', the invisible ecological flows between sectors, and it is through these linkages that ecological stability, sustainability and productivity under resource-scarce conditions are maintained. The invisibility of women's work and knowledge arises from the gender bias which has a blind spot for realistic assessment of women's contributions. It is also rooted in the sectoral, fragmented and reductionist approach to development which treats forests, livestock and crops as independent of each other.

(Shiva, 1993, pp.164–8)

For Shiva, the patriarchal world view is one of hierarchy and uniformity, in which gender bias leads to a reductionist approach that sees aspects of development as independent of one another, and the holistic connections sustained by women's work and knowledge are rendered invisible. By contrast, women's knowledge is attentive to diversity and the need for a holistic picture of the environment.

Put like this, the idea of a plurality of standpoints may seem an attractive one, especially when counterposed to the false universals of liberal or patriarchal ways of thinking that present a particular view of the world as universal. Equally, by paying attention to such diversity it is possible to make plain what is lost, as well as what is gained, by universalizing theories and the prescriptions that follow from them.

Nevertheless, are there distinct women's ways of knowing and acting as Shiva seems to suggest? And if so, do men and women reason differently? Do all women reason similarly, or are there differences among women of different cultures? We could go on. Commenting on the development of the idea of standpoint in feminist theory, Calhoun says that: 'Increasingly, the term standpoint came to denote not the search for a standpoint capable of offering universal understanding, knowledge, of guidance for action, but recognition of the divergence of standpoints rooted in different experiences' (1995, p.165).

We have suggested that claims to universality often encode certain identities, thereby presenting a partial view of the whole, including the perspectives of some while excluding those of others. But does this matter? Why not regard 'standpoint' as marking the fact that all forms of understanding, knowledge and recommendations for action are rooted in different experiences and social locations? Calhoun expresses this point as follows: 'Does not human life admit of – indeed necessarily produce – innumerable standpoints?' (1995, p.166). Correspondingly, G.A. Cohen has said that 'there is no way of being human which is not *a* way of being human' (2000, p.354). Before we consider some of the philosophical questions raised by these issues, we want to look at the idea of gendered concepts, specifically gendered conceptions of political identity.

3.3   Gender and political concepts

Consider, for example, the issue of political identity and the notion of 'citizenship'. During the seventeenth and eighteenth centuries when Hobbes, Locke, and even Kant, were writing, citizenship in European states was exclusively confined to males and, nearly everywhere, to property-owning males. Women's membership of the political community was mediated by the patriarchal family and household, in which men had political authority over women and children. Historically, ideas about gender, sexuality and family norms have played, and continue to play, an important role in defining national identities and in shaping the nature of cultures upheld by different communities. In turn, notions of citizenship and ideas about national cultures serve to constitute sovereignty in particular ways. Jacqui True argues that, historically, 'the boundaries of gender and the state have excluded women from domestic and international political life, and engendered international relations as the virtual preserve of men and as a primary site for the construction of masculinities through the control and domination of women' (1996, p.237).

More generally, True suggests that 'gender is a constitutive dimension of political identity' (1996, p.246). This is a difficult idea that we shall try to elucidate. True is pointing to the fact that social categories such as citizenship and sovereignty are themselves part of the social world – we 'identify *what* we do through an *account* of what we do ... in the sense that almost all socially significant human activity ... is identified as a certain *type of doing* through the accounts the agents and others give of that doing' (Benhabib, 2002, pp.6–7). Moreover, such accounts are always open to contrasting evaluations, competing narratives that involve normative assessments of those accounts. Thus, to say that 'citizenship', for example, is a gendered concept is to say that the accounts and evaluations given of the activities involved in being a citizen rest upon a distinct, socially and historically constructed, set of identities for women, men and children.

Question

Does citizenship entitle one to serve in the armed forces?

Norms of gender, sexuality, family and notions of citizenship may not be as blatantly patriarchal as in the historical past described by True but, for example, the continuing controversy over the role women play in the armed forces of many liberal democratic states indicates that these remain live issues. A central task of feminist theory in International Studies has been to examine the ways in which apparently genderless concepts – sovereignty, power, war and so on – have in fact been constructed in gendered ways, thereby making visible excluded identities and previously hidden relations of power. Cynthia Enloe, for instance, has argued that socially constructed, gendered accounts of concepts such as the state and citizen embody hierarchies of power, and that 'states depend upon particular constructions of the domestic and private spheres in order to foster smooth(er) relationships at the public/international level' (1989, p.131).

Thus far, we have seen that there are diverse forms of knowledge and ways of acting in the social world, and that many of the constitutive concepts of social and political life have been constructed in particular, gendered ways. Does this imply, finally, that the very idea of universalism is something we should dispense with?

3.4 What kind of universalism are we talking about?

Foundationalism
As used here, foundationalism refers to the idea that there are bare facts about human nature (including human reason) and its place in the world that provide the basis for agreement among individuals about questions of truth, beauty and what is considered to be right or good.

To answer the question just posed, it is helpful to distinguish two senses of universalism. There is, first, what is known as philosophical or metaphysical universalism, sometimes termed foundationalism. This is the belief that there are some defining facts about human nature (including human reason) and its place in the world that can ground claims to knowledge and understanding, whether it is in the sphere of science, art, morality or politics. Metaphysical universalism claims to identify something which guarantees that human judgements about what is true, beautiful or right and good will converge with one another.

In the sphere of practical reasoning about morality and politics, typical instances of metaphysical universalism include Kant's idea that all humans have an ability to recognize and act on universalizable moral principles or Hobbes's insistence that everyone is capable of discerning the natural law. This form of universalism has often underpinned the further claim to have identified a general political identity which all can reasonably be expected to subscribe to. When liberals present their accounts of political order in these philosophical or metaphysical terms, they are rightly open to the rejoinder that all such accounts can be shown to be a product of a particular history and culture, and to rest on taken for granted assumptions about political identity. Even if universal features of human nature and reason can be identified across cultures, these are too abstract and general to guarantee any serviceable convergence of opinion among differently located actors – as Hobbes, of course, was fully aware. In this debate, it seems that the advocates of political diversity have the upper hand, even if we grant the existence of universal morals and reason.

However, different standpoints have 'propositional content', that is, they make claims about the world and about the place of humans within it, they recommend some courses of action and not others, and so forth. Standpoints are not just talk, but they are ways of being and acting in the world. Conflicts among a plurality of standpoints can either be resolved by dialogue or by force (that is, the exercise of coercive power), or by the parties going their separate ways. We take it as given by history that, in a crowded and interdependent world such as ours, the latter is not a viable option. In any case, many of the most important of such conflicts, say, over the position and status of men and women in society, exist *within* (as well as between) given communities so that separation is not even possible. This leaves dialogue or force.

Dialogue as distinct from propaganda in the service of coercion presupposes that reasoning is a normative process, that is, an activity in which any given exercise of reasoning can be criticized, but only in the light of general criteria that themselves transcend present claims to knowledge and understanding. 'We can reasonably question any specific conception or deployment of reason', says Gary Gutting, 'but this will always have to be on the basis of some (unquestioned) broader conception or deployment of reason' (1999, p.175). A minimal list of the normative content of reasoning would include the following: 'Impartiality, objectivity, intersubjective verification of results, arguments and data, consistency of belief, and self-reflexivity' (Benhabib, 2002, p.27). Or, as Benhabib also says, 'All dialogue, in order to be distinguished from cajoling, propaganda, brainwashing, and strategic bargaining, presupposes normative rules' (2002, p.36).

This is the second form of universalism, sometimes called justificatory universalism. Note that unlike metaphysical universalism, it is explicitly anti-foundationalist: justificatory universalism does not presuppose any fixed philosophical or metaphysical foundations. Nor does it presuppose any fixed

Justificatory universalism
The idea that there is a normative content to human reason encompassing 'impartiality, objectivity, intersubjective verification of results, arguments and data, consistency of belief, and self-reflexivity' (Benhabib, 2002, p.27).

543

and final construction of social and political identities. As Adam Kuper has pointed out: 'The measure of human uniformity is our common ability to learn, to borrow, to assimilate. ... In a sense, it is what we share that produces the differences between us, which in turn depend on our interrelationships' (1999, p.243). Justificatory universalism argues that if we are to engage in dialogue between different standpoints, we must respect the normative aspects of reason. There is no one standpoint that speaks for us all, as many feminist theorists have rightly pointed out, nor are there any fixed foundations on which all claims to understanding, knowledge and action can be built. Nevertheless, there are things that distinguish dialogue from cajoling, and these must be respected if dialogue is not to be a disguised form of conflict. At some point, we may reach the limits of reason, that is, we agree to differ. Yet if separation is impossible, even an agreement to differ presupposes a continuing dialogue about how to handle differences, if it is not to degenerate into an exercise of force.

Of course, some have argued that not only are all particular claims to knowledge, understanding and action trapped in historically and culturally specific concepts and frameworks, but that the same is true of the core norms of rationality themselves. However, this seems to be a difficult position to hold with any coherence. (Furthermore, it is difficult to reconcile with what we know about processes of reasoning in a wide range of cultures.) If we are to assess the status of such claims, then we must assume that those who make them have not stopped reasoning; that they seek to convince us that we should take them seriously; and that we should ourselves believe in them. Nonetheless, in order to do this we must presuppose that there is a way things are in a publicly accessible realm, independent of our representations, even if alternative standpoints (or conceptual schemes) allow for different descriptions. As John Searle has said: 'If someone wishes to abandon normal understanding, he or she owes us an account of what sort of understanding is possible' (1995, p.189).

Thus, this second sense of universalism, justificatory universalism, is based on common norms of rationality that develop from the natural necessities of social life. Stuart Hampshire suggests we should think of it in terms of the kinds of adversarial 'reasoning typical of legal and moral disputes and disputes about evidence, rather than the formal deductions and proofs that are characteristic of logic and mathematics' (1999, p.88). We conclude from this that social science, especially critical social science, can happily dispense with the search for a universal identity from which to address the world, and that it has no need of fixed philosophical foundations on which to build its analysis and critique, but that it is hard to see how it can dispense with justificatory universalism, that is, the idea that reason has a normative content, operating as a regulative ideal (Nagel, 1997).

4 Marxism as a materialist theory of transformation

We seem to have come a long way from concrete theses about the potential for transformation of the international system. However, as our discussion of liberal and feminist ideas has tried to make clear, there is a close connection between theory as critique and the idea of transformation. The shared idea is that what currently exists may change because the ideas and attitudes that people hold about reality serve, in part, to constitute that reality. Accordingly, as those ideas change through a process of critique, so the previously invisible may be rendered visible, the previously taken for granted may be exposed as contestable relations of power. New forms of action and new understandings may then follow and therefore social 'reality' may change.

Yet in tracing the idea of critique from Kant's liberalism to the contemporary concerns of post-colonial and feminist critics, we have jumped over the single most important rival theory to liberalism that gained an organized embodiment in the modern international system, namely, Marxism. As you have seen, Kant sought to locate a universal standpoint in a conception of reason and the role that reason could play in human affairs. Marx, by contrast, sought the location of a universal standpoint in patterns of historical development, specifically in the class-divided character of the material production and reproduction of society. Rather than pursue the philosophical and theoretical character of Marx's thought and subsequent Marxism, we want to consider the idea that transformation may be the result of the material development of human society.

Question

How does Benno Teschke, in Chapter 2, account for the transformation of the absolutist states-system into the modern states-system?

We shall not recount Teschke's analysis in detail, but you may remember that he argues that the development and spread of the capitalist mode of production – first in seventeenth-century England, and later elsewhere in Europe and the rest of the world – transformed the nature of state sovereignty and geopolitics. The directly territorial form of political accumulation associated with absolutist states was replaced by a form of economic accumulation based on private property, wage labour and competitive markets, a form of accumulation that made possible, indeed required, a withdrawal of the state and politics from direct intervention in the economy.

Domestically, this implied that the state became the indirect guarantor of capitalist property and class relations based on the legal definition of property rights and contractual exchange. Internationally, it implied that states related to one another as economic but not territorial competitors, since economic expansion across borders no longer necessitated direct political control of property, labour and surpluses in other territories. In particular, Teschke contends that the features that are traditionally taken to define modern, sovereign states are products of an expressly capitalist form of development, one that makes possible, in truth demands, a novel form of separation of the 'economic' and the 'political'. Thus, Teschke's critique seeks to show that the modern (sovereign) states-system and the international capitalist economy are founded upon specifically capitalist social property relations, which express a certain pattern of class power.

Teschke refers to the structure of the international system produced by these developments as being socially uneven, yet geopolitically combined. This is a reference to Leon Trotsky's idea that Marxism has a distinct method for analysing international development and change in terms of 'uneven and combined development' (as you saw in Chapter 14). The dynamic features of capital accumulation, technological innovation and social and geographical expansion take place in a context of, and thus are bound up with, political and geopolitical relations that impart their own character to that development.

Uneven and combined development
Uneven development is the result of the interaction of all societies that have significant geopolitical relations with one another in circumstances in which the development of capitalist forms of economic and political power in one part of the world imposes the 'whip of external necessity' (Trotsky) on other parts. All subsequent development is 'combined development', both because other societies are forced, internally, to adapt to the changes wrought by capitalist development elswhere and because, in so doing, they embody a particular, external, relation to interstate and inter-societal processes of interaction.

Once established (according to Teschke, in seventeenth-century England), capitalist forms of economic and political power proved immensely superior to the pre-capitalist forms of political accumulation, thereby imposing an external pressure on other societies with direct implications for their internal reform or revolution. In his *History of the Russian Revolution* Trotsky referred to this as the 'whip of external necessity' produced by the fact of uneven development (1977, p.27). All subsequent development was 'combined development', both because other societies were forced, internally, to adapt to the changes wrought by capitalist development elsewhere; and because, in so doing, they embodied a particular, external, relation to interstate and inter-societal processes of interaction. Uneven and combined development was, therefore, a result of the interaction of all societies that had significant economic and geopolitical relations with one another. In fact, capitalism, especially industrial capitalism, proved so powerful that uneven and combined development soon became a feature of world, and not just European, development.

In terms of the framework we introduced in Section 1, these changes can be represented (albeit simplified somewhat) as shown in Table 15.4. A change in basic units of the international system, based in the economic and technological sector, transforms the nature of class reproduction, accumulation and state sovereignty – and hence the implications of these for geopolitics.

Table 15.4   Analysing international systems: Marxism

Elements of the international system	Sectors of the international system	
	Political sector of authoritative rule	Economic and technological sector of production, trade and innovation
Principal units in the international system	States; but the character of the state is directly bound up with the dominant social property relations in the society concerned.	Societies based on a dominant set of social property relations (e.g. feudalism, capitalism), giving rise to specific patterns of class relations and class struggle.
Structure of relations among units	Formally anarchy; but the logic of anarchy depends upon the character of the states that are subject to it and the configuration of uneven and combined development.	Uneven and combined development: different periods of history characterized by different configurations of uneven and combined development.
Interaction capacity		
Dominant processes of interaction	As capitalism develops and spreads, so pre-capitalist forms of political accumulation are replaced by economic accumulation, thereby transforming geo-politics from directly territorial forms of competi-tion over access to land and labour to economic forms of competition based on access to markets and capital.	Capitalism displaces and transforms pre-capitalist social property relations, both domestically and internationally, based on an in-built dynamic of capital accumulation, technological innovation and social and geographical expansion.

4.1   Marxism as a critical theory

Marxism is a theory of transformation that depends on social agency, principally on the collective agency of classes of agents sharing common relationships of ownership and non-ownership to the factors of production. Transformation of the international order – from the feudal geopolitics of the absolutist states to the capitalist geopolitics represented by eighteenth and nineteenth-century England – is the unintended result of these changes, just as the development of capitalism was an unintended consequence of the outcomes of class struggles in sixteenth and seventeenth-century England.

How does this image of transformation differ from that of Kant's?

While Kant was well aware of the material aspects of human history and their impact on political development, his theory of perpetual peace is explicitly a proposal derived from philosophical reasoning. Although he recognized that movement towards perpetual peace may only come about after a series of violent conflicts, Kant says that it is a 'step which reason could have suggested ... even without so many sad experiences'. Marx's view of historical transformation is less idealistic and more materialistic than Kant's, though it is as well not to overstate their differences in general terms. Marx rejected the view, which he attributed to Kant, that history is shaped by ideas and changes in ideas, in favour of the materialist claim that it is the social and historical circumstances that people encounter, including the inherited ideas of previous generations, that matter. 'Men make their own history', Marx famously said, 'but not of their own free will; not under circumstances they themselves have chosen but under the given and inherited circumstances with which they are directly confronted' (1973, p.146; first published 1852).

The historical transformation of the international system associated with the emergence and the subsequent uneven and combined development of capitalism is, for Marx as for Teschke, something that happens 'behind the backs' of those who are its agents. There is a discernible logic to this process, but it is not one that resides in the immanent development of ideas. Rather, the logic of the process of social development is located in the characteristic mechanisms generated by given sets of social property relations among people and the material world they must transform in order to live. Different social property relations interacting with one another in ways that are refracted through a pre-given geopolitical environment give rise to configurations of uneven and combined development that can be reconstructed historically, even if they cannot be predicted in advance.

In short, while Marxist theories of international order (and its transformation) recognize that there is a distinct level of geopolitics arising from a historically given plurality of independent political authorities, the specific focus of analysis for the modern international system is the uneven and combined development of capitalism on an increasingly worldwide scale. As Teschke points out, capitalism did not create a plurality of political authorities, nor was its genesis neatly confined within any one of them – though centred in England, the development of capitalism was, from the outset, a national, international and transnational process. Nevertheless, if Teschke's analysis is correct, capitalism did radically transform the nature of the states, anarchy and geopolitics that it inherited from the feudal and absolutist eras. Moreover, the task of a critical

Marxist theory today is still one of comprehending and explaining uneven and combined development as it now operates in the international system, as well as fashioning a political programme for a socialist transformation of that system.

In other words, Marxists have sought to analyse these configurations of uneven and combined development in order to formulate responses to them and, operating as a political ideology, Marxism seeks to shape that development in a socialist direction. As Marx once put it, in the eleventh of his 'Theses on Feuerbach', 'The philosophers have only interpreted the world, in various ways; the point is to change it' (quoted in McLellan, 1977, p.158). For example, Marxist theories of imperialism, briefly reviewed in Chapter 5, and Gramsci's observations on hegemony, were all linked to concrete recommendations for political action. Certainly, the relationship between theoretical understanding of a historical and materialist kind and socialist political practice has been a vexed question throughout the history of Marxism. Marx reckoned that the revolutionary transformation of (international) capitalist society – that is, socialist revolution – 'can only create its poetry from the future, not from the past' (1973, p.149; first published 1852). How to reconcile an emphasis on the historical and material shaping of the course of human history, on the one hand, with the political injunction to consciously and purposively appropriate that history and apply that knowledge to its collective transformation in the future, on the other, is perhaps the central unanswered question of Marxist politics.

It is important to see that it is also, as yet, an unanswered question for any other critique that seeks a purposeful transformation of the international order. Even those strands of analysis that try to distance themselves most emphatically from the substantive theses of Marxism – relating to the central role of the social relations governing material production in human history – do not deny that ideas and forms of social agency are, at least in part, shaped by their social and historical setting. Marx's comment about the making of history – that it is both a product of conscious human agency and that it takes place in circumstances directly confronted from the past – is now a commonplace of all forms of social analysis. The problems that confront a Marxist theory of politics are, in this respect, just as much questions for the advocates of perpetual peace, for those seeking to overcome patriarchal domination on an international scale, or for those who want to see a genuinely post-colonial world.

5 The cultural turn

As theories of international order, both liberalism and Marxism share certain features in common. They both recognize the importance of the geopolitical level in any analysis of the international system, but refuse to accept the realist contention that politics and geopolitics are sufficiently independent of other realms of social interaction to provide the basis for a self-sufficient theory of the international. Both seek to locate the basic components and dynamics of the international system elsewhere than in the striving for power in conditions of anarchy: for liberalism, in the private and collective action of socially located individuals conditioned by material scarcity, conflicting values and social influences; and for Marxism, in the dynamics and properties of social property relations and the kinds of class struggle, political as well as economic, with which these are associated.

Possibly because they share these features (while differing in many other respects, as you have seen), both have been criticized for being insufficiently attentive to the importance of culture, forms of symbolization, signification and representation in international affairs. What might be called the 'cultural turn' in International Studies rests on both a substantive claim about the importance of the politics of representation in the international arena and a theoretical challenge to modes of analysis that are alleged to be insufficiently attentive to the intersubjective constitution of social interests and identities. While constructivist theories of the international order provide an umbrella for much of the analysis that takes the cultural turn in the social sciences seriously for the purposes of analysing the international (see Chapter 14), the challenge goes much wider than that and can be found in many contributions that would not necessarily identify themselves as part of International Studies.

Question

Can you think of some examples of the importance of culture for understanding and analysing the international? Chapters 6, 7, 8 and 9 are particularly relevant in this context.

The contributions to Part 2 on the role of culture, rights and justice in the international system all contain instances of the importance of culture, and specifically of cultural differences, in international affairs. However, we want to highlight just three particular examples: Edward Said's celebrated critique of Orientalism and the culture of imperialism (which you haven't come across in this book in any detail); Samuel Huntington's notion of an incipient 'clash of civilizations' in the wake of the Cold War; and the cosmopolitan claims for the emergence of a transnational, global culture of human rights. Before you read any further, it would be a good idea to refresh your understanding of the two different ways that the term 'culture' is used in Chapter 6, on the one hand, and Chapters 8 and 9, on the other.

5.1 Edward Said and the politics of representation

In a famous critique of what he called 'Orientalism', the Palestinian cultural critic, Edward Said, argued that Western representations of the 'Orient' (essentially the contemporary Middle East) amounted to a form of cultural imperialism (1985; first published 1978). In a later work, *Culture and Imperialism* (1993), Said extended this critical analysis to the representation of the entire colonial and post-colonial world in the literature and art of the West.

Said's point of departure was the claim that Western discourses about the Orient constituted a set of statements and representations with their own internal procedures for validating knowledge and with an intrinsic relation to power. In fact, Said provided two rather different accounts of Orientalism. First, he traced a single, more or less unified cultural and intellectual Western tradition of thinking about the 'Orient', beginning with the Greeks and culminating in the Enlightenment, running from Aeschylus to Marx, which operated with a series of concepts based on a binary opposition between 'the Orient' and 'the Occident'. Sometimes these binary classifications were mapped onto those of 'race' as illustrated in Figures 15.3 and 15.4, although this is an area that Said himself never explored in any detail.

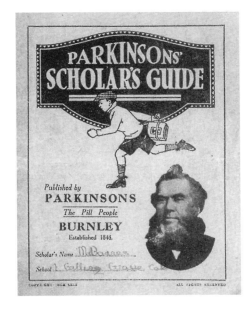

Figure 15.3 Racial classification in an imperial context from an English nineteenth-century textbook

The Races of Mankind.

WHITE RACE.

European Branch	Teutonic Family	Scandinavians, Germans, English.
	Latin	French, Spaniards, Italians.
	Slavonians	Russians, Finns, Bulgarians, Servians, Magyars, Croats, Tchecks, Poles, Lithuanians.
	Greek	Greeks, Albanians.
Aramean Branch	Libyan	Egyptians, Berbers.
	Semitic	Arabs, Jews, Syrians.
	Persian	Persians, Afghans, Armenians.
	Georgian	Georgians.
	Circassian	Circassians, Mingrelians.

YELLOW RACE.

Hyperborean Branch	Lapp Family	Samoiede, Eskimo, Koriak.
Mongolian Branch	Mongol	Mongols, Kalmucks, Buriats.
	Tunguse	Tunguses, Manchus.
	Turk	Turkomans, Kirghis, Osmanlis.
	Yakut	Yakuts.
Sinaic Branch	Chinese	Chinese.
	Japanese	Japanese.
	Indo-Chinese	Burmese, Siamese.

BROWN RACE.

Hindoo Branch	Hindoo Family	Sikhs, Jats, Rajpoots, Mahrattas, Bengalese, Cingalese.
	Malabar	Malabars, Tamals, Telingas.
Ethiopian Branch	Abyssinian	Abyssinians, Berabras, Gallas.
Malay Branch	Malay	Malays, Javanese, Macassars, Dyaks.
	Polynesian	Maoris, Tahitians, Marquesans.

RED RACE.

Southern Branch	Andian Family	Incas, Antis, Andians.
	Pampean	Patagonians, Puelches, Tobas.
Northern Branch	Southern	Aztecs, Mayas.
	North-eastern	Cherokees, Hurons, Iroquois, Sioux, Apaches, Creeks, Comanches.
	North-western	Chinooks, Digger Indians.

BLACK RACE.

Kafirs, Hottentots, Negroes, Papuans, Fijians, Andamans.

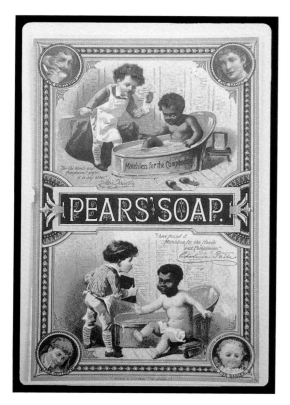 

Figure 15.4   The packaging of cultural difference

Said's first definition of Orientalism is in some danger of treating the 'West' in precisely the way that he complains about in the case of the 'Orient', simply inverting the terms of evaluation. Samir Amin, for example, has argued that the construction of the 'West' is as mythical as that of the 'Orient':

> The opposition Greece = the West/Egypt, Mesopotamia, Persia = the East is itself a later artificial construct of Eurocentrism ... the geographical unities constituting Europe, Africa, and Asia have no importance on the level of history of civilization, even if Eurocentrism in its reading of the past has projected onto the past the modern North–South line of demarcation passing through the Mediterranean.

(Amin, 1989, p.24)

There is a danger that Said's depiction of a Western tradition of Orientalism – more or less unchanged from the Greeks to the Enlightenment – falsely assumes a unity of representation and an intrinsic connection between power and knowledge.

Second, Said defined Orientalism as the culture of colonialism, as the set of representations bound up with the institutions and practices of European colonial rule in the Orient. Orientalism in this sense is:

> the corporate institution for dealing with the Orient – dealing with it by making statements about it, authorizing views of it, describing it, by teaching it, settling it, ruling over it: in short, Orientalism as a Western style of dominating, restructuring, and having authority over the Orient. ... The Orient was viewed as if framed by the classroom, the criminal court, the prison, the illustrated manual. Orientalism, then, is knowledge of the Orient that places things Oriental in class, court, prison or manual for scrutiny, study, judgement, discipline, or governing.

(Said, 1985, pp.3, 41; first published 1978)

What both these conceptions have in common is the fact that the Orient does not speak for itself; it is represented by others, particularly by others in positions of power. Perhaps most importantly for our purposes, Said went on to argue that so powerful was this process that 'the modern Orient ... participates in its own Orientalizing' (1985, p.325; first published 1978). That is to say, forms of discourse that privilege Western ways of acting and knowing as universal continue to dominate thought and action in the post-colonial world. One meaning of the term cultural imperialism is that representations which claim to be objective and universal, to be statements about the way things are, in fact embody distinct perceptions and identities that are the products of undisclosed relations of power.

This is a controversial argument, and we want to try to clarify what is at stake in Said's notion of the culture of imperialism. Central to Said's argument is not the unexceptionable claim that the imbalances in power between European societies and their colonial territories were reflected in the cultures, literatures and arts of the societies concerned, both in the metropolitan and colonial worlds. Nor is it the idea that these representations survived and continue to circulate in the post-colonial world. Instead, Said's basic contention is that the discourses and representations of Orientalism or, more generally, the European cultures of imperialism, were (and remain) essential features of the operation of those imbalances of power. In accounting for the longevity and impact of European imperialism, says Said, the representations of 'others' in the culture of the West 'played a very important, indeed indispensable role' (1993, p.267). Power operates in and through the politics of cultural representation as much as it comes from the barrel of a gun or the competitiveness of an economy. This is one of the central substantive claims of the cultural turn in International Studies (theorized most explicitly in constructivist accounts): the politics of representation matter because culture

Cultural imperialism
Cultural imperialism, according to Edward Said, is the way in which representations of 'others' in the cultures of the European imperial powers, that is, powers creating empires, played 'a very important, indeed indispensable role', serving as 'a vital, informing, and invigorating counterpoint to the economic and political machinery at the material centre of imperialism' (Said, 1993, pp.267–8).

is a medium of power. Challenging inequalities of power at the international level is, *inter alia*, about challenging representations.

This is a claim about the workings of the international system. It is an assertion that certain representations enable some courses of action and render others unthinkable. Consider, for example, the following piece by Jonathan Raban about the US-led war against Iraq of 2003.

> Whatever its immediate apparent outcome, the war on Iraq represents a catastrophic breakdown of the British and American imagination. We've utterly failed to comprehend the character of the people whose lands we have invaded, and for that we're likely to find ourselves paying a price beside which the body-count on both sides in the Iraqi conflict will seem trifling.
>
> Passionate ideologues are incurious by nature and have no time for obstructive details. It's impossible to think of Paul Wolfowitz curling up for the evening with Edward Said's *Orientalism*, or the novels of Naguib Mahfouz, or *Seven Pillars of Wisdom*, or the letters of Gertrude Bell, or the recently published, knotty, often opaque, but useful book by Lawrence Rosen, *The Culture of Islam*, based on Rosen's anthropological fieldwork in Morocco, or Sayyid Qutb's *Milestones*. Yet these, and a dozen other titles, should have been required reading for anyone setting out on such an ambitious liberal-imperial project to inflict freedom and democracy by force on the Arab world. The single most important thing that Wolfowitz might have learned is that in Arabia, words like 'self', 'community', 'brotherhood' and 'nation' do not mean what he believes them to mean. When the deputy secretary of defence thinks of his own self, he – like me, and, probably, like you – envisages an interiorized, secret entity whose true workings are hidden from public view. Masks, roles, personae (like being deputy secretary for defence) mediate between this inner self and the other people with whom it comes into contact. The post-Enlightenment, post-Romantic self, with its autonomous subjective world, is a western construct, and quite different from the self as it is conceived in Islam. Muslims put an overwhelming stress on the idea of the individual as a social being. The self exists as the sum of its interactions with others. Rosen puts it like this: 'The configuration of one's bonds of obligation define who a person is ... the self is not an artefact of interior construction but an unavoidably public act.'
>
> Broadly speaking, who you are is: who you know, who depends on you, and to whom you owe allegiance – a visible web of relationships that can be mapped and enumerated. Just as the person is public, so is the public personal. We're dealing here with a world in which a commitment to, say, Palestine, or to the people of Iraq, can be a defining constituent of the self in a way that westerners don't easily understand. The recent demonstrations

against the US and Britain on the streets of Cairo, Amman, Sanaa and Islamabad may look deceptively like their counterparts in Athens, Hamburg, London and New York, but their content is importantly different. What they register is not the vicarious outrage of the anti-war protests in the west but a sense of intense personal injury and affront, a violation of the self. Next time, look closely at the faces on the screen: if their expressions appear to be those of people seen in the act of being raped, or stabbed, that is perhaps closer than we can imagine to how they actually feel. The idea of the body is central here. On the website of Khilafah.com, a London-based magazine, Yusuf Patel writes: 'The Islamic Ummah is manifesting her deep feeling for a part of her body, which is in the process of being severed.' It would be a great mistake to read this as mere metaphor or rhetorical flourish. Ummah is sometimes defined as the community, sometimes the nation, sometimes the body of Muslim believers around the globe, and it has a physical reality, without parallel in any other religion, that is nowhere better expressed than in the five daily times of prayer.

The observant believer turns to the Ka'aba in Mecca, which houses the great black meteorite said to be the remnant of the shrine given to Abraham by the angel Gabreel, and prostrates himself before Allah at Shorooq (sunrise), Zuhr (noon), Asr (mid-afternoon), Maghreb (sunset) and Isha (night). These times are calculated to the nearest minute, according to the believer's longitude and latitude, with the same astronomical precision required for sextant-navigation. (The crescent moon is the symbol of Islam for good reason: the Islamic calendar, with its dates for events like the Haj and Ramadan, is lunar, not solar.) Prayer times are published in local newspapers and can be found online, and for believers far from the nearest mosque, a $25 Azan clock can be programmed to do the job of the muezzin. So, as the world turns, the entire Ummah goes down on its knees in a never-ending wave of synchronised prayer, and the believers can be seen as the moving parts of a universal Islamic chronometer.

In prayer, the self and its appetites are surrendered to God, in imitation of the prophet Mohammed, the 'slave of Allah'. There are strict instructions as to what to do with the body on these occasions. Each prayer-time should be preceded by ritual ablutions. Then, for the act of prostration, and the declaration of 'Allahu Akbar' (God is great), the knees must touch the ground before the hands, the fingers and toes must point toward Mecca, and the fingers must not be separated. Forehead, nose, both hands, both knees, and the underside of all the toes must be in contact with the ground. The body of the individual believer, identical in its posture to the bodies of all other believers, becomes one with the Ummah, the body of the Islamic community on earth. The abdication of self five times a day, in the company of the faithful millions, is a stern reminder that 'self-sufficient' is one of the essential and exclusive attributes of Allah, mentioned many times in the

Koran. Human beings exist only in their dependency on each other and on their god.

The physical character of this prayer is unique to Islam. Jewry and Christendom have nothing like it. The Ummah, a body literally made up of bodies, has a corporeal substance that is in dramatic contrast to the airy, arbitrary, dissolving and reconstituting nations of Arabia. To see the invasion of Iraq as a brutal assault on the Ummah, and therefore on one's own person, is not the far-fetched thought in the Islamic world that it would be in the west. ... It's no wonder the call of the Ummah effortlessly transcends the flimsy national boundaries of the Middle East – those lines of colonial convenience, drawn in the sand by the British and the French 80 years ago. Wolfowitz repeatedly promises to 'respect the territorial integrity' of Iraq. But integrity is precisely what Iraq's arbitrary borders have always lacked: one might as well talk about respecting the integrity of a chainsaw, a pair of trousers and a blancmange.

(Raban, 2003)

Question

How might Said's views on Orientalism or cultural imperialism, or Raban's arguments, be challenged?

You will have already noted that Said's first definition of Orientalism comes close to attributing a false unity to the West and 'its' representations. Does Jonathan Raban fall into the same trap? How convincing is Raban's distinction between Western and Muslim 'selves' and the meaning and place of religion in social life? Isn't Raban's depiction of Muslims and Islam precisely the kind of thing Said condemns – a view from the outside? Does Raban's argument fit with what you learned from Sami Zubaida in Chapter 8?

In regard to Said's general point about culture as power, Aijaz Ahmad, writing from a Marxist perspective, replies as follows:

What gave European forms of these [ethnocentric] prejudices their special force in history, with devastating consequences for the actual lives of countless millions and expressed ideologically in full-blown Eurocentric racisms, was not some transhistorical process of ontological obsession and falsity [Said's first definition of Orientalism] – some gathering of unique forces in the domain of discourse – but, quite specifically, the power of colonial capitalism, which then gave rise to other sorts of powers.

(Ahmad, 1992, p.184)

5.2 Samuel Huntington and the clash of civilizations

Samuel Huntington's argument about the competing values embodied in different civilizations, which you have encountered already several times (see Chapters 3, 6 and 8), is a very different use of the cultural turn to analyse change in international order. We do not want to repeat those arguments here, instead we want to see how Huntington's thesis provides another way of interpreting the (transformation of) international order.

Question

In terms of the framework we introduced in Section 1, how would you characterize Huntington's thesis about the clash of civilizations and the remaking of world order?

Huntington maintains that 'states remain the principal actors in world affairs' and that they pursue power and wealth as realist and liberal theories suggest, but also that their actions are 'shaped by cultural preferences, commonalities, and differences' (1996, p.21). Huntington says that 'Peoples and countries with similar cultures are coming together. Peoples and countries with different cultures are coming apart. ... Cultural communities are replacing Cold War blocs, and the fault lines between civilizations are becoming the central lines of conflict in global politics' (1996, p.125).

In other words, Huntington argues that the dynamics of the international system – seen in the first instance as a states-system in which states pursue wealth and power – is driven by relations between and among cultures or 'civilizations'. Moreover, it is an important feature of Huntington's argument that the fault lines of cultural conflict and co-operation are not coincident with the borders of states. 'In an age of civilizations', says Huntington, 'Bosnia is everyone's Spain. The Spanish Civil War was a war between political systems and ideologies, the Bosnian War a war between civilizations and religions' (1996, pp.290–1).

Question

What are the implications of clashes of culture and civilization for the states-system according to Huntington?

Countries with common cultures are drawing together – what Huntington terms the 'kin-country' syndrome – and countries divided by culture are 'torn' apart, 'fractured' or 'cleft'; civilizations encounter one another as potential rivals and enemies. This is a theory of international order seen from the socio-cultural sector of collective identities and competing conceptions of rights and justice. It is an account of culture as a set of shared values.

The era of superpower dominance, bipolarity and the Cold War (that is, the contours of the international system from the end of the Second World War to the fall of Communism in 1989–91) was, according to Huntington, one of Western dominance. The political and ideological conflicts of the Cold War were between two *Western* ideologies – liberal democratic capitalism and state socialism. Yet the epoch of Western dominance is now receding – 'the world is becoming more modern and less Western' (Huntington, 1996, p.57) – and, outside of the West, the culture of liberal democratic capitalism 'is probably shared by less than 50 million people or 1 per cent of the world's population and perhaps by as few as one-tenth of 1 per cent of the world's population' (Huntington, 1996, pp.57, 78). If this is so, then it is scarcely surprising that Huntington sees the contemporary reshaping of world order in terms of an 'emerging world of ethnic conflict and civilizational clash' (1996, p.310).

Activity 15.2

Complete the column in Table 15.5 headed 'Socio-cultural sector of collective identities and conceptions of rights and justice' in the light of Huntington's views.

Table 15.5   Analysing international systems: the clash of civilizations

Elements of the international system	Sectors of the international system	
	Political sector of authoritative rule	Socio-cultural sector of collective identities and conceptions of rights and justice
Principal units in the international system		
Structure of relations among units		
Interaction capacity		
Dominant processes of interaction		

Before turning to an alternative, cosmopolitan reading of contemporary cultural developments, we want briefly to note another possibility identified by Huntington – a descent into barbarism. After an extensive discussion of the coming clash of civilizations, Huntington concludes with a few sapient injunctions about the need for a *modus vivendi* between civilizations.

Huntington's recipe for a stable world order is almost the inverse of the liberal formula of multiculturalism at home and universalism abroad. In place of a cosmopolitan, multiculturalism within societies, Huntington advocates the renewal of civilizational identities: 'if the United States is de-Westernized [by the siren calls of multiculturalism], the West is reduced to Europe ... a minuscule and declining part of the world's population on a small and inconsequential peninsula at the extremity of the Eurasian land mass', and internationally he rejects the 'universality of Western culture' because 'it is false; it is immoral; and it is dangerous' (1996, pp.307, 310).

Different civilizations must find common ground, principally by 'renouncing universalism', by agreeing not to intervene in each other's 'internal' affairs, according to Huntington, because of the need to strengthen 'Civilization in the singular':

> Law and order is the first prerequisite of Civilization and in much of the world ... it appears to be evaporating ... On a worldwide basis Civilization seems in many respects to be yielding to barbarism, generating the image of an unprecedented phenomenon, a global Dark Ages, possibly descending on humanity.

(Huntington, 1996, pp.320–1)

Thus, Huntington never fully succumbs to the siren calls of international civilizational chauvinism, advocating at least a limited attempt to discover cosmopolitan values, for he says that 'people in all civilizations should search for and attempt to expand values, institutions, and practices they have in common with people of other civilizations' (1996, p.320).

The idea of a descent into barbarism is an image of dissolution rather than transformation, a world in which competing, overlapping authorities contend for popular loyalties, in which there are few, if any, stable arrangements for political order, and where anarchy means less the absence of authority among states and more the war of each against all in Hobbes's state of nature. Barbarism follows from the collapse of states as more or less independent political authorities capable of governing demarcated territories and populations. Although this is sometimes referred to, benignly, as 'neo-medievalism', it is as well to remember that the culture of the middle ages was one of unremitting war and economic stagnation.

5.3   A global, cosmopolitan culture – but so what?

Question

How convincing is Huntington's thesis of an incipient clash of civilizations?

Huntington's argument turns on a double misreading of the nature of cultural difference in the contemporary world. In the first place, all contemporary civilizations have been formed 'through complex dialogues with other cultures' and, in part as a consequence of this, 'in most cultures that have attained some degree of internal differentiation, the dialogue with the other(s) is internal rather than extrinsic to the culture itself' (Benhabib, 2002, p.ix). Second, it follows from this that:

> any view of cultures as clearly delineable wholes is a view from the outside that generates coherence for the purposes of understanding and control. Participants in the culture, by contrast, experience their traditions, stories, rituals and symbols, tools, and material living conditions through shared, albeit contested and contestable, narrative accounts. From within, a culture need not appear as a whole; rather, it forms a horizon that recedes each time one approaches it.

(Benhabib, 2002, p.5)

Huntington's view of culture is, we suggest, that of an outsider or, at best, that of an elite that claims to speak in a unified manner for what is in reality a diverse and often inchoate amalgam. There are certainly those who present international conflicts as conflicts of culture – one can readily imagine the popularity of Huntington's thesis among the denizens of Kandahar – but we need to have an ear for the other voices that contest those representations from within and that seek a common vocabulary across the world (see, for example, Christina Lamb's stunning memoir of her time in Afghanistan, *The Sewing Circles of Herat*, 2003).

Huntington makes much of what, following Ronald Dore (1984), he calls the 'second generation indigenization phenomenon', the turning away from Western secular ideologies towards indigenous religions and cultures by the masses and the second generation, post-independence elites. (In Huntington's reading, multiculturalism in the West, especially in the USA, represents exactly the same phenomenon.) These assertions of cultural difference are undoubtedly powerful and important developments, but how convincing is the image of a return to an indigenous culture? Dore himself has argued that to the extent that these second generation cultures cannot cope with the demands of modernization, which in popular terms now include many of the freedoms that Huntington takes to be specifically 'Western', they are in turn rejected or reworked by the subsequent generations.

To that extent, the culture of the 'West' has become global and universal, and the conflicts and negotiations around individual rights (including freedom of thought), the rule of law and pluralist forms of politics are now present within all civilizations. These observations are one starting point for the cosmopolitan thesis, that is, the idea that there are values and ideas rich enough and sufficiently widely shared to form the basis for a universal order among diverse individuals and groups.

For instance, Sami Zubaida argues that notions of individual rights and democracy are as pertinent to the Islamic Middle East as they are to Western Europe because they are, at root, ways of controlling the political power of modern states and ordering social life in the context of market capitalist economies (see Chapter 8). There are undoubtedly other ways of ordering social and political relations, but Zubaida contends that these are no longer relevant to the conditions established by the modernity of capitalism and the nation state. In relation to the Islamic Middle East, Huntington's thesis is an example of what Zubaida earlier called the temptation to 'read history backwards', that is, 'seeing the current [Islamic] "revival" as the culmination of a line of development of Islamic politics, rather than as the product of recent combinations of forces and events' (Zubaida, 1989, p.41). As Zubaida argues, after independence the dominant literate discourses of Middle Eastern states have been local adaptations of the social and political thought of the West. Islam is neither a culture nor a civilization, but a religion. Like all religions, it is socially indeterminate. It has only ever prospered as a political force when it has adapted to the terrain of modern political ideologies; political Islam was born when it adapted to the matrix framed by the sovereign state, to nationalism.

Alternatively, in Chapter 9 Jef Huysmans suggests that a global human rights culture is a source of political legitimacy which is 'powerful because it allows people to translate private desires or interests into public claims around which collective support can be mobilized. The emphasis is on the power of the discourse of rights for mobilizing subordinated people.' Huysmans accepts that this remains a 'contested' legitimacy and it is one that is appropriated in different ways in particular localities, 'but it does provide claims with a seriousness that they otherwise might not have had.' Huysmans (and Zubaida) base these contentions on a radically different notion of culture to that employed by Huntington; they reject the idea of culture as blocs of values and see it in terms of a contested field of meaning and action.

In reality, the central question for cosmopolitanism is not whether such values exist, but whether the notion of a political 'community' subject to common governance can be extended from kin, tribe, city and state to the world. That is, does the existence of a global, universalizing culture of human rights and democracy have a significant impact on relations among states? The predominant ideology of contemporary cosmopolitanism is liberal and from this point of view, as the interdependence and co-operation characteristic of relations within a given, politically bounded, society extend to relations between and among societies, so 'one might expect the emergence of a worldwide sense of community' (Brown, 1995, p.103). As we have seen, this is precisely what Kant, among others, anticipated.

Activity 15.3

What is the communitarian rejoinder to this argument? (See Raia Prokhovnik's discussion in Chapter 7.)

There is, however, a powerful objection to this line of argument available within the liberal tradition itself. It comes from Hobbes's unsurpassed argument about the importance of security to durable political order, an argument that many contemporary liberal theorists of a cosmopolitan world order are apt to forget. 'Hobbes differs from developed liberalism only, but certainly', says Leo Strauss, 'by his knowing and seeing *against what* the liberal ideal of civilization has to be persistently fought for ... Hobbes in an unliberal world accomplishes the founding of liberalism' (1996, pp.92–3). If Hobbes is correct in insisting that any notion of political community presupposes a resolution of the problem of security, then a genuinely cosmopolitan order – as distinct from widely shared values and ideas – would have to be built on the basis of a collective security arrangement for all states. This, as realists rightly point out, is a very long way from where the world currently is. Perhaps more critically, the resolution of this problem would have to go beyond that formulated by analogy to Hobbes's idea that establishing sovereignty solves the problem of the state of nature among *individuals* because no serious liberal thinker – not even, in the final analysis, Immanuel Kant – has ever advocated a *world* state (for the complexities of Kant's thinking on this and his ultimately unsuccessful attempt to escape the Hobbesian dilemma, see Cavallar, 1999).

6   Globalization as a transformation of the international system?

We have seen that all of the theories reviewed so far, with the partial exception of Kant's liberalism, have endorsed what we called the problematic of the international in Chapter 1 (after Rosenberg, 2000). Kant's idea of a universalization of cosmopolitan right does come close to transcending the problematic of the international, but even he eventually drew back from the idea of a world state, favouring instead a federation of liberal states. In *The Metaphysics of Morals*, Kant reluctantly concluded that '*perpetual peace*, the ultimate end of all international right, is an idea incapable of realization [principally because an ever larger state would become either despotic or ungovernable, or both]. But the political principles which have this aim, i.e. those principles which encourage the formation of alliances designed to approach the idea itself by a continuous process, are not impracticable' (1991c, p.171; first published 1797). For Kant, liberalism remained, in the end, a set of regulative ideals and empirical tendencies, not a utopia beyond all political differences. Coming from a thinker who more than anyone else fathomed the deepest currents of liberal good sense, we might do well to note these limits.

Nevertheless, the urge to transcend geopolitics is strong. It can be seen, for example, in some of the analyses of transformation that go under the heading of 'globalization' and we now explain why this should be the case. Thus far, we have more or less neglected the row of our framework concerned with the 'interaction capacity' of the international system. All the theories and models you have studied presuppose interaction capacity between and among the units of the international system, for without it the units could not sustain ordered relations and processes of interaction; they would not, therefore, form a system. Yet none of the models or theories we have reviewed places the technologies that facilitate interaction capacity at the centre of their analysis.

In contrast, the thesis that the contemporary international system is undergoing a transformation towards a global network society places interaction capacity right at the centre of its concerns. This thesis, which in Part 3 was illustrated with Manuel Castells's notion of the global network society, is one prominent example of a family of theories that can be grouped under the heading of globalization theories.

6.1   Theories of globalization or globalization theory?

At this point, we want to draw a distinction, introduced and employed by Rosenberg (2000), between 'theories of globalization' and 'globalization theory'. Let us define globalization for the purposes of this argument as a movement towards ever more extensive and intensive social relations of global scope (that is, worldwide social relations), operating at increasing speed – indeed, now in real time as a result of electronic communications – and with greater effect. 'Now, since no-one denies that "worldwide social relations" do indeed exist today in ways and to a degree that they never did before', Rosenberg avers, 'there can be no objection to calls for a theory of globalization, if that means an explanation of how and why these have come about' (2000, p.2).

To illustrate, Teschke's argument about the mutual constitution of capitalist forms of sovereignty, property and markets, and the ways in which these make possible a highly mobile and interdependent international economy is one (Marxist) theory of how economic globalization is entirely compatible with, or more accurately is made feasible by, the sovereign states-system.

Thus, a Marxist theory of globalization might be developed in terms of an account of the course of uneven and combined development, in which the universalization of capitalist relations of production and rule, socially and geographically, is explained as an outcome of the expanded reproduction of capitalism – this was precisely Marx's argument in the middle of the nineteenth century (as you saw in Chapter 14). Another example, pitched at the level of socio-cultural interaction, is the argument of Roland Robertson (1990) that cultural globalization can be explained in terms of the interaction and competition among diverse civilizational identities deriving from the world religions.

Whatever theory of globalization one opts for, it does not necessarily have any determinate implications for the transformation of the international system understood as the combination of a states-system, an international economy and a realm of socio-cultural interaction. Social relations may become ever more global in reach, by virtue of a change in interaction capacity, without fundamentally transforming the basic units of the system, the structure of relations among them, or even the dominant processes of interaction.

Globalization theory
Castells's work represents the latest in a line of theories which argue that globalization, understood as the worldwide distribution of ICTs, the networks of social relations built upon them, and the distributed 'action-at-a-distance' power operating in real time that is consequently made possible, itself explains the changing character of the modern world.

Globalization theory, by contrast, inverts the usual order of explanation in theories of globalization between *explanandum*, that which is to be explained, and *explanans*, that which does the explaining. Whereas a theory of globalization seeks to explain how global social relations come about, globalization theory posits 'globalization' as the *explanans*. In globalization theory, says Rosenberg, 'what presents itself initially as the *explanandum* – globalization as the developing outcome of some historical process – is progressively transformed into the *explanans*: it is globalization which now explains the changing character of the modern world' (2000, p.3).

What, then, is 'globalization' and what does it explain about the potential for transformation in the contemporary international system? There is no single answer to this question but a leading candidate is that 'globalization' refers to the worldwide distribution of ICTs, the networks of social relations built upon them, and the distributed 'action-at-a-distance' power operating in real time that is consequently made possible. Let us consider this in a little more detail.

The general thesis at work here, as expressed by Anthony Giddens (1984), is that the means or media of communication by which information is produced, stored, reproduced and distributed directly influence the nature of the social relations which they help to organize. Different media of communication (and transportation) facilitate different ways of organizing social activities in time and across space. Expressly, analysts such as Castells (1997) suggest that when digital media are sufficiently widely diffused, operating instantaneously across multiple locations and jurisdictions, a form of decentred, action-at-a-distance power comes to dominate all social activities, such that the process as a whole is beyond the control of any given set of hierarchically organized bodies. As you have seen, Castells argues that distributed digital media provide the basis for a step-change in the importance of one particular logic of social organization, namely, the network, a form of organization which is specifically capable of challenging relations of power founded on the hierarchies of the state.

Although these ideas attained a certain prominence in the 1990s, they are not especially novel. In many ways, the ideas of versions of globalization theory that came to the fore in the 1990s were anticipated by perhaps the first real globalization theory of the transformation of the international system – that of Marshal McLuhan in the mid 1960s. Announcing the coming of the 'global village', McLuhan (1994; first published 1964) argued that while mechanization in industrial society had expanded the power of the territorial and hierarchically ordered nation state, the coming of the electrical age would reverse this process:

> The stepping-up of speed from the mechanical to the instant electric form reverses explosion into implosion. In our present electrical age the imploding or contracting energies of our world now clash with the old expansionist and traditional patterns of organization. ... the alteration of social groupings, and the formation of new communities, occurs with increased speed of information movement. ... [centres of power appear everywhere in an] instant implosion and an interfusion of space and function.

(McLuhan, 1994; first published 1964, pp.47, 91, 93)

Traditional patterns of organization, specifically the hierarchically ordered territory of the sovereign state, are challenged by new centres of power, increasingly networked with one another by computer-mediated communications, so that 'we are witnessing in fact the diffusion of the power of surveillance and of violence ... into society at large' (Castells, 1997, p.301). The end result is that the authority of the state is fast becoming one node in a wider network of private and public, legal and illegal, powers. Since the modern international system is, in part, constituted by a plurality of more or less independent sovereign states, an unbundling of state power, and its redistribution across mobile, ever-shifting networks, would indeed represent a transformation of the system.

Unlike images of the dissolution of the state (Huntington's 'barbarism'), the idea that the authority of the state is being bypassed by network forms of organization is one in which order is sustained, but by new means. Order in the global network society arises not from the claims of sovereignty in relation to territories and populations, but from the social co-ordination achieved in networks. What James Rosenau has called 'sovereignty-free' actors operate in these networks more or less independently from the claims of the state (see Chapters 12 and 13). In a world of proliferating networks, states may survive only to the extent that they learn how to conform their institutions and activities to the logic of the former. Superficially, the political sector of the international system may continue to look like a states-system based on sovereign states, yet the reality is that transnational, and increasingly global, networks of co-ordination serve to shape practices of rule and governance.

It may be understandable that, given the radical nature of these claims, globalization theory is rather ambiguous about whether, first, globalization is in the process of transcending the problematic of the international or whether, secondly, it is one factor contributing to changes in its distinct form. Arguments of the first kind, as in the theory of cosmopolitan democracy associated with David Held (1995) and others, tend to rehearse many of the themes, and problems, we have explored in Kant's liberalism. The second contention must argue its case against those – realists and Marxists, for example – who insist on the underlying continuities in the structures of the modern states-system and international capitalist economy. Just how much difference do Information and Communication Technologies (ICTs) and an expansion of transnational, networked forms of co-ordination really make?

You may recall that in Chapter 12 Giles Mohan and Helen Yanacopulos expressed some doubts about how far processes of globalization and the rise of sovereignty-free actors had gone in challenging the sovereignty of states, thereby questioning many of the bolder claims about radical transformation.

Question

How does the rise of the global network society impact on technological change and the international economy?

These issues are discussed in some detail in Chapters 10 and 11, and we shall not repeat them here. Suffice to say that Suma Athreye, Roberto Simonetti and Grahame Thompson express a certain scepticism about the degree to which ICTs mark a qualitative shift either in the relationship of technological change to capitalist development or in the ways in which the international economy, including transnational corporations, are organized.

In Part 3, the thesis that a global network society is radically transforming the international order of either the states-system or the capitalist world economy was treated with considerable caution. None of the chapters there presented evidence or argument to support the idea of a transcendence of the problematic of the international. They even went so far as to cast some doubt on the impact of ICTs and transnational, potentially global, networks in making radically new forms of geopolitics.

Nevertheless, it is important to see what kind of theory of transformation is embedded in the claims of McLuhan, Castells, Giddens and many others. Essentially, these analysts are arguing that changes in the means and modalities of communication, particularly the advent of computer-mediated knowledge production and communication, are facilitating the emergence of transnational and global networks of co-ordinated social activity. In turn, these networks are said to be fundamentally reshaping the nature of political power and economic activity. That is to say, globalization theory seeks to explain what it identifies as a transformation of the international system by reference to changes in the *interaction capacity* of the system, specifically in terms of the distribution of ICTs and the networked forms of action and power that they facilitate. In its boldest formulation, globalization theory sees the global village of the digital age as a movement beyond geopolitics – hence the global *village*. In its weaker form, it identifies ICTs and the associated real time co-ordination of dispersed activities as a major force in reshaping geopolitics.

Activity 15.4

In the light of what you have learned about the global network society thesis in Part 3, complete Table 15.6. Assume the impact of a worldwide shift to ICTs as the dominant means of communication in the 'Interaction capacity' row.

Table 15.6   Analysing international systems: a global network society

Elements of the international system	Sectors of the international system	
	Political sector of authoritative rule	Economic and technological sector of production, trade and innovation
Principal units in the international system		
Structure of relations among units		
Interaction capacity		
Dominant processes of interaction		

7 Conclusion

This chapter has covered a great deal of ground and we make no attempt to summarize it here. We have tried to pull together material from the rest of the book in an attempt to respond, more systematically than Parts 1–3 were able to do, to our third framing question introduced in Chapter 1. That question was, 'Is the international system changing and, if so, by whose agency?' We have reviewed a range of ways of thinking about transformations in, and of, the international system from a wide variety of perspectives, some fairly conventional, others less so. Furthermore, we have tried to convey some of the richness of insight into these questions generated in International Studies. We have also explored the idea of theory operating as critique by looking at some of the taken for granted assumptions at work in different accounts of the international, since critique may itself lead to transformation. If any of this, including the rest of the book, encourages you to think about these matters in new ways, and with greater insight, our key objective will have been realized.

Further reading

For a balanced and careful review of the impact of globalization on the state and its implications for theories of international order, see Clark, I. (1999) *Globalization and International Relations Theory*, Cambridge, Cambridge University Press.

A bold, comparative and historical study of international systems that casts considerable light on the distinctive features of the modern international system can be found in Buzan, B. and Little, R. (2000) *International Systems in World History*, Oxford, Oxford University Press.

For a hugely informative and historically sensitive guide to a wide range of social and political thinking about international order and its transformation, see Boucher, D. (1998) *Political Theories of International Relations*, Oxford, Oxford University Press.

Answers to activities

Activity 2.1

Under feudal relations, increased personal gain for lords relies on political accumulation, particularly control over more land and a dependent peasantry. As the right of inheritance was limited to a lord's first born by around the year 1000, such accumulation could take place only through internal expansion (increasing the land under cultivation) or by outward expansion. The limits on further internal expansion from around 1050 meant that outward expansion was the only route open, particularly for the younger noble sons.

Activity 2.2

Feudal state formation in France was premised on weak organization of the ruling class leading to peasant freedom and the gradual, protracted and imperfect building of a feudal monarchy. Feudal state formation in England was premised on strong organization of the ruling class leading to the imposition and strengthening of serfdom and the consolidation of a centrally organized feudal monarchy.

Activity 2.3

This map illustrates three main characteristics. First, in comparison with Europe under the Carolingian Empire, Europe has become a multi-actor system. In the first map (Figure 2.2), Europe is dominated by the Carolingian Empire; in this map (Figure 2.3) it has become a system of mostly independent states. While those polities within the Holy Roman Empire did not achieve formal independence following the Peace of Westphalia and their 'sovereignty' remained legally strictly limited, some of them, notably the Austrian, Prussian, Saxonian and Bavarian dynasties, developed typically absolutist foreign policies. It is this multi-actor nature of the European states-system that realists and others point to when claiming Westphalia as a key turning point. Second, only one of these states – Great Britain – is a modern state. The map of Europe is dominated by absolutist states which have a geopolitical logic distinct from modern states. Third, the Peace of Westphalia itself was agreed primarily between absolutist states led by France and Sweden. England was the only major power *not* to be a signatory (Rosenberg, 1994).

The multi-actor nature of the European system remained up to the modern period (although the actual boundaries continued to shift through the Napoleonic wars, the revolutions and unifications of the nineteenth century and the First World War), but the nature of the states that constituted it and their patterns of conflict and co-operation were fundamentally transformed.

Activity 2.4

The completed table might look like Table 2.5 (overleaf).

Table 2.5   Feudal, absolutist and capitalist geopolitics compared

	Feudalism	Absolutism	Capitalism
Nature of sovereignty	'Parcellized sovereignty'; personalized and decentralized among lords sharing an oligopoly in the means of violence	Personalized and centralized in the monarch; the state is the private patrimonial property of the ruling dynasty	Centralized and de-personalized; residing in the state as an impersonal legal order with a monopoly in the means of coercion
Public and private/ political and economic	Political and economic: undifferentiated (fused)	Public affairs of the state directly linked with and fused to the private interests of the ruling dynasty	Separation in law between a private realm and a public sphere; differentiation between state and market
Relationship of the ruling class to the state	Ruling class *is* 'the state'; the feudal polity forms an ensemble of lordships or a 'state of associated persons'	Ruling classes directly connected to the state (the monarchy) in order to extract economic benefits	Ruling classes rely on the state indirectly to uphold their private rights to property and contract
Nature of accumulation	Political and geopolitical based on investment in the means of coercion	Political and geopolitical based on investment in the means of coercion	Economic competition on markets based on investment in the means of production
Economic development	Relatively lethargic and cyclical; governed by eco-demographic cycles	Relatively lethargic and cyclical; governed by eco-demographic cycles	Dynamic, self-sustaining, but crisis-prone; governed by permanent re-investment in the means of production

Military development	Dynamic; governed by permanent re-investment in the means of coercion	Dynamic; governed by permanent re-investment in the means of coercion	Conjunctural, sustained by dynamic market competition, but dependent on political conjunctures and threats to open world market.
Character of external policy	Feuding, territorial expansion, land reclamation, conquest, strategic marriages	Territorial-imperial expansion mediated by dynastic alliances, wars of succession, mercantile wars and strategic marriages	Dependent on the conjectures and crises of capitalism. Multilateral policies to promote and manage an international economy open to trade and investment among private parties, but also periods of economic nationalism and inter-imperialist war.
Nature of the balance of power	No balance of power	Big powers eliminate smaller powers, while a compensatory equilibrium maintains a dynamic balance among the big powers	Active balancing by Britain on the continent combined with imperial dominance of the oceans, followed by an extended period of geopolitically mediated, uneven development of capitalism on a worldwide basis
Form of territoriality	Shifting, fragmented, overlapping, non-contiguous, internally differentiated (marches)	Internally consolidated but shifting in scope	Bounded, fixed and uniform, but 'porous' regarding economic and other transactions

Activity 3.1

The answer is that:

1   The rules of deterrence are regulative rules – they regulate an already existing activity (threatening each other with nuclear weapons) among pre-existing independent actors (states exist before they possess nuclear weapons) around a shared interest (survival).

2   The rules of sovereignty are constitutive in this context – they serve to define the very possibility of international politics and define who the players in the game of international politics will be.

Activity 3.2

The clearest examples of constitutive rules from Sections 2.1 to 2.6 are (a) the principle of mutual recognition which in part defines the members of an international society as sovereign states, and (b) the balance of power as a maxim which in part determines how those states behave.

Activity 3.3

1   European interaction with the wider world, and the double standard on which it was based, was justified initially on religious grounds; and then on the liberal, secular terms of the lack of respect for individual rights and liberties among 'uncivilized' pre-political peoples. This in turn developed into racist justifications for the empire based on a belief in European superiority. Recognition of a right to national self-determination within Europe paved the way (in the wake of the Second World War) for the elevation of this right to the international level, accompanied by the recognition of universal human rights.

2   On one reading, the post-war creation of new universal norms was still a product of European expansion and, therefore, will always carry with it the particularism of its origins. However, against this, I would refer you back to the argument that I made in Section 2.3 that particular European origins do not prevent norms of international society from becoming universal, particularly if they are based, as Hobbes and others have argued, on reason rather than on power. In addition, we might note that the reconstruction of international society after the Second World War was, in some senses, based on the wreckage of European attempts to maintain the double standard of the colonial era. The contradiction of this double standard was hard enough to maintain with respect to the non-European world. When it came home to Europe, in the form of Nazism, the Western powers were forced to re-think.

Activity 4.1

The quotations contain two key liberal ideas:

1   that the liberalization of trade and commerce will have mutually beneficial effects for all

2   that freedom and democracy can spread across the world and increase the potential for international peace and co-operation.

The imperative for political action, therefore, is to pursue policies that liberalize economic relations and promote democracy and human rights internationally.

Activity 4.2

1   Deudney and Ikenberry seem to be arguing a case at the third level of transformation – that is, their claims about co-binding and semi-sovereignty imply a far-reaching change in the nature of relations among liberal states. This has displaced balance of power considerations among them and introduced a different conception of how sovereign power can be exercised collectively rather than individually (partly through the specific circumstances of German and Japanese reconstruction). However, it stops short of the fourth level in that clearly there is a non-liberal world (particularly the communist block) against which the liberal states continue to balance (see their discussion of NATO to reinforce this point).

2   You may also have noticed that, for the most part, Deudney and Ikenberry are discussing changes in the configuration of state preferences (Moravcsik's third assumption) among liberal capitalist states. In my presentation of their thesis it is largely taken for granted that liberal states share some common purposes (although they do in fact acknowledge that this is based on some common interests and norms among the populations of these states). However, note also that they share Moravcsik's emphasis on the importance of the nature of state institutions (his second assumption) in their argument about the US political system.

Activity 4.3

1   The hegemonic stability thesis ultimately rests on the view that it is the distribution of power across the system – particularly whether one state has a preponderance of power – which determines the character of the states-system. That is, it remains, like the realist view on which it is based, a top-down view. The states-system is anarchic internationally, and states ultimately have to think about their own survival. Relative gains therefore remain crucial and limit the degree of co-operation that is possible. While it accepts that state preferences are a factor (the hegemonic state has to see some benefits from economic openness in order to pursue it), its ability to realize this and its interest in this is ultimately subordinate to concerns of relative power and security.

2   The degree of transformation in the states-system that is possible is therefore inherently limited. At the very most a move towards the first level of transformation that liberals posit (that states with shared aims can co-operate in pursuit of those aims) might be possible. But even here, this is dependent on a state's security not being threatened by the relative gains of other states.

Activity 4.4

1   The key variables are:

   – liberals: state–society relations

   – hegemonic stability theory: the distribution of power resources

   – bipolarity thesis: the distribution of power resources

   – neo-Gramscian Marxists: state–society relations understood in terms of the development of the productive forces and class relations of capitalism.

2   You might expect the liberals to forecast the consolidation of the liberal order. Those focusing on power distributions tend to predict the re-emergence of power balancing against the USA. Marxists would expect shifts in the patterns of international accumulation to be reflected in changes in relations between the USA and its Western allies, and to see the spread of capitalism into formerly communist countries.

Activity 5.1

1   For Lenin, the crucial relationship is that between capitalist firms and 'their' home state, which translates economic competition into political and military conflict. For both ultra-imperialism and super-imperialism, the underlying idea is that the stability of the capitalist world as a whole depends upon the performance of certain global political functions – stabilizing the periphery, combating ideological challenges, solving conflicts of policy among the leading centres of capital accumulation – in order to uphold the common interests of different, and potentially rival, capitalist classes and states. Both ultra- and super-imperialism refer to co-operative relations among the leading capitalist powers (rather than rivalry), but for super-imperialism co-operation is enforced by the superior power of one state.

2   A number of themes are shared between these Marxist debates and those discussed in Chapter 4. Among these you might have noted the similarity between Lenin's and Cordell Hull's view of the destructive results of economic competition becoming politicized. The key difference is that, as a liberal, Hull thought that they could be kept separate, whereas Lenin saw the politicization of economic competition as an unavoidable consequence of capitalism. You could also draw parallels between the view of liberals and of Kautsky that shared interests in absolute gains can produce co-operation among capitalist states, as opposed to the realist and super-imperialist emphasis on the role of an over-arching hegemonic power in organizing such co-operation.

Activity 5.2

I argued that US power in the Atlantic arena was based on the first and third senses, roughly a combination of Gramsci's and Kautsky's views, and I suggested that US military dominance (its super-imperialist aspects) served to advance collective interests, not to pacify inter-imperial rivalries. In relation to China and Russia, by contrast, I argued that US super-imperialism remains important but that future relations will be governed by America's ability to mobilize Gramscian and Kautskian forms of power.

Activity 6.1

There is no answer to this activity because it is based on your own personal reflections. However, make sure to note some of the potential political consequences of different aspects of your identity.

Activity 6.2

There are a couple of ways in which this paradox was manifested. The first is the 'cartographers nightmare' of the principle of self-determination (a state for a people) meeting the reality of the mix of ethnicities, cultures and languages on the ground. The second is the resulting 'solution' of nation states proclaiming the right of self-determination and for a state to represent 'its' culture, which was constrained by the responsibility of the state to protect the rights of minority populations and cultures within its borders.

Activity 6.3

There is some evidence to support both views. Certainly, references to existing ethnic and cultural groups in Europe after the First World War and in Asia and Africa after the Second World War suggest a primordialist definition of nations onto which the political map is imposed. From this point of view, the problem of nation-building lies in how to match the boundaries of states to these pre-existing groups, and how to forge a national cohesion from the disparate cultures within a state. However, there is much to suggest a modernist view of nations as vehicles for, and arising out of, state creation. Indeed, many of the states, and the movements which formed them, were political creations, and in some nationalism was a tool to consolidate the new states and their leader's position within them. This point is encapsulated in the quotation from Massimo d'Azeglio in Section 3.2 about 'making Italians'.

Activity 7.1

You may recall that, in Chapter 3, Simon Bromley defended the idea of universal rights against the charge of Eurocentrism on the grounds that, although modern conceptions of rights were first formulated in Europe, they can still be relevant to people in other cultures. He also argued that the basic notions underpinning rights – essentially those of the moral equality of all human beings – can be found in many other cultures.

Activity 7.2

1   There is in fact sometimes no clear dividing line between principle and practice; that is, the line between the two criticisms is often blurred. Nevertheless, objections in principle might include the argument that universal rights are Western in origin and therefore cannot be universal (see Chapter 3 for a counter to this view). However, the related criticism that Western countries criticize others' human rights records and not their own is not an objection to rights in principle, just to the uses of rights discourse by Western states. Similarly, the criticism of DFID is about the non-fulfilment of rights in practice not principle. Similar distinctions can be made about the feminist critiques. The objection that women's rights are particularly hard to enforce is one of practice – a product of patriarchy. The argument that specifying universal rights obscures the different problems that women face is more of a principled objection to universal rights claims. The objection that rights at the international level create the problem of against whom rights should be claimed is a principled objection, although it leads to the practical problem that rights are not in fact realized for many people.

2   Criticisms that pertain particularly to the international level are the Western origin of rights, and the problem of against whom rights claims should be made. Feminist criticisms could apply to rights viewed entirely in the domestic sphere.

Activity 7.3

This one is difficult. You might find it helpful to work through the following argument of David Beetham.

> [I]t is difficult to see why we should accord equal respect to other cultures except on the basis of the equal human dignity that is due to the individuals who are members of those cultures. And if we accord them equal dignity, is it not as those capable of self-determination and as having a legitimate claim to an equal voice in their own collective affairs? To be sure, we have long since progressed from the simplistic Enlightenment assumption that equality denoted sameness. Indeed, the capacity for self-determination is precisely a capacity to be *different*, both individually and collectively, and a claim to have these differences respected by others. But that capacity also sets limits to the cultural practices that can be endorsed by the principle of equal respect. ... *Without* a strong principle of equal respect for persons, there can be no reason except power considerations why we should not treat cultural difference as a basis for exclusion, discrimination or subordination; *with* it, we are bound to take a critical attitude to those

cultural practices that infringe it, and not merely because we find them different and alien from our own.

(Beetham, 1999, p.15)

Activity 7.4

If all states uphold universal human rights, there is no tension between the claims of sovereign states to national self-determination and universal human rights. If some states do not uphold such rights, the claims cannot be reconciled. How competing claims can best be managed depends on one's evaluation of the weight of the respective claims. See the answer given to Activity 7.3.

Activity 8.1

1   The unity of Islam lies in the Quran, belief in the teachings and example of the Prophet, the rituals of worship and the role of the *Shari'a*. But note that even here different strands of Islam put different emphasis on these different elements and interpret their meaning in different ways. This diversity within Islam is further extended when one contrasts its political orientations – conservative, militant and reformist.

2   These dimensions in turn can be characterized by their social and political content: conservative Islam is socially authoritarian and reactionary and attracts support from many of the wealthier classes; militant Islam is directed against established 'infidel' authorities, which are often violently attacked; and reformist Islam is based on the reformist agendas of the intelligentsia and businessmen seeking to adjust Islamic practice to the needs of modern government and commerce. While the first two are opposed to notions of universal rights and emphasize obligations to authority and a patriarchally defined community, reformists seek different ways to accommodate rights and democracy in the context of upholding Islam.

Activity 8.2

It argues that international alignments and local political struggles shaped the public face of Islamic cultures, rather than vice versa. Which argument do you find more persuasive? Do they necessarily contradict each other?

Activity 9.1

The global propagation of rights is a cultural process in a double sense:

1   The specific sets of rights propagate particular kinds of values that can be contested by people that prioritize different values.

2   The propagation of sets of rights also propagates a rights culture, that is, a specific construction of self, sociality and agency. People define themselves and are defined by others as individual holders of rights and relate to others on the basis of the rights that they hold.

Activity 9.2

1   The section introduced two elements:

(a)   The imposition of human rights is resisted to protect traditional cultures. This argument rests on the assumption that claiming universal protection of human rights supports the global imposition of a Western liberal culture and destroys regional or local cultural traditions.

(b)   The imposition of human rights and resistance to it can also bear upon the economic and political power struggles between states. This argument assumes that culture is a political and/or economic power resource. Challenges to cultural identity then become challenges to a power resource of a state.

2   Useful elements that the section introduced are:

(a)   The protection of cultural identity is used to shield authoritarian governments from human rights that can encourage their population to resist them.

(b)   Individual freedom rights, such as free speech and the right of free assembly, are universally valuable because they allow individuals to articulate their values. This argument assumes that liberal rights cultures do not impose values as such but that they facilitate communication about cultural values among and between members of different cultures. In other words, they create conditions in which people can say what they value most instead of being told by governments what they should value.

Activity 9.3

Global rights can be powerful in three ways:

1   Through judicial and political institutions that have the capacity to make credible judgments and to enforce these judgments (an institutional approach to power). See also Chapter 7.

2   Through a great power or superpower that supports a consistent application of rights and their enforcement (a state power approach).

3   Through the capacity of rights discourse to provide those engaged in social and political contests in local and/or regional situations with a degree of legitimacy that depends on the international assertion of a global rights framework (a political–discursive approach to power that emphasizes the power of discourse or ideas). See also Chapter 8.

In the first two approaches the power of rights depends on the power of institutions and/or states to impose the application of rights. In other words, rights are seen as part of an international legal order made powerful either by powerful states or by international authority. In the third approach, the power of rights depends on the global legitimacy of rights and their local appropriation in the form of political mobilization in the name of these rights. In other words, rights are interpreted as a specific mode of political practice. The three approaches to the power of rights thus imply two different understandings of how rights function in world politics: imposition versus appropriation.

Activity 9.4

Two elements are important for your answer:

1   In the political–discursive approach to power the process of cultural globalization operates through local appropriation and the contesting of global rights, rather than through a global imposition of rights. The perspective changes from studying clashes between cultures in global international relations to studying how cultural globalization exists politically in local contexts.

2   This interpretation of the political encounter between global rights culture and local cultural tradition implies a change in the concept of culture. Interpretations of cultural globalization as a process of cultural imposition or a global clash between cultures often understand culture as a static, pre-given constellation of shared values. The reinterpretation in this section changes this homogenous and static concept of culture to a heterogeneous and dynamic concept. Cultures are not blocs of shared values but fields in which the 'inhabitants' of a cultural community contest hierarchies of values and acceptable patterns of life. In other words, cultures are always already contested from within. Cultural practice is thus not a static repetition of a shared cultural identity but a dynamic and contested appropriation and re-negotiation of values. This view makes it possible to interpret cultural globalization as a process that gains its political significance not simply from processes of the global imposition of and resistance to liberal rights culture, but also from its appropriation and contestation in always already contested and changing local cultural and political situations.

Activity 9.5

This is what I think this chapter does:

1   It starts from a cosmopolitan position that there is a global rights culture.

2   It moves away from a full endorsement of the cosmopolitan view by arguing that global rights work in practice by being appropriated in local cultures. In the process of local appropriation these global rights can become embedded in a local culture. They may change local values. At the same time the practical meaning of the global rights in that particular culture may change as well.

3   That means that this chapter – especially in the last two sections – develops a third position which is neither fully cosmopolitan nor fully communitarian. In the chapter I take the view that a cosmopolitan attitude to universal rights will, in practice, take account of communitarian concerns that emphasize that rights are cultural because:

(a) Rights are cultural products.

(b) Culture is mutable.

(c) Global rights discourses can and will be appropriated in different cultures, which is always at least partly a process of adapting both the appropriating culture and the meaning of global rights.

(d) The cosmopolitan culture of global rights has to exist for the process of appropriation of global rights to be possible.

Activity 10.1

US and German responses to the potential of electricity were different in the following respects:

■   The USA depended on its domestic market (connected by the railroad), and its large domestic market enabled it to grow in a broad-based way from producing consumer goods to capital goods. Germany depended on the European market and demand from the growing textile industry for chemical dyes to grow its industrial base.

■   An interesting development in the USA was the emergence of the machine tool sector as a specialized technology sector. The USA also developed a system of manufactures based on standardized components to exploit economies of scale.

■   German chemical firms pioneered the system of industrial R&D, and these firms had close links with the university sector. The lack of anti-cartel legislation also meant that firms had a greater tendency to co-operate with each other.

■   The two economies developed different forms of corporate finance to deal with the large-scale technology investments required during this period.

Activity 10.2

Investing in a brand name such as Virgin can confer both economies of scale and economies of scope. If there are significant fixed costs to advertising there will be economies of scale to be reaped. The costs of advertising a given product are very unlikely to rise in proportion to the number of units of that product that are sold. Equally, once a brand is established in the public mind for one product this may confer advantages in the sale of other products, thereby generating economies of scope.

Activity 10.3

The most striking result from Table 10.2 is that mass migration, capital flows and trade – all aspects of international economic integration – mattered for wage convergence. In Sweden, for example, the direct integration of factor markets – that is, markets in capital and labour – accounted for 45.9–51.4 per cent of the wage convergence on Britain and 58.6–75.4 per cent of the wage convergence on the USA. Mass migration, for example, accounted for all the wage convergence between Italy and Ireland on the one hand and the USA on the other. Portugal and Spain seem to have paid a high price for poor schooling. Notice also that trade seems to have been much less important than flows of labour and capital in explaining the convergence between leaders and followers.

Activity 11.1

1   The inequalities measured by these indicators are highest in Latin America, followed by Africa and the Pacific Rim, and are lowest in the rich OECD countries.

2   Broadly speaking these differences are confirmed on both measures. But the quintile ratio provides a more striking contrast than the Gini coefficient, for which the measures across regions are more similar.

Activity 11.2

1   You can check that the Theil index satisfies the additive decomposition property by adding together the Theil index for 'between countries' and the Theil index for 'within countries' for any given year. The result should be the same as the number for global inequality. Remember that the numbers may not be exactly equal due to rounding to three decimal places.

2   In 1998 the 'between countries' inequality Theil index was 0.513 and the global index was 0.716, so 'between country' inequality accounted for 71.6 per cent of global inequality ($0.513/0.716 \times 100 = 71.6$ to one decimal place). Within country inequality therefore accounts for the remaining 28.4 per cent.

Activity 12.1

For Peretti, micromedia (personal computers and the like) have the advantage of being widely accessible without the huge costs associated with mass media production. Contacting and connecting with millions of people, therefore, is possible for individuals and groups from all walks of life. Micromedia also enable access to 'democratic' media sites such as Plastic.com and Slashdot.com (the ones Peretti mentions) and thus a mass audience. Traditional, powerful media corporations can be bypassed.

Mass media clearly retain some advantages. Peretti notes that most email forwards die before they reach a critical mass, whereas mass media can reach the public domain without having to rely on the commitment of private individuals. And the media corporations that control the mass media, and the companies such as Nike that can access them, remain very powerful.

Activity 12.2

As Simon Bromley discussed in Chapter 3, Section 2.1, sovereignty is a claim made by states to a right to rule over a particular territory and population. The recognition of such claims by other states and actors makes them much more effective against rival powers, such as religious and economic organizations. In this sense, actors which are 'global', that is, free of any particular territory, could be said to be sovereignty-free as they are not subject to the rule of any particular state. This can be challenged in three ways, however. First, the extent to which any actors are really free of territory in this sense is highly questionable: people and groups have to live somewhere, companies have to have offices and production facilities, and even the Internet (which is discussed in Chapter 13) relies on servers and communications links that can be monitored and censored by governments. Second, such global actors may also be subject to regulation by the institutions of international governance, which may themselves owe their existence, authority and effectiveness to sovereign states. And third, even in the absence of international governance, states generally hold each other accountable for harmful actions originating on their territories.

Activity 12.3

■ *What political circumstances precipitated the need and desire to form or activate these networks?*

Globalization has seen an unprecedented level of flexibility in and integration of production, which has translated into stricter conditions in the factories of the developing world and a feminization of the workforce. This has, in part, been secured through political repression and neo-liberal policies, which make local activism hard. Hence labour activists worked with global trade union networks and multilateral organizations such as the ILO. These networks included NGOs, which together worked towards a form of 'social movement unionism'. These networks are less hierarchical and women are more active in them than they are in 'traditional' trade unions.

■ *How have the networks utilized ICTs to facilitate their campaigns and to what extent did the technology make a qualitative difference to their effectiveness?*

It is important to recognize that, alongside ICTs, more 'traditional' media such as TV (the CBS documentary) and books (Naomi Klein's *No Logo*) were also present. The networks were effectively loose coalitions based largely around websites and e-campaigning, although the trade union movement came to this new technology relatively late. We also saw in Section 1.1 how one piece of resistance – Peretti's 'sweatshop' emails – was quite spontaneous and uncoordinated.

■ *Given that networks are likely to form around shared values, what have been the tensions within networks over their goals and strategies?*

The most entrenched tension was the perennial trade-off between worker's rights and competition for investment, with too much activism scaring off investors. Second, there were issues of representation and debates about whether small organizations would lose identity if they became part of a large coalition. Third, there were tensions connected to sovereignty and the issue of whether transnational networks undermined national processes or effected a form of colonization by Northern campaigners. Finally, there were tensions over language and technology and the ability to frame issues in locally meaningful ways.

Activity 12.4

■ *What political circumstances precipitated the need and desire to form or activate these networks?*

The debt crisis from the 1970s onwards and the Structural Adjustment era of the 1980s generated significant national resistance. In the 1990s, in the lead up to the millennium, the debt issue became more co-ordinated. At one level this was about reframing the issue in moral terms: forgiveness, justice and equality. Much of this originated from the existing global network of churches but it involved a wide spectrum of organizations. The campaign targeted key global meetings (the G-7 and so on), but the eventual debt reduction required national agreement around HIPC and PRSPs from recipient governments.

■ *How have the networks utilized ICTs to facilitate their campaigns and to what extent did the technology make a qualitative difference to their effectiveness?*

The campaign mixed ICT-based activism with 'actual' protest (demonstrations, petitions and so on) as well as the involvement of high-profile celebrities. The debt cancellation lobby created dense networks of organizations engaged in lobbying and information exchange. This required the co-ordination of numerous local and national campaigns, which was only possible through ICTs.

■ *Given that networks are likely to form around shared values, what have been the tensions within networks over their goals and strategies?*

There were ideological differences over the outcomes, with some arguing for unconditional debt cancellation and others prepared to accept some conditionality (for example, over PRSPs). There were also tensions created by differences in the North–South agendas and questions of representation. Finally, there was debate about whether the debt issue represented a discrete campaign or part of an ongoing struggle against globalization and underdevelopment.

Activity 13.1

The completed table might look like Table 13.2.

Table 13.2

	Relationship of non-state actors to states	Tendencies to inclusion and exclusion	Sources of order and disorder
Merchants	The state can regulate private financial institutions through, among other things, the central banks, while global PFIs can utilize liberalized international currency and capital markets to develop new financial products and new sources of profit.	There are inequalities between countries exercising 'adequate prudential regulation' and countries that do not, those that are perceived to be attractive to foreign investment and those that are not.	Mobilize flows of investment and finance in the international economy leading to economic integration, while precipitating severe economic crises in many emerging markets.
Citizens	Social movements exist in the realm of civil society – a realm mutually constitutive with states (see Chapter 12). States regulate the civil realm, e.g. they attempt to control demonstrations, while social movements develop around a set of issues which both challenge state policies and develop across state borders.	States can restrict access to ICTs and can set up national firewalls. The distribution of ICTs is highly uneven, excluding those without access. Social movements often congregate around issues of exclusion in which inequalities and injustices are identified.	Social movement action (enabled by ICTs) occurs across state boundaries, and yet it is based within a national context, as evidenced by the Zapatistas and the dam movements in India. It can integrate social actors across the world while disrupting and challenging the actions of powerful states, companies and institutions.
Princes	Central element of the state, but military forces are increasingly networked among non-state, even anti-state, bodies.	Access to technology can allow less powerful actors to challenge more powerful national authorities, while technological development can strengthen the most powerful states' military capabilities.	National military agents have been given more surveillance and detention powers by new technologies, while control is also disrupted by the spread of such technology into the hands of insurgency groups.

Activity 14.1

This is not meant to be a comprehensive list by any means, but the following are an indication of some of the possible candidates. You might like to add more, or different, candidates yourself.

The completed table might look like Table 14.3.

Table 14.3   A framework for analysing (changes in) the international system (complete)

Elements of the international system	Sectors of the international system		
	Political sector of authoritative rule	Socio-cultural sector of collective identities and conceptions of rights and justice	Economic and technological sector of production, trade and innovation
Principal units in the international system	States (Ch. 2–5); civil society groups (Ch. 12, 13); social and economic interests (Ch. 2, 4, 6, 8, 9)	Cultures (Ch. 6, 8, 9); institutionalized norms (Ch. 3, 7, 9); people and peoples (Ch. 3, 6)	Classes (Ch. 2, 4); firms (Ch. 10–13); individuals (Ch. 4, 10, 11); networks (Ch. 11, 13)
Structure of relations among units	Anarchy and polarity (Ch. 2–5); networked relations (Ch. 12, 13); patterns of interdependence (Ch. 4, 5); patterns of uneven and combined development (Ch. 2)	Antagonistic and clashing or shared and universalizing (Ch. 3, 6, 8, 9)	Social property relations (Ch. 2); markets (Ch. 10, 11); patterned inequality (Ch. 11)
Interaction capacity	Military capabilities (Ch. 4, 5)	Formulation of rights claims (Ch. 7–9)	Economic development (Ch. 10, 11); development of ICTs and networks (Ch. 10–13)
Dominant processes of interaction	Balance of power (Ch. 3–5); territorial competition (Ch. 2); economic competition (Ch. 2, 4, 5, 10)	Contests over norms (Ch. 6–9)	Economic specialization, trade and international division of labour (Ch. 10–11)

Activity 14.2

For realists, authority is binding within states but not between them. Internally, the state's rule, expressed in its laws, is upheld by its monopoly on the use of legitimate force, which is the basis of state sovereignty. Between states there is no such authority and the ability to use force is dispersed among the states that make up the system. International law can, therefore, only ever be a weak constraint on state actions. States will not abide by international norms if they have an interest in breaking them, unless they are coerced to by more powerful states. To the extent that international law is upheld, it will thus be only a reflection of the interests of the most powerful states and their ability to coerce lesser states through threats and incentives to abide by such international norms. International laws will not be upheld when they cease to coincide with the interests of the powerful, or when other states want to break international conventions and think they can get away with it.

Activity 14.3

There are many examples in earlier chapters that you could bring in here. Situations in which preferences are in conflict could include the Cold War conflict; the antagonism between the revolutionary Iranian regime and the USA (Chapter 8); and the purported clash between the promotion of rights regimes by Western states and those in power in Islamic states looking to resist those norms (Chapters 7 and 9). Situations in which preferences are coincident might include the shared interests in economic liberalization among liberal capitalist powers in the post-Second World War era (Chapter 4). Situations in which there are a mix of coincident and conflicting preferences might include the relations between the USA and China: shared preferences over some economic issues and in curbing nuclear proliferation in the region, but conflicts over how dominant China might become in the region (Chapter 5). Note that in all these examples, it is what states are seeking to achieve – the curbing or spread of a particular brand of Islam; capitalism or communism; human rights; the aim of achieving higher economic growth based on freer international trade and investment; or the aim of maintaining stability in Asia – that determines both the extent of co-operation or conflict, and the content of that co-operation or conflict.

Activity 14.4

1   Possibly the most important dimension of international order that liberalism brings to the fore is the state–society relationship. Realism, especially in Waltz's version, defines this as outside the remit of a theory of the international system. Note that for liberals this leads to a weakening of the division between the domestic and the international, because domestic factors can have a determinate influence at the international level. In Waltz's model, this division is a rigid one and analysis operates at the international level only.

2   The most obvious dimension downplayed in the liberal account is the analysis of the balance of power in the system as a whole. Moravcsik argues that this is a secondary

consideration compared with what states seek to achieve. However, you might think that it remains important. Consider the impact on international order of a small country such as Tanzania pursuing its interests and the impact of a powerful state such as the USA doing the same. Maybe, even given the liberal approach, realism's focus on the great powers is still pertinent.

3   Moravcsik argues that the two accounts can be brought together, but only by putting the liberal account first. The liberal model sets the context in which it may be appropriate to apply a realist model: states whose aims threaten the survival of other states and which are locked in a zero-sum conflict. One example (in some accounts) would be the Cold War, where each state sought to overcome the other and measured gains and losses in the global battle in relation to the gains and losses of the other side. Nonetheless, for liberals this account is premised on the prior definition of each side's aims as being the destruction of the other or the triumph of its form of society (capitalism or communism).

Activity 14.5

The key to this is the nature of the relationships that have been constructed over time between the USA and the UK on the one hand and the USA and North Korea on the other. The UK and the USA share a long history of co-operation with many coincident interests and common identities; they both see themselves as liberal democracies, as members of 'the West', and as friends. By contrast, the USA fought a war against North Korea in the 1950s and has provided military and economic support to the North's main enemy, South Korea, ever since. North Korea sees the USA as one of the chief threats to its survival, and views itself as a communist state opposed to Western capitalist states. The identities that each holds of itself, and the ways in which these are defined in relation to the others, are consequently more important in analysing the international than who has how many guns.

Activity 14.6

A culture of enmity might include the conflict between the USA and the Soviet Union in the Cold War (Chapter 5); the conflict between the West and Islam in Huntington's clash of civilizations thesis (Chapter 6); US relations with Saddam's Iraq (Chapter 5) or post-revolutionary Iran (Chapter 8).

A culture of rivalry could include European international society (Chapter 3) or the types of relationship such as those between the USA, Russia and China (Chapter 5). The defence of the shared principle of sovereignty manifested in the UN's reversal of Iraq's invasion of Kuwait in the first Gulf War (1991) might also be an example of a culture of rivalry. The principles of self-determination and decolonization which were at the fore in the creation of many new states after the Second World War can also be seen, in some sense, as elements of a culture in which states remain rivals but accept each others' existence (see Chapters 3 and 6).

The leading candidate for a culture of friendship is the post-Second World War 'liberal' order among Western states (Chapter 4). Note that NATO (Chapters 4 and 5) constitutes the kind of collective security identity that Wendt talks about as being possible within a culture of friendship (in which an attack on one state represents an attack on them all).

Activity 14.7

Although Zubaida's account is not written from a Marxist perspective, his portrayal of the shaping of Islam shows some of the processes that Marxists are describing in talking about uneven and combined development. Zubaida points out how the process of modernization in states such as Turkey and Egypt took place in the context of the prior development of European states. The expansion of capitalist modernity, through economic and political means, impacted on the politics and culture of those societies and produced varying social and political formations – for example, the secular modernization in Turkey and reforms of Islamic law in Egypt. Zubaida also notes the rise of authoritarian and secular regimes in some of the countries of the region and the different ways in which Islam has been shaped by social forces opposing and supporting these processes.

Activity 14.8

The completed table might look like Table 14.4.

Table 14.4   Realism, liberalism, constructivism and Marxism compared

	What determines the actions of states?	What is the character of the relations between states?	What are the prospects for and bases of co-operation?	What part do other sectors of the international play in shaping international order?
Realism	The nature of the anarchical international system and their position within the balance of power. State preferences are fixed by the search for power.	Ultimately zero-sum across the system as a whole: gains for one lead to losses for others.	They are slim. States may co-operate in order to balance greater threats; or may co-operate if organized to do so in the interests of a dominant (hegemonic) power; but ultimately co-operation is subordinate to the requirements of self-help.	They are important in so far as they affect the power capabilities of states. For example, economic growth and technological leadership can feed into increases in military capabilities.

Liberalism	What states want. State preferences are exogenous to state–state relations and are shaped by state–society relations. But how states will pursue these aims will also depend on, and be constrained by, the preferences of other states.	It depends on the configurations of preferences – whether they are in conflict, in harmony, or a mixture of the two.	Mutual interests served by shared preferences or give and take bargaining over preferences that are in conflict.	(a) They help to shape state preferences (for example, economic actors). (b) They are the variety of arenas within which states pursue those interests (the world economy, an arena of co-operation or conflict over norms such as human rights, etc.).
Constructivism	The kind of 'subject identities' they have. These are formed by the history of interactions between states: enemies, rivals or friends. They are also formed by state–society relations (at least in part).	It depends on the nature of the shared ideas which constitute international order. States can see themselves and each other as enemies, rivals or friends, and relationships will vary depending on this.	Co-operation can develop, depending on the ideas that structure the system. In both 'cultures of rivalry' and 'cultures of friendship', co-operation can extend from shared norms such as sovereign recognition to extensive collective security arrangements.	Wendt's theory is primarily based on relations between states. However, he acknowledges that a considerable part of a state's identity is formed domestically and non-state actors play a role in this respect in a manner similar to a liberal model.
Marxism	Primarily, the form of society of which the state is a part. Capitalist polities will have a different form of geopolitics from absolutist ones. Among capitalist states, a combination of the overall management of the world capitalist economy and the particular interests of the domestic capitalist class will determine policies.	This depends on the nature of the societies (defined by their social property relations). Capitalist states have historically had a conflictual and/or transformatory impact on non-capitalist polities. Among capitalist societies, relations can be conflicting or co-operative.	Among capitalist societies, co-operation is based on the shared class interests of the dominant elements (in a manner akin to liberalism). Where these coincide in the joint management of capitalism internationally, capitalist states may act in an ultra-imperialist manner. Where rivalries between nationally based capitalisms come to the fore, conflict is likely.	The international capitalist economy is an integral part, along with national states, of international order. The changing nature of economic interests based on the uneven and combined development of capitalism as a social system is the primary determinant of international order.

Activity 15.1

The completed table might look like Table 15.7.

Table 15.7 Analysing international systems: liberalism (complete)

Elements of the international system	Sectors of the international system	
	Political sector of authoritative rule	Economic and technological sector of production, trade and innovation
Principal units in the international system	Individuals and private groups that use states to conduct political exchange and advance their collective interests	Firms (national and transnational) facing market incentives that create costs and benefits
Structure of relations among units	Interdependence, which may be positive-, zero- or negative-sum	Competitive in anarchic markets
Interaction capacity		
Dominant processes of interaction	Varies from harmony through bargaining to conflict, depending on the configuration of interdependent preferences	Specialization and the development of an international division of labour leading to increased interdependence

Activity 15.2

The completed table might look like Table 15.8.

Table 15.8 Analysing international systems: the clash of civilizations (complete)

Elements of the international system	Sectors of the international system	
	Political sector of authoritative rule	Socio-cultural sector of collective identities and conceptions of rights and justice
Principal units in the international system	States whose interests are defined in terms of civilizational identities	Collective identities, including notions of rights and justice, which are particular to different civilizations
Structure of relations among units	Anarchy + polarity + a thin international society	Some common elements shared by all civilizations relating to law and order but substantive conflicts of values between civilizations
Interaction capacity		
Dominant processes of interaction	Coming together of states sharing the same civilization and conflicts between civilizations	Civilizations are relatively bounded, unified entities in competition with one another

Activity 15.3

The communitarian rejoinder is that communities are not only grounded in more or less instrumental relations of interdependence and co-operation but also in more affective relations of belonging which are necessarily particular to a given culture and history.

Activity 15.4

The completed table might look like Table 15.9.

Table 15.9   Analysing international systems: a global network society (complete)

Elements of the international system	Sectors of the international system	
	Political sector of authoritative rule	Economic and technological sector of production, trade and innovation
Principal units in the international system	States reconfigured as networked states as in, for example, the European Union	The networked enterprise (including TNCs) + networks of technological innovation
Structure of relations among units	Co-ordination among the actors bound up in any given network; hierarchy and anarchy both transformed by global networking	Co-ordination among the actors bound up in any given network; market competition transformed by inter-firm collaboration
Interaction capacity	Defined by the flows of information and communication made possible by ICTs	Defined by the flows of information and communication made possible by ICTs
Dominant processes of interaction	Networking that serves both to include some and to exclude others; networks strengthen 'sovereignty-free' actors vis-à-vis states	Networking that serves both to include some and to exclude others; the network, rather than the firm, becomes the competitive unit

References

Achcar, G. (2002) *The Clash of Barbarisms: September 11 and the Making of the New World Disorder*, New York, NY, Monthly Review Press.

Ahmad, A. (1992) *In Theory*, London, Verso.

Amin, S. (1988) *Eurocentrism*, London, Zed Press.

Anderson, B.R.O'G. (1991) *Imagined Communities: Reflections on the Origins and Spread of Nationalism*, London, Verso.

Anderson, P. (1974) *Lineages of the Absolutist State*, London, Verso.

Anderson, P. (2002) 'Force and consent', *New Left Review II*, no.17, pp.5–30.

An-Na'im, A. (1990) *Toward an Islamic Reformation: Civil Liberties, Human Rights and International Law*, New York, NY, Syracuse University Press.

Anon (2001) 'Here comes the Barmy Army!: pink and silver on the warpath', *Do or Die*, vol.9, pp.12–14.

Archibugi, D. and Iammarino, S. (2000) 'Innovation and globalization' in Chesnais, F., Ietto-Gillies, G. and Simonetti, R. (eds) *European Integration and Global Corporate Strategies*, London, Routledge.

Archibugi, D. and Michie, J. (1997) *Technology, Globalisation and Economic Performance*, Cambridge, Cambridge University Press.

Arrighi, G. (1983) *The Geometry of Imperialism* (revised edition), London, Verso.

Athreye, S. (2004) 'Trade policy, industrialization and growth in India' in Bromley, S., Mackintosh, M., Brown, W. and Wuyts, M. (eds) *Making the International: Economic Interdependence and Political Order*, Milton Keynes, The Open University in association with Pluto Press.

Atkinson, A.B. (1999) *Is Rising Income Inequality Inevitable? A Critique of the Transatlantic Consensus*, WIDER Annual Lectures, 3 November, Helsinki, World Institute for Development Economics Research.

Baran, P. and Sweezy, P. (1966) *Monopoly Capital*, Harmondsworth, Penguin.

Barry, B. (1989) 'How not to defend liberal institutions' in *Liberty and Justice*, Oxford, Oxford University Press.

Bartlett, R. (1993) *The Making of Europe: Conquest, Colonization and Cultural Change, 950–1350*, Harmondsworth, Penguin.

Bassioumi, C. (1999) 'Policy perspectives favouring the establishment of the International Criminal Court', *Journal of International Affairs*, vol.52, no.2, pp.795–810.

Bauer, J. and Bell, D. (eds) (1999) *The East Asian Challenge for Human Rights*, Cambridge, Cambridge University Press.

Baugh, D.A. (1988) 'Great Britain's blue-water policy, 1689–1815', *International History Review*, vol.10, no.1, pp.33–58.

Beckett, J.V. (1990) *The Agricultural Revolution*, Oxford, Blackwell.

Beetham, D. (1991) *The Legitimation of Power*, Basingstoke, Macmillan.

Beetham, D. (1999) *Democracy and Human Rights*, Cambridge, Polity Press.

Beik, W. (1985) *Absolutism and Society in Seventeenth-Century France*, Cambridge, Cambridge University Press.

Bell, M. and Pavitt, K. (1997) 'Technological accumulation and industrial growth' in Archibugi, D. and Mitchie, J. (eds) *Technology, Globalisation and Economic Performance*, Cambridge, Cambridge University Press.

Bello, W., Bullard, N. and Malhotra, K. (2000) *Global Finance: New Thinking on Regulating Speculative Capital Markets*, London, Zed Books.

Benhabib, S. (2002) *The Claims of Culture*, New Jersey, NJ, Princeton University Press.

Bleiker, R. (2000) *Popular Dissent, Human Agency and Global Politics*, Cambridge, Cambridge University Press.

Bloch, M. (1961; first published 1940) *Feudal Society* (translated by Manyon, L.A.), London, Routledge.

Bloch, M. (1966; first published 1931) *French Rural History: An Essay on its Basic Characteristics* (translated by Sondheimer, J.), Berkeley, Calif., University of California Press.

Bobbitt, P. (2002) *The Shield of Achilles: War, Peace and the Course of History*, Harmondsworth, Allen Lane.

Bonnassie, P. (1991a; first published 1985) 'The survival and extinction of the slave system in the early medieval West (fourth to eleventh centuries)' in Bonnassie, P. (ed.) *From Slavery to Feudalism in South-Western Europe* (translated by Birrell, J.), Cambridge and Paris, Cambridge University Press and Maison des Sciences de l'Homme, pp.1–59.

Bonnassie, P. (1991b; first published 1980) 'From the Rhône to Galicia: origins and modalities of the feudal order' in Bonnassie, P. (ed.) *From Slavery to Feudalism in South-Western Europe* (translated by Birrell, J.), Cambridge and Paris, Cambridge University Press and Maison des Sciences de l'Homme, pp.104–31.

Brenner, R. (1985a) 'Agrarian class structure and economic development in pre-industrial Europe' in Aston, T.H. and Philpin, C.H.E. (eds) *The Brenner Debate: Agrarian Class Structure and Economic Development in Pre-Industrial Europe*, Cambridge, Cambridge University Press, pp.10–63.

Brenner, R. (1985b) 'The agrarian roots of European capitalism' in Aston, T.H. and Philpin, C.H.E. (eds) *The Brenner Debate: Agrarian Class Structure and Economic Development in Pre-Industrial Europe*, Cambridge, Cambridge University Press, pp.213–27.

Brenner, R. (1986) 'The social basis of economic development' in Roemer, J. (ed.) *Analytical Marxism*, Cambridge, Cambridge University Press, pp.23–53.

Brenner, R. (1987) 'Feudalism' in Eatwell, J., Milgate, M. and Newman, P. (eds) *The New Palgrave: A Dictionary of Economics: Marxian Economics*, London, Macmillan, pp.170–85.

Brenner, R. (1993) *Merchants and Revolution: Commercial Change, Political Conflict, and London's Overseas Traders, 1550–1653*, Cambridge, Cambridge University Press.

Brenner, R. (1996) 'The rises and declines of serfdom in medieval and early modern Europe' in Bush, M.L. (ed.) *Serfdom and Slavery: Studies in Legal Bondage*, London, Longman, pp.247–76.

Brewer, J. (1989) *The Sinews of Power: War, Money and the English State, 1688–1783*, New York, NY, Knopf.

Bright, C. and Meyer, M. (2002) 'Where in the world is America? The history of the USA in the global age' in Bender, T. (ed.) *Rethinking American History in a Global Age*, Berkeley, Calif., University of California Press.

Bromley, S. (1999) 'Marxism and globalization' in Gamble, A., Marsh, D. and Tant, T. (eds) *Marxism and Social Science*, London, Macmillan, pp.280–301.

Bromley, S. (2004) 'International politics: states, anarchy and governance', Chapter 5 in Bromley, S., Mackintosh, M., Brown, W. and Wuyts, M. (eds) *Making the International: Economic Interdependence and Political Order*, Milton Keynes, The Open University in association with Pluto Press, pp.95–129.

Brown, C. (1995) 'International political theory and the idea of world community' in Booth, K. and Smith, S. (eds) *International Relations Theory Today*, Cambridge, Polity Press.

Brown, C. (1997) *Understanding International Relations*, London, Macmillan.

Brown, C. (2001) 'Human rights' in Baylis, J. and Smith, S. (eds) *The Globalization of World Politics: An Introduction to International Relations*, Oxford, Oxford University Press.

Brown, C. (2002) *Sovereignty, Rights and Justice: International Political Theory Today*, Cambridge, Polity Press.

Brown, C., Nardin T. and Rengger, N. (eds) (2002) *International Relations in Political Thought*, Cambridge, Cambridge University Press.

Brown, K. (1995) 'Medical plants, indigenous medicine and conservation of biodiversity in Ghana' in Swanson, T.M. (ed.) *Intellectual Property Rights and Biodiversity Conservation*, Cambridge, Cambridge University Press.

Brownlie, I. (1984) 'The expansion of international society: the consequences for the law of nations' in Bull, H. and Watson, A. (eds) *The Expansion of International Society*, Oxford, Clarendon Press.

Brunn, S. and Dodge, M. (2001) 'Mapping the "worlds" of the World Wide Web', *American Behavioural Scientist*, vol.44, no.10, pp.1717–39.

Brunner, O. (1992; first published 1939) *Land and Lordship: Structures of Governance in Medieval Austria* (translated from the fourth edition by Kaminsky, H. and van Horn Melton, J.), Philadelphia, Pa., University of Pennsylvania Press.

Brzezinski, Z. (1997) *The Grand Chessboard: American Primacy and its Geostrategic Imperatives*, New York, NY, Basic Books.

Bull, H. (1995) *The Anarchical Society: A Study of Order in World Politics* (second edition), London, Macmillan.

Bull, H. and Watson, A. (eds) (1984) *The Expansion of International Society*, Oxford, Clarendon Press.

Bunting, M. and Burkeman, O. (2002) 'Pro Bono', *The Guardian*, 18 March, pp.54–6.

Buzan, B. (1991) *People, States and Fear: An Agenda for International Security Studies in the Post Cold War Era*, London and New York, NY, Harvester Wheatsheaf.

Buzan, B. and Little, R. (2000) *International Systems in World History*, Oxford, Oxford University Press.

Calhoun, C. (1995) *Critical Theory*, Oxford, Basil Blackwell.

Calleo, D.P. and Rowland, B.M. (1973) *America and the World Political Economy: Atlantic Dreams and National Realities*, Bloomington, Ind., Indiana University Press.

Caney, S. (2001) 'International distributive justice', *Political Studies*, vol.49, pp.974–97.

Carlsson, B. and Jacobsson, S. (1996) 'Technological systems and industrial dynamics: implications for firms and governments' in Helmstadter, E. and Perlman, M. (eds) *Behavioral Norms, Technological Progress and Economic Dynamics*, Ann Arbor, Mich., University of Michigan Press.

Cassen, B. (1995) 'Un concept sur mesure né à Singapour et à Kuala-Lumpur', *Le Monde Diplomatique*, August, p.2.

Castells, M. (1989) *The Informational City: Information Technology, Economic Restructuring and the Urban-Regional Process*, Oxford, Basil Blackwell.

Castells, M. (1996) *The Rise of the Network Society*, Volume 1 of *The Information Age: Economy, Society and Culture*, Oxford, Basil Blackwell.

Castells, M. (1997) *The Power of Identity*, Volume 2 of *The Information Age: Economy, Society and Culture*, Oxford, Basil Blackwell.

Castells, M. (2001) *The Internet Galaxy: Reflections on the Internet, Business and Society*, Oxford, Oxford University Press.

Cavallar, G. (1999) *Kant and the Theory and Practice of International Right*, Cardiff, University of Wales Press.

Cesaire, A. (1972; first published 1955) *Discourse on Colonialism*, New York, NY, Monthly Review Press.

Cesari, J. (2002) 'Global multiculturalism: the challenge of heterogeneity', *Alternatives*, vol.27, special issue. pp.5–19.

Chakrabarty, D. (2000) *Provincializing Europe: Postcolonial Thought and Historical Difference*, New Jersey, NJ, Princeton University Press.

Chandler, A.D. (1990) *Scale and Scope: The Dynamics of Industrial Capitalism*, London and Cambridge, Mass., Belknap Press.

Chandler, D. (2000) 'International justice', *New Left Review II*, no.6, pp.55–66.

Chandler, D. (ed.) (2002) *Rethinking Human Rights: Critical Approaches to International Politics*, Basingstoke, Palgrave Macmillan.

Chen, N. (2002) *Intra-National Versus International Trade in the European Union: Why Do National Borders Matter?*, CEPR Discussion Paper No.3407, London, Centre for Economic Policy Research.

Chesnais, F., Ietto-Gillies, G. and Simonetti, R. (eds) (2000) *European Integration and Global Corporate Strategies*, London, Routledge.

Clark, I. (1989) *The Hierarchy of States: Reform and Resistance in the International Order*, Cambridge, Cambridge University Press.

Cleaver, H. (1999) *Computer-Linked Social Movements and the Global Threat to Capitalism* [online]. Available from www.antenna.nl/~waterman/cleaver2.html [Accessed 17 October 2003].

Cline, W. (1997) *Trade and Income Distribution*, Washington, DC, Institute for International Economics.

Clinton, W.J. (1993) 'Remarks to the 48th Session of the United Nations General Assembly in New York City, 27 September 1993', *Public Papers of the Presidents of the United States, William J. Clinton, 1993, Vol. II*, pp.1612–18 [online]. Available from www.clinton-archives.gov/public_papers/public_papers.html [Accessed 11 February 2003].

Cohen, D. (2002) 'All the world's a Net', *New Scientist*, 13 April, p.24.

Cohen, G.A. (2000) *Karl Marx's Theory of History: A Defence* (expanded edition), Oxford, Oxford University Press.

Cohen, W. (2000) *East Asia At The Centre*, New York, NY, Columbia University Press.

Cohen, W. and Lenvintahl, D. (1989) 'Innovation and learning: the two faces of R&D', *Economic Journal*, vol.99, pp.659–99.

Collins, C., Gariyo, Z. and Burdon, T. (2001) 'Jubilee 2000: citizen action across the North–South divide' in Edwards, M. and Gaventa, J. (eds) *Global Citizen Action*, London, Earthscan.

Connor, T. (2001) 'Still waiting for Nike to respect the right to organize', *Global Exchange*, CorpWatch [online]. Available from www.corpwatch.org/campaigns/PCD.jsp?articleid=619 [Accessed 20 January 2004].

Cowan, J.K., Dembour, M.B. and Wilson, R.A. (2001) 'Introduction' in Cowan, J.K., Dembour, M.B. and Wilson, R.A. (eds) *Culture and Rights: Anthropological Perspectives*, Cambridge, Cambridge University Press, pp.1–26.

Cox, R.W. (1987) *Production, Power and World Order: Social Forces in the Making of History*, New York, Columbia University Press.

Cox, R.W. (1999) 'Civil society at the turn of the millennium: prospects for an alternative world order', *Review of International Studies*, vol.25, no.1, pp.3–28.

Crossley, N. (2002) *Making Sense of Social Movements*, Buckingham, Open University Press.

Cummings, B. (1991) 'Trilateralism and the New World Order', *World Policy Journal*, vol.8, no.2, pp.195–222.

David, P.A. and Bunn, J. (1987) 'Gateway technologies and the evolutionary dynamics of gateway industries: lessons fron electricity supply history' in Perlman, M. and Heertje, A. (eds) *Evolving Technology and Market Structure*, Chicago, Ill., University of Chicago Press, pp.121–56.

Davies, R. (1990) *Domination and Conquest: The Experience of Ireland, Scotland, and Wales, 1100–1300*, Cambridge, Cambridge University Press.

Della Porta, D. and Diani, M. (1999) *Social Movements: An Introduction*, Malden, Blackwell.

Dembour, M.-B. (2001) 'Following the movement of a pendulum: between universalism and relativism' in Cowan, J.K., Dembour, M.B. and Wilson, R.A. (eds) *Culture and Rights: Anthropological Perspectives*, Cambridge, Cambridge University Press, pp.56–79.

Department for International Development, UK (DFID) (1998) *Strengthening DFID's Support for Civil Society*, Consultation Paper, May [online]. Avaialble from www.dfid.gov.uk [Accessed 17 October 2003].

Department for International Development, UK (DFID) (2000) *Realising Human Rights for Poor People*, London, DFID Information Department.

Deudney, D. (1996) 'Binding sovereigns: authorities, structures, and geopolitics in Philadelphian systems' in Biersteker, T.J. and Weber, C. (eds) *State Sovereignty as Social Construct*, Cambridge, Cambridge University Press, pp.190–239.

Deudney, D. and Ikenberry, J. (1999) 'The nature and sources of a liberal international order', *Review of International Studies*, vol.25, no.2, pp.179–96.

Diebert, R. (2003) 'Black code: censorship, surveillance, and the militarization of cyberspace', paper presented at the International Studies Association Conference, Portland, Oregon.

Dobb, M. (1946) 'Capital accumulation and mercantilism' in Dobb, M. (ed.) *Studies in the Development of Capitalism*, London, Routledge, pp.177–220.

Donaghu, M. and Barff, R. (1990) 'Nike just did it: international subcontracting and flexibility in athletic footwear production', *Regional Studies*, vol.24, no.6, pp.537–52.

Donnelly, E. (2002) 'Proclaiming Jubilee: the debt and structural adjustment network' in Khagram, S., Riker, G. and Sikkink, K. (eds) *Restructuring World Politics: Transnational Social Movements, Networks and Norms*, Minneapolis, Minn., University of Minnesota Press.

Dore, R. (1984) 'Unity and diversity in contemporary world culture' in Bull, H. and Watson, A. (eds) *The Expansion of International Society*, Oxford, Clarendon Press.

Dosi, G. (1982) 'Technological paradigms and technological trajectories: a suggested interpretation of the determinants and directions of technological change', *Research Policy*, vol.11, no.3, pp.147–62.

Dosi, G. (1988) 'Sources, procedures and microeconomic effects of innovation', *Journal of Economic Literature*, vol.26, no.3, pp.1120–71.

Dosi, G., Freeman, C., Nelson, R., Silverberg, G. and Soete, L. (1988) *Technical Change and Economic Theory*, London, Pinter.

Doyle, M. (1986) 'Liberalism and world politics', *American Political Science Review*, vol.80, no.4, pp.1151–69.

Duby, G. (1953) *La Société aux XIe et XIIe Siècles dans la Région Maconnaise*, Paris, Librairie Armand Colin.

Duby, G. (1968; first published 1962) *Rural Economy and Country Life in the Medieval West* (translated by Postan, C.), Columbia, SC, University of South Carolina Press.

Duby, G. (1974; first published 1973) *The Early Growth of the European Economy: Warriors and Peasants from the Seventh to the Twelfth Century* (translated by Clarke, H.B.), London, Weidenfeld and Nicholson.

Duby, G. (1977; first published 1964) 'Youth in aristocratic society' in *The Chivalrous Society* (translated by Postan, C.), Berkeley, Calif., University of California Press, pp.112–22.

Dunne, T. and Wheeler, N. (eds) (1999) *Human Rights in Global Politics*, Cambridge, Cambridge University Press.

Dworkin, R. (1984) 'Rights as trumps' in Waldron, J. (ed.) *Theories of Rights*, Oxford, Oxford University Press.

Dworkin, R. (1997) 'The dragon as despot', *The Guardian*, 22 May, p.19.

Easterly, W. and Levine, R. (2003) 'It's not factor accumulation: stylized facts and growth models', *The World Bank Economic Review*, vol.15, no.2, pp.177–219.

Edwards, S. (1993) 'Openness, trade liberalisation and growth in developing countries', *Journal of Economic Literature*, vol.31, no.3, pp.1358–93.

Elliott, J.H. (1992) 'A Europe of composite monarchies', *Past and Present*, no.137, pp.48–71.

Elson, D. (1983) 'Nimble fingers and other fables' in Chapkis, W. and Enloe, C. (eds) *Of Common Cloth: Women in the Global Textile Industry*, Amsterdam, Transnational Institute, pp.5–13.

Emmott, B. (2002) 'Present at the creation: a survey of America's world role', *The Economist*, vol.363, no.8279, 29 June, special insert between pp.58–9.

Enloe, C. (1989) *Bananas, Beaches and Bases: Making Feminist Sense of International Politics*, London, Pandora Press.

Enos, J. and Park, W.H. (1988) *The Adoption and Diffusion of Imported Technology: The Case of Korea*, London, Croom Helm.

Fagerberg, J., Verspagen, B. and von Tunzelmann, N. (1995) 'The economics of convergence and divergence' in Fagerberg, J., Verspagen, B. and von Tunzelmann, N. (eds) *The Dynamics of Technology, Trade and Growth*, Cheltenham, Edward Elgar.

Feenstra, R.C. (1999) 'Facts and fallacies about foreign direct investment' in Feldstein, M. (ed.) *International Capital Flows*, NBER Conference Report, Chicago, Ill., University of Chicago Press.

Filipovic, M. (1997) *Governments, Banks and Global Capital*, Aldershot, Ashgate Publishing.

Fischer, M. (1992) 'Feudal Europe, 800–1300: communal discourse and conflictual practices', *International Organization*, vol.46, no.2, pp.427–66.

Fischer, S. (2003) 'Globalisation and its challenges', *American Economic Review*, vol.93, no.2, pp.1–30.

Fisher, J. (2001) 'Forward' in Blumler, J. and Coleman, S. (eds) *Realising Democracy Online: A Civic Commons in Cyberspace*, Swindon, IPPR/London Citizens Online Publications.

Fox, W.T.R. (1944) *The Superpowers*, New York, NY, Harcourt, Brace, Jovanovich.

Freeden, M. (1996) *Ideologies and Political Theory: A Conceptual Approach*, Oxford, Clarendon Press.

Freeman, C. (1997) 'The "National System of Innovation" in historical perspective' in Archibugi, D. and Michie, J. (eds) *Technology, Globalisation and Economic Performance*, Cambridge, Cambridge University Press.

Freeman, C. (2002) 'Continental, national and sub-national innovation systems: complementarity and economic growth', *Research Policy*, vol.31, pp.191–211.

Freeman, C. and Louçã, F. (2001) *As Time Goes By*, Oxford, Oxford University Press.

Freeman, C. and Perez, C. (1988) 'Structural crises of adjustment: business cycles and investment behavior' in Dosi, G., Freeman, C., Nelson, R., Silverberg, G. and Soete, L. (eds) *Technical Change and Economic Theory*, London, Pinter.

Frost, M. (2002) *Constituting Human Rights*, London, Routledge.

Fukuyama, F. (1992) *The End of History and the Last Man*, Harmondsworth, Penguin.

Ganshof, F. (1971) 'The institutional framework of the Frankish monarchy: a survey of its general characteristics' in *The Carolingians and the Frankish Monarchy: Studies in Carolingian History* (translated by Sondheimer, J.), London, Longman, pp.86–110.

Gardner, R.N. (1956) *Sterling Dollar Diplomacy: Anglo-American Collaboration in the Reconstruction of Multilateral Trade*, Oxford, Clarendon Press.

Garnham, N. (2000) *Emancipation, the Media, and Modernity*, Oxford, Oxford University Press.

Gereffi, G. and Korzeniewicz, M. (eds) (1994) *Commodity Chains and Global Capitalism*, Westport, Praeger Press.

Gerstenberger, H. (1990) *Die Subjektlose Gewalt: Theorie der Entstehung Bürgerlicher Staatsgewalt*, Münster, Westfälisches Dampfboot.

Giddens, A. (1984) *The Constitution of Society*, Cambridge, Polity Press.

Giddens, A. (1990) *The Consequence of Modernity*, Cambridge, Polity Press.

Gill, S. (1990) *America and the Trilateral Commission*, Cambridge, Cambridge University Press.

Gilpin, R. (1983) *War and Change in World Politics* (paperback edition), Cambridge, Cambridge University Press.

Gilroy, P. (2000) *Between Camps: Nations, Cultures and the Allure of Race*, Harmondsworth, Allen Lane.

Given, J. (1990) *State and Society in Medieval Europe: Gwynedd and Languedoc Under Outside Rule*, Ithaca, NY, Cornell University Press.

Goetz, H.-W. (1995) 'Social and military institutions' in McKitterick, R. (ed.) *The New Cambridge Medieval History, Vol. II, c.700–900*, Cambridge, Cambridge University Press, pp.451–80.

Goldstein, A. (2001) 'The diplomatic face of China's grand strategy: a rising power's emerging choice', *The China Quarterly*, no.168, pp.835–64.

Gong, G. (2002) 'Standards of civilization today' in Mozaffari, M. (ed.) *Globalization and Civilizations*, London, Routledge, pp.77–96.

Gowan, P. (1999) *The Global Gamble: Washington's Faustian Bid for World Dominance*, London, Verso.

Gowan, P. (2001) 'Neoliberal cosmopolitanism', *New Left Review II*, no.11, pp.79–93.

Gramsci, A. (1971) *Selections From the Prison Notebooks of Antonio Gramsci* (edited and translated by Hoare, Q. and Nowell Smith, G.), London, Lawrence and Wishart.

Green, D. (1995) *Silent Revolution: The Rise of Market Economics in Latin America*, London, Cassell.

Green, P. (2002) '"The passage from imperialism to empire": a commentary on empire by Michael Hardt and Antonio Negri', *Historical Materialism*, vol.10, no.1, pp.29–77.

Grzybowski, C. (1995) *Civil Society's Response to Globalization* [online]. Available from www.corpwatch.org/trac/feature/planet/gr-twn.html [Accessed 17 October 2003].

Gutting, G. (1999) *Pragmatic Liberalism and the Critique of Modernity*, Cambridge, Cambridge University Press.

Haldon, J. (1993) *The State and the Tributary Mode of Production*, London, Verso.

Halliday, F. (1990) 'The ends of the Cold War', *New Left Review I*, no.180, pp.5–23.

Halliday, F. (1994) *Rethinking International Relations*, Basingstoke, Macmillan.

Halliday, F. (1996) *Islam and the Myth of Confrontation: Religion and Politics in the Middle East*, London, I.B. Tauris.

Halliday, F. (2002) *Two Hours that Shook the World. September 11, 2001: Causes and Consequences*, London, Saqi Books.

Hampshire, S. (1999) *Justice is Conflict*, London, Duckworth.

Hardin, R. (1999) *Liberalism, Constitutionalism and Democracy*, Oxford, Oxford University Press.

Hawthorn, G. and Lund, C. (1998) 'Private and public in "late-modern" democracy' in Good, J. and Velody, I. (eds) *The Politics of Postmodernity*, Cambridge, Cambridge University Press.

Held, A. and McGrew, A. (2002) *Governing Globalisation: Power, Authority and Global Governance*, Cambridge, Polity Press.

Held, D. (1995) *Democracy and the Global Order: From the Modern State to Cosmopolitan Governance*, Cambridge, Polity Press.

Helmstadter, E. and Perlman, M. (eds) (1996) *Behavioral Norms, Technological Progress and Economic Dynamics*, Ann Arbor, Mich., University of Michigan Press.

Henderson, J. (1998) 'Danger and opportunity in the Asia-Pacific' in Thompson, G. (ed.) *Economic Dynamism in the Asia Pacific*, Milton Keynes, The Open University in association with Routledge.

Herod, A. (1998) 'Of blocs, flows and networks: the end of the cold war, cyberspace, and the geo-economics of organized labor at the fin de millenaire' in Herod, A., Tuathail, G.O. and Roberts, S. (eds) *Unruly World?: Globalisation, Governance and Geography*, London, Routledge, pp.162–95.

Hilton, R. (1976) 'Freedom and villeinage in England' in Hilton, R. (ed.) *Peasants, Knights, and Heretics: Studies in Medieval English Social History*, Cambridge, Cambridge University Press, pp.174–91.

Hilton, R. (1988; first published 1973) *Bond Men Made Free: Medieval Peasant Movements and the English Rising of 1381*, London, Routledge.

Hilton, R. (1990) 'Feudalism or *féodalité* and *seigneurie* in France and England' in *Class Conflict and the Crisis of Feudalism: Essays in Medieval Social History* (second edition), London, Verso.

Hirst, P. (2001) *War and Power in the 21st Century*, Cambridge, Polity Press.

Hobsbawm, E.J. (1991) *Nations and Nationalism Since 1780: Programme, Myth, Reality*, Cambridge, Cambridge University Press.

Holsti, K.J. (1991) *Peace and War: Armed Conflicts and International Order, 1648–1989*, Cambridge, Cambridge University Press.

Horowitz, D.L. (2000) *Ethnic Groups in Conflict* (second edition), Berkeley and Los Angeles, Calif., University of California Press.

Hume, D. (1994; first published 1752) 'Of the balance of power' in Haakonssen, K. (ed.) *David Hume: Political Essays*, Cambridge, Cambridge University Press.

Huntington, S.P. (1996) *The Clash of Civilizations and the Remaking of World Order*, New York, NY, Simon & Schuster.

Ibison, D. (1996) 'Mahathir insists West adopts more Asian values', *South China Morning Post*, 23 May, p.12.

Ibrahim, A. (1999) 'Young Asians will no longer allow the tiger of economic success to gorge on their human rights', *The Observer*, 18 April, p.26.

Ietto-Gillies, G. (2002) *Transnational Corporations: Fragmentation Amidst Integration*, London, Routledge.

Ignatieff, M. (2001) 'The attack on human rights', *Foreign Affairs*, vol.80, no.6, pp.102–16.

Ignatius, D. (1999) 'Policing hedge funds: who's in charge here?', *International Herald Tribune*, 22 February, p.6.

Institute of Development Studies (IDS) (2001) 'The value of value chains: spreading the gains from globalization' (edited by Gereffi, G. and Kaplinsky, R.), *IDS Bulletin*, vol.32, no.3, July.

Jackson, R. (2000) *The Global Covenant: Human Conduct in a World of States*, Oxford, Oxford University Press.

Jenkins, R. (1987) *Transnational Corporations and Uneven Development*, London, Methuen.

Jennings, I. (1956) *The Approach to Self-Government*, Cambridge, Cambridge University Press.

Jetin, B. and de Brunhoff, S. (2000) 'The Tobin Tax and the regulation of capital movements' in Bello, W., Bullard, N. and Malhotra, K. (eds) *Global Finance: New Thinking on Regulating Speculative Capital Markets*, London, Zed Books.

Johnson, C. (2002) *Blowback: The Costs and Consequences of the American Empire*, London, Time Warner Books.

Kaeuper, R.W. (1988) *War, Justice and Public Order: England and France in the Later Middle Ages*, Oxford, Clarendon Press.

Kagan, R. (2002) 'The power to divide' in *Prospect*, August, pp.20–27.

Kant, I. (1991a; first published 1795) 'Perpetual peace: a philosophical sketch' in Reiss, H. (ed.) *Kant: Political Writings* (second edition), Cambridge, Cambridge University Press.

Kant, I. (1991b; first published 1784) 'Idea for a universal history with a cosmopolitan purpose' in Reiss, H. (ed.) (1991) *Kant: Political Writings*, Cambridge, Cambridge University Press.

Kant, I. (1991c; first published 1797) *The Metaphysics of Morals*, extracted in Reiss, H. (ed.) (1991) *Kant: Political Writings*, Cambridge, Cambridge University Press.

Kant, I. (1993; first published 1871) *Critique of Pure Reason* (edited by Politis, V.), London, J.M. Dent.

Kapstein, E. (1994) *Governing the Global Economy*, Cambridge, Mass., Harvard University Press.

Kautsky, K. (1970; first published1914) 'Ultra-imperialism', *New Left Review I*, no.59, pp.41–6.

Keck, M. and Sikkink, K. (1998) *Activists Beyond Borders: Advocacy Networks in International Politics*, Ithaca, NY, Cornell University Press.

Keohane, R.O. (1984) *After Hegemony: Cooperation and Discord in the World Political Economy*, New Jersey, NJ, Princeton University Press.

Kepel, G. (2002) *Jihad: The Trail of Political Islam*, London, I.B. Tauris.

Khor, M. (2000) 'Why capital controls and international debt restructuring mechanisms are necessary to prevent and manage crisis' in Bello, W., Bullard, N. and Malhotra, K. (eds) *Global Finance: New Thinking on Regulating Speculative Capital Markets*, London, Zed Books.

Kidder, T. and McGinn, M. (1995) 'In the wake of NAFTA: transnational workers' networks', *Social Policy*, vol.25, no.4, pp.14–21.

Kindleberger, C. (1973) *The World in Depression*, Harmondsworth, Penguin.

Kissinger, H. (1957) *A World Restored: Metternich, Castlereagh and the Problems of Peace, 1812–22*, Boston, Mass., Houghton Mifflin.

Kissinger, H. (2002) *Does America Need a Foreign Policy?*, New York, NY, Simon & Schuster.

Klein, N. (2000) *No Logo: Taking Aim at Brand Bullies*, New York, HarperCollins.

Krugman, P. (2000) 'Downhill from here?', *New York Times*, 12 November.

Kuper, A. (1999) *Culture*, Cambridge, Cambridge University Press.

Lamb, C. (2003) *The Sewing Circles of Herat*, London, HarperCollins.

Landes, D. (1969) *The Unbound Prometheus: Technological Change and Industrial Development in Western Europe from 1750 to the Present*, Cambridge, Cambridge University Press.

Lee, E. (1999) 'Trade unions, computer communications and the New World Order' in Munck, R. and Waterman, P. (eds) *Labour Worldwide in the Era of Globalization: Alternative Union Models in the New World Order*, Basingstoke, Macmillan, pp.229–43.

Lenin, V.I. (1916) *Imperialism, the Highest Stage of Capitalism*, Peking, Foreign Language Press.

Levin, N.G. (1973) *Woodrow Wilson and World Politics: America's Response to War and Revolution*, Oxford, Oxford University Press.

Lieven, D. (2003) *Empire*, London, Pimlico.

Lipschutz, R. (1992) 'Reconstructing world politics: the emergence of global civil society', *Millennium*, vol.21, no.3, pp.389–420.

Lundestad, G. (1986) 'Empire by invitation? The USA and Western Europe, 1945–1952', *Journal of Peace Research*, vol.23, pp.1–23.

Lundestad, G. (1990) *The American 'Empire' and Other Studies of US Foreign Policy in Comparative Perspective*, Oxford, Oxford University Press.

Lundestad, G. (1998) *'Empire' by Integration: The USA and European Integration, 1945–1977*, Oxford, Oxford University Press.

Lyon, D. (1994) *The Electronic Eye: The Rise of Surveillance Society*, Cambridge, Polity Press.

MacCormick, N. (1999) *Questioning Sovereignty: Law, State and Nation in the European Commonwealth*, Oxford, Oxford University Press.

MacKinnon, C. (1993) 'Crimes of war, crimes of peace' in Shute, S. and Hurley, S. (eds) *On Human Rights: The Oxford Amnesty Lectures 1993*, New York, NY, Basic Books.

Mackintosh, M. (2004) 'Gaining from trade' in Bromley, S., Mackintosh, M., Brown, W. and Wuyts, M. (eds) *Making the International: Economic Interdependence and Political Order*, Milton Keynes, The Open University in association with Pluto Press.

Macleod, C. (1999) 'Negotiating the rewards of invention: the shop-floor inventor in Victorian Britain', *Business History*, vol.41, pp.17–36.

Maddison, A. (1982) *Phases of Capitalist Development*, Oxford, Oxford University Press.

Malcolm, N. (2002) *Aspects of Hobbes*, Oxford, Oxford University Press.

Mallet, V. (1994) 'Confucius or convenience?', *Financial Times*, 5 March.

Mandelbaum, M. (1991) *The Nuclear Revolution: International Politics Before and After Hiroshima*, Cambridge, Cambridge University Press.

Marx, K. (1970; first published 1867) *Capital: A Critique of Political Economy*, vol.1, London, Lawrence and Wishart.

Marx, K. (1973; first published in German 1939–41) *Grundrisse der Kritik der Politischen Ökonomie* (translated and with a forward by Nicolas, M.), Harmondsworth, Penguin.

Marx, K. (1973; first published 1852) 'The Eighteenth Brumaire of Louis Bonaparte' in *Surveys From Exile: Political Writings, Volume 2* (edited by Fernbach, D.), Harmondsworth, Penguin.

Marx, K. (1975; first published 1843) 'Contribution to the critique of Hegel's philosophy of law' in Marx, K. and Engels, F., *Collected Works*, vol.3, New York, NY, International Publishers, pp.3–129.

Marx, K. (1977; first published 1845) 'Theses on Feuerbach' in McLellan, D. (ed.) *Karl Marx: Selected Writings*, Oxford, Oxford University Press.

Marx, K. (1981; first published 1894) *Capital: A Critique of Political Economy*, vol.3, London, Penguin.

Marx, K. and Engels, F. (2002; first published 1848) *The Communist Manifesto*, Harmondsworth, Penguin.

Mayall, J. (1990) *Nationalism and International Society*, Cambridge, Cambridge University Press.

Mayer, T. (1963; first published 1939) 'Die Ausbildung des Modernen Deutschen Staates im Hohen Mittelalter' in Kämpf, H. (ed.) *Herrschaft und Staat im Mittelalter*, Bad Homburg, Gentner Verlag, pp.284–331.

Mazower, M. (1998) *Dark Continent*, Harmondsworth, Penguin.

McLellan, D. (ed.) (1997) *Karl Marx: Selected Writings*, Oxford, Oxford University Press.

McLuhan, M. (1994; first published 1964) *Understanding Media: The Extensions of Man*, Cambridge, Mass., The MIT Press.

Mearsheimer, J.J. (1990) 'Back to the future: instability in Europe after the Cold War', *International Security*, vol.15, no.1, pp.5–56.

Meehan, E. (1995) *Civil Society*, Swindon, Economic and Social Research Council.

Mehta, J. and Roy, R. (2004) 'The collective action problem' in Bromley, S., Mackintosh, M., Brown, W. and Wuyts, M. (eds) *Making the International: Economic Interdependence and Political Order*, Milton Keynes, The Open University in association with Pluto Press.

Meiksins Wood, E. (1995) *Democracy Against Capitalism*, Cambridge, Cambridge University Press.

Meiksins Wood, E. (2002) 'Infinite war', *Historical Materialism*, vol.10, no.1, pp.7–27.

Merry, S.E. (2001) 'Changing rights, changing culture' in Cowan, J.K., Dembour, M.B. and Wilson, R.A. (eds) *Culture and Rights: Anthropological Perspectives*, Cambridge, Cambridge University Press, pp.31–55.

Mill, J.S. (1873) 'A few words on non–intervention' in *Dissertations and Discussions*, New York, NY, HarperCollins.

Milward, A. (1992) *The European Rescue of the Nation-State*, London, Routledge.

Mitteis, H. (1975; first published 1940) *The State in the Middle Ages: A Comparative Constitutional History of Feudal Europe* (translated by Orton, H.F.), Amsterdam, North-Holland Publishing Company.

Montesquieu (1973; first published 1721) *Persian Letters* (translated by Betts, C.J.), Harmondsworth, Penguin.

Moravcsik, A. (1997) 'Taking preferences seriously: a liberal theory of international politics', *International Organization*, vol.51, no.4, pp.513–53.

Morganthau, H.J. (1978) *Politics Among Nations: The Struggle for Power and Peace*, New York, NY, Knopf.

Munck, R. (1999) 'Labour dilemmas and labour futures' in Munck, R. and Waterman, P. (eds) *Labour Worldwide in the Era of Globalization: Alternative Union Models in the New World Order*, Basingstoke, Macmillan, pp.3–23.

Nagel, T. (1986) *The View From Nowhere*, New York, NY, Oxford University Press.

Nagel, T. (1997) *The Last Word*, Oxford, Oxford University Press.

Nardin, T. (1983) *Law, Morality, and the Relations of Nations*, New Jersey, NJ, Princeton University Press.

Nelson, J.L. (1995) 'Kingship and royal government' in McKitterick, R. (ed.) *The New Cambridge Medieval History, Vol. II, c.700–900*, Cambridge, Cambridge University Press, pp.383–436.

Nussbaum, M. and Sen, A. (eds) (1993) *The Quality of Life*, Oxford, Oxford University Press.

Nye, J. (2002) *The Paradox of American Power: Why the World's Only Superpower Cannot Go It Alone*, New York, NY, Oxford University Press.

O'Brien, R. (2000) 'The difficult birth of a global labour movement', *Review of International Political Economy*, vol.7, no.3, pp.514–23.

O'Rourke, K.H. (2001) *Globalization and Inequality: Historical Trends*, NBER Working Paper No.8339, Cambridge, Mass., National Bureau of Economic Research.

O'Rourke, K.H. and Williamson, J.G. (2000) *Globalisation and History: The Evolution of a Nineteenth Century Atlantic Economy*, Cambridge, Mass., MIT Press.

Oakeshott, M. (1991) *Rationalism in Politics and Other Essays* (new and expanded edition), Indianapolis, Ind., Liberty Press.

OXF-1: Personal interview conducted by Helen Yanacopulos with Oxfam International, Washington, DC, 8 July 1998.

OXF-2: Personal interview conducted by Helen Yanacopulos with Oxfam International, Washington, DC, 4 September 1997.

Pagden, A. (1995) *Lords of All The World: Ideologies of Empire in Spain, Britain and France c.1500–c.1800*, New Haven, Conn., Yale University Press.

Pagden, A. (2001) *Peoples and Empires: Europeans and the Rest of the World from Antiquity to the Present*, London, Weidenfeld & Nicolson.

Parker, D. (1996) *Class and State in Ancien Régime France: The Road to Modernity?*, London, Routledge.

Payne, R. (2001) 'Persuasion, frames and norm construction', *European Journal of International Relations*, vol.7, no.1, pp.37–62.

Peretti, J. (2001) 'USA: my Nike media adventure', *The Nation*, 9 April [online]. Available from http://www.thenation.com/doc.mhtml?i=20010409&s=peretti [Accessed 22 January 2004].

Perez, C. (1989) *Technical Change, Competitive Restructuring and Institutional Reform in Developing Countries*, Strategic Planning and Review Discussion Paper No.4, Washington, DC, World Bank.

Perez, C. (2000) 'Technological change and opportunities for development as a moving target', paper presented at the 'High-level Round Table on Trade and Development, UNCTAD X', Bangkok, 12 February 2000.

Pettit, P. (2001) *A Theory of Freedom: From the Psychology to the Politics of Agency*, Cambridge, Cambridge, Polity Press.

Pfaff, W. (2000) 'Judging war crimes', *Survival*, vol.42, no.1, pp.46–58.

Pickerill, J. (2001) 'Weaving a green web: environmental protest and computer-mediated communication in Britain' in Webster, F. (ed.) *Culture and Politics in the Information Age: A New Politics?*, London, Routledge.

Piore, M.J. and Sabel, C.F. (1984) *The Second Industrial Divide*, New York, NY, Basic Books.

Pogge, T. (2002) *World Poverty and Human Rights: Cosmopolitan Responsibilities and Reforms*, Cambridge, Polity Press.

Polk, W. (1997) *Neighbours and Strangers*, Chicago, Ill., University of Chicago Press.

Pollard, R. (1985) *Economic Security and the Origins of the Cold War*, New York, NY, Columbia University Press.

Poly, J.-P. and Bournazel, E. (1991; first published 1980) *The Feudal Transformation, 900–1200* (translated by Higgit, C.), New York, NY, Holmes & Meier.

Porter, M. (1985) *Competitive Advantage: Creating and Sustaining Superior Advantage*, Basingstoke, Macmillan.

Porter, M. (1990) *The Competitive Advantage of Nations*, Basingstoke, Macmillan.

Pritchett, L. (1997) 'Divergence, big time', *Journal of Economic Perspectives*, vol.11, no.3, pp.3–17.

Raban, J. (2003) 'The greatest gulf', *The Guardian*, G2, Saturday 19 April, pp.1–2.

Rashid, A. (2001) *Taliban*, London, Pan Macmillan.

Rauch, J.E. (1999) 'Networks versus markets in international trade', *Journal of International Economics*, vol.48, pp.7–35.

Ravallion, M. (2001) 'Growth, inequality and poverty: looking beyond averages' in *World Development*, vol.29, no.11, pp.1803–15.

Reinert, E. (1995) 'Catching-up from way behind: A Third World perspective on First World history' in Fagerberg, J., Verspagen, B. and von Tunzelmann, N. (eds) *The Dynamics of Technology, Trade and Growth*, Cheltenham, Edward Elgar.

Reynolds, D. (2000) *One World Divisible: A Global History Since 1945*, London, Allen Lane Penguin.

Ribeiro, G. (1998) 'Cybercultural politics: political activism at a distance in a transnational world' in Alvarez, S., Dagnino, E. and Escobar, A. (eds) *Cultures of Politics, Politics of Cultures: Re-visioning Latin American Social Movements*, Colorado, Col., Westview Press, pp.325–52.

Risse-Kappen, T. (1995) *Bringing Transnational Relations Back In: Non-State Actors, Domestic Structures and International Institutions*, Cambridge, Cambridge University Press.

Robertson, R. (1990) *Globalization*, London, Sage.

Romer, P. (1993) 'Ideas and things' in 'The future surveyed', *The Economist*, vol.328, no.7828, 11 September, special insert between pp.68–9.

Rosenau, J.N. (1992) 'Governance, order and change in world politics' in Rosenau, J.N. and Czempiel, E.-O. (eds) *Governance Without Government: Order and Change in World Politics*, Cambridge, Cambridge University Press.

Rosenau, J.N. (1997) *Along the Domestic–Foreign Frontier: Exploring Governance in a Turbulent World*, Cambridge, Cambridge University Press.

Rosenau, J.N. (2000) 'Change, complexity, and governance in a globalizing space' in Pierre, J. (ed.) *Debating Governance: Authority, Steering and Democracy*, Oxford, Oxford University Press, pp.167–200.

Rosenau, J.N. and Czempiel, E.-O. (eds) (1992) *Governance Without Government: Order and Change in World Politics*, Cambridge, Cambridge University Press.

Rosenberg, J. (1990) 'What's the matter with realism?', *Review of International Studies*, vol.16, April, pp.285–303.

Rosenberg, J. (1994) *The Empire of Civil Society: A Critique of the Realist Theory of International Relations*, London, Verso.

Rosenberg, J. (1996) 'Isaac Deutscher and the lost history of international relations', *New Left Review I*, no.215, pp.3–15.

Rosenberg, J. (2000) *The Follies of Globalisation Theory*, London, Verso.

Rosenberg, N. and Frischtak, C. (eds) (1985) *International Technology Transfer*, New York, NY, Praeger.

Rösener, W. (1992) *Agrarwirtschaft, Agrarverfassung, und ländliche Gesellschaft im Mittelalter*, Munich, Oldenbourg.

Ruggie, J.G. (1986) 'Continuity and transformation in the world polity: toward a neorealist synthesis' in Keohane, R.O. (ed.) *Neorealism and its Critics*, New York, NY, Columbia University Press, pp.131–57.

Ruggie, J.G. (1998) *Constructing the World Polity: Essays on International Institutionalization*, London, Routledge.

Russett, B. (1993) *Grasping the Democratic Peace: Principles for a Post-Cold War World*, New Jersey, NJ, Princeton University Press.

Sachs, J. and Warner, A. (1995) *Economic Reform and the Process of Global Integration*, Brookings Papers on Economic Activity, Washington, DC, Brookings Institution.

Said, E.W. (1985; first published 1978) *Orientalism: Western Conceptions of the Orient*, Harmondsworth, Penguin.

Said, E.W. (1993) *Culture and Imperialism*, London, Chatto & Windus.

Sala-i-Martin, X. (2002) *The Disturbing 'Rise' of Global Income Inequality*, New York, NY, Columbia University Press.

Sassen, S. (2000) 'Excavating power, in search of frontier zones and new actors', *Theory, Culture and Society*, vol.17, no.1, pp.163–70.

Sassen, S. (2002) *Global Networks, Linked Cities*, London, Routledge.

Schelling, T. (1960) *The Strategy of Conflict*, Cambridge, Mass., Harvard University Press.

Schmidt, R. (2000) 'A feasible foreign exchange transaction tax' in Bello, W., Bullard, N. and Malhotra, K. (2000) *Global Finance: New Thinking on Regulating Speculative Capital Markets*, London, Zed Books.

Schmitt, C. (1996; first published 1932) *The Concept of the Political*, Chicago, Ill., University of Chicago Press.

Schroeder, P. (1994) 'Historical reality vs. neo-realist theory', *International Security*, vol.19, no.1, pp.108–48.

Schumpeter, J.A. (1934) *The Theory of Economic Development: An Inquiry Into Profits, Capital, Credit, Interest, and the Business Cycle*, Cambridge, Mass., Harvard University Press.

Schumpeter, J.A. (1942) *Capitalism, Socialism, and Democracy*, New York, NY, Harper.

Searle, J. (1995) *The Construction of Social Reality*, New York, NY, The Free Press.

Sen, A. (1997) *On Economic Inequality* (expanded edition), Oxford, Oxford University Press.

Sen, A. (1999) *Development as Freedom*, Oxford, Oxford University Press.

Sen, A. (2000) 'East and West: the reach of reason', *New York Review of Books*, 20 July.

Shaw, M. (1994) *Global Society and International Relations*, Cambridge, Polity Press.

Shiva, V. (1993) 'Women's indigenous knowledge and biodiversity conservation' in Mies, M. and Shiva, V., *Ecofeminism: Reconnecting a Divided World*, London, Zed Books, pp.164–73.

Shue, H. (1980) *Basic Rights*, New Jersey, NJ, Princeton University Press.

Silber, W. (1975) *Financial Innovation*, London, D.C. Heath.

Simonetti, R. (1998) 'Technological change' in Simonetti, R., Mackintosh, M., Costello, N., Dawson, G., Himmelweit, S., Trigg, A. and Wells, J. (eds) D319 *Understanding Economic Behaviour: Households, Firms and Markets*, Block 5, *Firms*, Milton Keynes, The Open University.

Simonetti, R. (2001) 'Technological change' in Himmelweit, S., Simonetti, R. and Trigg, A. (eds) *Microeconomics: Neoclassical and Institutional Perspectives*, London, International Thompson Business Press.

Smith, A.D. (1999) *Myths and Memories of the Nation*, Oxford, Oxford University Press.

Smith, D. (1998) 'The Asian tigers turn tail', *Sunday Times*, 24 May, pp.8,12.

Spence, J. (1999) *The Search for Modern China* (second edition), New York, NY, W.W. Norton & Co.

Standage, T. (1998) *The Victorian Internet: The Remarkable Story of the Telegraph and the Nineteenth Century's On-Line Pioneers*, New York, NY, Walker and Company.

Stedman Jones, G. (1972) 'The history of US imperialism' in Blackburn, R. (ed.) *Ideology in Social Science: Readings in Critical Social Theory*, Glasgow, Fontana/Collins.

Stein, P. (1999) *Roman Law in European History*, Cambridge, Cambridge University Press.

Steiner, H. and Alston, P. (2000) *International Human Rights in Context. Law, Politics, Morals: Texts and Materials*, Oxford, Clarendon Press.

Strange, S. (1998) *Mad Money*, Manchester, Manchester University Press.

Strauss, L. (1996) 'Notes on Carl Schmitt, the concept of the political' in Schmitt, C. (ed.) *The Concept of the Political*, Chicago, Ill., University of Chicago Press.

Suganami, H. (1984) 'Japan's entry into international society' in Bull, H. and Watson, A. (eds) *The Expansion of International Society*, Oxford, Clarendon Press, pp.185–99.

Temple, P. (2001) *Hedge Funds*, Chichester, John Wiley and Sons.

Teschke, B. (1998) 'Geopolitical relations in the European middle ages', *International Organization*, vol.52, no.2, pp.325–58.

Teschke, B. (2002) 'Theorising the Westphalian system of states: international relations from absolutism to capitalism', *European Journal of International Relations*, vol.8, no.1, pp.5–48

Teschke, B. (2003) *The Myth of 1648: Class, Geopolitics, and the Making of Modern International Relations*, London, Verso.

The Economist (2003) 'Economics focus: catching up', *The Economist*, 21 August [online]. Available from http://www.econ.jhu.edu/courses/101/StanleyFischeronGlobalization.pdf [Accessed 26 January 2004].

The Polish Treaty (1919) Treaty between the principal Allied and Associated Powers and the Republic of Poland, signed at Versailles on 28 June 1919 [online]. Available at http://www.ucis.pitt.edu/eehistory/H200Readings/Topic5-R1.html [Accessed 18 November 2003].

The Versailles Treaty (1919) The Versailles Treaty, signed 28 June 1919 [online]. Available at: http://history.acusd.edu/gen/text/versaillestreaty/vercontents.html [Accessed 18 November 2003].

Thompson, G. (2003) *Between Hierarchies and Markets: The Logic and Limits of Network Forms of Organization*, Oxford, Oxford University Press.

Tomlinson, J. (1999) *Globalization and Culture*, Cambridge, Polity Press.

Touraine, A. (2002) 'The importance of social movements', *Social Movement Studies*, vol.1, no.1, pp.89–95.

Trotsky, L. (1977) *The History of the Russian Revolution*, London, Pluto Press.

True, J. (1996) 'Feminism' in Burchill, S., Devetak, R., Linklater, A., Paterson, M., Reus-Smit, C. and True, J. (eds) *Theories of International Relations* (second edition), Basingstoke, Palgrave.

Truman, H.S. (1963) *Public Papers of the Presidents of the United States, Harry S. Truman, 1947*, Washington, DC, US Government Printing Office.

Tuck, R. (1999) *The Rights of War and Peace*, Oxford, Clarendon Press.

Tully, J. (1995) *Strange Multiplicity*, Cambridge, Cambridge University Press.

United Nations (1948) *Universal Declaration of Human Rights* [online]. Available from http://www.un.org/Overview/rights.html [Accessed 6 January 2004].

United Nations (1951) *UN Convention Relating to the Status of Refugees*, Washington, DC, United Nations.

United Nations (1992) *CEDAW General Recommendation 19: 1*, Washington, DC, United Nations.

United Nations (1995a) *Our Global Neighbourhood: The Report of the Commission on Global Governance*, Oxford, Oxford University Press.

United Nations (1995b) *Beijing Declaration and Platform for Action: Platform 3* (Official Documents: D (sec.119)), The IV World Conference on Women, 1995, Beijing, China.

United Nations Conference on Trade and Development (UNCTAD) (1998) *Trade and Development Report 1998*, Geneva, United Nations Conference on Trade and Development.

United Nations Development Programme (UNDP) (1999) *Human Development Report*, New York, NY, United Nations.

United Nations Development Programme (UNDP) (2001) *Human Development Report: Making New Technologies Work for Human Development*, Oxford, Oxford University Press.

USA Today (1991) 'USA at war: the world could wait no longer', *USA Today*, 17 January, p.11.

van der Pijl, K. (1984) *The Making of an Atlantic Ruling Class*, London, Verso.

van der Pijl, K. (1998) *Transnational Classes and International Relations*, London, Routledge.

Vidal, G. (2002) *Perpetual War For Perpetual Peace: How We Got to Be So Hated, Causes of Conflict in the Last Empire*, Edinburgh, Clairview Press.

Vincent, R.J. (1984) 'Racial equality' in Bull, H. and Watson, A. (eds) *The Expansion of International Society*, Oxford, Clarendon Press.

von Clausewitz, C. (1976; first published 1832) *On War*, New Jersey, NJ, Princeton University Press.

Wade, R.H. (2002) 'Globalization, poverty and income distribution: does the liberal argument hold?', paper presented at conference 'Towards a New Political Economy', University of Sheffield, Political Economy Research Centre.

Wade, R.H. and Wolf, M. (2002) 'Are global poverty and inequality getting worse?', *Prospect*, vol.72, pp.16–21.

Walt, S.M. (2000) *Keeping the World Off Balance: Self-Restraint and US Foreign Policy*, Faculty Research Working Papers Series No.00–013, Cambridge, Mass., JFK School of Government, Harvard University.

Waltz, K.N. (1959) *Man, the State and War: A Theoretical Analysis*, New York, NY, Columbia University Press.

Waltz, K.N. (1979) *Theory of International Politics*, New York, NY, Random House.

Waltz, K.N. (1993) 'The emerging structure of international politics', *International Security*, vol.18, no.2, pp.44–79.

Waltz, K.N. (2000) 'Structural realism after the Cold War', *International Security*, vol.25, no.1, pp.5–41.

Waterman, P. (1999) 'The New Social Unionism: a new union model for a new world order' in Munck, R. and Waterman, P. (eds) *Labour Worldwide in the Era of Globalization: Alternative Union Models in the New World Order*, Basingstoke, Macmillan, pp.247–59.

Watkins, K. (2002) *Making Globalization Work for the Poor*, Oxford, Oxfam.

Watson, A. (1984) 'Russia and the European states system' in Bull, H. and Watson, A. (eds) *The Expansion of International Society*, Oxford, Clarendon Press.

Webb, M.C. and Krasner, S.D. (1989) 'Hegemonic stability theory: an empirical assessment', *Review of International Studies*, no.15, pp.183–98.

Weber, M. (1968; first published 1922) *Economy and Society: An Outline of Interpretive Sociology* (edited by Roth, G. and Wittich, C.), New York, NY, Bedminster Press.

Weber, M. (1991; first published 1920) 'Author's introduction' in *The Protestant Ethic and the Spirit of Capitalism* (translated by Parsons, T. and introduced by Giddens, A.), London, HarperCollins.

Wendt, A. (1992) 'Anarchy is what states make of it: the social construction of power politics', *International Organization*, vol.46, no.2, pp.391–425.

Wendt, A. (1999) *Social Theory of International Politics*, Cambridge, Cambridge University Press.

Westphal, L., Kim, L. and Dahlman, D. (1985) 'Reflections on the Republic of Korea's acquisition of technological capability' in Rosenberg, N. and Frischtak, C. (eds) *International Technology Transfer*, New York, NY, Praeger.

Wheaton, H. (1836) *Elements of International Law: With a Sketch of the History of the Science*, Philadelphia, Pa., Carey, Lea & Blanchard.

Wickham, C. (1994) 'Making Europes', *New Left Review I*, no.208, pp.133–43.

Wight, M. (1966a) 'The balance of power' in Butterfield, H. and Wight, M. (eds) *Diplomatic Investigations: Essays in the Theory of International Politics*, London, Allen and Unwin, pp.149–75.

Wight, M. (1966b) 'Why is there no International Theory?' in Butterfield, H. and Wight, M. (eds) *Diplomatic Investigations: Essays in the Theory of International Politics*, London, George Allen and Unwin, pp.17–34.

Wight, M. (1986) *Power Politics* (second edition), Harmondsworth, Penguin.

Wohlforth, W. (1999) 'The stability of an international world', *International Security*, vol.24, no.1, pp.5–41.

Wood, E. (1991) *The Pristine Culture of Capitalism: A Historical Essay on Old Regimes and Modern States*, London, Verso.

World Bank (2000) *Consultation with Civil Society Organisations: General Guidelines for World Bank Staff*, Washington, DC, NGO and Civil Society Development Unit, The World Bank.

World Bank (2002) *World Development Indicators 2002*, Washington DC, World Bank.

Yanacopulos, H. (2002) 'Think local, act global: transnational networks and development' in Robinson, J. (ed.) *Development and Displacement*, Oxford, Oxford University Press.

Young, I.M. (1990) *Justice and the Politics of Difference*, New Jersey, NJ, Princeton University Press.

Young, R.J.C. (2001) *Postcolonialism: An Historical Introduction*, Oxford, Blackwell.

Zubaida, S. (1989) 'Reading history backwards', *Middle East Report*, no.160, pp.39–41.

Index

Note: an index reference in **bold** type indicates a marginal note.

Acknowledgements

Grateful acknowledgement is made to the following sources for permission to reproduce material in this book.

Every effort has been made to contact copyright holders. If any have been inadvertently overlooked the publishers will be pleased to make the necessary arrangements at the first opportunity.

Text

pp.381–4: Wade, R. and Wolf, M. (2002) 'Are global poverty and inequality getting worse?'. This material first appeared in the March 2002 issue of *Prospect* magazine. pp.419–20: Peretti, J. (2001) 'USA: my Nike media adventure', reprinted with permission from the 9 April 2001 issue of *The Nation*. For subscription information, call 1-800-333-8536. Portions of each week's *The Nation* magazine can be accessed at http://www.thenation.com. pp.443–4: Bunting, M. and Burkeman, O. (2002) 'Pro Bono', *The Guardian*, 18 March 2002, © The Guardian. pp.54–6: Raban, J. (2003) 'The greatest gulf', *The Guardian*, G2, 19 April, © Jonathan Raban.

Tables

Table 10.1: from Freeman, C. and Louçã, F. (2001) *As Time Goes By*. Reprinted by permission of Oxford University Press.

Figures

Figure 11.1: from *Human Development Report 2001* by United Nations Development Programme, © 2001 by the United Nations Development Programme. Used by permission of Oxford University Press, Inc. Figure 11.4: Atkinson, A.B. (1999) *Is Rising Income Inequality Inevitable?*, WIDER Annual Lectures, 3 November 1999, United Nations University World Institute for Development Economics Research (UNU/WIDER). Figure 15.1: Tuan, Y.-F. (1974) *Topophilia*, Pearson Education Inc. Figure 15.2: Tuan, Y.-F. (1974) *Topophilia*, Pearson Education Inc. Figure 15.4: © The Robert Opie Collection.

Photos

Cover image © Photodisc Europe Ltd. p.15, top: © Copyright The British Museum. p.15, bottom: © Eric Draper/Associated Press. p.69: © G. Samoilova / Associated Press. p.85: © Hulton Archive. p.97: © Associated Press. p.113: © Thomas D. McAvoy / Time Life Pictures / Getty Images. p.115: © Richard Drew / Associated Press. p.120: From Richard N. Gardner (1956) *Sterling Dollar Diplomacy: Anglo-American*

Collaboration in the Reconstruction of Multilateral Trade, Oxford University Press. p.152, left: © Bildarchiv Preussischer Kulturbesitz, Berlin. p.152, right: © Novosti, London. p.177: © EPA / PA Photos. p.205: © Hulton Archive. p.221: © Saleh Rifai / Associated Press. p.228: © United Nations Photo Library. p.283: © Bettmann / Corbis. p.308: © EPA / PA Photos. p.322: © Tariq Aziz / Associated Press. p.457: © Nick Ut / Associated Press. p.466: © Jerome Delay / Associated Press.